THE DEMOCRACY PRINCIPLE

FARMER CO-OPERATIVES IN TWENTIETH CENTURY AUSTRALIA

Gary Lewis

The Democracy Principle: Farmer Co-operatives in Twentieth Century Australia is
published by the author, Gary Lewis of Wamboin, NSW, under the auspices of the
Co-operative Federation of NSW Ltd. Funding for printing was provided by the New
South Wales Registry of Co-operatives and Associations Co-operatives Development
Grants Program.

ISBN 0-646-46587-2

Cover and book design by The Magic Lantern Company, Melbourne
Typeset by The Magic Lantern Company, Melbourne
Printed by BPA Print Group, Melbourne

FOR CATHY

Contents

THE DEMOCRACY PRINCIPLE
FARMER CO-OPERATIVES IN TWENTIETH CENTURY AUSTRALIA

Acknowledgements

Largely self-funded, *The Democracy Principle* has been written independently of tertiary institutional support. Periodic employment or consultancy over many years in the co-operative sector allowed work to proceed. In this regard special mention should be made of the New South Wales Registry of Co-operative Societies Co-operative Development Branch, Ricegrowers' Co-operative Limited, Credit Union Services Corporation (Australia) Limited, the Australia-Pacific Co-operative Training Centre, *National Co-op Update*, the Australian Centre for Co-operatives Research and Development (ACCORD) and Gateway Credit Union Ltd.

The help and encouragement of many colleagues is gratefully acknowledged, in particular Garry Cronan, Bruce Freeman, Ray Ison, Tim Dyce, Tony Gill, Chris Greenwood, Lawrie Dooley, Wayne Ryan, Race Matthews, Jill Jordan, Anthony Esposito and the late Bill Rawlinson, Kevin Yates and John Gill. Garry's abiding belief in the practical value of co-operatives' history helped sustain the motivation over many years. Thanks also to Geoffrey Bartlett of the Australian National University History Department (retired) for his unwavering belief in the research and to the National Library of Australia Oral History Department, the (former) Co-operative Federation of Australia, the Co-operative Federation of Victoria and the Co-operative Federation of Western Australia for their support at key moments.

The kind assistance of Norco Co-operative Limited, Nambucca River Co-operative, Bega Co-operative Society Limited, Murray-Goulburn Co-operative Company Limited, Australian Co-operative Foods Limited, Co-operative Bulk Handling and the Battye Library, Perth, Western Australia in making photographs available for use in the book is greatly appreciated. The photographs are arranged more or less randomly and add an interesting historical flavour to the book.

Special thanks to the Board of the Co-operative Federation of NSW Ltd and in particular, Executive Officer Helen McCall, for graciously sponsoring an application to fund the printing of this book and for their assistance and efforts in bringing it to print readiness.

Without the generous support of the New South Wales Registry of Co-operatives and Associations Co-operatives Development Grants Program, which provided funding to print this book, it simply would not exist. I am greatly indebted to the Registry and its officers.

Nothing would have been possible without the sterling efforts of Maureen Clarkson, who worked above and beyond the call of duty to word-process and manage the development of a large and complex manuscript – my deepest appreciation, again, Maureen.

Finally, without my wife's patience and understanding through years of unpaid research for the co-operative sector, the book would never have seen the light of day. Thanks Lida.

Gary Lewis
Wamboin NSW
October 2006

Abbreviations

AAC	Australian Association of Co-operatives
AAP	Australian Associated Press
AAPBS	Australian Association of Permanent Building Societies
ABC	Australian Broadcasting Commission/Corporation
ACCC	Australian Competition and Consumer Commission
ACCoRD	Australian Centre for Co-operative Research and Development
ACDL	Australian Co-operative Development League
ACF	Australian Co-operative Foods
ACFA	Australian Canning Fruitgrowers' Association
ACMAL	Amalgamated Co-operative Marketers (Australia) Limited
ACT	Australian Capital Territory
ADFF	Australian Dairy Farmers Federation
ADIC	Australian Dairy Industry Council
AFCUL	Australian Federation of Credit Union Leagues
AFFO	Australian Farmers Federation Organisation
AFIC	Australian Financial Institutions Commission
AFP	Australian Farmers Proprietary Limited
AFR	Australian Financial Review
AFWCF	Australian Farmers' Wholesale Co-operative Federation
AGM	Annual General Meeting
AIDC	Australian Industry Development Corporation
ALP	Australian Labor Party
AMP	Australian Mutual Provident Society
APCTC	Asia-Pacific Co-operative Training Centre
APF	Australian Premium Foods
APRA	Australian Prudential Regulatory Authority
APWCF	Australian Producers' Wholesale Co-operative Federation
ASC	Australian Securities Commission
ASX	Australian Stock Exchange
ATO	Australian Taxation Office
Australian CWS/CWS	Australian Co-operative Wholesale Society
AWB	Australian Wheat Board
Berrima District	Berrima District Farm and Dairy Co-operative
BHP	Broken Hill Proprietary
BP	British Petroleum
CASGU	Centre for Co-operative Studies in Agriculture (Griffith University)

CBH	Co-operative Bulk Handling
CCA	Co-operatives Council of Australia
CCC	Co-operative Community Council
CCF	Christian Co-operative Fellowship
CCP	Core Consistent Provisions/Common Core Provisions
CCUs	Co-operative Capital Units
CDA	Co-operative Dairy Association of New South Wales Limited
CDB	Co-operative Development Branch
CDF	Co-operative Development Fund
CDP	Co-operative Development Programme
CDS	Co-operative Development Services Limited
CDS	Co-operative Development Society
CDU	Co-operative Development Unit
CEO	Chief Executive Officer
CER	Closer Economic Relationship
CFA	Co-operative Federation of Australia/Commonwealth Co-operative Federation of Australia
CFG	Co-operative Farmers' and Graziers' Direct Meat Supply
CFNSW	Co-operative Federation of New South Wales
CFQ	Co-operative Federation of Queensland
CFSA	Co-operative Federation of South Australia
CFV	Co-operative Federation of Victoria
CFWA	Co-operative Federation of Western Australia
CIC	Co-operative Insurance Company of Australia
CIS	Co-operative Insurance Society UK Limited
CNWP	Co-operatives National Working Party
COD	Fruit Marketing Committee of Direction
COR	Commonwealth Oil Refineries
CSR	Colonial Sugar Refinery
CSU	Charles Sturt University
CUQ	Co-operative Union of Queensland
English CWS/CWS	English Co-operative Wholesale
CWSQ	Co-operative Wholesale Society of Queensland
DFG	Dairy Farmers' Group
DFMC	Dairy Farmers' Milk Co-operative Limited
DFT	Department of Fair Trading
DLP	Democratic Labor Party
DMS	Domestic Market Support Scheme
DOPIE	Department of Primary Industry and Energy
Edunda Farmers'	Edunda Farmers' Co-operative Society Limited

EEC	European Economic Community
EEU	European Economic Union
FACE	Family and Community Empowerment
Farmers' and Settlers'	Farmers' and Settlers' Co-operative Company Limited
FIF	Franked Income Fund
FSA	Farmers' and Settlers' Association of Western Australia
G & N	Gippsland Butter Factories Co-operative Produce Company/ Gippsland and Northern Co-operative Company Limited
GATT	General Agreement on Trade and Tariffs
GST	Goods and Services Tax
HISCOL	Herd Improvement Services Co-operative Limited
	Industries Assistance Commission
ICA	International Co-operative Alliance
ICPA	International Co-operative Petrol Association
ICTO	International Co-operative Trading Organisation
IEL	Industrial Equity Limited
LA	Legislative Assembly
LC	Legislative Council
LEED	Local Economic and Enterprise Development
Ltd	Limited
MACC	Ministerial Advisory Committee on Co-operation
MENA	Maleny Enterprise Network Association
MINCO	Ministerial Council for Corporations
NBFI	Non-Bank Financial Institutions
NCP	National Competition Policy
NCU	National Co-op Update
NGCs	New Generation Co-operatives
NRMA	National Road Motorists Association
NSW	New South Wales
NSW CWS	New South Wales Co-operative Wholesale
NSWCUL	New South Wales Credit Union League
NT	Northern Territory
Overseas Farmers	Overseas Farmers' Wholesale Co-operative Federation
PD	Parliamentary Debates
PDS	Producers Co-operative Distributive Society Limited
PIBA	Primary Industry Bank of Australia
PIVOT	Phosphate Co-operative of Australia
PLC	Proprietary Limited Company
£	pound
PP	Parliamentary Papers

PPA	Primary Producers Association
PPU	Primary Producers' Union
Primaries	Queensland Primary Producers' Co-operative
Q/Qld	Queensland
QUD	Queensland United Dairies Association/Unity Dairy Foods Co-operative Association
RCL	Ricegrowers' Co-operative Limited
Red Comb	Poultry Farmers' Co-operative Society
RIDC	Rural Industry Development Corporation
SA	South Australia
SAFCU	South Australian Farmers' Co-operative Union
SCA	Standing Committee on Agriculture
SCAG	Standing Committee of Attorneys-General
SCAGWP	Standing Committee of Attorneys-General Working Party
SCAWP	Standing Committee on Agriculture Working Party
SEP	Social Enterprise Partnership
SMAs	Statutory Marketing Authorities
South Coast and West Camden	South Coast and West Camden Co-operative Company
Tas	Tasmania
UDFV	United Dairy Farmers of Victoria
UK	United Kingdom
USA/US	United States of America
UTS	University of Technology Sydney
VCA	Victorian Co-operative Association
VCCA	Victorian Credit Co-operatives Association
VCP	Victorian Producers' Co-operative Company
VFCHS	Victorian Federation of Co-operative Housing Societies
Vic	Victoria
VPC	Victorian Producers' Co-operative Association
WA	Western Australia
WACP	Western Australian Country Party
WCWS	Wesfarmers Co-operative Wholesale Section
Western District	Western District Co-operative Produce Company
Westralian Farmers/Wesfarmers	Westralian Farmers' Co-operative Company Limited
WOCCU	World Council of Credit Unions
WTO	World Trade Organisation
YCW	Young Christian Workers
YOGI	Young Organic Growers Group

Foreword

I *am very pleased to be writing a foreword for what is, I hope, an important contribution to the revival of the co-operative movement in Australia.*

Although we are in the middle of preparing accurate statistics of the world co-operative movement, we are undoubtedly much bigger than we ourselves or outsiders think. With over 800 individual members and providing over 100 million jobs worldwide, co-operative enterprise is a big player on the global economic stage. Many cooperatives today compete very successfully with some of the largest multinational conglomerates.

Any examination of the movement shows however the predominance of agriculture. Whether it gives itself more naturally to co-operation or not is an interesting question – and one tackled in this book. Farmers are paradoxically both individualistic and collective; conservative and radical – so no answers there! But the sharing of equipment and marketing strategies seemed to lend themselves very readily to co-operation.

I am not sure I understand why the Australian movement seems to have been overcome by the empty promises of demutualisation which offer nothing except bigger salaries for the CEO's. Australia , like many co-operative movements' countries, has a fine progressive and socially democratic tradition, not unlike your near neighbour in New Zealand which has one of the most vibrant co-operative economies in the world.

I rather agree with the author's emphasis on the democracy principle. Of all the values, that surely is the one that differentiates us from traditional capitalistic-based enterprise. Of course it can be interpreted differently, but essentially it means that no matter what is your personal stake, it gives you no extra influence in the organisation. I fail to see therefore why that means, to some, a weakening of business acumen or a deterrent to commercial success.

Cooperatives are often confused for 'not-for-profit' enterprises. This is wrong. We are for profit, but profit which is used on an unexploitative and socially just basis. We have plenty of examples worldwide of co-operative organisations that are very successful commercial businesses. Capital acquisition is not a problem for them but they don't acquire it at the expense of their co-operative ideals.

This book, I hope, will help to encourage Australia back towards its natural home – an ethically sound and commercially successful co-operative economy.

Iain Macdonald
Director General
International Co-operative Alliance
Geneva, September 2006

Mr S.W. Sargent and Mr & Mrs George Braid at the Sargent
dairy near Corndale (just outside Lismore) c1910.
Photo courtesy of Norco Co-operative Limited.

Preface

THE DEMOCRACY PRINCIPLE

'Democracy principle', as used here, refers to an idea held by Australian farmers that it is possible in a capitalist society to democratically own and control a business on a one-member-one-vote basis made all the more remarkable by the fact that for over a century, many have done so through thousands of co-operatives. In its purest expression the democracy principle is about participation and means, literally, the active involvement of members in key business and policy decisions. The book has been written in the belief that a capitalist democracy is incomplete and immature in the absence of a robust 'third sector' comprising democratic associations and businesses such as co-operatives, mutual societies and community organisations.

In co-operatives, the owners and users are identical (the mutuality principle). Traditionally, primary co-operatives have been structured on the basis of one-member-one-vote (regardless of how much a member has invested in the share capital), limited return on share capital and a share of surpluses proportionate with a member's contribution to business (the patronage principle). No matter how young or old a co-operative, how large or small, in what industry, state or nation, how variegated, how selective in applying co-operative principles, whatever the method of capital-raising, or purpose, it shares at least one quality in common with all others – the democracy principle. A co-operative may have other reasons for existence, including providing services for members, employment and creating wealth, but none more intrinsic than the one-person-one-vote principle and, apart from this, has no real claim to a distinctive identity. The democracy principle is truly the co-operative 'difference'. In this book we are concerned with the principle in so far as it relates to primary (individual) co-operatives, rather than secondary (associated) or tertiary (federated) co-operatives, which may employ other democratic voting methods.

There are almost as many definitions of co-operation and co-operatives as there are commentators. H H Bakken, for instance, speaks of co-operation as:

> ... a resultant system of economics. It is a synthesis combining the desirable qualities of the laissez-faire economy and planned economy. In so far as it is possible, the undesirable features inherent in the two older systems are not transmitted to the new system of co-operation. Its natural range of application or latitude extends from a position in which private initiative and freedom of action are preserved in a large measure to one in which the member sacrifices some individualistic functions in co-ordinating his efforts with others to attain certain ends.

Studying co-operation in animals, the evolutionary biologist Lee Alan Dugatkin describes co-operation as a 'self-interested refusal to be spiteful ...quasi-altruistic selfishness' and concludes that this can be either an *achievement* in itself; something a group does; or a *behaviour* designed to achieve co-operation:

> Co-operation is an outcome that, despite potential relative costs to the individual is 'good' in some appropriate way for the members of a group and whose achievement requires collective action.

The International Co-operative Alliance (ICA) defines a co-operative as:

...an autonomous association of persons united voluntarily to meet their common economic, social, and cultural needs and aspirations through a jointly-owned and democratically-controlled enterprise.

Co-operatives are based on the values of self-help, self-responsibility, democracy, equality, equity and solidarity. In the tradition of their founders, co-operative members believe in the ethical values of honesty, openness, social responsibility and caring for others.

ICA Co-operative Principles (1995) contemplate:

Voluntary and Open Membership

Co-operatives are voluntary organisations, open to all persons able to use their services and willing to accept the responsibilities of membership, without gender, social, racial, political or religious discrimination.

Democratic Member Control

Co-operatives are democratic organisations controlled by their members, who actively participate in setting their policies and making decisions. Men and women serving as elected representatives are accountable to the membership. In primary co-operatives members have equal voting rights (one member, one vote) and co-operatives at other levels are also organised in a democratic manner.

Member Economic Participation

Members contribute equitably to, and democratically control, the capital of their co-operative. At least part of that capital is usually the common property of the co-operative. Members usually receive limited compensation, if any, on capital subscribed as a condition of membership. Members allocate surpluses for any or all of the following purposes: developing their co-operative, possibly by setting up reserves, part of which at least would be indivisible; benefiting members in proportion to their transactions with the co-operative; and supporting other activities approved by the membership.

Autonomy and Independence

Co-operatives are autonomous, self-help organisations controlled by their members. If they enter into agreements with other organisations, including governments, or raise capital from external sources, they do so on terms that ensure democratic control by their members and maintain their co-operative autonomy.

Education, Training and Information

Co-operatives provide education and training for their members, elected representatives, managers, and employees so they can contribute effectively to the development of their co-operatives. They inform the general public – particularly young people and opinion leaders – about the nature and benefits of co-operation.

Co-operation among Co-operatives

Co-operatives serve their members most effectively and strengthen the co-operative movement by working together through local, national, regional and international structures.

Concern for Community

Co-operatives work for the sustainable development of their communities through policies approved by their members.

The origins of the Australian farmer co-operative movement can be traced back to the Rochdale Equitable Pioneers of Lancashire, England, who, in 1844 opened a shop in Toad Lane, Rochdale, applying principles which became the basis of a great international co-operative movement. (A history of the Rochdale consumer movement in the antipodes is found in the present author's *A Middle Way: Rochdale Co-operatives in New South Wales, 1859-1986*.) Rochdale idealists sought to create a 'Co-operative Commonwealth', a democratic, social-economy rising from a decentralised network of consumer co-operatives (shops) linked to primary producer co-operatives through a giant co-operative wholesale trading entity creating capital to fund other co-operative enterprises in the services, manufacturing and tertiary sectors, coordinated and governed by a Co-operative Union, a grand 'parliament' of democratic organisations. An elegant theory, Rochdale consumerism came unstuck at key points, for example: the inability of co-operative consumers and producers to co-operate; the trouncing of idealism by pragmatists; the failure to educate; and a propensity to fritter dividends rather than invest surpluses in co-operative development. By the 1970s, the Rochdale consumer movement was largely a spent force in Australia, but elements of its theory, which originally inspired farmers to co-operate, survived in the agricultural co-operative movement.

The Australian farmer co-operative movement began in the late nineteenth century, almost certainly in dairying on the south coast of New South Wales. Borrowing from Rochdale ideas, farmers constructed co-operatives for the handling and processing of commodities as the basis of their movement, not shops. Periodically farmer leaders argued for co-operation as a way of life; a distinctive, transformative philosophy suited to rural life and superior to aggressive, competitive capitalism. Some even argued for a 'Co-operative Commonwealth' and were seriously listened to around the turn of the twentieth century. Their voice was lost, however, in the approach to Federation in 1901 and in disagreements with consumers which saw unruly markets develop before World War I, requiring governments to enter the field of industry organisation. Nineteenth century co-operative idealism seldom resurfaced in the farmer co-operative movement thereafter, but, even as statutory regulation seized agriculture in the interwar period, some leaders continued to argue for the co-operative organisation of industry, describing co-operation as a higher calling, superior to capitalism or socialism – a 'middle way'. Traces of idealism were still evident in the movement until quite late in the century. For instance, Producers' Distributive Society (PDS) Co-operative General Manager G A J Beytagh told the 1974 Co-operative Federation of Australia (CFA) convention:

> *People will stay with something they call a movement so long as it serves a deep social and psychological hunger as well as a physical need... Be successful, but be different! [The co-operative mission is]...contributing to social reform, human betterment, the quality of life and a just, compassionate Australian society'.*

While co-operatives were businesses, traditionalists like Beytagh insisted they were not solely about making money but also about 'self-help', service, economic democracy, autonomy and independence. Such views waned somewhat after the 1980s when a new brand of co-operative leaders emerged to focus farmer co-operatives on individual wealth accumulation and market competitiveness arguing that co-operative philosophy was purely a commercial philosophy with no higher meaning. No matter how defined, co-operatives represent farmers' determination to achieve just reward for their labour and other investments and were created to drive out 'middle men' and to supply farmers with goods and services of the required quality at competitive prices. They have enabled aggregated farmer-members to pool resources, minimise input costs, maximise the value of products and share profits from value-added processing, distribution and consumer sales. The purposes and structure of Australian farmer co-operatives and co-operative companies have varied over time and across jurisdictions but essentially they serve to receive and dispose of members' produce, process or market rural produce and provide other services to farmers including, herd or crop improvement, the purchase of farm requisites such as seed, fertilisers and chemicals and services like transport, grading, packing, storage, promotion, wholesaling and exporting. Australian farmer co-operation has normally extended to post farm-gate activities and little evidence of on-farm co-operation has been found.

While co-operatives like any business must be economically viable, theoretically the goal of a co-operative is not simply profitability but the long-term benefit of members and the community. Key phrases in understanding traditional co-operative philosophy are 'self-help through interdependence' and 'collective stability is more important than individual gain'. In co-operatives it is generally agreed that member interests always come before institutional efficiency. Throughout Australian co-operatives' history, co-operators have frequently subordinated pure business considerations to co-operative principles, producing policies often more about farmer 'intuition' or 'heritage' than economic rationality. This has been a function of the democracy principle.

As organisations set up to prove a common benefit to members, co-operatives often refund surpluses to members and provide services at cost but are normally not required to service shareholder value. Co-operatives are similar in some ways to corporations, however, in that they have limited liability and objects and powers embodied in the structure but are unique in that the business is democratically owned and controlled. Some argue that apart from this, there is no compelling economic reason for co-operatives to exist. In addition, co-operatives have been impelled by uniform taxation and business compliance laws to apply a corporate structure with prescribed rules and regulations, including the 'mutuality principle' for taxation purposes (at least 90 per cent of business done with members). Co-operators normally elect a board of directors and may provide share capital, some of which may be retained for business development and for ensuring continued control of the co-operative by its owners. Ideally, farmers support the co-operative with their business, invest in it, nourish a bond of association and uphold equitable, democratic principles, which emphasise the importance of the *individual in unity with others and not his or her capital power*.

Co-operating farmers hold that ownership and control of the inputs, supply, processing and marketing of farm products is the only dependable way of underpinning the value of their basic business (the family farm), maintain farm profitability, adjust production to demand, provide healthy competition for private-profit merchants and processors and ride out adverse trading conditions (particularly in international markets). Historically, this has been important for marketing co-operatives, particularly wholesale traders in perishable commodities such as fruit, fish and fresh milk, or where prices are volatile. By eliminating 'middle men' from the economic cycle and providing a dependable vehicle for distribution of commodities to markets, co-operatives have given farmers a greater sense of security and confidence, especially in periods of gluts, economic downturn or drought and flood, to which much of Australia is prone. They have also helped farmers exercise quality control and to achieve crop variety and herd improvements, enhancing productivity. Processing and manufacturing co-operatives have enabled farmers to add value to commodities through the supply chain, thereby exerting market force, operating in their interests. Supply co-operatives have helped protect individual farmers against market forces which would impose upon them a price-taker role, positively influencing post farm-gate price leadership by encouraging open markets in so far as for-profit merchants and processors must compete for supplies with them and are not free to set prices independently. In this way, farmer co-operators hold, co-operatives deliver effective competition, keep market participants 'on their toes' and ensure they stay 'honest'.

Looking across the Wilsons River at the Norco Lismore factory (present day).
Photo courtesy of Norco Co-operative Limited.

In the broader political economy, co-operatives have served to decentralise industrial ownership (to a limited degree) and have been employed by governments with mixed success for purposes of immigration, rural settlement, encouraging new industries, improving farm productivity, developing international trade, jobs creation and as vehicles for the dismantling of statutory marketing authorities (SMAs).

The United Nations estimated in 1994 that the livelihood of nearly three billion people, or half of the world's population, was enriched through co-operatives. In 2003, over 760 million people were members of co-operatives around the world. At time of writing the Geneva-based ICA involves 219 member organisations in approximately ninety countries.

The exact figures for Australian co-operatives are not known, because no authoritative statistics exist, but it seems clear they do not compare favourably with other Organisation for Economic Co-operation and Development (OECD) nations. Following an extensive takeover and demutualisation phenomenon beginning in the 1970s it was estimated early in the new millennium that somewhere between 2600 and 2800 co-operatives operated in Australia, registered under co-operatives law, together with eight large mainly Victorian co-operative companies registered under company law. Excluding financial co-operatives and co-operative companies they produced an annual turnover of approximately $5 billion and held total assets of around $3 billion. Over 300 small to medium-sized agricultural co-operatives were also operating. In addition mutual financial co-operatives (of which there were 213 credit unions and eighteen building societies) held $35.5 billion in total assets.

Over 90 per cent of all Australian co-operatives were in the three eastern states – Victoria, New South Wales and Queensland. In the largest and most diverse of the Australian states co-operative movements, New South Wales, Jayo Wickremarachichi and Andrew Passey tell us that in 1999/2000 the annual turnover of co-operatives amounted to approximately $4.36 billion, excluding 'foreign' (interstate) co-operatives and co-operative companies. This accounted for approximately 85 per cent of total Australian co-operative sector turnover! The sector was asymmetrically developed physically with a handful of farmer co-operatives comprising 39,791 members in dairying, fishing, fruit and vegetable, grains, cotton, livestock, sugar, rice and miscellaneous primary industries accounting for most economic activity. Most co-operatives were very small, with 76.2 per cent holding assets of less than $1 million and only 4.1 per cent holding assets exceeding $10 million. Over 75 per cent of co-operatives produced an annual turnover of less than $1 million. Excluding financial co-operatives, New South Wales' 849 general co-operatives had 1.29 million memberships, but just one co-operative (a consumer co-operative) accounted for 892,920 of this. While the aggregate number of Australian co-operatives compared unfavourably with OECD nations, thirteen co-operatives were listed in the top 1,000 of Australian businesses, albeit some already well advanced in a demutualisation process:

CO-OPERATIVES AND CO-OPERATIVE COMPANIES IN TOP 1000 AUSTRALIAN BUSINESSES 2000	
	Ranking
Dairy Farmers' Group (New South Wales)	119
Murray-Goulburn (Victoria)	133
BONLAC Foods (Victoria)	144
Ricegrowers' Co-operative Limited (New South Wales)	276
Namoi Cotton (New South Wales)	323
Mackay Sugar (Queensland)	467
Capricorn Society (Western Australia)	674
Australian Unity Friendly Society (Victoria)	747
Co-operative Bulk Handling (Western Australia)	787
Warrnambool Cheese and Butter (Victoria)	803
Tatura Milk (Victoria)	840
Norco (New South Wales)	846

New co-operatives were forming, particularly in 'niche' and 'boutique' markets in fields previously dominated by SMAs, but the rate of co-operative formations was slowing and it was uncertain whether co-operatives would dwindle or experience an unexpected renaissance.

In seeking to understand how the democracy principle has operated and was adapted over time it is important to understand its vital relationship with that other co-operative imperative – capital adequacy. Co-operative capital traditionally has been employed for mutual, rather than individual, benefit and has been drawn from two main sources: members, either by subscription or deposits, including retained rebates; or debt. Markets, however, determine the value of scarce resources in capitalist economies, including capital. The increasing capital intensive nature of value-adding processes involving greater volumes, technological sophistication and market differentiation, together with improved competition, placed immense pressure on the capital position of commercially-oriented co-operatives after the 1980s. For example, processing milk was no longer a simple separator technology but a complex and expensive biotechnological activity requiring sophisticated plant – and capital to fund this. Large, agricultural co-operatives were also competing against immense, vertically-integrated agribusinesses with ready access to capital in addition to negotiating with huge supermarket chains in a ruthless 'auction' for market share. An insatiable hunger for capital gave rise to a 'co-operative dilemma', centring upon the tension in co-operative structure between democracy and capital adequacy, which dominated co-operative politics late in the century. An exploration of this dilemma forms a major theme of the book.

Co-operatives have tended to be very conservative in their financial structure, in that member-contributions to equity are low, particularly direct capital contributions to funding assets, and they generally have relied on borrowings. Revolving fund schemes were not uncommon but, with financial institutions reluctant to fund organisations with poor earnings records, deferred or long-term debt was not a feature of Australian agricultural co-operatives for most of the century. Generally speaking, for much of the century farmers were content to receive government-regulated prices for commodities *plus* dividends rather than to fund their co-operative adequately. Indeed, co-operatives tended to minimise taxation liability by distributing surpluses, weakening the asset base and dissipating funds which might have been used for growth and investment. Some directors argued for fund retention and exposure to corporate taxation, but very few – members would not let them! Farmers preferred 'money in the pocket' and to offset income against farm investments. The resultant lack of investment in co-operatives, with some notable exceptions, often saw them reliant upon outmoded equipment and plant, not keeping pace with technological advancements and becoming less efficient than competitors – or even their own farmer shareholders! For much of the century, in regulated markets, this was tenable but with deregulation and improved competition, capital had to come from somewhere, and quickly. There were real limits to how much farmers could or would invest in their co-operatives, applying a brake to co-operative competitiveness while strengthening a case for radically altering co-operative structure, making it more flexible for fund-raising purposes.

Farmers reluctant to relinquish the democracy principle in locating capital found themselves pitched on the horns of the 'co-operative dilemma'. New leaders argued that if ownership capital was to be restricted to members, they should be *obliged* to provide it themselves. The alternative was being driven out of business! Compulsory bonus share schemes, however, in many instances did not resolve the dilemma and gave rise to a 'management-crisis' where experts, hired more for business skills than an understanding of co-operation, were required to manage members' capital profitably, not necessarily coinciding with traditional member-expectations or co-operative values. Questions also arose about how to raise member expectations in respect of investments without creating shareholder 'classes', which might dilute the vital bond of association, and how to redeem compulsorily-subscribed shares in a downturn. Farmer-investors needed to feel confident that they could redeem equity when exiting farming and to accept that they probably could not sell or borrow against such investments, possibly placing them in further debt to retain farm ownership while investments remained locked up in a co-operative. This required a mighty act of faith. Who was to say, anyway, that a cohesive bond of association was not more important in matching competition than amassing capital?

In some cases new breed managers urged farmers to *share* ownership with external investors and *separate* the roles of farmers as custodians of democracy from investors in 'hybrid' organisations, jeopardising the democracy principle. Farmers generally believed that democratic ownership *and* control were indivisible, for the leverage this gave in markets and could not exist in a shared ownership arrangement. Sceptical farmers demanded to know how leaders proposed to reward external ownership *without* losing control because, inevitably, investors would push a case serving their interests. The rejoinder was to challenge members to solve the riddle of keeping control *and* retaining ownership if this meant being driven out of business. But why would anyone invest in something the primary purpose of which was to enhance member returns, and not have a vote? (Torgerson) And, if a co-operative could not raise sufficient capital from members to serve their needs adequately, why should it *not* convert to a company? (Munkner) Certainly, solving the 'co-operative dilemma' was vital by the 1990s or, many co-operative leaders believed, commercial co-operatives could be a thing of the past. Consequently, in seeking to radically reinvent themselves, some co-operatives assumed a border line not-for-profit designation and experienced an identity crisis: what did co-operatives really stand for – providing services or accumulating capital?

The book began life in the early 1980s in the Australian National University History Department as part of doctoral research, a substantive element of which was published in *Middle Way*. Additional data were located in recorded interviews conducted through the National Library of Australia Oral History Department, with the co-operation of the Co-operative Federation of Australia (CFA), the Co-operative Federation of Victoria (CFV) and the Co-operative Federation of Western Australia (CFWA) and in an extensive archive held by the (recently disbanded) Australian Centre for Co-operatives Research and Development (ACCoRD). Repeated requests made to the co-operative sector for information to assist the study yielded very few contributions, a clue to general apathy and low priority given to education.

A central question motivating research was, why in liberal-capitalist Australia has democracy been largely confined to party politics and has not extended extensively to economics? While *Middle Way* explained why the Rochdale consumer movement failed to make a significant impact upon the Australian political economy, I was curious to know whether this was the same for farmer co-operatives operating upon an infinitely greater economic base. Certainly, in a national economy characterised for much of the period by a rural division of labour, agricultural co-operatives made an immense contribution to economic and national development and warrant study for this reason alone. Perhaps they would also provide evidence challenging the conventional wisdom that 'democracy and business do not mix'. A longitudinal study considering the experience of farmer co-operatives across a century of tumultuous change might shed light on why farmers formed co-operatives and help answer the question: if the democracy principle is such a good idea why did farmer co-operatives not make a greater impact upon Australian social and economic affairs?

Notwithstanding the title, the book considers not only farmer co-operatives; although primarily so; but also rural communities in which co-operatives have served, public policy affecting co-operatives' development and co-operative movement politics, where unity perennially has been elusive. It was difficult to discover a key to the interlocking nature of a 'higgledy-piggledy' co-operatives' history and several models were tried. While the present arrangement has deficiencies, in so far as events considered at state level often require restating briefly in the national context, and vice versa, and discussion on the dairying co-operative movement needed to be broken into broad industry and case study 'book ends', for example, the framework integrates the content well and permits useful analysis. Numerous strands relevant to individual co-operatives, specific industries, legislation, regulatory regimes and federal, state and regional co-operative movements are interwoven with mainstream political and economic events, to weave the tapestry of the story.

Where the histories of the consumer and producer co-operative movements intersect, occasionally information found in *Middle Way* is reiterated.

It is important to note at the outset that no such thing as a rural 'co-operative movement', as such, has ever existed in Australia, although several attempts have been made. The term is used figuratively for convenience. State and federal 'co-operative movements' organised in federations have existed over time, generally poorly supported and often operating on a weak mandate. Indeed, ruinous disunity is a recurrent theme in discussion.

Another important distinction to be made is that between 'co-operatives' and 'co-operative companies'. Essentially, for most of the century, the former had no fixed capital, subscribed strictly to the democracy principle and were described in co-operatives law, whereas the latter were registered mainly under company law, often varied the democracy principle to accommodate investor interests and subscribed to the mutuality principle, not necessarily for philosophical reasons, but for taxation benefits conferred. Nevertheless, to the degree co-operative companies have applied the democracy principle and influenced co-operatives' history, they are included in discussion.

The study has been necessarily selective as sources (and resources) became available and it has not been possible to be as comprehensive as one would wish. Unfortunately, resources did not extend to a treatment of Aboriginal co-operatives, Tasmania or the Territories, Papua-New Guinea and Pacific Island co-operation (in which Australia played an important role), or to the fishing industry. The treatment of farmer co-operatives in South Australia and Queensland is rudimentary, but sufficient to demonstrate the great diversity of the Australian rural co-operative movement. Much discussion on Victoria occurs in the context of the dairy industry. For the same reason a bibliography is not provided but extensive notes will guide the reader in this regard. The author apologises in advance for such 'sins of omission' while noting the desirability of leaving something for other researchers. Unless otherwise stated all monetary figures are in Australian dollars.

Ideally, to write such a history one needs to be a lawyer, economist, politician, accountant and farmer. The present author is none of these things but a social historian with an interest in co-operatives and the idea of economic democracy. It is a story which needed to be told before the data are lost, key personages pass away and an extraordinary chapter in Australian rural history disappears forever. The book celebrates the vision and courage of farmer co-operators dedicated to the democracy principle while offering a sobering reminder that powerful forces inside and outside the co-operative movement do not share this vision. It is thrown into the torrent of public debate as a 'message in a bottle' to contempories and future generations who might have an interest in co-operation and wish to know how and why the Australian farmer co-operative movement took the shape it did in the twentieth century.[1]

Part I

DAIRY

*L*and pressures and technological change in the 1880s saw dairy farmers on the south coast of New South Wales and elsewhere establish co-operatives to drive out 'middle men' and assert farmer control over produce. The co-operative idea rapidly spread throughout Australian dairying districts. Disagreements developed between 'bogus' and 'genuine' co-operatives and free-trade and protectionist co-operatives over market access and marketing models, especially in New South Wales and Victoria, weakening co-operative unity.

By World War One the dairy co-operative movement boasted noteworthy physical development at a regional level but doubts had arisen about the merits of voluntary co-operation as a suitable basis for organizing industry. Increasing calls for government intervention from within the movement and from unions were boosted by emergency wartime regulations, which lasted until 1921.

After the war nineteenth century notions of co-operation as an economically and socially transformative philosophy gave way to a more utilitarian view of co-operatives as a practical business model suited to rural settlement schemes and the enhancement of agricultural productivity. Between the wars, co-operation as a basis for industry self-regulation was superseded by regulatory models, reducing the field for co-operative development and confining co-operatives to relatively simple economic functions in supply, handling, processing and distribution. The Great Depression and the return of war in 1939 simply accelerated this process of market socialization, driving dairy co-operatives to the margins of economic relevance in heavily regulated markets.

Industry rationalization and corporate raids saw much of the traditional agricultural co-operative movement's heartland disappear in the 1970s. When deadlines were set in the early 1990s to deregulate the dairy industry, co-operatives avidly sought capital for growth and market share, creating a 'co-operative dilemma' in balancing the capital and democracy imperatives in co-operative structure. In 2000, when the Australian market milk industry was deregulated, the few remaining co-operatives were required urgently to reappraise their rationale and modus operandi.

The cream boat "Sunshine II" with a load of cream cans for the factory.
Photo courtesy of Norco Co-operative Limited.

Chapter One

The New South Wales And Victorian Dairy Co-operative Movements To World War I

Introduction

As far as we know, farmer supply co-operatives emerged on the south coast of New South Wales in the 1880s designed to eliminate 'middle men' and improve returns. The co-operative idea spread with migrating dairying families and co-operative creameries and central processing co-operatives were formed extensively throughout dairying districts. With improvements to transport and refrigeration the fledgling dairy co-operative movement sought to enter exports, until then the jealously guarded domain of proprietors, developing trade with the giant English Co-operative Wholesale Society (CWS). In a contest for this trade, 'bogus' and 'genuine' co-operatives vied with each other. 'Bogus' co-operatives were investor-controlled and 'genuine' co-operatives, farmer controlled. After the takeover of a 'genuine' co-operative by a 'bogus' co-operative company, Charles Meares championed voluntary co-operation as a basis for organising industry and led the formation of a co-operative processor which survives today, albeit much transformed: Dairy Farmers Limited.

Meanwhile, Victorian dairying co-operation was developing along different lines, more amenable to government involvement, less doctrinaire in the interpretation of co-operative principles and influenced more by protectionist thinking. Inevitably, states-rights issues and disagreements between the northern free-traders and southern protectionists over marketing models, spilled into co-operative politics.

Federation saw co-operatives remain cemented in inadequate ex-colonial legislation, hampering unity and development. In the first decade of the new century, the dairying co-operative movement failed to unite around common objectives or construct stable national marketing and industry bodies, leaving an organisational vacuum for governments to fill and setting the shape of the modern movement.

With calls for government intervention coming from consumers, trade unions, trading partners and some sections of the co-operative movement itself, the Commonwealth Government tentatively entered the field of dairy industry export quality control under constitutional external powers. World War I and the imposition of emergency regulations delivered a fillip to government intervention, including the statutory pooling of commodities, which created a precedent for a centralised orderly marketing regime. After the war, it would no longer be a case of co-operative advocates like C E D Meares resisting regulation, for that was an established fact, but of constructing a model superior to it.

Early co-operation in the New South Wales Dairy Industry

In the late 1870s and early 1880s dairy farmers on the south coast of New South Wales collaborated in purchasing expensive new technology and organised to eliminate 'middle men', that is commission agents and merchants interceding in the economic cycle between producer and consumer, reducing returns to farmers.

South coast dairying communities in the Illawarra region south of Sydney around Albion Park and Kiama were close knit, sharing many characteristics with urban industrial communities where Rochdale consumerism also flourished in the late nineteenth century. Both were communities familiar with hard work and adversity, where a strong work ethic prevailed and a close bond of association forged in shared experience tied families and communities together. Urban industrial and rural dairying communities also shared a Victorian ethos of self-reliance and defiance of anyone contriving to steal rewards legitimately theirs. There was little time for leisure and, as in mining communities where Rochdale co-operatives proliferated, the church, predominantly Protestant, particularly Methodist or Presbyterian, played an important role in community life. The beautiful coastal harbour town of Kiama, around which the dairy co-operative movement began, had more churches than pubs in 1867: five to two. Stuart Piggins has observed that while churches in the region were conservative in theology and social and moral values helping to influence a conservative, religious society, this was not paralleled in the community's politics where a strong radical clerical tendency existed seeking to build bridges between capital and labour. This is where co-operation flourished.

Most dairy farms ranged in size between 80 and 160 acres and women played a major role in their management. While the men were engaged in clearing, ring-barking, ploughing, fencing and other back-breaking work, women would run the household (normally caring for up to eight children), drive the herd, milk the cows twice a day, sterilise utensils, tend poultry and vegetable gardens, and climb out of bed at two in the morning in summer months to prepare butter in the cool, for market. In poorer families, women slogged alongside men with the manual work, too.[1]

At the same time, the 'system' – as a network of agents and merchants operating in Sussex Street, Sydney, was commonly referred to by dairy farmers – combined through informal patronage and conspiracy to drive down returns to primary producers with no benefit to consumers. These 'middle men' were widely perceived by farmers as the main reason for a failure to share in the general prosperity of the period before the 1890s depression. Given improvements in refrigeration and transport, farmers began seriously to consider the possibility of co-operation as an alternative to the existing marketing 'system'.

Farmer discussion turned to democratic methods of industry self-regulation along lines suggested by the then burgeoning Rochdale retail store consumer movement but, preoccupied with the practical running of farms and with limited resources, farmers were unable to organise effectively. Moreover, a radical, urban-based idea like Rochdale co-operation, essentially a consumerist theory, was viewed askance by many primary producers, suspicious of urban theorists. Farmers remained non-committal until technological innovation virtually compelled co-operation.

John Weston, the editor of *The Kiama Independent*, who was well acquainted with co-operation in Lancashire, sustained a vigorous editorial campaign through the late 1870s, canvassing the idea of co-operatives for farmers. Learning of this, Sussex Street agents immediately transferred advertising from Weston's *Independent* to competitors and visited farms carrying gifts, promises and horrific tales of alleged co-operative failures in Britain. One farmer wrote:

> When visiting the various districts these plenipotentiaries of the 'system' developed a marked tendency towards devoutness and made a point of attending divine worship on Sundays where the opportunity of meeting a number of farmers at once was too good to miss. It was remarkable the effect these continual visits had upon many farmers. They proved effective brakes to the wheels of slow progress that was being made by the great Co-operative Movement.

Weston persisted and, in 1879, organised a meeting in the Old Temperance Hall, Kiama, which brought together dairy producers from Wollongong to the Shoalhaven River and from up on the adjacent tableland. Roundly denouncing the 'system', farmers appointed representatives to tour dairying districts and locate support for 'self-help co-operation'.

The South Coast and West Camden Co-operative Company

The first known co-operative company in New South Wales, and possibly Australia, for the disposal of farm and dairy produce was formed from this action: the South Coast and West Camden Co-operative Company. Registering under New South Wales' company law, since no useful co-operative legislation existed, South Coast and West Camden opened selling floors in Sussex Street, Sydney, in June 1880. Immense consignments were immediately withdrawn from the 'system' by farmers and sent to the fledgling co-operative. T C Kennedy describes the opening day.

> The only dairy produce which came to Sydney by rail came from Camden, Campbelltown and Berrima districts, or by steamers twice a week. Mondays and Thursdays steamers arrived from Wollongong, Kiama and Shoalhaven. One steamer a week worked from Merimbula and Bega and one from Moruya. The principal consignments of dairy produce were for the [Co-operative] Company. It has been detailed how the agents' carts returned from the wharf early in the morning empty. Carrier after carrier had to be engaged to convey the butter, bacon and cheese to the Company's floor while many agents along the street had nothing else to do but stand outside their doors and watch what was going on at the Company's premises. There was quite a dislocation among the grocers. They came as usual to the particular agents for supplies of butter, et cetera, but the agents had hardly any to sell. This led to a kind of stampede for the Company's floor where, not only the staff was going as hard as it could, but even a number of the directors were there to lend a hand. It was a trying day because the Company did not know anything of the financial standing of their clients and thus a certain risk was undertaken in opening accounts. Notwithstanding the fact that the consignment was large the Company closed its doors on the evening of the opening day with clear floors and an advance of three pence per pound in the price of butter, a refutation of the old tale the 'system' used to spin about glutted markets and unsaleable consignments. Succeeding days' business showed further improvement and by the third day the price of butter advanced from five pence to nine pence per pound and the store closed each day with clear floors. So much for the beginning.[2]

Co-operative factories

After the centrifugal (cream) separator was introduced into New South Wales from Denmark in 1881 (where a burgeoning dairy co-operative movement had begun); ironically reducing farmer returns through unregulated market discounting; farmers in the Kiama, Robertson, Candelo, Burrawang and Camden districts in a south-west arc around Sydney co-operated to buy this expensive machinery. In this context, discussion turned to co-operative butter and cheese processing factories.

Pointing to South Coast and West Camden's success as proof that co-operation worked for *distribution*, John Weston now advocated establishment by farmers of co-operative butter factories for *production*. Interested farmers from Kiama, Jamberoo and surrounding areas clubbed together in 1884 to send D C Dymock to Denmark to study co-operative production there. After studying Dymock's report, farmers contributed £2,000 and developed a co-operative butter factory at Albion Park in 1885: the Pioneer Co-operative. Farmers simply delivered produce to the roadway and the co-operative did the rest. This rationalisation produced an outcry from local shopkeepers, alarmed that now only *one* man would be required to carry farmers' produce to town for treatment instead of several, potentially harming businesses. Rumours spread about disease, cheating and waste at the factory, but Pioneer Co-operative survived and was popular with farmers.

Other co-operative factories soon sprang up. In 1887 the Woodstock Co-operative Dairy Factory started at Jamberoo with others following at Gerringong, Berry, Jasper Brush, Kangaroo Valley, Barrengarry, Robertson, Wooragee, Jindyandy and elsewhere.

Further improvements to refrigeration made storage and the export of dairy products practicable and helped to reduce seasonal cycles of gluts and scarcities and destabilising price fluctuations. Pasteurisation in 1899 brought new sophistication and marketing potential to the industry, aiding further rationalisation while permitting more people to enter dairying. The industry was further stimulated by the introduction of improved centrifugal separators in the late 1880s, the Babcock Test in 1892 (which accurately measured the butter fat content of milk), the completion of the railway link from Sydney to the Shoalhaven River in 1893, the introduction of improved pastures, better milking shed design and herd improvement programmes. These improvements exacerbated land pressures and contributed to a Diaspora of dairying families from the Illawarra region along the east coast north and south and into other colonies, carrying with them co-operative ideas and practical knowledge of co-operation.

Aided in many cases by Sou'coasters (as migrants from the region were known) as they took up new properties, more co-operatives started through the Hunter, Clarence, Manning and Richmond river systems to the north, into Southern Queensland and up onto the Atherton Tableland, and south into the Bega Valley and Gippsland region of Victoria. Dairy co-operatives developed in many areas where sou'coasters settled: at Wauchope for example (1887), at Singleton and Ulmarra (Clarence River Pioneer Co-operative, 1899) and others soon after at Osterley, Koyuga and Bowthornes. By 1894 co-operative dairy factories were well developed in the big scrub (littoral rainforest) stretching from Byron Bay inland, possibly the first of these developing at Seccombe's Farm on the Ballina Road in 1888. Twenty more co-operative factories formed in various parts over the next six years with sou-coasters prominent in the development of many. Some regional newspapers, for example *The Northern Star* at Lismore, regularly published south coast news in 1888; special articles for sou'coaster settlers; and broadcast information on co-operation in the Illawarra and adjacent regions. Some historians dispute the influence of sou'coasters on the spread of dairying co-operation and no doubt co-operative factories were independently established in districts where sou'coasters were not well represented.[3]

Central processing co-operatives

Attempts in the early 1890s to establish central co-operative creameries to process milk, however, failed to attract sufficient capital in the economically depressed conditions and farmers, therefore, remained dependent upon private-profit enterprise for processing. However, in 1893 settlers in the Richmond River region of the north coast, many of them sou'coasters, initiated a successful attempt to rationalise the proliferation of co-operative factories dotting the landscape: North Coast Fresh Food and Cold Storage Co-operative Limited (later, North Coast Co-operative Company [Norco]), which opened a central creamery in Byron Bay in 1893. Norco, well placed climatically and geographically to serve both Brisbane and Sydney markets when southern production seasonally declined, quickly developed into one of New South Wales' most successful dairy co-operatives and is still operating at time of writing.

Soon after Norco began, the Illawarra Central Co-operative Factory opened at Albion Park on the south coast and other coastal creameries followed at Nowra and Milton.

An attempt to enter exports

By the early 1890s South Coast and West Camden was the largest dairying agency on Sussex Street. However, it was caught between the need to capitalise the handling of greater volumes attending productivity gains, on the one hand, and depressed markets, on the other. Carrying debts of £48 000, rumours spread about the co-operative's imminent collapse.

Responding to these rumours, South Coast and West Camden directors announced plans to trade out of difficulties by entering export markets, until then the jealously guarded precinct of private traders, and appealed for farmer solidarity in a determined drive to rid the export industry of speculators and commission sharks. Private traders, in turn, attempted to woo supplier co-operatives and shareholders away from South Coast and West Camden with offers of better spot prices. Some farmers, including Norco members, elected to trade independently of South Coast and West Camden and to accept the best prices available, precipitating acrimonious exchanges between co-operatives, which were not soon forgotten. Meanwhile, cold climate farmers in the Berrima district on the highlands south west of Sydney, who were formerly associated with private operators and now faced severe economic hardship, decided to co-operate independently, opening a rival selling floor to South Coast and West Camden in Sussex Street: the Berrima District Farm and Dairy Co-operative (hereafter, Berrima District).

Unable to unite the co-operative ranks and controlling insufficient of the market to make exports feasible, South Coast and West Camden's export-led recovery plan lost momentum. Certainly this first known instance of a co-operative-led export drive was premature. Australian rural co-operation was still primitive and disorganised, financially strapped and with no stable institutional machinery to support farmer-controlled exports. Of greater import for the future of Australian co-operation was the apparent reluctance of co-operatives to co-operate, preferring to develop opportunistically along regional lines. The fierce 'localism' this induced, admirable as it might have been for community building, was not conducive to co-operative unity or to sensible industry rationalisation.[5]

Developing co-operative trade: the English CWS in Australia, 1896

Learning that representatives of the giant British Rochdale consumer co-operative, the English Co-operative Wholesale Society (English CWS), would tour the colonies in 1896 and concerned that local co-operatives were poorly placed to capitalise on trade opportunities, the New South Wales Department of Agriculture appealed to producers to co-operate. In what may be the first instance of an Australian government encouraging co-operative development for economic advancement, the department broadcast, 'Co-operation is good for farmers…producing a better feeling among farmers…instead of a close and often jealous and selfish feeling.'

The English CWS was truly enormous, consisting in 1895 of 250,000 members producing an annual turnover of £16 million Sterling and with depots in Montreal, New York, Copenhagen, Hamburg and Aarhis, which it plied with a fleet of six ships. Having invested £100,000 in the construction of the Manchester Canal, which was completed in 1894, the CWS was keen to recoup this outlay through trade with foreign and colonial primary producers linked co-operatively with its vast network of northern English and Midlands' consumer co-operatives. CWS trade with the colonies had already begun before the visit, in tallow for soaps and leather for shoes. Australia was now to play a key role in the giant multi-national's expansionary trading programme. The question was whether the rudimentary colonial 'co-operative movement' was capable of participating in this coherently?[6]

John Plummer, a buyer for the Sydney Civil Service Co-operative, a department store, spoke at many public meetings promoting the English CWS tour and prepared numerous journal articles calling upon Australians to 'co-operate with the old country'. The English CWS was hungry for Australia's dairy products, Plummer said, and a direct *barter* system involving colonial primary products and CWS manufactured goods would advantage both parties. There was one condition, however: trade should occur only through *co-operative* organisations. For colonial farmers to access British consumer markets through CWS, therefore, they would have to do so through co-operatives, or some semblance of a co-operative.[7]

The rural press was full of stories about the visit, reporting that a Central Co-operative Board had been set up in Melbourne to orchestrate the 'Great International Co-operative Movement'.[8]

Arriving first in Adelaide, CWS delegates spoke of the 'humane and godlike principles of co-operation and the joyful marriage between labour and capital' it theoretically embodied. After touring the fruit growing regions of South Australia delegates moved on to Victoria to meet representatives of co-operatives and a 'Co-operative Dairy Distribution Society' (discussed below). Wherever they went, the visitors emphasised that they were interested only in 'orderly' marketing, ideally occurring through co-operative associations, but where this was impossible, co-operative trade under the auspices of state instrumentalities would do. Delegates also pointed out that, while they represented British consumers, in the colonies producers were their 'starting point'.[9]

In Sydney press reports spoke of the visit 'shaking the colony to its foundations'. Delegates were afforded a civic reception in the Town Hall, inspected South Coast and West Camden selling floors and were introduced to the New South Wales Board of Exports. Playing on colonial jealousies, the visitors referred to the 'excellent quality of Victorian butter'. The CWS officials called for a Grand Co-operative Alliance of colonial producers to join in the 'international brotherhood of co-operation'. Indeed, a Co-operative Alliance did form, designed to encourage 'productive and distributive co-operation in their various forms' and to devise a plan for New South Wales producers to co-operate with the English CWS. How, or whether, this functioned is unknown.[10]

Delegates then moved on to Queensland, New Zealand, Canada and the USA before returning to Manchester, establishing a pattern which continued for much of the twentieth century: English CWS officials touring the world, courted by producers, lauded by governments, waxing lyrical on Rochdale rhetoric, arriving from somewhere 'highly competitive', en-route to a potentially superior, alternative supplier.[11]

'Bogus' and 'genuine' co-operatives in the NSW dairy industry, 1896-1906

Lured by the promise of a special trading relationship, not only farmers were drawn to the idea of co-operating with the Manchester co-operative movement. Many proprietary companies with rural interests added 'co-operative' to their title after the English CWS visit. No law prohibited usage of the term or defined a co-operative. In this context a contest for most-favoured relationship with Manchester arose between 'bogus' and 'genuine' co-operatives and, in the decade after the 1896 visit, the fledgling New South Wales' dairy co-operative movement was racked with dissension and scandal, damaging the credentials of co-operation as a genuine democratic social movement and driving a wedge between dairy co-operators in New South Wales and Victoria, which was disastrous for co-operative unity in the long term.

'Bogus' co-operatives proliferated in New South Wales. In 1923, when the *Co-operation Act* was passed (discussed in Chapter Two), no fewer than 240 companies used 'co-operative' in their title, 125 of them engaged in dairy production!

The Woolgrowers' Co-operative Association is a good example of a 'bogus' co-operative. Forming soon after the English CWS visit, this company was owned by a small group of mainly Sydney-based pastoralists and operating on a capital of £60,000, was in no real sense a producers' organisation. Painting itself, nevertheless, as a 'Rochdale co-operative', the Woolgrowers' Co-operative published a journal, *The Co-operator*, which claimed to be the 'official journal of the co-operative movement...an eclectic cosmopolitan journal devoted to the interests of the people [promoting] productive and distributive co-operative on the Rochdale model.' Emphasising the pecuniary advantages of co-operating, *The Co-operator* said co-operation:

> *...improved the material condition of all, halved selling costs, brought higher prices, eliminated taxes, commissions, promoter shares, director fees, bogus charges; incurred no debt or liability; paid a dividend on the value of shares [sic] and allowed autonomous producer control where small and large growers were democratically equal.[12]*

Organising trade with the English CWS

The first English CWS agent to be stationed permanently in Australia, R J Fairbairn, arrived in January 1898, establishing headquarters in Sydney. Fairbairn was briefed by his employers to organise the ill-formed colonial co-operative movement, consign premium quality primary produce to the Manchester parent and indent CWS goods for sale through existing colonial co-operatives and kindred outlets. To this end Fairbairn reconvened the Co-operative Alliance and, with the assistance of the New South Wales Board of Exports, developed a Co-operative Advisory Council, to assist the government conduct co-operative trade with Manchester. Here is the genesis of a special relationship between successive New South Wales administrations and the rural co-operative movement, which would continue until very late in the twentieth century.

Fairbairn lectured on co-operation throughout the colonies, including New Zealand, and in association with the New South Wales Department of Agriculture, organised a primary production conference at Bathurst. There, the Co-operative Advisory Council was formally constituted, consisting of representatives from the South Coast and West Camden, the Woolgrowers' Co-operative Association and the Farmers' Fruitgrowers' Co-operative. A general wholesale, the Farmers' and Settlers' Co-operative Company Limited (hereafter, 'Farmers and Settlers'), was formed for the purpose of exporting primary produce and importing English CWS goods. Farmers and Settlers included as shareholders Fairbairn, representatives of the co-operatives mentioned above and, significantly, directors of proprietary pastoral houses, underling the fact that CWS was not averse to co-operating with proprietors provided this occur through some semblance of a co-operative intermediary.

A registered company, there still being no suitable legislation for co-operatives, Farmers and Settlers was commonly referred to by Fairbairn and associates as the 'Farmers' Co-operative'. It published a monthly, the *Farmers' Co-operative News*, which peddled a blend of Rochdale rhetoric, eulogies to the English CWS, market information extolling the virtues of 'international brotherhood through co-operation with Manchester' and urged farmers to 'combine and unite labour and capital to secure for the worker under co-operation the whole fruit of his labour and break the exploiter and monopolist'.[13]

The collapse of South Coast and West Camden

It must be acknowledged in fairness to Fairbairn that the task of constructing a genuine co-operative link to Manchester, if ever this was intended, was complicated by the weak state of colonial rural co-operation. South Coast and West Camden was struggling financially and faced mounting rumours of insolvency. The *Sydney Morning Herald* speculated cruelly on the co-operative's imminent collapse, alleging extravagant entertainment expenses and exorbitant dividends and, most damaging, linking these to rising consumer prices. Whether the *Herald* charges were justified, or not, is unknown but rumour had the same effect as fact and in January 1900 South Coast and West Camden's bankers foreclosed, appointing as trustees Fairbairn and Farmers' and Settlers' director, former colonial treasurer and liberal free-trader, \.

Fairbairn and McMillan set about restructuring South Coast and West Camden and, in incorporating it into Farmers and Settlers, offered shareholders spot cash amounting to £15,000, well below the co-operative's real value. The alternative, McMillan said, was long marketing delays and interruptions to income. As farmers deliberated on what may be the first corporate take-over of a co-operative in Australia, Fairbairn and McMillan attracted the ire of a former South Coast and West Camden executive who was to have a mighty impact on the shape of Australian co-operation: Charles Edward Devenish Meares.[14]

Charles Meares

Charles Meares (1861-1934) was born on a dairy farm in the Omega district, near Kiama. His father was an Anglican clergyman from Wollongong and his mother was a daughter of J M Tooth the brewer. A thickset, forceful man Meares was a ball of energy, a strong driving personality who could win loyalty in those around him and make enemies. His biographer, R S Maynard, tell us:

> He never suffered from an inferiority complex. He had a good opinion of himself and an absolute faith in the all powerfulness of co-operation. Anything that attempted to stand in the way of co-operation was swept aside with an amused contempt. At times he carried this…into circles where it was not appreciated, even in his own organisation.

A passionate supporter of the British Empire, Meares believed it could 'save the world' and that co-operation was the agent to make this possible. In 1879 Meares began as a bookkeeper in Sussex Street. Two years later he joined the staff of the newly-formed South Coast and West Camden Co-operative, rising to a senior management position. In the McMillan restructuring he was shifted sideways to become little more than a commercial traveller. Meares resented this and in the *Kiama Independent* alleged that McMillan and his cohorts were the enemies of co-operation and were 'bogus' co-operators. He urged farmers to reject the take-over offer, revealing that W and A Macarthur of Camden Park Estate were involved in the bid and were seeking access to the 'co-operative barter system with English CWS to overcome an exchange disadvantage damaging their importing business'. Meares told farmers that McMillan and the Macarthurs together would hold 460 of the 952 shares in the restructured company and called upon them to support the 'genuine' co-operative dairy industry.[15]

Embarrassed by such publicity Fairbairn sought to dissociate himself from the McMillan offer, declaring in the *Farmers' Co-operative News*:

> I did not authorise the inclusion of my name in the trustees of the farmers' co-operative company.
> I do not want the public to think that the [English CWS] has any monetary interest in any co-operative association in these colonies.

The agent stopped short, however, of actually denying that he or English CWS did have a monetary interest in Farmers and Settlers or that he had assisted in the take-over of South Coast and West Camden. There is no direct evidence, however, linking Fairbairn to the bid, although subsequent events beg the question.[16]

At a meeting in the Temperance Hall, Kiama, dairy farmers accepted McMillan's takeover offer overwhelmingly, even though it represented a return to them of less than twenty shillings in the pound (£). The meeting, which saw Meares in a hopeless minority, also saw co-operation in disrepute.

T C Kennedy, a dairy farmer, journalist and staunch co-operator, attended that Kiama meeting. He left dejected and downcast and wandered down to the Kiama Blow Hole, where the ocean snarls through a crack in igneous rock and explodes skywards. He and a friend sat in the gloom on a bench and listened to the unsympathetic hiss and roll of the sea. A solitary figure approached out of the dark and sat next to them. It was Meares. Kennedy finally managed to break the silence with a general comment about the meeting. Meares said nothing. Then Kennedy expressed the view that co-operation had been hit hard that night. Without turning Meares stiffened and replied, 'You think so do you? Co-operation this night is on a safer and sounder footing than it ever has been. You will hear a good deal more in a few days.' Meares left Kennedy with the feeling that he was already plotting to destroy the McMillan operation and reaffirm 'genuine' co-operation.[17]

Co-operation's credibility is dented

What did the collapse of South Coast and West Camden mean for rural co-operation? First, it confirmed a perception among sceptics that co-operators were incapable of adequately capitalising operations and that his was a fatal flaw in co-operative methodology. Secondly, it demonstrated the vulnerability of co-operatives to rumour, particularly in periods of market instability and a proneness of co-operatives to 'insider' take-overs. Third, the co-operative's demise reinforced a growing public perception, valid or otherwise, that a direct link existed between rural co-operation and rising consumer prices, deepening a rift already growing between consumer and producer co-operatives, on the one hand, and producer co-operatives and the labour movement, on the other. Fourth, McMillan and associates took over valuable co-operative assets at below par value while appearing, like 'White Knights', to rescue co-operation from its own inadequacies. Fifth, the restructure represented a take-over of a genuine co-operative by mainly urban-based 'dry' (non-producer) shareholders with rural connections and there was nothing in law to prevent this. Sixth, the take-over demonstrated the vulnerability of co-operatives to attack by ideological enemies with ready access to capital. Finally, co-operation's credibility as a legitimate basis for organising industry, already dented by trade union scepticism, the failure of state-sponsored co-operative settlement schemes and the collapse of building societies in the 1890s depression, was dealt a further blow.[18]

Federation changes nothing

Federation of the Australian Colonies, to form the Commonwealth of Australia in 1901, changed nothing for co-operatives. The Constitution was silent on co-operation or co-operatives, which remained subject to a mosaic of archaic or unsuitable states' laws, which failed in most cases even to receive improvements in imperial legislation. Inadequate and incompatible states' co-operatives legislation would characterise Australian co-operative development for virtually all of the ensuing century.

A dreadful drought, at the turn of the century, peaking in 1902, and the worst economic depression in the nation's history to that time through the 1890s, however, impelled many farmers towards co-operation. Economic sluggishness continued for much of the first decade of the new century, through which the dairying industry was wrought by further technological change and market innovation which, while enhancing productivity, exerted strong land pressures and forced many young dairying families to relocate, some to the other side of the continent. The idea of dairying co-operation spread over vast distances in a fragmentary and piecemeal way focused on industry sectoral concerns and not co-operative institutions, setting the pattern for the rest of the century.

Coastal Farmers' Co-operative Dairy Company and the Producers' Distributive Society

Seeking support for a 'genuine' co-operative to challenge 'McMillan's', as he insisted upon calling Farmers and Settlers, C E D Meares encountered scepticism wherever he went about co-operatives' capacity to function in a federal setting and managed to raise only £250 after months of effort. With this meagre sum, however, he enticed away from McMillan's executives who, like Meares, had suffered in the restructuring, and led the formation of Coastal Farmers' Co-operative Dairy Company (later, 'Dairy Farmers' Milk Co-operative Company Limited') for processing and production. Later, Producers' Distributive Society (PDS) was formed, for the distribution of dairy and primary products.

At a meeting in Albion Park Town Hall in January 1900, convened by Meares, producers from all parts of the south coast resolved '…to emancipate themselves and initiate a new company whereby their milk could be marketed to the best advantage. The time has arrived for the formation of a milk company upon pure co-operative lines.' A subsequent meeting at Kiama saw farmers give the Coastal Farmers' Co-operative Milk Company Limited a resounding endorsement.

In March 1901 Coastal Farmers began publishing *Coastal Farmers' Gazette*, a monthly newspaper broadcasting industry information, attacking McMillan's and urging farmers to abandon 'bogus' co-operation and support 'genuine' co-operation:

> *Co-operation is an industrial effort of a body of people on the same plain with interests in common seeking to better their interests. True co-operation is power from within, not without… something created and carried on by [people] themselves. Anything giving to monetary institutions or capitalists a voice in its government is not co-operation.[19]*

Meares saw co-operation pragmatically as a device to 'better interests' and eliminate 'middle men' through the democratic self-regulation of industry. He dismissed any idea of social transformation through co-operation, as preached by Rochdale idealists, and promoted a conservative, sectional co-operation confined wholly to primary producers and conferring upon consumers the obligation to co-operate in their own interests. Meares was certainly not interested in a Rochdale-style Australian co-operative wholesale linking Australian consumers and farmers in domestic markets, arguing that this would give too much market power to consumers: producers organised to *sell* at the best price; consumers organised to *buy* at the best price – the market should determine outcomes, not cosy 'co-operative' arrangements. Far from a co-operative wholesale linking co-operators in a 'Co-operative Union', Meares called for a 'Co-operative Butter Council' and a 'co-operative government of prices' achieved through a voluntary network of *farmer*-owned co-operative distributive associations exerting market influence. Such a system, he believed, co-ordinated by a *farmer-owned* wholesale, would produce surpluses for diversification into such fields as co-operative marketing (but not co-operative banking, to which Meares was opposed), would defeat 'bogus' co-operation, pre-empt government moves to regulate dairying and extract just rewards for farmer labours.

McMillan's and the CWS

Meanwhile, CWS Agent Fairbairn had travelled to Manchester for briefings, returning in 1901 with instructions to expand business and to investigate bulk wheat handling (a directive which would see a great trade develop between Manchester and the South Australian and Western Australian wheat industries). Purchasing six acres of land on the Alexandria Canal in Sydney on behalf of English CWS, Fairbairn supervised the construction of processing works for oil, tallow, soap, bone, dust and manures, which were to be run as wholly-owned CWS subsidiaries trading under the name 'Wheatsheaf'.[20]

Then, suddenly, in December 1901, Fairbairn '…left the lucrative position of the Australian representative for the English CSW to join Farmers and Settlers at the special request of Sir W McMillan.' It is not known why Fairbairn left. It may have related to allegations of corruption surfacing in a Royal Commission into the Victorian Dairy Industry (1902-1904), discussed below.[21] It may simply have been a response to an excellent offer. Whatever, the move formalised a relationship between the agent and McMillan's which had existed since the take-over of South Coast and West Camden and did not involve any interruption of supplies to the English CWS. The appointment did, however, mean that Manchester no longer had a representative on the New South Wales Co-operative Advisory Council. When English CWS officials again toured in 1902, therefore, they were anxious to find a replacement for Fairbairn and considered Meares a possibility. Indeed Meares and the English visitors were seen together frequently around Sydney.[22]

Coastal Farmers struggles

The fact was, Coastal Farmers was already struggling, posting losses in its first two years of operation. Indeed the co-operative would have wound up had not a rain deluge prevented shareholders from forming a quorum to effect this. Meares called for 'public spirited action from shareholders' and farmers rallied to the call, backing the original guarantors to the bank for finance necessary to carry on trading. Still under-capitalised, it is reported that the co-operative was obliged to levy growers on the gallon-age of milk supplied, with shares allocated to suppliers as their contributions accumulated. If this is so, it would not be the last time the co-operative resorted to this practice.[23]

With Coastal Farmers in difficulties, no progress was made on Meares' 'co-operative government of prices' idea, which most farmers saw as grandiose and impractical, particularly as they continued to squabble over quality margins and regional differences. Voluntary co-operation might be good for harnessing local initiative, but as a basis for industry organisation it seemed to be lacking.

Meanwhile, a powerful Victorian dairying co-operative movement was emerging, one which would ultimately dominate Australian dairying, and it is to this that our attention now turns.

Early dairying co-operation in Victoria

The first clear evidence of dairying co-operation in Victoria appeared in 1888 when the Cobden and District Pioneer Cheese and Butter Factory and the Warrnambool Cheese and Butter Factory commenced operations, registered under company law as no suitable co-operatives' legislation existed. Prior to that time the manufacture of butter and cheese was carried out on farms under very primitive conditions. When news of the Danish centrifugal separator reached the colony, however, the government urged farmers to form co-operatives and develop a dairy industry on the Danish model. From the very beginning in Victoria, the state took a prominent role.

The formation of other co-operatives quickly followed, for instance: the Swan Pool Dairy Co-operative Limited (1889), the Colac and Camperdown Cheese and Butter Company (1893) and the Shepparton District Butter Cheese and Ice Factory (1894). The last, which subsequently developed into IBIS Milk Products, is a good example of an early small-holder co-operative. The co-operative consisted of 126 farmer shareholders operating within daily delivery distance of the factory. Supplier members carted untreated milk to the factory door and returned with skimmed

Dairy transport in early pioneering days.
Photo courtesy of Norco Co-operative Limited.

milk for use with their pigs. Shares in the co-operative were so organised that no individual bloc could gain control, but apparently did not conform strictly to a one-person-one-vote principle.

Co-operation and Victorian protectionism

Shepparton's success, and the experience of New South Wales Sou'coasters migrating into the Gippsland region, saw support for co-operation grow. Co-operative creameries rapidly developed throughout Victoria. The expansion of production which followed exceeded Victorian requirements and soon saw pressure build to place surpluses in foreign markets. 'Foreign' could mean interstate or international markets and, theoretically, after Federation, constructed on a Constitution guaranteeing free-trade between states, there would be nothing preventing either. With refrigerated vessels now available for transportation throughout Australia and overseas, the Victorian government assisted farmers financially to build and equip factories and provided export bonuses to lead a Victorian milk-producer export charge.[24]

Like their New South Wales counterparts, these early Victorian co-operatives were obliged to register as companies. Indeed, the 1876 *Industrial and Provident Societies Act*, which contemplated co-operatives but made no provision for primary producers, was not amended usefully until 1928, long after New South Wales had legislation for co-operatives. Early Victorian dairy co-operatives developed also in a period of economic depression in the 1890s, unlike some in New South Wales which had operated for almost a decade before the economic downturn. It is possible that these factors, in addition to the colony's prevailing protectionist sentiment, influenced Victorian dairy farmers in seeking government intervention and adapting co-operative principles in ways unacceptable to 'genuine' free-trader dairying co-operatives in New South Wales. Certainly, strained relations between the New South Wales and Victorian dairy co-operative movements helped shape twentieth century Australian co-operation.

Organising a Victorian dairy co-operative movement

In the approach to the English CWS visit in 1896, W G Nuttal, an ex-CWS director and then a gentleman farmer in Victoria, and W Bateman, 'a co-operative expert [who] knew co-operation in Argentina and New Zealand', delivered hundreds of lectures around the colony on the subject of co-operation, urging the development of a Co-operative Dairy Distribution Society 'to co-ordinate trade with the British consumer movement'. Bateman was sent by the Victorian government to greet the CWS visitors when they disembarked in Port Adelaide and he escorted them through their Victorian itinerary, including a visit to Warrnambool and to Nuttal's property.

As noted earlier, a Melbourne-based Central Co-operative Association emerged from the CWS visit, led by Rochdale enthusiasts John Ross and his protégé, T M Burke. Ross and Burke argued for a Rochdale-style wholesale linking Victorian consumers *and* producers and trading independently of the proprietary system with English CWS. Burke travelled extensively throughout Victoria, Western Australia and Tasmania seeking support for this idea. John Ross lectured and published on a 'Co-operative Union of Farmers and Consumers' with independent co-operative banking and finance facilities and the co-operative manufacture of farming implements – an embodiment of the Rochdale 'Co-operative Commonwealth' idea. There was some interest, as evidenced by the large number of audiences Burke and Ross addressed, but farmers generally dismissed the scheme as impracticable. Nevertheless, a company, the Victoria Butter Factories Co-operative (Limited) did form from these meetings, designed to rationalise costs and co-ordinate the efforts of proliferating small co-operative factories. This co-operative company was quickly infested with profiteers and speculators, however, and was required to alter its articles of association to prevent an immediate take-over by 'dry' shareholders.

English CWS Agent R J Fairbairn, meanwhile, also toured the colony canvassing support for a distribution house similar to Farmers and Settlers in New South Wales and reaching a supply arrangement with some co-operative and proprietary butter factories in north eastern Victoria and the Gippsland region. No further details have come to hand. We do know, however, that by 1905 there were approximately 100 co-operative dairy factories operating in Victoria and a great exporting industry had begun.

State governments investigate co-operative dairying

With no stable co-operative agency in place to supervise export product grading and quality control, however, CWS officials looked to government for market support, communicating this in New South Wales through the Co-operative Advisory Council. The New South Wales Dairy Industry Bill followed in late 1902, a landmark in the regulation of New South Wales' primary industry. Significantly, the impetus for this came from sections of the co-operative movement itself, responding to English CWS demands. Charles Meares personally opposed the Bill, but with Coastal Farmers faltering, the Victorians stealing a march in exports and anxious not to offend potential customers, he quickly fell into line. Already, the state was moving into an organisational void left by the co-operative movement and the intervention could only expand.[25]

Acting on a Victorian precedent, a few weeks later the New South Wales Government announced plans for a state-owned experimental dairy factory at Berry on the south coast to produce a 'standard quality' butter, and appointed Fairbairn as manager. A journalistic war erupted between Meares and the English CWS agent with Meares accusing the government of attempting to 'invade the producers' realm', a phrase he often used, and to 'muddle co-operation with regulation, the way it is developing in Victoria.' He blasted Fairbairn for litigating against South Australian wheat growers for allegedly supplying inferior grain, charging that such 'slander against farmers' was the price of dealing with 'bogus' co-operators who pandered to government intervention. Responding to these allegations, Fairbairn offered a large reward to anyone who would help him find 'the culprit' and employed a private detective to follow Meares.[26]

With fierce competition between butter marketers now developing, including co-operatives, the *Melbourne Age* kept up a scathing attack on malpractice in the dairy industry, demanding that governments do something. A Victorian Royal Commission into the dairy industry, which reported in 1904, unmasked a system of 'secret rascality [by which] a number of harpies were strangling dairy men...of their just profits', and recommended support for 'genuine' co-operatives to rid the industry of this 'secret circle'. The Royal Commission linked Fairbairn and New South Wales and Victorian shipping agents to a system of secret rebates to secure cargoes and price fixing, in which some operators were acting both as agents and merchants, with absolutely no benefit to consumers. Commissioners described grave irregularities in the management of co-operatives, where 'shady business practices' existed and recommended that the government introduce a bonus scheme to encourage the establishment of butter factories and cheese factories to promote exports. Acting on this recommendation, the Victorian government channelled £233,000 directly into supporting the dairy industry, setting a precedent for government intervention in co-operative development and clearly at odds with Meares' autonomous industry self-regulation position. The New South Wales and Victorian dairy co-operative movements were splitting along 'free-trade – protectionist' lines, a division which would prove to be disastrous for Australian co-operative unity.

Fairbairn, who had initially sought to use the Victorian Royal Commission as a platform from which to hurl abuse at Meares, now found himself answering charges that the P & O Shipping Company had been paying McMillan's and other agents (unnamed) a 3 per cent commission for butter cargoes. The former CWS agent had been exposed as simply another 'middle man'. Fairbairn countered that this had 'only become necessary [because] Meares and his cohorts [were] bribing away factories and engaging in peculiar and questionable tactics damaging to the co-operative movement.' Meares replied that McMillan's had nothing to do with co-operation and demanded that the New South Wales premier, the Liberal free-trader Joseph Carruthurs (later, an architect of the 1923 *Co-operation Act*), conduct an independent inquiry in Sydney.

The ensuing inquiry confirmed that a 'possible fraud had been perpetrated by the representative of the Manchester CWS under instructions from Farmers' and Settlers' Co-operative Society,' implying strongly that McMillan's had operated to the disadvantage of producers but concluding vaguely, 'We regret that we are unable to further investigate'.[27]

Here was a scandal: the former disciple of 'international co-operative brotherhood' linked to possible fraud and co-operation described by Victorian Royal Commissioners and a Sydney inquiry as something manipulated by a 'secret circle' to the detriment of both consumers *and* producers.

Revelations from the Victorian Royal Commission and New South Wales inquiry rocked the dairying co-operative movement obliging Meares to move quickly to rally the 'genuine' co-operative troops. The general manager called a meeting at Berry where he declared 'Fairbairn, not co-operation' to be a failure, alleging that over £10,000 had been spent trying to discredit him and the 'genuine' co-operative movement. To a standing ovation Meares announced that Coastal Farmers had overhauled McMillan's as the major butter exporter to Britain. Meares and co-operation received three rousing cheers. He intensified calls for an 'Australian Committee' to defend the interests of 'genuine' Australian producers in Britain, implying that the consumer-dominated English CWS could not be trusted to do this:

> *Relations between the two great bodies [the English CWS and Australia dairy producer co-operatives] are limited in extent and ultimately they have opposite interests. One produces food to sell and one buys food to consume. A direct relationship between these opposites reduces competition and ultimately reduces prices, which is not in the interests of the producer.*[28]

The Western District Co-operative Produce Company

From out of the turmoil of the Victorian Royal Commission and revelations that the industry was rife with corruption and malpractice, a new and influential Victorian marketing co-operative arose: the Western District Co-operative Produce Company (hereafter, 'Western District'). Six companies at Colac, Grassmere, Framlingham, Koroit, Warrnambool and Rosebrook became shareholders in the co-operative which was formed:

> *...to undertake the marketing of dairy produce within Australia and overseas [and to]... refrain from speculation, to rely wholly upon consignment commissions for income, to maintain legitimate values and to bring producers and consumers closer together, [while] giving the laws of supply and demand free play.*

The co-operative's policies included ethical business practice, one week's credit (no more), direct selling by-passing proprietary agents, weekly cheques to farmers and, in the interests of solidarity, a refusal to accept divided consignments from suppliers. By steadying markets, Western District hoped to suppress the speculative control of prices then prevailing, which was destabilising the industry and producing unpredictable and inequitable returns to producers. Harry Osborne was appointed manager.

Harry Osborne and Western District

Harry W Osborne was the son of British immigrants who had been lured to Victoria by gold. He worked as a journalist, editor and a municipal secretary in the Warrnambool Shire. Osborne was appointed manager *precisely* because he had had nothing to do with the industry and because he was known and trusted by some of the new co-operative's directors.

Osborne's immediate task was to launch the co-operative. This was not straightforward. The Commercial Bank would only finance Western District if directors accepted 'joint and several' responsibility for security, a risk which farmer-directors were unwilling to take. A way was found through the impasse involving a 'mutually beneficial arrangement', the nature of which is unknown. We do know, however, that Osborne and his directors were compelled to provide 'greater security' for investors, who, by 1905, included wealthy pastoralists with an interest in dairying – 'dry' shareholders. A new charter was drawn up and although this appears to have been basically co-operative in complexion, no clear reference was made to voting practices and it is not known whether the restructured co-operative operated on a weighted voting system or on a one-person-one-vote basis. The point for our discussion is that the co-operative would almost certainly have failed to operate if purely co-operative principles had not been waived.[29]

Leading Melbourne agents and merchants refused to take Osborne or the new co-operative company seriously and were determined to drive Western District out of business. Osborne found it impossible to distinguish friends from enemies with proprietary agents and distributors courting him and offering inducements to deal with them. When this did not work they sought to undermine Osborne's credibility among shareholders and customers. Proprietors approached individual farmers, offering to pay them more than the co-operative for consignments. Farmers knew why they were being offered more – because the co-operative existed, and they held firm! Proprietors engaged a private detective to follow Osborne's every move. Wherever the manager alighted in his travels, an agent would be on the next train. Osborne spent much of his time refuting 'insidious attacks by agents who resorted to all means possible to create distrust and suspicion of the co-operative' and was repeatedly offered bribes:

> *I was constantly on the war path, stirring to build up business in Melbourne and rushing off to the country to meet a threatened breakaway. I stated that we were fighting for the principles of Co-operation and against proprietary-ism and that we were at war with a system which had proven to be detrimental to the interests of a great industry...Every ton of butter given to proprietary interests was so much ammunition in the hands of enemies of co-operative marketing. I addressed many meetings and wrote articles to many newspapers advocating the principles of co-operation.[30]*

In Melbourne seeking sales rooms, Osborne was treated to a 'warm' reception by agents and wholesale merchants who made jokes about the new co-operative:

> *One firm had placed whiz bangs and crackers under the door and these exploded as we entered their office. Of course we were startled and then there were roars of laughter from the principals and staff. This was one example of the contemptuous regard for the 'invaders', as one of them explained it.*

The Western District executive was required to exercise great caution in recruiting because it was known that agency firms were trying to infiltrate the co-operative to gain 'insider' knowledge and to foment distrust and suspicion among shareholders. Indeed, the co-operative did have enemies within, including the export agent, employees of which were quietly seeking to derail it. When Western District withdrew all business from the company, it countered by seeking to obtain consignments direct from individual factories. Again farmers held firm. Subsequently the offending company lost its butter business and closed down all of its dairy produce branches throughout Australia.[31]

Returns to farmers supplying Western District improved appreciably, amounting to hundreds of thousands of pounds over the next thirty years. Producers elsewhere in Victoria emulated the model, for example the Gippsland Co-operative Produce Company and even proprietary competitors, including the Victorian Butter Factories Co-operative, which adopted the co-operative's policy of selling direct to retailers.

The Gippsland Butter Factories Co-operative Produce Company Limited

In 1906, the Gippsland Butter Factories Co-operative Produce Company Limited (later, Gippsland and Northern Co-operative Company Limited, [hereafter, G & N]) was formed, assisted by Western District. Earlier, five Gippsland factories had entrusted butter sales to Western District but the quality of butter supplied did not match the latter's standards, affecting prices. With proprietary agents exploiting disagreements between suppliers, some Gippsland farmers returned to them. Agents then circulated rumours that Western District was losing business because it could not afford to pay market rates. In response, Harry Osborne suggested that Gippsland farmers form their own co-operative to beat 'city speculators'. They did so, but, soon, G & N was faltering in Melbourne markets. Western District again assisted, making space available on its selling floors,

Leongatha Butter & Cheese Factory (early 1900s)
Photo courtesy of Murray Goulburn Co-operative Co Limited.

bringing G & N into association with a network of buyers. Soon the new co-operative took off, ably guided by General Manager A W Wilson of Mirboo North, who remained manager until 1948. A grain department was added and later sections for seeds, livestock, land sales, merchandise (including co-operative oil from the United States), farm machinery and a seed cleaning plant. In 1911 G & N purchased headquarters in Flinders Lane, Melbourne, and later joined with Victorian Butter Factories Co-operative and Western District in a joint box-manufacturing complex at Yarraville. In 1914 the co-operative was renamed G & N Co-operative Selling and Insurance Company Limited and began publishing a weekly, *The G & N Co-operator*.[32]

Disagreement over co-operative marketing models: 1906–1910

In New South Wales, meanwhile, C E D Meares' grand vision of a 'co-operative government of prices' in domestic markets, to be achieved through the co-operation of farmer co-operatives and an Australian Committee in London for exports had failed to attract much support. With regard to domestic markets, most Victorian producers were suspicious of any Sydney-based scheme and many farmers, particularly Western District suppliers, were now openly endorsing direct government intervention in the dairy co-operative movement – an absolute anathema for Meares. G & N was drawn to Meares' idea but doubted the capacity of farmers to organise such a thing. The northern New South Wales co-operative, Norco, was non-committal, considering an independent marketing system linked to a proposed co-operative shipping line carrying north coast New South Wales produce out of the Macleay River. The cold climate Berrima Co-operative Society in the southern highlands was not interested. The *Sydney Morning Herald* doubted also that sufficient support would ever be found for Meares' export proposals, even if co-operators could agree, because the scheme would offend 'certain interests', specifically private merchants who would resist any attempt to weaken their hold on overseas marketing.

The Commonwealth Government enters the field

In 1905 the Commonwealth Government, flexing new constitutional muscle under external powers, passed the *Commerce Act*, by which it entered the field of export product quality control.

In April the following year the government convened a major exports conference in Melbourne, bringing together manufacturers, importers, exporters and co-operative dairy producers to review the legislation. Here, W E Pleasants of the Victorian Co-operative Association (the renamed Central Co-operative Association) argued for an amalgamated (producer *and* consumer) Australian Co-operative Wholesale on the English model, assisted by government export subsidies and income stabilisation schemes, with production and marketing retained in co-operative hands. The proposal seems to have been an attempt to reach a compromise between Meares' (free-trade) and Western District's (protectionist) positions. Pleasants called for government aid in establishing a European (Raiffeisen)-style co-operative bank for financing co-operative production, marketing and other co-operative enterprises, including the manufacture of farm implements. He spoke of an independent Australian co-operative sector built upon the economic foundation of primary production, uniting consumers and producers in a mutually beneficial economic relationship through a giant wholesale creating a true 'Co-operative Commonwealth of Australia'.

Meares would not have a bar of it. He told the conference co-operation was about 'bettering interests', not reducing farmer returns through co-operating with consumers. Moreover, he had no quarrel with private banks and government intervention of any form was simply unacceptable.

Why was Meares so opposed to a co-operative bank? Perhaps he believed it would be repugnant to English CWS, which already had a Co-operative Bank, and jeopardise plans for an Australian Committee in London in association with the Manchester giant. Perhaps he was protecting other financial interests or concerned that such a bank would be Melbourne-based, conferring an advantage on Victorian producers and possibly leading to financial domination of the co-operative movement by 'protectionist' Melbourne. Maybe he was merely acknowledging that in New South Wales co-operative banking had been outlawed since 1865 by dint of the *Industrial and Provident Societies Act*. Whatever the reason, Meares' opposition to a co-operative bank and a co-operative wholesale of producers and consumers must be taken into account in assessing the significance of his role in Australian co-operatives' history.

The Australian Co-operative Wholesale Society

Within weeks of the 1906 federal conference, T M Burke of the Victorian Co-operative Association organised another conference where draft plans were drawn up for an Australian Co-operative Wholesale along lines suggested by Pleasants, but 'without any other intervening agents', a pointed reference to Meares' proposed Australian Committee. Burke and John Ross promoted the idea throughout rural districts and, at a conference in Warrnambool, called for a Co-operative Union of Producers and Consumers to eliminate merchants and agents through the 'co-operative middle way', combining primary, secondary and tertiary economic sectors in a glorious 'Co-operative Commonwealth'.[33]

An Australian Co-operative Wholesale Society (Australian CWS) formed from this Warrnambool meeting but attracted little farmer support. Nevertheless, it served as a forum for national co-operative debate before World War I, convening annually, normally around the time of the Melbourne Agricultural Show, and bringing together rural and urban co-operators. However, in 1912, following the collapse of the Civil Service Co-operative of Victoria, with which T M Burke was associated, Australian CWS disintegrated, the first in a long line of short-lived attempts to achieve a cohesive federal co-operative umbrella organisation representing all sections of the co-operative movement.

The Unity Conference 1909

Charles Meares, meanwhile, left no stone unturned in advancing his Australian Committee idea. A major obstacle was removed in 1908 when McMillan's Farmers' and Settlers' was declared bankrupt. The general manager quickly organised a long-planned 'unity' conference, with the purpose of creating an independent Australian producer co-operative selling floor in London. Such an entity, Meares argued on a tour of eastern states and New Zealand, would achieve co-operation's goals and 'beat the commission operators...fend off government and...link [us] with the British consumer movement'.

The Unity Conference was convened in July 1909 and involved co-operatives from New South Wales, Victoria and Queensland. Queensland delegates announced that they were ready to join with Coastal Farmers in an overseas marketing venture, but Norco, concerned that a Sydney axis might compromise its market position, agreed only to 'investigate the idea further'. The Victorian co-operatives present consented only to a pilot scheme for the promotion of Australian products and the researching of market potential abroad.

Armed with this weak mandate, Meares left for Britain in 1910 seeking to realise his grand vision – an Australian Committee of Co-operative Producers trading into English markets.[34]

Calls for government intervention grow

Support for direct government intervention in dairying was growing, however, both within the industry and inside the federal Fisher Labor Government. In 1911 and again in 1913 the Commonwealth Government sought powers through referenda to regulate trade between the states. Unsuccessful, it looked to strengthen control of export quality and packing standards through external powers. In 1912, the government appointed a Royal Commission to inquire into the food industry, which recommended government-sponsored produce departments in all states for the conduct of exports. Nothing concrete came from this before World War I, but the recommendations were a clear indication of federal thinking.

A federal tendency toward intervention was reflected at state level. In New South Wales a Holman Labor Government Royal Commission into profiteering in the wool industry in 1913 attributed this to the absence of a single co-ordinating pricing authority. Commissioners recommended that the New South Wales Department of Agriculture take a more active role in the affairs of distributive agencies, including co-operatives, foreshadowing regulation. Thereafter, the department was more pro-active in the affairs of rural co-operatives, developing Agricultural Bureaux as part of a general thrust towards a 'more planned and better organised economy'. Although progress was slow before the war, Agricultural Bureaux proliferated after 1918, forging close ties between the department and rural co-operatives (discussed in Chapter Two).

Co-operation is criticised

As these events unfolded, in London Meares' embryonic 'Australian Committee' was coming under fire from the Australian High Commissioner Sir George Reid, who accused the committee of 'associating with proprietary agents in a way that is nothing short of a scandal' and of butter blending and profiteering to the detriment of Australian producers. Unsubstantiated allegations resurfaced of 'secret circles' in the co-operative movement, who had combined to drive up prices, prompting unionists and newspaper editors to demand government intervention. Meares responded by attacking 'union aggression', condemning government intervention in industrial relations and advocating co-operation as a 'middle way' between the extremes of market corruption and political extremism. Only through co-operation, Meares argued, could farmers retain control of their industries and not forfeit this to bureaucrats and proprietors.

Following a successful trade union submission to the Arbitration Commission (for industrial relations), resulting in a pay increase for rural workers, Meares joined with the Chamber of Commerce to 'fight socialistic and governmental encroaches on liberty'. Union leaders counter-charged that price fixing was rampant in the dairy industry where co-operatives predominated, arguing that it was anomalous, anyway, for the co-operative movement to be free to set prices while the *price of labour* itself was regulated by an independent tribunal.

Then Meares was embarrassed by an incident involving Coastal Farmers' Leeton canning operation, which collapsed. The government rescued the plant for nakedly political reasons. Meares did not complain. Clearly he did see a place for government intervention where the absence of it meant financial ruin. Equally, the experience eloquently demonstrated to government that co-operation was no panacea in developing rural production.[35]

The Victorians organise

As Meares organised in London, Victorian co-operative companies proceeded independently in developing British markets and a 'co-operative government of prices' for domestic markets. Both Western District and G & N had agents acting on their behalf in London before World War I. Indeed, Victorian domestic markets were governed by the parity of prices ruling in London (including transport costs and other fees) with prices set at regular Friday afternoon meetings between Western District, G & N and Victorian Butter Factories, where market conditions were discussed and prices for butter and cheese fixed for the following week. Other agents generally accepted prices so fixed. Later, proprietary manufacturers were invited to join this committee, in which co-operative companies held the whip hand. In New South Wales, on the other hand, the marketing of dairy products was still very much a free-for-all, ironically, making the need for regulation even greater.

Significant achievements on the eve of war

By the eve of World War I the eastern Australian dairy co-operative movement, barely thirty five years old, could boast noteworthy achievements. More than 70 per cent of all dairy products were processed in co-operative factories and marketed and distributed through co-operative agencies. Co-operatives had weathered sustained attacks by ideological and market rivals and had driven competitors from the field. Communities had developed around hundreds of dairy co-operative factories, scattered along the coast and hinterland and elsewhere throughout Australia. Selling floors in major cities had been established providing producers with better returns and eliminating middle men. Progress had been made in engaging British markets, particularly the English CWS. But now wartime emergency regulations suspended co-operative development for seven years, to 1921. Everything was about to change.[36]

Co-operation through World War I: emergency regulations set a precedent

The Commonwealth War Precautions Act of 1914, which imposed compulsory conditions on export trade, was complemented by state legislation committing governments to the maintenance of supplies and in some cases the regulation of prices. For the dairy industry this meant that surplus butter was purchased by the imperial government at prices arranged by Prime Minister W M Hughes often without consultation with the industry. No objection was raised at the time out of a sense of patriotic duty, but market conditions were quite chaotic, especially for shipments of butter and cheese.

Severe drought in the eastern states in 1914 and 1915 saw farm production plunge. Milk prices nose-dived, local shortages developed and allegations of profiteering in the dairy and wheat industries intensified, forcing governments to act more determinedly in the control of prices and supply. As charges of malpractice grew, the co-operative movement continued to disagree on how to counteract this, creating a policy vacuum. Seeking to assist a beleaguered industry, the federal government created the Federal Butter Advisory Committee to provide guidance on production. Various states passed legislation to assist farmers obtain credit. A march of regulation was beginning which would eventually engulf co-operative development.[37]

C E D Meares had no quarrel with advisory and financial assistance, announcing that he was prepared to co-operate with governments in 'solving problems too big for the industry to solve itself'. Meanwhile, however, he organised conferences to 'unite producers in safeguarding the industry against the desire of governments to get control'.

Charges of commodity profiteering in the dairy industry peaked in 1915. The *Sydney Morning Herald*, for example, declared:

> *The leaders of the butter industry have taken the law into their own hands…Consumption is to be checked by higher or prohibitive prices…The law is ignored for the butter industry is a law unto itself…The co-operative principle as practised by the butter industry is a sham… Co-operative control today attempts to dictate to parliament and the public alike.*

Meares sued the *Herald* claiming that it implied that he was 'incompetent, used underhand tactics, had conspired to deceive, was given to untruth, had taken advantage of the drought and had flouted the law'. But a court and a court of appeal declared that the defamation had been against *co-operation*, not Meares.

As prices continued to soar Melbourne unionists struck in January 1916 to prevent further exports of wheat and butter. In response the Hughes Government passed the *War Precautions (Prices Adjustment) Regulations Act*, establishing a Commonwealth Price Adjustment Board, which consisted of a commissioner from each state armed with a brief to 'prevent a rise in prices to export parity'.

It is difficult to know whether the co-operative dairy industry had been profiteering, and if so to what extent. Certainly higher prices were being demanded of local consumers as crammed cargoes left for Britain, but whether this related to imperial war-time demand, drought, dislocated shipping channels and lost cargoes, or all or some of these, is uncertain. Nevertheless, community outrage and parliamentary passions had been aroused by a combination of shortages and high prices and farmers, including co-operative farmers, were identified with this. Indeed, co-operation in the dairy industry was now linked in the public mind to higher prices for food, providing a rationale for further state intervention in agriculture and, as a corollary of this, interference in co-operative affairs. A central point for discussion is that governments were simply responding responsibly to allegations of malpractice in acting to regulate and were not invading the field as Meares would suggest, a field left vacant in any event by divisiveness and vacillation in the rural co-operative movement, particularly tetchiness between New South Wales and Victorian dairying co-operatives.[38]

The Primary Producers' Union

Adamant that the Price Adjustment Board was a tyrannical encroachment upon the freedom of farmers to organise their own industry, and seeking improved producer representation, Meares worked with farmers, mainly in northern New South Wales, to form the Primary Producers' Union (PPU) to 'defend and put forward an independent farmer view' and oppose any legislation which interfered with existing export market arrangements. The PPU forged close links with the Dairy Farmers' Association and the Farmers' and Settlers' Association. Farmers were discovering a political voice, eventually taking the form of the Country (National) Party (discussed in Chapter Two).

'Orderly Marketing'

Not surprisingly, relations between the dairy co-operative movement and the New South Wales Labor government deteriorated dramatically in 1916 when, after importing butter from the United States to meet production shortfalls, the government found itself with a heavy carry-over of inferior quality butter, which it was forced to sell at a loss. The government reacted by appointing a Royal Commission to investigate rural industry and trade. This recommended that 'orderly marketing' be achieved legislatively and that legislation specifically for co-operatives be enacted. The summations of the Royal Commission and a complementary Federal Royal Commission were that voluntary systems were *unworkable* in a federal setting, particularly as co-operatives were hamstrung by states' laws. Constitutional doubts surrounding these recommendations, however, prevented the commonwealth from acting and, with state governments confined by war-time regulations, a stalemate was reached. Nevertheless, a rationale for the post-war statutory regulation of markets existed and legislation for co-operatives was seen as part of this. Whether voluntary co-operation and statutory regulation were actually *compatible,* however, remained unclear.[39]

The pooling of commodities

The tendency towards government intervention in rural industry accelerated in late 1916, when the Hughes Government, responding to union calls for a more planned economy, convened a Melbourne conference to discuss constitutional methods of pooling shipping to overcome interruptions and shortages. This agenda was broadened by Western Australian delegates W D Johnson (Labor MLA), a Rochdale consumer movement stalwart (discussed in Chapter Six), and G L Sutton of the Western Australian Department of Agriculture, to include the pooling of *whole commodities*, co-ordinated by uniform (statutory and co-operative) national handling and marketing authorities. Johnson saw no contradiction between statutory pooling and the co-operative voluntary principle, arguing that it was simply a matter of *farmers* retaining democratic control over the entire process. However, many farmers; dairy farmers in particular; were opposed, fearful of pooling's impact on reputations and premiums for regional quality. C E D Meares persisted in opposing *any* government involvement, on principle.

Farmer concerns were allayed somewhat when Prime Minister Hughes announced that his government would *guarantee* funds to develop a national pooling scheme. He also assuaged doubts about 'creeping socialism' by emphasising that co-operative autonomy would be respected, provided co-operatives observed a 'public responsibility'. Hughes also foreshadowed a Commonwealth Pools Committee comprising representatives of the sugar, wheat and dairy industries to assist in the drafting of a *Commonwealth Pools Act* to regulate the scheme. The proposed legislation would specifically prevent co-operative factories and mills from exporting *until* a quota of best quality produce had been allocated for local consumption and would form the basis of government-to-government trading between the Australian and British governments.

Again, it might be noted that the initiative for statutory control came from elements of the co-operative movement, specifically W D Johnson supported by the (Victorian) Western District Co-operative and was not simply the machination of power-hungry governments.[40]

Acting promptly upon recommendations from the 1916 conference, T M Burke, representing the Victorian Butter Factories Co-operative, organised a Co-operative Butter and Cheese Conference to plan for a national dairy produce pool, which would give expression to the *Commonwealth Pools Act*. Meares, predictably, objected, continuing to argue for voluntariness, free-trade and the co-operative regulation of industry and prices. It was clear by now, however, that he was out of step with industry opinion and, again, the Victorians, specifically T M Burke and Harry Osborne of Western District, carried the debate. An old world nineteenth century view of co-operation as a transformative philosophy and basis for voluntary industry self-regulation was giving way to a twentieth century concept where co-operatives simply functioned as one stakeholder along with proprietors and governments in a regulated 'orderly marketing' regime.

The Commonwealth Dairy Produce Pools Committee

A Commonwealth Dairy Produce Pools Committee, 'upon which each state and all interests would be represented, also nominees of the federal government', was established briefed to function for the duration of the war and until three years after. Its objectives were to stabilise prices and equalise returns to producers in both local and overseas markets. T M Burke was elected chairman. Complementary state legislation was to be enacted to establish Advisory Boards, co-ordinating the pools' operations. Dairy factories, including co-operatives, were required to 'contribute their quota' to the local market and provide information *assisting* the determination of prices. Subsequently the British government agreed to take all Australian surpluses at satisfactory prices.

Here was Meares' 'co-operative government of prices' in a nutshell, but it was neither industry-regulated nor voluntary. On the contrary, it was state-regulated and compulsory. Furthermore, the Dairy Produce Pools Committee included *all* interests: co-operative; proprietary and government; in what amounted to their *mandatory* co-operation in assured markets. In effect, the *Pools Act* contemplated a tripartite division of labour: supply, processing and distribution for co-operatives; manufacturing, marketing and services for proprietors; and underwriting, regulation and administration for governments. Historically, the act simply institutionalised relationships which had existed informally for years and for which co-operation had no answer, while extending to governments a power which they had not previously possessed. The question now was: would governments vacate the field in 1921? Certainly Meares was adamant that they should, engaging in what Harry Osborne described as 'underground engineering' to have T M Burke removed as chairman and the powers of the Pools Committee truncated.[41]

A weak co-operative legacy

By the end of World War I the shape of the twentieth century Australian rural co-operative movement was set. Already a deep antagonism divided rural co-operatives, on the one hand, and consumer co-operatives and the labour movement, on the other, from which Australian co-operation would never recover. Doubts had arisen about co-operation's theoretical *bona fides*, which had only been selectively applied by farmers for their exclusive benefit. Co-operation was linked in the public mind with 'secret circles' and rising consumer prices, inviting government intervention. A credibility gap existed between co-operation's grandiose claims and its practical achievements, for instance, 'international co-operative brotherhood', which was perceived to be simply rhetoric. The geographically-dispersed dairy co-operative movement was parochial, sectional and, apart from a few enthusiasts in Victoria, unconcerned with the interests of consumer co-operatives. A limited co-operation had taken root in dairying, narrowly focused, utilitarian and wholly dedicated to farmer betterment. Already co-operatives had revealed capitalisation problems, vulnerability to sudden change and had been confined to the relatively simple economic functions of supply, handling, processing and distribution. Opportunities to establish a co-operative domestic marketing system and co-operative banking, manufacturing and retail operations had been squandered, largely because the co-operators could not agree on their desirability. The case for federal co-operatives' legislation and a Co-operative Union promoting co-operation to governments and the public had been put and lost. Poorly served by legislation, co-operatives remained a states' responsibility in a federal environment, where free-trade between states was constitutionally guaranteed. How could farmer co-operatives construct a strong movement on these fragile foundations?

For co-operative campaigners like C E D Meares after 1921, when war-time regulations lapsed, it would no longer be a matter of resisting government intervention, for that was an established fact, but of constructing superior models to state-managed ones. The historical evidence so far suggested that the co-operative movement lacked a capacity for this.

Chapter Two

A March Of Regulation:
Farmer Co-operatives In The Inter-war Years

Introduction

In the period between the world wars a nineteenth century idea of co-operation as a form of transcendental voluntarism of high moral order gave way to a more practical view. The change had begun before the war and was simply accelerated by it. Co-operatives came to be seen by governments and farmers alike as merely useful business structures for enhancing agricultural productivity and developing new primary industries often linked to ambitious rural settlement schemes associated with British immigration and investments. Increasingly, co-operation became something governments *legislated* for rather than an autonomous self-help movement, a tendency aided by the co-operative movement's own disunity and inability to sensibly manage markets and stabilise prices and incomes at industry level. Voluntarism was shown to be not up to the task of regulating industry, paving the way for statutory marketing authorities (SMAs) and other protectionism.

Resistance to regulation by co-operative advocates was essentially a rearguard action for the precedent of government intervention established during the war was a relatively easy one to continue and extend. Primary producers, particularly those in new industries or in post-war rural settlement schemes, became accustomed to price stabilisation and market controls in the seasons to 1921, when wartime emergency regulations were removed and the idea that government intervention was *desirable* gained widespread support. In the process, Charles Meares' pre-war dream of industry self-management through a 'co-operative government of prices' was converted into a powerful example of Australian agricultural socialism. As Meares predicted SMAs severely narrowed the scope for co-operation, limiting it to relatively simple economic functions, retarding development and confining co-operation to a state-based level of operations.

The following chapter explores facets of this process with particular reference to dairying including:

- ❖ partially successful efforts by co-operators after World War I to co-operatively organise overseas markets;
- ❖ the re-shaping of co-operation by emergent farmer political groups;
- ❖ the failure of voluntary co-operative schemes to regulate the domestic dairy industry and the fillip this delivered to SMAs;
- ❖ efforts to encourage co-operation as an alternative to SMAs in New South Wales and how legislation to achieve this confined co-operatives while doing nothing to stem the march of regulation; and
- ❖ how Australian co-operation was retarded at the end of the period as another world war began.[1]

(i) The Co-operatives Organise Overseas Markets
The Australian Producers' Wholesale Co-operative Federation 1918

A May 1918 Melbourne co-operatives' conference, inspired by Western Australian Labor MLA W D Johnson, brought together twenty-five co-operatives and co-operative companies from all Australian states and New Zealand with the idea of forming a national producers' wholesale for exports. Co-operatives, co-operative companies and proprietary companies represented at the conference included:

Victoria:

❖ Victorian Producers' Co-operative Company;

❖ Western District Factories' Co-operative Production Company;

❖ G & N Co-operative Selling and Insurance Company;

❖ Victorian Butter Factories Co-operative Company;

❖ Victorian Orchardists' Co-operative Association;

❖ Geelong District Farmers' Co-operative Association;

❖ Western and Murray Co-operative Bacon Curing Company;

❖ Goulburn Valley Industries Company; and

❖ Wimmera Inland Freezing Company;

New South Wales:

❖ Coastal Farmers' Co-operative Union; and

❖ Farmers and Settlers Co-operative Grain Company;

South Australia:

❖ South Australian Farmers' Co-operative Union (SAFCU); and

❖ Farmers Producers' Co-operative Limited;

Queensland:

❖ Downs Co-operative Bacon Company;

❖ Queensland Co-operative Fruit-growers' Company;

❖ Rural Industries (Queensland) Limited; and

❖ Queensland Cheese Manufacturers' Association;

Western Australia:

❖ Westralian Farmers;

Tasmania:

❖ Tasmanian Orchardists' and Producers' Co-operative Association; and

❖ Farmers, Stock-owners and Orchardists' Association.

Pre-war disagreements over co-operative development strategies quickly resurfaced, with most Victorian delegates seeking retention of the existing pooling system and, predictably, Meares and the free-trade camp opposed, arguing that it would be unconstitutional and calling for a strengthened 'Australian Committee' of co-operative producers in London with links to the English CWS. The situation was complicated by disagreements among the Western Australians. While W D Johnson was not averse to government aid for co-operatives, seeing this as not necessarily inconsistent with self-help, other Western Australians, notably Basil Murray of Westralian Farmers, supported Meares. On the other hand, benefiting from sympathetic state legislation, which many easterners thought encouraged 'bogus' co-operation, Westralian Farmers' delegates flatly rejected calls for national co-operatives' legislation, which Meares now supported, while strongly supporting the

The Bega butter factory (c1950s).
Photo courtesy of Bega Co-operative Society Limited.

idea of a Raiffeisen-style bank for rural industry, to which Meares remained implacably opposed. It would ever be thus – a fractious Australian co-operative movement unable to agree on the key issues of national representation, federal legislation or a co-operative bank.

Nevertheless, the conference passed a resolution to form a provisional committee of an 'Australian Producers' Wholesale Co-operative Federation' (APWCF), designed to replace government-run commodity pools in the post-war period and build trade with the British co-operative movement and other Empire markets. Significantly, the Victorian co-operative companies, Western District and Victorian Butter Factories, dissented, signalling an intention to press for the maintenance of pools. A provisional committee for a 'Co-operative Federation of Australia' was also formed but only the Western Australians acted on this with any resolve, forming the Co-operative Federation of Western Australia (CFWA) in 1919 (discussed in Chapter Six).[2]

When the APWCF was formally constituted in Melbourne in 1919, the organisation included affiliates from all mainland states. The federation's objectives included: establish direct trading links between the 'Australian Primary-Producer Co-operative Movement' and the English CWS; build a co-operative basis for collective sales purchases and distribution of produce and requisites in rural production (to replace pools); and safeguard and advance co-operative enterprise, including adequate representation on any government pool or board. The charter extended to trading, shipping, merchandising and manufacturing but there was no mention of a co-operative bank or co-operative principles.

The Co-operative Insurance Company (CIC)

In 1918, G & N joined with Western District to establish Co-operative Insurance Company (CIC) of Victoria. Within a year 1,000 farmers had transferred policies to the new company and 160 agencies had been established in butter factories throughout Victoria. The company's name was changed to CIC (Australia) Limited in 1919 when the South Australian Farmers' Co-operative Union (SAFCU) and the Victoria Butter Factories took shares. Tough negotiations between the APWCF provisional committee and recalcitrant Victorians continued through 1919. Finally, in 1921, in order to get Victorian dairy producers into the federation, Meares applied for 3,000 shares in CIC, bringing in the Producers' Co-operative Distributive Society Limited (PDS), which had formed from an amalgamation of Coastal Farmers' and Berrima District Farm and Dairy Company. CIC branches were later opened in Brisbane and Hobart.

Reluctantly conceding to Melbourne APWCF's national headquarters, Meares insisted that the Victorians cease calling for government involvement in primary industry after 1921, when war time regulations would lapse. The Victorians ambiguously consented.[3]

Overseas Farmers' Wholesale Co-operative Federation

Meares and Basil Murray of Westralian Farmers then travelled to England to negotiate APWCF's affiliation with the English CWS. There they encountered Western District's Harry Osborne, sent by the Commonwealth Dairy Produce Pools Committee to seek accreditation and access to British markets through the pools. Furious, Meares joined with New Zealand delegates, who were also attending the British Government, to undermine Osborne by broadcasting that the pools would be unconstitutional after 1921. Following acrimonious exchanges between the Australians, Osborne returned with no progress to report. Clearly, the co-operative ranks, particularly in dairying, were bitterly divided.

In Manchester Meares and Murray met with English CWS officials and representatives of other empire co-operative movements to form the Overseas Farmers' Wholesale Co-operative Federation (hereafter, Overseas Farmers), described as a 'mutual purchaser system of direct indenting'. Overseas Farmers included as shareholders English CWS, APWCF (the biggest single shareholder), the Federated Farmers' Co-operative Association of South Africa Limited and the Farmers' Co-operative Wholesale of New Zealand. Rhodesian primary producers affiliated soon after. A E Gough, of English CWS, was appointed manager, organising branches in nine British cities and elsewhere in Europe. A subsidiary company, Empire Dairies Limited, opened a selling floor in Tooley Street, London, handling Canadian, Rhodesian, Irish, New Zealand and Australian dairy produce and operating a telephone link-up providing futures trading information and monitoring changes in money values.[4]

There is no question but that APWCF and Overseas Farmers were successful. By the late 1920s the annual turnover of Empire Dairies amounted to Sterling £10 million. It was the largest butter exchange in the world handling one-fifth of the total New Zealand and Australian output with Australian producers accounting for about 80 per cent of this. By 1929 the English CWS was reported to be the largest individual purchaser of primary produce in the world with Australia its biggest supplier, most of this trade passing through APWCF, particularly wheat, dairy products and fruit. Approximately 80 per cent of business handled by Overseas Farmers also originated in Australia. Australian processed produce – with value added in English CWS factories (not Australian factories) – was retailed through Overseas Farmers in 8,000 Rochdale co-operatives throughout Britain and Europe. In return, English CWS manufactures and processed goods reached many thousands of Australian households through rural societies and trading co-operatives, agricultural bureaux, produce stores and pastoral agencies. Trade items included farm implements, tools, hardware, cement, fertilisers, processed foods, tea, drapery, household items and a host of other items. Between 1920 and the early 1970s, Overseas Farmers handled approximately Sterling £1 billion of produce for APWCF and for various commodity boards, including the Australian Wheat Board, the Australian Dairy Products Board and the Australian Dried Fruits Board, in a trade cycle heavily favouring Australian producers.[5]

Too little, too late

Significant as these achievements were, and a testament to Charles Meares' tenacity, this co-operative response to the precedent of war-time pools came as too little too late. The APWCF's capacity to market produce varied inversely as Overseas Farmers' ability to absorb it, a capacity limited by the participation of other empire producers and limits to the ability of British consumer co-operatives to actually retail products. Further, the market share of English CWS, immense as it was, seldom rose above one-seventh of total British consumption and its giant subsidiary, Empire Dairies, could only ever account for about one-fifth of all Australian output. The extent of export market penetration possible, therefore, via the co-operative system, was limited. Improving rural productivity in Australia and in other producer nations, achieved through greater participation, co-operation, government assistance and technological advances, inevitably meant that additional marketing arrangements needed to be made, particularly in domestic markets where producer and consumer co-operatives, patently, were not co-operating.

The APWCF, too, developed in feverish, speculative markets exposing wool, wheat and dairy producers to large carry-overs. Then recession gave way to the Great Depression (1929-1934) and a weak, patchy recovery before World War II. Voluntary co-operation was ill-suited to these unstable conditions. Farmers required practical assistance in the orderly marketing of surpluses and dealing with erratic prices and return and governments were well-qualified to do this, if not for economic good management then for political survival.

There was another sense in which APWCF came as 'too little'. The indenting relationship with English CWS presupposed a division of labour where the federation exported commodities and imported goods. Implicit in this equation was the assumption that APWCF would do nothing to encourage indigenous production co-operation which might compete against Manchester's manufactures. That is precisely what happened. Australian farmer co-operatives, with few exceptions, stayed aloof from local consumer co-operatives and CWS showed little interest in its Australian clone, the Newcastle-based New South Wales Co-operative Wholesale Society (NSW CWS), while cultivating a mutually beneficial trading relationship with farmers. This may help to explain why the Rochdale consumer movement languished while a handful of agricultural co-operatives achieved immense size, giving rise to an asymmetrical development of the Australian movement.

(ii) Co-operation and Farmer Politics
The Australian Farmers' Federation

Through the war and in the immediate post-war period farmer political groups made progress in all states and at the federal level incorporating co-operation into their platforms while moulding it to match political realities. In late 1916 the Australian Farmers' Federation Organisation (AFFO) was formed from state farmer groups. The AFFO resolved to run or support political candidates who would assist farmers and returned servicemen, encourage rural-related manufacture, ensure that producers were represented on commodity boards, encourage British immigration, swear unswerving loyalty to the King, affirm that farmers produced all wealth, argue for a Living Wage for Rural Workers and *support co-operation*, not class warfare, in the establishment of a solid yeomanry 'rooted in the soil'.

The Massey-Greene Scheme

The AFFO co-operated with the Nationalist Party (after Billy Hughes defected from Labor) through the war. At a December 1919 election, however, eleven rural representatives: eight from Victoria and three from the Farmers' and Settlers' Association; were elected to the federal parliament, most on an AFFO platform. Unable to govern in their own right, a rural representative, W Massey-Greene, formerly a dairy farmer from the Richmond River region of New South Wales, was appointed Minister for Trade and Customs. Massey-Greene campaigned for a commonwealth scheme based on national (state) legislation for standards control underpinning co-operative enterprises in the handling and marketing of primary produce. These were to take over from war-time pools and SMAs in 1921. A government agency drawn from co-operative organisations was to be empowered to administer rural industries, issue and withhold licences, regulate brand names, control the purchase of all supplies used in manufacture relating to primary production and assist farmers in financing operations. The proposed agency would also co-ordinate and assist co-operative production and marketing while ensuring that primary industry proceeded on a voluntary, self-regulating footing. The resonance with Meares' position is clear.

Calls for an Australian Producers' Co-operative Party

There were calls in New South Wales at this time for an Australian Producers' Co-operative Party, to promote legislation establishing a National Co-operative Wholesale, modelled on Meares' Coastal Farmers' Co-operative, handling all imports and exports in the interests of primary and secondary industry. Secondary workers were to have access to federal funds to finance production-co-operatives and a network of retail co-operatives would distribute products. The proposed Co-operative Party was dedicated to decentralisation, doing away with 'too many governments, too many middle men, too many money lenders, strikes and a wasteful legal system'. Such a 'Co-operative Commonwealth' as the party proposed would embody principles of Christian brotherhood and abolish a system where 'stealing is the rule'. Nothing more is heard of the plan.[6]

Co-operation and marketing boards: the Australian Country Party

Following a Melbourne conference instigated by N Earle Page early in 1920, however, the Australian Country Party was formed, embracing some features of the Massey-Greene scheme but more directly influenced by Victorian protectionist thinking. Elected leader in 1921, Earle Page foreshadowed a Nationalist–Country Party Coalition. He also proposed a national co-operative marketing scheme for primary produce which would 'place industry in the hands of statutory tribunals on which producers will have a majority', similar to war-time pools, but voluntary associations run along business lines with no government interference. A 'land bank' would be created to 'make advances on broad acres assisting co-operative finance and supporting fodder and grain reserves'. Co-operation was being more closely drawn into mainstream politics.[7]

British immigration, co-operation and the '£34 Million Agreement'

In February 1923 the Bruce–Page Nationalist–Country Party Federal Coalition formed a 'businessman's government of men, money and markets'. A fairly stable period of federal politics followed during which time the government refurbished pre-war imperial links in what has been described as an 'Indian summer of neo-colonial mercantilism'. One element of this was the *Empire Settlement Act*, by which British and Dominion governments would 'formulate and co-operate in carrying out agreed schemes for joint assistance to suitable persons in the UK to settle in any part of overseas dominions'. British investors undertook to support the development of rural production and related public works in co-operative settlements populated by British immigrants. Land settlement schemes, run by the states, were to be financed by Australian primary produce exports. Agricultural productivity would be enhanced by 'improved' co-operation, scientifically promoted by governments in tandem with co-operative associations. Increasingly, co-operation was becoming something administrations employed to advance policy objectives rather than an autonomous movement.

The act led to the Anglo–Australian Agreement of 1925, the '£34 Million Agreement'. State governments vigorously competed for preferred treatment in this agreement and related rural reconstruction programs. Although the agreement largely failed to materialise, in feverish monetary conditions Australia became a major repository for British investment and, on a per capita basis, one of the most highly capitalised nations on earth. Much of this went into politically opportunistic rural-related infrastructure programs supporting co-operative settlement schemes, not necessarily founded on sound economic principles – unviable railway lines, for example.[8]

(iii) Dairy Co-operatives and Regulation in the Post-war Period
Unruly Markets

The sale and distribution of butter by the British Government after the war was what Harry Osborne of the Western District Co-operative (Victoria) described as 'a shocking mess', with disastrous results for dairy farmers throughout the world. After relinquishing control of foodstuffs, the government sought to dispose of all stocks on hand, precipitating chaotic market conditions and a disastrous plunge in prices. Meanwhile, rationing continued as a 'butter mountain' accumulated in cool stores. Then, when the Commonwealth Dairy Produce Pools Committee was unable to raise finance to purchase the surplus and staunch a price collapse, the British Government dumped butter at 'ruinous prices' to distributors and wholesale merchants, who realised fat profits. The impact of glut dumping impacted on world markets for dairy products for nearly a year and saw a wholesale price collapse. In this context, Osborne and other critics of Meares' voluntary co-operation thesis became more determined than ever to secure government assistance.

Meares had never accepted the 1916 Commonwealth Dairy Produce Pools Committee, arguing reasonably that it prevented the co-operative movement from advancing into marketing and gave proprietors disproportionate representation on boards which were subject to political manipulation. Immediately the war ended, Meares sought the pool's dismantling, applying political and constitutional pressure through the Primary Producers' Union (PPU) to have the committee's powers reduced to an advisory role while resuming a campaign to develop a national co-operative wholesale for *export* marketing and improved legislation for rural co-operatives, providing for easier access to capital. Notwithstanding Meares' rousing rhetoric imploring farmers to control their own destiny, it was widely understood by the mid 1920s that Victorian producers, blessed with favourable production conditions, had the potential to *flood* national markets with produce and the New South Wales industry, for one, was vulnerable. The fear of a 'foreign' invasion by southerners drove the orderly marketing debate more than anything Meares had to say about voluntary co-operation and free-trade. If regulation and protectionism could stem the invasion, and co-operation could not, then, farmers reasoned, let it happen in whatever form was politically achievable.[9]

'Voluntary schemes are unworkable': the Joint Stabilisation Committee

Certainly, continuing conflict in the dairying industry compelled governments to act. Preparing for the termination of war-time regulations in 1921 some state governments enacted legislation to regulate product standards and prices. In response, the Queensland and New South Wales dairy co-operative movements, led by Charles Meares, developed a Joint Stabilisation Committee, an income stabilisation scheme designed to levy producers voluntarily and equalise returns across the industry. The idea was not supported in other states, however, and following producer disagreements over regional quality differences, different processing standards and prices, the scheme fell apart.

Interventionists in the Western District Co-operative pointed to this failure as further proof that voluntary schemes were unworkable, arguing to the federal government that *more* statutory boards should be created and protection extended to primary producers as a 'bonus', along the lines of the Federal Tariff Board for Secondary Producers. The Commonwealth Dried Fruit Board, set up soon after the war, was touted as a model for dairying. Constitutional uncertainty lingered, however, which Meares exploited strenuously in opposing the idea, continuing to promote a co-operative domestic marketing arrangement along the lines of APWCF for exports.[10]

Another model considered by primary industry and government officials at the time was the Sapiro Co-operative Scheme, which was becoming popular in some American states. Named after Aaron Sapiro, the system involved compulsory membership and contracted supply and distribution arrangements and was favoured by some large scale, single commodity co-operatives. It was thought that the Sapiro Scheme's compulsoriness would be 'politically unpalatable' in Australia, however; repugnant to the Country Party and to trades practices laws; and the idea was scrapped. In 1923, however, an exemption from the *Monopolies Act* of primary producer combines in instances where a public interest could be demonstrated (the public interest test) boosted support for SMAs.

Following a Melbourne conference in August 1923 the dairy industry endorsed a Western District Co-operative proposal calling for a commonwealth-regulated prices and income stabilisation scheme for dairy exports under federal external powers co-ordinated through the 'voluntary association of marketing authorities in the states' (to circumvent constitutional difficulties). The proposal, which envisaged restructuring the industry into a 'co-operative' of commonwealth and state boards, received broad industry support, although C E D Meares remained sceptical. Again it might be noted that the initiative came from sections of the co-operative movement and not government.

The Dairy Produce Control Board

The Commonwealth Government duly passed the *Dairy Produce (Export) Control Act* setting up the Dairy Produce (Export) Control Board to control the export of butter and cheese to Britain. The federal board included twelve representatives of co-operatives and proprietary companies empowered to regulate prices and levy producers to achieve income stabilisation across the industry.

Meares urged New South Wales farmers to boycott the board, describing it as 'practically proprietary in outlook and decision'. Following threats from New South Wales co-operatives to withdraw from CIC (Australia) and intense political engineering through the Country Party, the Dairy Produce (Export) Control Board was restricted to an advisory role. But the issue was far from resolved. For many producers, the act did not go far enough and, as London prices for butter fell through the 1920s and competition for domestic markets intensified, pressure was kept on the Commonwealth Government to act to equalise returns and stabilise prices within and between domestic and export markets. Victorian and New South Wales dairying co-operatives were at loggerheads on the issue.

A 'descendant of co-operation': The Patterson Scheme, 1926–1934

Meanwhile, the regulatory juggernaut gathered momentum. In January 1926 the Commonwealth Government created the Australian Butter Stabilisation Committee, known as the 'Patterson Scheme', named after a Country Party member for Gippsland. Western District's Harry Osborne is credited as the architect of this scheme, which was painted as an 'improved system of voluntary regulation, a descendent of co-operation'. The committee's object was to 'give producers a return more in keeping with Australian living standards' by paying a *bonus* to producers for butter exported and *equalising* returns between domestic and external markets. Producers were levied to finance the committee's operations. The rub for Australian consumers was that local prices were to be adjusted by the amount of the export bonus and maintained to this degree *above* London parity. In other words, Australian consumers would subsidise the competitiveness of Australian producers abroad.

The Patterson Scheme was a classic example of economic feather-bedding, demonstrating that what Australian dairy farmers meant by 'stabilisation' was the raising of prices to the highest possible level at all times. Consequently, local consumers paid an average of 4.5d per pound for butter above market prices. By 1929 Australian dairymen had reaped £6.5 million from the scheme, a figure rising to £20 million by 1934. The point for our discussion is that the scheme did more than stabilise the dairy industry, it *superseded* voluntary co-operation while legitimising regulation. Again, the inspiration came from a section of the co-operative movement.

The Imperial Economic Conference, Ottawa, 1932

During the Great Depression nations sought to restrict imports by creating tariff walls and quotas while seeking free entry for their own goods in foreign markets. Germany and France, for example, flooded UK markets with dairy products. With UK protectionism on the rise, Harry Osborne of Western District Co-operative and a contingent of Australians, including Major J Russell King, soon to replace an ailing Charles Meares as general manager of the PDS-Dairy Farmers group, travelled to Canada for the 1932 Ottawa Imperial Economic Conference. The outcome was that the British Government agreed to impose substantial duties and quotas on imports from foreign countries for butter, cheese, condensed and dried milk, honey and eggs, apples and fresh fruit, and guarantee a preference for empire trade for three years, to be reviewed thereafter. The arrangement saw strengthened government intervention in agriculture and by dint of that, in co-operative affairs.[11]

The Patterson Scheme disintegrates

In 1933 the Patterson Scheme began to disintegrate when 'disloyal' factories, both private and co-operative, refused to pay the industry levy while continuing to enjoy higher domestic prices available through the scheme. The system became counter-productive when, not withstanding the Ottawa agreement, increasing British protectionism and disintegrating export markets saw export surpluses actually reducing local prices to *less* than London prices, less shipping. Aggressive discounting and border price wars developed, pitting co-operative against co-operative. For instance, after Norco opened a rival selling floor in Sydney, a bitter price war erupted between the northern co-operative and PDS. If co-operative unity could not be found in dairying, where could it be found?

In May 1934 the Patterson Scheme was abandoned. Critics pointed to its voluntariness as a central weakness and:

> *Industry leaders then decided that the solution was to maintain local value irrespective as to what exports promised to realise by a system of quotas giving a fair share of the market to each producer together with a system of price equalisation…The leaders speedily decided that it was hopeless to expect that this result could be achieved by a voluntary arrangement.*[12]

A new scheme, modelled on an international wheat agreement, which imposed import and export quotas and regulated production and marketing in an orderly fashion, was seen as a desirable option. The day had arrived for production quotas and zones compulsorily regulated by state-based

SMAs co-operating in a 'gentleman's' agreement to circumvent constitutional difficulties in respect of free-trade. For the dairy industry, and the co-operatives within it, six decades of heavy regulation began.[13]

Dairy Produce Equalisation Committee Limited

With unruly markets continuing, however, and New Zealand and Australian dairy products exceeding the capacity of UK markets to absorb them, prices tumbled. In late 1933 the Commonwealth Government passed the *Dairy Produce Act*, creating the Dairy Produce Equalisation Committee Limited. (This was subsequently restructured as the Australian Dairy Produce Board [later 'Corporation'] after the Privy Council ruled the act unconstitutional and the commonwealth was reduced to acting through its customs and trade description powers, with state governments 'assisting'.)

Operating under the aegis of the Commonwealth Government, the Dairy Produce Equalisation Committee was co-ordinated by state shareholders nominated by state dairy boards set up under complementary legislation (eight from Victoria, New South Wales and Queensland and four from each of the other states). Essentially a national commodity monopoly, this corporate hybrid was registered under company law as no suitable co-operatives law existed. State dairy board shareholders comprised government officials, proprietors and co-operatives, 'co-operating in a government of prices'. The Equalisation Committee was empowered to 'oblige every manufacturer to accept the principle of sharing markets equitably and remove any incentive to impair value by engaging in any unhealthy competition [*sic*] on any particular market'. The committee was designed to establish a quota system, fix prices, market produce, sequester inequitable returns from producers who breached the committee's charter, meet transport costs and levy producers for the costs of maintaining the scheme. Co-operatives, which were now producing more than 80 per cent of the national dairy output, were given better representation than previously under the Dairy Produce (Export) Control Board. The fact remained, however, that co-operatives in a political sense were virtually auxiliaries of SMAs.

Meares accepts government intervention

After the New South Wales *Dairy Products Act* was passed to complement commonwealth legislation, the New South Wales Milk Board became that state's shareholder of the Dairy Produce Equalisation Committee. Even C E D Meares, in a retirement speech where he regretted the failure of co-operatives to move further into marketing, acknowledged that under the depressed economic conditions there was no real alternative but to accept government intervention. The Equalisation Committee was necessary, he said, for the survival of 'established' producers and this could only be achieved through a system of quotas. The formula, he believed, exercised through a system of licences and quota shares, would have the effect of eliminating excess capacity and would drive market irritants (he had NSW CWS in mind) and 'disloyal' producers from the industry. It was, he now believed, 'hopeless to expect that this result could be achieved by voluntary arrangement'.

Here was the result of more than thirty years' effort by Meares and 'genuine' co-operators to put the Australian dairy industry on a co-operative basis: a company comprising state SMA-shareholders setting production quotas and prices in one of the most regulated markets in the English-speaking world. A national poll taken to constitute the Equalisation Committee produced a fifty to one vote in favour. Within five years, following a series of amalgamations and takeovers, only two registered Milk Board metropolitan suppliers remained in New South Wales: Dairy Farmers and Norco. NSW CWS had been driven from the field. The vanquishing of the consumers, however, was really a pyrrhic victory for farmers, as would become evident six decades later, when the industry was deregulated (discussed in Chapter Three).[14]

(iv) New South Wales, Co-operation and Butter Wars

While national and international events saw government intervention in production, marketing and trade on the increase, in free-trade New South Wales a deliberate attempt was being made by the state to encourage co-operation in the form of the *Co-operation Act* (1923). Victoria would not have co-operatives legislation for another thirty years. Queensland had co-operatives legislation but it was about 'compulsory' co-operation, an anathema in Charles Meares' home state. Western Australia would soon have co-operatives legislation but as a sub-section of company law and, easterners believed, this simply encouraged 'bogus' co-operation. The New South Wales *Co-operation Act* was held up as the 'show piece' of co-operatives legislation, something unique in Australia, an act permitting 'genuine' co-operation and supporting co-operatives without commandeering them. The problem was that the legislation was anything but what sponsors claimed it to be. Far from encouraging co-operatives as an alternative to SMAs, the act enmeshed them in regulation and complicated their organisation.

The New South Wales *Co-operation Act*

The political purpose of the New South Wales *Co-operation Act*, which formed part of the *Empire Settlement Act* vision, was to woo back to the Nationalist-fold the recalcitrant Progressives (County Party). The economic and foreign policy purpose was to tie the New South Wales rural economy back into a pre-war imperial order built on British capital investments, agricultural exports and British immigration.

Beginning life as the 'Co-operation, Community Settlement and Rural Credit Bill', the *Co-operation Act* was passed by a Nationalist Government with Progressive support. Introducing the bill into the Legislative Assembly in October 1923 Liberal (Progressive) Attorney-General T R Bavin described it as the most important bill that session adding that co-operation had potential to transform society fundamentally 'without standing on its head'. Capitalism was flawed, Bavin continued, and co-operation was superior. A Labor parliamentary colleague interjected that Bavin must be in the wrong party. Co-operation would assist trade with Britain, the attorney-general continued, and 'above all, we are trying to develop a large class of small producers [and] co-operation tends to make that less expensive'.

Following intense cross-party debate on the *meaning* of co-operation Bavin dropped a bombshell by announcing that a ban on co-operative banking going back to 1865 was to be augmented by a prohibition on co-operative *insurance*. The political purpose appears to have been to pre-empt plans by the Victorian-based Co-operative Insurance Company (CIC) to extend operations into New South Wales as a co-operative eligible for taxation exemption under the bill's provisions, thereby improving competition. The government appears to have caved in to objections from New South Wales insurance companies, including the Farmers' and Graziers' Co-operative Grain, Insurance and Agency Company Limited, a 'bogus' co-operative controlled by a consortium of Sydney-based insurance and pastoral houses, representatives of which had complained that they would be disadvantaged by co-operative insurance unless they too enjoyed the bill's taxation provisions. The government's solution was to ban co-operative insurance altogether, and, in so doing, strike at the heart of co-operative financial autonomy. CIC would have to operate in New South Wales as a company, not a co-operative.

The insurance prohibition provoked uproar in the house, with Labor charging that the bill would be useless. How could a co-operative movement ever evolve without financial autonomy? Banks could foreclose at any time, said Labor, to crush a co-operative which showed any signs of real competition against private companies. Leading Labor, P F Loughlin said he would 'test' the house on the issue of co-operative finance, seeking to drive a wedge between the Progressives and Nationalists and bring the government down. The house divided. Loughlin's motion that *both* co-operative insurance and banking be included in the bill was defeated.

Then H Main ('True Blue' Progressive, Cootamundra), a farmer and grazier, moved to extract another concession from the Nationalists for supporting the insurance prohibition, moving that 'other persons' be added to paragraph (a) of clause 7, Rural Societies, so that it read: 'A rural society may…dispose of the agricultural products or livestock of its members or other persons'. J T Lang (Labor, Parramatta) exploded:

You will kill co-operation…A small group may call themselves a co-operative – but never get new members and become general traders selling not only their own stock or goods or produce – but [those] of everybody else in the district. Co-operation [would become]…a huckstering concern…with taxation exemption.

H V C Thorby ('True Blue' Progressive, Wammerawa), a farmer and grazier, said that the amendment was necessary to ensure the continuance of one of the '…largest co-operatives in New South Wales…the Farmers' and Graziers' Co-operative Grain, Insurance and Agency Company Limited'. T L F Rutledge ('True Blue', Progressive, Goulburn), a grazier, said that 'other persons' doing business with a co-operative would derive rebates, learn about the benefits of co-operation and become members. The amendment was necessary, he said, to the survival of many well-established rural co-operative companies.

The amendment was passed along party lines. Its effect was to extend to patrons of a co-operative, shares in the co-operative if the board so decided together with the option of dividends on tax-exempt services. This amounted to a discount subsidised by tax-payers and acted as an inducement to 'bogus' co-operation subject to the influence of 'dry' (non-producer) shareholders while reducing further the incentive to 'genuine' co-operation. This was only possible because no definition of co-operation along Rochdale lines, for example, was included in the bill, despite persistent Labor calls for this.

The bill proceeded to the Legislative Council where it was further amended enabling rural co-operative companies registered *before* the act and choosing *not* to employ the bill's provisions to continue to use 'co-operative' in their title. The 'bogus' co-operatives had won another reprieve.

In this form the *Co-operation, Community Settlement and Rural Credit Act* came into force on 3 January 1924. Under its provisions, a co-operative society could be formed with a minimum of seven members. Other than extant co-operative companies, only new societies registering under the act were permitted to include 'co-operative' in their title. The legislation compartmentalised co-operation into eight business structures: rural societies, trading societies, rural credit societies; urban credit societies, building societies, investment societies, community advancement societies and co-operative settlement societies. The functions of the various co-operative types were subject to a doctrine of *ultra vires*, the effect of which was to complicate co-operation between different types of co-operatives. As an instance of this, trading and rural societies operating in the same building and involving virtually identical personnel in Bega were prevented from registering as a single entity, putting the Bega Co-operative (dairy) to additional expense and duplicating administration.

Only societies of the same 'type' could form a Co-operative Association to 'supervise the affairs of and render services to its component parts'. Only two or more such co-operative associations could form a 'Union of Co-operative Associations' to promote co-operation in general and supervise its component parts. Combinations outside these provisions, even if 'co-operative' in a Rochdale sense, were 'unlawful'. Indeed, as parliamentarians on both sides of the House had predicted, the provision became a 'dead letter'. Only two weak Co-operative Associations formed before the Great Depression, not withstanding the registrar's enthusiastic encouragement, and not one Union of Co-operative Associations was formed.

The Co-operative Advisory Council, which had first been set up in the 1890s, was refurbished, however, providing better representation for the various co-operative 'types' while keeping a tight government rein. The council continued to be dominated by agricultural co-operatives and, by the second half of the 1920s, had become a political lobby for farmers and a battlefield for co-operative producers and consumers, with the latter resenting the government's favoured treatment of the former.

The Registrar of Co-operative Societies created by the act headed a registry administering co-operatives with a brief to foster co-operation. In reality the position became a political appointment and the registry more an administrative policeman regulating co-operation in accordance with prevailing ideologies and party political dictates. The first registrar, H A Smith, emerged from a background in the Statisticians Department and was concerned primarily with farmer co-operatives.

The act also detailed 'model rules' and regulations for co-operatives, ostensibly to assist with development, but these were of such a technical nature that they required often expensive legal and accountancy counsel to interpret, curbing spontaneous co-operation. An under-staffed registry also saw long delays develop in processing applications with Registrar Smith noting that, 'Any larger increase in the number of societies rendered it impossible for official inspectors to give the small societies the individual attention and assistance they required'.

The legislation strengthened directors' powers by enabling them to withhold dividends against regulated reserve levels. It also allowed co-operatives to enter into temporary contracts of exclusivity with suppliers, which improved their contractual position but, as this was kept on a voluntary basis (to circumvent trades practices regulations), it did nothing to prevent private merchants from wooing producer-suppliers away with better spot prices or farmers demanding 'cash-in-hand' from their co-operatives. The *Co-operation Act* was intended to give co-operatives a stronger legal personality to encourage investment but patterns of investment hardly varied with farmer-members continuing to invest the bare minimum, preferring to offset income against investments in the prime asset, the home farm.

The democracy principle was strictly applied to credit societies but (over time) other societies were able to allot up to two additional votes in accordance with business done or the number of shares held by a member. Proxies were permitted, a maximum of five per member. Capital-raising, however, was confined to funds from members, loans against a mortgage, bonds and deposits. Certain taxation exemptions were extended to 'eligible co-operatives' (that is, co-operative companies not within the act's jurisdiction) provided that 90 per cent of business was conducted with members – the mutuality principle.

Approximately 160 rural societies registered under the act before the Great Depression arrested further development. Most 'co-operation', however, actually occurred *outside* the act through Agricultural Bureaux, which proliferated, sponsored by the Department of Agriculture.

Agricultural Bureaux permitted a more flexible combination of functions, proscribed by the act. Essentially departmental field outposts, Bureaux were described by a departmental officer as 'little co-operative worlds in themselves', organising social, technical, commercial, farming and selling activities and providing administrative and technical support for local co-operatives, which the fractious co-operative movement seemed incapable of providing for itself.

By 1935 there were more than 300 Agricultural Bureaux, most linked informally to rural and trading co-operatives and enjoying, by dint of that, taxation benefits while effectively *beyond* the registrar's jurisdiction. Registrar Smith repeatedly voiced concern at the scope for taxation abuse this *ad hoc* arrangement permitted but was powerless to act and no government was prepared to face the rural backlash a challenge might precipitate. It should be stressed that no evidence linking Agricultural Bureaux or co-operatives mentioned in discussion to taxation avoidance has been found but the registrar's long-term concern that tax abuse was rife must raise the question.

Perhaps the most serious shortcoming, as far as national co-operatives' development was concerned, was that the act did nothing to assist co-operatives trading, or wishing to trade, on a commonwealth basis. In the absence of compatible co-operatives' legislation in other states, or uniform legislation facilitating national membership, trading under the act was confined to New South Wales for the very practical reason that the state's co-operatives, bound by the mutuality principle for purposes of taxation consideration, were precluded from accepting business beyond the act's jurisdiction where such trade exceeded 10 per cent of turnover, while remaining a co-operative for purposes of the act's provisions. The subaltern was that a 'foreign' (interstate) co-operative seeking business in New South Wales was exempt from the act's provisions and therefore eligible for taxation. In this way, the *Co-operation Act* served as a 'firewall' to keep other co-operatives out of New South Wales, particularly Victorian dairying co-operative companies, already rattling at market doors.

In the name of encouraging co-operation, the *Co-operation Act* precluded co-operative financial autonomy, gave comfort to 'bogus' co-operatives, complicated co-operative organisation and hampered interstate trade.[15]

'Assisting self-help': statutory marketing authorities in New South Wales

In September 1927 the Department of Agriculture convened a conference in Bathurst representing consumers and producers to plan for collective marketing boards. Notwithstanding the *Co-operation Act*, the department had concluded that voluntary schemes of industry regulation simply did *not* work, at least not quickly enough to meet government economic and social objectives. When Registrar of Co-operative Societies H A Smith complained that the government was going too far and intruding upon co-operative autonomy, the Lang Labor Government appointed an information officer to 'assist' him.

The proposed marketing boards, modelled loosely on Queensland examples (the 'McGregor Scheme', discussed in Chapter Five), were to be clothed with powers to *expropriate* commodities, which would be 'vested' in boards. A Primary Producers' Organisation Bill would provide legal machinery for the scheme, which would be extended to primary industries where (only) 60 per cent of producers approved the constitution of a board. The government justified the proposal by saying that it was necessary to 'assist primary producers in the processes of self-help...to give consideration to their problems and to devise ways of solving them, encouraging co-operative associations and enterprise on non-party lines, uniting these with private organisations into a national body'. The inference was that the co-operative movement, left to its own devices, was incapable of this.

Predictably Lang's 'red' Labor plan to unite the interests of producers and consumers received short shrift from the Primary Producers' Union (PPU) with C E D Meares to the fore:

A conference inspired by political altruists was convened,…the ostensible object being to consider and devise ways and means of bringing the producer and consumer closer together… Representatives of the retail co-operative houses, which in the main represent and cater for the benefit of an industrial clientele, sought to bridge the gap which was alleged to yawn between producer and consumer by an attempt to deal direct with the factories…To representatives of the producers the brainy brilliant idea did not appeal in the least [for] they realised that if [it] materialised it would mean the end of the co-operative distributing business which had been initiated and carried on largely through the employment of producers' capital. The idea of being asked cheerfully to cut the throat of…their co-operative undertakings did not appeal to them. The conference therefore proved abortive and nothing good or evil came from it.

An angry correspondent to the NSW CWS journal, *Co-operative News*, from an anonymous APWCF executive (possibly Meares) said:

The producer does not matter a tuppeny dump. All he is asked to do is send his surplus butter… and permit the consumer, be he Novocastrian or Australian, or a Londoner and English, to buy it at a bedrock price and subsequently to be further rewarded by the return of surpluses. The producer…is expected to hand over his butter, bacon and cheese so that the Australian or British industrialist may get cheap food…The management of the [NSW CWS] must have a very poor conception of the mentality of the average producer if he thinks the dairy farmer…is likely to entertain a proposal which while not benefiting him one penny will inevitably destroy not only his co-operative distributing houses in Australia but will give a final coup de grace to the Overseas Farmers' Federation.[16]

In mid 1927 the Lang Government passed the *Marketing of Primary Products Act*. The act was not to become effective for one year during which time polls would be taken to identify industries seeking application of its provisions. In the interim, however, Labor lost office. The incoming Bavin Coalition Government (1927-1930) preserved the legislation but *abolished* consumer representation on boards! In this form the New South Wales *Marketing of Primary Produce Act* became a model for Victoria, South Australia, Tasmania and Western Australia.

Meat, butter, millet and fresh fruit producers all rejected proposals for SMAs, however, as constitutional uncertainty lingered. Registrar Smith, meanwhile, continued to promote co-operative associations as an alternative to boards under the *Co-operation Act*. Indeed, with Smith's help, a Co-operative Poultry Council and the Young (Prunes) Co-operative Association were formed as alternatives to the statutory model, but their poor performance did little to advance the co-operative cause. Producers in newer and smaller agricultural industries, facing difficult economic conditions, voted to establish boards, for example, the Murrumbidgee Irrigation Area Rice Growers' Co-operative in 1928. Boards were also formed for bananas, ginger, potatoes and honey. An attempt to form an egg marketing board was unsuccessful. The honey board was dissolved in 1932. The economic fact was that, in the Great Depression, markets simply did not exist to justify the existence of co-operative marketing systems *or* SMAs.

A 'butter war'

The *Marketing of Primary Produce Act* did nothing to improve relations between producer and consumer co-operatives. Protesting the Bavin government's removal of consumer representation from boards in 1929, the consumer co-operative movement withdrew its representative from the Co-operative Advisory Council. Then, when the government amended the *Co-operation Act* to permit companies using 'co-operative' in their title to come under the act while placing limits on what they could borrow, consumer co-operators lambasted this as 'slaughter with a vengeance', accusing primary producer co-operatives of being an actual 'grave danger to Rochdale'. The NSW CWS launched a 'butter war', securing the agency rights of the proprietary Hunter–Gloucester District Butter Factory Association and dumping butter on the New South Wales south coast, the heartland of the dairying co-operative movement:

> *Newcastle threw down the gauntlet against the owner-producer milk monopoly…Sydney has failed. Newcastle must safeguard democracy. If it hurts primary producers we can't help it. We are free to sell wherever we want. Primary producers should not name call. Time will tell which one of us is right.*

The New South Wales Milk Board

In response, the Lang Labor Government, which was returned to power in October 1930, constituted the New South Wales Milk Board, set up to take charge of unruly markets in Sydney and Newcastle. All milk from registered producers in defined zones was to be vested in the board, which appointed five existing distributive companies as agents, including two co-operatives, Dairy Farmers and Norco. The NSW CWS repeatedly and unsuccessfully sought a distributor's licence from the board and to have consumer representatives reappointed to it. Registrar Smith supported NSW CWS in its fight with the dairy co-operatives, concerned that the latter had 'demonstrated a limited amount of loyalty to the principles of co-operation'. Smith also supported NSW CWS President and Labor Parliamentarian George Booth in calls for a 'shared market arrangement', joining producers and consumers in a national wholesale, marketing Australian co-operative primary produce through co-operative retail stores. How else, Smith asked, could an integrated co-operative movement ever develop?

When D P McEvoy, who was also sympathetic to consumer co-operatives, replaced Smith as registrar in 1933, he saw to amendments to the *Co-operation Act* permitting trading societies and rural societies to affiliate and helped NSW CWS in an application to the Milk Board for a distribution licence. McEvoy also urged the minister to bring the now numerous agricultural bureaux under his jurisdiction. This led in 1936 to the formation of Agricultural Bureaux Co-operative, which McEvoy then sought to affiliate with NSW CWS to form one large co-operative wholesale, joining producers and consumers and paving the way for a NSW CWS Milk Board licence. The Agricultural Bureaux Co-operative board flatly refused to have anything to do with NSW CWS and that was that. Nothing could get the producer and consumer co-operators to co-operate, not even government agency support.

The NSW CWS demanded a royal commission into the dairying industry, alleging that the Charles Meares' PDS–Dairy Farmers Co-operative group was *not* co-operative and therefore unsuitable to act as an approved marketing agent for the Milk Board. The Rochdale wholesale contended that Dairy Farmers, as it was then constituted, did not apply a one-person-one-vote principle and was effectively controlled by a small group of mainly 'dry' shareholders, adding that it had 3,300 members holding 168,000 one pound shares. 'Dry' shareholders were admitted by a majority vote to attend general meetings where five shares allowed one vote, twenty-five to one hundred shares allowed two votes and more than one hundred shares allowed four votes! In addition, any one member could proxy for up to *twenty* other members. This was not economic democracy, Rochdale leaders complained – Dairy Farmers was virtually a joint stock operation. They demanded that the government take 'bogus' co-operatives in hand.

This war between sections of the co-operative movement and the collapse of the Young (Prunes) Co-operative Association, which underlined the unreliability of voluntary systems, strengthened the government's resolve to proceed with statutory regulation. Indeed, Registrar McEvoy was reluctantly obliged to acknowledge that SMAs only existed *because* of co-operation's deficiencies.[17]

(v) Co-operation is Retarded
Individualism brakes co-operation

Writing in the *Annuls* of the American Academy of Political and Social Science in 1931, the academic, F R Mauldon, noted how the fierce individualism of Australians was acting as a brake on co-operative development. All attempts to unite co-operatives, he wrote, had been repeatedly frustrated by parochialism. In Australia, business instincts were demonstrably stronger than the co-operative impulse and a fierce competitiveness existed between co-operatives, which were purely commercially-oriented. There was 'no buoyant idealism' in Australian primary producer co-operatives, scarcely any surplus was dedicated to co-operative education and a general indifference prevailed among members and management about the importance of cultivating a virile faith in the co-operative ideal. The result, Mauldon said, was 'sore disappointment' to those Australians who had 'caught the vision of co-operation and sought to spread welfare through co-operation'.[18]

Failure to live up to expectations

New South Wales State Marketing Board Director A A Watson described SMAs as the 'logical extension of the co-operative movement…their grandchildren'. Former Registrar of Co-operative Societies H A Smith, speaking from retirement, disagreed, but conceded along with Registrar McEvoy that the co-operatives had failed to live up to expectations in regulating, equalising or stabilising markets and had paved the way for them. While two-thirds of Australian dairy factories were co-operative, Smith said, Australian co-operation was retarded relative to similar nations and was still quite insignificant in the Australian economy. Co-operation extending beyond the borders of any state was almost entirely unknown. Despite several interstate conferences, still no permanent, inclusive national umbrella organisation existed to advance the co-operative cause. No co-operative credit facility existed and the joint purchasing of goods and services through co-operatives was still in its infancy. Unlike many other countries, Smith continued, organisations which had been developed under government control to handle rural products had failed to develop into co-operatives, or even quasi-co-operatives, with the possible exception of the voluntary wheat pools:

> *The lack of cohesion between the co-operative organisations of the various states, and the limited amount of loyalty of co-operators to the principles upon which they work, have gone far to defeat the true success of co-operative endeavour. Having introduced price cutting and competition, not only interstate but between societies in the same state…producers have failed to gain complete control over marketing…and butter is still in some measure a speculative product of which the marketing is only partly organised. Of course this condition of affairs is rightly attributable in large measure to the vagaries of the seasons. But the fact remains that although the nature of the dairying industry affords peculiar advantage for co-operative manufacture and marketing, much remains to be done in Australia before the industry is placed upon a truly co-operative basis.[19]*

Smith saw the absence of suitable legislation as a key problem retarding the co-operative movement. Nearly all states had copied English laws but had failed to amend them so that they had become antiquated. Most primary producer co-operatives, therefore, had *necessarily* adapted joint stock laws to their own ends. Only in Queensland and New South Wales had any real progress been made in the co-operatives' legislation area, Queensland for agricultural co-operatives (the *Queensland Primary Producers' Co-operative Associations Act*) and New South Wales for general co-operatives (the *Co-operation Act*). The former registrar observed:

> *The greatest drawback in most forms of voluntary co-operation is that the benefit to any particular individual is rarely sufficient to induce him to undertake the risks of loss of time and money which the promotion of a society involves.*[20]

Having demonstrated an inability to create a workable system of voluntary industry self-regulation or to co-operate the interests of producers and consumers, it was proper, indeed inevitable, Smith concluded, that governments should move to regulate markets, further narrowing the field for co-operative endeavour.[19]

The return of war

The return of emergency war-time regulations in 1939 simply accelerated this process of market socialisation which had begun in the inter-war period and for which co-operation had no answer. This was a much more powerful Commonwealth Government than the one which had moved tentatively into pooling during World War I, resolving:

> *...to acquire at any time any part of the output of any manufacturer which the minister might deem it necessary to acquire...The minister will not hesitate to use the fullest extent if necessary of the power conferred upon him.*

These sweeping powers remained in force until 1948, three years after the war ended, confirming and consolidating the shape of Australia's highly regulated marketing system for primary products. Indeed, war-time arrangements agreed by the Australian and British governments lasted until 1955, boosting Australian productions while engendering a culture of dependence and apathy among cosseted farmer-suppliers and their co-operatives, who grew accustomed to this.

Chapter Three
_____

'It is time to deregulate the sacred dairy cow': THE POST-WAR DAIRY CO-OPERATIVE MOVEMENT

Introduction

Having considered in the previous chapter how *regulation* came to ensnare co-operatives in the dairy industry, our attention now turns to how *deregulation* was achieved and the part played in this by co-operatives.

In the approximately three decades between the end of World War II and the mid-1970s deregulatory pressures built within the Australian dairy industry, in which co-operatives were well represented. This produced ructions within individual co-operatives and between the co-operative movements of different states, particularly those of New South Wales and Victoria. Memories were not so short as to have forgotten the unruly free-for-all which had preceded regulation in the inter-war years. To disband regulation would require a very convincing argument. Nevertheless, pressure for deregulation continued to build, raised, in the main, by Victorian co-operative milk processors.

In the end, however, it was not economic rationalism which set the deregulation clock ticking, but decisions taken by a foreign government and local consumers – Britain's entry into the European Economic Community (EEC) in 1973 and a shift by consumers from butter to margarine consumption. From early in the century British markets were seen by dairy farmers as a 'sink' for the absorption of most of Australia's dairy exports. Now the 'sink' was plugged while Australian butter consumption plummeted. The ramifications would reverberate throughout the industry for at least a decade. Disbarred by a Commonwealth Dairy Produce Equalisation Committee 'gentlemen's agreement' between state governments from participating in interstate markets, co-operatives geared to exports were required to adjust or go out of business, particularly in Victoria, where supply far exceeded local demand. Equally, co-operatives accustomed to comfortable trading conditions in protected fresh-milk markets were required to defend those markets or be driven from the industry by superior Victorian competition. The alternative was for the dairying co-operatives to co-operate – but they could not. Instead, there was a scramble for capital to fuel growth and competitiveness heralding a 'co-operative dilemma', where co-operatives struggled to bring democracy and capital adequacy into balance.

Some, like the Murray-Goulburn Co-operative (Victoria), which invested in developing new products, export markets and infrastructure, looked enviously at protected domestic fresh-milk processors, including co-operatives, which enjoyed reliable conditions in lucrative metropolitan markets and wondered how to enter those markets. Inevitably, friction developed between co-operatives in the processed (manufactured) and market (fresh) milk segments of the industry, spilling into national co-operative affairs and shattering all attempts at unity. That this should occur in an industry where co-operatives were so well represented was calamitous for Australian co-operative development, confounding all attempts at unity when this was so vital in capturing post-war opportunities.

Because the deregulatory debate in dairying was driven primarily by Victorian co-operative companies; ironically, given their role in constructing the regulated regime in the first place between the wars; discussion first considers developments in that state before moving on to a broader consideration of mounting deregulatory pressures in the final two decades of the century, with elements of the dairying co-operative movement proactive and others resisting. We will consider various federal schemes to slowly nudge the industry towards deregulation to the degree this was politically achievable, including the imposition of National Competition Policy (NCP) and pressure building within the co-operative movement to solve the 'co-operative dilemma' to a point where some co-operatives sought external investments and prepared for listing. Dairying co-operatives passed through what one leader described as the 'most difficult position in history' when perceptions of co-operatives changed and the traditional nexus between co-operatives and members was altered forever in a deregulatory 'big milkshake'.

Industry Background

Discussion does not pretend to be a history of the Australian dairy industry in the period for that would require specialist research beyond the brief of a general study on agricultural co-operatives. It is useful to keep in mind, however, that we are concerned with *two* industries – one for manufactured milk; which was generally export-orientated; and another for fresh (liquid) market milk, for daily consumption in domestic markets. Various commonwealth and state systems which had evolved in the inter-war years, designed to pool production, set quotas, designate supply zones, set prices and equalise returns across the industries through cross-subsidies, bounties and levies, operated throughout the period and reference is made to these in so far as they shed light on the operations of co-operatives.

Fresh milk was sold in separate state markets, regulated by state authorities applying various state rules. Interstate markets were effectively 'foreign' markets, notwithstanding constitutional guarantees of free-trade, and were a testament to the political influence of dairy producers at state and federal levels. Milk boards controlled production, distribution and pricing in metropolitan areas. Particular suppliers and vendors were linked to particular processors in exclusive distribution zones. Generally speaking fresh milk producers in regulated zones received much higher prices; as much as double; as producers in areas outside the zones, or selling into manufactured milk markets. Not surprisingly these inequities translated into producer dissatisfaction and volatile dairy industry politics.

In 1950 there were 82,479 dairy farmers in Australia. By 1996 that number had fallen to 13,888, two-thirds of them in Victoria. In the same period Australian dairy production rose from 5,630 mega litres to 8,716 mega litres, about 65 per cent of this produced in Victoria. The number of dairy farms was halved in one decade alone; the 1970s; when the number of dairy cows more than halved. In 1972 there were 400 dairy factories in Australia. By 2002, following intensive rationalisation, there were fewer than 150, about 70 per cent of them co-operatively based. Of the five major processors, processing almost 75 per cent of all milk, three were co-operative or co-operative companies: the Murray-Goulburn Co-operative and Bonlac Foods (Victoria) and the Dairy Farmers' Group (New South Wales); which between them handled 60 per cent of all milk processed. Victoria was by far the greatest Australian dairying state with 60 per cent of all dairy farms producing 62 per cent of national product, 93 per cent of this in the form of manufactured milk. The next largest dairying state was New South Wales accounting for a mere 13 per cent of national production, over 50 per cent of this, market milk. Asymmetrical productive capacity and disputes over market access drove the deregulation debate and, coincidentally, deeper divisions in the rural co-operative movement.

On the eve of the new century Australian dairy farmers produced 2 per cent of the world's milk (10.85 mega litres), 82 per cent of this manufactured milk and 18 per cent, fresh milk. Australia was the world's third largest dairy exporter after the European Union and New Zealand, exporting liquid, powdered milk, butter, cheese and other manufactured goods and Australian dairy farms were among the most productive in the world. After nearly a century of domination, however, co-operatives lost the ascendancy in fresh milk processing to proprietors in 1993.[1]

NUMBER OF DAIRY FARMS AS AT 30 JUNE							
Year	NSW	Vic	Qld	SA	WA	Tas	Aus
1950	16,685	27,975	21,475	7,751	4,432	4,161	82,479
1970	8,733	19,803	8,931	4,111	1,656	3,232	46,460
1975	4,805	14,920	4,622	3,064	961	2,229	30,601
1996	1,853	8,275	1,693	791	457	819	13,888

WHOLE MILK PRODUCTION (MEGA LITRES)							
Year	NSW	Vic	Qld	SA	WA	Tas	Aus
1950	1,420	2,133	1,278	406	225	168	5,630
1996	1,114	5,482	751	513	342	514	8,716

DAIRY FOOD PROCESSORS 2000*	
Murray-Goulburn*	Tatura Milk Industries*
Bonlac Foods*	NORCO*
Dairy Farmers' Group*	Peters and Browns
National Dairies	Bega Co-operative*
Nestlè Australia	Lactos
Parmalat (Italy)	Capel
Kraft	De Chicco
Cadbury	Hastings Co-operative*
Warrnambool Cheese and Butter*	

Indicates co-operative/co-operative company.

Arguments for and against deregulation

Critics of the existing regime charged that it shielded producers from market signals, encouraged a culture of dependence and 'rent-seeking' and served as a disincentive to market-driven efficiencies, because producers received an average price *regardless* of quality, efficiency or the market effort made. The system was also susceptible to political manipulation, amounting to economic feather-bedding and 'back-door' protection, which discouraged improved production quality and marketing effort, especially in overseas markets. Regulation, the detractors said, encouraged special interest agreements between politically powerful farming lobbies and pliant governments who conspired to extract money from consumers through a myriad of regulatory bodies and subsidies, which kept prices artificially high. Others said the regulated system was simply unnecessary and redundant, given productivity increases at farm level and improvements to transport, treatment and storage technologies.

Defenders of the regulated system pointed to its egalitarian roots, which, they said, confirmed the solidarity necessary to build and retain control of an industry. Without the protection regulation gave, Australia could never have built a great internationally competitive dairy industry and major food exporter. The regulated system had helped to develop thriving rural communities built around the family farm and centred on the co-operative beyond the farm gate. No free market could have produced the immensely valuable social and economic assets created by the regulated dairy industry, simply because profits would have been creamed off to serve city interests. While it was true that the system was centrally driven and not market driven, producers enjoyed a level of security and control through ownership of co-operatives and representation on statutory marketing authorities (SMAs), which was impossible in a free market situation. Regulation had a proven record of positive achievement and the onus lay with critics to prove that any real alternative to central planning existed in Australia's special circumstances. Certainly, voluntary, self-regulatory free-market systems touted by C E D Meares and others before World War II had been tested and found wanting.[2]

The problem for the pro-regulation camp was that much of its case related to *past* events. The basis to these assumptions disappeared following Britain's entry into Europe and oil price hikes, which saw the emergence of a wholly new world financial order.

Notes on the Victorian Co-operative Dairy Industry
(i) Murray-Goulburn Co-operative Company drives the deregulation debate.

An excellent account of the history of the Murray-Goulburn Co-operative is found in Catherine Watson's *Just a Bunch of Cow Cockies: The Story of the Murray-Goulburn Co-operative* and it is not intended to repeat detail of this here. It is important, however, to sketch what became after World War II one of Australia's greatest and most important dairy co-operatives and a key player in the deregulation debate.

Originally known as the 'Murray Valley Co-operative' (the name was changed in 1961), the Murray-Goulburn Co-operative grew from a 1949 public meeting at Katunga, the centre of a soldier settlement, where fourteen settlers guaranteed supplies and subscribed 17s 6d (less than $2) in a hat. The fledgling co-operative took a year to organise, but by 1951 almost sixty suppliers had undertaken to supply it; 264 by 1956. Commonwealth and state governments assisted with lines of credit and irrigation programmes and it is fair to say that without these supports the co-operative, and the local industry which sustained it, could not have developed. The co-operative had the advantage of a relative youthful membership with no 'hang-ups' about co-operation or co-operatives. A superb choice of manager was made in the form J J (Jack) McGuire, a 'no nonsense' practical man, absolutely committed to co-operation, who insisted that 'management manage'. McGuire regularly participated in what he called 'missionary work', broadcasting his co-operative's (then) motto:

> *Co-operation, a way of life…Co-operation is more than a business – it is a way of life. Carried to its ultimate conclusion co-operation can bring the world Peace – Prosperity – and Contentment. But the individual must play his part in the plan. Co-operation is based on Christian service. Each for all and all for each.*

By 1965 the Murray-Goulburn Co-operative had 1,300 shareholders and, following a period of amalgamations, became Victoria's largest dairy company. The new co-operative dealt with the usual problems: proprietary resistance; agents bribing suppliers away; parochialism; personality clashes; sectarianism; and passive resistance from vested interests. Riding a wave of prosperity in the 1950s and early 1960s, however, Murray-Goulburn went from strength to strength, restructuring from butter production to more lucrative powdered-milk and cheese markets, previously monopolised by proprietary interests. The co-operative's expansion into the Southern Riverina of New South Wales and the Western District of Victoria, however, saw leaders of established factories in those districts – co-operative and proprietary – grow suspicious, concerned about possible takeover, the closure of existing facilities and vanishing jobs. Gippsland dairy factories, for instance, began to rationalise and merge, specifically to fend off Murray-Goulburn's charge.[3]

By 1969 Murray-Goulburn, now comprising some 49,000 shareholders, was the largest exporter of Australian dairy products to Japan, the United States and South-East Asia and was exporting to fifty countries. By the early 1970s, it was Australia's largest producer and manufacturer of processed dairy foods, with a turnover of more than $100 million. McGuire, understanding the seriousness of Britain's proposed entry into the EEC and Australian gluts which would develop when the 'sink' was closed off, now became more involved in industry politics, determined to give bureaucracy a 'shake', seeking to 'drag [the industry] into the modern world' and overcome the 'nightmare [of] bickering and posturing', which, he believed, industry bodies had become.[4]

Even though Murray-Goulburn was the largest producer of its kind in Australia, accounting for 48 per cent of national output, McGuire reasonably protested, the co-operative still had only *one* vote on industry representative bodies, the same as the tiniest proprietary or co-operative company. Moreover, McGuire continued, the existing commonwealth price equalisation scheme acted as a disincentive for quality production in butter, cheese, whole milk powder and casein pools and had become bureaucratic and illogical. Bureaucrats lacked vigour, had no incentive to get out and sell and that was why 'over production' existed; simply to maintain a bureaucratic *status quo*. The existing system was propping up inefficient producers in areas which were not 'natural dairying areas' but fortunate enough to be near metropolitan zones.

Regarding parliamentary and media questions concerning national bounties paid to dairy farmers (25 per cent of which were paid to Murray-Goulburn, reflecting its contribution to production), McGuire said that while he was sympathetic to complaints about the 'rigid, bureaucratic, regimented, regulated system which dominated the industry' he would defend the family farm, farmer control and 'the co-operative vision' to the death. However, he believed that the so-called 'democracy' of the established co-operative dairy industry was a sham for, almost without exception, Victorian dairy co-operative companies were not only *technically* not co-operatives but not co-operative in *spirit*, a point McGuire and the co-operative's chairman, Joe Curtis, often made in addressing farmer groups appealing to supplier loyalty in the endless merger and amalgamations game.[5]

With the last shipments of Australian bulk butter to pass through the Australian Producers' Wholesale Co-operative Federation (APWCF) leaving for Europe, McGuire now looked to the Co-operative Federation of Australia's (CFA) International Co-operative Trading Organisation (ICTO) strategy (discussed in Chapter Ten) as a possible alternative to what he saw as inadequate existing Australian marketing arrangements. However, ICTO was ineffective and McGuire was obliged to return to the task of dismantling the panoply of regulatory bodies choking free markets, as he saw it.

With disappearing British markets seeing gluts appear, McGuire welcomed a re-jigged Commonwealth Dairy Produce Equalisation Scheme in 1972, which was designed to sort out returns from various world and Australian markets and allocate quotas to dairy associations in order to equalise returns. He remained convinced, however, that the existing marketing system was stifling not only his co-operative but the national industry and persisted in protesting that while co-operatives controlled most production and processing they were still poorly represented on industry boards and committees, which were dominated by proprietary interests. In a rare show of co-operative solidarity, McGuire was elected to represent co-operative factories on the Australian Dairy Produce Board (later, the 'Dairy Produce Corporation'). There, he harangued the board, saying that the existing system was essentially pessimistic and restricted production while demand was growing for Australian products in new markets in Asia and the Pacific Rim. The true productive capacity of the industry, particularly the Victorian industry, was being thwarted by regulations, especially those prohibiting access by efficient producers to domestic markets.[6]

The Murray-Goulburn Co-operative continued to expand through the 1970s. This was a slow, painful and secretive process occasionally provoking angry reactions from farmers and managers affected by it and creating problems with the co-operative's democratic structure and taxation position. In response to the democracy question, the co-operative introduced a delegate system of representation through twenty zones, each divided into districts, which sent 'grass roots' delegates to a central board. Districts elected delegates to zones on the basis of production – the more production, the more delegates. Delegates in turn elected zone directors, who attended monthly meetings in Melbourne. The system naturally acted as an incentive to production but great care was taken to ensure that the main producing areas did not dominate.

So prepared, the Murray-Goulburn Co-operative flagged an intention to enter New South Wales markets in a 'scale never seen before'. The co-operative gained a quota from the New South Wales Dairy Industry Authority (which had recently replaced the Milk Board) via Murray-Goulburn's Finley factory in the Riverina district of south-western New South Wales. Murray-Goulburn also sought a quota for the growing Australian Capital Territory (ACT) market, centred on Canberra. In 1973 the Cudgewa Co-operative at Corryong, on the New South Wales-Victorian border, joined Murray-Goulburn and milk from that factory was sold in Sydney. This 'southern invasion' sparked an angry response from New South Wales co-operatives, particularly Dairy Farmers and the Bega Co-operative, which resented Murray-Goulburn's renunciation of the Equalisation Committee's 'gentlemen's agreement'.[7]

Murray-Goulburn proceeded, purchasing Nederveen and Company, a Melbourne general and dairy products exporter, and calling in 1974 for an Australian-wide dairy products marketing co-operative, 'a co-operative of co-operatives', with each constituent co-operative holding equal shares in an entity possessing exclusive marketing rights for members' produce. The federal government strongly supported the proposal, which, unfortunately, like so many rational co-operative development proposals, fell foul of interstate co-operative politics and the absence of national co-operatives' legislation. Parochialism and inadequate legislation therefore *obliged* Murray-Goulburn to proceed unilaterally while the *status quo* remained intact, a point not lost on New South Wales producers fearing deregulation.[8]

The year 1975 was a difficult one for the dairy export industry with US and European subsidies corrupting markets, gluts, collapsing world markets for skimmed milk, production costs climbing, butter fat returns plunging, a cholesterol scare reflecting adversely on dairy products and margarine making further inroads into markets. Proprietors began picking off productive suppliers from co-operatives, including Murray-Goulburn.

Employee Jim Flanagan supervising the loading of butter onto rail trucks (date unknown). The Norco factories were built on the railway to expedite the transport of butter in refrigerated trucks to the ships.
Photo courtesy of Norco Co-operative Limited.

With Murray-Goulburn personnel to the fore, Victorian dairy farmers organised demonstrations in Melbourne demanding a dismantling of the regulated system and a marketing and price distribution system equitable for *all* farmers. Murray-Goulburn issued a manifesto, which thousands of producers signed, calling on state and federal governments to take steps to restore farmer incomes and pointing out that Victorian dairy farmers were the most efficient in Australia, yet their incomes had fallen by 33 per cent since 1971, while average earnings in other occupations had risen by 58 per cent! Thousands of farmers faced bankruptcy and governments needed to help if the Australian dairy industry was to survive. The manifesto demanded a stable and effective system of domestic and export product and returns stabilisation, including an *enlargement* of the existing equalisation scheme, which would give producers of whole-milk powder and other processed milk an equitable share of the fresh-milk market.

Murray-Goulburn's determination to demolish regulation was strong. In 1976, however, it was in a weak trading position, operating on a $16 million bank overdraft, carrying other large loans and facing 'vicious rumours' concerning its liquidity. Membership fell following the impost upon members of fees, which were reluctantly introduced simply to continue operating. Largely due to Jack McGuire's immense energy and drive, however, the co-operative won a huge Venezuelan contract for full cream, replacing Nestlè and Unigate, and secured markets in Russia, Sri Lanka and Romania. The co-operative became the major Australian exporter of full-cream milk, a position previously occupied by proprietors, who complained bitterly to the Commonwealth Government that Murray-Goulburn was 'selling below world prices'. Murray-Goulburn installed the world's biggest spray drier at Maffra, the world's most modern Gouda cheese factory and built Australia's first fully-automated cheddar cheese processing plant at Cobram. Purchasing the New South Wales distributing rights of Norco, the Victorian co-operative company now controlled 70 per cent of the

Australian butter market and nearly *all* of the New South Wales butter market, opening depots at Bankstown in Sydney, Wollongong and Canberra.

After Jack McGuire retired in 1979, however, the co-operative began rapidly to lose suppliers: 1,500 in twelve months. Some of this was due to natural attrition but also because the co-operative was resented in some districts as a 'conglomerate, gobbling up everything' and allegedly manipulating the system to its advantage. Young farmers, not concerned with co-operative principles and with no idea of the struggle involved in creating the co-operative, were prepared to supply the organisation, *only* if prices paid exceeded those offered by competitors. The new general manager changed the co-operative's style, reduced dividends to suppliers to service loans and made a determined move into marketing. McGuire recalls:

> *A whole lot of new people came in. I don't want to make a point of it. We are dependent on supply, without it our plant is nothing. Some of them (farmers) are ornery buggers but farmers have a lot of sense that a lot of people don't give them credit for. They will stick together but expect efficiency. A co-operative has got to earn its right to lead but modern man forgets this. They see themselves a super beings looking down at the 'illiterate' farmer. That's all wrong – that's where the strength is – at the base with the farmer. Without their milk flowing through our plant what are they worth – nothing!* [9]

In a less than unanimous decision, McGuire was brought back from retirement in 1981 to resume duties as general manager, staying on until 1984. The dairy industry was now at rock bottom and Murray-Goulburn appeared to be heading for ruin. Drought, pessimism, declining commodity prices, disaffection and the exit of many suppliers saw the co-operative balanced on a knife edge. There was a real possibility in 1981 that Murray-Goulburn would have to be sold off to repay loans, which were no longer negotiable. Many believed that the organisation had lost its way, had become proprietory in outlook and philosophy and was 'soft' on deregulation. Indeed, the co-operative had acquired several proprietary subsidiaries in the milk, cheese, butter, distribution, hardware, retail and general trading fields. A New South Wales subsidiary, Berriquin Dairy Company Limited, was registered under Company Law, not because Murray-Goulburn sought this but because the New South Wales *Co-operation Act* made it difficult for an interstate co-operative company to register as a co-operative in that state.

Over the next three years McGuire savagely pruned operations to reduce costs. Murray-Goulburn was at a cross-road. Farmers were still leaving in droves, even though farm productivity was improving and production was climbing. It was all very well to be making inroads into Asian, Middle-Eastern and North American markets but McGuire remained convinced something had to be done about accessing domestic fresh-milk 'fortress' markets. The membership remained far from united on the issue of deregulation, however, and even those who saw it as inevitable and necessary remained uncertain on the way to proceed or the timing.

Under McGuire's firm hand suppliers returned and by 1983 the co-operative's profits were rising, debt was more than halved and prices paid to farmers had increased significantly. The turnaround did not come, however, without great strain between McGuire, directors and management and bitterness between loyal supporters and 'deserters' who had returned. The vexed question of access to interstate fresh-milk markets also remained unresolved. [10]

(ii) Bonlac Foods Limited

Not only New South Wales' producers were alarmed by Murray-Goulburn's expansion through the 1960s. Annoyed by the dynamic new co-operative's jibes that the old Victorian co-operative companies were undemocratic, controlled by city investors, 'tired' and simply existed to attract favourable taxation treatment, and determined to retain a local identity, co-operatives and co-operative companies attached to Shepparton Co-operative Butter and Stanhope Co-operative Butter amalgamated to form IBIS Dairy Products. Then, in 1967 co-operatives in the Traralgon, Wangaratta, Warragul, Warrnambool, Yarram, Bendigo, Dandenong, Leongatha, Orbost and Shepparton districts formed Amalgamated Co-operative Marketers (Australia) Limited (ACMAL), comprising:

- ✤ Western District Co-operative Limited.
- ✤ Gippsland and Northern Company Limited;
- ✤ Amalgamated Marketers Cold Storage Limited;
- ✤ G & N (NSW) Proprietary Limited (Albury and Casino);
- ✤ Co-operative Insurance Company of Australia (CIC); and
- ✤ Co-operative Box Company of Victoria Limited.

The ACMAL board included three directors from each of three Victorian zones and three directors from New South Wales. ACMAL later added facilities for seed storage, cheese-processing and opened new operations in Warrnambool and Casino (New South Wales). After vacating the stock and station business, in 1976 ACMAL-BEN Marketing Limited opened Singapore offices, later diversifying into travel, property, real estate and pleasure craft.

In the early 1980s IBIS and Colac and Camperdown co-operatives considered merging. In a secretive operation, officials approached every co-operative in Victoria – except Murray-Goulburn – with a view to forming a 'mega' marketing co-operative. In 1982 this group of co-operatives and ACMAL merged to form Bonlac Foods Limited, a co-operative company. Other co-operatives or companies to subsequently join Bonlac included Cobden, Victorian Butter Factories, Drouin, Midland Milk and Australian Frosty Boy. The Bega (southern New South Wales) and Tasmanian Unity co-operatives were invited to join but demurred. NEDCO, consisting mainly of north-eastern producers, joined Murray-Goulburn. Bonlac was now second only to Murray-Goulburn in size and, with the latter, accounted for 70 per cent of all Victorian milk production.[11]

(iii) Tatura Milk Industries Limited: 'Small is Beautiful'

Tatura Milk Industries Limited, a Victorian processor which was formed in 1907, proceeded independently. While Murray-Goulburn and Bonlac grew and rationalised operations to achieve economies of scale ('Get Big or Get Out'), Tatura subscribed to a 'Small is Beautiful' philosophy. Registered under Corporations Law, Tatura served an homogenous group of farmers; 80 per cent of them operating in a 20 kilometre radius around the co-operative; enshrined co-operative principles in framing the articles of association; and used a simple, traditional co-operative structure including:

- ✤ modest entry costs;
- ✤ active members only;
- ✤ new members as markets permitted;
- ✤ 90 per cent of business with members;
- ✤ a rotating directorship;
- ✤ internal funding only;
- ✤ no public share-trading;
- ✤ limits on shares held by a member;

❖ 75 per cent approval by active members for a co-operative sale or takeover;

❖ periodic bonus shares;

❖ premium prices related to quality; and

❖ competitive dividend on farmer investments.

Local producers coveted membership of Tatura Co-operative and shares in it were highly valued, with farmers confident that they would be redeemed. Tatura developed a reputation as a high quality, low cost, reliable supplier co-operative, built strategic alliances with marketers leaving marketing to the experts and, in so-doing, overcame many agency problems and capital and governance difficulties associated with traditional co-operative structure. Focused on building *farm* value, the co-operative company developed a reputation for innovative product development, value-adding and carefully-focused expenditure.

(iv) Victorian Artificial Breeders' Co-operative

No background to the Victorian dairy co-operative movement would be complete without reference to the Victorian Artificial Breeders' Co-operative. This co-operative was formed in 1958, appropriately, jesters quipped, in a hay barn at Werribee. Assisted by a £20,000 grant from the Bolte Liberal Government, the herd-improvement service co-operative worked with other artificial insemination co-operatives to form the Artificial Breeders and Herd Improvement Association. By the mid-1970s, the co-operative was exporting semen overseas and interstate. After trading losses in the mid-1970s, relating to a downturn in the beef-cattle and dairy industries, a marketing survey in 1979 led to a dramatic turnaround and, restructured as Herd Improvement Services Co-operative Limited (HISCOL), the co-operative enjoyed renewed success and was a key element in the success of the Victorian dairy industry.[12]

Against this background, our attention now turns to key events in the approach to deregulation in 2000 and the role co-operatives and co-operative companies played in this.

Deregulatory pressure grows, 1975–1983

With the Whitlam Federal Labor Government (1972–1975) ending subsidies for surplus production, cutting tariffs, whipping away bounties and other concessions and, with wages and inflation soaring, the capital position of many agricultural co-operatives was vulnerable, particularly as they adjusted to Britain's entry into the EEC and changes in consumer habits. Corporate raiders successfully moved on many co-operatives at this time, seriously eroding the rural co-operative movement. The only sensible way forward, many co-operative leaders believed, was more rationalisation, more mergers and acquisitions and more markets: a 'Get Big or Get Out' philosophy.

Not only Victorian producers protested the inequity of the existing regulated system. Some New South Wales' co-operatives were also calling for reforms to remove unfair trading conditions, the north coast co-operative, Norco, for example, which was locked out of southern metropolitan fresh-milk markets.

The recalcitrants' position was strengthened by a High Court decision in October 1975 ruling that the New South Wales *Dairy Industry Authority Act* could *not* prevent interstate milk flowing into New South Wales markets. The decision provoked a hornet's nest in New South Wales where protected dairy farmers fully expected markets to be inundated with cheap Victorian milk.

Industries Assistance Commission (IAC) reports in 1975 and 1976 recommended a levy to equalise payments across fresh and manufactured milk markets and the placement of production limits on manufactured milk. The levy idea was generally acceptable to the industry but Victorian producers would not accept production caps, demanding access to domestic fresh-milk markets and an extension to a national level of an existing Victorian scheme established to share returns equitably between markets. Producers in states geared to fresh-milk production (particularly New South Wales, Queensland and Western Australia) flatly refused to open their markets unless Victoria introduced production ceilings. Though far from unanimous, Victorian producers then demanded a national liquid milk pool in which market-share was allocated relative to the *size* of each state's industry. Victoria, with an industry three times the size of New South Wales, would clearly be the chief beneficiary. The New South Wales Dairy Industry Authority dismissed the idea. A stalemate was reached and the regulated system continued with relations between interstate dairy co-operatives and co-operative companies severely strained.[13]

After sweeping to power in 1975, the Fraser Federal Coalition Government reduced the pressure somewhat by ending the Commonwealth Dairy Produce Equalisation Committee Scheme and replacing it with a stabilisation payment scheme collected by Canberra and redistributed to producers through the Australian Dairy Corporation. State governments simultaneously adjusted regulations, removing geographic boundaries to milk zones and permitting more producers access to metropolitan markets. In 1976, for example, the New South Wales Wran Labor Government repealed Sydney Milk Zone legislation, dropped regulations dividing producers into 'classes', ended quota negotiability and introduced measures to allow a more equitable share of fresh-milk trade. These reforms were widely seen as the first step towards deregulation in that state. It would be some time before this was achieved, however.[14]

The Hawke Labor Government drives deregulation

With the election of the Hawke Federal Labor Government in 1983, industry restructuring, deregulation and other macro- and micro-economic reforms became urgent policy imperatives. With breathtaking speed the government deregulated the financial system. Industry policy was redefined and focused on national objectives, seeking to make the Australian economy internationally competitive. In ensuing years, a hurricane of deregulation swept through Australian primary industry affecting particularly the citrus, dried fruit, banana, apple, pear, cotton, vegetable, wheat and dairy industries. Still disorganised and described in generally inadequate states' laws, however, co-operatives were poorly positioned to exploit opportunities (as co-operatives) in the new circumstances.

Dairy farmers in all states were nervous about impending deregulation. Nevertheless, most recognised that the existing pooling system, stabilisation levies and equalised prices were interrupting market signals and helping to preserve inefficiencies, which were unsustainable in world markets. Equalisation, notwithstanding a commendable egalitarianism, patently discriminated against efficient, high-quality farmers. Producers confined to less lucrative manufactured-milk markets also were perennially jealous of the privileged position enjoyed by suppliers in metropolitan fresh-milk markets where sometimes double the returns were being achieved. Nevertheless, farmers dealing with mortgages, risky financial gearing and soaring interest rates, were generally loathe to surrender the benefits of regulation, particularly with international butter prices depressed and a European Union (EU) butter 'lake' glutting markets. A world trend to dairy industry rationalisation was also knocking on Australia's door as the federal government negotiated a Closer Economic Relationship (CER) with New Zealand, paving the way for entry into Australian markets of the most efficient dairy industry in the world and the world's second largest dairy product exporter. It was no longer simply a case of southern 'foreigners' invading protected markets. Much more alarming – Kiwis!

The Industry Assistance Commission Inquiry 1983

An IAC inquiry and report in 1983 triggered a deregulatory tsunami which engulfed the dairy industry. The report uncompromisingly attacked state regulation of market milk, rejected production controls, noted the efficiency of manufactured-milk suppliers, argued that state borders should 'disappear' in marketing and recommended that pooling for exports should continue for only *three more years* and be terminated.

Not surprisingly, the report outraged fresh-milk interests accustomed to regulation, particularly in the New South Wales industry, who flagged that they would not give up without a fight. Senior dairy industry figures, however, such as Chair of the Australian Dairy Industry Council (ADIC) Pat Rowley (Queensland), urged a compromise and convinced the federal government that the industry, particularly in New South Wales and Queensland, needed a 'breather' to adjust to new circumstances.

ADIC subsequently recommended the placing of a levy on *all* milk to subsidise exports. The main beneficiaries, obviously, would be Victorian manufactured-milk suppliers but state ministers would be empowered to *terminate* payment of the levy in the event of any break down in orderly marketing, that is, any incursion by interstate processors into established marketing arrangements. Essentially, the concept was to deliver manufactured-milk producers 'protection money' to desist from selling milk interstate while 'buying time' for market-milk producers in less efficient dairying industries to prepare for deregulation. The Australian Agricultural Council, comprising federal and state agricultural ministers, agreed with the proposal which became the basis of the federal government's Kerin Plan.[15]

The Kerin Plan

In 1987 the Commonwealth Government launched the Kerin Plan, named after the Federal Minister for Primary Industry and Energy John Kerin, a poultry farmer and co-operative advocate. The five-year plan, which was to terminate in June 1992, placed a levy on *all* milk to support exports while product pooling was phased out and the industry was placed on a more competitive footing. The government undertook to direct payments to producers at world parity prices, plus the market support levy. Canberra hoped that the scheme would provide a buffer between states' dairy industries, reducing friction, while initiating a progressive unwinding of regulated market-support systems.

While the Kerin Plan went some way towards resolving industry tensions, Victorian processors, particularly Murray-Goulburn Co-operative, continued to drive for deregulation and were highly critical of what they saw as a denial of equal opportunity, arguing that Victorian producers could realise better returns in free markets, competing on a 'level playing field'. Critics also said that protected milk simply encouraged excess production which either *displaced* milk produced more efficiently elsewhere or *depressed* prices, overall. Improved transport methods and technologies had long ago done away with the need for regulated supply zones, which were a relic of a by-gone era. Farmer rallies were held in Canberra protesting that the Kerin Plan 'heralded the end of the industry'.

By late 1987 the scheme was on shaky ground as Victorian fresh milk poured into Sydney supermarkets at retail prices well below the regulated price. The New South Wales and Victorian governments managed to keep a 'lid' on this impending 'milk war' by permitting a variation to the 'gentlemen's agreement', allowing small shares of interstate markets in exchange for agreements on production levels and compensation for the transfer of milk quotas. With the constitutionality of this uncertain, however, Victorian milk continued to flow into New South Wales markets.[16]

Victoria pushes the pace

The Victorians were at least five years ahead of their northern counterparts in the business of industry rationalisation and building strategic alliances. Murray-Goulburn was already co-operating with Nestlès in transport, and with Tatura Milk, Nestlès and Kraft in a milk-collection scheme in central northern Victoria and the Gippsland region. Twelve more co-operatives had merged with Bonlac Foods. Murray-Goulburn and Bonlac gave greater attention to product diversity, brand awareness, customer loyalty and marketing. Already United Dairy Farmers of Victoria (UDFV) was conducting an investigation into the possibility of creating a 'super co-operative' of all farmer-owned dairy companies with a view to achieving the necessary operational scale and marketing leverage to compete with multinationals, particularly the New Zealand Dairy Board. Along with Murray-Goulburn, UDFV complained that domestic fresh-milk processors in other states were dragging their feet on deregulation and were mired in self-interest. The Victorians were rationalising energetically in preparation for deregulation while other states were biding time, bracing themselves for the onslaught.

Everything was accelerated by the collapse of the Soviet Union and the flooding of world markets with cheap former Soviet Bloc dairy products, which impacted adversely upon Victorian exports. The economic situation of dairy farmers was further worsened by recession, international turbulence in Iraq and Yugoslavia and by one of the worst seasons on record in 1990/91, affecting particularly exporters. In addition, *all* Australian producers faced vigorous new competition from New Zealand as the CER proceeded to ratification. New Zealand producers, benefiting from a low New Zealand dollar, a competitive advantage derived from the Kerin Plan export levy and with only one government to deal with; not *nine* as in Australia; were several years ahead of their Tasman neighbours with a sophisticated national marketing scheme while the Australian industry remained segmented at different points of production, distribution and consumption. Australian manufactured-milk producers' fear of the impact upon foreign markets of New Zealand competition was matched only by the fear of Australian fresh-milk producers of an impending post-deregulatory 'invasion' by southern processors.

'It is time to deregulate the sacred dairy cow'

In September 1989 the Victorian government proposed further deregulation of the industry in that state, virtually to farm-gate level by 1993. 'It is time to deregulate the sacred dairy cow', the *Australian Financial Review* (*AFR*) declared in February 1990; time to lift the whole panoply of regulated farm-gate prices, levies, tariff quotas, supply zones, export controls, underwriting, marketing boards and subsidies. Another 'milk war' was looming between Victorian and New South Wales producers and the reason for this was simply frustrated attempts by more efficient Victorian producers to sell fresh milk interstate. The New South Wales industry was the most regulated in Australia and, the influential newspaper wanted to know, why was the conservative Greiner Coalition government not applying:

> *...its revered principles of free-market forces and good management to its own dairy industry...*
> *The New South Wales government needs to disprove suspicions that it is a slave to its rural constituents and immediately take steps to free the milk market.*

The government had deregulated bread and eggs and SMAs were under review, the paper queried, so why not the dairy industry? Western Australia had already deregulated beyond the farm gate. The Victorian government had years earlier deregulated the production chain to stimulate competition between processors and vendors, but had kept the farm-gate price. South Australia controlled only the price of whole milk. New South Wales had done *nothing*. The AFR charged that in New South Wales the processing and distribution of milk:

> *...is controlled by a system of geographic monopolies. Individual vendors are given a monopoly over the distribution of milk in key areas and are contractually tied to specific processors who monopolise sales in specific areas. Therefore United Dairies and Dairy Farmers control 90 per cent of Sydney metropolitan sales and about 75 per cent of state sales. Seventy other processors account for the rest! This is a ridiculous situation and must end. It is time for the government to cut its ties with the dairy industry and deregulate it.*

It was inevitable, AFR added, that some processors would disappear, mainly those which had been 'spoon fed' by the government, not those which were entrepreneurial and, the paper concluded, 'good riddance'.[17]

The New South Wales Deregulation Task Force

Responding to such criticism, the Greiner Coalition cabinet applied pressure to National Party Minister Armstrong to expedite matters. A Deregulation Task Force was assembled with Australian Co-operative Foods (ACF) (Dairy Farmers) Chairman Ian Langdon (who was identified with the anti-deregulation camp) engaged to oversee this. Langdon spoke of a need to get the processor-vendor 'mix' right and to break down old habits and attitudes in preparing for a gradual 'managed' deregulation process. The gist was to move cautiously enabling the New South Wales' industry to prepare for deregulation – the alternative was the possible destruction of the states' dairy industry (discussed in Chapter Fifteen)!

The Crean Plan

With New South Wales' processors, vendors and producers taking profit cuts to meet competition and exporters facing difficult world markets, all sections of the industry understood that a collapse of the export support system would precipitate a scramble for domestic markets and not all processors would survive. Accordingly, the faltering Kerin Plan was again stitched up in a deal between state governments involving a complicated pricing formula tied to a Victorian base price for market milk and permitting interstate competition, where margins rose beyond the costs of transportation. This was seen within and outside the industry for what it was: a shaky truce between the states and political horse-trading which had nothing to do with economic rationality.

In mid-1991, twelve months ahead of schedule, the Hawke Government replaced the Kerin Plan with the Crean Plan (named after the incumbent minister). This envisioned reducing market support over (another) five years, ostensibly to comply with General Agreement on Trade and Tariffs (GATT) requirements. The Kerin Plan's essentials were retained, however, in a politically-motivated appeasement of embattled dairy producers in marginal electorates where a 'rural revolt' was under way.[18]

The deregulation timetable is set

In November 1991 an IAC hearing set deadlines to end legislative support for the dairy industry in three stages:

- ❖ removal of post-farm gate regulations by mid-1996;
- ❖ a phased reduction of support for manufactured-milk by 1996; and
- ❖ ending all farm-gate regulation by mid-1999.

Western Australia had already virtually achieved post-farm gate deregulation. Tasmania did so by the middle of 1993. Victoria began the process in 1992 and completed it in 1995. South Australia completed the process by 1995. In New South Wales, however, following representations to the minister from dairy industry leaders seeking the maintenance of the regulated margin in fresh-milk markets long enough for farmers to 'sell to someone prepared to take the risk of deregulation or at least amortise their investment and enter deregulation without debt', the government continued to move slowly on post-farm gate deregulation. Not until late 1993 was a timetable set in Sydney and that was not to mature until 1 July 1998, two years later than the IAC timetable. The situation was much the same in Queensland.

Co-operatives still cannot co-operate

The dairy industry atmosphere festered with rumour. Smear campaigns and speculation continued in the media about possible mergers and acquisitions, takeovers or the demutualisation of co-operatives. Bonlac Foods, for example, which was planning a $20 million public share issue, was painted as 'selling out' the co-operative ideal. Murray-Goulburn hotly denied any talk of a merger with Bonlac, which it described disparagingly as an 'investor organisation', while the former was a 'defender of the co-operative ideal'. With co-operatives in all states seeking a national profile in preparation for deregulation and embarked upon serious rationalisation, ructions erupted within and between co-operatives. Efforts by co-operatives to achieve a rational allocation of resources were repeatedly stymied by emotion, parochialism, states' rivalries, old 'tribal' grudges and a fear of domination and loss of 'identity'. Subjective factors were exacerbated by structural barriers, particularly a capital shortage, legislative impediments to cross-border mergers, taxation implications for merged entities, trades practices legislation in respect of supply agreements and the slowness of co-operatives' democratic decision-making, which, some executives complained, meant directors and managers had to govern 'with one hand tied behind the back'. A combination of human failings and structural impediments was draining the dairy co-operative sector's vitality, dividing and confusing it precisely at a time when unity was crucial in dealing with deregulation and competition policy (discussed below). Unable to coalesce around a core of common objectives, co-operatives and co-operative companies proceeded unilaterally towards the greatest shake-out dairying had ever known in a grim contest to determine who would be the 'last man standing', the antithesis of co-operation.

The Bonlac share issue 1992

Further debt was not an option for the Victorian dairy co-operative company, Bonlac Foods in 1992 but, like most dairy processors, it did require funds hurriedly for expansion and rationalisation. In order to resolve this 'co-operative dilemma', Bonlac launched a public issue of shares seeking $25 million on a non-voting basis and set a precedent in the dairy co-operative movement. This was the first public share issue of its type in Australia for a major co-operative company and set a precedent in the dairy co-operative movement. The 1992 Annual General Meeting authorised directors to create two classes of shares: investment shares; and supplier shares. Investment shares were transferable and redeemable (or renewable) after five years, held no voting rights except on issues that affected the terms and conditions specifically of the investment share issue and were not publicly quoted (to retain the mutuality principle in respect of taxation liability). The issue of additional bonus shares tied to company performance was anticipated and directors were authorised to issue shares with varying terms and conditions, reflecting demand which might exist in capital markets from time to time. Supplier shares were designed to protect the co-operative company's 'heritage', held full voting rights at all meetings and were a prerequisite to trading with the co-operative.

Bonlac's investment shares were pounced upon by investors and massively over-subscribed. However, reflecting a general reluctance by farmers to invest in co-operatives, members subscribed to only half their allocation (20 per cent had been reserved for them). Successful as the issue was, the co-operative company was placed on a footing where investor expectations became important. Could Bonlac afford to service these expectations and still retain farmer control? Many observers doubted this.[19]

National Competition Policy

In 1991 Australian governments agreed to a national approach to competition policy and began a process of examining existing statutory arrangements in so far as these affected competition. SMAs came under special scrutiny. An Independent Committee of Inquiry (the Hilmer Committee) was commissioned to find ways of improving national economic efficiency, while enhancing community welfare and choice. In 1995 all Australian states and territories agreed to National Competition Policy (NCP) pursuant to *Hilmer Report* recommendations that all barriers to free and open competition between states' industries be removed. State governments could grant industries exemptions where a 'public interest' test was satisfied, and stiff penalties existed for non-compliance. The Australian Competition and Consumer Commission (ACCC) was established to supervise the agreement. The implications for co-operatives slavishly tied to SMAs were obvious – their special privileges would soon be swept away, bringing new urgency to the matter of solving the 'co-operative dilemma'.

'The most difficult position in history'

Speaking of these developments, ADIC and Australian Dairy Farmers Federation (ADFF) Chairman Pat Rowley said that co-operatives were now placed in the most difficult position in their history. In order for co-operatives to comply with NCP guidelines they would in many respects have to operate in *direct conflict* with co-operative principles. NCP and co-operation, potentially, were antithetical (for further discussion see Chapter Eleven).

Delaying deregulation: the Domestic Market Support Scheme

Coincidentally, the federal government introduced the Domestic Market Support Scheme (DMS), adjusting the Crean Plan to comply with (recently formed) World Trade Organisation (WTO) obligations. The DMS, to expire by June 2000, was established ostensibly to support domestic markets but actually served to prop up export markets, amounting to 'back door' protection. The scheme levied producers on the *fat and protein content* of milk supplied, rather than on the basis of *which market* the milk was intended for. State governments still controlled sourcing, distribution, quotas and pricing of market milk but a revised IAC ruling called for post-farm gate deregulation to be completed by June 1999 (three years later than originally intended) and all export subsidies to be removed by 2001.

Critics attacked the DMS as preventing a truly national market for drinking milk and economic feather-bedding for producers at consumer cost. The scheme, they charged, also continued to give a competitive advantage to foreign (New Zealand) competitors, who were unencumbered by the levy, disadvantaging local producers, particularly Victorians.

Victorians continue to press the issue

It was clear to even the strongest opponents by 1995 that deregulation was inevitable and Victorians were pressing the issue. Victorian producers called upon state and federal governments to leave the industry to markets – co-operatives and their industry needed to be *market-driven* and attuned to the market place, not coddled. While it was true that all states wanted farm-gate prices retained for milk it was also true that if Victoria deregulated, the rest of the country would be obliged to follow as no constitutional basis existed to bar 'foreign' milk.

The Murray-Goulburn Co-operative continued to drive for full deregulation, arguing that even though the industry milk in-flow in Victoria was three times that of Queensland and twice New South Wales, the southern state held only 7 per cent of the national fresh-milk market! This was a terrible distortion of available markets! The Australian Dairy Corporation was ignoring Murray-Goulburn, the co-operative's officials complained, even though it accounted for 25 per cent of total Australian in-take, 40 per cent of total dairy exports, was approaching a $1 billion annual turnover and was Australia's leading exporter of processed foods. The co-operative company was perfectly suited to a deregulatory environment, officials said, and sceptics, who doubted the ability of co-operatives to raise sufficient capital to remain competitive in post-deregulatory markets, were talking nonsense. Success was contingent not simply upon raising capital but a matter of *co-operating* and building *strategic alliances* and *joint ventures*. Murray-Goulburn Chairman Frank Stewart deprecated the slowness with which deregulation was proceeding in some other states, saying this was 'threatening the Victorian industry' and causing an unacceptable loss of markets to interstate and overseas competitors. Meanwhile, New South Wales co-operatives were 'up-scaling' operations in Victoria and 'dumping' products, which were cross-subsidised by regulated premium prices for fresh milk, and throwing up every obstacle possible in their own markets. Now, giant multinationals like Italy's Parmalat were setting up operations in Australia as a springboard to Asia, targeting co-operatives for take over and playing a waiting game. They could afford this while Australian co-operatives squabbled, dithered and accentuated self-interest before co-operation in determining the way ahead. *All* Victorian co-operatives, big and small, Murray-Goulburn officials said, wanted deregulation and *all* Victorian producers genuinely wanted a 'level playing field' and a national dairy industry that was truly competitive. Some southerners believed that removing regulatory props from New South Wales and Queensland processors would see many 'fall over' and that was why northerners were playing such an obstructionist game, harming the industry *and* the co-operative movement at this crucial time in its history when virtually everything co-operation stood for was under attack in the NCP.

Jittery New South Wales and Queensland dairy industries, however, continued to argue for 'partial deregulation', a 'half pregnant' approach, which was inconsistent with NCP and most farmers knew it. The strategic purpose was simply to delay deregulation as long as possible while producers located capital in an attempt to remain competitive and readied themselves for the inevitable southern and New Zealand invasion.

The 'co-operative advantage'

Notwithstanding such difficulties faced by dairy co-operatives and co-operative, prominent market analysts acknowledged that co-operatives were the 'real quiet achievers of the food industry', particularly in exports of semi-processed and processed foods into Asia, pointing to sales and profit growth for three major co-operatives and co-operative companies as evidence:

	Sales 1991 $Million	Sales 1994 $Million	Profit Growth 1991-4
Bonlac Foods Limited (Victoria)	$629	$826	149%
Murray-Goulburn Co-operative Company Limited (Victoria)	$504	$782	83%
Australian Co-operative Foods Limited (ACF) (New South Wales)	$407	$548	432%

Some commentators believed that these spectacular results were achieved precisely because co-operatives had a distinct *advantage* over proprietorial competitors and, in particular:

...patient shareholders. The co-operative capital structure allows management a long-term planning horizon unknown to publicly-listed food producers. Co-operative managers know that their shareholders will put up with a decline in earnings for one or two years, if the end result is a bigger market share.

The AFR believed it was now 'crunch time', however, if dairy co-operatives were to maintain this record. Co-operatives would have to find 'new *permanent* capital'. ACF and Bonlac had already appointed advisers to 'assist in lining up some new form of equity capital over the next twelve to eighteen months', the AFR reported, and ACF would likely see 'a firm proposal for capital-raising, possibly using non-voting shares for non-supplier shareholders, within a few months'. Almost gleefully, the newspaper anticipated tension between supplier-members and external shareholders.[20]

Solving the 'co-operative dilemma'

The question was: how could co-operatives access 'permanent capital' without recourse to external investors and compromising the democracy principle? As the deregulation clock ticked down, dairy co-operative leaders sought an answer to this conundrum at numerous conferences. Perhaps there was none. Nevertheless, in ensuing years the great debate in co-operative movement politics was capital adequacy almost to the exclusion of other important matters impinging upon co-operative development (see Chapters Nine, Fifteen and Sixteen).

ADIC Chairman Pat Rowley agreed with much of ACF Chairman Ian Langdon's thesis that co-operatives must provide *incentives* to invest so that they might develop a scale of operations necessary to compete. He agreed also that this was complicated by archaic co-operatives' legislation, which made mergers across borders difficult and unnecessarily complicated operations. Rowley warned, however, against the folly of soliciting *external* investors, saying that co-operatives were very attractive targets for corporate raiders and pointing to Parmalat, which was targeting Australian co-operatives as deregulation proceeded. Even if external investors did not capture control through *ownership* they would organise to fulfil *dividend expectations*, thereby driving down prices to farmers. Rowley's solution to this 'co-operative dilemma' was external *directors,* not external *capital* and he pointed to the Bonlac and Murray-Goulburn models, where public companies had been formed for manufacturing and marketing with the co-operative holding a controlling interest.

United Dairy Farmers of Victoria Administrative Director Terry O'Callaghan also argued that farmers needed to invest more in their co-operatives if they were serious about retaining control because, he said, outside investors 'don't give a damn what your milk price is – they only want a dividend'. Farmers invested four and a half times more in their farms than they did in their co-operatives and this situation had to change or, inevitably, they would lose control of their industry. Farmers simply must invest more in co-operatives!

Frank O'Connor, Chairman of the National Co-operatives' Council of Australia (a forerunner of the Co-operatives Council of Australia [CCA], which replaced the Australian Association of Co-operatives [AAC], discussed in Chapter Twelve) said that Australian trades practices legislation presented real problems for traditional co-operative agreements and supported those opposing any dilution of the democracy principle through concessions to external capital. External investors were simply 'dry' shareholders in another guise, O'Connor argued. Co-operatives should build strategic alliances and joint ventures with co-operatives and other companies (on the Murray-Goulbourn model) and grow scale this way.

Co-operative Federation of NSW Ltd (CFNSW) Chairman Jordan Rigby was also strongly opposed to outside investors, cautioned against co-operatives accepting advice from the corporate world and joined the chorus of opinion calling upon co-operative members to invest more.

First Business Finance Managing Director James Evans said that the democratic nature of co-operatives ruled out development finance available through conventional equity investors because investors wanted *both* control *and* return. Therefore, co-operatives had to access capital some other way. Their capital-raising capacity was hampered, however, by regulatory barriers, a limited return on capital, incompatible states' legislation, negative perceptions of co-operatives in the finance world and the unfortunate fact that co-operatives seemed forever prone to conflict. Evans suggested a variety of possible equity devices and was non-committal on the external equity option.

Monash University's Michael O'Keefe, who had recently led a group of co-operative leaders on overseas study tours aided by Rabobank, argued views similar to Ian Langdon's in a paper commissioned by the New South Wales Registry of Co-operatives. O'Keefe believed the key to co-operative development was developing *member relationships* as co-operatives developed a marketing orientation and a 'member-as-investor' consciousness. This would require an 'unbundling' in co-operative structure of the price paid for raw material from investment returns. Many traditionalists saw this as an anathema – co-operatives existed to improve returns to farmers by maximising payments and minimising costs, not to tie up farmer capital in investment schemes.[21]

Disastrously for co-operative unity, dairying co-operatives and co-operative companies could not agree on a common approach to the 'co-operative dilemma' and generally proceeded independently. There was really no alternative given the fractious state of the movement and the absence of an effective umbrella organisation, a co-operative bank arranging sympathetic finance or federal or national co-operatives' legislation.

Bonlac restructures and lists on the Australian Stock Exchange

Press speculation continued on the likelihood of Bonlac Foods and ACF listing on the Australian Stock Exchange (ASX), a rumour strenuously denied by ACF Chairman Ian Langdon (ACF was now known as 'Dairy Farmers Group' [DFG]). Bonlac, operating on a $1 billion-annual turnover, was preparing to develop a $150 million dried-milk facility, the biggest project ever undertaken in Australian dairying history, and, in examining capital-raising alternatives, considered a 'split-up' or 'hybrid' option, sharing ownership with external investors. Farmer shareholders, however, were adamant that they would under no circumstances surrender control. A comprehensive Macquarie Bank report, nevertheless, recommended a radical operational restructure. Accordingly, the co-operative company was split into two parts: a traditional milk-manufacturing business owned by farmers; and a dairy company operation with ready access to capital for value-adding. Bonlac issued $100 million of listed non-voting perpetual capital notes, geared to return 9.5 per cent interest for five years (complying with a 'sunset clause' in respect of the democracy principle in ASX rules). The Bonlac listing provided a precedent for the boards of other co-operatives also seeking rapid expansion, including DFG. To some observers, however, it was only a matter of time before the co-operative company, on the 'slippery slope' to capitalist orthodoxy, was devoured by investors. This theme is resumed in Chapters Eleven and Thirteen.[22]

A Victorian ultimatum

As the tortured co-operatives' capital adequacy debate rambled on and possible ways of modifying co-operative structure to suit investors were explored, the deregulatory clock was ticking. In July 1998 (seven years after Western Australia) the New South Wales government finally deregulated post farm-gate market-milk prices. The fresh-milk industry, however, remained regulated.

With DFG still opposed to full deregulation, along with National Foods and Parmalat, Victorian producers resolved to *force* the deregulation timetable, agreeing in 1998 to co-ordinate the cessation of regulation in their industry by 30 June 2000 and to seek a federal government compensation package.

In acknowledging this ultimatum, ADFF Chairman Pat Rowley observed that deregulation was now inevitable and would hurt many producers who would be driven from the industry. Victorian prices would determine prices for the rest of Australia and Victorian milk would intrude into other states' markets. There would be fewer producers, fewer processors and a need for *federal* legislation to reflect the new order.

DFG Chairman Ian Langdon berated Victorian dairy industry leaders alleging they were confusing the industry and overwhelming farmer organisations. Nevertheless, while he said he would 'choke on the words', Langdon agreed to promote the idea in states where DFG operated, although he remained convinced the co-operative movement was not yet ready for deregulation. Vigorously dismissing any idea that his co-operative would 'fall over' when deregulation came, as some southerners believed, Langdon still hoped that co-operatives in different states would find ways of co-operating but seriously doubted their ability to achieve this (discussed in Chapter Sixteen).

Perceptions of co-operatives change

Throughout this period of manoeuvring for market position in the approach to deregulation, rumours flew in a climate of mistrust between producers and processors, including co-operatives. The perception of co-operatives was changing and the sense of ownership and loyalty to them was being reframed. Once, co-operatives were seen as an extension of the farm, but now to many farmers it seemed that co-operative executives were obsessed with *growth* and *capital* while members, as always, were primarily concerned with *control*. Co-operatives increasingly were seen by members as a province of managers, insider cliques, secretive elites and investors. Rather than eliminating 'middle men', some co-operatives seemed hell-bent on becoming one themselves in replacing SMAs or were being 'fattened up' by managers with a view to liquidating their assets or handing marketing over to corporate experts. Members were being divided into shareholder 'classes': long-term and new suppliers; large and small suppliers; and those exiting or staying in the industry, post-deregulation. Many members believed that co-operatives were now no different from investor firms and were unrecognisable from what they had been in earlier years. Farmers were particularly concerned that a quiet consensus appeared to be developing between processors and giant retail chains. Some

Staff at a 100 box (2.5 ton) wooden butter churn at the Norco Lismore factory (1960s).
Coutesy of Norco Co-operative Limited.

asked if investments for growth and perpetual control *really* were reconcilable or would the former inevitably destroy the latter? Was a 'Get Big or Get Out' philosophy really the only way forward for co-operatives or was it a case of maintaining a strong, cohesive bond of association resting on the democracy principle? There was little time to reflect on these questions for, on 30 June 2000, the Australian fresh-milk industry was deregulated.

Deregulation: June 2000

After almost seven decades of Byzantine regulation, it was back to the rules of the market in dairying with no SMAs determining who could supply milk and how much to pay for it. A 'take it or leave it' $1.78 billion Commonwealth Government structural adjustment package (the Dairy Industry Adjustment Bill 2000) became effective, spread over eight years. This was the second largest agricultural adjustment package in Australian history and was to be paid for by a levy of approximately eleven cents per litre on packaged milk for retail sale and collected by the processor. The package was designed to make an average compensation pay-out per farm of $118,192, but this varied significantly between states. The average in Victoria, for example, was $95,000, in New South Wales it was $169,408 and in Western Australia, $240,000!

The traditional member-co-operative nexus is broken

Deregulation effectively divided the dairy industry into a farm industry and a post-farm industry and, in the process, revolutionised the traditional relationship between dairy farmers and processor co-operatives. Members now *demanded* their co-operatives match on-farm efficiency gains in adding value to raw materials. Co-operatives, on the other hand, like all processors, were free to pay market rates for milk supplied as opposed to the previously existing premium rates. Both farmers and processors were obliged by market forces to sell wherever the best prices could be fetched, introducing a new element of rivalry between farmers, on the one hand, and between farmers and processors, on the other. The old 'contract' between producers and co-operatives no longer automatically existed and they no longer necessarily shared common interests. The motivation to defend farmer co-operatives as unique and intrinsically valuable was unravelling and, in this context, the idea of accessing a co-operative's assets to aid members adjusting to deregulation or exiting the industry was more appealing. More than a century in the making, the Australian dairy co-operative movement faced its greatest identity crisis ever. This theme is explored further in Chapters Fifteen and Sixteen, by way of a case study of DFG.

The 'big milk shake'

The press enjoyed journalistic licence in describing deregulation as the 'big milkshake'. In *The Australian*, writing under the by-line, 'Welcome to Globalisation', journalist Paul Kelly explained that the regulated dairy industry had collapsed from within after Victorian producers 'pulled the plug'. Kelly applauded deregulation as 'good riddance to Australia's sacred cow disease' and celebrated the demise of the 'cash cow'. With regard to the Dairy Industry Adjustment Bill, Kelly said:

> It is the price all Australians are paying to demolish the Gothic horror of government interference in the economy that masqueraded as agricultural policy...for generations...Comfortable on the public teat, the dairy industry in most states, notably New South Wales, Western Australia and Queensland, let things go on as they always had. The problem was that the Victorian industry with greater pasture and greater efficiencies of scale could produce more milk than it could sell in that state.

A huge transfer of economic power from dairy farmers and processors to retailers occurred in the immediate post-deregulatory period. Between June and December 2000, $750 million was transferred from producers *and* consumers to supermarkets, which realised windfall profits equivalent to an asset reduction among dairy farmers Australian-wide of $3.7 billion. Within six months of deregulation 180 Queensland dairy farmers and 200 New South Wales dairy farmers had left the industry and the number of farmers staying in the industry had fallen below 1974 levels. Between one-third and one-quarter of dairy farms were not expected to survive, especially in New South Wales, Queensland and Western Australia.

In August 2000 Australia's largest supermarket chain, Woolworths (Woolies), put its house-brand milk supply contract out to tender. Business and financial journalist Robert Gottleibsen reported:

> ...In a brief but breathtaking display of market power Woolies reworked the entire dairy industry in a matter of months...It wasn't a deliberate bid to cripple [the] industry but the drastic economies imposed on dairy farmers and processors were consequences of the predictable behaviour of two powerful duopolists (Coles joined Woolworths) driven by competition to provide low prices to customers and also to pay more dividends to their shareholders.

Gottleibsen reported that Woolworths extracted $500 million 'out of the pockets of its suppliers' and passed some of this on to customers, pocketing the rest for shareholders. The tendering exercise damaged brand names built up over many years by the three major processors: DFG, National Foods and Paul's; which between them accounted for 63 per cent of the Australian fresh-milk supply. The giant retailers, Gottleibsen said, simply watched as processors 'cut their throats to get the business'. Sales of processors' brands plummeted by 75 per cent over the next two years as generic brands achieved acceptance.[23]

It is only possible to conjecture how different the situation might have been if earlier in the century producers and consumers had co-operated in creating a national co-operative wholesale, as Rochdale theoreticians had argued, or if dairy co-operatives and co-operative companies had been able to identify common ground and co-operate.

Part 2

STATES

*D*iscussion on the states' co-operative movements has been affected by the variable *quality and availability of sources. The consideration of South Australia and Queensland, for example, offers only an outline and discussion does not extend to Tasmania or the Territories, rural indigenous co-operatives or the fishing co-operative movement. Unavoidably, some co-operatives and events have been omitted. Nevertheless, sufficient evidence exists to illustrate the heterogeneity of co-operative movements in Australian states.*

South Australia has one of the oldest co-operative traditions in Australia, going back to the 1860s and is notable for the rich variety of co-operatives which took root there.

Co-operation began quite early in Queensland but developed slowly and was characterised by powerful state intervention. The concept of 'compulsory' co-operation was minted in Queensland and exported to other states in the form of statutory marketing authorities.

The Western Australian chapter provides a detailed case study of a struggle between an immensely successful co-operative company and defenders of the democracy principle and how, in this context, traditional co-operative principles were 'adapted' in that state.

Much of the debate on Victorian co-operation occurs in the context of the dairy industry and Chapter Seven focuses on the consequences of inadequate co-operatives legislation in that state until very near the end of the century, governmental attempts to 'kick start' the movement and poor support given to co-operative federations.

The two chapters dealing with New South Wales consider first how the movement lost opportunities to unite and forge a powerful presence after World War II and secondly how a depleted and asymmetrically-developed movement turned more to government for support after the 1980s.

Midland Saleyards 1939.

*(Courtesy Battye Library 023351PD. No further reproduction may be made
from this copy for any purpose without the written permission of the
Library Board of Western Australia)*

Chapter Four

The South Australian Co-operative Movement:
An Outline

Introduction

South Australia has one of the oldest co-operative traditions in non-indigenous Australia. As early as 1864, the British *Industrial and Provident Societies Act* was received into the colony and, two years later, a South Australian Co-operative Association was formed. By 1868 the Adelaide Co-operative Society had opened for business, quickly growing into one of the largest Rochdale stores in Australia, developing a lively trade with the English Co-operative Wholesale (CWS) in tea, sugar, soap and cocoa. The co-operative operated for nearly a century. Inspired by a visit by CWS delegates to the colony in 1896, other Rochdale stores were formed including the Port Adelaide Co-operative Society (1897), which was formed by railway workers in Vincent St, Adelaide, ran a shop in Commercial Road, took over the Sussex Hotel and developed a bakery in Lyons Street. In 1906 Rowley Campbell led the formation of the Millicent Co-operative Society and later the Wallaroo Co-operative in the wheat port of that name. The Wallaroo Co-operative's monthly newspaper, *Wheatsheaf,* was adopted in 1921 by the New South Wales Co-operative Wholesale Society (NSW CWS) as the official journal of the Australian Rochdale co-operative movement. Re-named *Co-operative News*, the journal was published monthly until 1959 and provided an important source of information for this study. By World War I there were at least seven Rochdale co-operatives in South Australia in addition to those already mentioned, including co-operatives at Mt Gambier, Angaston and Eudunda. What follows is a sketch of the South Australian rural co-operative movement but sufficient to hint at its success and diversity.

The Farmers' Mutual Association

It appears that South Australian rural co-operation evolved first among wheat growers. In 1887 farmers around Lyrup near Berri on the River Murray met to consider ways of breaking a stranglehold on their industry held by agents and also methods of rationalising costs. A Farmers' Mutual Association later formed in the northern wheat fields at Crystal Brook, east of Port Pirie, which explored methods of improving prices for commodities and marketing conditions, including political activism and co-operation. Falling commodity prices and successful wage claims by rural workers saw new urgency enter farmer debates.

A pamphlet by H S Taylor was circulating at this time discussing successful co-operative enterprises, in particular the English CWS, the Adelaide Co-operative Society and New Zealand producers' co-operatives. Farmers at Quorn north east of Port Augusta met to consider the Taylor pamphlet and possible ways of co-operating to cut costs. They decided to experiment by leasing small sidings from the Railway Department and pooling the crop. Farmers could not capitalise the operation adequately, however, and it was soon taken over by a private company, Treleven and Brown. Nevertheless, the experience taught wheat farmers that by *pooling* produce they could command better prices and wield greater market 'leverage'.

At a Farmers' Mutual Association Annual General Meeting in February 1888 three issues emerged for consideration: land reform; improved access to rural credit (via a state bank); and co-operation through a 'farmers co-operative union'. Delegates from Jamestown, east of Port Pirie, and nearby Caltowie, including Thomas Mitchell and John Pearce, were particularly enthusiastic about co-operation.

Concerned that 'private interests' – meaning proprietors *and* unionists – would attempt to sabotage the proposed 'self-help co-operative scheme', farmers held meetings secretly in the first half of 1888. Catching wind of this, sections of the press speculated on the 'risky venture'. The Registrar of Friendly Societies warned farmers against attempting such a thing and even the Farmers' Mutual Association was cool to the idea, seeing it as 'radical' and influenced by urban-consumer ideas. Other small co-operatives already operating, including those at Baroota and Terowie, were not interested.

The South Australian Farmers' Co-operative Union

John Pearce and supporters scoured the countryside seeking shareholders. They were successful in locating 103 confirmed producers who subscribed £288. Only thirty of these attended an inaugural meeting early in 1888 to form the South Australian Farmers' Co-operative Union (SAFCU), and only by the narrowest of margins voted for the co-operative to commence business. From this shaky start one of Australia's greatest and most progressive co-operative companies grew.

Modelled on the New Zealand Farmers' Co-operative Association, SAFCU was established at Jamestown in June 1888. The co-operative existed to handle, store, sample, grade, issue certificates, establish agencies, protect crops, cover risks, forward and deliver and direct on board the produce of regional wheat growers. Its objectives included:

> ...the fostering of local industry, united action of matters of national importance, combining for mutual self-help on the principle of Co-operation by buying in bulk and distributing the commodities at the lowest possible price [and] combining to place large quantities of produce on the market thereby securing the best prices for its members.

This was an heroic vision considering SAFCU's headquarters at the time consisted of a twelve by fourteen foot (3.6m x 4.2m) tin shed in Jamestown. As no suitable legislation existed, SAFCU was registered under Company Law. No Rochdale idealism illuminated SAFCU's objectives, which was established purely as a farmer buying and selling group with all benefits flowing to producers. It waived the Rochdale principle of limited interest on share capital, accepting money on deposit at 6 per cent, well above prevailing bank rates. Directors did not hesitate to take legal action against shareholders who neglected to subscribe to unpaid capital, arguing that it was better to get rid of 'non-co-operators' than carry them, *gratis*.

Three seasons passed before SAFCU was established soundly. The first two deliveries of bulk wheat were disastrous; one lost to rain and the other to mice. Directors were forced to meet losses from their own pockets and John Pearce was obliged to leave his farm to manage the co-operative full-time. Slowly, however, the co-operative company established a reputation for yielding better returns and, by 1891, some larger wheat farmers in established growing districts, also driven by a need to rationalise costs in depressed markets, began redirecting crops through SAFCU.

Two years before English CWS delegates visited the colony, in 1894 the first shipment of SAFCU wheat left for England on board the *Glennifer*, a great leap forward for the co-operative company. Thereafter SAFCU developed a close and lucrative trading relationship with CWS, exporting primary products and importing super-phosphate, farm machinery and vehicles in a direct indenting arrangement. Soon after, the co-operative company opened agencies in the Yorke Peninsula, in the southern and south-eastern growing districts and began an extensive programme of shed construction. Consistently paying growers better prices for produce than proprietary competitors, SAFCU was frequently approached to do business with non-members but strictly confined dealings to shareholders, who rewarded the co-operative with unswerving loyalty.

Rapid expansion stretched the co-operative's capital position, however. Then it received potentially a 'knock out blow' when an agent defalcated with two-thirds of the capital! SAFCU was by now a very attractive investment proposition and had no difficulty in locating funds but these tended to be at premium rates and available only from 'dry' (non-producer) investor-shareholders. How re-financing the operation affected its democratic nature is not made clear by the sources, but we do know that SAFCU was awash with capital at the turn of the century when many co-operatives in the wheat and other agricultural industries were struggling, particularly in the eastern states.[1]

In the period before World War I, SAFCU became a tremendously influential wheat exporter, moving also into wool, lamb, barley, oats, potatoes, skins, manures, corn sacks, general merchandise, stock, land and estate agencies and later hardware, groceries, dairy, drapery and the conduct of banking accounts for shareholders. From 1904 onwards SAFCU published *The Farm*, an industry journal providing valuable market information (but little in the way of co-operative education).

In 1906 SAFCU appointed English CWS as its agent in Britain. The following year, however, for unknown reasons, but possibly relating to litigation mounted by CWS Australian Agent R J Fairbairn over an alleged supply of sub-standard wheat, SAFCU switched to Berry Barclay and Company, an old established and widely-known firm of brokers. E B Young, a South Australian resident in London, was retained to organise the co-operative's lamb trade in Britain. In 1909 Clement Giles, a former SAFCU secretary and manager, in association with brokers Berry Barclay, was appointed as the co-operative's first full-time representative in London. After the business was presented with a large British taxation demand, however, the export branch was shut down. Giles then began arguing for a wholly farmer-owned and independent Australian co-operative marketing agency in Britain, the genesis of what would become after World War I the Australian Producers' Wholesale Co-operative Federation (APWCF), (discussed in Chapter Two).

By 1914 the co-operative's turnover exceeded Sterling £1 million and it operated substantial headquarters in Franklin Street, Adelaide. Like most businesses SAFCU went into suspended animation through the war when government-to-government arrangements were in place. Many farmers enlisted in the army. Drought, mice and weevil plagues saw production plunge and business almost at a standstill. In 1915 the co-operative company was influential in having the South Australian State Wheat Pool formed as part of the war effort. SAFCU favoured the continuation of pooling after the war so long as this was organised co-operatively, and saw the co-operative movement's role as 'bringing the producer and consumer (English CWS) into closer touch with each other, reducing the cost of living and minimising the industrial unrest which is so prevalent'.[2]

The South Australian rural co-operative movement received a boost from the (state) 1917 *Loans to Producers' Act*, enabling the government to make long-term loans to primary producer organisations registered under the 1864 *Industrial and Provident Societies Act*. Loans were repayable over twenty years and seven years for machinery for the construction of factories, packing sheds and related infrastructure. The act did not affect SAFCU directly, which was registered under the company code, but permitted the rapid expansion of the dairy industry and other primary industries in which SAFCU had an interest. Certainly the co-operative company utilised the act in purchasing two proprietary dairy businesses, a huge central processing plant and a chain of factories in the South Australian dairy districts, linked by a fleet of river craft. Seeking to capture other business opportunities, SAFCU offered preference shares at 7.5 per cent. This was a controversial move with critics inside and outside the co-operative describing the offer as 'unco-operative'. The combination of state loans to producers and attractive investment conditions, however, saw SAFCU poised to capture post-war opportunities and geared for rapid growth.[3]

After the Bank of Adelaide refused to have anything to do with a SAFCU proposal to commence co-operative insurance, the co-operative company took shares in CIC (Australia) Limited, an outgrowth of the Victorian dairy co-operative movement. A separate company, South Australian Farmers' Co-operative and Executors' Trustees Limited was established at the same time, about which no information has come to hand but which probably underwrote the interests of investors in primary industry co-operatives.

After war-time regulations were suspended in 1921, SAFCU was instrumental in establishing a voluntary wheat pool designed to resume trade on a co-operative basis. SAFCU also took a lead in seeking improved long-term credit arrangements for farmers through commonwealth loans guarantees and later entered submissions to a Commonwealth Government inquiry which saw taxation consideration extended to co-operatives under a mutuality principle (discussed in Appendix One). As in the east coast dairy industry, however, the voluntary wheat pool could not deliver orderly markets, with growers breaking ranks to take higher prices and resorting to the pool only when prices were depressed, opening the way for statutory regulation.

The most extensive co-operative movement in Australia

Visiting South Australia in 1924, the newly appointed New South Wales Registrar of Co-operative Societies, H A Smith, described SAFCU as the most comprehensive co-operative organisation in Australia and a model for many other co-operatives, noting that this had all been achieved *without* co-operatives legislation! Lamenting the fact that the broader Australian co-operative movement lacked vision and cohesion and was hamstrung in most cases by obsolete laws, Smith applauded South Australian farmers for building the most advanced co-operative movement in the commonwealth adding that, on a per capita basis, more people were involved in co-operatives in South Australia than anywhere else in Australia.[4]

By World War II, SAFCU had 14,000 shareholders, operated on a £5.3 million annual turnover and held £1 million in capital and £1.76 million in assets. The co-operative company, which had never held a mortgage, was the largest manufacturer of cheese in Australia, South Australia's largest exporter of butter, cheese and eggs, the state's largest handler of wheat and milk, the only manufacturer of condensed milk in South Australia and had over 400 agencies and branches throughout metropolitan and rural districts.

SAFCU was lost to the co-operative movement in the 1970s (discussed in Chapter Ten).[5]

Eudunda Farmers' Co-operative

The land around Eudunda, 110 kilometres north of Adelaide, was being cleared of mallee bush for settlement in the 1890s and store keepers and merchants were selling wood for fuel in Adelaide and elsewhere. When economic depression saw prices and demand for wood plunge, many pioneer farming families were reduced to penury. Store keepers began paying farmers in goods for wood supplied and merchants gave store keepers cash in exchange for cart delivery notes, which farmers used as currency.

The Fashion Department Store, one of the five retail divisions owned by the
Barossa Community Co-operative.
Photo courtesy of The Community Co operative Store (Nuriootpa) Ltd.

Led by Henry Mucklow, a former wood buyer, farmers discussed co-operation at several meetings in Sutherlands on the Murray Flats. At a meeting in the Eudunda Hotel on Boxing Day 1895, called by licensee A E Mann, who was keen to develop the region and his business, farmers and woodcutters formed the Eudunda Farmers' Co-operative Society Limited (hereafter 'Eudunda Farmers').[6]

Eudunda Farmers opened wood yards at Eudunda and Sutherlands. In the first three weeks ninety-one wood carters delivered 517 tons of wood. Two other yards were opened at Bower and Mount Mary. The co-operative leased railway stacking yards and a tiny office was opened in Adelaide. A reluctant local bank manager was cajoled into extending the co-operative £200, allowing Eudunda Farmers to open its first retail store, at Sutherlands, in 1897. Set on twenty-five acres, the shop had a weighbridge for wood deliveries and sold household goods and farm requisites to members. A full-time manager, Mrs Lynch, was appointed. Other stores soon followed at Bower and Eudunda.

When local proprietary store keepers began underselling the co-operative in Adelaide wood markets, it was obliged to revert to the old currency system, issuing suppliers with cart notes and requesting voluntary work. Many shareholders withdrew. Settlers left the district and the bank refused to honour the co-operative's cheques. By 1902, in the midst of a terrible drought, Eudunda Farmers was near collapse. A proprietor offered to buy the co-operative's stores but members refused:

> *It was a period when the principles of co-operation were on trial, when the future of the co-*
> *operative movement throughout the rest of the state depended largely upon the success or failure*
> *which attended the efforts of its pioneers on the Murray Flats. Although it might not have been*
> *realised at the time, it was a period of tantalising trial when any mistakes…might have been*
> *fatal to the future of the movement.[7]*

A private loan was negotiated, the details of which are unknown, and the co-operative survived. Eudunda Farmers appears never to have strayed from the democracy principle, however, strictly operating on a one-member-one-vote basis.

A railway line reached the mallee country as far as Pinnaroo in 1904 and, after the seasons improved, the co-operative entered a phase of sustained growth. Eudunda Farmers put the river steamer, *Pyap*, into service in 1908, operating along the Murray River at sixty landings. The co-operative began to buy out proprietary competitors and established substantial wholesale headquarters in Adelaide. In 1915 it began extending selective credit to members of good standing in the community. This policy, necessary to a business serving primary producers during a war, was contrary to the Rochdale movement's insistence on cash trading and sparked a long stand-off with the consumer co-operatives.

Eudunda Farmers dissociated itself from the Rochdale co-operative movement, the rhetoric of which directors described as 'anti-capitalist propaganda'. East coast Rochdale consumers, Eudunda Farmers' leaders believed, were: 'prejudiced by a class consciousness and political in intent whereas, in Eudunda Farmers'…people of all classes co-operated; the wealthy and the poor.'

For their part, Rochdale traditionalists criticised Eudunda Farmers for an alleged 'bureaucratic and centralised style' and for exercising 'an iron grip on branches' which, they argued, should be autonomous. Farmers were co-operating with Eudunda Farmers, purists charged, because they were 'acquisitive' and not at all interested in spreading the co-operative idea beyond their narrow sectional interests. In this way, the farmer-consumer schism, which so divided co-operatives in other states, carried into the South Australian movement.

Development stalled through World War I but thereafter growth was spectacular. Membership rose from 3,500 to over 11,000 in the five years to 1923 when the co-operative's annual turnover exceeded £500,000. It regularly paid employees a bonus and returned 6 per cent on shares, 2.5 per cent above prevailing bank rates! By 1924 Eudunda Farmers was the largest consumer co-operative in Australia with twenty-nine stores and functioned virtually as an independent co-operative wholesaler, untrammeled by Rochdale orthodoxy. The co-operative conducted a lively education programme in its journal, *Home Circle* and, in 1925, introduced the first superannuation scheme for co-operative employees in Australia. By the end of the Great Depression, Eudunda Farmers was the largest co-operative of its type in the southern hemisphere and one adult in thirty in South Australia was a member – one in six families!

In a spirit of post-war reconciliation Eudunda Farmers was a principal architect of a Rochdale Centenary Congress held in Adelaide in 1944, which brought together SAFCU, the Berri Co-operative Union, the Murray Producers' Co-operative Wholesale, CIC (South Australia) and Rochdale consumer co-operatives. Relations with the consumer movement were seldom cordial, however, and all efforts by east coast Rochdale leaders to develop a South Australian wholesale as part of a national 'One Big Society' strategy were vigorously resisted by Eudunda Farmers, which saw itself as already fulfilling this role and deplored interstate meddling.

By 1948 Eudunda Farmers had grown to include forty-five stores covering half of the state with almost 50,000 members and a £7 million annual turnover. With sound investments in Commonwealth Bonds and in Bank of Adelaide fixed deposits the co-operative was on a firm capital base. It had returned £673,000 in dividends to members since its inception. A decade later the co-operative had nearly 70,000 members and was consistently returning high dividends. It also defied a trend evident in the Rochdale movement and continued to grow and prosper through the 1960s and 1970s. By the early 1980s Eudunda Farmers had more than 90,000 members, employed over 500 people, held $1.4 million in reserves, produced a turnover of more than $28 million and was involved in an extensive warehousing operation with Associated Grocers.[8]

The Murray River Village Settlements

In conjunction with the 1893 *Crown Land Act (Village Settlements)*, the South Australian government released 46,900 acres of land adjacent to the Murray River in the north east of the state. The political objective was to reduce a potential for radical activism by removing the unemployed from Adelaide streets. The economic objective was to intensively settle land and bring it to production for exports. In addition to the extant Renmark settlement, twelve settlements were begun at Murtho, Lyrup, Pyap, New Residence, Moorak, Kingston, Holder, Waikerie, Gillen, New Era, Morgan and Lake Bonney.

Although most of these state-sponsored settlements did not involve experienced farmers and many were based on collectivist rather than co-operative principles, and failed, some did serve as nuclei for subsequently successful farming communities, particularly in the fruit and vine industries and, as such, warrant brief attention here.

The Murtho settlement, consisting of 200 acres opposite Renmark, was founded on Henry George principles with land held in common. Government credit was made available for its development. Lyrup consisted of 16,000 acres of mixed farming. A 'semi-communistic' association consisting mainly of Australian settlers, community coupons were used as currency, alcohol was banned, a 'school under the trees' was conducted and frequent, often fiery, meetings were held in a canvas hall. The Pyap community consisted of hand-picked tradesmen and families, mainly of Anglo-Celtic background, holding 16,000 acres in common for mixed farming. With women disenfranchised while men were free to demand a ballot on any issue, Pyap was racked with dissension, discontent and leadership struggles. New Residence, sponsored by the Workers' Education Association, was a small settlement of mainly unskilled workers from the Port Adelaide area familiar with Rochdale co-operation. By 1898, however, settlers were planning to divide the acreage into individual plots and develop co-operation in the fruit industry. Moorak consisted of 3,500 acres on which twenty-four families, mainly from Port Adelaide with close neighbourhood ties. They developed mixed farming as 'a combination of communism and co-operation seeking a better, freer, healthier life away from wage servitude and landlordism'. Moorak settlers contracted an experienced farmer to work the land and abandoned a coupon system of exchange used in some other settlements as too 'radical'. At Kingston approximately 100 mainly unskilled labourers from Port Adelaide and a sprinkling of Swedes, French, Italians and Americans, worked 4,000 acres on a communistic principle (but with no vote for women!). Holder consisted of 10,000 acres but that community, too, was torn with dissension. At Waikerie arguments between married and unmarried settlers over food shares saw a splinter group leave to establish an alternative settlement at Ramco, describing themselves as 'failures as co-operators' but anxious to prosper as individuals (with government support). Residents at Gillen were apparently given to drink and laziness, while those at New Era were hopelessly in debt. No details have come to hand for other settlements at Morgan and Lake Bonney.

Travelling by steamer along the Murray River in 1896 English CWS officials dispersed Rochdale literature among settlers, describing their enterprises as the 'Mississippi' of Australia. A South Australian Royal Commission in 1900, however, described the settlements as a failure. Only seven survived and they were struggling. Recommending that land be sub-divided into individual blocks and rented and that government assistance be directed to the development of co-operative fruit marketing, commissioners believed that, '…prosperity, harmony and equity as automatic by-products of co-operation on communally owned land is romantic and Utopian. Human nature defeats co-operation'. By 1913 only the Lyrup settlement survived.

The confusion of collectivist and co-operative principles embodied in the settlements, and their failure, damaged co-operation's reputation in South Australia at the turn of the century, as did similar failures in other colonies. The scheme, however, did see a significant transmigration to the Murray River basin. Many settlers stayed, developed fruit and vine industries and, later, co-operatives.[9]

Co-operation in the fruit and vine industries

The first evidence of co-operation in the South Australian fruit industry which has come to hand occurred in 1901, when the Renmark Fruit Packing Union joined with the Mildura Raisin Trust to organise the co-operative sale and distribution of the region's dried fruit. Proprietors resisted all the way to the Privy Council and it was not until 1907 that the Australian Dried Fruits Association (ADFA) was able to form for the control of dried fruit nationally. As no suitable national legislation existed, however, the association was obliged to operate on a voluntary basis permitted by the Australian Constitution, a far from satisfactory business arrangement.[10]

The tiny settlement of Berri, originally a re-fuelling point for River Murray steamers, was in 1906 a dusty scatter of buildings perched on an arid sheep run. A government-sponsored irrigation scheme in 1910, however, brought water for horticulture to a forty-one square mile area. As was common in such schemes at the turn of the century, no attention in planning was given to markets, so that settlers had to watch the depressing sight of fruit rotting on trees and vines. Seeking a practical solution, settlers organised a distillery and, in 1918, the Berri Co-operative Winery and Distillery Limited was formed for the production of fortified wine, later becoming the largest of its kind in the southern hemisphere.

The establishment of soldier settlements along the River Murray and elsewhere after World War I saw fruit production soar. In 1919 the Renmark Fruitgrowers' Co-operated (later, 'Co-operative') Limited formed out of the Packing Union to receive produce, weigh and grade fruit, furnish dockets, make door payments and provide requisites, repairs, finance, insurance and transport. Intensely loyal to Rochdale principles, Renmark Fruitgrowers' was registered under the 1864 *Industrial and Provident Societies Act*, operated on a one-person-one-vote basis, issued non-tradable shares of unchanging value which were cancelled or refunded on the death of a shareholder and strictly observed the patronage principle (dividends proportionate with a member's use of services).

In 1923 the Renmark Fruitgrowers' Co-operative and the Berri Co-operative Packing Union were instrumental in having the *Industrial and Provident Societies Act* overhauled, extending its application from 'any labour, trade or handicraft, except banking' to 'any industry, business or trade, wholesale or retail, except banking'. The revamped legislation placed restrictions on usage of the word 'co-operative' in a company's title and the Registrar of Industrial and Provident Societies established by the act was given sweeping powers of determination.

Murray River Wholesale Limited

Better suited to the needs of primary producers, the rewritten act allowed the development of the Murray River Wholesale Limited, a co-operatively-structured fruit growers' export arm based in Renmark and involving twenty-eight co-operative packing houses along the Murray River. Murray River Wholesale made arrangements with Overseas Farmers (discussed in Chapter Two) and with

Packers' (Australia) Proprietary Limited to handle the river area's produce overseas and joined with growers' co-operatives in Victoria and New South Wales to form the Co-operated Dried Fruit Company, for non-British exports.

Statutory regulation

With fruit production expanding rapidly in the inter-war period, a fierce competition between ADFA affiliates and proprietors for market-share saw prices plunge. After ADFA and proprietary companies co-operated to eliminate such 'unhealthy' competition, however, critics described this as a cartel and called for the statutory regulation of markets. Accordingly, in 1924 and 1926 South Australian licensing and control boards were established for dried vine produce and canned fruit, respectively. The Commonwealth Dried Fruits Control Board took control of exports and state boards, established under complementary legislation, set quotas and regulated the operations of packing sheds. In this way another important industry where co-operation might have flourished nationally aided by federal legislation for co-operatives, succumbed to state authority. It is fair to say, however, that South Australia, generally-speaking, was not so prone to regulation as other states, with the exception of Western Australia, and farmers were generally more inclined to seek co-operative solutions than to lean on the state.[11]

The South Australian Grape Growers' Co-operative (Kaiser Stuhl)

During the Great Depression grape growers in the Barossa Valley found themselves in a disastrous situation. To assist, the *Commonwealth Wine Overseas Marketing Act* (1929) established the Australian Wine Board to control domestic and export markets. With the market trough continuing, however, growers came to understand that the only dependable solution lay in their own hands.

The Barossa Wine Growers' Association held regular meetings in the Victoria Hotel, Tanunda, seeking a way through the marketing crisis. At one meeting wine makers, including Tom Hardy, Hugo Gramp, Leslie Penfold-Hyland, Sam Tolley and Oscar Seppelt, told the audience that prices paid to growers needed to be reduced by 30 to 40 per cent! Over 200 growers decided to form a co-operative.

The South Australian Grape Growers' Co-operative Limited was launched in February 1931. Early development was shaky in the depressed economic conditions. With plans for a winery on hold the co-operative faltered, meaning that the first vintages had to be processed by Tolley, Scott and Tolley, and Penfold's Kalimna. Then World War II saw port and dry red wine (Nurivin) exports disappear and the co-operative facing an uncertain future with serious liquidity problems, unable to raise sufficient finance to receive and process the 1942 vintage, for example.

Post-war sales surged, however, particularly sweet wine, port and bulk wine. By the mid 1950s port was out of favour as markets changed and sherry became popular. The co-operative did not have available sherry grapes and new irrigators entering the industry began to claim markets. The response was to introduce half-gallon flagons of dry red and five-gallon kegs of wine largely for consumption by Italian migrants in Melbourne.

The industry was revolutionised in 1956 when Orlando introduced sparkling 'Barossa Pearl' wine products, which won wide acceptance. The South Australian Grape Growers' Co-operative soon moved into the field. In 1961 Wolf Blass, a young German wine maker, joined the co-operative and the product range was expanded on domestic and export markets. Fruit was now also brought in from Langhorne Creek and the Coonawarra districts.

In 1976, following a series of amalgamations which saw the South Australian Grape Growers' Co-operative transformed, the Barossa Co-operative Winery, Berri Co-operative Winery and Distillery, Renmano Wines Co-operative, Loxton Co-operative Winery and Distillery and Waikerie Sellers' Co-operative combined to form Kaiser Stuhl, named after three hills in the Barossa Valley. Kaiser Stuhl was then Australia's largest winery commanding 7.7 per cent of the total market. Its exit from the co-operative movement is discussed in Chapter Ten.[12]

Berri Fruit Juices Co-operative Limited

In 1943 the Berri Co-operative Packing Union Limited purchased a small but expensive extractor plant to process citrus juices for US military personnel in the Pacific campaign. After World War II, as citrus fruit production expanded rapidly in soldier settlement schemes, the co-operative cultivated a domestic market. This was insignificant until the late 1950s and growers instead directed capital into the Riverland Fruit Producers' Co-operative Limited for the canning of quality fruit. In 1954, however, several co-operatives in the Upper Murray region around Waikerie, Kingston, Loxton, Renmark, Barmera, Moorook and Ramco, together with the Berri Co-operative Winery and Distillery and some proprietary companies, formed Berri Fruit Juices Co-operative Limited.

In 1961 Berri Fruit Juices installed a large extractor plant for lower grade fruit including oranges, grapefruit, lemons, tomatoes, stone fruit and grapes. Beginning as a side line for producers seeking a return on waste and surplus fruit, the fruit juice business grew rapidly into a spectacular success. By the late 1960s fruit juice was a major wealth earner for producers in the area and the industry employed 750 people throughout Australia. By the 1980s the Berri Fruit Juices Co-operative had branches in every Australian capital city, Newcastle and Wollongong and was involved in a joint venture with a Japanese company based in Berri. Commonwealth and South Australian industry development agencies supported the co-operative, renamed Berrivale Orchards Limited. Through the nineties, the co-operative company was financially restructured to permit external shareholders and the resultant company, Berri Ltd, moved headquarters from Adelaide to Melbourne.[13]

Community hotels

The first known co-operative hotel in Australia, based on the German Gothenberg system, whereby profits from alcohol consumption were ploughed back into community development, opened in Renmark in 1897. The Renmark Community Hotel was formed at the recommendation of a local Anglican priest concerned by the impact upon local communities of beer sprees when passing steamers called. By 1949 the hotel had contributed almost £150,000 to local welfare projects including a war memorial, a hospital, an irrigation trust, schools, sporting facilities, parks and tourist complexes. Other community hotels were formed at Waikerie, Barmera, Berri, Loxton and Nuriootpa.

Nuriootpa: a co-operative township

Nuriootpa, a small township about 75 kilometres north of Adelaide, drew upon strong traditions of community work going back many years. In 1925, for example, the community constructed a memorial community hall including a library, a stage and a cinema. As noted elsewhere, a co-operative winery and distillery was established in the township in 1931. Many co-operative horticulturalists lived in or around the town. In 1933 the community worked together to build a rotunda for band practice and in 1936 established an eighteen-acre centennial park, including dressing rooms, a playground and a camping area. The local community also persuaded the government to build a local high school.

A community hotel, the Vine Inn, was developed in the township in 1937 for '...promoting and fostering the interests of the town of Nuriootpa and surrounding districts and for the improvement of the town and district and its amenities'. In the decade to 1947 the Vine Inn distributed more than £7,000 throughout the township and district, contributing to the development of a swimming pool, a bowling green, croquet and tennis facilities, a golf course, playground, gardens, parks, kindergarten, a theatre, an assembly hall for the local band, a fire brigade and a hospital. The co-operative did have critics, however, with some residents concerned at the affects of the 'demon drink' on the township, but most townsfolk saw community ownership of liquor outlets as a reasonable solution to the problem of traffic in alcohol:

> It may turn the curse of alcoholism into a blessing of good neighbourliness, turning its profits back into the community for its betterment instead of taking them out of the community for private gain.

A new community centre was established in the township in 1944; a recreation and services club on forty acres, with some of the land donated. The community centre developed a child-care centre, a babies' clinic, a youth club, new residential building blocks, a native flower sanctuary, camping cabins, community forest and gardens and had plans to develop an open-air theatre, a youth hostel, a leadership training centre, picnic grounds and district archives. In the same year F W Hopman, a doctor, and Arthur Reusch launched a campaign to purchase the town's largest store, which was for sale, and run it co-operatively along Christian lines:

> The striving for unity and a fuller life based on the INFLUENCE OF EXAMPLE [sic]...the Nuriootpa community ideal is based upon the Christian principle of 'suffer the little children to come unto us'...If [the family] can work together...then the children will grow up to be good citizens and splendid neighbours. Human character and the example of Jesus Christ are the first qualities called upon in the devotion of time and service.[14]

Post-World War II 'New order' sentiment saw the Nuriootpa model lauded throughout Australia as an antidote to totalitarianism and centralised systems of government. For example, Co-operative Federation of Australia (CFA) Councillor T H Bath told Nuriootpa residents:

> I remind you again that you are pioneers. What you succeed in doing if it covers even a part of your plans will not only be of great importance and benefit to yourselves here and to Australia but of great and invaluable importance to the whole survival of democracy. In doing it as pioneers although your difficulties will be greater, I am sure your satisfaction will also be greater because if you manage to reach a point by your own vigorous activity then you will be ensuring not only the completion of your own plans but will also be opening the way for the developing of similar centres in other parts of Australia.[15]

Several community development committees were formed in Nuriootpa immediately after the war including the National Fitness Committee, the Armed Forces Welfare Fund Committee and the Post-War Planning Inquiry Committee, working with established groups to further develop the town. The Vine Inn ran a passenger coach, took children to kindergarten free, conducted a tourist information centre, purchased a dairy in 1948 and developed close links with the South Australian Fruit Growers' Co-operative, based in the same town. By the late 1940s the community hotel had 1,400 members and was open to anyone in the ward. By 1958, three-quarters of the local population were also members of the co-operative store, which had already returned £82,000 to the township.[16]

A conscious effort was made to educate the town's young people in the ways of co-operation through a 'Rainbow Club', where children were exposed to:

...witty verses full of co-operative education. These radiant white-clad youngsters proudly bearing their rainbow flags are being excellently trained for future membership and leadership under the Rainbow Flag and as their special co-operative song clearly showed.[17]

Nuriootpa, the most co-operatively organised town in the commonwealth, became widely celebrated throughout rural Australia and attracted much media and academic interest:

Nuriootpa looks as if it will be one of those nurseries of local self-government which Australia so badly needs...Here in Nuriootpa is being engendered through voluntary local self-government just the sense of political responsibility which we [currently] lack.

With Arthur Reusch and Allan Tonkin of Barmera to the fore, the South Australian Community Development Association was formed to seek funding for regional development along co-operative lines and committees were formed to this end. It is reported that dozens of towns in the region and elsewhere in Australia 'came alive to the benefits of community action,' inspired by the Nuriootpa example.

In 1965 the Nuriootpa co-operative store opened one of the state's first (Foodland) supermarkets. The hardware division was expanded in 1978 and a furniture division was opened in 1987, by which time membership exceeded 12 000. In 1994 the co-operative purchased a large tract of land including a spacious hardware store. Four years later it opened a regional shopping centre containing a large IGA Foodland supermarket and specialty shops. An electrical division followed in March 1999. With 250 employees working in modern amenities, the Nuriootpa co-operative store adhered to the Rochdale tradition of returning dividends to member-consumers, when possible.[18]

Chapter Five

The Queensland Co-operative Movement:
AN OUTLINE

Introduction

As for South Australia, resources available to this study unfortunately have not extended to a detailed account of the Queensland rural co-operative movement. The brief discussion offered, however, highlights the distinctiveness of Queensland co-operation insofar as the concept of 'compulsory co-operation' was minted in that state, an exemplary poultry co-operative (Red-Comb) played an important role in national co-operatives' affairs and education and, more recently, the Maleny co-operative movement has shown new standards of leadership.

Co-operation began quite early in Queensland but developed only slowly. It is believed the first Rochdale-style co-operative store in Australia opened its doors in Queen St, Brisbane in 1859, the same year as the colony was separated from New South Wales and only fifteen years after the Toad Lane store began in Lancashire, England. There is a report also that in 1873 a Darling Downs Farmers' Co-operative existed, establishing a flour mill at Warwick, but no corroborating evidence has been found. A Brisbane Co-operative Baking Society, the Peak Downs Mutual Society at Copperfield and the Queensland Civil Service Co-operative are reported to have been operating in the same year. By 1884 other co-operatives were functioning, including the Central Queensland Co-operative and Baking Society in Rockhampton, the West Moreton Co-operative Society at Booval, with a branch later at Ipswich, and Co-operative Cash Stores Limited.

We know that co-operation was promoted by W C Ruthnig, who in 1888 published *A Word to the Farmers of Queensland: Co-operative and the Produce Trade* and lectured extensively throughout Queensland to farmer and business groups. Ruthnig advocated local associations of farmer co-operatives and the pooling of capital to finance production along the lines of Schulze-Delitzch (German) credit co-operatives. Nothing more is heard of the plan.

The New Australia Co-operative Settlement Association

In the late 1880s and early 1890s journalist William Lane wrote in *The Boomerang* and Queensland *Worker* about 'ideal' communities, lionising the Australian bushman and railing against the Queensland Government for failing to assist striking shearers assembled in 'co-operative' camps around Clermont, Barcaldine (Blue Bush Swamp), Winton, Muttaburra, Hughenden, Capella, Isisford, Charleville, Cunnamulla, Saint George and Mungindi. Shearers in some of these camps, where it is commonly believed the Australian Labor Party (ALP) was born, formed informal co-operatives; more collective in inspiration than co-operative; to supply basic requisites and to tender for shearing contracts. Co-operative contracts were frowned upon by some union leaders for allegedly reducing overall piece rates available to workers, bringing co-operation into disrepute in sections of the labour movement.

In late 1891, disenchanted with Australia, Lane formed the New Australia Co-operative Settlement Association and, in July 1893, set sail from Sydney Harbour with 220 emigrants, a few tools (and a grand piano!) on the *Royal Tar* bound for Paraguay, where the government had made land available. By 1896, the failure of Lane's grand scheme was common knowledge in the colonies, further harming co-operation's credentials. For an excellent account of Lane's adventure see Gavin Souter's *A Peculiar People*.

The Communities Land Act 1893

Sensitive to the possible political consequences of 'people being forced from these shores', in 1893 the Queensland government passed the *Communities Land Act*, similar to legislation contemporaneously enacted in New South Wales, Victoria and South Australia. The act enabled the development of twelve co-operative settlements involving 2078 settlers: three in the Roma district (one at Rockybank); Reliance Co-operative at Springsure; the Mizpah Group at Chinchilla; the Protestant Unity Group at Cooran; Monmouth, Lake Weybar and Burrum groups; Nil Desperandum and Excell groups at Emerald and; the Alice River Group at Barcaldine. Similar to state-sponsored rural settlement co-operatives in other colonies, these largely failed.

The early Queensland dairy industry

Early development in the Queensland dairy industry was retarded somewhat by the capacity of northern New South Wales' farmers to supply most of that colony's needs. However, after migrating southern dairying families began farming the Darling Downs and Moreton districts in southern Queensland and moved along the coast to Burnett, Dawson, the Callide Valley and the Atherton Tableland, a government adviser was appointed in the late 1880s to accelerate dairy production. Ian Stewart's *A History of Dairying on the Atherton Tableland* provides a good account of some of these developments.

By 1893 there were butter and cheese factories operating in South Brisbane and Yangan, but it is not clear if they were co-operatively structured. We do know that by 1898 the Lockyer Farmers' Co-operative Association had established links with Sydney-based English Co-operative Wholesale Society (CWS) Agent R J Fairbairn. By 1899 a Queensland Agriculturalist Co-operative Dairying and Supply Company Limited was marketing butter and cheese. In the early 1920s there were forty-three co-operative butter factories in Queensland producing 98 per cent of the state's butter and more than seventy co-operative cheese factories producing over 90 per cent of the state's cheese. Apart from these few details, no further information on the early Queensland dairy industry has come to hand.[1]

Co-operatives and the sugar industry

The *Queensland Land Act* (1876) assisted hundreds of 'yeoman' small-holder farmers into the sugar cane industry. The industry was then dominated by plantation owners who monopolised cane-crushing equipment and refineries and exploited indentured Melanesian labour. North coast New South Wales cane growers, migrating to the cane-growing districts of Queensland, carried with them ideas of co-operation learned from dairy farmers. However, small-holders were unable to compete with large plantation owners, frustrating government plans to develop self-sufficient rural communities of British stock.

Struggling cane growers organised a petition in 1885 and presented this to the Griffith Liberal Government. The petition called for a ban on non-European labour after 1890 and the development of state-sponsored co-operative mills to break the planters' monopoly. An 1889 Royal Commission into the sugar industry found that the industry was generally depressed because London and Melbourne capital was flooding into land (rainforest) clearing and not into the sugar industry's technological and infrastructure needs, keeping the industry on a primitive labour-intensive basis.

Cutting green cane at Broadwater, 2003
Photo courtesy of Helen McCall

The 'Griffith Plan' emerged from this, by which the government undertook to finance two central mills at North Eaton and Racecourse, both in the Mackay region. Growers were required to reimburse government loans over fifteen years.

The scheme ran into immediate problems when growers were unwilling to invest in the scheme, considering the risk too high, and some declined to participate for ideological reasons, believing the idea 'socialist'. Mechanical failures at the mills and administrative inexperience saw the enterprises almost collapse, but both survived. Racecourse is reported to have been the first mill to crush cane and it is believed North Eaton was the first to be owned co-operatively.

The take-up of the 'Griffith Plan' was poor among growers, however, with only 25 per cent actually subscribing to shares, obliging the government to carry the remainder. Most growers were still dependent on plantation owners for refining and many farmed as poor tenant farmers, often on incomes lower than their labourers, caught between mill owners paying as little as possible for cane and trades unions demanding as much as possible for labour. In the Bundaberg region, 90 per cent of small holders failed outright. Those who did not survived on less remuneration than employees. While small-holder 'cocky' farmers and unionists were generally sympathetic to each other's situation, no alliance was possible as growers faced being permanently 'blackballed' by the proprietary mills if they were seen by owners to co-operate with unionists.

'Compulsory co-operation': The *Sugar Works Guarantee Act*

With many small growers facing ruin, the *Sugar Works Guarantee Act* was passed in 1893, introducing for the first time in Australia and possibly the world the idea of 'compulsory co-operation'. This was theoretically a contradiction in terms in that co-operation assumes voluntary association in autonomous entities but it was practical in so far as the act permitted the government to galvanise a still quite primitive industry. The Queensland government provided £500,000 for the construction of more co-operative crushing mills with growers required to give the government a lien over their land and *guarantees* that they would take shares in the co-operatives. As there were no penalties for non-compliance, however, in most cases growers simply acquitted mortgages and serviced other debts rather than finance the co-operatives, which remained largely the burden of taxpayers.

Nevertheless, government sponsored co-operative mills developed at Marian, Pleystowe, Plane Creek, Mackay, Prosperine, Mulgrave, Cairns, Mossman, Port Douglas District, Gin Gin, Bundaberg, Isis, Childers, Mount Bauple, Maryborough, Moreton, Nambour, Nerang, South Port and elsewhere in Queensland. In addition, wholly state-owned mills were developed at Babinda, South Johnstone and Tully.[2]

In 1914 the *Co-operative Agricultural Production and Advances to Farmers Act* was passed to help break a city-based investor stranglehold on capital flows and enable cane growers to raise finance to take shares in their co-operatives. Thereafter, under wartime emergency conditions to 1921, the industry was established on a more or less stable footing.

The McGregor Scheme: 'compulsory co-operation'

The Queensland *Industrial and Provident Societies Act* of 1920, which sought to clarify the legal personality of co-operatives, was generally poorly utilised by farmers. The Theodore Labor government, therefore, unencumbered by an Upper House (the Legislative Council having abolished itself in 1921) and looking to the successful precedent of the *Sugar Works Guarantee Act*, launched into a sweeping reorganisation of Queensland primary industry, informally referred to as the 'McGregor Scheme', after Queensland Director of Marketing L R McGregor.

McGregor, previously an employee of the Perth-based Westralian Farmers (discussed in Chapter Six), had been sent to London by that co-operative company to organise its shipping business. While in Britain, McGregor studied the co-operative movement in detail and was tutored by English CWS officials in wheat dealing. McGregor understood co-operative theory and respected it but also had observed the endless niggling and quarrels in co-operative movement politics, a general lack of cohesiveness among farmer co-operators and the slowness and unpredictability of voluntary methods in delivering practical results. In assuming the position of Director of Marketing, McGregor resolved that the only way of achieving the government's objectives lay not through working with an immature co-operative movement but through deliberate government intervention. The Labor government had no problem with that, seeing rural co-operation as a politically and economically important part of a centrally-planned, regulated economy. It authorised McGregor to proceed with a comprehensive regime of regulated commodity markets.

In 1922 the *Queensland Wheat Pool Act* established a marketing board for that commodity, without any consultation with growers. There were some rumblings from sections of the industry but the scheme's demonstrable effectiveness and the orderliness it brought to markets, following on from the war-time pools, persuaded growers and they approved of the board (88 per cent) in a subsequent poll.

The *Agriculture Bank Act*, by which the government undertook to make advances to co-operatives and co-operative associations for the construction of infrastructure and purchase of machinery and other agricultural requisites, superseded the 1914 *Co-operative Agricultural Production and Advances to Farmers Act*. Any chance of a co-operative bank ever emerging in Queensland, remote as that prospect was, was eliminated in this state-socialist scheme.

The *Fruit Marketing Organisation Act* followed, initially to assist pineapple and banana producers dealing with gluts and falling returns. Fruit and vegetable growers were grouped in local associations and organised in electorates. Sectional group committees elected by local associations were created for different types of produce. To be reviewed at three-yearly intervals and revitalised if a majority of growers so decided, the act constituted the Fruit Marketing Committee of Direction (COD), comprising two members from each sectional committee. L R McGregor presided over the scheme.

The *Primary Producers' Organisation Act* was then passed to assist farmers '…give consideration to their own problems and devise ways and means of solving them'. For purposes of the act, the State of Queensland was divided into nineteen districts. Built on the COD model, the act envisaged a hierarchical chain of command based on local producer associations rising to district councils, a Council of Agriculture and finally a grand supervisory body, the Queensland Producers' Association. Local producer associations were empowered to elect delegates to the appropriate district council. Each district council appointed one member to the Council of Agriculture (whose membership included six representatives appointed by the government). Standing committees within the Council of Agriculture represented the interests of various primary industries.

While the purpose of the *Primary Producers' Organisation Act* was orderly marketing, its objects included the 'encouragement of co-operative associations and co-operative enterprise on non-party lines and the unification of these and private organisations into a national body'. The state undertook to bear establishment costs for the first two years during which time various commodity boards would be constituted, pending the consent of producers. The government also undertook to absorb half the costs of operating the scheme for a period of two and a half years after the establishment phase.

The *Primary Producers' Organisation Act* precipitated a violent reaction from the Canned Fruit Agents' Association, which formed a 'League of Freedom' to fight what it described as the Theodore Government's 'creeping socialism'. There was also disquiet among farmers about the scheme's heavily centralist nature but this gave way to overwhelming support as producers saw gluts cleared, sales expand, incomes improve and industries stabilise. Regulation worked![3]

Building on the success of the *Wheat Pool Act* the government enacted the *Primary Producers' Pools Act* in 1922 enabling the formation of statutory marketing authorities (SMAs) under the *Primary Producers' Organisation Act* to 'meet the necessities of organised marketing where the voluntary system is shown to be inadequate'. While primary producers were not *compelled* to constitute SMAs, the government undertook to 'educate' farmers to the desirability of so doing, applying strong coercion.[4]

To criticisms from the Rochdale co-operative movement that 'compulsory co-operation' put a brake on genuine co-operative development and was only 'partially co-operative', McGregor replied that the old voluntary system had demonstrated that primary producers were conservative and wary of change. Experience in the wheat and fruit-growing industries had shown that compulsory co-operation materially improved farmers' economic position. Farmers were now loathe to return to the competitive and speculative pre-war conditions, for which co-operation had offered no antidote. To further allegations that a simple majority vote compelled a sizable dissenting 'oppressed' minority to channel production through a commodity board, McGregor replied:

> *It is true that voluntary co-operation gives more individual freedom but this individual freedom frequently brings about frustrations of co-operative objectives. Moreover, voluntary co-operation can [consolidate growers] into a fairly firm position as a business corporation whether 100 per cent or 50 per cent efficient, whereas compulsory co-operation is constantly on trial by reason of the arrangements for a vote having to be taken at intervals…Under the voluntary system the experience has been that the burden of finance has fallen on the enthusiastic minority while the majority have benefited by the work and experience of the minority. There is no state*

control [in the McGregor Scheme] but the government has afforded the necessary protective legislation as well as sympathetic and practical help and encouragement for self-help. As a result the produce of a minority cannot be used to break down such organisation as the majority may set up.[5]

The *Queensland Primary Producers' Co-operative Associations Act*

The *Queensland Primary Producers' Co-operative Associations Act* (1923), which was modelled on South African legislation, however, did seek to address some of the Rochdale co-operative movement's complaints. It was designed to unify and organise Queensland primary production by assisting the development of co-operatives among the many producer associations which had formed from the *Primary Producers' Organisation Act* (over 700 with 18,300 members). The act created a Queensland Registry of Co-operative Associations for Primary Industry, described model rules for co-operative formation and restricted use of 'co-operative' in the title of organisations to those where a one-person-one-vote principle applied and to where at least two-thirds of the members were suppliers to the co-operative. New societies complying with these criteria were required to register under the act. Extant co-operative companies registered under company law were exempted. The scheme was to be funded from levies upon producers, where the consent of a simple majority in an industry existed.

While the act envisaged federations of co-operative associations forming from producer associations, the thrust was clearly towards boosting agriculture through scientific marketing, the stabilisation of prices, better methods of production and improved credit facilities for producers. The act also allowed a number of quasi-co-operatives to enjoy the taxation benefits of co-operatives while withholding dividends from members and operating 'contract' co-operation on the US Sapiro model, by which members were compulsorily required to sell a portion of their crop for a specified period through a co-operative. For this reason the *Primary Producers' Organisation Act* was bitterly opposed by 'old world' exponents of voluntary industry organisation, particularly C E D Meares' New South Wales PDS Co-operative, which operated in Queensland and saw the act as tolerant of 'bogus' co-operation.

The Theodore government dismissed such complaints, describing the act as a 'stepping stone to co-operation'. Indeed, while the legislation did not directly influence the New South Wales *Co-operation Act*, which was contemporaneously being developed (discussed in Chapter Two), it did inspire legislation for commodity boards in other states, including New South Wales, later in the twenties. In this way, Queensland 'compulsory co-operation' influenced the shape of the Australian co-operative movement for much of the twentieth century.[6]

The McGregor Scheme's democratic complexion, however, was transitory. The *Primary Producers' Organisation Act* was amended in 1925, altering the structure of the Council of Agriculture, reducing the number of district councils from nineteen to eight, with only one representative from each council eligible for election to the Council of Agriculture. The position of commodity boards was strengthened (already, eight boards were operating) and the reformed Council of Agriculture, which included four government representatives, was now presided over by the Minister for Agriculture and Stock, not the Director of Marketing as previously. The government was taking a much stronger hand.

The *Primary Producers' Organisation and Marketing Act*

Then in 1926 the *Primary Producers' Organisation Act* and the *Primary Producers' Pools Act* were merged into the *Primary Producers' Organisation and Marketing Act*. The Council of Agriculture was again reconstituted – on a purely commodity-basis. Local producer associations were retained but district councils were dissolved. Marketing boards, now numbering ten, each sent a representative to the Council of Agriculture on which *five* government delegates now served. In effect, the grass-roots representation and inbuilt checks and balances of the two original acts, which preserved some semblance of the McGregor Scheme's democratic nature, were cancelled. While the 1926 act paid lip-service to voluntary association; allowing dissenting producers an avenue for the airing of grievances, for example; it was really a mature example of state socialism and had little to do with co-operation or the democracy principle.

In 1932 the Moore Country-National Progressive government amended the *Primary Producers' Organisation and Marketing Act* to allow for a better balance on the Council of Agriculture between commodity boards and geographical representation. The amendments also permitted improved participation by local producer councils, which were still outnumbered by statutory board and government representatives. The ensuing Forgan-Smith Labor government abolished local producer associations altogether in 1938 and placed the Council of Agriculture again on a purely commodity basis with no brief to 'encourage co-operative enterprise as such. [Instead] the functions of the council shall be to co-operate with the department any board, or boards, and any other approved bodies or persons'. An executive committee was constituted to give effect to these amendments. The Queensland Council of Agriculture, now directed by this committee, remained constituted on this basis until the 1970s.

What had begun in the early 1920s as an attempt to creatively blend voluntary co-operation with statutory obligations, by World War II had been converted into a bureaucratically-controlled, compulsory commodity marketing system in which co-operatives functioned essentially as ancillaries. By 1939 there were sixteen commodity boards in Queensland for arrowroot, Atherton maize, barley, broom millet, butter, canary seed, cheese, cotton, eggs, fruit, honey, pigs, peanuts, plywood veneer and wheat. Local producer associations, originally conceived by L M McGregor as nurseries of co-operation, were virtually extinct.[7]

The Poultry Farmers' Co-operative Society: 'Red Comb'

Notwithstanding such state-socialist intervention, a Queensland co-operative was formed in the early 1920s which played an important role in shaping Queensland and Australian co-operation: the Poultry Farmers' Co-operative Society ('Red Comb').

In 1922 eighty-five members of the Queensland branch of the Utility Poultry Breeders' Association, which had been running a voluntary grain and feed distribution service, met to form a co-operative for the bulk purchase of requisites and the pooling of production. Known by members as 'Red Comb', the Brisbane-based co-operative, which initially involved producers operating close to the metropolitan area, was not formally constituted until 1925 when it was registered as Poultry Farmers' Co-operative Limited, directed by R H Woodcock, who also served as manager, secretary, store man and clerk, virtually on an honorary basis.

After a disastrous sortie into export eggs marketing, Red Comb decided to leave marketing to the Queensland Egg Board and for a time no longer received eggs, concentrating on feed and production requisites. Indeed, the co-operative established the first mass production and storage plant for poultry farmers in Queensland. In so doing, it met strong resistance from proprietors who organised boycotts, obliging Red Comb to *import* wheat from New South Wales, assisted by NSW CWS. This experience taught Red Comb the importance of co-operation between co-operatives and forged a long and cordial association with the Rochdale consumer movement, making it one of very few Australian producer co-operatives in this regard. Red Comb's leaders were well versed in Rochdale theory, genuinely sought to develop a broad, cohesive co-operative movement, not limited to sectional interests, and conducted possibly the most energetic co-operatives' educational programme in Australia at the time.

In 1928 the co-operative purchased property in Roma Street, Brisbane, and immediately established a sick-benefit fund for members and employees. Weathering the Depression tolerably well, in 1932 Red Comb entered the export cold-storage chicken market to Britain, adding grocery and hardware departments and benefiting from close links with English CWS, coordinated through NSW CWS.

The co-operative received a mighty boost from large contracts to victual allied troops in the Pacific basin during World War II and rapidly grew into Queensland's largest co-operative numerically, with 18,500 members. By the end of the war, Red Comb ran five feed mills, abattoirs, a frozen food division, lucerne exports and later added seed cleaning and grain buying departments, a veterinary lab, a bakery, a terminating building society, a credit union and other services.[8]

After the war Red Comb became a leader of Queensland and Australian co-operation, consistently producing some of the movement's finest leaders including Stan Lloyd, Clem Kidd and William (Bill) Kidston. Lloyd and Kidd made important contributions to the 1943 Co-operative Congress in Canberra from which the Co-operative Federation of Australia (CFA) emerged (discussed in Chapter Ten), arguing co-operation as an antidote to all 'isms', particularly communism and fascism – a 'middle way' between capitalism and socialism. Kidd issued a pamphlet, *Economic Democracy: The Role of Co-operation*, arguing self-help at community level through co-operation in developing a people's democracy created from the 'grass roots up'. Co-operators, Kidd believed, should never rely on governments of either left or right persuasion and could only trust themselves.

Maintaining good relations with consumer and producer sections of the co-operative movement, Red Comb became influential in co-operative politics, establishing *Co-operative Press* and regularly publishing *Co-operation*, a magazine carrying information on co-operation in Australia and abroad and which, for educational value, was rivaled only by the Rochdale movement's *Co-operative News*.

The Co-operative Union of Queensland

Red Comb organised formation meetings in March 1945 for what became the Co-operative Union of Queensland (CUQ), established 'to organise co-operative effort and to educate people in co-operative principles with a view to the ultimate establishment of a universal co-operation'. CUQ supported the NSW CWS line that a national co-operative wholesale, 'One Big Society'; was the 'common ground on which agricultural and consumer co-operators could in fact co-operate', putting it at odds with the Western Australian and South Australian co-operative movements, which would have nothing to do with the scheme, unless they controlled it. A dynamic new leader, Bill Kidston emerged at this time, throwing his enormous energy as CUQ Assistant Secretary into organising co-operative conferences and calling for new legislation because 'present legislation is trampling on us, preventing consumers and producers from uniting'.[9]

In 1946, at the behest of CUQ, the *Industrial and Provident Societies Act* was amended allowing co-operatives to 'carry on a business, industry or trade...dealing in land, receiving deposits or lending'. While no definition of 'co-operative' was included, the amendments did permit more flexible development and easier co-operation between producer and consumer co-operatives than was possible in New South Wales, for instance.

Many new co-operatives were registered in the post-war boom. Fifty-five societies formed in two years to 1948 and forty-nine of them affiliated with CUQ. By 1950 there were 125 farmer co-operatives in Queensland in the dairying, sugar, fruit and other primary industries in addition to scores of co-operative stores with over 100,000 members, nearly 6,000 employees and producing £56 million in turnover.

Bill Kidston saw to the development of the Co-operative Wholesale Society of Queensland (CWSQ), designed to become the Queensland section of 'One Big Society', joining producers and consumers to their mutual benefit Australia-wide, as Rochdale movement disciples had been arguing for decades. In the post-World War II euphoria, CUQ's enthusiasm for an integrated co-operative movement abolishing 'isms' and joining primary producers, consumers, manufacturers, banking and insurance companies, credit unions and building societies in a 'co-operative commonwealth', was well received by Queensland Labor Premier E M Hanlon, who said:

> ...in all seriousness and with all the emphasis at my command that the day is fast approaching when farmers and workers will be solidly united in a bond of common interest in the advancement of this country towards a real Co-operative Commonwealth.[10]

The government also supported the idea of a co-operative ministry. However, after T H Bath, who was a Westralian Farmers' Director and Honorary Secretary of the Co-operative Federation of Western Australia (CFWA), visited the state and disapproved of the proposal, it was dropped. Instead, a Co-operative Advisory Council was constituted.

At a Co-operatives Round Table Conference called by CUQ in 1948, there was no evidence of the deep divisions between primary producer and consumer co-operators evident in other states, especially New South Wales and Western Australia. On the contrary, a tolerant eclecticism characterised debates involving diverse co-operative groupings, including a new and energetic generation of co-operative building society and credit union supporters. A CUQ Co-operatives Development Committee was formed to foster co-operation in all fields, *Co-operative Press* issued a stream of articles and pamphlets on co-operation and CUQ officials broadcast frequently on radio, publicising the benefits of co-operation.

With Cold War tensions peaking in the early 1950s, dividing co-operators along ideological lines, tensions which had split the Australian Labor Party and CFA at national level spilled into Queensland co-operative politics. At the 1951 CUQ Congress, which was attended by NSW CWS leaders and the CFWA's Tom Bath, it became apparent to CUQ affiliates that the visitors saw Queensland as something of a 'prize' in a contest for leadership of the national co-operative movement. CUQ resolved to strike an independent course and not be drawn into debilitating arguments separating consumers and producers in other states.

The Co-operative Federation of Queensland

By now, the fortunes of the Queensland co-operative movement had changed. The deaths of Stan Lloyd in 1952 and Clem Kidd in the following year coincided with a sharp contraction in co-operative retail business, badly affecting CWSQ. Dividends dwindled, co-operative membership declined and rifts between Rochdale 'socialists' and farmer 'reactionaries' began in the CUQ. In 1954 CUQ changed its name to the 'Co-operative Federation of Queensland' (CFQ), removing 'union' from the title, which some affiliates found offensive. By 1955 CFQ membership comprised mainly primary producers although a few building societies and credit unions remained affiliated.

Under Kidston's influence, and with Red Comb's continued support, CFQ became a hub of east-coast co-operation as the New South Wales Rochdale movement declined. Between 1958 and 1963 CFQ conferences were the most representative of all Australian co-operative gatherings, joining primary producers, consumers and building society and credit union supporters. The

CFQ played host to national and international co-operative conferences and in association with the Commonwealth Government played a key role in developing co-operation in Papua New Guinea and the South Pacific. CFQ conferences routinely involved delegations of co-operative guildswomen from the ailing New South Wales Rochdale movement along with leaders of the building society and credit union movements, including E H Tytherleigh of the Australian Association of Permanent Building Societies (AAPBS) and Keith Young of the New South Wales Credit Union League (NSWCUL). At a CFQ conference in 1960 a 'unifying symbol' for Australian co-operation was chosen, a North American image preferred by the New South Wales' credit union movement - twin pine trees on a circular golden background. (It was not widely accepted.) CFQ managers' conferences were regularly held concurrently with membership conferences where well-researched papers on marketing, international trends in co-operation, taxation and other matters of co-operative development were discussed.[11]

Questioning Rochdale orthodoxy

Bill Kidston was now openly questioning the cogency of Rochdale consumer theory and pointing more to North American co-operative models, where a pragmatic, business-oriented philosophy prevailed and managerial efficiency had subsumed what some saw as 'sentiment' and 'grandiose theory'. Not prepared to discard Rochdale theory entirely, however, Kidston sought to *improve* it by ridding the co-operative movement of a 'small store' mentality and a doctrinal inflexibility and preciousness which tended to exclude other co-operative forms. Staying on an independent path, Kidston agreed with CFWA centralists John Thompson and Tom Bath and with Sydney-based English CWS Agent A F J Smith that it was necessary for co-operatives to compete effectively in the commercial world to survive, let alone grow. He was adamant, however, that democratic ownership *and* control were at the heart of co-operation and rejected any adaptation of co-operative principles diluting the democracy principle, which he believed was fundamental to an understanding of co-operation.[12]

Lethargy

With much of the Rochdale consumer movement decaying through the 1960s despondency crept into Kidston's voice. He pointed to lethargy, the 'great danger to the co-operative movement':

> Lethargy has crept into our movement at the very time when our co-operatives need creative powers more than ever before. The co-operative movement is drifting from one conference to another through a series of pious resolutions. Could it be that the time is later than we think? Could it be that instead of talking of the challenge of the future we should really wonder if even we have a future? Can we really expect business ethics enunciated at the dawn of the industrial revolution to be effective in the jet age of the 1960s?

The CFQ activist maintained an energetic co-operative education programme, including a *Co-operative Study Course*, one of only a few attempts in Australia to include co-operatives' history in a managers' training course. In a stream of pamphlets and newsletters Kidston spoke of 'second and third generation co-operators' who, because of the established movement's neglect of education, knew nothing about co-operation or the great social and economic achievements of an earlier generation of co-operators:

> Co-operatives which do not change will go the way of the small store. [Their] days are numbered. Eventually [they] become a shrine and not an economic benefactor. Co-operators without ideology are dead...education!

Rochdale principles, Kidston argued, remained basically sound but membership alienation had to be acknowledged and ponderous boards weighed down by outmoded ideas needed to step aside:

> The co-operative concept has within itself the seeds of its own destruction. Co-operatives fail to adapt their appeal to cultural changes or the way people think in the present day affluent society. No clear concept of co-operation is projected and the existing range of educational materials fails to make it clear. A 'special' co-operative language is used. Co-operators take themselves too seriously. Many think they are out to save the world...Others think co-operation is for saving pennies...Others for assisting the struggling and the down at heel. Some think it is for farmers only. Instead we need to appeal to the modern family's love of the 'good rich life'. Our educational materials do next to nothing to establish a clear consistent appealing image. They sound virtuous but dull, lacking humour. We rely too much on plain facts. When we do not resort to emotional appeals it is usually in the glittering righteous tones of old-fashioned evangelism. Indeed we still represent ourselves as a farm-based movement. We still speak in the proletarian prose of the thirties when the people we need most to reach think of themselves as educated middle class. We have failed to interest the un-churched. We must help people to understand that co-operatives are special places, not just places to save money. We must present opportunities for people to project their own image into their business enterprise. We must strengthen the bond between co-operatives and members [and] develop a sense of ownership and responsibility.[13]

Two philosophies

Kidston continued to see co-operation as a 'middle way' between 'the impossible alternatives of communism and economic fascism', but not as a philosophy directed towards social transformation, as Clem Kidd and Stan Lloyd had believed; he thought people had lost faith in that idea. Rather, the mission of co-operators was to construct a powerful co-operative sector countervailing the extremes of the private-profit and public sectors. The co-operative movement, however, Kidston believed, was 'resting on its laurels [with] no sound political platform, no education explaining its meaning and offering no middle of the road ideology'. He spoke of 'two philosophies of co-operation':

> There are those who believe that the original dream of the Rochdale pioneers of an ultimate Co-operative Commonwealth is still attainable. To these people therefore their local co-operative is but a stepping stone [to this]. They foresee the expansion of the principles of co-operation to all other spheres of human endeavour until the competitive system is completely replaced by a Co-operative Commonwealth.
>
> The other school of thought agrees that co-operators must aim to extend their influence and ownership through all stratus of commercial enterprise [but] believes that co-operative enterprise will always flourish in competition with non-co-operative enterprise. They see the co-operative movement not as a replacement for other types of business but as an alternative regulating factor which by its open and free competition will benefit the community at large. This philosophy is the one to which co-operators in this state generally subscribe.[14]

Despondency grows

With the demise of NSW CWS evidencing Rochdale's shortcomings in modern business, a great malaise afflicted CFQ as the 1960s drew on, more serious than simply poor public relations or theoretical problems, serious as these were. CFQ conference resolutions were not being acted upon.

For instance, two resolutions from the 1962 conference calling for a centre for the exchange of co-operative shares and a central secretariat 'under the co-operative rainbow flag' saw no action whatsoever. Affiliates were becoming disillusioned about the economic value of CFQ membership. Red Comb Co-operative, long a CFQ mainstay, was becoming impatient with propping it up. Business continued to drift away from CWSQ as affiliates ceased trading or deserted the wholesale, preferring private-profit competitors. Fierce arguments erupted between CFQ affiliates calling for the amalgamation of co-operatives into a centralised grand-national unit and those defending local ownership, co-operative autonomy and strong membership interaction. So torrid were some debates that delegates at the 1963 CFQ conference, for instance, were reminded of fines for drunkenness, refusing to leave, or striking or fighting another member.

Bill Kidston despaired. The radical fervour of co-operation had passed, he believed, replaced by pragmatism. Co-operative development was slow; too slow; and now history was speeding past, leaving co-operation on the margins of mainstream events. Post-war affluence had caused many to question the need for co-operation – people were too busy becoming prosperous. Rochdale theory and practice, Kidston believed, needed to be 'wrapped in modern garb' and co-operation's supporters needed to clearly differentiate in the public mind co-operative enterprise from private-profit enterprise. They seemed too sheepish to do this. Why? Was not co-operation an admirable philosophy with its own integrity? Co-operation needed to be presented as a 'fulfilment of people's needs' and the social aspect needed to be stressed – integrity, purity, friendliness:

> *The universal appeal of the co-operative movement lies in the fact that it offers us a Christian alternative to the excesses and abuses of state communism on the one hand and the practical answer to extreme capitalism on the other. It provides us with a channel wherein without quarrelling with anyone else's beliefs or methods of business operations we can combine and work out our own economic destiny. It is a movement which revives our faith in our own abilities, which generates charitableness to all humanity. In the midst of this trilogy of faith, hope and love, we must inevitably accept the challenge to perpetuate its principles and hand them on proudly and untarnished to a generation to follow.[15]*

The CFQ went into rapid decline after the mid-1960s as primary producer co-operatives disaffiliated, demutualised or acted unilaterally and the credit union and building society movements hived off to develop independent umbrella organisations. The CWSQ was reduced to merely arranging 'deals' for a dwindling membership. Kidston devoted himself largely to CFA and South Pacific Commission work and, working with Australia's Foreign Aid Programme through the South Pacific Commission, took a prominent role in the development of co-operation in Papua New Guinea, Fiji, the British Solomons, New Hebrides, the Cook Islands and Tonga.

By the end of the decade, there were seventy-seven co-operative stores operating in Queensland attached to primary producer co-operatives with 57,000 members and a further 50,000 members of Rochdale-style co-operative stores. Most co-operative development, however, was occurring in mutual buying groups; many hundreds of them; tied contractually to a private wholesale grocery and not recognised as co-operatives either by the co-operative movement or the act.

With Kidston's health deteriorating (suffering a severe stroke in the late 1970s), neither he nor CFQ made notable contributions to CFA federal conventions in the 1970s (discussed in Chapter Ten). In 1980 Red Comb was taken over by Fielder Gillespie Limited and CFQ quickly declined, never recovering anything like its former glory.

The Maleny co-operative movement

As so often in co-operatives' history as one flowering of co-operation withered another was blooming, a remarkable instance of community-based rural co-operation: the Maleny co-operative movement.

In 1979 a group of so-called 'hippies', determined to live life less dominated by conventionality and more communally and closer to nature; 'back to basics'; started the Maple Street Co-operative, a consumer co-operative in the township of Maleny, about 150 kilometers north-west of Brisbane in the Sunshine Coast hinterland. The Maleny community was then suffering from a severe downturn in traditional rural industries, especially dairying, and townsfolk were drifting away. New settlers found it philosophically agreeable and affordable to relocate from mainly urban areas to that beautiful place. With Jill Jordan to the fore, a constellation of co-operatives and co-operatively-run associations was formed. In 1984 the Maleny and District Credit Union began and, along with the Maple Street store, became an important employer and financial hub in the township and environs. Crystal Waters Co-operative, a community settlement co-operative was formed in 1986, followed a year later by an unincorporated local employment trading system, LETS. In 1989 Wastebusters Co-operative, a community advancement co-operative and Mountain Fare Co-operative, a co-operative for women, were formed. These were followed in 1991 by Barung Landcare (an environmental association), Maleny Enterprise Network Association (MENA) Inc and two community settlement co-operatives, Cedarton Foresters Co-operative and Manduka Co-operative. The Ananda Marga River School, Black Possum Publishing Co-operative and Peace of Green (an arts and craft collective association) were formed in 1992. Between 1993 and 1995, five more co-operatives or associations were added to this remarkable record of achievement including the Maleny Film Society, the Waroo Performance Arts Co-operative, the Maleny Co-operative Club, Green Hills Incorporated (an environmental planning association) and the Booroobin Valley Learning Centre Educational Cooperative. LEED (Local Economic and Enterprise Development) Co-operative was formed in 1997 and a family support services association, FACE (Family and Community Empowerment), in the following year. Other groups emerged including YOGI (Young Organic Growers Group) (1999), Hinterland FM Radio Community (2000) and, in 2001, the Maleny Community Forum (a discussion group), the Booroobin Bush Magic Workers' Co-operative and an intra-and inter-regional networking and buying association. The Maleny Cultural Learning Exchange and the Maleny Working Together Strategic Planning Project (an alliance of older traditional and 'new-age' co-operatives in the region) followed in 2002 and 2003, respectively. Though many of these entities were tiny and, significantly for our discussion, not registered as co-operatives due to a perceived structural unsuitability and legislative complications, each formed part of a broad social ferment employing co-operative methodologies and, in particular, the democracy principle.

The Co-operative Community Council

Maleny was not alone in forging new co-operative growth in Queensland. The Cooperative Community Council (CCC) was founded in April 1990 as an independent co-operative association supporting south-east Queensland's community-based cooperatives. Focused on co-operatives' education, inter-cooperative co-operation and networking, regional development issues and political and legislative matters impinging particularly upon community cooperatives, the CCC played an important part in informing the Queensland government's preparation of 1997 co-operatives legislation. At time of writing, CCC continues to run lively annual co-operatives' educational weekends which, like earlier CFQ conferences, provide a valuable forum for innovative co-operators.

Other Developments

Other Queensland developments included the formation in 1984 of Capgrains Co-operative Association Limited for chick pea, cotton, mung bean, sorghum, wheat and other grain producers, inland between Mackay and south of Gladstone. Like earlier generations of co-operators, farmers understood that their future security depended on an ability to *control* commodities through to the end user buyer, whether local or international. Capgrains quickly developed a reputation for marketing and technological innovation.

Another successful new co-operative, the Blue Gum Co-operative, joined specialised grass-fed beef companies in central and south-west Queensland. Through strategic alliances, Blue Gum became a significant shareholder in a Brisbane-based company supplying meat-foods to hotels and restaurants in and around Brisbane.

In 1988, several co-operative raw sugar mills in the Mackay region, at Marian, Racecourse, Cattle Creek, North Eton and Farleigh, some of them almost a century old, combined to form Mackay Sugar Co-operative Association Ltd. Mackay Sugar quickly grew into Queensland's second largest producer of raw sugar accounting for 20 per cent of national production and involving 1100, intensely co-operatively-minded growers.

There were also attempts, as in other states, to employ co-operatives as vehicles in the privatisation of SMAs. For instance, in 1992 Queensland coarse grain growers involved in SMAs for barley, grain, sorghum, wheat and bulk grain voted unanimously to form a super co-operative. The proposed co-operative was to be owned by grower shareholders and would consist of three subsidiaries for marketing, handling and commercial services, including government relations. It was hoped that the Queensland government would assist by allowing the co-operative to retain SMA suppliers, wave stamp duties and financially assist the co-operative in the establishment phase. Many growers, however, doubted that a merger of entities involved in such disparate industries would be feasible and the government was uncertain about assisting such an organisation. The vexed issues of 'dry' shareholders, disclosure and intellectual property also bedeviled the conversion process, which quickly passed through a co-operative phase before being converted to corporate structure.[16]

In 1997 the Queensland *Co-operatives Act* was passed, substantially similar to Victorian and New South Wales acts, and forming part of a Common Core Provisions (CCP) national legislation scheme (discussed in Chapter Fourteen). The act removed an old obstacle to co-operatives formation in Queensland by reducing the number of people and 'natural persons' required to form a co-operative from twenty-five, to five.

The business of developing the legislation, preparing regulation and administering a complex new statute, however, siphoned public resources away from general co-operative development leaving much of the burden for this with CCC and the Maleny co-operative movement.

At time of writing approximately 250 co-operatives, both local and 'foreign' were registered in Queensland operating in such fields as Aboriginal and Torres Strait Islander community advancement and housing, banana, cotton, sugar, dairy, beef, cattle-breeding, grain, organic food, lucerne, olive, flower, avocado and potato production and marketing, forestry, fishing, water management, harvesting, sale-yards and stockyards, health, hospital, social welfare, aged-care, job creation, trading, recycling, environmental management, arts, crafts and performance, engineering, travel, wine consumption, rescue response, bus runs, vintage railway, heritage conservation, clubs and taxis.[17]

Chapter Six

'Democracy Tomorrow':
THE WESTERN AUSTRALIAN CO-OPERATIVE MOVEMENT

Introduction:

The following discussion examines the relationship between a hugely successful agricultural co-operative company, which had a towering influence on Western Australian and Australian co-operation: Westralian Farmers' Co-operative Company Limited (hereafter, 'Westralian Farmers'); and the Western Australian co-operative movement. It is offered by way of a case study considering how the democracy principle was moulded in a protracted struggle between a company adapting co-operative methodologies for commercial purposes and defenders of 'genuine' co-operative principles.

Registered in 1914 under company law and with its original wealth built upon wheat handling and storage, in the inter-war period and after, Westralian Farmers entered wool broking, livestock sales, fertiliser distribution, farm merchandise distribution, skin and hide processing and distribution, rural land and property sales, finance, dairy processing, packaging and distribution, fertiliser manufacturing, domestic and industrial gas and appliance marketing, road transport, retail store keeping, printing, stationery and publishing, shipping and travel, insurance underwriting and broking, among many other activities. The co-operative company developed lucrative trade links with Britain, Europe, the Middle East and South East Asia, was a prominent player in Australian coastal and international shipping and consistently produced the Australian co-operative movement's boldest entrepreneurs; albeit selective in the application of co-operative principles; who displayed clear-sightedness in commercial dealings every bit as daring as proprietorial competitors, which the company consistently out-performed. 'Co-operative' was added to the company's title in 1946.

Until Westralian Farmers was publicly listed in 1984 (Wesfarmers Limited), it was truly a major force in Australian co-operation. The co-operative company was instrumental in organising the Australian Producers' Wholesale Co-operative Federation (APWCF) and Overseas Farmers after World War I (discussed in Chapter Two), for many decades largely funded the most effective of the nation's co-operative federations; the Co-operative Federation of Western Australia (CFWA) (1919); and was a co-founder of the Co-operative Federation of Australia (CFA) (1943) (discussed in Chapter Eleven). For many years Westralian Farmers' personnel served as surrogate Australian representatives to the International Co-operative Alliance (ICA).

In analysing the ten best and ten worst corporate decisions in the decade to 2002 the distinguished market-analyst, Robert Gottleibsen, considered the extraordinary success of the Perth-based conglomerate, Wesfarmers, which at time of writing, was a major hardware retailer (Bunnings), a leader in the provision of rural services (Dalgety), one of Australia's top six coal producers operating in three states, a major gas distributor, a prominent fertiliser and chemicals distributor, ran large engineering, forest industry, transport and construction products operations and was one of Australia's largest and most profitable companies. In explaining Wesfarmers' success Gottleibsen said that it derived in large measure from a 'legacy structure' inherited from its origins as a farmer co-operative, which had allowed the development of a performance culture in a decentralised system where associated businesses functioned as autonomous profit-centres. Gottleibsen also believed that Wesfarmers' exemplary capital management programme, which fuelled development, had its origins in the *patience* of farmers:

> *It is not in the nature of farming people to look to the short term. It was their support that allowed Wesfarmers' capital management techniques to flourish [and] meant that Wesfarmers was rarely pressured to deliver short-term gains or to repel the threat of being broken up by raiders…Based on the success of companies like Wesfarmers market watchers are now beginning to realise that 'conglomerate' is not a dirty word.*[1]

The decentralised performance culture, to which Gottleibsen refers, originated in the historical relationship between Westralian Farmers and CFWA where the former provided wholesale 'backroom' services, including legal, treasury and business development, and the latter co-ordinated the trading operations of affiliates and served as a communications link. The relationship was not always harmonious, as discussion will attest, with frequent and passionate disagreements over a proper observance of the democracy principle. Generally speaking, the company argued for the pragmatic adaptation of Rochdale principles to suit local conditions; which included vast distances and capital shortages; while federation affiliates demanded greater respect for co-operative principles. The relationship generally worked, nonetheless, producing a dynamic Western Australian co-operative movement which was unique in Australia and very successful. Aided by flexible company legislation for co-operatives, Westralian Farmers pursued commercial goals unfettered by limitations placed on 'pure' co-operatives by legislation elsewhere in Australia, particularly New South Wales. The flexible adaptation of co-operative principles this permitted allowed the co-operative company to adopt a 'backwards integration' policy in developing agriculture-related businesses within a co-operative framework extending to wholly-owned agencies, acquisitions, alliances and joint ventures with co-operative and non-co-operative partners.

Not surprisingly Rochdale purists objected that Westralian Farmers was a 'quasi' co-operative. In *A Bunch of Pirates: the Story of a Farmer Co-op – Wesfarmers*, however, Kevin Smith refutes any idea that Westralian Farmers (referred to as 'Wesfarmers') was not a co-operative:

> *From time to time, farmers who are not closely associated with Wesfarmers have criticised the company for not being truly co-operative. The word is then used with quasi-religious significance rather than in its true economic meaning. They allege that co-operation is merely a way to avoid taxes. Such innuendoes are based on false premises. Wesfarmers is a co-operative within the meaning of the Co-operatives Section of the Companies Act and does pay its taxes. Some of the subsidiaries are not co-operative [and] also attract the proper taxation.*[2]

Westralian Farmers historically was more about *engendering* co-operation than *complying* with co-operative principles *per se* and, in this sense, was able to be more innovative than 'genuine' co-operatives confined by rigid legislation.

Certainly Westralian Farmers had a towering influence on the shape of Australian co-operation, achieved through the pivotal role it played in trade with the English Co-operative Wholesale Society (CWS). Major co-operatives and co-operative companies in other states looked enviously upon the giant co-operative company's commercial freedom with admiration. So immense was the sway of Westralian Farmers in national co-operative affairs, that when the company exited the movement in 1984 the vacuum it left was such that the Western Australian (and Australian) co-operative movements never fully recovered.

There is no denying Westralian Farmers' material success of or its mighty influence on Australian co-operation. In assessing the company's historical *bona fides* in respect of the democracy principle, however, it is important to examine its relationships with other players including the Rochdale consumer movement, CFWA, the Western Australian Wheat Pool, the Wheat Growers' Union, Co-operative Bulk Handling (CBH) and English CWS. There have been other large Australian agricultural co-operative companies which might be scrutinised in the manner here, but few have been as prolific in providing sources, or as seminal in influencing events. I am indebted to CFWA for practical support of the research, which in 1984 included permission to inspect historical documents in the T H Bath Memorial Library, Perth, where an anonymous 'Green Folder' was located, offering clues to Westralian Farmers' history varying from official accounts such as J Sandford's *Harper and the Farmers* and Kevin Smith's *A Bunch of Pirates*, referred to above.[3]

Charles Harper and the Western Australian Primary Producers' Union

In 1887 the Western Australian colonial administration appointed a Royal Commission into that colony's rural industry on which Charles Harper (1814-1912) served. Harper was born at Toodyay. As a young man Harper went north, contracting, pearling and making money. A pious, conservative philanthropic man, Harper encountered Rochdale co-operation in Britain in the 1870s. He returned to Australia to purchase 250 acres at Woodbridge, near Guildford and ran an orchard and nursery as a retired gentleman farmer. He entered parliament and became a proprietor of *The Western Mail*, a weekly newspaper for farmers. The recommendations made by Charles Harper's Royal Commission would have a major influence on the shape of Western Australian co-operation and, by dint of that, upon the emerging Australian co-operative movement.

In 1891, the Royal Commission recommended 'co-operation on the Anglo-European model and on the model recently adopted in the east coast dairy industry in order to improve rural productivity'. Harper was appointed chairman of the Department of Agriculture's Agricultural Bureaux, authorised to implement the commission's recommendations. He supervised the development of co-operatively-funded railway sidings in established fruit and wheat growing districts, involving considerable sums of his own money in indemnifying loans. Here was the genesis of a peculiar adaptation of co-operative principles which followed.[4]

The Western Australian *Homestead Act* (1893) saw many more settlers take up freehold land and agriculture spread over a wider area. In 1894 the *Friendly Society Act* was received into the colony from Britain and a Registrar of Friendly Societies was appointed. The act however, which contemplated cash trading, did not suit the longer-term credit needs of primary producers and was poorly utilised. In the same year, Harper served on a committee with a brief to develop an agricultural credit bank along Raiffeisen (German) lines but this lapsed when the government introduced legislation for a rural bank. How the course of Australian co-operative history might have been altered by the existence of a co-operative bank in Western Australia can only be imagined.

As more settlers, who now included diggers vacating the gold fields, moved into farming Charles Harper toured the state extensively as chairman of the Agricultural Bureaux promoting the idea of co-operation, particularly with regard to railway sidings for handling and consigning produce. Impressed by the South Australian Farmers' Co-operative Union's (SAFCU) direct indenting arrangement with English CWS, Harper also toured USA, Europe and Britain to learn more about co-operation. After returning he helped form a Primary Producers' Co-operative Union (which appears to have functioned under various names, including the 'Union of Agricultural Producers' and the 'Producers' Co-operative' and the 'Farmers' Co-operative', before dropping 'co-operative' in 1904 to become simply the 'Primary Producers' Union' [PPU]).

W D Johnson and the *Co-operative and Provident Societies Act*

In 1901 W D Johnson (MLC, Labor, Kalgoorlie and later Guildford), a Rochdale co-operative stalwart, introduced the Industrial and Provident Societies Bill into the Western Australian parliament. The radical tenor of the bill, which included a definition of co-operation and emphasised cash trading, consistent with Rochdale theory, was wholly unpalatable to rural conservatives in parliament and it lapsed. The legislation was reintroduced in 1903, however, as the Co-operative and Provident Societies Bill, drawing upon the *Friendly Society Act*. The resultant *Co-operative and Provident Societies Act* was still seen by many farmers and rural businesses to be unsuitable for their purposes and only a few co-operatives, mainly urban co-operatives of a Rochdale orientation, registered under it before World War I. Nevertheless, the act remained virtually unchanged until 1974. Most Western Australian agricultural co-operatives and co-operative companies were registered outside its jurisdiction.

Co-operation and the wheat industry

With the acreage under wheat in Western Australia expanding six fold between 1905 and 1906 and that commodity poised to displace gold and wool as a major export, in 1905 Charles Harper's PPU began exporting wheat parcels to Britain. In the following year the PPU formed Producers' Markets Co-operative Limited. This brought Harper into conflict with a rival merchant, M H Jacoby, who described Harper as a 'bogus' co-operator and said that farmers, by co-operating with him, were confusing philanthropy with self-help. Calling for a genuinely democratic co-operative along SAFCU lines to handle wheat exports, Jacoby alleged that farmers were 'wrong to trust city-based financiers, the only people they could count on was themselves – co-operate!'

In this exchange can be seen elements of what became a protracted struggle between politically powerful 'St George's Terrace farmers' (Perth-based merchants and speculators with rural interests), on the one hand, and co-operative advocates, on the other, for control of the co-operative movement, especially the burgeoning wheat industry. Both camps exhorted the virtues of co-operation but meant entirely different things.[5]

The Farmers' and Settlers' Association

Following a punishing drought in 1911/12 and a successful Amalgamated Workers' Union log of claims, including a demand to bring Western Australian rural workers into the new commonwealth arbitration system, a farmers' conference was convened seeking ways to unite farmer ranks. This led to the formation of the Farmers' and Settlers' Association of Western Australia (FSA) in June 1912.[6]

One of FSA's primary goals was to develop a 'strong central co-operative to expedite trade, to reduce the dependence on humanised labour and to rationalise production and handling costs'. The plan was to link members of Harper's PPU (now numbering 1,300) with the Farmers' Mercantile Union, a consortium of merchants, shipping agents and 'St George's Terrace farmers', including M H Jacoby and insurance agent Basil Murray. 'Central Organisation' would take over from PPU in developing co-operative bulk-handling infrastructure for the wheat industry, which would *demonstrably* be owned by farmers, not investors.

Contemporaneously, the Western Australian Country Party (WACP) was formed on a platform including the abolition of tariffs, improvements to the state's water and irrigation supply and preferential voting. Seeking to lure Labor's rural vote, WACP also championed democratic co-operation as an alternative to state-controlled models of industry management.[7]

Walter Harper and the democracy principle

After Charles Harper died in 1913 his son, C W (Walter) Harper (1880–1956) took control of PPU, now with approximately 3,000 members.

At a FSA meeting in March 1913, called to form a 'central co-operative' to absorb PPU's assets, M H Jacoby and Walter Harper clashed on the proposed structure. Jacoby repeated allegations that co-operating with 'philanthropists' and 'bogus' co-operators was risky, urging farmers to apply 'self-help' co-operative principles and not rely on city-based investors. Harper replied coolly that he was there 'to protect the capital of those who have blazed the co-operative trail in Western Australia', meaning PPU associates. He insisted that the one-person-one-vote principle would need to be waived if the proposed farmers' co-operative was to have any chance of attracting sufficient capital to operate. Denouncing this '…curious departure from the co-operative tradition which seems to have been forgotten in this "bogus" co-operation', Jacoby said he would have nothing to do with the proposal and moved that FSA members do the same. They concurred.

Without PPU's financial support, however, FSA was able to raise only £7,000, insufficient to finance the handling and distribution of that season's crop. In this context, and dealing with successive poor seasons and rising labour costs, FSA affiliates were persuaded to Harper's view and agreed to waive the one-person-one-vote principle. Thus was the democracy principle varied at the very inception of 'Central Organisation'. Shareholders holding up to forty-nine shares were permitted one vote; those holding between fifty and ninety-five shares were permitted two votes; and those with more than one hundred shares, three votes.

Immediately £60,000 of capital was forthcoming from PPU to finance a co-operative under the auspices of FSA to receive and handle the wheat crop. So began a contest between investors and producers for democratic control of the wheat industry lasting to World War II.

Westralian Farmers' Co-operative Limited, 1914

Westralian Farmers' Co-operative Limited was registered under company law on 27 June 1914. The company was forbidden, initially, from using 'co-operative' in the title pursuant to the *Co-operative and Provident Societies Act* but this did not stop company officials from referring to the business as the 'farmers own co-operative company'. Commencing operations in November in three small rooms in Harper's buildings in Howard Street, Perth, Westralian Farmers employed a staff of three with a very simple objective: 'To supply farmers with requisites'.[8]

The company began in the midst of drought, when wheat production had fallen to 1904 levels. Indeed, wheat was being imported into the state from Argentina! It also coincided with the introduction of emergency war-time marketing controls, including the pooling of commodities, an idea reported to have been suggested to the federal government by W D Johnson. When the Western Australian Labor Government appointed several agents, including the company, to serve as merchants for the Western Australian Wheat Pool, however, Westralian Farmers protested and, through its WACP friends in parliament, who held the balance of power, succeeded in impressing upon the government the possible political consequences of not giving the company a larger quota next season.

Westralian Farmers secures sole rights to the crop

The 1915 crop was a bumper one with many farmers foregoing the fallow to recoup losses from the previous year. After Westralian Farmers, now cashed-up by the addition of Mercantile Union capital, announced plans to seek *sole* rights to the war-time crop, an ugly disagreement began

Westralian Farmers Exhibit Royal Show, Perth 1923

with FSA, which was concerned at the way 'non-producers are lining up with the co-operative movement and making far-reaching changes to its nature'. The FSA conducted a poll indicating that most farmers favoured a *government* run-pool linked to the Australian Wheat Board and guaranteeing a fair share of the market to all. The minister responsible, W D Johnson, however, wanted the crop handled on a *co-operative* basis but saw Westralian Farmers as neither co-operative nor sympathetic to consumers or trade unions. With his government party on a political knife-edge in parliament, however, the minister sought a compromise whereby Westralian Farmers would adopt a 'genuine' co-operative constitution (on a one-person-one-vote basis) in exchange for the government allocating it a larger share of the crop. This would not be the last compromise the minister was obliged to make.

Westralian Farmers' executives Walter Harper, Deane Hammond and Basil Murray flatly refused Johnson's offer and broke from FSA to 'concentrate on the company'. About one quarter of farmers previously supporting Westralian Farmers withdrew their harvests from the company, which was appointed but one of several government-authorised agents to handle the 1915 crop. Returning from a Melbourne Commonwealth Government conference considering pooling arrangements, Johnson appointed F Mann, formerly a Dreyfus Company employee and a well-known critic of Westralian Farmers, as overseer of the proposed Western Australian Wheat Marketing Board.[9]

Meanwhile, Walter Harper, Deane Hammond and Basil Murray toured the state's wheat fields promoting what they described as the 'voluntary co-operative alternative to the compulsory socialist scheme' and creating a network of 'independent co-operative units' designed to supply 'Central Organisation', as Westralian Farmers was commonly referred to. In parliament, WACP succeeded in delaying Johnson's bill to constitute a wheat board and saw to the appointment of a Special Committee of the Legislative Assembly to 'investigate the relationship of the government and certain millers'. Already seriously split on the conscription issue, Labor backed down, convinced of the 'inadvisability of appointing Mann' and allocated Westralian Farmers two-thirds of the crop for the following season.[10]

The cave-in provoked an outcry from the Department of Agriculture and from rival firms, that one organisation should be so favoured for reasons of political expediency. It did not help Labor, though, for in a fractious political environment, the government fell in 1916 and WACP switched allegiance to the Liberals.

Meanwhile, Westralian Farmers' officials, Murray, Hammond and Sterling Taylor continued to organise meetings in FSA strongholds and to form 'independent co-operative units' pledged to serve as agents for the 'farmers own co-operative company':

> *The farmer who is content in these times and in the times that are ahead to plough the lone furrow and to hold aloof from Westralian Farmers' Limited and Co-operation can be written down as blind – commercially blind.*

By 1917 Westralian Farmers' tied network of 'independent co-operative units' numbered forty-nine agencies; ninety-two by 1921.[11]

Sole right to the crop

Seeking to arrest a slide of votes to WACP, W D Johnson undertook to approach contacts in federal parliament to have viewed favourably the company's claim to the *entire* wheat pool for the 1917/18 season on the understanding that Westralian Farmers would restructure along Rochdale lines, including one-person-one-vote and limited interest on capital. In addition, Johnson sought the creation of a co-operative federation to supervise the company's transformation to a democratic organisation and to develop a co-operative wholesale joining producers and consumers, ownership of which would eventually revert to members, forming the basis of a Co-operative Union.

In a tightly worded response, Westralian Farmers agreed to sponsor a federation and a 'collective purchasing agency' which would revert to *producer* ownership at 'some future date'. This ambiguous promise was the best Johnson could hope for. On this basis, and to the vociferous protests of market competitors alleging a monopoly, Westralian Farmers was awarded sole right to the 1918 crop.

The FSA immediately demanded a Royal Commission to inquire into Westralian Farmers' competency to handle the crop. Wheat farmers involved with the company's network of 'federated co-operatives' also demanded shares, so as to immediately begin coming to own the company. Westralian Farmers' parliamentary friends stonewalled calls for a Royal Commission but the company did endorse a FSA resolution to create 'One Big Society', a wholesale which farmers would eventually own, along lines suggested by W D Johnson but with *no* consumer representation.[12]

The English CWS link

By the end of World War I Westralian Farmers had achieved total control of the wheat pool and was strategically placed to capture post-war opportunities. As noted in Chapter Two, in 1918 the company was instrumental in organising a Melbourne conference of co-operative companies from which the Australia Producers' Wholesale Co-operative Federation Limited (APWCF) emerged. There was talk at this conference of a national co-operative federation and a national credit extension scheme for co-operatives but, protesting the alleged 'socialist' tendencies of east-coast co-operators, Westralian Farmers' delegates showed no interest. It was the beginning of a long stand-off between Western Australian and eastern coast co-operators which would have serious consequences for the national co-operative movement.

Westralian Farmers Managing Director Basil Murray was elected a director of APWCF and a Westralian Farmers' staffer, L M McGregor, (who later played a key role in Queensland co-operation, discussed in Chapter Five) was sent to the UK to be tutored in the wheat trade by English CWS officials. Murray and A J Monger toured Britain inspecting markets and developing links with CWS, officials of which indicated strong interest in direct barter trade through Overseas Farmers involving CWS manufactures and Australian wheat, similar to the long-standing arrangement with SAFCU. There was one problem however – CWS dealt only with co-operative agencies and Westralian Farmers was not one!

In this context Westralian Farmers became more amenable to demands by W D Johnson and the FSA to take steps to democratise the Western Australian co-operative movement and to establish a co-operative federation, truly controlled by farmers.[13]

The Co-operative Federation of Western Australia

The first meeting of the Co-operative Federation of Western Australia (CFWA) was convened by Westralian Farmers in October 1919. Representatives from seventy-one rural co-operatives and Westralian Farmers' units attended. It was a lively affair. Conference Secretary R C Dunman, a Westralian Farmers' employee since 1916, said that the proposed federation's purpose was to 'co-operatively co-ordinate trade between rural affiliates and Central Organisation [Westralian Farmers] and spread the co-operative word'. FSA delegates objected. The real issue, they said, was *democratic control* of the wheat crop and curbing the influence of 'dry' shareholders in the Wheat Pool. Westralian Farmers' blatant anti-Labor, pro-Country Party stance, they said, made a mockery of the company's talk about democracy. The FSA demanded a *statutory* basis to the Wheat Pool guaranteeing rights and spelling out the responsibilities of all stakeholders.

Seeking to calm proceedings and perhaps reach another compromise, W D Johnson pointed out that a statutory body was politically impossible in the current parliament. The WACP simply would not permit it. The politician therefore called for continued producer support of Westralian Farmers' pool *if* the company undertook to support CFWA's affiliation with the Australian Co-operative Union, being developed by Rochdale co-operators in the eastern states, and the formation of a CFWA Central Council comprising five democratically-elected representatives from co-operative zones throughout the state, a central objective of which would be the creation of an Australian co-operative wholesale linked to the Co-operative Union. It was pure Rochdale theory. In a 'spirit of patriotism' the company agreed and Westralian Farmers' grip on the crop stayed.[14]

The CFWA's jurisdiction was divided into five regional groups providing for Rochdale co-operatives, producer co-operatives, suburban co-operatives and Westralian Farmers Central Organisation's 'federated co-operatives', which by now were numerically powerful. There is a report that CFWA affiliates undertook to conduct all dealings with Central Organisation through the federation, as was required by English CWS. It appears, however, that many affiliates assumed this was on a voluntary basis, consistent with co-operative theory, while the company saw it as a compulsory commercial arrangement, with CFWA simply co-ordinating business. Whether this was a genuine misunderstanding or dissembling is unknown. However, it subsequently became apparent that Westralian Farmers had no intention of supporting the Rochdale movement's Co-operative Union or the proposed national co-operative wholesale society. Harper penned a curt letter to Sydney-based Reverend Frank Pulsford, then the Rochdale movement's chief strategist, telling him pointedly to 'desist' from urging Westralian Farmers to adopt a genuine co-operative structure – the company was as co-operative as it could be!

Westralian Farmers consolidates

Resignations from the federation followed and demands for a statutory basis to the Wheat Pool increased. Indeed, W D Johnson again sought unsuccessfully to steer a Wheat Pool Bill through parliament. The fiercely Rochdale-orientated Collie Industrial Co-operative, based in the coal-mining town of that name east of Bunbury, called for a conference in Perth, independent of Westralian Farmers, to create a co-operative wholesale linked to 'genuine' producer co-operatives as an alternative to 'Central Organisation'. Collie's proposal was supported by disaffected wheat growers, particularly in the Lake Grace district, concerned at the hold 'dry' shareholders had gained on the industry.

The Westralian Farmers' controlled CFWA Central Council formally reprimanded Collie but waived further action. Instead, it created a CFWA metropolitan sub-committee on which Collie was entitled to be represented. As a quorum of three was sufficient for this sub-committee to make executive decisions and with rural councillors prevented by distance and work pressures from attending executive meetings, however, authority stayed effectively with the Perth-based group.

In May 1920 CFWA affiliates voted unanimously to support Westralian Farmers' conduct of the Western Australian Wheat Pool until 1921, when war-time arrangements would lapse. So it was that as APWCF commenced operations in London in 1920, Westralian Farmers had the infrastructure, suppliers and network through CFWA in place to be ready to capture lucrative post-war trading opportunities with English CWS. The Western Australian wheat industry, nonetheless, remained divided over whether to continue supporting the co-operative company after war-time regulations ended or press for a statutory Wheat Pool.

'Admirable theory': the democracy principle

A Westralian Farmers' instigated Grain Growers' Co-operative Elevators Limited was formed soon after the war ended but quickly liquidated for want of support. The episode, which caused resentment on Westralian Farmers' side, also deepened suspicion in some wheat grower districts over the direction in which the company was taking the co-operative movement. At a 1920 CFWA conference the company came in for harsh criticism with regard to centralist tendencies and the failure to act on 1919 undertakings in respect of a co-operative wholesale and support of the Co-operative Union. After a motion of no confidence was put, Walter Harper argued that democratic committees might be admirable in theory but small business-like committees were superior in achieving industry goals. Democratic committees were unwieldy and expensive, he continued, and, as for a co-operative wholesale, Harper believed that the Westralian Farmers' agency network was adequate and there was no need for a Rochdale-style entity, which would simply divert capital from farmers' real needs. In any event, Harper added, the company was now more interested in bulk handling wheat and planned to invest in that area rather than in wholesaling. Harper then said coolly that he would stand down as CFWA secretary if the federation found his position untenable, implying that this would entail a withdrawal of Primary Producers' Association (PPA) investments in the forthcoming Wheat Pool. The motion of no confidence lapsed. Harper agreed to meet dissidents and discuss the issues but it was clear where the real power lay.[15]

Walter Harper, Basil Murray and L M McGregor then negotiated directly with English CWS to finance the handling and export of the season's crop. Keen to secure as large a quota of Australian wheat as possible when post-war regulations ended, English CWS appears to have been less concerned now about Westralian Farmers' co-operative credentials than with its inability to secure the indemnification of loans raised to fund the pool. Who or what would guarantee loans – government or business interests?

Here was a strange situation: W D Johnson, Labor politician and Rochdale champion, seeking a statutory Wheat Pool in parliament, while the heirs of Rochdale orthodoxy turned a blind eye to Westralian Farmers' investor-orientation and the company extolled the virtues of voluntary co-operation as an antidote to 'socialism'. Exploiting factional fights in parliament, Westralian Farmers succeeded in having the government extend war-time controls for another year, until 1922, making Western Australia unique in the commonwealth in this regard and leaving sole wheat crop agency rights in the company's hands.[16]

Pressure to democratise the pool builds

When Overseas Farmers Executive Officer A E Gough visited Perth in October 1921, he noted intense friction in CFWA centred upon the influence of Westralian Farmers' 'dry' shareholders. Only forty-three of the federation's ninety affiliates endorsed the company's continued control of the post-war pool. Gough heard the company censored for failing to act on 1919 undertakings to create a Rochdale wholesale and to adopt a democratic structure. He noted protests about the company's habit of poaching membership in areas already served by co-operatives and heard applause when Mr Capel demanded that Westralian Farmers stop competing with genuine co-operatives. The visitor observed CFWA affiliates demanding that Westralian Farmers 'distribute profits in the recognised co-operative way' and Basil Murray counter bluntly that there was *not* going to be a Western Australian CWS and that an Agency Agreement with Central Organisation was, as far as the company was concerned, adequate. A delegate demanded to know what *was* Central Organisation? The CFWA? Westralian Farmers? Central Committee? The Country Party? He was never sure which of the 'Siamese twins' was being referred to when company executives spoke. There was ironic laughter. Another delegate moved that two, not one, CFWA directors sit on the company's board. A lengthy and inconclusive debate followed.

On the following day W D Johnson put another compromise motion to the federation. Delegates agreed to ratify the Agency Agreement with Central Organisation for the handling of that year's crop in exchange for the company calling democratic elections for the board and eliminating 'dry' shareholders. Grumbling continued, however, for few believed that Westralian Farmers had any intention of acting on the undertaking. Meanwhile, however, there was a harvest to shift. Talk of a democratic co-operative movement must wait.[17]

Indeed, as some delegates at the CFWA October meeting had predicted, no democratic election for company directors proceeded. Westralian Farmers did agree, however, in November, to elections for the CFWA executive and to establish district councils for Metropolitan, South Western, Northern, Lower Southern, Eastern and Central zones, which would be empowered to rule on *local* issues. All matters crossing zone borders, however, would automatically be referred to CFWA Central Council. It was a tangible concession to democracy but Westralian Farmers' control of the wheat crop remained intact. Moreover, while Basil Murray and W D Johnson were interstate over the summer of 1921/22, attending Reverend Frank Pulsford's Co-operative Union Conference in Melbourne, the federation's Perth-based Central Council collaborated with the Metropolitan Sub-Committee to alter the articles, neutralising any democratic effect the zonal scheme conferred. Under the new articles any organisation whose activities 'overlapped' Central Organisation's official policy could be disqualified from participation in the Wheat Pool and Central Organisation would be authorised to take over the business of the offending body! On this basis elections for the CFWA executive were held.[18]

A howl of protest came from CFWA rural affiliates and more resignations followed. Visiting Trayning Co-operative, Harper and Murray received a stormy reception. The Central Organisation executives, however, were unrepentant, signalling a preparedness to deal harshly with critics. The Trayning Co-operative was *deregistered* from CFWA and from participating in the Wheat Pool. The company also threatened to set up a rival receival system in the town if the co-operative did not fall into line. In addition Central Organisation blocked applications for CFWA membership from organisations whose operations allegedly overlapped the company's, for example the Helena Co-operative and the Urban Co-operative.

Fed up with eastern-state criticism of the company's disregard for co-operative principles, company executives now also openly dismissed as impractical the idea of a Co-operative Union and saw to further CFWA rule changes dissociating the Western Australian co-operative movement from 'socialist' Rochdale ideas while affirming that Central Organisation would give expression to co-operation in its *own* way, not slavishly, in some theoretically hidebound way, as they alleged occurred on the east coast. The prospects for Australian co-operative unity seemed bleak.[19]

The Trustees of the Wheat Pool

After the Commonwealth Government undertook to guarantee loans to voluntary pools, if they undertook to avoid competition driving up prices, in March 1922 a Primary Producers' Association conference voted to establish a voluntary wheat pool in Western Australia. At a CFWA meeting later in March, however, Harper announced that English CWS money was now available to finance the company's handling of the crop. This had come about after Walter Harper, Basil Murray (now general manager of Westralian Farmers and director of the Mercantile Union) and A J Monger (chairman of the Western Australian Meat Export Company) had agreed to underwrite loans *personally*. The guarantors, to be known as 'The Trustees of the Wheat Pool', were described as courageous souls who were risking everything to fend off the 'socialist' challenge embodied in W D Johnson's Wheat Pool Bill, the constitutionality of which in any event was doubtful. If the Trustees were prepared to risk so much in support of farmers, farmers really should support them.

CFWA delegates undertook to support The Trustees of the Wheat Pool for the 1922/23 season on condition a fourth trustee was appointed; a government nominee (possibly Johnson); and a government-regulated Wheat Pool Advisory Board was constituted, including producer representatives, to monitor the pool's management. This was agreed.

The Western Australian Coalition Government duly appointed The Trustees of the Wheat Pool as sole agent for the receiving and handling of wheat in Western Australia. Trustees appointed Nicholls Proprietary Limited as stevedores and joined with APWCF affiliates and wheat pools in South Australia and Victoria to open an expanded selling floor in London, employing Overseas Farmers and the brokerage company, Berry Barclay and Company.

'At issue is the co-operative principle'

Notwithstanding this coup by Trustees and the success of the company's pooling arrangements, disquiet continued in sections of the wheat belt, where a perception persisted that city-based interests, not farmers, had gained ascendancy in the industry through 'dry' shareholder control of Westralian Farmers. Many growers were concerned particularly by the close identification of Trustees with the company. The independence of Trustees, although absolute, was unclear and some believed the arrangement could lend itself to abuse. Rumours continued that the company was juggling sales to its own advantage and to the detriment of the pool. Indeed, Westralian Farmers continued to trade in premium quality bagged wheat independently of the pool while the company and Trustees shipped grain to England conjointly. It appeared as if the company was securing all of the profit for some of the crop and some of the profit for the remainder. Did this serve farmer interests?

Then, when Central Organisation appointed Primary Producers' Association Executive Sir John Teasdale as the fourth Trustee, CFWA affiliates protested that the appointment was superfluous, had not been referred to the Growers' Council (the renamed Wheat Pool Advisory Board) and contravened a CFWA resolution that the additional Trustee be a *government* appointee. W D Johnson accused the company of stacking the pool and complained to the press. Central Organisation (or 'Central Council of the CFWA', the distinction is often unclear in the sources) censured Johnson, disputing his right to act as CFWA spokesman.

At an emergency CFWA meeting in August 1922 Harper and Johnson clashed. The parliamentarian demanded that the company honour an earlier undertaking to redraft CFWA rules and give growers greater control of the Wheat Pool, not the company's self-appointed Trustees. Growers, Johnson said, were voluntarily aligning themselves with Trustees and the company therefore should show proper respect for democratic process. He demanded that the company implement a CFWA resolution to include a federation nominee on its board. In a swipe at Harper, Johnson said that the chairman should be the managing director of Central Organisation, and that the federation should be the peak democratic body of the co-operative movement, determining and enforcing policy – not the company!

Much debate followed on the rules – whether farmers should own the company or the company should continue to control Central Organisation. Johnson and Basil Murray jousted over different understandings of 'socialism'. *Everything*, Johnson accused, was 'socialist' if the company did not agree with it – state regulation *or* Rochdale co-operation. W Gayfor (Corrigan Co-operative) supported Johnson. 'At issue', he said, 'is the co-operative principle and this conference demands sounder respect for co-operative principles'.

Again indicating where the real power lay, Basil Murray calmly moved that CFWA immediately take over the pool and finance it! There was no seconder. Notwithstanding their protestations, growers were not prepared to fund the pool, certainly not while Johnson's Wheat Pool Bill was bogged down in parliament. Frustrated, Johnson had to be content with a CFWA motion censuring Westralian Farmers.[20]

John Thompson

At this stormy August 1922 CFWA conference Basil Murray introduced a young man who would have a major impact on Western Australian and Australian co-operation: John Thompson. Formerly a tea-broker in Britain before migrating to Western Australia and losing his farm to fire, Thompson brought prodigious energy and entrepreneurial flair to the company and to the co-operative movement. Known as 'Tearing Tommy' for his unbridled energy and habit of roaring about farms on a motorbike, tyres often filled with rags, inspecting wheat for the war-time pool, Thompson possessed detailed knowledge of the tea business which was useful in negotiations with English CWS, which operated extensive tea plantations in Ceylon and India and wished to expand this trade into Australia.

The CFWA falters

The 1922/23 harvest proceeded uneventfully and was well-managed by The Trustees of the Wheat Pool, a point not lost on farmers. However, resignations from CFWA continued and many growers broke from the pool to accept spot-cash from competitors (which included Westralian Farmers!).

Fractiousness in the wheat industry and the fact now obvious to many affiliates that Westralian Farmers had no intention of constructing a democratic co-operative wholesale along Rochdale lines, saw CFWA almost fall apart in 1923. It was important to the company that this not happen because the federation was the co-operative 'glue' joining it to the vital English CWS trading relationship.

T H (Thomas) Bath

With Harper out of the state for several months the federation fell moribund until a Special Meeting in June 1923, when its future was considered. At this meeting a quiet, diffident man was introduced: T H (Thomas) Bath. Bath had come from the east seeking gold. A Labor Party stalwart in earlier days, he won the seat of Hanan for Labor in 1902 and succeeded Charles Harper as Chairman of Committees. Bath briefly led Labor in opposition in 1905, steering the party through a difficult reorganisation process. He held ministerial portfolios for Lands, Education and Agriculture. Losing his seat to a FSA nominee, Bath retired from politics, became a farmer, studied accountancy and operated a wool store. A reserved, some said 'stodgy' man, Bath was converted to co-operation in 1916 while holidaying in Tammin and began to read and espouse Rochdale ideas.[21]

With Labor credentials, farming experience, administrative skills and detailed knowledge of Rochdale theory and practice, Bath was well qualified to perform an 'honest broker' role in CFWA and arrest eroding farmer support for The Trustees. This was especially so as internal Country Party squabbles saw a split in November 1923 and Labor sweep back to power in March 1924. Now Johnson's Wheat Pool Bill might become a reality!

It is not known whether Bath was appointed CFWA secretary by Central Organisation or was elected, but he declared upon assuming office that he was determined to democratise the Western Australian co-operative movement and to restructure Westralian Farmers' country units so they would be in a position *eventually* to own the company. In this he appears to have been at odds, at least initially, with Walter Harper who continued to support policies of district councils, controlled by CFWA Central Council, and a tight executive. Bath had no quarrel with this to the extent that he approved of strict central auditing, sensible rationalisation, improved efficiency and educating managers and directors in modern business practice and co-operative principles, but his determination to democratise the movement appears to have been genuine.

CFWA reforms 1923–1924

The CFWA's fourth annual conference in August 1923 was an exercise in compromise. The purpose was to achieve reforms consistent with English CWS expectations that trade occur only through genuine co-operative organisations. Rules governing the appointment of the federation's Executive Council were altered to establish seven districts, each with voting rights. Westralian Farmers was given powers to appoint representatives and visit District Council meetings with costs covered by members of that district. The 1919 undertaking to create a co-operative wholesale was reaffirmed and assurances were repeated that ownership would be transferred to shareholders – in time. Compulsory agency agreements with Central Organisation were dropped and affiliates were authorised to purchase autonomously wherever members' interests were best served. In a popular move, Bath was appointed as CFWA delegate to the Westralian Farmers' board and made editor of the *Westralian Farmers' Gazette*, a company newspaper designed to educate people in co-operative principles and philosophy and broadcast industry news.

Meanwhile, exploiting political fissures in parliament, Westralian Farmers' parliamentary friends sought an amendment to the *Companies Act* enabling the company to distribute bonus shares (rather than dividends) to farmers consigning through the Wheat Pool. The amendment was passed. Tom Bath approved. A very real prospect now existed that ownership of the pool would gradually transfer to growers. (The amendment was found to be illegal in 1929 but, in the interim, the company retained control of wheat marketing and its rural agencies still numerically controlled the CFWA Central Executive.)

'Wealth creators' and 'divvy hunters'

Despite these reforms, relations between the company and the Rochdale movement continued to deteriorate. Australian Co-operative Union Honorary Secretary Tom Shonk demanded to know who really *owned* the Western Australian co-operative movement – the co-operatives or Westralian Farmers? Tom Bath made his position clear in *Westralian Farmers' Gazette*, lionising English CWS and drawing a line between western 'wealth creators' involved in primary industry and east-coast 'divvy hunters' in consumer co-operatives. No 'wise man of the east' was going to tell Western Australian co-operators how to run a co-operative movement![22]

Nevertheless, in 1924 the future of the Western Australian co-operative movement came under a CFWA microscope. The issue was again Westralian Farmers' domination versus democratic ownership and control along Rochdale lines. Affiliates remained deeply concerned by broken promises and the very close relationship between the company, investors and WACP. The CFWA resolved to join the Australian Co-operative Union, subscribe to *Co-operative News* (the journal of east-coast Rochdale 'radicals') and join easterners in fighting a tax challenge affecting co-operatives. A Wholesale Committee was also formed to press the company to fulfil its undertaking to launch a co-operative wholesale.[23]

On the basis of these understandings The Trustees of the Wheat Pool negotiated a Sterling £18 million loan at 4.5 per cent through English CWS to finance the conduct of the Western Australian Wheat Pool through CFWA for the ensuing *six* seasons. The Trustees appointed Westralian Farmers sole agent. The company also continued to trade as an independent wheat merchant 'because of the need for a co-operative channel for farmers who wanted to sell part or the whole of their crop rather than pool them'. The arrangement meant that Westralian Farmers continued to perform as both buyer *and* seller for non-pooled premium grade wheat while managing marketing for the pool.[24]

Co-operative Wholesale Section (CWS) Limited

A row erupted when the CFWA Wholesale Committee announced plans for Co-operative Wholesale Section (CWS) Limited, which, far from a democratically-owned and controlled entity, was to be a wholly Westralian Farmers'-owned department in 'partnership' with rural co-operatives and the company's trading units. John Thompson, preparing to take over from a terminally ill Basil Murray as Westralian Farmers' General Manager, described the proposal as a sensible move because it was necessary to 'wait and see' whether English CWS would favour the eastern consumer co-operative movement or Western Australia in establishing headquarters for a national wholesale. Whatever the case, Central Organisation would 'in time' relinquish ownership and control of the department to co-operatives. Tom Bath also endorsed the scheme saying that it made good economic sense for country co-operatives to 'co-operate with Westralian Farmers in a compulsory purchasing scheme involving a tied insurance system'.

A separate loan was organised through English CWS to finance a warehouse in Perth, where the company's CWS Department headquarters was to be based. It appears that the facility might also have been used to store premium grade un-pooled wheat purchased by the company for sale to English CWS, but the sources are unclear.

When John Thompson became General Manager of Westralian Farmers and Secretary of the Wheat Pool he was responsible for a staff of approximately 300 in addition to external agents, organisers, commercial travellers, wheat inspectors and machinery service staff. With ample finance arranged through English CWS and almost total control of the wheat crop, Westralian Farmers was poised to enter a period of sustained growth.[25]

After Basil Murray died Tom Bath was appointed a Trustee of the Wheat Pool, a popular move with farmers, who were still suspicious of the company's motives. Managers of most rural co-operatives, however, refused to have anything to do with CWS Department, which languished.

Only thirty-seven delegates from seventy affiliates attended the CFWA sixth annual conference in October 1925, many openly questioning the federation's practical value. Farmer resolutions were repeatedly ignored, disconsolate delegates said, and only the veneer of co-operation existed, opportunistically framed to entice farmers and co-operatives into the company's Wheat Pool while satisfying English CWS co-operative trading requirements.

Occupying the chair at this meeting, Walter Harper used all of his persuasive powers to emphasise that the federation was important and that co-operation with Central Organisation was real. There were big savings to be made in bulk handling and only the federation and co-operation could achieve this and fend off a 'socialist' alternative of a commodity marketing board. Growers must pull together, Harper insisted, for already 'socialists' in the Railway Department were refusing to guarantee tenure of railway sidings used by the Wheat Pool, exposing the company to high risks.

Tom Bath urged affiliates to support the company's CWS Department which, he said, was really a collective buying agency in a co-operative purchasing scheme involving direct indenting through English CWS. Using the facility co-operatives could skirt rationing quotas and save big money through volume purchasing items such as tea and machinery.

Frank discussion followed indicating deep distrust of the company's motives in seeking to tie co-operatives compulsorily into the CWS Department's trading and insurance arrangements. Co-operation, the critics said, was about *voluntary* association and the company would not be seeking such terms if it were a genuine co-operative. New legislation must be enacted, delegates insisted, to draw the company into line as a co-operative. The conference called for a completely new co-operation act to replace existing legislation and urged W D Johnson to lobby for this in parliament.[26]

Westralian Farmers grows rapidly, 1924–1930

Aided by good seasons, ample finance and astute leadership, Westralian Farmers and the Wheat Pool made a lot of money for shareholders in the period to the Great Depression. The company posted unprecedented progress, augmenting wheat and stock sales with wool brokerage and storage functions. Westralian Farmers launched the first radio station in Western Australia, 6WF, which broadcast from the top floor of the company's Perth headquarters, known as the 'House of Co-operation'. The company moved into livestock and skins 'reluctantly', executives said, because there was 'little money in it', taking over Graziers Limited. Machinery was added to the range of services and in 1924 the company began investigations which led to The Trustees of the Wheat Pool taking a two-thirds share and Westralian Farmers a one-third share in Australian Outturns Proprietary Limited, a cargo supervising firm. The Trustees used a Growers' Pool Reserve Fund (accumulated from a levy on wheat deliveries) to effect the purchase. In 1926 Westralian Farmers pioneered the shipping of wheat from the port of Esperance, representing a significant saving to growers and later bought Nicholls Proprietary Limited, a stevedoring company. The 'two co-operatives', as The Trustees of the Wheat Pool and Westralian Farmers were described by company executives, also became part-owners in 1927 of Berry Barclay and Company Limited, grain sellers of London, in association with co-operatives from New South Wales, South Australia and Victoria.[27]

The company later diversified into printing, honey and fruit, bought out H J and J Simper Food Exporters with depots in South-East Asia and a network of packing sheds in south-eastern Australia and, in so doing, won a long-standing battle with M H Jacoby for control of the state's fruit export markets. Westralian Farmers bought a factory for milk pasteurisation, cheese and butter production from Pascomi and gained access to the Perth fresh-milk supply market, becoming embroiled in the process in a long dispute with dairy co-operatives in the south-west of the state. In perhaps the boldest and riskiest move, a subsidiary company known as Westralian Farmers' Super-phosphate Limited, comprising Westralian Farmers' directors and members of the FSA Executive Council, bought shares in Cuming Smith and Company Proprietary Limited and Mount Lyell Farmers' Fertilisers Limited in direct competition with the Adelaide-based Cresco Phosphate Company. The Westralian Farmers–FSA consortium took up 40,000 shares and urged farmers to purchase 360,000 more. Plant was constructed at Geraldton and Bunbury but, with the first shocks of the Great Depression now being felt, farmers were reluctant to subscribe to shares and many disapproved anyway of the co-operative company's obvious enthusiasm for joining with proprietary companies.[28]

Disillusionment with Central Organisation

So long as Westralian Farmers and the Wheat Pool were profitable, growers in general were happy to direct business through the 'two co-operatives', notwithstanding some farmer and independent co-operative board resentment at their allegedly domineering ways. Nevertheless, CFWA membership dwindled through the 1920s and the company's CWS Department stalled. Managers of autonomous rural co-operatives boycotted Central Organisation, deprecating its habits of poaching business from established stores, appointing managers to country stores without even advertising the positions and demanding 'loyalty' while failing to act on undertakings, especially placing the wholesale on a democratic footing.

After English CWS executives touring Australia in 1926 announced that headquarters for a Wholesale Co-operative linked through an indenting arrangement with the Manchester parent would be based in the eastern states, but that Westralian Farmers could continue to manage its own operation, John Thompson again urged country co-operatives to sign a 'loyalty' pledge with Central Organisation to direct all of their business through CWS Department and 'realise big savings'. Most country co-operative stores flatly refused to do so, demanding that the company pay greater heed to co-operative autonomy and the democracy principle.[29]

The CFWA annual conference in 1927 was conspicuous by the absence of Westralian Farmers' directors. Delegates discussed W D Johnson's proposed Co-operation Bill, which remained subject to a Country Party filibuster in parliament and demanded Central Organisation establish a wholesale co-operative 'under the ownership and control of the federation' to promote the:

> ...uniform and sound practices in the co-operative movement and friendly relationships in all matters of business to better co-ordinate the movement and to ensure that the movement acts as one united body on all matters of common interest.[30]

Central Organisation had no such intention and, through 1928, discussions between the company and democratic elements in CFWA reached a stalemate.

Deteriorating terms of trade

Meanwhile, economic buoyancy was giving way to eroding markets and falling prices. Recession was deepening. Noticing sluggishness in wheat markets when visiting the United States, Tom Bath upon his return urged production cuts and warned against entering into further debt. The Westralian Farmers' board ignored him and, after the CFWA Secretary, who appears not to have been quite in favour at this time, insisted, he was told to be quiet. Then overseas markets collapsed. Suddenly, domestic markets and the moribund CWS Department became very important to Westralian Farmers.[31]

The Companies (Co-operatives) Act
Soon after, in 1929, W D Johnson, then Speaker of the House in the Collier Labor Government, introduced the Co-operation Bill, as a private member. The new legislation, he said, was necessary to protect the co-operative movement against attack from 'dry' shareholders and to ensure that ownership and control of co-operatives stayed in the hands of those who produced the wealth. It is clear that the bill was targeted specifically at Westralian Farmers' subsidiary 'partnerships' competing with established co-operatives, which many saw simply as 'stooge' co-operatives delivering the company numerical control of CFWA. Johnson's bill was framed also to confine usage of the word 'co-operative' in a business name to organisations operating on a one-person-one-vote basis and place limits on shareholder dividends, restricting this to a maximum of 5 per cent per annum in excess of bank two-year term deposit rates. All surpluses would be divided strictly on a patronage basis, proportionate with trade carried on with a co-operative. Safeguards against the engineered winding up of a co-operative by 'dry' shareholders were included, requiring the approval of three-quarters of all shareholders. As for new federal taxation provisions for agricultural co-operatives engaged in productive activities in the public interest, Johnson argued that these should be confined to *genuine* co-operative organisations applying a mutuality principle (90 per cent of business with members). Clearly, Johnson's bill was a frontal attack on Westralian Farmers' domination of the Western Australian co-operative movement.

In a fraught political environment, which included a campaign to have Western Australia secede from the Commonwealth of Australia, Labor lost to the Mitchell National-Country Party Coalition in April 1930. Westralian Farmers' parliamentary associates quickly moved to steer Johnson's Co-operation Bill into the *Companies Act*, specifically Section 108, Clause 8. The affect was to disallow further registration of co-operatives under the 1903 *Co-operative and Provident Societies Act* and to permit co-operatives registered *after* passage of the amendments to come under company law, preventing shareholders in such co-operatives from *withdrawing capital at will*. To Johnson's loud protests that this fixed-capital idea made a mockery of co-operation, the Attorney-General replied that much of the 1903 legislation was already duplicated in the proposed Companies (Co-operatives) Bill in any event and Johnson should acknowledge this or run the risk of his bill being scuttled altogether.

The resultant *Companies (Co-operatives) Act* meant that Westralian Farmers' wholly-owned subsidiaries and 'partnership' agencies could now by a simple resolution qualify as co-operatives for affiliation with CFWA and be eligible to vote in Federation elections and send delegates to Central Council and federal conferences. 'Democratic' control of the federation now simply required an executive majority of delegates from co-operative zones where Westralian Farmers' subsidiaries, partnerships and agencies predominated. This, while locking into the company's Wheat Pool bonus shares and other farmer investments. It was a political masterstroke delivering the company more power in the co-operative movement than it had ever had before.

Recalling these events years later, Johnson acknowledged that he had been tricked:

> It was a private bill drafted for the Co-operative Federation by a private firm of solicitors and a member of that private firm was the Federation adviser…We all remember the year 1929…Things were in a very bad state and it is not pleasant to recall the circumstances that necessitated the hasty passing of the 1929 legislation (sic). Certain developments were taking place and that caused great anxiety and when the House was asked to pass the measure it did not contain the provisions I would have like to see included. It was really a compromise. I was under the impression that I had discussed it with a certain member of parliament in his capacity as member, not as a member of the legal firm that was advising the…federation. There was a difference of opinion between us at the time. I would not claim that I always see eye-to-eye with Mr C W Harper. Mr T H Bath at times differs from both of us…[and] when the 1929 bill was under discussion we were not all agreed as to the provisions it should contain. I did not like Clause 8 but it was the product of the Co-operative Federation.[32]

Many CFWA affiliates described the *Companies (Co-operatives) Act as* a joke, alleging that the company had engineered the legislation simply to satisfy the requirements of a major creditor, English CWS. The act, they said, did nothing to advance genuine co-operation and everything to consolidate Westralian Farmers' grip on the co-operative movement and wheat industry. As a sop, perhaps, to a parliamentarian who had been outmanoeuvred, or as a concession to outraged CFWA affiliates, whose continued support was so important, W D Johnson was nominated as a Westralian Farmers' director and permitted an ex-officio role in the CFWA Central Council.

The 1929 CFWA annual conference was postponed, ostensibly for reasons of cost. The combined affects of economic depression and the company's apparent disregard for co-operative principles saw a further decline in CWS Department business, which was now vital following the collapse of British and foreign markets. On the eve of the Great Depression Western Australian trading co-operatives, most in rural districts, had 60,000 members producing an annual turnover of £1.1 million. By 1933, these figures had fallen to 40,000 and £627,000, respectively. Meanwhile, Westralian Farmers' indebtedness to English CWS under the 1924 six-year wheat-for-manufactured-goods indenting agreement, loomed large.[33]

Westralian Farmers and the Depression

Westralian Farmers now entered a troubled period lasting until 1935. The company was dangerously over-extended financially and the Wheat Pool held large carry-overs. After incurring losses, Radio Station 6WF was sold to the Commonwealth Government and became part of the Australian Broadcasting Commission (ABC) network.

At the March 1930 CFWA annual conference there were again spirited calls for democratic reforms in the co-operative movement. Not surprisingly, given the company's level of indebtedness, English CWS officials present told the assembly that this was not the time for such niceties. Rural co-operatives *should* support the company's CWS Department and Westralian Farmers *should* 'tighten its reins' and trade out of difficulties. The English CWS *would not* assist the company with any additional finance which, the visitors asserted, clearly *was not* a co-operative, notwithstanding, the *Companies (Co-operatives) Act*, and anyone asserting that English CWS had had anything to do with that legislation was mistaken. Moreover, tariff barriers now made it impossible for English CWS manufacturers to compete in Australia and it was incumbent upon the Western Australian co-operative movement, the English officials continued, to find some solid basis for a trading relationship with Manchester and loyally abide by this. Under current circumstances a direct indenting arrangement appeared to be the only way of achieving that.

Characteristically, W D Johnson argued for a compromise, moving that Central Council should have powers to inspect co-operatives and ensure compliance with trade goals, but *only if* Westralian Farmers allowed direct representation of zone directors on its board with a view to autonomous co-operatives eventually controlling the organisation, when conditions improved. The motion was deferred.[34]

Under administration

With wheat prices falling catastrophically and Westralian Farmers deeply in debt, the E S & A Bank appointed an administrator to supervise the company's accounts. Then, when the company began foreclosing on debtors for advances made, growers reacted violently, accusing the company of 'gambling' on speculative wheat futures markets and of paying producers less than market rates in its capacity as a private buyer. Indeed, a 1930 Royal Commission on Stored Wheat in the 1929/30 season confirmed that the company had incurred heavy losses dealing in wheat futures and said that this was not in the interests of growers.

The Wheat Growers' Union

Again calls arose for a statutory marketing authority (SMA) to conduct the Wheat Pool. A Wheat Growers' Union formed, led by I G Boyle, a Lake Grace farmer. By 1933, the Wheat Growers' Union had 6,500 members, approximately the same number as CFWA, and was publishing a journal, *The Wheat Grower*, which called upon growers to boycott The Trustees of the Wheat Pool, demand legislation for a SMA and to deplore the 'remote control' of independent co-operatives exercised by Westralian Farmers through CFWA. It was impossible, the journal alleged, to unseat Westralian Farmers' directors from the Wheat Pool because most producers were unable to attend general meetings, and the company knew it, delivering effective control to Central Organisation and its agents. *The Wheat Grower* said that the company had thwarted all promises of democracy contained in the *Companies (Co-operatives) Act* and it was now time to exercise a statutory option – no more promises!

An emergency meeting: reorganise the co-operative movement

An emergency meeting was held on 30–31 July 1930 bringing together representatives from Westralian Farmers, the Wheat Pool, the Wheat Growers' Union, English CWS and 116 delegates from forty-one CFWA affiliates. The stated purpose of the meeting was to reorganise the co-operative movement. This translated into an English CWS directive to cement an Agency Agreement allowing Westralian Farmers to trade out of difficulties under various heads of agreement in a compulsory arrangement with Manchester involving the direct indenting of English CWS manufactures and foodstuffs, especially tea. The company was to immediately reactivate the CWS Department and CFWA affiliates were *expected* to place all trade through it. The English CWS would send 'samples' on a ninety-day payment basis to avoid tariffs, as high level international talks (the Ottawa Conference, discussed in Chapter Two) proceeded with a view to improving the tariff situation. All requests for English CWS to reduce the existing rate of interest on outstanding loans were to cease. Clearly, when it came to outstanding debt, the heirs of Rochdale were as pragmatic as any other businessmen. For their part, Wheat Growers' Union representatives at the emergency meeting were no less resolute, announcing plans to introduce a Wheat Pool Bill into parliament designed to wrest control of the Wheat Pool from Westralian Farmers.[35]

A growers revolt looms

Allegations from disgruntled, hard-pressed wheat growers that Westralian Farmers was behaving like a 'profiteering, mercantile corporation', paying prices below those fetched at time of sale, continued through 1931 and 1932. The fact that the Wheat Pool was not properly constituted or representative of growers unsettled many. Westralian Farmers countered that no company could pay better than market prices prevailing, with world commodity prices plunging, and alleged that growers were actually 'striking'; holding back supplies; in an attempt to force up prices in markets that did not exist.

Angry letters appeared in the press doubting the value of the company's services and CFWA's true democratic nature and threatening a revolt. Wheat growers demanded real change to the composition of The Trustees of the Wheat Pool. Elections had been discontinued, correspondents said, and it was impossible to unseat directors. The co-operative nature of the Wheat Pool was a sham. Westralian Farmers was still controlled by 'dry' shareholders. The company had 6,900 shareholders but only 4,336 of them were growers! The Primary Producers' Association had 6,500 members and fewer than 5,000 were active growers! The Wheat Growers' Union, on the other hand, now with approximately 6,000 members, consisted entirely of genuine growers.

Tom Bath replied dryly that the antidote to any perception that the federation was not democratic and simply a company puppet, was to participate. At least, he said, he was prepared to publish letters in the *Gazette*. Wasn't that democracy? Tariffs were to blame for the company's plight, he continued, advocating the formation of a co-operative loan society for farmers and a farmers' advisory service. He blasted the co-operative consumer movement which, he said, was 'not concerned with producers' interests and [has] gone off to chase political phantoms' and lampooned allegations that CFWA, Westralian Farmers and the Wheat Pool were all 'one and the same'.[36]

Soon after, the co-operative company discontinued the *Gazette*, ostensibly as a cost-cutting exercise. Instead, a simple information sheet was periodically issued, edited by Walter Harper.[37]

A bulk handling experiment

After litigation (Chapman *versus* Verco) established that the Wheat Pool was indeed not formally constituted, early in 1932 the Farmers' and Settlers' Association, the Primary Producers' Association and the Wheat Growers' Union met to form a joint committee to consider bulk handling. Westralian Farmers General Manager John Thompson announced that money for such a scheme was available in London, in the event that government guarantees were forthcoming, to finance the building of holding bins at receival points at Fremantle, Albany, Bunbury and Geraldton.[38]

It is clear, however, that English CWS was not prepared to extend Westralian Farmers further finance and, when Thompson visited England he was told bluntly by Manchester officials that a 'new breed' now controlled the wholesale's executive determined to advance *consumer* co-operation and who regarded the 'various efforts among producers to assist themselves by mutual aid as being only a counterfeit of co-operation'.[39]

Nevertheless, with industry pressure building to rationalise costs, including the high cost of bags (£872,000 per annum by 1933), the company proceeded with plans to experiment with bulk handling, locating finance in the Prudential Assurance Company (United Kingdom). Experimental bulk handling installations were developed at five sidings for the 1931/32 season, which was a bumper crop, three times the previous harvest, with many farmers foregoing the fallow. Volumes were now four times what they had been in 1920! The magnitude of the crop and the demonstrable savings achieved through pooling convinced many farmers that bulk handling was the way forward, but still the vexed question of ownership and control of the infrastructure remained unresolved. Who should control this, growers or the company?[40]

The Wheat Pool Bill

In 1932 the Western Australian Wheat Pool Bill entered parliament for a first reading to 'constitute and incorporate The Trustees of the Wheat Pool...to regulate the appointment of trustees and to define their powers and authorities' and allowing for Wheat Growers' Union participation. New Wheat Pool guidelines were drafted. The legislation provided *inter alia* for the division of wheat fields into twenty districts with elected pool councillors from each district vested with powers to elect trustees each four years. Producers were limited to one vote each, companies to two and partnerships to four. The powers of a reformed Growers' Advisory Council were to be clearly articulated with regard to monitoring a Pool Reserve Fund.

By the time the bill entered parliament for a second reading in October 1932, however, it had been so amended by Country Party members that Westralian Farmers' domination of the Wheat Pool remained largely intact. Moreover, the rewritten legislation included a provision that the state indemnify loans raised in converting the industry to bulk handling![41]

The government had no intention of providing such guarantees, however, so that when The Trustees of the Wheat Pool proceeded with installing a bulk handling system for the 1932/33 season, they employed the Wheat Pool Reserve Fund, unsecured.

Westralian Wheat Farmers' Limited

Early in 1933 a bill sponsored by Westralian Farmers and The Trustees of the Wheat Pool entered parliament seeking to confer monopolistic powers on a co-operative bulk handling scheme to be known as 'Westralian Wheat Farmers' Limited', formed by the Trustees in April. The bill contemplated government guarantees for loans raised in financing the scheme. Directors included A J Monger, C W Harper, T H Bath and J S Teasdale. Westralian Wheat Farmers' Limited planned to take over all existing plant and leases (fifty-three units) with securities for investments given by means of debentures over the new company's assets.

A growers' revolt

Wheat Growers' Union affiliates in the Lake Grace district revolted and formed an independent pool with fifty sidings. This 'strike' (as Westralian Farmers' Official Historian J Sandford describes it) began on the Koorgabencubbin line and spread to more than one hundred sidings where picket lines stopped deliveries to the Wheat Pool.

Westralian Farmers took legal action against the Wheat Growers' Union. Parliamentary faction fights erupted between elements of the Country Party and Labor, contributing to Labor's win at the April 1933 election, ousting the Mitchell Coalition. (Coincidentally, a state referendum saw strong support for Western Australia seceding from the Commonwealth, which was subsequently rejected as unconstitutional by a House of Commons [UK] Joint Select Committee [1935].)

With the Wheat Growers' Union journal, *Wheat Grower,* repeating allegations that CFWA was not a democratic organisation, that Westralian Farmers' bulk handling scheme was a 'club' with practically no shareholders at its AGM, that directors were appointed rather than elected when a vacancy occurred and that The Trustees of the Wheat Pool had no authority to speak for

Western Australian wheat growers, the Lake Grace breakaway group attracted further support in the 1933/34 season when it organised 170 sidings.

Some pressure was taken off growers and the company at this point by a Commonwealth Government assistance package flowing from an Ottawa Conference agreement for preferential trade in respect of British Commonwealth agricultural commodities, including wheat, and an International Wheat Agreement which set export quotas to protect markets. In line with this a Commonwealth Royal Commission into the Wheat Industry in 1933 recommended financial assistance for wheat growers in the form of super-phosphate subsidies, taxation concessions, debt adjustment grants and long-term loans (which were eventually written off).

A store managers' revolt

With each returning cargo from England, however, Westralian Farmers faced the problem of compulsorily merchandising CWS lines through a recalcitrant rural store co-operative movement. The company revamped its CWS Department, which was renamed the 'Collective Purchase Department', and dissolved existing partnerships with country stores in exchange for *guarantees* that they would take fixed quotas of CWS manufactures and foods. Predictably, store managers complained that such press-gang tactics were an absolute denial of co-operative principles. Tom Bath, who was given the task of appeasement, painted the arrangement as a 'voluntary co-operative middle path [between] the anarchist individualism of private capital [and] state dependence'. Wherever he travelled, however, Bath encountered deep cynicism and fewer than twenty co-operatives agreed to trade with Collective Purchase Department. The CFWA Secretary advised Central Organisation to further soften its partnership policy to an 'advisory director scheme' and records, without explanation, that co-operatives in some districts '...were pressed into a more active policy of business getting for Westralian Farmers'.

At an angry meeting of country co-operative store managers and representatives later in 1933, Westralian Farmers was accused of 'devouring the democratic co-operative movement through pernicious poaching practices'. A motion was carried to form a democratic wholesale along Rochdale lines (as agreed in 1919!) and a committee was formed to act on this, comprising W D Johnson, Westralian Farmers Assistant General Manager W Arnott and the company's administrator, E V Jukes. The meeting also demanded that Westralian Farmers stop trying to *control* co-operatives and constitute a proper democratic process for electing boards and administrative machinery to enable this. In exchange, *if* the company acted in good faith on these demands, store managers and directors undertook to urge CFWA affiliates to *voluntarily* support the company's bulk wheat-handling pool and wholesale operation. Participating co-operatives would lodge rebates in Collective Purchase Department by way of a *loan* to Westralian Farmers with a view to future democratic ownership of the entity. Co-operative managers also demanded more autonomy in selecting lines. The terms were agreed.

Many country co-operative store managers thought the agreement did not go far enough, however: Collective Purchase Department was still housed in the same building as Central Organisation and had no independent legal personality; its success still depended upon the company's goodwill and good faith; and, far from democratically-elected boards, the 'advisory director scheme' amounted to 'company plants' on co-operative boards, smoothing compliance with Central Organisation. There was no true voluntary democracy in the arrangement, critics said, particularly as the company continued to build its network of units registered under the act as 'co-operatives' but which were really nothing more that company outposts.

The company outmanoeuvres the federation

Deftly side-stepping these protests, Westralian Farmers now demanded that *all* federation affiliates 'legally' trade through Collective Purchase Department *before* the company would take any further steps to convert the department to a genuine co-operative structure! Another stalemate ensued – Westralian Farmers unable to secure guarantees of 'loyal' trading from independent CFWA affiliates, who, in turn, were helpless to stop the company from expanding its network of retail satellites. By 1936 Westralian Farmers' retail network consisted of three wholly-owned country branches, thirteen directly-controlled subsidiaries, eighteen private agencies with contracts of exclusivity and fifteen agencies financed by groups of local farmers sympathetic to the company. This total of forty-nine company satellites matched *exactly* the number of independent co-operative stores represented in CFWA, most of them ailing. The company was again in a position to dominate federation policy.[42]

The dispute widens

At a stormy public meeting convened by the Fremantle Businessmen's Association in late 1933 to protest The Trustees of the Wheat Pool's planned bulk scheme (Westralian Wheat Farmers' Limited), the Lumpers' Union, business interests from Perth, bag suppliers, merchants and the Wheat Growers' Union joined in a chorus of protest saying that the scheme amounted to nothing but a private monopoly with government guarantees. If that was so, Tom Bath replied defiantly, it was 'a compliment' because growers could not possibly perpetrate a monopoly against themselves. That was not received well at the meeting. While growers were far from unanimous on how the industry should be structured, the Wheat Growers' Union made it plain that it would support the Lumpers' Union in proposed industrial action and repeated demands that any bulk handling scheme be placed on a proper statutory footing.

Emphasising that the new Labor administration was sympathetic to state-ownership of a bulk scheme and supported dock workers and the Wheat Growers' Union in their dispute with Westralian Farmers, the government threw out the proposed bill to constitute Westralian Wheat Farmers' Limited, suspended all experiments with bulk handling, stopped the granting of railway siding licences to the Wheat Pool and appointed another Royal Commission to inquire further into allegations that Westralian Farmers had 'gambled' on stored wheat futures in the 1929/30 season.[43]

As Labor's Royal Commission deliberated, Westralian Farmers executives, including Tom Bath, travelled throughout Wheat Growers' Union strongholds addressing gatherings of farmers, dispersing literature justifying the company's actions, reaffirming Westralian Farmers' identity as a 'co-operative' and urging farmers to resist the 'compulsory socialist' model allegedly embodied in Labor's proposed bulk handling scheme and support the 'voluntary co-operation' option offered by Westralian Farmers.[44]

A Deed of Trust

The Royal Commission dismissed allegations that Westralian Farmers had traded on the wheat futures exchange deliberately to the detriment of growers, but recommended a tightening of contractual arrangements in the industry, ruling that the company prepare a Deed of Trust *guaranteeing* the handing over to growers of any bulk handling system which it developed within a designated period (fifteen years) and that a copy of this deed be posted at every receival point.

Co-operative Bulk Handling

The company moved quickly. Still £600,000 in debt, Westralian Farmers accessed finance available in London and negotiated an overdraft extension sufficient to finance forty-eight new bulk bins, bringing the total under the company's control to fifty-three. Westralian Farmers contributed £60,000 to construction costs and a further £90,000 was located in the Wheat Growers' Reserve Fund. It was proposed that a toll on commodity deliveries would accumulate, enabling growers to buy out the bulk handling scheme within the set period. A skeleton company, Co-operative Bulk Handling (CBH), was formed comprising mainly Westralian Farmers and Wheat Pool personnel and with *no* Wheat Growers' Union representation on its board. The CFWA negotiated the formation process.[45]

Charging that wheat growers had not been consulted in the process, Wheat Growers' Union President I G Boyle said the scheme was designed to benefit the few at the expense of the many and questioned the company's motives: Why were shares in CBH not offered to farmers? Why was CBH not representative of farmers? What was Westralian Farmers' real role in the Pool? Was CBH just another 'middle man' serving the company's interests? Wheat growers watched CBH's development intently.

A disastrous season

The 1933/34 season, the first generally handled in bulk, was disastrous, hit by a combination of depressed markets and torrential rains. Much of the crop was ruined by rain and mice. Errors in handling also proved extremely costly and prompted bitter disagreements and recrimination. In June 1934 the *Wheat Grower* published pictures of the sodden crop, describing Westralian Farmers' bulk handling bins as utterly inadequate 'pig pens' and accusing the company of 'hoodwinking' producers. The Wheat Pool, Westralian Farmers' and CBH, the journal alleged, were all one and the same and the idea that farmers owned any of them was a myth.

A showdown looms

Westralian Farmers sued the *Wheat Grower* and the journal had costs awarded against it. More litigation followed prompting the Wheat Growers' Union to issue a circular:

> *Stand firm. We are under attack. From the outset there has been an incessant campaign to defeat us. If farmers fail now to stand up to the movement they started they will never again have the opportunity to build their own organisation.*

The breakaway Lake Grace district wheat pool, however, fared no better than the CBH operation and failed to produce a dividend. The Wheat Growers' Union wound up the pool and appointed a private merchant to run an organisation known as 'Grain Pool', operating independently from CBH.[46]

Westralian Farmers' executives again toured the state extensively through 1935 seeking a reconciliation. Tom Bath wrote prolifically in (a resumed) *Gazette* broadcasting Rochdale rhetoric, arguing against 'a state-socialist operation' and warning growers against giving in to 'anarchic individualism', as he characterised the Lake Grace breakaways. The CFWA Secretary lambasted Labor, his old party, which he said was 'anti-co-operation', lampooned W D Johnson's faith in the state, which 'only looked after itself', and sought to rally farmers behind an attack on the labour movement, which was 'antagonistic to the co-operative movement'. This was evidenced, Bath alleged, by unions refusing to accept bulk wheat at railway sidings and passive resistance on the wharves.[47]

Historical bulk load being received.
Photo courtesy Co-operative Bulk Handling Limited

The *Bulk Handling Act* 1935

The Wheat Growers' Union persisted with allegations that Westralian Farmers and CBH, as it was currently constituted, were 'putting it over farmers' and demanded a government-regulated wheat board. Opposition to the company's CBH initiative also mounted in both houses of parliament.

In 1935 the Collier Government recalled the 1933 Royal Commission into Westralian Farmers' futures trading, extending the brief to encompass the entire wheat industry. The restructured commission deliberated for six months, calling farmers, ship masters, government department, merchants, unions, politicians and representatives of the co-operative movement to give evidence. The report noted that the system as currently constructed represented *no benefit* to the Harbour Trust, railways, workers, consumers, merchants or stevedores. On the other hand, farmers stood to benefit from a taxation-subsidised system on which there was no public representation! The report recommended that CBH proceed, but on a legislative basis, and that the company should state the terms of future sale to growers more clearly.

With W D Johnson enthusiastically assisting, a Bulk Handling Bill was introduced into parliament, predictably meeting fierce opposition from the Country Party, which delayed it through committees until late 1935. When finally the Bill did pass, according to one report, it was 'so amended by political friends of Westralian Farmers that it was impossible to understand'. Essentially the bill allowed the continuation of Westralian Farmers' virtual monopoly of bulk wheat handling, subject to legislative controls. The new scheme, however, was confined to active growers (allowing two years' interruption in supply), making it more difficult for 'dry' shareholders to control things and provided a *legislative* basis for handing CBH over to growers. Democracy at last? Maybe so, but it was enshrined in a state-socialist model.[48]

Westralian Farmers turns the corner

With the wheat pool imbroglio sorted and CBH on a solid legislative footing as economic conditions improved, Westralian Farmers revived in earnest a diversification program begun in the early 1920s and interrupted by the Great Depression. Robust trade with English CWS resumed with Manchester delegates again eagerly courting business. Westralian Farmers' Transport Limited was formed, providing direct services for producers in Western Australia, New South Wales, Queensland, Victoria and South Australia and with a subsidiary based in London. The company chartered fifteen ships for wool exports in addition to wheat activities and also chartered specially designed ships for Atlantic trade, helping to open new markets in Britain, Europe and Palestine for fruit, eggs, lamb and barley. Ships returned to Australia crammed with cargoes of machinery, tractors, sulphur, newsprint, cement, groceries, tea and other English CWS lines and carried passengers both ways. The shipping operation was highly profitable and well-supported, dramatically reducing freight costs, estimated at savings of £500,000 a year for the first three years. Westralian Farmers' Transport Limited also handled the London end for APWCF affiliates associated with Overseas Farmers and handled commodities for the Australian Wheat Board (AWB) and the Commonwealth Government. Westralian Farmers General Manager John Thompson's son-in-law, K W (Ken) Edwards, a former AWB senior officer, was appointed general manager of the transport arm (Outturns), which traded successfully until it was taken over by the Commonwealth Government during World War II.[49]

By 1937 Westralian Farmers was Australia's largest wheat exporter. The company had retired all of its debt to English CWS and, interlocking with CBH and the Wheat Pool, now handled 83 per cent of the Western Australian wheat harvest. Quite apart from CBH, the company produced an annual turnover of £1.24 million, owned three country branches and thirteen agencies, engaged eighty-three other general agencies and seven machine agents and co-ordinated a network of forty-nine trading co-operatives through Central Organisation (CFWA). The company's Collective Purchasing Department was thriving, its fortunes further enhanced when in 1938

Westralian Farmers was appointed the first distributor in Western Australian country districts for Commonwealth Oil Refineries (COR).

In a popular gesture of good will, bad debts amounting to £350,000 outstanding to the company were written off by CFWA (representing Central Organisation), helping the majority of rural co-operative units and agencies, still reeling from the Depression, to recover.

Improved economic conditions also saw cordiality return to relations between CFWA and counterparts in other states. With English CWS executives stressing the importance of commonwealth-wide co-operative trade *beyond* the parochial level, the *Gazette* carried more articles on consumer co-operation and interstate co-operation. Western Australian personnel travelled more frequently to eastern states studying co-operative developments there and entering a new dialogue on the possibility of launching a national co-operatives' wholesale. But squabbling continued and talks stalled on disagreements over copyright to the English CWS 'Co-op' Label, to which the New South Wales consumer co-operative felt entitled as 'true' heir to the Rochdale mantle, but which Westralian Farmers had secured in a deal with CWS Agent H Marsland *en route* to Sydney to take up general manager duties for the Manchester wholesale! Moreover, calls by easterners for national co-operatives' legislation and a co-operative bank were consistently rejected by CFWA, which eschewed anything interfering with the *Companies (Co-operatives) Act* and was satisfied with existing financial arrangements. This provoked some friction between country co-operative store managers and Tom Bath, who reprimanded the former, demanding that they be 'better co-operators' and 'be loyal'.[50]

Meanwhile W D Johnson renewed calls for a national co-operatives' representative body (the genesis of the Co-operative Federation of Australia, discussed in Chapter Ten) *and* a national co-operative wholesale joining Australian producers and consumers in a mutually beneficial trading relationship capable of developing the co-operative movement on a broader front. In 1936 Johnson travelled to New South Wales to attend a conference organised by the Hawkesbury Agricultural College, where he studied the New South Wales Agricultural Bureaux system and met Rochdale consumer-movement leaders. There is a report in the *Gazette* of a 'Co-operative Federation of New South Wales' forming at this time, described as an 'eastern district council of CFWA' and comprising six co-operative units with support from dairy co-operatives. No further information on this organisation has been located and it is probable that it did not function.

The return of war

Although Westralian Farmers had entered a new phase of prosperity, daunting problems lay ahead. The wheat market was dull in 1938 and prices tumbled. It was a shocking year and growers, still recovering from the Depression, eagerly sought additional government assistance (through the *Wheat Industry Assistance Act*, for example). The slump was not helped by a record crop in 1939 and the cessation of Commonwealth Government super-phosphate subsidies. Then the outbreak of World War II saw a return to emergency regulations. All talk of a federal co-operatives advisory body, national co-operatives legislation, a co-operative bank and an Australian co-operative wholesale ceased, not to resume until near the end of the war.

Federation Trusts Limited

Westralian Farmers executives occupied key positions in the war-time apparatus. Prime Minister Menzies appointed John Thompson General Manager of AWB, based in Melbourne. Assisted by son-in-law, Ken Edwards, Thompson provided honorary service to the Commonwealth Ships Chartering Service, which commandeered twenty-eight ships, including Westralian Farmers' vessels, to carry wheat for AWB. Walter Harper was appointed head of the Western Australian Districts Contracts Board from which position he organised a Wheat Management Board for AWB, Federation Trusts Limited, consisting of Harper, Tom Bath, W D Johnson and J H Worthington. Federation Trusts organised all wheat agencies other than CBH, which continued as part of Westralian Farmers' corporate structure, and ran a preservation fund to help co-operatives in trading difficulties. CBH was appointed sole receiver of bulk wheat in Western Australia and Westralian Farmers sole receiver of bagged wheat, plus shipping. CBH and the Wheat Pool were appointed brokers for AWB in government-to-government trade. When wheat shipments to the UK and Europe virtually ceased due to the war, the company moved into exporting barley, tinned fruit, eggs and butter. With wool much in demand for military apparel, prices soared and producers and the company prospered.

CBH is transferred to growers

In October 1943 Westralian Farmers passed control of CBH to growers, five years ahead of schedule. There was no altruism in this – CBH was virtually inactive and had been expensively storing wheat for three seasons due to war interruptions. For Westralian Farmers, seeking to concentrate on marketing and services to take full advantage of prevailing conditions, the move made good commercial sense. So it was that, finally, after a protracted and sometimes acrimonious battle between the company and wheat growers centred on the democracy principle, the ownership and control of bulk wheat handling infrastructure in Western Australia passed to farmers. Tom Bath, the only director of the Wheat Pool to survive a grower election for the directorate, was made CBH vice-president, holding this position until 1948 when war-time regulations lapsed. Albeit moribund through the war, CBH was now responsible for handling 99 per cent of the Western Australian wheat crop.[51]

Post World War II: 'backwards integration'

Having been dragged to the altar of democracy in a marriage of convenience with CBH, Westralian Farmers largely lost interest in wheat dealing in the immediate post-World War II period, particularly after the *Commonwealth Wheat Industry Stabilisation Act* placed wheat marketing on a national statutory basis and as marketing boards were created for oats, barley and other grains. There were alternative opportunities. The company resumed a diversification programme based on 'backwards integration', that is ownership and/or control of agriculture-related enterprises, co-operative and non-co-operative, all the way through the supply chain from farm gate to the point of consumption, essentially a 'top-down' inversion of Rochdale methodology with producers at the apex. In the post-war period, this would become the dominant farmer co-operative paradigm nationally, driven robustly by Westralian Farmers.

'Co-operative' by name and improved representation

To comply with the requirements of (still) its largest trading partner, English CWS, Westralian Farmers added 'Co-operative' to the title in 1946. Then, responding to renewed criticisms from CFWA affiliates that the co-operative company was undemocratic and dominated by city-based shareholder-investors, in 1947 it began drawn-out moves to introduce a new system for electing directors. The delay was prolonged by the death in 1948 of W D Johnson, long a driving force in efforts to democratise the Western Australian co-operative movement.

By 1951, however, the new system had been perfected and gave farmers significantly improved representation. Previously, directors (seven elected, two nominated by Westralian Farmers and two non-voting associate directors appointed by directors) had been elected mostly by proxy at the co-operative company's AGM in Perth. Under the new arrangement the state was divided into sixteen zones with shareholders in each zone electing a representative to the board. In addition five general directors were elected by *all* shareholders, wherever they resided. An executive board was elected by the full board. All voters and directors were required to be *bona fide* producers, proxy voting and nominee directors were disallowed and postal voting was permitted.

Seeking capital

Gearing up for the lifting of war-time regulations in 1948, the co-operative company began a sustained capital drive employing a very successful revolving fund scheme. Westralian Farmers made major property purchases and revived the defunct Collective Purchase Department, reshaping this as Westfarmers' Co-operative Wholesale Section (WCWS), which it saw as the hub of an Australian co-operative wholesale linked to English CWS (a role which NSW CWS and Eudunda Farmers [South Australia] also coveted) and a spear in the 'backwards integration' campaign. Issuing 100,000 preference shares to private investors, WCWS purchased a clothing and soft goods proprietary company, opened a Melbourne branch in Collins Street, took a 75 per cent holding in Evans and Couts and ran retail mail-order, travel currency and land agency departments.

The co-operative company entered Asian trade, opening an office in Singapore, and developed new markets in Malaysia and Indonesia. Ken Edwards managed Australian Farmers' Transport Limited in London and represented the Co-operative Federation of Australia (CFA) at ICA conferences in Scotland, France and Stockholm. The company entered more joint ventures with proprietary companies, for example Tutt Bryant, Master Dairies, a timber mill at Coppinup and a flour mill. It bought Ashburton Transport Company and Amalgamated Gascoyne Trading Proprietary Limited, entering the road transport and banana haulage business. A long-running tussle with the South-West Dairy Co-operative resurfaced over access to Perth markets. The company continued to conduct a robust trade with English CWS, recruited managers from the UK, built homes for them, introduced long-service leave conditions, conducted a young managers' programme (assisted by CFWA), organised tours by Western Australian co-operative farmers to the UK and ran an air-charter service facilitating trade with its British co-operative partner. Westralian Farmers joined the English CWS International Co-operative Petrol Association (ICPA), participated with Gippsland and Northern (Victoria), PDS (New South Wales), Queensland CWS and South Australian Farmers' Co-operative Union (SAFCU) in co-operative oil conferences in Melbourne and Perth and began marketing Co-operative Motor Oil in Western Australia in 1948.[52]

Refurbishing CFWA

CFWA Honorary Secretary T H Bath worked assiduously to rebuild the federation, aided by English CWS officials, and again squared up to the east-coast Rochdale consumer movement in a tussle for most favoured relationship with Manchester and control of CFA (discussed in Chapter Ten). To CFWA affiliate complaints that Westralian Farmers was re-positioning itself to take over the co-operative movement and behaving like a despot, Bath and General Manager John Thompson replied that under Western Australian conditions, where co-operators in isolated rural districts simply did not have access to capital or services necessary to build an industry, there was no alternative but to rely upon Central Organisation until farmers were in a position to form autonomous co-operatives.

By 1950, CFWA affiliates included Westralian Farmers' Central Organisation and eight branches, the Producers' Marketing Co-operative and one branch, two dairy co-operatives, the

Honey Pool, one Rochdale co-operative, fifty-one rural storekeeping co-operatives, thirty-four Westralian Farmers' agency co-operatives, one fish co-operative, a poultry co-operative and the Trayning Farmers' Co-operative. The Trustees of the Wheat Pool, CBH and WCWS joined soon after. There were then ten agricultural co-operative companies in Western Australia, with 32,600 members (6,305 of them Westralian Farmers' shareholders) producing an annual turnover of £11.4 million.[53]

'The democracy principle is not essential'

There was no doubting Westralian Farmers' commercial success but Rochdale purists persisted in criticising the company for an 'un-Rochdale' departure from co-operative principles. One such critic was the newly-appointed New South Wales Minister for Co-operative Societies C E Martin; the only such minister in Australia; who in 1950 addressed CFWA speaking as an 'Australian citizen', receiving a drubbing for his pains. Martin noted the 'slightly unusual way' in which primary producer co-operatives had developed in Western Australia, adding that they were nevertheless ahead of the rest of Australia. Western Australia, the minister continued, 'mingles producer and consumer co-operatives in a way that is impossible in New South Wales and it is farmers who fund the CWS, not consumers'. While Westralian Farmers was 'unique' in Australia, however, Martin added, the company's ownership of branches at Waroona, Narembeen, Belka, Corbel and Carnarvon was wholly outside the minister's understanding of co-operative principles. 'You can't impose co-operation. It must come from the grass roots,' Martin went on, adding that Western Australia really should have a co-operation act to enable funds to be ploughed back into general co-operative development and not simply swallowed up by Central Organisation:

> You should pressure government to treat you as something apart from a normal company...The transfer of shares to beneficiaries of estates is an appalling breach of co-operative principles – legal under company law but not so co-operative law. People living in other states are shareholders of Western Australian co-operatives, which [I find] appalling.

John Thompson rounded on the minister.

> The honourable minister complains about Waroona. This is not the first time wise men of the east have told us we are not co-operative. For example, they said it about our wheat buying organisation (the Pool). The prime minister would not finance us because it wasn't co-operative. I went to the United Kingdom and organised finance with the CWS. The chairman of the CWS said our buying and selling of wheat on the Rochdale plan was good co-operation but the pools were not co-operative and they didn't like them. It seems to me that there is a fundamental principle of co-operation which is the real test...that people join together to perform functions without a profit being extracted from them. Rochdale returns profits while pools carry on at cost. Both are co-operative. Tacked on to this, however, there are a number of principles which are held to be inviolate, for example one-man-one-vote. I do not require this as a principle of co-operation [Thompson's emphasis]. It is democratic and a very fine safeguard in a co-operative organisation. In ninety-nine out of a hundred cases it is sound, but in the hundredth case there may be some good reason otherwise.[54]

Thompson said that an Oat Pool, for example, would simply be too costly and cumbersome operating on a democratic basis and that was why the government had chosen 'four good men and true' to be Trustees of the Wheat Pool which *was* co-operative, as this term was understood in Western Australia, because profits went back to the participants. The Rochdale plan was fine as a measuring stick of efficiency in relation to the performance of individual units, but Martin was wrong about Waroona and other company branches, which were simply part of Westralian Farmers' general trade with the farming community. Shareholding clients participated in profits derived exactly as in any other department of the company. Thompson was adamant that a co-operation act and ministry for co-operatives would simply introduce rigid rules like those existing in the eastern states and would hamper development. The Australian co-operative movement needed to take after the United States co-operative movement and not the European because, 'European co-operation is largely socialistic in its ideas…and this is something we in Australia and people in America cannot all accept'.[55]

Martin had supporters in the Western Australian co-operative movement, however, the South-West Dairy Co-operative, for example, and a handful of Rochdale-inspired stores, including the Collie Industrial Co-operative. Long thorns in Westralian Farmers' side, they persisted with calls in CFWA for the movement to be placed on a truly democratic footing guaranteed by new co-operatives' legislation and hounded the company over its centralist policies. Thompson would not have a bar of it, repeatedly dismissing Rochdale co-operation as 'socialistic' and insisting that Westralian Farmers would continue to trade with private enterprise and raise capital from external investors to suit an expansionary agenda, unfettered by restrictive co-operative legislation.

Seeking to mollify the debate, CFWA President Walter Harper agreed that the Western Australian co-operative movement's material progress had been good, 'but I still feel the spiritual and educational side…is only just so'. Good service by itself was not enough for a co-operative movement to succeed, Harper said, and the movement must find people with 'courage, determination and missionary spirit' to build up an appreciation of the 'ethical values of co-operation':

> We work happily in this federation. In some states there is not such a happy feeling – big producer co-operatives look upon it as being a little 'infra dig' to associate with smaller consumer co-operatives and this looking down from high places…produces no fellow feeling among co-operators…We have to convince people that we have a way of life that is superior to all other systems.[56]

CFWA's Rochdale purists and commercial pragmatists would never agree on what constituted appropriate co-operative development but the latter could readily point to the formers' inability to organise CFA and, after the mid-1950s, to the general decline of the consumer co-operative movement. Idealism was losing and pragmatism was winning, Tom Bath and John Thompson argued, because of 'flaws' in Rochdale theory. Rochdale principles needed to be *adapted* to suit the special conditions of environments in which co-operatives functioned. The 'divvy-hunters' of the east could 'fritter surpluses' if they wished, but Western Australian co-operatives would secure capital for growth.

Westralian Farmers continues to grow

Westralian Farmers and its growing stable of subsidiaries and agencies went from strength to strength. In 1951 Westralian Buildings Proprietary Limited bought a Perth theatre and a hotel and acquired more country stores, running them as general retailers. Later the company entered the finance field through Discount Proprietary Limited. In 1955 AWB entrusted the company's subsidiary, Australian Outturns Proprietary Limited, with the superintendence of practically the whole of the board's wheat shipments to Europe. In the following year Westralian Farmers was appointed state distributor of liquefied petroleum gas for industrial and domestic purposes. Kleen Heat Gas Proprietary Limited was formed two years later as a subsidiary company to handle this business. A huge warehouse and wool store was built in South Fremantle and wool sales began at Albany.

Through the 1960s the company launched operations in Esperance, the Ord River District and Hamersley iron ore towns in the Pilbara. By 1964 Westralian Farmers was marketing skins, livestock, milk, fresh food, seed and cotton, in addition to supplying farm merchandise, fertilisers, chemicals, stock feed, farm machinery and tractors, pre-cut houses, hardware, household needs and general merchandise. The company was providing services for insurance, land sales, transport, ship chartering, tax advice, printing, general travel and seasonal finance. It was grooming a new generation of managers through a training and scholarship scheme, quickly computerised and, by the end of the decade, was handling almost 25 per cent of the wool produced in Western Australia and 25 per cent of the state's fruit exports to twenty-six countries. This was in addition to an important export role in vegetables, fruit, livestock and dairy products. In 1971 the company bought Blue Cross Products Proprietary Limited, a manufacturer of horticulture products and pesticides with an interest in meat exports. With Britain's entry into the European Economic Community (EEC), however, trade with English CWS declined rapidly as a proportion of the company's business.

A changing of the guard

Meanwhile, there had been a changing of the guard. In 1956 Walter Harper and Thomas Bath both died. The following year John Thompson retired, replaced as general manager by Ken Edwards, who served until 1973. E T (Sir Thorley) Lotan became chair of Westralian Farmers and of CFWA and, like Bath and Thompson before him, defended the co-operative nature of Westralian Farmers which, he said, had simply adapted Rochdale principles in unorthodox ways to achieve commercial success.

With Bath's passing, however, CFWA lost momentum. It was not until Bill Rawlinson was appointed executive officer in 1965 and honorary secretary of CFA based in Perth, that the federation again took a prominent role in Australian co-operation, promoting 'backwards integration' in the conduct of trade through the International Co-operative Alliance's (ICA) International Co-operative Trading Organisation (ICTO) (discussed in Chapter Ten).[57]

By 1972 the co-operative company's turnover exceeded Sterling £100 million per annum and it employed 2,000 people. In that year Westralian Farmers took 50 per cent equity in Wesdelf Limited, a merchant bank, in association with the Bank of New York (25 per cent) and Development Holdings Company Limited (25 per cent) (formerly Development Finance Corporation of Sydney, involving Ron Brierley). By 1973 Westralian Farmers (renamed 'Westfarmers' through this period), with 16,400 farmer shareholders and an annual turnover of $220 million, was considered to be the largest agricultural co-operative company in Australia.

'A giant corporate monolith'

After Keith Edwards retired in 1973 John Bennison was appointed general manager. The impressive development continued. Westfarmers' Europe Limited (London) and Westfarmers' Export Company (Melbourne) co-operated in manufacturing wool tops in Bradford, England, in 1975. A new insurance brokering company, Glanville West Proprietary Limited (later, Jardin Westfarmers' Insurance Brokers Proprietary Limited) opened an office in Tehran. Westfarmers' Stores Proprietary Limited (a descendant of the old wholesale department) became Farmers' Stores Proprietary Limited and began live-sheep exports to the Middle East using chartered ships. Through 1977 and 1978 the co-operative company mounted one of the largest takeover bids in Australian corporate history to that time, attempting to absorb Cumin-Smith (super-phosphate) of

Melbourne. The *Australian Financial Review* reported that the bid, if successful, could '...develop into a threat to part of Australia's corporate heritage'. Ron Brierley's IEL and others, including media magnate Kerry Packer, made counter offers. Elders-GM, British Petroleum (BP), Western Livestock and the Trades Practices Commission opposed the bid, giving rise to lengthy and expensive litigation in the Victorian Supreme Court. Certainly it was not a popular bid in some sections of Western Australian agriculture. The Western Australian Farmers' Union, for example, criticised the idea, repeating allegations that Westfarmers was in no sense a co-operative but in fact '... a giant corporate monolith'. Finally the company secured only limited control of the super-phosphate market.

The making of Wesfarmers Limited

The company did not stay co-operative in any sense for much longer. With new CEO Trevor Eastwood at the helm, annual sales of approximately $700 million and performing as one of Australia's largest agribusiness enterprises, rivalled only in Western Australia by Robert Holmes-à-Court's Bell Group and Bond Corporation, in 1984 Westralian Farmers' Co-operative prepared to list on the Perth Stock Exchange.

Westralian Farmers' Co-operative initially held a 58.51 per cent (later reduced to 50.1 per cent) controlling interest in the listed company, Wesfarmers Limited, which was one of the top sixty corporations in Australia. A board of sixteen included thirteen farmers, one of whom was the chairman. Of the 20,000 company shareholders, 99.9 per cent were farmers, 90 per cent of them holding fewer than 5,000 shares. Wesfarmers' ownership and control scheme was complex, involving interlocking jointly-owned holding companies and a Franked Income Fund (FIF) Scheme (which was listed in 1988). Broadly speaking, FIF unit holders were entitled to dividends from Wesfarmers after co-operative shareholders had been paid a 10 per cent dividend on their co-operative holdings, sourced from a retained interest in Wesfarmers and preference shares held in the jointly-owned FIF intermediary. While the co-operative's dividend was initially constant it was anticipated that the leverage of FIF unit holders would increase significantly as Wesfarmers' dividends rose in the future.

Reflecting a conservative farming heritage, Wesfarmers determined to remain domestically-based and concentrate on industries in which Australia was internationally competitive. The company was one of the first to introduce a placement scheme, to limit dividend cash outflows while maximising franking benefits to co-operative shareholders, as noted above, and was a pace-maker in developing a shareholder information service. Wesfarmers' rapid development into Western Australia's top stock falls outside our brief. Suffice it to say that in 1987 the company took a stake in Bunnings, a Western Australian timber company with a small hardware operation, in order to head off a raid by Ron Brierley. Two years later Wesfarmers bought Western Collieries and participated in a bonanza in the eastern-state coal industry. In 1994, under CEO Michael Chaney, Wesfarmers acquired all of Bunnings shares, laying the groundwork for a quick and hugely successful expansion into the eastern states and New Zealand.

Wesfarmers made a bid for Howard Smith's BBC Hardware in 2001. In the ensuing deal the Westralian Farmers' co-operative pedigree was abandoned because, Robert Gottleibsen notes, '...the institutional shareholders of Howard Smith would not have agreed to the takeover offer if [the co-operative] still held the controlling stake'. The giant co-operative company, which for so long had dominated the Western Australian and national agricultural co-operative movement, was no more.[58]

Decline of the Western Australian co-operative movement

The number of co-operatives operating in Western Australia declined in the 1990s to around seventy; twenty of them agricultural and all but two registered under the Companies (Co-operatives) Act. The CFWA, severely impacted by Westralian Farmers' departure, slowly rebuilt, running conferences, providing training and advice services and seeing to amendments to the act in 1994. By the mid-1990s, 95 per cent of co-operatives in the state were affiliated. Adamant that existing legislation was a major advantage to co-operatives in that state and that 'any change in the situation would be hotly contested by our co-operatives', CFWA's role in the nationally uniform co-operatives' legislation debate is discussed in Chapter Fourteen.

Early in the new century, CFWA, now trading as 'Co-operatives WA', had forty eight affiliates, representing approximately 70 percent of the co-operatives and co-operative companies registered in the state in such diverse fields as primary producer services and requisites, newsagents, grain handling, carob growing, dairying, travel, water management and irrigation, lobster, fishing and inland fisheries, taxi services, timber, forestry and milling, packaging, meat, fruit, banana and poultry production, haulage and community services. At time of writing, the state's biggest co-operative company, CBH, which had been investigating possible demutualisation since 1999, contributed $2 billion to the Western Australian economy, from a total $2.75 billion contributed by the overall co-operative movement. Only one co-operative was not registered under the *Companies (Co-operatives) Act*, which still remained partially incompatible with legislation for co-operatives in other states.

United Farmers Co-operative Company Limited

It would be remiss to conclude our discussion of the Western Australian farmer co-operative movement without reference to United Farmers.

In 1992 five Western Australian farmers facing poor commodity prices, increasing farm input prices, concern over the family farm and the loss of farmer competitive advantage in markets contributed $5,000 to form United Farmers Co-operative Company Limited, a fertiliser and chemical products co-operative servicing producers in the grain industry. Within a year the co-operative had 600 members. By the end of the decade it had 3,000 members, had developed a nationwide focus and was widely seen as a dynamic new leader of the Western Australian co-operative movement. United Farmers joined NETCO, a co-operative of co-operatives in the grains industry, which was established to achieve national economies of scale while enabling members to remain responsive to local conditions. NETCO included such interstate co-operatives and co-operative companies as: Capgrains Co-operative Association; Gilgandra Marketing Co-operative; Australian Producers' Co-operative; Shepherds Producers' Co-operative; Mirrool Creek Grain Co-operative; Moulamein Grain Co-operative; Southern Quality Produce; and Walgett Special 1 Co-operative.

Chapter Seven

'Is Anyone Out There?'
THE VICTORIAN CO-OPERATIVE MOVEMENT 1944–2000

Introduction

Because Victoria is the heartland of the Australian dairy industry, much of our discussion on co-operation in that state occurs in the context of dairying, considered in Part I. For much of the twentieth century dairying and co-operation were virtually synonymous in Victoria and if any Australian jurisdiction had the potential to develop a cohesive and powerful co-operative movement built upon the foundations of a great industry it was that state. Melbourne was the political capital of Australia until 1927. For much of the period the headquarters of the Australian Producers' Wholesale Co-operative Federation (APWCF) and the Co-operative Federation of Australia (CFA) were based in Melbourne (discussed in Chapter Two and Chapter Ten, respectively). Yet for of all of this the Victorian co-operative movement failed to achieve anything like its potential. Indeed, after World War II, Rochdale consumer movement leaders unkindly referred to Victoria as the 'weak link in the Australian co-operative chain'.

Leaving aside sectoral divisions between general co-operatives, credit unions and building societies, which were common to each state and territory, the problem for co-operative development in Victoria, historically speaking, was that several huge players were not registered as co-operatives *per se* but as *co-operative companies* under company law. The significance of this is reflected in the fact that for much of the period a handful of co-operative companies accounted for over 90 per cent of Victoria's total general co-operative activity, not including credit unions and building societies. Notwithstanding many common elements, 'genuine' co-operatives tended to dismiss co-operative companies as 'bogus', while the latter tended to characterise the former as ideologically hidebound and unsuited to modern business practice. It was as if the two forms were from different 'planets', and in a sense they were, with 'genuine' co-operatives concerned with a raft of economic and social issues and not averse to government support while co-operative companies were preoccupied with commercial and sectional industry concerns in competitive markets and were often churlish about government intervention. Pragmatically, co-operative companies generally adopted co-operative principles for the taxation benefits so bestowed and the measure of commodity control they conferred, while utilising flexible corporations law for capital-raising purposes, acquiring subsidiaries and forming joint ventures. Though they often shared a common regard for the democracy principle, at a practical level 'genuine' co-operatives and 'quasi' co-operative companies really had very little else in common; especially in the matter of co-operative development. The result, historically speaking, was a splintered, under-developed Victorian co-operative movement, notwithstanding the immense size and market power of some co-operative companies. That this should occur in a state where co-operation was so deeply embedded in a great national dairying industry was a disaster for Victorian and national co-operation. (For more detail, see the Co-operative Federation of Victoria Ltd's Web Site *www.australia.coop*.)

The following discussion considers landmarks in post-World War II Victorian co-operative development, highlighting efforts to unite the movement, divisions between 'genuine' and 'quasi' co-operatives, events which harmed co-operation, the slow development of suitable legislation and a general unwillingness by the sector to unequivocally support co-operative umbrella organisations.

The Victorian Co-operative Association

Over the summer of 1944 W D Johnson of the Co-operative Federation of Western Australia (CFWA) toured Victoria seeking support for the newly formed Co-operative Federation of Australia (CFA) (discussed in Chapter Ten). Johnson was adamant that CFA affiliates should be 'genuine' *bona fide* Rochdale organisations. Not only were 'bogus' agricultural co-operative companies, which flourished in the state, illegitimate and unacceptable, Johnson said, but the Rochdale consumer movement would also refuse to recognise the Christian Co-operative Fellowship (CCF), the Young Christian Workers (YCW) or the Victorian Co-operative League. These tiny, enthusiastic co-operative development organisations, comprising mainly young radical activists, Christian socialists, returned services personnel and idealistic remnants of the pre-war Rochdale movement, were particularly interested in credit unions along Antigonish (Canada) lines and building societies. As far as Rochdale purists were concerned, building societies and credit unions were merely 'capitalistic window dressing'. Instead, Johnson contrived a 'Victorian Co-operative Association' (VCA) from a few Rochdale trading stores operating at Cheltenham, Wonthaggi and elsewhere, anointing this as the 'legitimate' CFA affiliate, eligible for membership of a proposed national co-operative wholesale designed to capture post-war opportunities and launch the Rochdale movement onto a new growth cycle.

As expected, the Melbourne-based APWCF, with which several large Victorian agricultural co-operative companies were affiliated, refused to have anything to do with VCA or CFA. Consequently CFA failed to function in Victoria, prompting New South Wales Co-operative Wholesale Society (NSW CWS) President George Booth to describe the state scornfully as the 'weak link in the Australian co-operative chain'.

With shortages and rationing continuing after the war, however, several Victorian agricultural and rural trading co-operatives did affiliate with NSW CWS to take advantage of a barter-trading arrangement with English CWS, which circumvented rationing. A brief rapprochement with APWCF followed, negotiated by CFWA, and VCA was restructured to permit the affiliation of co-operative companies. As shortages eased and the importance of English CWS trade lessened, however, interest in VCA faded. By 1955 NSW CWS had withdrawn from Victoria and the VCA had fallen apart. Meanwhile, APWCF had seized control of CFA for the licence this gave to British and international trade through the International Co-operative Alliance (ICA).

The Victorian *Co-operation Act* 1953

Responding to lobbying from YCW, the Victorian Co-operative League and credit co-operative and building society advocates, the government began moves in 1949 to formulate discrete co-operatives' legislation. There were then approximately thirty-eight agricultural co-operatives and co-operative companies in Victoria, mainly in the dairy industry, consisting of 20,157 shareholders with £2.5 million of assets, producing an annual turnover of £14.5 million. Only a few of these were registered under the *Industrial and Provident Societies Act* (1876). Most were registered under company law.[1]

It took nearly four years, but in 1953 Minister for Education A E Shepherd introduced into parliament the Victorian *Co-operation Act*, modelled largely on the New South Wales *Co-operation Act* (1923).

Korumburra Dairy factory (1954)
Photo courtesy of Murray Goulburn Co-operative Co. Limited.

In the Cold War hysteria of the time, the bill provoked a storm in the Upper House where the legislation was described absurdly by one politician as 'calculated to set up a Soviet-style society and lead to a Union of Soviet Socialist Societies'. The act made provision for a Co-operatives' Advisory Council and contemplated government guarantees for loans raised by community advancement co-operatives, along the lines of those existing for building societies in New South Wales. Significantly, the legislation enabled co-operatives and co-operative companies registered under other acts either to retain 'co-operative' in their title *or* register under the new law. Not surprisingly, few long-established rural co-operative companies bothered to register under the *Co-operation Act* and only one agricultural co-operative did so. A handful of trading societies, community advancement and credit union co-operatives, however, did use its provisions.

Upon retiring in 1956, Registrar of Co-operative Societies R T Ebbels described the *Co-operation Act* as 'wholly inadequate' and urged state governments to discard states-based laws for co-operatives and frame uniform *federal* co-operatives' legislation. Two years later the act was redrafted, permitting more flexible trade between primary producer and trading co-operatives, but still big co-operative companies ignored the legislation, considering it 'useless'.

The Co-operative Development Society

With building society and credit union activists Ted Long and Bob Maybury to the fore, in February 1961 YCW formed the Co-operative Development Society (CDS) with the object of building new co-operatives and spreading the understanding of co-operative principles. Open to anyone with an interest in co-operative development and with a strong emphasis on education, CDS published the quarterlies *Co-operator* and *Development Bulletin* between 1961 and 1970, developed a library and conducted seminars and education sessions. The society precipitated a brisker registration of co-operatives and by 1970 there were 858 co-operatives in Victoria with 158,715 members, mainly community advancement co-operatives (for schools) enjoying government guarantees for loans raised, but also including seventy primary producer co-operatives and co-operative companies with 40,000 members (not all registered as co-operatives). With rationalisation of the dairy industry in full swing, however, registrations slowed thereafter. By 1983 there were sixty-eight agricultural co-operatives registered under the act, seventeen large co-operative companies in the dairy, fruit and phosphate industries under company law and one co-operative under industrial and provident societies' legislation – only nine more co-operatives and 5,200 more members than there had been thirteen years earlier![2]

Co-operatives Registered Under the Victorian *Co-operation Act*, 1964–1982					
December	1964	1969	1974	1979	1982
Melbourne	4	5	5	8	6
Metropolitan	3	3	2	2	1
Urban – Geelong, Ballarat and Bendigo	2	3	4	4	4
Country	50	58	53	57	56

VICTORIAN CO-OPERATIVE COMPANIES, 1985	ANNUAL TURNOVER $MILLION
Amalgamated Co-operative Marketers (Australia) Limited (ACMAL)	11.9
Ardmona Fruit Producers' Co-operative Company	10.3
Camperdown-Glenormiston Dairy Company	26.8
CIC (Australia)	21.6
Colac Dairy Co-operative Limited	16.2
Ibis Milk Products	43.08
Mildura Co-operative Fruit	12.7
Moe Co-operative Dairy	2.9
Murray-Goulburn Co-operative Limited	39.6
North East Dairy Company	8.8
Phosphate Co-operative Company Australia Limited	101.538
Robinvale Producers' Co-operative	2.7
SPC Limited	15.6
Tatura Milk Products Limited	11.1
Victorian Producers' Co-operative Company	7.8
Warrnambool Cheese and Butter Factory	2.9
TOTAL	335.518

The Co-operative Federation of Victoria

Stimulated by CDS, efforts began to create a more representative co-operative umbrella organisation. Protracted discussions continued through much of the 1960s and finally, in October 1970, the Victorian Federation of Co-operative Housing Societies (VFCHS), the Credit Co-operative Association (CCA), the Victorian Trading Co-operative Association and a few co-operative companies agreed on the terms of an industry association to be known as the Co-operative Federation of Victoria (CFV).

The CFV, which supplanted CDS, was a voluntary association of co-operatives designed to encourage the application of co-operative principles in distribution, marketing, housing, health insurance, credit and other services with a view to co-ordinating the different types of co-operatives and integrating and rationalising co-operative sector resources. The federation ran educational, advisory, advocacy and publishing sections and other services designed to support efficiency and uniformity in the conduct of members' business. Led by John Mason (VFCHS) and Bob Maybury (CCA), CFV affiliated with CFA and, between 1971 and 1974, published *Co-op Digest* (adopted by CFA in 1972 as its official journal), which had a circulation of around 500.

Victorian co-operatives' activist David Griffiths notes four themes in CFV's development over subsequent decades: a mission to achieve improved co-operatives' legislation; an emphasis upon education in retaining ownership and control of co-operatives by members; an ambivalent relationship with government; and an ongoing struggle to attract and retain members.

From the outset the federation was poorly supported. Many co-operatives doubted the need for it. Several co-operative companies looked to industry bodies outside the co-operative movement for representation and support. Rural co-operatives were suspicious of the federation's urban roots. The building society and credit union movements developed independent associations. A few large agricultural co-operative companies did support CFV, however, including the Phosphate Co-operative Company, the Victorian Producers' Co-operative Company and the Murray-Goulburn Co-operative, which were all keen to explore trade opportunities through CFA with the ICA's International Co-operative Trading Organisation (ICTO) as Britain prepared to enter the EEC. Under the aegis of CFA, directed by Bill Rawlinson, CFV and the Co-operative Federation of New South Wales (CFNSW) co-operated in advancing the ICTO strategy (discussed in Chapter Ten).

After ICTO failed to deliver practical results, however, and as 'milk wars' erupted between Victorian and New South Wales dairy farmers over access to fresh-milk markets, this promising collaboration dwindled and with it much of the rationale for CFA and CFV. After CFA's Canberra secretariat was closed, Rawlinson relocated to Melbourne and in 1978 was seconded to CFV as secretary on a part-time basis.

The Co-operative Development Programme

With sector support waning, CFV looked more to government for support in co-operative development initiatives, meeting with some success. When in 1981 the Victorian Department of Employment and Training established a job-creation scheme, the Co-operative Development Programme (CDP), the department made funds available to the federation to run workshops and other activities relating to worker co-operatives.

Soon after the Cain Labor Government took office in April 1982, Bill Rawlinson challenged the new administration through the Co-operatives' Advisory Council to really get behind the co-operative movement and help it realise a greater potential. The CDP, Rawlinson argued, was disproportionately focused on just *one* element of co-operation; worker co-operatives; when there was much more to Victorian co-operation. The co-operative movement was big business in the state, he said, a major player in processing and marketing dairy products and a significant player in herd improvement, fresh and canned fruit-processing and the marketing of fertilisers, livestock, eggs and fish. Yet the public hardly knew anything about co-operatives and both the ministry and registry had very low profiles in government. Many people were looking for a 'middle road between the public and private sectors [but] have a hazy idea of the co-operative way and lack a detailed knowledge of what a co-operative is'. Rawlinson called upon the government to support a major co-operative education initiative and to completely overhaul co-operatives' legislation to include a definition of co-operatives as a 'business or society based on the fundamental values of equity (capital), equality (one-person-one-vote) and mutuality (service for members)'. The existing legislative arrangements for co-operatives and co-operative companies were a mess, Rawlinson argued, tolerating several 'pseudo' co-operatives and the Co-operatives' Advisory Council was completely ineffective. The CFV secretary also called upon the state's co-operatives to get behind the CFV and support it adequately.[3]

By 1984 it was evident that the CDP was dysfunctional. The CFV was concerned about the scheme's bureaucratic control and administrative delays, which were causing cash-flow problems for target co-operatives and hampering operations. Federation personnel, most volunteers or engaged in time-consuming support work for the department for which no on-going practical outcomes were apparent, argued that the CDP should be run by professional business organisers, not bureaucrats.

Co-operative Farmers' and Graziers' Direct Meat Supply

Meanwhile, the inadequacy of Victorian co-operatives' legislation had been painfully demonstrated in an imbroglio involving the Co-operative Farmers' and Graziers' Direct Meat Supply (CFG), which attracted much media attention and reverberated as far the Commonwealth Government Cabinet. CFG, a huge meat processing, distributive and retailing operation, was established in 1950 by Leslie Bett with a view to raising prices for producers, cutting prices to consumers and competing with private-profit enterprise. Registered under the *Co-operation Act*, by March 1960 the co-operative had 1,350 members in Victoria, South Australia and the Riverina. By the mid-1960s it was a pace-setter in the industry, exporting to the United States and Japan, providing exemplary working conditions and enjoying good industrial relations.

In 1967, however, the co-operative recorded a loss of $871,000. After banks stopped payment on the co-operative's cheques, in 1968 the Victorian Dairy Farmers' Association, the Australian Primary Producers' Union, the Victorian Wheat and Woolgrowers' Association and meat industry employees assisted with a capital injection. The co-operative's general manager, L P (Les) Smart, was appointed administrator and given sweeping powers approved by the Supreme Court. Under Smart's rigorous hand the co-operative climbed out of difficulty. The Australian Industry Development Corporation (AIDC) assisted with additional finance, allowing the co-operative to purchase abattoirs at Ballarat and Bendigo. After a severe downturn in meat prices in 1974, however, and strikes, the co-operative was shut down for nine days, occasioning losses in excess of $1 million. The co-operative again approached AIDC for assistance and was refused. Four meat works were closed and 1,300 workers lost their jobs. The popular press attacked co-operatives for 'fooling' workers, being 'slack in administration' and so 'stacked' with cronies that they were 'laughable'.

General Manager Smart advised AIDC to put the co-operative up for sale on the international market because, in his view, producer shareholders were not up to the task of running such a business. He then resigned. AIDC was left to bail out the co-operative. When AIDC accepted a $10.25 million offer from Protean Holdings, however, the co-operative's members revolted,

Washing cream cans at the Maffra dairy factory (date unknown).
Photo courtesy of Murray Goulburn Co-operative Co. Limited.

charging that it was behaving like a 'loan shark' and asserting that CFG was worth three times that amount:

> *Shareholders, politicians, farmers then came out of the woodwork in droves demanding to know why a works operating profitably should be the victim of a forced sale. The farmers feel something very strange and grave has happened and the co-operative is not being given a chance.*

Producers took legal action for which there was no precedent in Australia and Smart entered a counter claim. The Supreme Court stopped the Protcan Holdings takeover bid, pending CFG's ability to raise $9 million in government-guaranteed loans, which was possible under the act. When the Federal (Fraser Coalition) and Victorian (Hamer Liberal) governments agreed to guarantee loans to the co-operative, a media storm erupted:

> *Now it is the Fraser Gravy Train. The government is opening itself to the charge of cavalier dispensation of public funds and the risk of raising the public's suspicion of corrupt dealings.*

Under the headline, 'Co-operative Farmers' and Graziers' leads Hamer and Fraser to Slaughter', the *Primary Industry Newsletter* said that the government must 'believe in miracles putting good money after bad'. A Victorian government inquiry revealed glaring anomalies in the *Co-operation Act*, which was described as 'vague', co-operative rules were described as wholly inadequate and the Registry of Co-operative Societies was '…simply not equipped to cope'.

Details of the co-operative's long and painful demise fall outside the ambit of our discussion. Suffice it to say that the crash was the biggest company collapse in Victoria for many years, Smart was imprisoned and the controversy tarnished co-operation's credentials in Victoria at precisely a time when CFA and CFV were attempting to build bridges to the Fraser and Hamer governments on numerous issues including ICTO, a co-operative bank, a farmers' co-operative service in the Department of Primary Industry and uniform national co-operatives' legislation, none of which eventuated.[4]

The Act is rewritten

In the wake of the CFG scandal the Hamer government moved to tighten and clarify the administration of co-operatives. The *Co-operation Act* was again comprehensively rewritten in 1981, clarifying rules for primary producer, trading, community advancement and community settlement co-operatives, credit unions and associations and federations of co-operatives. A prohibition was placed on usage of the word 'co-operative' in the title of a registered co-operative or society formed *after* 1953 which was incorporated under legislation other than the *Co-operation Act*. At least sixteen co-operative companies formed before that date and regulated by company law, however, were free to continue using 'co-operative' in their names. The redrafted act drew within its jurisdiction about fifty small to medium-sized co-operatives, involving over 45,000 shareholders, but did nothing to promote co-operative unity or release resources for co-operative development or education, issues which were seen as the responsibility of the co-operative movement.

Responses to the 1981 amendments were contrastive with some critics describing them as 'restrictive', 'excessively regulatory', 'legalistic and suffocating', on the one hand, or 'vague', 'loose' and allowing co-operation to 'wallow aimlessly' while tolerating 'pseudo-co-operatives', on the other. Most critics agreed, however, that the Registry of Co-operative Societies had become hidebound by regulation and seemed to exist more for protecting organisational forms and imposing penalties than providing a flexible framework encouraging co-operative development. CFV officials believed that co-operatives were now in real danger of losing a distinctive identity and a public profile in Victoria and were being 'hacked into pieces' by a plethora of legislation, which now included the *Co-operation Act*, the *Companies Code*, the *Industrial and Provident Societies Act*, the *Co-operative Housing Societies Act* and the *Associations Incorporation Act* (1981).[5]

The Ministerial Advisory Committee on Co-operation (MACC) 1984

The Cain Labor Government responded by establishing the Ministerial Advisory Committee on Co-operation (MACC) in February 1984, within the Ministry for Housing, substantially supported by the Minister for Employment and Training, which hosted the CDP. MACC's brief, focused on a possible role for government in co-operative development, was to review the *Co-operation Act* and identify suitable strategies for developing the co-operative sector ('movement' was now hardly ever used). Of the committee's ten members, only three came from the co-operative sector – from CFV and the credit union movement. Nevertheless, MACC personnel made important contributions to Victorian co-operative development over the ensuing years, including CFV activists Tony Gill and David Griffiths, and Race Mathews, a former Whitlam Labor Government Parliamentary Secretary to the Prime Minister and then Minister for the Arts and Minister for Police and Emergency Services in the Cain government.

In December 1984 Bill Rawlinson retired from CFV, having earlier resigned as CFA secretary in June 1983. Tony Miller became CFV Executive Officer.

MACC's terms of reference sought to determine the degree to which co-operative philosophy and principles were embodied in different forms of co-operatives and co-operative companies operating in Victoria and how co-operative development might coincide with government priorities in employment, worker rights, work-place democracy and occupational health and safety. The committee consulted widely with the Victorian co-operative movement, organised a major Co-operatives' Seminar in Melbourne, which attracted over 500 people, engaged in overseas and interstate fact-finding missions and established consultative working parties for legislation, education and training, finance and to examine the asymmetrical physical development and fragmented nature of the Victorian movement.

In July 1986 MACC released a well-presented report which included thirteen pages of recommendations – sixty-three in all. Couched in intense, advocatory language the report noted that only just over half of the 2,714 co-operatives with 736,000 members operating in Victoria (including building societies and credit unions) were registered under the *Co-operation Act*. While seventy-nine agricultural co-operatives with 45,000 members were registered under the act, twenty-nine rural co-operatives holding $13 million in assets remained under the *Industrial and Provident Societies Act* and sixteen major agricultural co-operative companies with assets of $726 million (including subsidiaries) operated under the *Companies Code*.

A close reading of the MACC Report suggests that there were deep ideological differences between working parties established for the farmer co-operative companies and urban co-operatives, respectively. Paraphrasing these, the Primary Producer Working Party:

❖ emphasised individual action and self-help;

❖ sought variations to the one-person-one-vote principle to allow a system of democratic membership that was not 'a disincentive to raising equity share capital [such as] a limited proportional voting system';

❖ demanded the inclusion of a definition of 'co-operative company' in any proposed legislation;

❖ was divided on the inclusion of ICA principles;

❖ sought strengthened directors' powers (not greater registry power);

❖ suggested the periodic revaluation of co-operative assets to reflect inflation;

❖ recommended an equitable bonus share system including variations to existing surplus distribution provisions to include the buy-back of shares in order to rid co-operatives of 'dry' shareholders; and

❖ opposed direct government financial assistance, recommending that this should be confined to loans and government guarantees via the registry.

The Worker Co-operative Working Party, on the other hand, emphasised:

❖ collective action;

❖ strict observance of one-person-one-vote democracy principle; and

❖ direct government help for co-operative development.

The report was almost silent on the subject of co-operative companies, saying only that their 'specific sector requirements' were inconsistent with the committee's remit and recommendations, especially with regard to variations to the democracy principle, which MACC would not countenance, and also with regard to public share-raising, low minimum membership and taxation.[6]

The report was the most comprehensive analysis of co-operatives completed to that time in Australia and was a genuine attempt to construct productive bridges between government and co-operatives. Noting the uneven physical development of the Victorian co-operative movement, consisting of a few agricultural giants of 'uncertain' co-operative credentials and a swarm of minnows performing multitudinous functions, and emphasising differences between co-operatives, private-profit enterprise and government agencies, MACC urged the Cain government to:

> ...*encourage, befriend and occasionally directly assist co-operatives consistent with their autonomy principle in developing a comprehensive integrated Victorian co-operative movement by the year 2000.*

The report called upon the government to regard co-operatives, not as just another form of small business in which co-operative principles were seen by some as a *hindrance*, but the embodiment of a noble philosophy – an exemplar of economic democracy– and posited four options for the government in developing co-operatives:

❖ do nothing, and provide simply a facilitative legislative framework;

❖ take an active interest in co-operatives without domination;

❖ directly organise and control a co-operative movement; or

❖ positively discriminate in favour of co-operatives.

The report argued that the lopsided physical development of Victorian co-operatives meant that each sector had different support requirements and that a practical role for government lay in assisting the development of sector associations. Some co-operative sectors, for example worker co-operatives, required direct government financial inputs, whereas many larger primary producer co-operatives, given to principles of autonomy and self-help, would not welcome this. MACC called upon the government to issue a statement of support for the co-operative movement and to urgently integrate and co-ordinate the existing fragmented administrative framework for co-operatives. In arguing that co-operatives should be more accountable to government, the report recommended the formation of a completely new Co-operatives' Council empowered to advise the government on co-operative development, the creation of a Co-operative Development Unit in the Department of Labour and a ministerial portfolio directing an Office of Co-operatives, established to co-ordinate co-operative development. New, flexible legislation was a priority, allowing for the inclusion of co-operative principles:

> ...*a deregulatory, enabling instrument with appropriate prudential standards and accountability provisions, defining a co-operative as a group of people who voluntarily come together on a basis of equality, self-help and mutual aid with the purpose of promoting their socio-economic well-being in a democratic manner while adhering to the principles of co-operation incorporated within the act.*

The MACC Report also called for a Co-operative Education and Training Authority to develop curriculum for co-operatives' education and stimulate informed public debate. Credit co-operatives should be encouraged to become financial brokers for the co-operative movement. For larger wholesale loans, however, the co-operative movement as a whole should investigate the setting up of a national financial facility, separate from credit co-operatives – a co-operative bank. It was vital that co-operatives and trade unions should re-establish a healthy dialogue. The co-operative movement needed to unify, establish sector associations delivering appropriate services and representation for the movement and never, ever subordinate ethical ideas to business techniques, for then 'the movement has no basic satisfactory reason for its existence'.

Incandescent with enthusiasm, the MACC Report, if acted upon could have formed the basis of a cohesive, purposeful co-operative movement in Victoria. Little of ongoing practical benefit issued from it, however. The Victorian Attorney-General's Department did conduct a review of the *Co-operation Act*, noting with some concern how co-operative companies were structured to qualify for taxation benefits and how difficult it was to monitor their actions. A Co-operative Development Unit (CDU) was set up within the Victorian Registry of Co-operatives in 1986 with six staff, consolidating co-operative development resources, but it did not last long.[7]

David Griffiths later described the MACC process as:

> *A frustrating experience...bogged down in ideological battles and administrative inertia, despite the earnest attempts of CFV to build a practical and supportive government approach to co-operatives. The time and effort directed towards MACC by CFV has been at the cost of direct member contact and services...MACC lingered on until May 1992 but neither its report nor its recommendations influenced government decision-making and its existence finally ended with [a] state election.*[8]

Indeed, the time-consuming involvement of CFV personnel in the MACC process meant that the immediate needs of federation members were unavoidably neglected. An affiliate reaction began and CFV membership plunged.

The Victorian Division of the Australian Association of Co-operatives

After the Co-operative Federation of New South Wales (CFNSW) resigned from the CFA in 1986 and withdrew secretariat support, announcing plans for an Australian Association of Co-operatives (AAC) (discussed in Chapter Twelve), CFV was undecided about what to do. Concerned about falling membership, the lack of progress and a work burden falling on a few shoulders, the federation actually considered closing down altogether. After Tony Miller resigned as executive officer, CFV personnel met AAC officers and in December 1987 suspended the federation's operations and established a Victorian Division of the AAC in May 1988. In January the following year Tony Gill became CFV secretary and executive officer. Only twenty-seven CFV affiliates which were still operating made the transition to AAC. Over the next five years, however, the Victorian division arrested the decline in affiliation and improved relations with the government and departments in a determined bid to formulate radically new legislation for Victorian co-operatives (which, by 1993, numbered 1,300 with 235,000 members, excluding credit unions and co-operative companies).[9]

The Victorian Co-operatives Bill 1999

Tony Gill and colleagues prepared a detailed submission for the government and, in July 1989, a draft Co-operatives Bill, which drew upon MACC recommendations, a review of the New South Wales *Co-operation Act* and contributions from major co-operative companies, was released for public comment. The draft bill proposed:

- ❖ a *single* type of primary co-operative rather than the seven co-operative types which currently existed;
- ❖ a minimum membership of three persons, including 'natural persons' (corporate bodies);
- ❖ an easier formation process;
- ❖ different classes of shares;
- ❖ bonus shares;
- ❖ proxy voting;

❖ the removal of upper limits on the number of directors permissible on a co-operative board;

❖ flexible decision-making rules;

❖ active membership provisions;

❖ improved accounting and auditing requirements;

❖ restrictions on the sale of co-operative assets;

❖ limits on a maximum shareholding to 20 per cent;

❖ strengthening the registry's discretionary powers;

❖ a new schedule of penalties for non-compliance; and

❖ a new Co-operatives' Council to advise the Attorney-General on co-operative matters.

An important purpose of the proposed legislation was to include co-operative companies within its jurisdiction while exempting them from compliance with the act's provisions for up to five years and permitting 'long-term flexibility to restructure'. The bill's authors also hoped that the bill would become a template for nationally uniform co-operatives' legislation, '...a legislative framework that will enable the co-operative movement to be a strong viable third sector'.

The draft bill passed through an extensive consultative process. Supporters argued that the proposed legislation would bring a proper balance of flexibility and prudential discipline to co-operatives, would help to fend off corporate raiders, expel 'dry' shareholders and open up innovative fund-raising options without surrendering control to investors. Detractors complained that it did not go far enough, would do nothing to help co-operatives become a genuine third sector capable of competing equally with companies and multinational co-operatives, and would not facilitate self-management and self-regulation by co-operatives:

> ...if the government is serious about advancing the cause and benefits of co-operatives, it must recognise that co-operatives need to be given full corporate powers with minimum interference from government.

Other critics claimed that the bill went *too far* and was essentially protectionist and re-regulatory in spirit in a rapidly deregulating, free-trade, global economy. There were also old complaints about the bill's alleged 'socialist' complexion which, some said, insisted upon promoting co-operation as the antithesis of capitalism and an improvement to it. Finally, the Victorian Division of the AAC recommended eighty-six amendments to the exposure bill.

Heavily amended, the Victorian Co-operatives Bill was introduced into parliament for a second reading in March 1990. The timing was terrible. An Australian-wide economic recession was affecting Victoria more than other states and rates of unemployment, bad debts and bankruptcies were high. With rumours circulating about the solvency of some non-bank financial institutions (NBFI), including credit unions and building societies, in June 1990 the Geelong-based Pyramid Building Society (Farrow Group) collapsed, precipitating a run on deposits. A few other NBFI collapsed or were forcibly merged, including the Bendigo-based North West County Co-operative, the Moe Credit Union and the Bentmore Credit Union in the south-east of Melbourne. The Pyramid collapse in particular, which caused hardship for thousands of people around Australia, was widely reported in the media and gave rise to public and government alarm about a perceived slackness in NBFI administration. The government began an intensive review of regulatory arrangements for NBFI and kindred organisations, focused on prudential arrangements and capital adequacy. This was not an ideal time to be introducing new legislation for co-operatives into parliament.

The Co-operatives Bill was withdrawn for amendment in December 1990, particularly with regard to including stronger prudential and regulatory controls, and lay suspended in events surrounding the invention of new national prudential arrangements for NBFI (the Australian Financial Institutions Commission [AFIC]), details of which fall outside our brief. Suffice it to say a concerned Victorian government urgently commissioned consultants to report and they recommended draconian draft legislation to tighten controls. The report noted that the Registry of Co-operative Societies had forty-eight staff to administer 250 NBFI *plus* over a thousand general co-operative societies. It was impossible with such inadequate resources to effectively administer this large and diverse clientele, particularly with constant staff changes, a short average tenure of employment in the registry and an appalling lack of bureaucratic knowledge and experience in the field. Staff resources were wholly inadequate to provide a suitable quality of prudential regulation ensuring that deposits with institutions were safe. The report recommended *inter alia* in respect of NBFI: a ban on commercial lending; tighter prudential controls; closer supervision; increased reserves held by NBFI; and separate registries for NBFI and general co-operatives. The Victorian Credit Co-operatives Association (VCCA), the Australian Federation of Credit Union Leagues (AFCUL) and Labor Minister Race Mathews opposed many of the recommendations arguing that they struck at the heart of NBFI autonomy. The issue bogged down in Labor Caucus Committees, dragging the draft Co-operatives Bill into a political mire. Meanwhile, the press continued to speculate on 'risky' NBFI and kindred organisations, such as co-operatives.

Two further attempts were made to reintroduce the amended Co-operatives Bill (one in August 1992) but these were derailed, first by objections to the alleged regulatory 'overreaction' to NBFI failures, second by the government's wish to postpone action while passage of the New South Wales Co-operatives Bill was observed, third by Premier John Cain's resignation and replacement by Joan Kirner, and finally by the dissolution of parliament and election of the Kennett Coalition in late 1992.

There the draft bill lay marooned for years as protracted talks continued between state regulators exploring the possibility of national uniform co-operatives' legislation based on the New South Wales *Co-operatives Act* (discussed in Chapters Nine and Fourteen). In the light of these inconclusive discussions, and difficulties some jurisdictions had with accepting the New South Wales act, the Kennett government decided to draft a completely *new* Co-operatives Bill. The Co-operative Development Unit was closed down and its resources and functions were absorbed by other sections of the registry, with more staff redeployed to NBFI administrative duties. In January 1993 the AAC received a commitment from Attorney-General Jan Wade that the government would proceed with new co-operatives' legislation. Again, the timing was dreadful because in March that year AAC went into voluntary liquidation! (Discussed in Chapter Twelve.)[10]

The Co-operative Federation of Victoria is reactivated

In May 1993 the former AAC Victorian Division Chairman John Gill (Victorian Producers' Co-operative Company [VCP]) (no relation to Tony Gill) convened a Future Directions Forum for Victorian Co-operatives. From this meeting the Co-operative Federation of Victoria (CFV) was reactivated in July, chaired by Brian MacIntosh (Gippsland Tip-Truck Co-operative) and later by John Gill. The reconstituted CFV had a simple objective: 'to develop and promote the co-operative movement as a means of satisfying the economic and social needs of people'. Tony Gill was engaged part-time as secretary, operating on a tiny budget, often subsidised by unpaid work, and supported administratively by VPC and Phosphate Co-operative Company.

In December 1993 the federation met to discuss the proposed new co-operatives' legislation. CFV was focused on legislative reform but the federation also introduced new taxation and insurance services, affiliated with the 'National Co-operative Council' (a forerunner of the Co-operatives Council of Australia [CCA]) (discussed in Chapter Twelve), published *Victorian Co-operative News* and later helped establish a Co-operative Opportunities Project led by Vern Hughes, which was established to explore new possibilities for co-operatives in electricity, health and local government. Again, support from the sector was poor, with only fourteen co-operatives and co-operative companies previously associated with CFV initially affiliating; many former affiliates having ceased trading or dissolving in the previous six years. Only the federation's legislation agenda was able to proceed with any confidence and only after the federation had convinced the government that CFV was indeed the legitimate voice of Victorian co-operatives.

Over the next few years, CFV membership grew steadily. Approximately sixty eight co-operatives and co-operative companies affiliated in the six years to 1999 from diverse trading and non-trading co-operative backgrounds including agriculture, forestry, child care, housing, health, retail and group purchase, broadcasting, water supply and transport. By September 1999 CFV had eighty four members and had formed alliances with providers of education and training, legal, insurance, taxation and business services and provided a telephone hotline and lobbying service. The federation arranged meetings, seminars and itineraries for overseas visitors, conducted training, prepared submissions to inquiries and departmental reviews, represented co-operatives on committees, produced educational materials and assisted the government in developing and implementing new co-operatives legislation (discussed below), which subsequently became a model for Australia.

The Victorian *Co-operatives Act* 1997

In May 1994 the Kennett Government invited CFV to review the New South Wales *Co-operatives Act*. The federation recommended fifty changes! Late in 1995 the government formally committed to new co-operatives' legislation, drawing on the New South Wales act and recommendations made by the Standing Committee of Attorneys-General Working Party (SCAGWP) and Ministerial Council for Corporations (MINCO) (discussed in Chapter Fourteen). In January 1996 a draft co-operatives bill was authored by a four-person team, appointed by the attorney-general, which included Tony Gill. In April Attorney-General Wade appointed an officer to achieve inter-governmental support for the bill and in July an exposure bill was released to federal, state and territory governments.

Wade introduced the Victorian Co-operatives Bill for a second reading in October 1996 'with pride', she said, because it was '...a milestone in Australian Corporations Law...a triumph', which enjoyed cross-party support. Commenting upon how the New South Wales act had failed to win widespread support and how earlier Victorian attempts to develop co-operatives' legislation had fallen foul of 'philosophical differences within the parliamentary [Labor] party', the attorney-general noted that there were now 1,026 co-operatives registered in Victoria; forty-seven had registered in the previous year alone; and that most of these were community advancement and trading co-operatives. Remarking on the prominent role co-operatives played in the Victorian dairying, tobacco, egg, fishing and irrigation industries, Wade was optimistic about the future development of co-operatives in Victoria, and pointed specifically to provisions in the bill designed to overcome limitations to cross-border trade. The bill, which repealed the 1981 *Co-operation Act* and Part 6 of the 1983 *Housing Act*, incorporated the best features of New South Wales legislation, which also had been enacted by a conservative government, Wade remarked, and included new initiatives:

- ❖ allowing any 'natural person' to form a co-operative;
- ❖ giving co-operatives wider corporate powers;
- ❖ removing *ultra vires* limits on a co-operative's objectives;
- ❖ enshrining active member provisions as a bulwark against hostile takeovers;
- ❖ requiring co-operative operational standards similar to those of corporations;
- ❖ presenting co-operatives with a wider range of capital-raising options;
- ❖ permitting co-operatives to appoint external directors (one-third of a board); and
- ❖ freeing up merger, transfer of engagement and sale provisions between Victorian co-operatives.

While granting co-operatives greater commercial flexibility, Wade continued, the bill also strengthened the registry's inspection powers. The attorney-general noted with pride how the bill embodied national Core Consistent Provisions (CCP), as requested by the Commonwealth Government, to allow a roll-back of Corporations Law permitting co-operatives to operate fully under state and territory legislation (discussed in Chapter Fourteen), adding that she felt certain the bill would become a base document for a nationally uniform scheme of co-operatives' legislation, with Victoria 'the lead state'. The bill also included recently revised ICA co-operative principles, including 'concern for community' (discussed in the Preface), and contemplated:

- ❖ two simple categories of co-operatives: trading (return on capital); and non-trading (non-return on capital, which could operate with or without share capital);
- ❖ beneficial and non-beneficial shares for purposes of disclosure; and
- ❖ shares in trading co-operatives to be held by members only (which helped simplify the Co-operatives-Corporations Law interface and aided the CCP process).

As for the democracy principle, voting remained strictly on a one-person-one-vote basis with a simple majority for ordinary resolutions, a two-third majority for special resolutions and 75 per cent of actual votes for certain special resolutions. Wade noted that the bill had deliberately excluded New South Wales provisions for Co-operative Capital Units (CCUs), because, she said, they complicated the CCP scheme. The Victorian legislation relied instead upon subordinated debt.

Debating the bill Mr Pandazopoulos (Labor, Dandenong) spoke of the close links which he believed existed between his party and the co-operative movement and how Race Mathews had earlier championed the co-operative cause in parliament. He referred to the twenty-nine Aboriginal co-operatives which existed in the state and to new co-operatives in the egg, tobacco, pea, timber, electricity, rental housing and irrigation industries. Mr Carli (Labor, Coburg), describing the previous legislation as prohibitively restrictive, also spoke of the strong relationship which, he said, existed between his party and the co-operative movement, asserting that the bill actually emerged from this tradition and arguing that co-operatives could triumph in a deregulated environment, creating a viable 'third sector'.

> *...while we often think of democracy as being time-consuming and wasteful, co-ops are actually more productive. Whatever you consume in a democratic process you gain in terms of a greater, more productive, more inclusive workplace. The economic participation of shareholding and equality of voting are also important...It doesn't matter what your capital is, you have the same vote: that is fundamental.... [Co-operatives] in tackling the distortions...of the market, allow for a response from ordinary people...Although political ideologies may be different, the belief in co-operation is the same...I commend the bill...[which] may become important legislation in renewing Australia's interest in co-operation in the economics of civil life.*

The bill becomes a national template

With most large Victorian co-operative companies regulated under company law, unlike the situation in New South Wales where they were registered under co-operatives' law, the Victorian *Co-operatives Act* was not so powerfully influenced by the concerns of beleaguered farmer co-operatives as the New South Wales *Co-operatives Act* of 1993 had been. Consequently, Tony Gill believes, Victorian legislation was less prescriptive than in New South Wales and avoided much of its 'bureaucracy', particularly the centrally-driven Co-operatives' Council. Essentially, Gill believes, the Victorian legislation devolved more on the notion of stiffer penalties with less regulation and government intrusion than its northern equivalent. Certainly the act was a strong contender for national CCP legislation, quickly finding support in South Australia, Queensland and the Northern Territory. Even New South Wales incorporated Victorian improvements and CCP provisions in amending legislation in 1997 (discussed in Chapter Nine).[11]

Co-operatives decline

Finally, after decades of abortive efforts and false starts, Victoria possessed comprehensive, well-framed legislation for trading and non-trading co-operatives. The CFV conducted numerous educational seminars explaining and promoting the act and supported the Co-operatives Investigation Services Section, set up under the act, in efforts to rationalise and reorganise the splintered co-operative movement. This met with only limited success. Despite the improved legislation and a few positive signs, including the formation of new co-operatives in niche markets for agricultural products, natural fibres, organic horticulture and energy, co-operatives were dwindling in Victoria. In the four years to 2000 the number of Victorian co-operatives registered under the act fell from 1,026 to 883. Many co-operatives (168) had still not registered and faced possible legal action. As seriously, more formative groups were choosing alternative structures, especially incorporated associations. For instance, the Victoria Department of Human Resources, investigating collaborative options for the delivery of health services, actually recommended *against* co-operatives, describing them as complicated, slow and unwieldy with decisions made on a collective rather than a corporate basis, unsuited to rational management in a competitive tendering environment and ultimately leading to a loss of independence of agencies.

The Monash University Agribusiness Seminars

The CFV also helped to develop the Australian Agribusiness Research Centre in the School of Marketing at Monash University, which became an important forum for integrating the agricultural co-operative sector (including co-operative companies) with agribusiness. Led by Director Dr Lawrie Dooley and Executive Officer Michael O'Keefe, the centre developed executive training programmes, conducted and commissioned research, provided a consultancy and led tours to North America and Asia between 1993 and 1998, which exposed Australian co-operative leaders to overseas innovations and helped develop links with The Netherlands Co-operative Bank (Rabobank). Supported by CFV with Commonwealth Government funding made available through the Rural Industry Development Corporation (RIDC), Monash University began a series of annual agribusiness co-operative director seminars, initially emphasising capital-raising and structural issues. This quickly developed into a prestigious forum for national and international debate on practical issues affecting agricultural co-operatives and co-operative companies and a source of practical information and knowledge-sharing.

National Co-op Update

Supported by CFV and with New South Wales Co-operative Development Branch (CDB) (discussed in Chapter Nine) assistance, *National Co-op Update* (*NCU*), a pithy, practical overview of Australian and overseas co-operative developments, was launched in Victoria in 1995, edited by Chris Greenwood, a journalist with experience in the dairy industry. Until the newsletter ceased publication in 2002, another victim of co-operative apathy, NCU served as the only national publication devoted to news of the co-operative movement in Australia, providing a forum for the exchange of views, information exchange and going some way toward filling the void in national co-operatives' communication left by the absence of an effective third-tier organisation.

Co-operative Development Services Ltd

Again, CFV fell upon hard times with some large affiliates leaving the movement or disaffiliating, dissatisfied with the federation's services. After leaving CFV, Tony Gill formed Co-operative Development Services Ltd (CDS), described as a practical hands-on 'grass roots' co-operatives' formation and advisory service working in the field with new and potential rural co-operatives, defending the co-operative business model and critiquing social-economy theorists who would reduce co-operatives to 'vintage class'. CDS worked with formative co-operatives and produced a useful internet guide to Australian co-operatives.

Mutuality Australia

In 1999 Vern Hughes, who had earlier been associated with CFV in promoting co-operatives for electricity, forestry, health and local government services delivery through the Co-operative Opportunities Project, convened Mutuality Australia. This Melbourne-based 'think tank', formed in a Christian-Socialist mould with links to the Fabian Society, with which Race Mathews was associated, brought together diverse public interest groups motivated by a desire to improve current social structures, compensate for a centralisation of economic power and mitigate the shortcomings of markets and political processes. It sought to inform public debate on mutuality, the social economy and such ideas as civil society, social capital, social entrepreneurship, social partnerships and ethical investment. Mutuality Australia looked for inspiration to the Canadian Antigonish Co-operative Movement and the Mondragon Co-operative Movement in the Basque Region of Spain and sought to 'build community, co-operation and civil society' by tapping into 'networks' and 'partnerships'. In a vision which drew upon British New Labor's 'Third Way', co-operatives were seen as but one type of business model functioning alongside local organisations, voluntary associations, philanthropic bodies, clubs, church congregations, neighbourhood groups and other not-for-profit organisations; part of a 'third sector' seeking new solutions and alternatives to the problems of big government, economic rationalism, unemployment, powerlessness, social fragmentation, social exclusion, managerialism and a loss of a sense of community. Mutuality Australia interpreted 'co-operation' generically as an abstract noun – an impulse to work together – rather than something intrinsic to co-operative structure theoretically released by observing certain principles. The group's social-theorist architects, while referring to the co-operative model, deliberately broke free of structural confines in seeking something less constrictive, more amenable to spontaneity and suitable for bringing together fluid networks of people, communities and institutions, for which the co-operative option, as it was currently configured in Australia, seemed poorly suited. Emphasising 'relationships' between government, industry and community sectors, which would 'empower stakeholders' through active participation in enterprises integrating social and economic objectives, Mutuality Australia resisted the 'demutualisation syndrome' then sweeping through the not-for-profit sector (discussed in Chapter Thirteen), demanding a top level public inquiry to arrest this 'piracy' of mutual assets. Consistent with earlier MACC recommendations, Race Mathews and supporters sought to build links between the credit union movement and regional mutual institutions, seeking to harness savings for deployment in local investment and the aggregation of local purchasing power. There was still little interest in the credit union movement. A well-attended Social Entrepreneurs' Conference, brimming with optimism, was convened by Mutuality Australia in Sydney in November 1999. This tapped an enormous reservoir of community good will but produced little in the way of practical results.

Distributism and Social Enterprise Partnerships

Some of Mutuality Australia's ideas were reflected, however, in *Mutualism: A Third Way for Australia*, authored by Federal Labor Parliamentarian and later briefly Leader of the Opposition, Mark Latham, who argued *inter alia* that many big, established co-operatives had become institutionalised and had lost their true identity, particularly the characteristic of participatory governance, and had become private-sector hierarchies by another name, rarely fostering mutual ideals. Co-operatives needed to be rejuvenated so that they might once more 'practice social mutualism [and] economic distributism' (a political philosophy minted in Victorian and Edwardian Britain holding that the ownership of the means of production, distribution and exchange should be as widespread as possible). In *Jobs of Our Own: Building a Stakeholder Society*, Race Mathews put the case for distributism as an alternative to the market and the state and realisable through mutual assurance societies, building societies, credit unions and co-operatives.

Vern Hughes went on from Mutuality Australia to create Social Enterprise Partnerships (SEP), a network-co-ordinating bureau designed to support the development of a 'third sphere'. Hughes believed that, while markets and governments played vital roles in Australian life, by themselves, they were incapable of creating vital, inclusive and prosperous communities and required a:

> ...*third sphere of initiative-taking and relationship-forming activity to interact with strong civil society in which people; as individuals, families, communities, associations and businesses; interact to form partnerships and generate ventures to achieve social purposes.*

'Is anyone out there?

With more co-operatives exiting the co-operative movement, CFV membership continued to decline. As in the mid 1980s, the federation again became critically concerned about a lack of member involvement and dissatisfaction with services. This identity crisis was symbolised in practical form by a poorly attended 'Future Directions' workshop in 2000, which lasted all of three hours and posed more questions than it provided answers. In a *Victorian Co-operative News* article published later in the year CFV Executive Officer Graham Charles raised serious doubts about the federation's future and asked if anybody was really concerned. 'Is any one out there?' he implored.

> *The CFV survives at time of writing, however, and, in 2002, launched www.australia.coop, reported to be the first coop country portal in the world, providing useful information and conducting a lively debate and news service for co-operatives, a commendable achievement, albeit in virtual reality.[12]*

Chapter Eight

A Movement Adrift:
NEW SOUTH WALES CO-OPERATIVE DEVELOPMENT 1944–C1987

Introduction

In the more than forty years to the mid-1980s the New South Wales general co-operative movement drifted, indifferently supporting peak bodies and impacted upon by dramatic changes in the mainstream economy. After a promising start, by the end of the period agricultural co-operatives were more agents for the delivery of government economic and social programmes than part of an autonomous movement with a distinctive identity. Co-operatives remained divided on a raft of issues, including co-operative principles, federal support, uniform national legislation and capitalisation.

The following discussion traces key moments in this meandering progression including the rise and fall of the New South Wales Co-operative Institute, the creation of a ministry for co-operatives, increasing government involvement, legislative reforms and the emergence of the Co-operative Federation of New South Wales (CFNSW) and the Australian Association of Co-operatives (AAC). Some material unavoidably echoes *A Middle Way: Rochdale Co-operatives in New South Wales, 1859-1986*; where the paths of consumer co-operatives and agricultural co-operatives intersect.

A Co-operative 'New Order': The New South Wales Co-operative Institute

Four months after the Co-operative Federation of Australia (CFA) was formed in Canberra, in March 1944 (discussed in Chapter Ten), New South Wales Registrar of Co-operative Societies Alf Sheldon sought to galvanise the co-operative movement for the creation of a 'New Order' following the war, flagging changes to the *Co-operation Act*, which, he believed, 'sectionalised co-operation', complicated co-operatives' operations and limited the role they could play in the broader economy. Priorities in co-operative development, Sheldon said, were federal co-operatives' legislation and a national co-operative tribunal with binding powers in determining policies:

> The time is rapidly approaching when the co-operative movement in Australia will face the parting of the ways. One way will lead to a proper appreciation of the part it is capable of playing in post-war years. The other part will lead to its relegation to a very minor place in the social and economic life of the state. It will rest largely with the co-operative movement…as to what role it will take.
>
> In the past the co-operative movement has been satisfied to develop unobtrusively by a process of evolution. In fact it, too, "Like Topsy, just growed". Stark Necessity was its strongest motivation. It was regarded by capitalistic interests in the nature of a poor relative – to be patronised and even encouraged when it could serve a useful purpose in a sphere unprofitable to those worshipping at the shrine of private profit…In certain states half-hearted attempts have been made by governments to make proper use of co-operative methods. The press has given faint praise from time-to-time [because] the principal newspapers are the products of either the capitalistic or non-capitalistic interests [in the Labour Movement] which have regarded co-operatives with a degree of suspicion as being a potential rival political force.

The co-operative movement in Australia must wake up and become a real live power. It must not regard itself as an adjunct or supplementary to some other economic philosophy. It is a philosophy in itself. It must think beyond making butter, selling groceries or providing homes. It must regard itself as one positive force that can claim to eliminate the weaknesses and evils both of the extreme capitalistic state and also of the extreme socialised state. It can and does use the best points of each. It is the one economic and social theory that is completely reconcilable with the professed basis of the New Order.[1]

Assisted by Sheldon's department, in June 1944 the New South Wales Rochdale consumer movement convened a Centenary Co-operative Congress in Sydney to commemorate a century of Rochdale co-operation. This brought together unionists, all sections of the co-operative movement, English Co-operative Wholesale Society (CWS) representatives and government officials. The most notable feature, however, was the lack of agreement on the scope or purpose of a post-war co-operative 'New Order'.

In September Sheldon convened another Co-operative Round Table Conference where a provisional committee of a 'New South Wales Co-operative Institute' was formed. Sheldon's hope was that this would affiliate with the newly formed CFA as New South Wales' official member. The institute drew on a wide spectrum of co-operative opinion, including dairy, vegetable, potato, fruit, grazing, community advancement and marketing co-operatives, building societies, English CWS, the New South Wales Co-operative Wholesale Society (NSW CWS), Christian pioneers of the fledgling credit union movement, government officials and media figures.

Sheldon appealed to co-operators to work together through the Co-operative Institute to achieve unity and drive co-operative development at a *national* level:

Co-operation cannot continue as in the past to be an expedient to fill in the gaps in our economy and social set-up, in effect the recipient of crumbs from the rich man's table...Co-operation must be the major segment or it will cease to count at all. No one will do it for us. We must put our house in order and present a united front. It is idle to think that there will not be conflict, but whilst the movement dissipates its strength in pursuing these differences and...conflicts instead of composing and reconciling them, it will get nowhere...If we adopt the defeatist attitude that the producers and consumers will never get together we might as well right now abandon any hope of playing an important part in post-war affairs...The Co-operative Institute marks a red letter day in the history of Australian co-operation. All co-operative units should support it however successful their activities. We [the registry] have been accused of not being co-operative...but this is only because we have not been able to engage ourselves more completely in the wider co-operative movement. The institute must not be sectional.

Still, the co-operators could not agree. The Rochdale consumer movement, for example, wanted a co-operative bank on the English CWS model. Farmer co-operatives were divided, some seeking a financial institution on the (German) Raiffeisen model while others were content with existing institutions. Rural co-operatives were united, however, in their opposition to an English CWS-NSW CWS proposal for a new co-operative insurance society to rival the farmer-sponsored Co-operative Insurance Company (Australia) (CIC). *Everyone* agreed that co-operative education was important but few were prepared to invest in this. It would ever be thus. Most accepted that 'co-ordinated' co-operatives' legislation was critical to the movement's future but could not agree on whether this should be federal or state-based legislation. They never would. All that could be achieved was a vague recommendation to the New South Wales Co-operative Advisory Council that CFA should investigate issues raised by the congress 'as a matter of urgency'.

The Co-operative Institute appears to have wallowed until late 1945. Then Kevin Yates, a young co-operative idealist recently returned from air-force duty in North America, where he had studied credit unions in Antigonish, was appointed publicity officer. Yates energetically sought to unite the squabbling movement. It was a daunting task with NSW CWS officials dismissing credit unions as 'window dressing', the building society movement rejecting any idea of a co-operative bank and primary producers livid that NSW CWS seemed obsessed with setting up another 'parochial' insurance co-operative. Moreover, NSW CWS flatly refused to recognise the Co-operative Institute as the CFA's 'legitimate' affiliate, supported in this by the Co-operative Federation of Western Australia (CFWA), which fiercely opposed federal or nationally uniform co-operatives' legislation, which NSW CWS supported.

While NSW CWS ignored the institute, however, farmer co-operatives utilised its framework to recommend changes to the *Co-operation Act,* including provision for non-members to serve as directors, powers to retain surpluses by a simple majority and an extension of government indemnification of loans (applying to community advancement and community settlement co-operatives) to loans raised for farmer purchases. After much of this agenda was obtained, however, many agricultural co-operatives also abandoned the institute, which began to fall apart.

Disillusioned by what he saw as the narrow commercial concerns and endless squabbling of the co-operative movement, Yates redirected his energy to the fledgling credit union movement and went on to become one of that movement's great pioneers. The building society movement also proceeded independently. Now torn by 'Cold War' polemics in the early 1950s, the institute floundered.

A minister for co-operatives

At national level, a battle continued between the farmer-based Australian Producers' Wholesale Co-operative Federation (APWCF) and the Rochdale consumer movement for control of the CFA (discussed in Chapter Ten). Consumers stole a march in October 1949 when NSW CWS stalwart and Labor parliamentarian George Booth succeeded in having appointed the first minister for co-operatives in Australia, C E Martin. Booth made no secret of the fact that Martin was 'his man' and that the position existed to 'counter Advisory Council and Registry influence', where primary producers held sway.

Martin immediately placed a watchdog on the Co-operative Advisory Council to 'protect co-operation', he said, a move bitterly resented by farmer co-operatives. Bowing to pressure from rural interests in parliament, where a fragile political balance existed, however, in September 1950, Martin created *separate* advisory councils for agricultural co-operatives and general co-operatives, administratively recognising a schism which had long dividing the movement.

Divisions deepened when arguments erupted between NSW CWS and the building society movement over the latter's plans for a 'socialist' co-operative bank. The row spilled into Labor Party politics, then polarised by 'Cold War' issues. Following a Labor split and the formation of the Democratic Labor Party (DLP), Martin was dumped as minister and replaced by C E Evatt, a pro-building society man. In 1954 Evatt resigned after differences with the premier on the issue of building societies versus public housing and other issues and was replaced by C A Kelly, who administered a crowded portfolio, which saw co-operatives effectively downgraded.

Registrar Sheldon's dream of a post-war co-operative 'new order' was fading. Preparing for retirement, he blasted 'trouble makers' in the movement and deplored opportunists, he said, who paid lip-service to co-operation for personal advantage without ever guessing at its substance.[2]

Agricultural co-operatives make progress

Not withstanding unbridgeable gaps between credit unions, building societies and agricultural co-operatives, each sector continued to make strong progress. Not so the Rochdale consumer movement, which slid into decline, hit by superior competition, capital deficiencies, changing consumer habits and a calcification attending doctrinal rigidity.

Indeed, the New South Wales agricultural co-operative movement was flourishing. Approximately 104 new rural co-operatives had formed since the war, bringing 40,000 new members into the movement. By 1950 there were 199 rural societies operating in the state, with 91,004 members and an annual turnover of £41.42 million (rising to £147 million over the following decade).

REGISTERED AGRICULTURAL CO-OPERATIVES, NEW SOUTH WALES, JUNE 1950	
Dairy	57
Fish	16
Farm machinery	22
Distribution (linseed, bananas, poultry, livestock, vegetable, prunes, dairy products, fruit, rice, etc)	20
Meat (abattoirs and bacon)	10
Handling (cool storage, packing, canneries, marketing, rice mills, etc)	14
Weighbridges	7
Electricity sales	3
Farm merchandise and trade items	43
Pigs and bacon	6
Water reticulation	1
Seed potato	1
Sawmill	1
Shearing shed hire	1
Veterinary	1
Derrick	1
Miscellaneous	15

Five primary-producer co-operative associations were operating: Young Co-operative Nurseries; Kiama Animal Health Co-operative; Gosford Co-operative Association; Irrigation Co-operative Societies Association (Griffith); and Growers' Co-operative Sales (Sydney). In 1956 potato and pumpkin growers also formed an association. A union of co-operative societies, the Prune Growers' Co-operative Union Limited (Sydney), linked producer associations in the Griffith, Young and

Packing and freezing Ice Cream during the 1970s at the Norco Lismore Factory. Norco started producing Ice Cream in the 1950s as margarine increasingly replaced butter amongst consumers.
Photo courtesy of Norco Co-operative Limited

Yenda districts. Scores of rural advancement co-operatives functioned, providing goods and services for farmers. A handful of co-operative settlements existed, for example, Cumnock at Narrabri.[3]

A corporate raid in 1961 on the Dairy Farmers' Co-operative mounted by a consortium of powerful Sydney businessmen (discussed in Chapters Three and Fifteen), however, underlined how vulnerable to 'dry' (non-producer) shareholders farmer co-operatives were. Through the Advisory Council, agricultural co-operatives saw to amendments to the act, allowing for the more flexible operations of trading and rural societies and introducing safeguards against 'dry' shareholder sell-outs.[4]

The Co-operative Federation of New South Wales

With numerous agricultural co-operatives forming in the early 1960s, in 1964 a group of mainly farmer co-operatives met at Kempsey in the north of the state, resolving to form a federation similar to the CFWA, recognised as the most effective co-operative federation in the country. Development was slow, but by 1965 more than fifty-five co-operatives in the dairy, fruit and cannery, meat and fishing industries, plus a handful of consumer and building societies, had affiliated. By 1967 more than seventy co-operatives had joined. Seeking to overcome 'the luxury of splendid isolation and parochial attitudes', CFNSW began issuing a newsletter in 1967, which appealed for unity and provided advice on taxation, trade practices and related matters, fund-raising options and discussions on national (not federal) co-operatives' legislation and a co-operative bank.

Another proposal for a co-operative bank

After a banking licence became available in 1969, CFNSW activists, including credit union pioneer Tom Kelly, mounted a spirited campaign to combine the financial resources of the co-operative and credit union movements, registered associations, clubs and trade unions and link these with a German co-operative bank. Rochdale co-operatives and the credit union movement, however, could still not agree on what form the proposed bank should take, the trade union movement would only support a development led by it, federal Labor forgot electoral promises and the plan went awry. It would not be the last attempt to attain the 'Holy Grail' of co-operative financial autonomy, but it was the last real chance in the twentieth century of obtaining it.

A 'siege' mentality

Not withstanding a sustained membership drive, by the early 1970s it appeared that CFNSW would go the same way as the Co-operative Institute and wither from lack of support. Meanwhile, with corporate raids on co-operatives increasing, a siege mentality gripped the farmer co-operative movement, particularly after an 'icon' of the movement, Producers' Distributive Society (PDS), was taken over by the brewer, Tooth. Increasingly, this infused farmer co-operative debate, which became focused *less* on broad co-operative development issues and *more* on individual, industry-specific problems, particularly a perceived need for greater operational flexibility, especially for capital-raising. With many rural co-operatives exiting the movement (discussed in Chapter Ten), surviving co-operatives increasingly acted unilaterally or looked more to government for support, urging ministers to utilise co-operatives in decentralisation and regional development programmes, for instance. This was risky for a self-professedly autonomous movement – but there was no real alternative for co-operatives failing to unite around common objectives and speak coherently to government or the public.[5]

'Operation Rescue Co-operation'

The new Registrar of Co-operative Societies David Horton, a barrister, soon after his appointment in 1972, launched into a vigorous co-operatives' development programme known as 'Operation Rescue Co-operation'. Horton impressed upon the government and the public the important economic and social roles co-operatives performed, supported CFNSW in developing agricultural co-operatives, appointed deputy registrars for credit unions and building societies, revamped the Advisory Council to make it more representative, convened meetings in rural communities, initiated a staff training program, clarified the registry's role in relation to the 'national' (New South Wales) economy, gathered statistics demonstrating the scale of co-operatives in the economy and held discussions with the International Co-operative Alliance (ICA) on the possibility of overseas trade with New South Wales co-operatives. In numerous articles in the CFNSW newsletter, Horton detailed the diversity of New South Wales rural co-operatives, pointing to rural co-operatives for clubs, business services, local and community services, water reticulation, wheat storage and cleaning, rice milling, film distribution, TV equipment, tourism, arts and crafts, bakeries, retail stores, agricultural factories, abattoirs, hospitals, medical services, housing, financial services, recreation, community advancement and heritage preservation.

Responding to the registrar's recommendations through the Advisory Council, the New South Wales Askin Liberal-Country Party Government made available $3 million to assist sugar-cane growers set up three co-operative mills in the north of the state after the CSR monopoly pulled out, possibly the first ever direct funding specifically for co-operative development in the state.[6]

There was no denying the government's support for particularly agricultural co-operatives, but those who knew co-operatives history were concerned – the initiative was coming more from the bureaucracy than from the co-operative movement itself. Co-operatives were losing ground to superior competition and corporate raiders while co-operative development became more a matter of political patronage than something driven by an autonomous, integrated social movement.[7]

Ministerial changes

The registry carried an enormous administrative burden in a cluttered portfolio, which, by the mid 1970s included the Housing Commission, the Rent Control Office, the Strata Titles Office, the Builders' Licensing Board and the Board of Architects of New South Wales. In addition to agricultural and general co-operatives, the registry also administered credit unions, permanent building societies and friendly societies. Complicating things further, there were constant changes to political masters. In 1973 S T Stephens (Country Party, Byron) retired as Minister for Co-operatives and Housing and was replaced by J C Bruxner (Country Party). Bruxner was replaced later in the year by L M McGinty (Willoughby), who was replaced soon after by W J Crabtree. In 1975 Crabtree was replaced by Ross Griffith. The *Co-operation Act* was also regularly amended and was becoming decidedly shabby. Indeed David Horton, like Sheldon before him, believed the act 'fossilised co-operation' and urged a radical overhaul, perhaps a complete replacement.[8]

Tension between the registry and the co-operative movement

It appears that the matter of legislative reform contributed to a cooling of until then cordial relations between the registry and CFNSW. There had previously been some resentment over the former's 'policeman' role while, for its part, the registry was finding the burden of co-operative development work growing 'out of hand'. Co-operative development, Horton reasonably argued, was a matter for the co-operative movement. The registry existed to *supervise* co-operatives, not *rescue* them. Some co-operators were also concerned about a 'watering down' of co-operative principles after Horton wrote on the 'necessary evil' of 'dry' shareholders because co-operatives were simply not in a position to refund them as they left an industry. The registrar also recommended that active shareholders should be given weighted votes to counteract any takeover bid by 'dry' shareholders, advised co-operatives on ways to amass capital, for example converting shares to interest-bearing debentures, and spoke on methods for retaining dividends and converting these to bonus shares (with Advisory Council approval). Horton argued for the appointment of external directors on co-operative boards, saying that the expertise and objectivity they would bring were necessary in the new competitive, commercial environment. Much of what the registrar had to say was an anathema to defenders of traditional co-operative 'faith', but it was a pointer to the future.

Seeking to improve communication between his office and co-operatives, the registry seconded a CFNSW officer (J A Ashe) for six months and promoted the formation of co-operative associations 'to work together and share costs' in co-operative development. Horton implored the movement's leaders, 'Let us for goodness sake maintain a vital movement, which is doing what it should be doing, and not one which has lost its way!'[9]

Bruce Freeman activates CFNSW

Changes in the management committee of a financially strapped CFNSW in 1974 saw the federation draw closer to the dairy co-operative movement, then facing a major Victorian challenge in the regulated fresh-milk market (discussed in Chapter Fifteen). A full-time executive officer (Colin Littlemore) was appointed but left soon after. It was not until Bruce Freeman, formerly an employee of GRAZCOS Co-operative (a victim of a corporate raid involving 'dry' shareholders) became executive director in 1975 that the federation showed signs of permanence. Freeman immediately amended the federation's rules to allow easier affiliation and revamped the management committee to embrace a wider cross-section of co-operative interests.

Support for the federation remained poor, however. Not withstanding a sustained membership drive aided by the registry in 1975 fewer than fifty co-operatives were affiliated with CFNSW when there were approximately 1,000 general co-operatives in the state! Then some co-operatives disaffiliated, concerned by the federation's ambitious agenda, particularly a banking service (the Australian Financial Administrative Group) operating on a commission basis in an effort to achieve financial independence, and possibly by Freeman's hard line on the importance of eliminating 'dry' shareholders. The number of affiliates fell to forty-one.

The minister calls for a 'missionary campaign'

The recently-elected New South Wales Wran Labor Government (ending nearly twelve years of Liberal-National [Country] Party rule), separated the co-operatives' portfolio from the housing portfolio in 1976, linking it to consumer affairs. The new minister, S D (Syd) Einfeld (Bondi), passionately supported co-operatives, was familiar with Rochdale theory and chaired twenty-four terminating building societies. Enthusiastically proclaiming that *one-third* of the state's entire adult population belonged to co-operatives the minister also expressed disappointment at the movement's failure to develop further and called upon co-operatives and his department to launch a 'missionary campaign' to revive co-operation's fortunes.

Directed by the minister, the registry circulated a needs survey to every co-operative in the state. Only twenty-one responses were received! At a CFNSW seminar in Newcastle in 1977, to which only ninety co-operatives, 40 per cent of them non-affiliates, sent affiliates, Einfeld excoriated the assembly for fractiousness and apathy, for turning the co-operative movement into what he described as a 'tax dodge'. Foreshadowing sweeping legislative changes which would take co-operation 'in hand', Einfeld said:

> *The International Co-operative Alliance adopted six essential principles in 1966 which were based on those laid down by the Rochdale Pioneers. One of those six principles goes something like this – All [Einfeld's emphasis] co-operative organisations in order to best serve the interests of their members and their communities should actively co-operate with other co-operatives at local, national and international levels in every practical way. This means that it is not enough to have a vague feeling of ambition for a co-operative. It is not enough to feel a cosy sense of mutual protection from being a member of a co-operative. It certainly isn't enough to confine the aim of a co-operative to making a profit for itself, for its own special co-operative, at the end of the year.*

'The system has made suckers of you'

At the CFNSW annual conference later in the year, the letters editor of the *Sydney Morning Herald* and credit enthusiast John O'Hara tore into the co-operative movement. He held little, if any, hope for the future of co-operation in Australia since, he said, it consisted almost entirely of a loose-knit collection of introverted, conservative, mutually self-interested groups serving specific purposes of convenience. Co-operators mouthed the cause of co-operation but failed to co-operate themselves. The movement was stale, flat and unprofitable, steeped in parochialism and bereft of imagination and initiative because it had suffocated its dynamic co-operative idealists and driven away popular support. The movement was not merely apolitical but conservative, largely because of a rural psychology infusing it which endorsed co-operation only to the extent that it did not interfere with but reinforced the property-based sanctity of the capitalist system. The rural co-operative movement, O'Hara continued, was frequently merely an extension of farmers' native hostility to the city. Now misguided leaders were inviting government into the movement and allowing politicians to imprison co-operation:

> The system has made suckers of you. The co-operative movement has blindly and meekly dedicated itself to a role much like that of the bird that pecks at the teeth of the crocodile...You are in the same situation as the undeveloped nations against the developed...You have no one to blame but yourselves... You drift and drift waiting for the current.

Further amendments to the act

Einfeld saw to changes to the *Co-operation Act*, incorporating many of Registrar Horton's recommendations which:

- ❖ gave co-operatives greater flexibility in lending and borrowing;
- ❖ clarified the functions and powers of directors and other co-operatives' personnel;
- ❖ allowed for loans by members to co-operatives in an effort to improve their capital position;
- ❖ described ways of rewarding investments through bonus shares;
- ❖ insisted that 90 per cent or more of business be conducted with co-operative members in order to qualify as a co-operative for taxation purposes; and
- ❖ sharpened the registrar's powers by detailing a new schedule of penalties for non-compliance.

The Co-operative Development Trust Fund

The government also made available a $3 million Co-operative Development Trust Fund over three years for the development of 'service-orientated' co-operatives, in particular worker co-operatives through a Youth Work Co-operative Scheme and gave CFNSW an administrative role in this. The irony was that as Einfeld legislated to give co-operatives greater operational flexibility, made resources available for co-operative development and reined in 'bogus' co-operatives, he was bolstering bureaucratic intervention and compromising 'self-help'. The fractious state of general co-operatives, however, meant that no sensible alternative existed – certainly, the co-operative movement had not produced one. As if to underline the point, share and loan provisions in the act designed to improve co-operatives' capitalisation were poorly utilised, with only about fifty co-operatives employing them over the next decade, farmers preferring a 'divvy' in the pocket for investments in the farm, to equity in their co-operative.

Why a federation?

The rationale for having a co-operative federation came under close scrutiny at a CFNSW seminar in Coffs Harbour early in 1978. Sceptics argued that governments now operated small-business agencies duplicating many of the federation's functions, which co-operatives were reluctant to fund. For the sake of unity, however, and largely due to Bruce Freeman's persuading, the assembly agreed that CFNSW should continue and actually *broaden* its role to include an award and industrial service, an employment agency, a superannuation fund, a travel service, a financial administration division, a tax adviser, a trade directory, an education programme, a management consultant, accounting, bookkeeping and secretarial services. This was a splendid wish list, and fundamental to a serious 'self-help' movement, but who would pay? The federation was starved for funds.

The following year Freeman reported that the federation's centralised banking arrangement was working reasonably well and making valuable investments in authorised trustee securities but, he added, affiliation was still paltry and he acknowledged that the federation had failed to bring the movement together.[10]

'We must recognise the failures of the past'

The new Minister for Co-operative Societies Terry Sheahan did not mince words when he addressed the CFNSW annual conference. 'Co-operatives,' he said, 'whatever their original concept, now serve purely economic ends.' The new minister believed retail co-operation had no future and even the future of rural co-operation was 'cloudy'. Building societies and credit unions were flourishing, however, and Sheahan was convinced that the future of the movement lay in worker co-operatives and small community-based service co-operatives. A fundamental conflict existed between co-operative philosophy and the realities of the competitive world, the minister said, adding:

> The co-operative movement is…returning to its basic concept – the provision of common services to relatively few groups under honorary or low cost management…There is unlikely to be any major future development of large scale commercial co-operative societies which evolved and flourished in a past era. This is not the time for soothing words…we are witnessing a situation where segments of what might be described as…the backbone of the[rural] co-operative movement…are going out of existence one by one. We must recognise the failures of the past.

Speaking as a private citizen CFA Executive Officer Bill Rawlinson chided Sheahan for a narrow perception of co-operation and for overlooking the rural co-operative movement's many successes. He doubted that the New South Wales government was sincere in efforts to bolster co-operatives, describing the government's intervention as 'creeping socialism', which would eventually engulf the movement. Rawlinson was correct, for consecutive ministers strengthened the role of the bureaucracy in directing co-operative development, but the CFA official might have been just as concerned about 'creeping capitalism', for it was the corporate sector which was devouring the movement and would continue to do so for much of the remaining century. As for the co-operative movement, it was just 'creeping', unable to achieve a consensus on any big issues and, with each supportive step the government took, the sector's capacity for self-management receded.

'Time to act'

The minister introduced further amendments to the act in 1980, sharpening the registrar's power and authorising him to *direct* any society to transfer engagements to another society or appoint an administrator to any society. At the October 1981 CFNSW Annual Conference, which was entitled 'Time to Act' and involved fifty-four delegates, Minister Sheahan told the assembly that co-operatives needed to break out of 'outdated and restrictive' principles and procedures and that only radical legislative change could achieve this. The consumer co-operative movement was irreversibly in decline and the time for talking airily about co-operative development had ended. Co-operatives urgently needed improved, modern management skills and had to co-operate in sharing 'back room' costs, for example, accounting and insurance-purchase expenses. Sheahan said co-operatives needed to find new ways of attracting capital, perhaps even accessing *external* sources, and ways of polishing up a tarnished co-operative image. Confined by narrow objects, co-operatives were just not reaching young people and were bogged down in old ways, the minister concluded.

Executive Director Bruce Freeman reminded delegates how GRAZCOS had been taken over by a hostile raid targeting 'dry' shareholders. Education was vital to the movement's future and he repeated an oft-quoted adage, 'A co-operative which does not educate will last a generation

Norco display at the Sydney Royal Easter Show in 1948.
Photo courtesy of Norco Co-operative Limited.

and a half!' The federation was on a reasonable financial footing with the centralised banking service working well, he said, but an urgent need existed for practical workshops to debate and solve specific problems endemic to the movement and have recommendations from these carried forward into legislation. The co-operative movement was losing its 'memory' and a new breed of leaders was entering the sector, ignorant of and with little respect for traditional co-operative principles.[11]

With approximately $35 million per month now passing through CFNSW's centralised banking service and New South Wales government funds for worker co-operatives and common ownership feasibility studies circulating through the organisation, the federation's financial position was strengthened through 1983 allowing it to computerise, prepare government submissions and extend a training programme. Some large agricultural co-operatives which had already refused to participate in the banking service, however, disaffiliated, apparently objecting to the federation assuming a 'national' brief, specifically calls for federal or nationally uniform co-operatives' legislation and a federal minister of co-operatives. Others, including the Dairy Farmers' Co-operative, were concerned at the federation's determination to expel 'dry' shareholders at a time when co-operatives were struggling with capital adequacy problems. A growing rift between Bruce Freeman's CFNSW (and its successor, the Australian Association of Co-operatives (AAC) (discussed in Chapters Nine and Twelve) and powerful sections of the farmer co-operative movement would seriously hamper co-operative development in ensuing years.

The Ministry is discontinued

As sections of the co-operative movement disagreed and broke from the federation, the 'profile' of co-operatives in government was diminishing. The Ministry of Co-operatives was discontinued in 1983, although the *title* remained with the minister. The registry's capacity to administer co-operatives was also compromised by staff reductions and a function-shedding rationalisation, which obliged the office to discontinue data gathering and statistical analysis. Consequently, the quality of advice reaching the minister suffered. With the Labor Government focused on community-based service co-operatives, including Aboriginal welfare, childcare, school development and alternative lifestyle co-operatives, farmer co-operatives reasonably protested that insufficient attention was being paid to them as more capital-starved co-operatives succumbed to corporate raiders.[12]

'New initiatives for co-operative development'

In 1984, the new Minister for Youth and Community Affairs with responsibility for co-operatives, Frank Walker, promised new initiatives for co-operative development. The corner stone of public policy would be meticulous planning of co-operative development strategies ensuring the continued democratic control of co-operatives by members while curbing predation by corporations upon 'dry' shareholders. With a view to assisting farmer co-operatives solve pressing financial problems, Walker examined the democracy principle closely, concluding that *control* by members would always be the bedrock of co-operative structure but *ownership* might possibly be *shared* with external investors if legislative means for achieving this could be found, consistent with co-operative principles. He urged agricultural co-operatives to rid themselves of 'dry' shareholders or, if they were not prepared to do this because of the impact upon the capital base, at least give 'dries' voting rights, perhaps by introducing two classes of shares: one for members and one for investors.

External investments and classes of shares were repugnant to traditional co-operators in CFNSW, however, who complained to the minister that they were wholly outside the spirit of co-operation since ownership and control were *indivisible* in co-operatives, shares in which did *not* exist for capital gain but as a 'ticket' to participation in the organisation.

The minister agreed with farmer co-operatives that *service* alone was insufficient in a contemporary business environment to guarantee the success of any business venture, co-operatives included. Co-operatives now had to achieve the technical and operational sophistication of corporate competitors or 'recent difficulties would see their ruin'. Walker agreed also that the registry's 'policeman' role was 'contentious', sometimes preventing co-operators from acting on democratically agreed decisions, but affirmed that the government would continue to take a strong regulatory hand in the matter of co-operatives' administration. To criticism that his department was doing little to encourage new forms of co-operation, Walker replied that the co-operative movement should put its *own* house in order before telling departments what to do.

'No intention to "run" the co-operative movement'

Minister Walker and his successor, Bob Debus, saw to amendments to the *Co-operation Act* through 1985-1987 clarifying directors' duties and responsibilities, further sharpening the registrar's powers, detailing fees and penalties, strengthening active membership provisions and including ICA principles, the application of which by co-operatives was optional.

Minister Debus began a major review of the department and the act in March 1986. To repeated criticisms from sections of the movement, including CFNSW, that the government was taking too high a hand in co-operative affairs, the minister replied that traditions of co-operation were not deep in Australia and needed encouragement. His department had no intention to 'run' the co-operative movement, only to provide the right public policy environment and incentives to facilitate, encourage and co-ordinate the 'self-help' movement's development, which was now in an emergency 'catch-up' phase. Reiterating previous ministers, Debus observed that the co-operative movement did not operate in a vacuum, co-operatives had to compete successfully to survive, co-operative development should be consistent with the government's economic development strategy and the Co-operatives' Department needed to be more attuned to the needs of other sectors of the economy, particularly overseas marketing. If co-operatives could no longer make a tangible contribution to the economic and social life of citizens, they had no reason for being.

CFNSW and the Australian Association of Co-operatives

The CFNSW resigned from CFA at this time (discussed in Chapter Twelve) and with Bruce Freeman to the fore aided by James McCall of the Co-operative Federation of Victoria (CFV) and some co-operatives in Queensland, in July 1986 formed the Australian Association of Co-operatives (AAC).

From the start AAC's development focus was broader than some major farmer co-operatives thought desirable. Agricultural co-operatives were primarily concerned with flexibility in capital-raising, growing market share in the approach to deregulation, adapting co-operative principles to modern trading conditions and facilitative legislative reforms facilitating this. The AAC, on the other hand, equally concerned that established co-operatives remained competitive, insisted this could only be achieved through *faithfully* applying co-operative philosophy and practice.

There was nothing fundamentally wrong with co-operation, Bruce Freeman argued, not withstanding the criticisms of corporate consultants and some in the movement, who simply did not know how to apply it. A stickler for the democracy principle, limited return on shares, commitment to member service and the patronage principle, Freeman mistrusted not only 'dry' shareholders but those who argued their case and insisted that many current co-operative movement leaders (in and out of government) did not understand or value co-operative traditions. How could they when co-operative education had for so long been neglected, weakening the movement's 'memory' and obliging co-operatives to turn to 'white knights' in government and the corporate sector to bail them out? Whatever happened to 'self-help'? The AAC was focused on active membership, internal co-operative finance (not external investors), federal or national uniform co-operatives' legislation, a federal co-operatives development service, adherence to ICA co-operative principles, co-operation between co-operatives (including the ICA) and education. Freeman made it plain to anyone who would listen that he and AAC would do everything in their power to 'protect the co-operative commercial environment from any attempt to water-down legislative protection'. The AAC was also concerned with developing *new* co-operatives relevant to contemporary economic and social issues and would definitely not confine itself to the commercial and sectoral concerns of long-established agricultural co-operatives and co-operative companies; the co-operative 'establishment'. Indeed Freeman denounced those farmer co-operatives which were taking unilateral action instead of co-operating with other co-operatives and which were adopting a predatory style, mimicking corporations and neglecting general co-operative development and education. Co-operation, Freeman emphasised, was about economic democracy, working together, and not just making money for a few shareholders.

Not surprisingly relations between AAC and some large New South Wales farmer co-operatives, particularly in the dairy industry, were strained. Increasingly the latter went *direct* to government via the Advisory Council, bypassing the association, doing nothing for co-operative unity and sending confusing signals to the administration (also discussed in Chapter Fifteen).

The Ministerial Council of Future Directions for Co-operatives 1986

As AAC took shape, in October 1986 Minister Debus created the Ministerial Council of Future Directions for Co-operatives. This was briefed to make recommendations for co-operative development consistent with the government's Economic Development Strategy, which had been launched in July, centred on deregulation, investment, growth, structural change, economic progress and employment. Essentially, the plan was to directly link economic development with co-operative development. The minister announced plans to comprehensively restructure his department and create a small 'enterprise' unit to work 'hand-in-hand with the co-operative sector' to assist the development of an integrated, co-ordinated co-operative movement providing better services and 'products'. The registry's role would also be enhanced, broadening the focus from prudential regulation to pro-active facilitation in developing the sector. The state was moving into a vacuum left by the co-operatives.

Chaired by the minister, the ministerial council included over thirty representatives drawn from AAC, worker co-operatives, credit unions, buildings societies, housing co-operatives, friendly societies, the Co-operative Advisory Council and government departments. It is not clear from the sources whether farmer co-operatives were directly represented, or via the Advisory Council. Seven working parties were established: legislation (briefed to review the act); research and statistics; education; co-operation between co-operatives; fund-raising; marketing; and the role of co-operatives in the broader economy. The registry provided secretariat support for working parties, which were to report regularly to the Council of Future Directions, which met three times a year.

Critics complained that the Ministerial Council was too interventionist and duplicated AAC's work. Not so, departmental officials replied, AAC existed for *national* co-operative development; the Council was for *New South Wales*!

'Plan 88'

In May 1987 Minister Debus' department released 'Plan 88', a co-operatives' future directions policy statement incorporating much of the AAC platform and some recommendations from a 1986 (Commonwealth) Standing Committee on Agriculture Working Party (SCAWP) Report (discussed in Chapter Twelve). The SCAWP report said co-operatives could be the answer to many of Australia's agricultural problems, noting the importance of co-operatives in the rural economy but how they had not kept pace with change, and called upon state governments to assist with their development. In line with this, 'Plan 88' called for a federal agricultural co-operatives extension service similar to those in Canada and the United States, inclusion of ICA co-operative principles in all relevant acts, greater co-operation among co-operatives, particularly in international trade and, interestingly, uniform legislation for *each* of the co-operative sectors. The plan called upon the New South Wales government to make representations to Prime Minister Hawke to create a federal ministry with responsibility for the co-ordination, promotion and development of the co-operative sector. 'Plan 88' appears not to have made any specific reference to uniform national legislation, innovative fund-raising, or co-operative banking, all recommendations in the SCAWP report, but this is not clear from the available sources.

Amending the act to expel 'dry' shareholders

The Co-operation Act was again amended in October 1987 to strengthen provisions for active membership and banish 'dry' shareholders, preventing them from selling shares to outsiders. The Dairy Farmers' Co-operative, a corporate raid upon which had prompted the government to act (discussed in Chapter Fifteen), was ambivalent about these reforms, understanding the need to protect co-operatives against raids but complaining that the approximately *80 per cent* of its shareholders who were 'dries' represented a cheap source of capital and were sentimentally valued as part of the co-operative's 'family heritage'. Driving them out could mortally wound the co-operative.

Dairy Farmers General Manager Murray Mead proposed a two-class share system to overcome the problem; with voting rights for suppliers and non-voting for 'dries', keeping them in. This was strongly opposed by AAC, which persuaded the government to amend the act further allowing co-operatives to *compulsorily* redeem the shares of former producer members who had not supplied the co-operative for two years, expelling them, and for this to be phased in over one year to assist Dairy Farmers' capital adequacy problems. The alternative, Bruce Freeman argued, was almost certainly the takeover of the co-operative by corporate interests, either immediately or incrementally. The issues of 'dry' shareholders and 'watering-down' co-operative principles to accommodate the expectations of external investors sparked a long-running disagreement between AAC and the Dairy Farmers' Co-operative, with serious consequences for the New South Wales and Australian co-operative movements (discussed in Chapter Fifteen).

The Co-operative Development Branch

Later in 1987 Minister Debus established the Co-operative Development Branch (CDB), reflecting the registry's changing role from 'regulatory policeman' to 'one of pro-active involvement in the development control (*sic*) of the co-operative sector in this state'. Commencing operations early in 1988 the CDB was designed as an 'enterprise' unit working closely with the co-operative sector to 'grow' it through the administration of a Co-operative Development Fund (CDF), amounting to $350,000 per annum. (With a state election looming it appears that the immediate deployment of the CDF was delayed. The sources do not always clearly distinguish between the Co-operative Development Trust Fund, specifically for worker co-operatives, and the CDF, for general co-operative development.)

The Windschuttle Report

CDB commissioned academic Keith Windschuttle to examine the economic significance of the co-operative sector in New South Wales and recommend policies for future growth. Windschuttle concluded that the future role of co-operatives depended upon their ability to adapt to changing circumstances. Agricultural co-operatives held significant market share in New South Wales in 1987: seafood 80 per cent; fruit 40 per cent; cotton 82 per cent; rice 100 per cent; sugar 100 per cent; dairy 91 per cent; and meat 5 per cent; but farmer co-operatives urgently needed to modernise if they were to continue to play an important role in economic restructuring. Windschuttle argued that co-operatives could be useful in smoothing the path to deregulation, replacing statutory marketing authorities (SMAs), particularly for 'value adding' and international trade. On capitalisation for growth, the report recommended against external investors, favouring internal funding schemes including cross-investments from the different sectors of the co-operative movement (presumably through a co-operative bank, which did not exist, or a centralised banking service, such as the AAC's).

Registry officers cross-referenced recommendations from the Windschuttle Report with State Development Strategy priorities and identified opportunities for co-operative growth. It was precision planning, but what would the co-operative movement make of this centrally-driven process and how would it alter the nature of co-operative development? There was little time to think about this, however, as Labor was ousted in March 1988 and the Greiner Liberal-National (Country) Party began a seven year rule.

Conclusion

In approximately four decades from the end of World War II to 1987, the New South Wales general co-operative movement drifted from a position where it was held to be the possible basis for a 'new order' to one where government was obliged to mount a rescue operation. Great credit union and building society movements had developed in the period but general co-operatives, split along producer-consumer lines and incapable of agreeing on such vital issues as a co-operative bank, uniform legislation, federal involvement in development work, capitalisation models and the democracy principle, continued to shamble along. If 'Plan 88' were ever to bear fruit, it would be under the aegis of a conservative government and a National Party minister sympathetic to a rural constituency.[13]

Chapter Nine

'Co-ops 2000':
NEW SOUTH WALES CO-OPERATIVE DEVELOPMENT 1988-C2000

Introduction

When the Greiner Liberal-National Party Coalition Government took power in Sydney early in 1988 the New South Wales rural co-operative movement was asymmetrically developed, characterised by a few economically and politically significant co-operatives, particularly in the dairy, rice, cotton and sugar industries. In rural electorates a political backlash was building against economic-rationalist policies introduced by federal and state governments of all hues, which were contributing to a run down in rural infrastructure and business, social amenities, services and jobs. It was not surprising, therefore, that a close link should develop between the new government and rural co-operatives and that this should be reflected in public policy for co-operatives. Whether the narrowly-focused commercial agenda which agricultural co-operatives, besieged by deregulation, globalisation and corporate raiders, brought to the debate was appropriate to broader co-operative development was less obvious, however, as the sector entered a most challenging period, when threats and opportunities existed in equal measure.[1]

Gerry Peacocke: Minister for Co-operatives

The new minister for co-operatives, Gerald (Gerry) Peacocke, (National Party, Dubbo), a lawyer, was a strong co-operative advocate in the old agrarian-socialist mould, vestiges of which survived in the National Party. A fierce states-righter and opponent of anything smacking of 'centralist-socialist Labor', Peacocke served in a cabinet noted for deregulatory enthusiasm and economic pragmatism, a difficult position for a politician whose constituents were directly exposed to the extremes of such policies. As new ministers seeking to put their mark on things are wont to do, Peacocke stopped action on 'Plan 88' and Labor's proposal for new legislation as he familiarised himself with the portfolio and the landscape of co-operative movement politics. In doing so the minister discerned several 'voices' proffering sometimes conflicting advice: the Australian Association of Co-operatives (AAC) (discussed also in Chapters Eight, Twelve and Fifteen), his own department's recently formed Co-operative Development Branch (CDB) and the Co-operative Advisory Council, reflecting industry sectoral opinion and, in particular, commercial agricultural co-operatives.

'A little man's way to capitalism'

The new minister seized the portfolio with relish. Publicly declaring his strong support for co-operatives, Peacocke restructured the Department of Co-operative Societies, merging it with the Department of Business and Consumer Affairs (and in 1991, the Department of Local Government and Co-operatives) and set about working with AAC to overcome what he saw as a rural 'prejudice' against co-operatives, which he believed had been spawned by the previous 'socialist' administration:

Under the previous Labor Government the co-operative movement was administered by left-wing ministers. As a consequence, many country residents regard co-operatives as a radical communist scheme...I see them as the little man's way to capitalism.

With Victorian dairy producers assailing New South Wales fresh-milk markets, the minister agreed to extend a 'breathing time' given by the previous administration to enable dairy co-operatives to prepare for deregulation. Peacocke also assisted a 'reasoned compromise' in a Panfida takeover bid for Dairy Farmers' Co-operative (discussed in Chapter Fifteen), helping to slow a drain on the co-operative's capital base caused by the exit of 'dry' shareholder funds pursuant to active membership provisions enacted by Labor. At the same time the minister foreshadowed sweeping new co-operatives' legislation allowing societies greater capital-raising flexibility while tightening accountability regulations.

Gerry Peacocke was determined to revitalise what he saw as a 'moribund co-operative movement' and encourage its development into a formidable third sector in the business world, powerful enough to deliver a real challenge to public and private industries. There were, he explained, 4,000 co-operatives in Australia; 1,200 of them in New South Wales; and 350,000 members of agricultural co-operatives throughout Australia, holding $2.5 billion in total assets. If financial co-operatives were included, the minister continued, there were 6,000 Australian co-operatives with six million memberships holding $35 billion in assets! Co-operatives were an important force in Australia's economic and social fabric and had the potential eventually to do away with social welfare and see the development of a resourceful, independent 'yeomanry'. The government's proposed dismantling of statutory marketing authorities (SMAs) was a golden opportunity for local co-operatives, Peacocke believed, especially in the grains industry. In this context he floated the idea of regional co-operative movements linked to local investor co-operatives, marshalling capital for rural economic development. An appalling ignorance of co-operatives needed to be overcome, the minister said, and this could be achieved by introducing co-operative studies into schools. Clearly, Peacocke had done his 'homework', assisted by AAC and CBD, and was well informed and enthusiastic about co-operatives. The movement could not have hoped for a better minister but Peacocke's empathy with the agricultural co-operative 'establishment' was a matter of concern to some observers who thought it unlikely that a broad co-operative renaissance was possible while under this influence.

The minister and AAC

Relations between the minister and AAC appear to have been initially cordial. Peacocke dropped an inquiry into the association's finances begun by the previous government. An appreciative association warmly noted the minister's enthusiasm for co-operatives and the gusto with which he had accepted the portfolio. Peacocke transferred the Co-operative Development Trust Fund from a floundering Worker Enterprise Corporation, established by Labor, to AAC, for use with general co-operatives, enabling the association to form its own Co-operative Development Unit (CDU), managed by Jim McCall of AAC's Victorian division, supported by Reg Nichols. How CDB officers viewed this potential rival is unknown. Nevertheless, in August 1988 the CDB and AAC jointly organised a Co-operative Week and Trade Fair to showcase co-operatives and 'encourage the co-ordination of the co-operative movement'.

It appears that tensions between the department and AAC on policy direction first arose over the latter's strong support for a Commonwealth Government Standing Committee on Agricultural Working Party (SCAWP) recommendation for a national Agricultural Co-operatives Service to expedite deregulation by promoting co-operatives as an alternative to SMAs, which had been accepted in Labor's 'Plan 88'. A prerequisite for this was federal, or at least nationally uniform, co-operatives' legislation. Some New South Wales agricultural co-operatives were sceptical, however, understanding that the Western Australians would never agree to this and concerned secondly at the fillip uniform legislation might give 'foreign' (interstate) competitors before New South Wales was ready for deregulation. Certainly the Co-operative Federation of Western Australia (CFWA) bitterly opposed any idea of regulation by Canberra. The minister himself took a jaundiced view of any arrangement surrendering control to 'centralist-socialists' but appears not to have been opposed *per se* to nationally uniform co-operatives' legislation, envisaging proposed New South Wales legislation as a model for this. Peacocke was also attentive to calls by some agricultural co-operatives for the freeing up of capital-raising options for co-operatives, even to the point of external investments, something to which AAC was implacably opposed.

Notwithstanding these latent tensions, the minister and AAC worked well together in 1989, developing the Yeoval Community Co-operative Hospital, situated in Peacocke's electorate. The AAC loaned the embryonic co-operative $100,000. AAC Executive Director Bruce Freeman served as vice-chairman on the co-operative's board and finance committee. This successful project, driven by strong community support, saw the development of a seven-bed hospital, a seven-bed nursing home and, later, other improvements. AAC also assisted in the development of a co-operative roller-skating rink in the nearby town of Wellington, the idea being to use this much-needed amenity for young people to return profits to the community for further community development works. The association also assisted in converting a refrigeration supply operation, which was surplus to Dairy Farmers' Co-operative needs, into an employee-owned enterprise.

It appears, however, that some strain entered the relationship after AAC, aided by federal moneys through the Export Marketing Development Scheme, set up Co-operative Trade Australia Proprietary Limited, and CDU Manager Jim McCall broadcast prospects of a 'staggering $600 million deal' through the International Co-operative Alliance (ICA) with the Soviet Union, which, he believed, would break the stranglehold of proprietary companies on Australian–Soviet trade. Even so, with New South Wales agricultural co-operatives standing to benefit materially from the proposed AAC–ICA relationship, which promised preferential trade for co-operatives in seventy-one nations, the relationship stayed positive.[2]

As the department prepared for a major review of the *Co-operation Act*, however, friction became evident. After CDB officers presented Peacocke with options for the review, AAC urged upon the minister the importance of the *co-operative movement* taking the initiative in any proposed co-operative development programme, not bureaucrats or private consultants. The association was adamant that co-operative values should *not* be diluted in any legislative reform and warned against any attempt to 'water down' the democracy principle, active member provisions or the established share-capital basis of co-operatives, which might permit 'back door' entry by 'dry' shareholders and eventual investor control.

Faced with occasionally conflicting advice from departmental officers, AAC and the Co-operative Advisory Council, the minister decided to engage 'neutral' experts, at arms length from the co-operative movement and the government, to review the *Co-operation Act*.[3]

The Co-operative Development Fund is activated

At the same time the minister activated Labor's Co-operative Development Fund (CDF), an annual allocation of $350,000 direct from Treasury through the CDB. The fund, unique in Australia, was created initially to conduct feasibility studies and develop business plans for new and existing co-operatives 'in a competitive environment' and for education and research consistent with government priorities. The co-operative movement simply did not have access to such resources and the CDF delivered CDB considerable power in the public policy debate.

Aided by the fund, CDB took a more prominent role in New South Wales and subsequently, national co-operative development. Over time the CDF's purpose was expanded to include developing strategic plans, training, evaluation, product development, co-operative formations, development policy, publishing, information dissemination, seminars and conferences and supporting such councils and sub-committees formed by the minister as 'would develop national and international networks'. Substantial grants were made through the fund over the next decade for research and policy projects, including submissions to Industries' Commission inquiries into SMAs, papers on capital options for co-operatives and discussion forums, conferences and seminars exploring opportunities for co-operatives in a deregulatory environment. The CDB ran a library, a general referral service for co-operatives, issued a newsletter, supported research, brought to Australia several international co-operative experts and CDB officers regularly travelled to international congresses and made fact-finding visits to Spain, Italy, China, Malaysia, India, the United Kingdom, USA and elsewhere. The CDF was deployed in funding a major CDB-orchestrated co-operative development initiative, *Co-ops 2000* (discussed below), helped to launch a national newsletter (*National Co-op Update*), supported the development of the Asia-Pacific Co-operative Training Centre (APCTC), assisted an ICA-Registry international trade project and helped the Co-operative Federation of NSW Ltd to form in 1993, among other projects.[4]

Certainly, while Peacocke held the reins and CDB was pro-active, co-operative development in New South Wales accelerated. Between 1988 and 1992, 138 new co-operatives were formed, aided by CDB (and the CDU), and only thirteen failed, well below the rate for general business.

Still the sector's physical development was deformed. In 1992 five New South Wales agricultural co-operatives (Australian Co-operative Foods [Dairy Farmers], Ricegrowers' Co-operative Limited, Namoi Cotton Co-operative, Norco and the New South Wales Sugar Co-operative), with 5,426 members from a total general co-operative membership of 1,028,612, produced $1.36 billion of a total annual general co-operatives' turnover of $1.77 billion. That is, less than 1 per cent of the co-operators produced around 80 per cent of the total co-operative turnover. Moreover, due to rationalisation, there were thirty-five fewer agricultural co-operatives in 1993 than there had been a decade earlier and the 'big five' now accounted for $772 million of the state's total $1.028 billion of general co-operatives' assets.[5]

The *Co-operation Act* is reviewed, 1989

In February 1989 Minister Peacocke appointed a solicitors' firm, Blake, Dawson, Waldron, and the investment bankers, Dominguez, Barry, Samuel, Montagu Limited, to conduct a review of the 1923 New South Wales *Co-operation Act*. The need for new legislation, the minister said, was underlined by the recent (unsuccessful) Panfida raid on Dairy Farmers' Co-operative. Peacocke called for a report and recommendations to be on his desk by May, for circulation among the 'co-operative community' by the end of June with a view to introducing new legislation by the end of the year. It was a very short lead time.

The AAC questioned the suitability to the task of solicitors and investment bankers, who, the association said, knew nothing of co-operative culture, and complained that the hectic schedule precluded considered debate. The minister replied that there was an urgent need for action, particularly so as the co-operative sector appeared not to be able to speak with a single voice, a reference to the fact that AAC and some farmer co-operatives held different views on co-operative development policy.

Outside the Bega Butter Factory (employee identity and date unknown).
Photo courtesy of Bega Co-operative Society Limited

At a New South Wales Dairy Industry Association Annual Conference, the minister told how the review had been briefed to consider the whole question of capital formation for co-operatives and the nature of co-operative shareholding with a view to identifying *alternative* forms of fund-raising and debt-financing:

> It is no secret that the dairy industry generally, and in New South Wales in particular, expects to face considerably increased competition as a consequence of the closer economic ties between Australia and New Zealand...The industry is proceeding as a consequence of the Langdon Report [discussed in Chapter Fifteen] and, I am sure also as a consequence of the Review of the Co-operation Act, to meet this challenge.[6]

The consultants received over 100 detailed submissions and the minister's office an additional 200. A special forum was held, involving consultants, the Co-operative Advisory Council, AAC officials, representatives of major co-operatives and departmental officers. It is clear that by now AAC was perceived by the minister to be but one stakeholder in the development process with no mandate to speak for all co-operatives.[7]

The consultants' report recommended a complete replacement of the *Co-operation Act* by a new act in 'simple readable form', accessible to members of all co-operatives, embodying and reflecting co-operative principles while providing adequate prudential standards and government regulatory powers to 'assist, rather than hinder co-operative development'. Principally about fund-raising, the review's recommendations reflected corporate values and challenged traditional views on co-operation and co-operative principles.

On capital formation the report questioned established notions of co-operative ownership, recommending the *separation* of membership from shareholding and the issuing of bonus shares for the purpose of *equating* members' nominal interests with the asset values of a co-operative. This radical departure from traditional co-operative practise was in line with a submission from sections of the dairy industry. The consultants argued that active members' shares should be an equitable representation of each member's interests in the on-going economic activity of a co-operative and issued on a standard basis relative to anticipated business, with further contributions in proportion to members' actual transactions with the co-operative. Consultants emphasised that, in the event of a co-operative being wound up, members should be entitled to participate in its assets. The legislation should also streamline the means by which surpluses might be turned into loans in the form of revolving funds, *without* the approval of the Advisory Council, guided purely by the principle of giving members a greater claim upon a co-operative's resources.

On the contentious matter of external equity, the report said that legislation should make easier existing provisions for co-operatives to create subsidiaries, unit trusts and to enter joint ventures, recognising the realities of the capitalist, competitive market system in which co-operatives functioned. In vague language the report said the proposed act should enable projects to be kept financially independent in the matter of *accessing funds*, while a co-operative maintained *control* of a project's assets. 'Dry' shares might be converted by the consent of members to interest-free deposits, donations or to a new quasi-equity vehicle to be known as 'Co-operative Capital Units [CCUs] [which are] not unlike preference shares'.

The report said it was imperative that such new forms of capital contribution be allowed as the present requirement for *one class* of share capital within a co-operative was illogical in current commercial conditions. Therefore, the traditional requirement for co-operative capital to consist *solely* of contributions by active members should be varied to permit the issue of CCUs, which would allow *external risk capital* to become available through legal structures, co-ordinated and controlled by, but external to, the co-operative. Co-operatives should be permitted to issue CCUs, which were to be freely transferable, on a one-vote-per-share basis. While CCU holders would not be deemed members of a co-operative they would be entitled to all correspondence sent to members. The rights of unit holders could be varied, but only with the consent of 75 per cent of CCU holders.

Debt capital could also be made easier by abolishing the doctrine of *ultra vires* so that if a co-operative invited non-members to subscribe to CCUs, or deposit with, or lend money to a co-operative, standard company laws would apply. A co-operative should simply state its primary objects in the rules and be endowed with full corporate powers in pursuit of those objects in a manner consistent with the Companies Code. Co-operatives should have the full powers of a 'natural person' under the control of internal management, guided by scrupulous and transparent accountability principles and the Companies Code, which, consultants believed, would strengthen security in dealings with co-operatives and *mitigate any perceived loss of democratic control*. The idea essentially was to attract investor interest in co-operatives without members losing control, on the assumption that these elements were compatible.

Also, the report continued, co-operatives should be allowed to incur subordinated debt, which would rank ahead of equity on winding-up, but after other unsecured creditors. Greater use should be made of government tax-deductible loans, as was common in some other jurisdictions. Co-operatives should also be free to incorporate *without* share capital and to convert to, and from, this form of limited liability.

As to mergers, the consultants recommended the retaining of existing provisions for intrastate mergers, providing that all members were properly informed and 75 per cent of those voting approved. Recommendations dealing with the merger of a New South Wales co-operative with an *interstate* co-operative, however, involved a complex administrative process and approval by the New South Wales Supreme Court. The review said that interstate co-operatives should be free to pursue their objects in New South Wales, as co-operatives, rather than being required to register under the Companies (NSW) Code, provided they disclosed *all financial information* relating to their operations, equivalent to that available in respect of New South Wales co-operatives. With manoeuvring for market share, take-overs and mergers then in full swing in agriculture, particularly dairying, it was unlikely that interstate co-operatives would consider such transparency strategically wise, effectively preserving the *status quo*.

The report was largely silent on the question of uniform national co-operatives' legislation, other than to say:

> There may be further need for the New South Wales government to make arrangements with other states for compatible co-operative legislation with a view to seeking reciprocity along the lines achieved by the Companies Code.

On the question of a co-operative converting to a company the consultants recommended that the minister's approval need *not* be required for it was up to members to choose to sell or not sell the assets or undertakings of a co-operative:

> The term "takeover" has emotional connotations, particularly in a co-operative context. However, properly regulated to ensure full information to members, equal opportunity to participate, adequate time to assess a proposal and, most importantly, member determination of the fate of the proposal, a takeover proposal need not differ significantly from other forms of rearrangement of a co-operative's affairs. The above recommendations are directed towards the primacy of member self-determination subject to overriding guidelines of fairness as between all members.

The report said that while the position of directors should be elevated, boards should be made more *accountable* for decisions and directors *personally liable* for a breach of duty. The registrar should have powers to enforce directors' duties and remedies should exist for breaches, for example, indemnity insurance. External directors with 'expertise in making profits' should be permitted to sit on co-operative boards.

As for ICA co-operative principles, which were enshrined in existing legislation, albeit as an optional extra, consultants said that these were more suitable to small co-operatives than to large commercially-driven co-operatives and needed to be 'modified':

> *We accept that co-operative principles can apply successfully to co-operatives of all sizes, but note that as co-operatives become larger in size many of the classic issues of corporate regulation arise. For example, with growth co-operatives tend to exemplify the typical divorce of ownership from management control that is the foundation of many of the rules and regulations of companies. In this regard recommendations of our Review motivated by this tendency are designed to enhance members' control, thereby reinforcing co-operative principles albeit in a modified or more complex form.*

Referring to co-operative development, the report believed it was important for the functions of the minister, the registry and the Co-operatives' Advisory Council to be clarified. The minister should have a clear mandate for policy-making and the registry should be clothed with inspection powers similar to those existing under the Companies Code, including powers to obtain court orders to enforce directions. A Co-operatives Council should replace the Co-operatives Advisory Council and become the 'meeting place' of government and the co-operative movement:

> *The mid-point on specific decision-making involving exercising discretions for particular co-operatives should be placed in a representative body with experience and knowledge of co-operative principles, some element of accountability and removed from a person of administrative functions. The Co-operatives Council [should]…review decisions of the registrar upon request of a person aggrieved [and] delegate any discretions vested in it to the registrar with directions as to matters to be taken into account in exercising the delegation. The majority of members should be appointed by the minister, thereby importing an element of ministerial accountability. However, the minority members should be a wide variety of representatives of co-operatives appointed by the Australian Association of Co-operatives and other representative associations. The registrar should report to, be entitled to attend meetings of, but not be a voting member of the Council. The minister [or delegate] should be entitled to attend council meetings as he chooses and to chair meetings if he chooses.*

These recommendations, if proceeded with, would deliver far greater central control of co-operative development policy than ever before. An entity chaired by the minister or his delegate with a majority of members appointed by the minister and with only minority representation from 'other co-operative associations' could in no real sense be described as a co-operative representative body. Clothed with powers to review registry decisions, delegate tasks to the registry and brief the bureaucracy on the means of completing tasks, the proposed Co-operatives Council, potentially, could become a ginger group influencing the public policy agenda disproportionately.

It seems clear that consultants were recommending far more than simply an overhaul of existing legislation. They were advocating the radical re-engineering of co-operative principles and structure in corporate image. Every tenet of co-operative identity was to be tested: the democracy principle; the notion of shareholding; limited return on shares; the patronage principle; even 'dry' shareholders could be acceptable in another guise – CCU holders. The report concluded:

The above reforms to co-operative law are designed to enhance the business efficiency of the operation of co-operatives while valuing and protecting the control by members of co-operatives and applying co-operative principles in a systematic way. A heightened harmony between these two objectives is in the interest of achieving members' mutual objectives.[8]

'We do not want to be carved up by city lawyers and investment bankers'

In June 1989 the *Co-operation Act* review discussion report was made public for two months before final recommendations were to go to the minister. Copies of an executive summary of the recommendations were mailed to every co-operative in New South Wales. Press releases spoke of the review as a major overhaul of the co-operative system; the first in over sixty years; to bring co-operatives into line with other companies and give them the flexibility to compete while maintaining basic co-operative principles. The proposed legislation would help to improve efficiencies in co-operatives and allow them wider corporate powers to pursue their own objectives and determine their own destinies with less government intervention and more responsibilities for managers and directors.[9]

The AAC, however, questioned the government's motives in seeking to impose such radical change on the co-operative movement. While the association endorsed the idea of making co-operatives more flexible, officials were deeply concerned about the stronger role the government proposed for itself in co-operative affairs:

We believe there needs to be freeing up, but freeing up from the bureaucracy, from the paternalism, from the control of government that has been there for some sixty-odd years. Co-operatives need the freedom to operate as co-operatives, not in a paternalistic environment, but rather in a business-like environment that allows them to compete in the market place.

Many New South Wales rural co-operatives, Bruce Freeman said, were alarmed that the co-operative movement could be completely *dismantled* by the proposed legislative changes. The *Co-operation Act*, as it stood, was *not* out of date and did *not* need revitalisation. New South Wales co-operatives were 'vital and vibrant' and because of that were a target for takeover, not because they were ailing or inadequate in a business sense, as the report implied. The AAC was critically concerned that active membership provisions were being 'watered down' and viewed askance proposals for CCUs, the treatment of surpluses, takeover provisions, directors' responsibilities (especially in relation to community co-operatives), the imposition of additional regulation while the rest of the economy was *deregulating*, and the consultants' apparent fixation with external investments and shareholder *value*. Freeman alleged that the review's organisers 'are also the organisers of business seminars on how to take over co-operatives' and said, without detailing the allegation, that speculation was rife in the movement about the government's motives for so speedily seeking to rewrite the act. The co-operative movement had fought for many years to have active membership provisions included in the act and now the review was recommending the entry of *private investors* into co-operatives and so restructuring them that they would effectively *cease* to be co-operatives in any sense understood by genuine co-operators. Recommendations, purporting to *build up* co-operatives, were actually about *tearing them down* and, if the minister accepted them, they would have the reverse affect of stimulating new growth, almost certainly triggering a takeover by private investors of co-operatives. That was the real, hidden danger, Freeman protested, in the so-called 'freeing up' of co-operatives canvassed by the draft report. The AAC planned to visit rural co-operatives to discuss the proposals but, Freeman complained reasonably, there was '…little time to formulate a considered position before the deadline (16 August)…It's a very rushed thing'.

Responding to the discussion report, Legislative Councillor P B V Pezzuti said that an entrenched public service bureaucracy was unlikely to let the existing system change if that meant less opportunity for its people to interfere and empire build. Successive governments had been manipulated very carefully and skilfully by the public service and there was no reason to think otherwise now. Pezzuti was convinced that co-operative principles were about to be 'mangled' by vested interests and power consolidated in the hands of an entrenched and inbred co-operative leadership. The proposed restructuring of the co-operative sector would create '...a monolithic monopoly which is basically bureaucratic in nature and which will allow its controllers to divest, quite legally, substantial resources at farmer expense.' Farm ownership was already dangerously concentrated in corporate hands, Pezzuti continued, and 'mega' co-operatives, which were touted as desirable in the consultants' report, would concentrate decision-making further in metropolitan areas as dairy factories continued to be closed in rural districts in obeisance to 'economic rationalism'. The so-called 'overhaul' of the co-operative system was nothing but a grab for power by vested interests and would benefit controllers, not farmers.

There were other critics. The board and members of the Independent Liquor Group Co-operative Limited, for instance, were opposed to any watering down of active membership provisions and believed that CCUs were simply a ploy to usher in the gradual takeover of co-operatives:

> We certainly do not want the takeover provisions included. We are alarmed that the directors could be subject to court actions if present exclusions for liability are discontinued. The report was supposed to ensure efficient business operations of co-operatives and to enable them to maximise their objectives. Instead the report contradicts itself. Why introduce investment shares or CCUs when the full report says co-operatives have no problems raising capital generally.
>
> Our co-operative adheres to the principle of one-member-one-vote regardless of shareholding. When it does come time to count the numbers it ensures all members have an equal say. It is not efficient to have two types of shares, one seeking the long-term stability of the co-operative, the other short-term profits.
>
> Retain the active membership provisions. Co-operatives have just completed this and now it is suggested that this should be reversed in a takeover situation. Do not make optional the disclosure of relevant interest in shares and ensure the Premier keeps his promise to retain the active membership provisions.
>
> The substance of the existing act is serving co-operatives well. Why does the registrar need provisions for special investigations? Minister, please ensure the interests of co-operatives and those who work in them are upheld. We do not want to be carved up by city lawyers and investment bankers.

The widely respected, straight-talking Ricegrowers' Co-operative Limited Secretary Bruce Caldwell thought that consultants seemed 'obsessed' with restructuring co-operatives and had 'erroneously' concluded that the service-based co-operative concept was outmoded. Why were they so preoccupied with building up the *value* of capital held by shareholders in a co-operative? His co-operative disputed the logic of CCUs and the whole idea that for co-operatives capital-raising was a problem. Raising capital for co-operatives was *not a problem* – any profitable co-operative could readily raise capital. Only unprofitable co-operatives had problems in raising capital.

Some co-operatives also felt 'discomfort' about the proposed reporting and voting arrangements for CCUs, which they believed were not an appropriate instrument for co-operatives to raise capital. CCU holders, they believed, would in time exert influence conflicting with the interests of co-operative shareholders. 'Dry' shareholders, for example, could demand CCUs as equity when exiting a co-operative, bringing to bear intolerable capital strain on an organisation. Directors endeavouring to administer the proposed units would be put in a difficult position, particularly in the light of penalties for breach of duty being proposed.

A response from the Norco Co-operative noted:

> ...*in almost every instance where a matter of some substance is sought to be reviewed, the recommendation is to adapt a company law principle to solve the perceived problem. As a consequence, a number of provisions may well become part of a new act, which have no specific relevance to co-operatives.*

The Norco submission noted the report's inordinate attention to CCUs, which were 'irrelevant' to nearly all co-operatives other than a few agricultural co-operatives seeking growth. CCUs would achieve no purpose, would create more problems than they solved and would introduce difficulties in the treatment of surpluses, exposing co-operatives to takeover. Why would provision for CCUs need be included in an act ostensibly dedicated to co-operative development?[10]

The review is delayed

Administrative upheaval attending the calamitous crash of the (Victorian) Pyramid Building Society in 1990, the hasty invention of a nationally uniform prudential regulatory scheme for non-bank financial institutions (NBFI) under the Australian Financial Institutions Commission (AFIC) scheme, to which the minister was strongly opposed, and the advent of National Competition Policy (NCP), which required a review of *all* legislation to ensure consistency, brought the co-operatives legislation review process to a standstill. The proposed bill did not find its way into parliament until late 1991, was not passed until mid-1992 and not promulgated until May 1993, four years after the consultants' draft report!

Bruce Freeman: 'A co-operative movement in mortal danger'

In the interim, relations between the minister and AAC deteriorated notwithstanding Bruce Freeman's departure from the association in 1989 due to of poor health. Freeman did not leave quietly, however, warning that where the public and corporate sectors predominated, as was becoming the case in New South Wales, co-operatives inevitably would be squeezed and, where co-operative goals of self-help and democratic control were compromised, a co-operative movement was in mortal danger. The retiring co-operator said that many pseudo co-operatives in Australia were grooming themselves for take over at farmer expense and that moneyed interests were seeking legislative changes in respect of ownership and control to smooth the way. Freeman was utterly opposed to demutualisation believing, 'It is totally immoral that, at any point in time, members or shareholders or both can gain a capital gain at the expense of future generations.' The solution to a so-called 'co-operative dilemma', as some insisted upon characterising co-operatives' limited fund-raising ability, was a co-operative bank which understood and respected co-operative principles and did not constantly attack co-operative structure, like some 'so-called co-operative leaders with the government's ear'. The AAC and its predecessors had long argued for a unified, national co-operative development strategy educating the public and representing co-operatives in a co-ordinated, consistent way to federal government, Freeman added, but great and powerful farmer co-operatives had quietly opposed nationally uniform co-operatives' legislation. Why, he asked? Was it because they were concerned wholly with their own fortunes and not with general co-operative development? Government-centred co-operative development agendas, Freeman concluded, were a furphy and would lead the co-operative movement into a blind alley.[11]

There were few left in the New South Wales or Australian co-operative movements in the early 1990s with Bruce Freeman's passion and understanding of traditional co-operative values and their vulnerability to bureaucratic control, on the one hand, and corporate hybridisation, on the other. His departure left a huge gap in the movement's already depleted leadership ranks as government intervention and the priorities of commercially-orientated agricultural co-operatives became more prevalent.

CDB takes the lead in co-operative development

In late 1989 the minister flagged new directions for the CDB. The branch would now be focused on regional development and decentralisation in the contexts of a review of SMAs and NCP. Public policy in respect of co-operatives now comprised three strands: employing co-operatives for community-based regional development; constructing an alternative to SMAs; and enhancing agricultural co-operatives' competitiveness in preparation for deregulation.

With regard to the regional development strand the minister planned a co-operative bond scheme to encourage investment in local rural economies compensating for the closure of banks and other businesses and the withdrawal of government services. The department commissioned a consultant to explore the possibility of links with credit unions and building societies in micro-financing regional development through co-operatives, but there was little interest as NBFIs were preoccupied with the new AFIC scheme. CBD officers travelled extensively throughout rural districts advising farmers and community groups on how to form co-operatives. Facing significant staff cuts (as personnel were shifted to AFIC), however, the department was unable to process in a timely fashion the flurry of applications which arrived, a clue to the limitations of centrally-driven co-operative development programmes.

The Branch seconded a marketing specialist from the Department of Agriculture and Fisheries, Jim Manwaring, to develop co-operatives as an alternative to SMAs. Known affectionately by farmers as 'Mr Co-operatives' for his enthusiasm for the business model, Manwaring believed that SMAs were still suitable for mass commodities like wheat, wool and milk, but 'niche' markets like lamb, super-fine wool, beef, grain legumes, horticulture, oysters and goat meat would benefit from specialised marketing bodies; either co-operatives or other farmer-owned businesses. The marketing specialist set about educating farmers accustomed to regulation on how to co-operate, pointing to nine 'quality' strategies:

- research (feasibility studies);
- capital investments of significant sums of money (up to $1,500 per member);
- commitment and strict discipline;
- skilled directors, including external directors;
- competent managers;
- market (not production) driven economic goals and consumer focused marketing strategies ensuring a dependable supply to the co-operative;
- excellent communication;
- ongoing strategic planning; and
- rigorous organisational analysis including the development of new products.[12]

Aided by a $30,000 grant jointly provided by the CDB's Co-operative Development Fund, shire councils and a voluntary producer levy, Manwaring directed a grain legume marketing co-operative feasibility study undertaken by consultants to investigate the possibility of establishing a co-operative for pulse crops at Coonamble, in the minister's electorate in central western New South Wales. This was to be a prototype for the dismantling of SMAs employing the 'co-operative option' – a centrally-driven exemplar.

AAC is sidelined in New South Wales

The AAC wondered why the department seemed so intent upon developing a regional development capacity 'in direct competition to the various participating associations, who for many years have successfully operated such services', and why an officer had been engaged to promote co-operatives as an alternative to SMAs and the rural bond investment scheme when the AAC and the co-operative movement were fully qualified to do this. As far as determining public policy for New South Wales co-operatives, however, it seems the department had reached a view that AAC existed for national and international issues and had no particular mandate for co-operative development in the state.

The ICA Asia–Pacific Ministerial Co-operatives Conference and Exhibition 1990

Indeed, AAC was embarked upon an ambitious international co-operative trade agenda. In February 1990 the association convened the ICA Asia–Pacific Ministerial Co-operatives Conference and Exhibition at Darling Harbour, Sydney, designed to showcase the diversity of Australian co-operatives and encourage trade in 'value-added' primary products between co-operatives in the region. Describing co-operation as a 'middle way between capitalism and regulated state-ownership systems', Federal Minister for Primary Industry and Energy John Kerin called upon the rural co-operative movement to seize opportunities in domestic markets as governments dismantled SMAs, while expanding export markets. In both instances, the minister believed, the prospects were hampered by the absence of nationally uniform co-operatives' legislation. Kerin urged the co-operative movement to *agree* on this vital issue, and quickly, or opportunities would be lost forever.

Recommendations from the conference included one to establish a Federal Ministerial Council for Co-operatives with powers to drive a comprehensive co-operative development strategy, 'harmonise' states' co-operatives' legislation and better inform the public about co-operatives. The AAC also undertook to examine the feasibility of establishing a co-operative bank. (Discussion on these issues is resumed in Chapter Twelve.) The point here is that AAC was embarked on a national co-operative development strategy emphasising traditional co-operative principles and federal or uniform co-operatives legislation, while the New South Wales department was focused on state-rights issues and legislative reforms radically altering co-operative principles and structure to enhance fund-raising and the competitiveness of major agricultural co-operatives. Inevitably, these agendas would cut across each other.

The Ministerial Council on Future Directions for Co-operatives is revived

New South Wales seemed more determined than ever to proceed unilaterally in the business of co-operative development. With the Co-operatives Bill on hold, the minister's attention turned to the matter of the general long-term development of the 'co-operative sector', as the co-operative movement was now commonly called. In line with this the Ministerial Council on Future Directions for Co-operatives, first convened by Labor in 1986, was reconstituted, chaired by former Dairy Farmers' Managing Director Don Kinnersley.

Two months after the AAC-ICA Darling Harbour Conference, this council convened a 'Marketing for the '90s' seminar at Charles Sturt University, Bathurst. The tenor of the meeting suggests that New South Wales had no intention of leaving all of the initiative in overseas co-operative trade with the AAC–ICA agreement. Soon after, Minister Peacocke and thirty New South Wales business representatives and departmental officers left for the United States, Canada and UK in a *tour de force* seeking business links for New South Wales' rural co-operatives. The minister also represented the Australian co-operative movement at the World Council of Credit Unions (WOCCU) Convention in Canada.

Not surprisingly, rumblings emanated from sections of the co-operative movement and not only AAC that the government was driving into co-operative development issues too hard and fast and questions arose about New South Wales' self-appointed national mantle, for which it was unqualified. The fact was, however, AAC's financial position was again the subject of registry scrutiny and the association itself did not enjoy a national mandate.[13]

Pressure on departmental resources

Following the Greiner Coalition's re-election in March 1991, the Premier's Department determined to propel deregulatory change, believing that the industry consultative process was taking too long. The government launched a fundamental review of all programmes, the most ambitious ever undertaken by a government in that state, designed to flush out programmes with 'no clear definition of who the client is or what the outcome should be'. Departments were directed to become 'outcomes orientated [in ways] which the public can legitimately expect' and agencies were challenged to consider the rationale for their continued existence. A Management Council was established to conduct a forensic review of all government functions. In a ministerial shuffle, Gerry Peacocke was made Minister for Local Government and Minister for Co-operatives, accepting a mighty work load. Following an Electoral Commission redistribution, however, the minister's seat of Dubbo was significantly reshaped and the number of Lower House MPs was reduced, disappointing Peacocke, whose cabinet seat was now in doubt.

With a Victorian inquiry into the collapsed Pyramid Building Society proceeding, highlighting a serious lack of resources available to the regulator, a New South Wales inquiry indicated a similar situation while noting that prudential standards were generally better in that state than elsewhere in Australia:

> *Currently the resources of the Registry of Co-operatives within Business and Consumer Affairs are barely adequate to satisfy the immediate statutory requirements of the registry and certainly do not permit the registry to fully discharge its range of duties. This is evidenced by the backlog in a number of areas and by the numbers of approved programmes deferred through lack of resources, in particular its lack of human resources.*

Approximately twenty of the registry's forty-nine staff positions were about to be transferred to AFIC and, as mentioned above, already a work backlog existed, including numerous applications from interstate co-operatives, credit unions and friendly societies, which could not be quickly processed. The office was prevented from making field visits to assist troubled or new co-operatives and from conducting sector studies or performing inspections at a time when many new co-operatives were forming or seeking guidance on forming. (250 new co-operatives were formed over the next eight years!) The most demoralising aspect of the restructure from a staff point of view was that the registry was now being shunted 'from pillar to post' across different locations in Sydney. The portfolio was losing profile.

The Bega Butter Factory 1978
Photo courtesy of Bega Co-operative Society Limited

The Australian Co-operative Development League

Faced with resource difficulties, in August 1991 the minister redirected the Co-operative Development Trust Fund from AAC to support co-operative development work within the registry. Some of this work was to be undertaken by a new quasi-independent industry advisory body, the Co-operative Development League (later Australian Co-operative Development League [ACDL]). The official rationale was that AAC's future was under a financial cloud and it was therefore 'not fit to lead co-operative development impacting on New South Wales co-operative affairs'. Registered as a community-advancement co-operative under the *Co-operation Act*, ACDL staff included Jim Manwaring and former AAC staffers Jim McCall and Reg Nichols. Jim McCall was appointed ACDL Director Co-ordinator and Ministerial Policy Adviser.[14]

ACDL assumed responsibility for the AAC–ICA international trading agreement and duplicated many of the association's functions. Jim Manwaring was sent by the government to the United States to study New Generation Co-operatives (NGCs), modern funding models for co-operatives and innovative marketing methods for agricultural co-operatives. ACDL also developed Manwaring's earlier work, advising farmers (including interstate farmers) on how to form a co-operative, for example, Bundaberg (Queensland) producers interested in tomato marketing and farmers interested in cotton ginning at Warren, wine and grape marketing in the Hunter Valley and fruit and vegetable markets on the Southern Tablelands. ACDL also provided taxation advice, once a province of AAC, and issued a newsletter.

The *Co-ops 2000* Strategy

With ACDL in place, the department prepared for one of the most ambitious co-operative development programmes ever mounted in Australia; *Co-ops 2000*; which grew from the Ministerial

Council on Future Directions for Co-operatives. A *Co-ops 2000* Co-operative Development Strategy Steering Committee was formed, chaired by Don Kinnersley with CDB Manager Garry Cronan serving as executive officer. Essentially a policy to action programme, the declared purpose of *Co-ops 2000* was to provide the government with a strategic planning blueprint for co-operative development in the approach to the millennium. Garry Cronan noted:

> *The task of Co-ops 2000 is to provide an overall planning umbrella so that the relevance of individual initiatives can be fully considered in the broader context so a judgement and an assessment as to what is necessary for strategic sustainable development of co-operatives in New South Wales can be made.*

Five working parties were created, directed by the Ministerial Council and the *Co-ops 2000* steering committee: funding and regional development; value-adding and exports; education and training; legislation and micro-economic reform; and social responsibility. Fifty representatives of the co-operative movement, private enterprise, government departments, professional advisers, researchers and universities were invited to participate in the working parties, the focus of which extended to:

- ❖ trends affecting co-operative development;
- ❖ capital-raising for value-added processing and manufacture through co-operatives;
- ❖ international trade;
- ❖ joint ventures;
- ❖ regional development and funding opportunities for co-operatives;
- ❖ the relationship between *Co-ops 2000* and other government strategies;
- ❖ appropriate legislation at state or federal level;
- ❖ education and public awareness;
- ❖ training for co-operatives;
- ❖ strategies for the integration of co-operative sectors;
- ❖ successful case studies;
- ❖ opportunities in deregulation;
- ❖ a national co-operative database; and
- ❖ the type of development infrastructure needed in New South Wales to bring about sustained development of the co-operative sector – government department, statutory authority, foundation or an industry-based association?

Working parties were required to submit interim reports by December 1991 (when the Co-operatives Bill entered parliament for a first reading). It was envisaged that reports would form the basis of a Green Paper for circulation and discussion, leading to a White Paper briefing the government by August 1992. Australian Co-operative Foods (ACF) (the result of a merger between Dairy Farmers, Hunter Valley and Shoalhaven co-operatives) Chairman Ian Langdon was commissioned to conduct a survey of co-operatives 'to confirm the issues identified by the steering committee and working parties', that is, ownership and funding, legislation, education and promotion. A *Co-ops 2000* Implementation Committee was formed, described as a sub-committee of the 'Co-operatives Council' (which presumably did not yet officially exist as the Co-operatives Bill had not been promulgated), comprising ministerial appointments nominated by sector 'stakeholders'.

AAC questions the *Co-ops 2000* Strategy

AAC Education and Training Manager Tim Dyce wanted to know what particular problem *Co-ops 2000* purported to fix. Was it perhaps a solution in search of a problem? Dyce thought the strategy's policy-to-objectives-to-responsibility process was strange and 'insufficient motivation in itself to ensure a commitment to achieving objectives'. *Co-ops 2000* was purely a 'governmental initiative and the co-operative movement…still has to pick it up fully, own it and work with the government better to prepare it for use by the rest of the country'. Dyce also noted adroitly how AAC was struggling to fund educational work, while *Co-ops 2000* seemed amply resourced.

The minister introduces the act

In December 1991 Minister Gerry Peacocke carried his 243 page, 466-section Co-operatives Bill into the New South Wales Lower House and set about reading the massive document, taking nearly two hours and ten minutes to do so. The purpose of the bill, the minister said, was to replace the 1923 *Co-operation Act*. Co-operative housing societies, Starr-Bowketts (interest-free building societies), non-terminating building societies and several existing (unnamed) societies, however, would be permitted to continue under the old act for the time being. Essentially, Peacocke told parliament, the bill was designed to encourage co-operative development, the philosophy of co-operation, co-operative self-management, the integration of the co-operative sector, remove the old act's paternalism and introduce greater disclosure, accountability and flexibility for co-operatives. A key feature was the abolition of the doctrine of *ultra vires*, affording co-operatives a legal capacity similar to that of corporations. Aspects of Corporations Law were included in the act because:

> *Current thinking in public policy leads me to the belief that at a number of levels there is considerable reappraisal occurring regarding the types of ideas which this country needs to pursue to be successful in an increasingly competitive world environment. One response to these needs can occur through the further development, strengthening and expansion of the co-operative movement. A set of beliefs perhaps loosely defined as co-operative beliefs will I believe play an increasingly important role in the identification of opportunities for growth in this state.*

The minister said that he was no less enthusiastic than New South Wales Nationalist Attorney-General T R Bavin had been when introducing the *Co-operation Act* in 1922. Bavin had described his legislation as the most important bill to come before parliament that session and Peacocke believed the current bill was no less portentous with potential to 'transform society fundamentally'. General co-operatives in New South Wales, he told the House, produced an annual turnover of $2.2 billion; mainly in primary industry; held $1.2 billion in assets, had 822,000 members and were dominant in the dairy, fish, sugar, rice and cotton industries and prominent in horticulture, stone fruit, bananas, meat and eggs. He had not accepted all of the review consultants' recommendations, he said, and would continue to 'work closely both personally and through the office of the Registry of Co-operatives with the AAC'; which, the minister claimed, now fully supported the bill; and would work with 'others' to ensure the success of the act. He was particularly heartened 'by the wide spread acceptance the exposure bill received from co-operatives generally'. The bill was one element of other initiatives being taken by the government to develop a broad strategic plan for the co-operative sector in New South Wales (*Co-ops 2000*), which would herald a new beginning, a new phase of robust growth for co-operatives. The strategy would help co-operatives to improve efficiency, enhance export performance and move further into value-adding areas so that they could assume their rightful place in the state's mainstream of economic and social activity. In one of many hints that the minister hoped his legislative reforms would carry into the national arena, Peacocke described the bill as the most up-to-date legislation for co-operatives in Australia, adding that New South Wales would continue to take a leading role in the development, operation and supervision of the co-operative sector.

Under the bill's provisions, the minister continued, co-operatives would have enhanced corporate powers '…providing them with the powers of a natural person, a situation equivalent with corporations'. Any 'natural' person could become a member of a co-operative, whether a corporation or private enterprise. A corporation could be registered as a co-operative if it functioned in accordance with co-operative principles included in the bill. Five corporations, for instance, could form a co-operative if they abided by those principles. By abolishing the doctrine of *ultra vires* in application to co-operatives entities they would be freed from rigid, confining objectives and could simply declare primary activities in the rules for purposes of determining active membership.

Voting would continue to be on a one-member-one vote basis and there would be restrictions on the voting rights of a member who held shares in which another person had an interest. Proxy voting was limited to five votes. However, former members ('dry' shareholders) would be entitled to share in any surplus from a winding-up or sale of a co-operative for up to *five* years (later changed to three years but not *two*, recommended by AAC) after forfeiting shares, if purchased by an organisation *other than* a co-operative. Similarly, if a co-operative converted to a company, was wound-up, or became a subsidiary, former members were to be notified. Any decision to sell, wind-up or convert a co-operative would have to be agreed to by at least 75 per cent of active members.

With regard to capital-raising (the most controversial aspect of the bill), the proposed legislation gave co-operatives a '…clearer range of alternatives in determining the optimal capital structure to best service the needs of the members'. In addition to powers to incur subordinated debt and raise funds through member shares, entry fees, periodic charges to members, the retention of profits from trading and debt-finance raised externally, co-operatives were to have a new fund-raising option, a form of *non-active member* capital to be known as 'Co-operative Capital Units (CCUs)'. Co-operative surpluses could as usual be distributed by way of rebates, dividends and bonus shares but the bill did not prescribe ways of treating unallocated reserves; that was a matter for members to decide.

The legislation contemplated co-operatives *with* or *without* share capital, the latter pertaining to non-pecuniary organisations, and allowed for a variety of shareholder models. Shares were to be of one class, but two or more persons could hold shares jointly (with only one vote) if the rules allowed. Shares could be issued at a premium but not at a discount, were transferable to active members and capable of devolution by will or the operation of law subject to a co-operative's rules. A member could buy or sell shares to other members but any relevant interest was not to exceed 20 per cent of the nominal value of the issued share capital of a co-operative. (The new supreme policy-setting authority, the Co-operatives Council, however, could '…increase the maximum percentage in a particular case or approve of a special resolution increasing the maximum percentage'.) With a board's consent shares could be sold to any person if there were 'reasonable grounds for believing' that that person *would be* an active member. Shares in a co-operative could also be transferred to a person if that person's offer was approved by 'holders of at least 90 per cent of the nominal value of the shares concerned (within four months)'. A co-operative could *compulsorily* require members to take up additional shares provided proper disclosure measures were taken.

Co-operatives would be free to invest in other bodies, corporations, unit trusts, joint ventures and partnerships and in certain circumstances could engage in exclusive dealings. For example, a member could be required to have specific dealings with a co-operative for a fixed period and to enter into a contract for that purpose 'even though in restraint of trade' because of the unique character of co-operatives. Exemptions for purposes of the *Trades Practices Act* might in special circumstances be granted. (This provision was subsequently repealed.)

Up to 25 per cent (one in four) of a board could be other than an active member. Corporations Law standards would apply to directors and, in line with this, co-operatives would be required to take appropriate insurance. Greater director responsibility involved greater accountability and there were severe penalties for punishable offences. Co-operatives would have similar business reporting standards to those which applied to corporations and all directors of 'reporting entities' would be legally responsible for the same standard of reporting requirements as applied to commercial entities. Co-operatives could apply to the registrar for a less onerous reporting regime.

The legislation would facilitate the merger or acquisition of co-operatives whether interstate or local with another co-operative or corporation and recognise the separate registration and operation of interstate co-operative organisations in New South Wales. Part 12 described how, in the case of an amalgamation between a local and interstate co-operative, the resulting co-operative would, as far as New South Wales was concerned, be able to select the place of registration and domicile. Co-operatives from outside New South Wales could register as foreign co-operatives and would have *largely* the same powers as local co-operatives but they were required to comply with certain (unspecified, probably disclosure) conditions if they solicited for members in New South Wales, or provided certain services to members resident in New South Wales, or carried on business in the state. Mergers, transfers and reconstructions involving foreign (interstate) co-operatives would be permitted but provisions were limited to the extent of the legislative power of the State of New South Wales and subject to complementary legislation being enacted in the foreign jurisdiction. (That is, they would not be impossible, but difficult, costly and contingent upon legislative reform.)

Part 13 detailed a complex process for dealing with arrangements and reconstructions. A co-operative would be free to convert to come under corporate law, but, while converting to some other form of business model meant it would cease to be registered as a co-operative, '...the new body established is to be treated as a continuation of the co-operative'.

The bill retained the six ICA co-operative principles included in the *Co-operation Act*: voluntary association and open membership; democratic control; limited interest on capital; equitable division of surplus; co-operative education; and co-operation among co-operatives. As was the case in the *Co-operation Act*, however, their application was not obligatory, but the principles would be applied when interpreting the law with a view to enabling a 'co-operative' outcome.

Provision existed for associations and federations of co-operatives. An association of co-operatives could involve two or more co-operatives or, if an association had fifty or more members, a body 'which is incorporated under any other law (whether or not of New South Wales) may become a member of it'. Such organisations, even though not necessarily co-operative, would be required to function in accordance with co-operative principles.

The bill allowed co-operatives greater freedom from registry intervention but sharpened that office's powers in respect of investigation and enforcement. The registrar could no longer refuse the registration of co-operatives but retained powers to transfer the engagements of a co-operative to another entity.

A Co-operatives Council was to replace the old Advisory Council. The new council would consist of nine members appointed by the minister for up to five years, four of them to be persons nominated by co-operatives and selected by the minister together with representatives from AAC, ACDL, the ICA representative in Australia or other departmental officials. The registrar would be entitled to attend and chair Co-operatives Council meetings or appoint a deputy. A clear chain of command was articulated: the minister determined policy; the registrar implemented policy; and the Co-operatives Council had regard to the minister's policy in exercising functions. The registry was empowered to provide secretariat and administrative support for the Co-operatives Council.[15]

Launching *Co-ops 2000*

Anticipating prompt passage of the bill, Minister Peacocke officially launched *Co-ops 2000*. The co-operative movement, he said, must look to the future and bridge a communication gap with the community. It was vital that co-operative development was consistent with the government's priorities and, the minister added, 'the government's role should be to help facilitate development by providing the necessary structures within which the co-operative movement and the broader community generally can agree on a future sense of direction and purpose'.

The CDB began having 'visions' and issuing 'mission statements', then popular in the business world. The wording was finessed over time, but essentially *Co-ops 2000* was focused on economic performance and designed to achieve a co-operative movement, which by the year 2000 would be:

- ❖ materially greater, meeting the economic and social needs of members;
- ❖ more actively involved in a wider range of industries;
- ❖ financially strong with easier access to capital-raising;
- ❖ fewer in number but stronger and adding value to exports in accordance with international best practice;
- ❖ occupying a major market share of exports to Asia;
- ❖ forming a growing market segment of viable businesses in Australia;
- ❖ comprising decentralised agricultural groups and domestic-based service providers and industries;
- ❖ focused on sustainability;
- ❖ exploiting well-researched market opportunities through developed products and services to meet customer needs;
- ❖ better understood and respected by all sectors of government and commerce for having created additional employment;
- ❖ benefiting from the services of a market-driven Registry of Co-operative Societies funded on a fee-for-service basis;
- ❖ making a significant contribution to the state's economy; and
- ❖ the New South Wales *Co-operatives Act* would form the basis of nationally consistent legislation for co-operatives.[16]

The ACDL co-operative bank initiative

One of ACDL's most ambitious projects at this time, pursuant to the *Co-ops 2000* Strategy, was an attempt to launch a co-operative bank. A feasibility study, originally initiated by AAC, was picked up and developed. A questionnaire was circulated among co-operatives noting, in almost evangelical language, that co-operative finance was at a crossroads and inviting co-operatives and kindred organisations to participate in forming a new bank:

Some old guards have powerful positions to protect, many will have genuine misgivings, some will regard [the idea] as all too much hard work, whilst others will argue the time is not right. There can be no birth without pain. Therefore, co-operatives must grasp the nettle now cast before them or miss the opportunity that will surely be lost to them for decades to come...The aspirations of thousands of co-operators [are] on trial...with many convinced that the sleeping giant can spring from its slumber to take its rightful place in the community.

The ACDL proposed 'a co-operative bank operation' for ordinary people, small businesses, mutual business and the rural sector, based on European models, particularly Rabobank, which drew upon a credit union pedigree and was The Netherlands' third largest bank. The proposed bank would consist of a consortium of credit unions, building societies, grain and other co-operatives and mutual organisations, which would apply for a banking licence from the Reserve Bank. Building societies and credit unions would continue operating separately under AFIC legislation but would introduce a co-operative banking agency into their operations.

In January 1992 the minister invited the Association of New South Wales Credit Unions (ANSWCU) to a meeting with ACDL to consider the proposal. ANSWCU was cool to the idea, not having been involved in the feasibility study and protesting that insufficient time and documentation existed to make a sensible decision. The proposal also came at a bad time as NBFI were still preoccupied with AFIC issues and the co-operative bank idea simply complicated things and distracted attention. Unsubstantiated rumours spread that the department and the bank's backers were using the proposal to undermine confidence in the AFIC scheme. The minister vociferously denied these 'conspiratorial rumours' arguing that his department's primary concern was possible injury to New South Wales' co-operatives and credit unions through 'weak' prudential standards, possibly inferior to New South Wales' standards and noting that he was supported in this view by Victorian Attorney-General Keenan, who was also opposed to AFIC legislation. The minister also denied that the co-operative bank proposal was intended 'to undermine the lending base of the State Bank of New South Wales', which the government was preparing to sell, and cut across the business of Australia's (then) largest building society, St George, which was preparing to apply for a banking licence. With the New South Wales government distancing itself from any idea that it would financially support the proposed bank (and with a controversy building in the government's ailing Homefund Scheme, constructed on co-operative housing societies), the ACDL proposal lapsed for want of support, joining a long list of failed attempts to create a co-operative bank (discussed in Appendix Two).[17]

The Coonamble Wool Processing Co-operative Project

Meanwhile, with AAC struggling, the association's trading arrangement with ICA lost momentum. In 1992 a Chinese co-operatives' delegation representing co-operatives with 114,000,000 members and 4,000,000 employees visited Australia. Delegates complained that they had been negotiating with Australian groups for several years seeking joint ventures and this was a 'final effort'. The minister and departmental officers personally assisted the delegation and were successful in brokering an agreement with the All China Federation of Supply and Marketing Co-operatives and the Jiangsu Provincial Union of Supply and Marketing Co-operatives for the supply of scoured, cleaned and topped wool for manufacture. This was a marvellous opportunity for Australian co-operatives.

The agreement came after the Coonamble Shire President approached the minister and ACDL Policy Adviser Jim McCall with a view to finding co-operative solutions for hard-pressed wool growers facing deregulation and a collapse in world wool prices. A feasibility study funded through the Co-operative Development Fund recommended a 'value-added' co-operative, selling directly to manufacturers and employing modern marketing techniques. The Coonamble Wool Processing Co-operative was duly formed as a pilot project to demonstrate 'appropriate' government promotion of co-operatives for regional development, assisted by the registry and with the department providing on-going support. If successful, the co-operative would serve as a model for wider application in rural New South Wales and Australia, linking agricultural co-operatives to a 'huge global network' through the ICA and other co-operative agencies. The plan was to market in Europe, Israel and Japan, clothing and other woollen goods manufactured by China Inter-Co-op.

Other co-operative pilot projects

The ACDL conducted further negotiations with Korean and Japanese co-operatives, seeking investments in feed-lot facilities and abattoirs in the Coonamble area for value-added products to be marketed by a Feed Lot and Meat Marketing Co-operative through Uni-Co-op (the Agricultural Union of Japan). The department also funded the continued presence in Australia in 1993 of an ICA representative briefed to work closely with the minister and ACDL in realising the full potential of the wool-scouring and feed-lot co-operatives at Coonamble and other *Co-op 2000* projects and to assist with direct co-operative-to-co-operative trade. ACDL opened a 'world class' international co-operative retail and trade exhibition centre in The Rocks, Sydney to serve as a 'showcase' of co-operative excellence. *Co-ops 2000* appeared to be delivering practical results.[18]

'Wealth and income': the Co-operatives Bill receives a second reading

In a political environment where legislation was coming under scrutiny for consistency with National Competition Policy, further refinements were necessary before the Co-operatives Bill entered parliament for a second reading in April 1992. (62 pages of additional regulations and standard rules were subsequently added.)

The bill passed with bipartisan support and general congratulations to the minister from both sides of the House. Much commentary in the debate, which was characterised by glowing oratory attesting co-operation's virtues, alluded to the sheer *size* of the legislation. Apart from a few questions about the minister's frequent references to capital problems allegedly afflicting co-operatives and external investors, however, support for the bill was generally uniform contrasting with torrid debates of the 1920s when cross-party diatribes of an ideological nature centred on co-operation reverberated around the chamber. In the 1990s co-operation was something both sides of the House saw simply as a legitimate business model with distinctive characteristics enhancing competitiveness and of no threat whatsoever to the status quo.

Mr Amery (Labor, Mount Druitt) led debate for the Opposition. Amery was more than pleased to support the bill, which, he said, had met with the approval of the co-operative movement 'by and large' although some in the sugar industry still had reservations. The legislation was virtually a 'rule book' for co-operatives and, he said, formed a basis for optimism about the future. Amery spoke of the economic force of the state's co-operatives, describing them as 'flourishing' in industries other than those already noted by the minister, including beef, veal, lamb, pork, processed foods, printing, saw-milling, insurance and job creation. He referred to the long-established and intensely co-operative-minded Curlewis Farmers' Co-operative which was returning record profits to the community in a recession, due to strong community support. The Egg Producers' Co-operative, he continued, had rescued the government from an 'irresponsible blunder' in deregulating the industry. But, Amery noted, there were real concerns in sections of the co-operative movement about CCUs, about external investors who could buy in and sell out at will, and the possible financial destabilisation this could cause, precipitating a takeover. The Opposition would monitor the operation of CCUs very carefully.

Mr Jeffrey (National Party, Oxley), a rice farmer, said, 'Without doubt the minister will go down in history as one of the greatest ministers ever for the co-operative movement in Australia.' Jeffrey welcomed the registrar's increased powers because, he said, some co-operatives were becoming very large and complex commercial business structures. He saw a future for co-operatives in giant corporations forming co-operatives, for example Broken Hill Proprietary (BHP) and cement companies co-operating to compete with overseas tenders in building toll roads.

Mr Martin (Labor, Port Stephens), the son of a dairy farmer and knowledgeable about agricultural co-operatives, referred to the twenty-four fishing co-operatives in the state as exemplars of orderly marketing in an industry facing imminent deregulation. However, he saw problems for the co-operative movement 'down the line' because it was being *re-regulated* while industries in which co-operatives operated were *deregulating*. Co-operatives ran the risk of being 'squeezed by regulation and at the other end by deregulation'. That was 'dangerous' and the co-operative movement could find itself in 'big trouble'. It was *easy* to destroy a co-operative movement and '… there are many destroyers in our community'. The minister and his colleagues, Martin said, were:

> …*driven probably by a more narrow view than a more overall view of the industry [and] whole industries rather than just co-operatives or marketing units should be considered…In industries which are being squeezed, mavericks may want to break away for a quick gain for a few individuals and this can ruin a co-operative movement.*

Mr Fraser (Coffs Harbour) congratulated the minister who 'eats, drinks, breathes and sleeps co-operatives'. In fact, in addition to co-operatives in a crowded portfolio the minister had also to think about council rates, swimming pools, flags, sewerage, pollution, motor vehicle and property maintenance, roads and road safety, town and country planning, farmer conservation, growth centres, land rezoning and town and country planning, among other issues. The bill, Fraser believed, obviously with commercial co-operatives in mind, put co-operatives on a 'level playing field' with corporate competitors. With regard to CCUs, however, Fraser urged the minister to quickly develop 'appropriate guidelines at a very early stage after the commencement of this act', the inference being that the financial instruments could be a threat to continued farmer control of co-operatives.

Mr Small (Murray), who had grown up with the rice industry, congratulated the minister who 'has done his homework', saying that he supported any move to assist farmers. He referred to the 'rice industry parliament – the Rice Industry Executive Committee, which consisted of Ricegrowers' Co-operative Limited, the Ricegrowers' Association and the Rice Marketing Board – as a 'shining example of economic democracy in action'. Rice growers, he reminded the assembly, ran the industry democratically and owned every nut and bolt in it. Growers leaving the industry could recoup money which they had contributed for its development and 'I have never seen another industry work in that way'. He hoped that the bill would help co-operatives in other industries to develop similarly.

Acknowledging the many compliments, Minister Peacocke emphasised that the bill was about primary production, value-adding, exports and *wealth* and that he saw the legislation as a blueprint for the nation:

> *This piece of legislation is extraordinarily important for those of us who believe in freedom and the rights of ordinary people in society to have the mechanisms and opportunities to create*

wealth, to improve their own standards of living and to be able to operate economically in a free society. We have the ability through the co-operative sector to transform the economy of the state and of the nation. Using every ability I have and every tool available to me I intend to see that the development of value-adding to our primary produce takes place in Australia creating new wealth, new jobs and new prosperity for our ordinary people...The range of co-operative opportunities is vast – almost limitless. Co-operatives are a way in which ordinary people like all of us here can co-operate with one another to create wealth and to improve our income and what we can do....Never has there been a greater window of opportunity for the development of new co-operatives in this state than there is today...Co-operatives will be the way of the future in Australia as government intrusion is reduced and the ability of people to control their own destinies is enhanced...This liberating legislation will enable co-operatives to expand.

The minister said that Australian co-operation was retarded relative to the vast, integrated movements of Japan, North America, Western and Eastern Europe, South America, China and the UK – just about anywhere in the world but Australia. He referred to the 'Coonamble co-operative experiment' being conducted in his seat of Dubbo, which, if successful, would be replicated throughout the state. Dismissing criticisms of CCUs, Peacocke believed they would be a major success in promoting the co-operative movement.

The Co-operatives Bill passed through the Legislative Assembly in May 1992. Another year would pass before it was promulgated, however, as the time-consuming task of drawing up regulatory detail and model rules consistent with the legislation and NCP continued in a resource-depleted registry.[19]

'Hybridising' Co-operatives': The *Co-operatives Act*

The name said it all – *'Co-operatives Act'*. This legislation was not about a philosophy called co-operation, as its predecessor ostensibly had been, but about a business model with peculiarities – a determination by users to control their business. Garry Cronan, whose difficult task it was to 'market' the omnibus act to general co-operatives, said it could help them become an important third sector enhancing regional development, exports, value-adding and industrial self-management and self-regulation. He strongly endorsed the abolition of *ultra vires* for co-operatives and applauded the greater commercial flexibility the act provided through provisions for mobilising capital, transparency and disclosure, takeovers, conversions, winding-up and co-operative principles. Nevertheless, Cronan acknowledged that the legislation's 'hybrid' corporate-co-operative interface was potentially confusing:

One way to characterise the Act is that for matters of internal governance such as voting and co-operative principles, co-operative legislation has been the main source. On the other hand Corporations Law has been the model...for matters predominantly concerned with external or third parties. The Act is an attempt to balance the convenience of using a well-developed and widely understood set of procedures drawn from the body of company law with the need to develop and maintain unique co-operative practice... Corporations Law also has an affect on co-operatives if they operate outside their home state. If a co-operative seeks to undertake fund-raising or to significantly carry on business with members outside its state it will generally find that it needs not only to comply with its home state's legislation, but probably the co-operative legislation in the other state or states as well as Corporations Law itself.[20]

Donald Margarey, a principal in the law firm which had conducted the minister's review of the *Co-operation Act* and author of *A Guide to the Co-operatives Act*, commissioned by the New South

Wales Registry of Co-operatives, described the legislation as 'a departure from earlier legislation' in that it sought to promote the self-regulation of co-operatives 'with accompanying enhanced disclosure and accountability provisions and the encouragement of greater commercial freedom in the management of co-operatives'. The act existed, he said, to promote *disclosure* rather than to *regulate* choices. Major reforms lay in the fields of capital-raising, the abolition of *ultra vires*, defining directors' responsibilities and distribution of power in the Co-operatives Council. Jenni Mattila, a lawyer associated with the *Co-ops 2000* Strategy (and later with the drafting of Victorian co-operatives' legislation), said that the act allowed co-operatives greater freedom consistent with co-operative principles while providing a more appropriate and enhanced regulatory and supervisory framework. Dairy Farmers Official Historian Jan Todd believed the Act was 'designed to bring co-operative culture and operations into closer alignment with the corporate sector [and] acknowledge that, a century on, co-operatives still had a capital problem'.[21]

Indeed, the *Co-operatives Act*, which was concentrated on structural, administrative, procedural and compliance issues, sought to mould co-operatives in a corporate image while preserving vestiges of distinctive co-operative identity. As such it was a genuine attempt to resolve the 'co-operative dilemma' residing in co-operative structure between the contesting imperatives of capital adequacy and the democracy principle and potentially useful for large trading co-operatives. Focused on the economic functions of co-operatives, particularly the competitiveness of agricultural co-operatives, the act was preoccupied with takeovers, mergers, control and, above all and unashamedly, capital accumulation and wealth creation. Legitimate as these concerns might be for commercial co-operatives, they were largely irrelevant to small, not-for-profit community and service-based co-operatives, the heartland of the co-operative movement. The act was about making commercial co-operatives more competitive in industries where they were economically and politically strong, especially dairying, rice and sugar, and efficient vehicles for the achievement of government economic and political priorities. There was nothing new in this. The *Co-operation Act* had been forged in a similar crucible: woo the rural vote; attract foreign investment; improve investor confidence; encourage the export of farm products; and accelerate regional development. The grafting of corporate law onto the co-operative stem, however, was new and there was no guarantee that the hybrid would 'take'.

The *Co-operatives Act* was nevertheless truly momentous in Australian co-operatives' history, politically transforming co-operatives from membership organisations to partly membership–partly investor entities. The act put a new spin on the old co-operative 'middle way' idea in that co-operatives were no longer seen as vehicles for striking a democratic path between state-socialism and *laissez-faire* capitalism, but simply business models negotiating a legalistic tightrope between co-operatives' and corporate law.

'Members come last'

The act's critics complained that ordinary members now seemed to come last. For example, in order to alter a co-operative's rules it was necessary first to seek the registrar's approval *before* putting the proposed rule change to a special resolution. The Co-operatives Council could *order* a co-operative to change its rules regardless of members' wishes. A co-operative was required to report to the registrar at least a *fortnight* before reporting to members at the AGM! Registry inspectors were clothed with sweeping powers to inspect a co-operative's books under twelve headings, many of which only accountants and lawyers could understand, for example capital adequacy provisions. Although a co-operative had all the powers and legal capacity of a natural person, it could not act by itself – only *agents* could act for it, and they were required by the rules to have a detailed knowledge of laws governing business and commerce while exercising a duty of care, for which fidelity bonds and insurance were mandatory. Where was the autonomy and democracy in this? How could small, community-based co-operatives possibly cope with this highly technical blunderbuss and the expense and risk it implied?

Cross-border trade

The act also did nothing, critics said, to overcome costly compliance issues hampering the interstate operations of New South Wales cross-border operations. Interstate regulators were understandably wary of accepting into their jurisdiction co-operatives affected by the application of Corporations Law in respect of interstate and capital-raising functions. The need to disclose commercial-in confidence information was also seen as strategically 'inappropriate' in positioning co-operatives for interstate mergers or acquisitions. On the other side of the equation, interstate co-operatives seeking to operate in New South Wales as co-operatives were subject not only to that state's law but to complementary legislation enacted in each foreign jurisdiction. Until such legislation existed (and there seemed little immediate prospect of this) it was virtually impossible for a foreign co-operative to merge with a New South Wales co-operative and continue to trade in that state as a co-operative. Moreover, a new co-operative entity, for instance one made up from a merger of two existing interstate co-operatives, faced hefty capital gains taxation. How was this going to facilitate national co-operation?[22]

A 'top down' Co-operatives Council

The previous Co-operative Advisory Council established under the *Co-operation Act*, in theory, enlisted a representative cross-section of co-operatives, endeavouring to bring balance to co-operative development. In practice the council had come to be dominated by large agricultural trading co-operatives. The new Co-operatives Council, by contrast, was centred upon a triumvirate of the minister, departmental officers and nominated representatives of co-operatives appointed by the minister. There was no pretence of this being an independent co-operative movement 'parliament' advising the government at arm's length on policies suitable for general co-operatives development. Rather, the Co-operatives Council was a 'top down' policy machine for driving the co-operative movement in directions determined by the government of the day. Critics complained that the council's two sub-committees; the Legislative Review Sub-Committee and the *Co-ops 2000* Sub-Committee; were merely instruments of political control. Certainly, their administration was consuming considerable CDB resources, which might alternatively have gone into supporting broader co-operative development. Most importantly for national co-operative progress, the bureaucratic nature of New South Wales co-operative development was repugnant in some jurisdictions and became a stumbling block in negotiations for nationally uniform co-operatives' legislation (discussed in Chapter Fourteen). Certainly, the New South Wales co-operative movement was now more centrally-driven than ever before in its history.

Sectioning ownership and control

The democracy principle in co-operatives pertains to ownership *and* control on a one-member-one-vote basis. The owners, controllers and users of the business are identical and equal. The *Co-operatives Act* challenged this understanding, seeking to *disengage* ownership from control on the assumption that the latter could exist where the former was shared with investors. The notion of *equal* ownership was replaced by one of *equitable* ownership based on a direct relationship between supply and investments – the more you used a co-operative the more you owned it. The patronage principle had traditionally meant that a member *benefited* from using a cooperative's services *proportionate* with the use of those services: the greater the business, the greater the share of surpluses. This was now turned on its head. Where members agreed, the act permitted a co-operative to compulsorily require a member to subscribe to bonus shares commensurate with business done. Rewards for membership could now relate not only to business done but to *investments* made.

Supporters argued that issuing bonus shares instead of, or as well as, distributing dividends would overcome the 'co-operative dilemma' and represent a fractional interest in the (assumed) increasing value of a co-operative's assets, better reflecting a member's financial interest and engaging them more. So long as investments came from members themselves, the new equitable mode of ownership mooted could not possibly jeopardise control.

There were problems with the thesis, however. By linking shareholding to business done, the act could permit 'classes' of shareholders to evolve: big and small suppliers; new and old suppliers; for instance. Far from strengthening the traditional cement binding co-operatives together – the collective bond of association – the *Co-operatives Act* could dilute this by segmenting membership. For instance, taking a dairy industry analogy, a 'member' could be a 'natural person', anyone from Farmer Brown, thirty years a co-operative supplier-member with fifty milkers, to newly-admitted member, Cowboys Proprietary Limited, a corporation bigger than the co-operative itself commanding thousands of milking cows. Under the revised patronage principle Farmer Brown and Cowboys would quickly accumulate significantly disparate levels of shareholdings. Applying corporate logic, this was financially equitable, but how long would Cowboys tolerate equal representation with Brown? Inevitably, a few large-volume suppliers could amass a greater financial stake, and sway, in the co-operative than numerous small suppliers. This could have serious ramifications for a co-operative's stability in a rapid growth phase, preparing for deregulation, for example. Sectional interest groups might form, introducing into membership divisive cross currents of opinion. While limits existed on the upper limits of shares a single member could hold, potentially five 'natural persons' (the minimum number required by the act to form a co-operative) could control a co-operative's capital base, policy-making machinery, markets and brands. 'Loyalty' was now defined not in terms of a member's philosophical commitment to co-operation and practical support of a co-operative's business, identity and bond of association, but by the *volume* of business done and commensurate *investments* and whether these were more financially rewarding than doing business another way. Moreover, realising value on shares was contrary to everything 'genuine' co-operatives had stood for a century. The issue of bonus shares relative to supply might whet an appetite for access to a co-operative's assets in certain circumstances; a takeover bid for instance; or suppliers getting out of the industry; creating tensions between members wanting to 'cash in', on the one hand, and those who wanted to remain in the industry, supported by a competitive co-operative. There was nothing really new in this, agricultural co-operatives had always been an extension of a farmer's core business and farmers were pragmatists, but what was different was the *nature* of ownership and how this might impinge upon farmers seeking to maintain some measure of commodity control in markets.

While there were plenty of theories, no one really knew what impact the accumulation of shares in fewer hands would have on the democracy principle or how future boards might redeem bonus shares in a downturn. Now, a co-operative might be so structured as to make it practically a pseudo-borrowing scheme. Who would repay? As always, in any business, everything hinged on sound direction and successful management. Management judgement in funds investment was still crucial in ensuring that surpluses were available to redeem shares at the appointed time. Again, there was nothing new in this. Successful co-operatives like Ricegrowers' Co-operative Limited and Namoi Cotton had long used revolving loans to fund growth – but this had not been linked to *ownership*. The new scheme gave managers vastly greater flexibility but exposed members to considerably greater risk. What if management failed to provide adequately for the redemption of bonus shares? Might that not precipitate a sale of co-operative assets to the highest bidder, almost certainly a proprietary rival? The full value of a co-operative's brands, its supply and distribution networks and marketing infrastructure, might by stealth or mismanagement fall into the hands of investors or corporate raiders exactly as Labor Member for Port Stephens Martin had intimated debating the bill in parliament and Bruce Freeman had predicted years before. True, there were checks and balances against 'imprudence' in the issuing of bonus shares; including appropriate disclosure, approving each issue by special resolution and annual limits on the total nominal value of shares issued, upon all of which members had the right to vote; but, equally, members at any time had the prerogative to determine the *value* of retaining control and who should share in the fruits of ownership. It was not impossible to conceive of a set of circumstances, possibly orchestrated by a management obsessed with shareholder value, to present the sale of co-operative assets as virtually a *fait accompli*.

Nevertheless, there was a harsh logic in the new legislation. By exposing the democracy principle to market forces, the *Co-operatives Act* challenged co-operators to *value* their co-operatives and acknowledge that, like everything else in a market economy, democratic control came at a price. The partitioning of ownership and control allowed by the act challenged co-operators to finance the former and value the latter. How much was democracy worth?

'A class of property *sui generis*': Co-operative Capital Units

Co-operative Capital Units (CCUs) were the most controversial element of the act's implementation phase. Before a co-operative could issue CCUs the rules were required to authorise the issue in line with minimum requirements contained in the act. Ostensibly created to allow co-operatives a flexible external fund-raising instrument without jeopardising member control or diluting co-operative principles, a CCU was personal property; an interest in the capital, but not the *share* capital, of a co-operative; essentially, a profit-share instrument with attributes similar to redeemable preference shares. CCUs could not be construed as being member shares conferring the rights of membership and holders had none of the rights or entitlements of a member. However, they did have the same rights as debenture holders with regard to receiving notices of a co-operative's meetings and other documents. Each unit holder was entitled to one vote only at meetings of CCU holders. Such rights could be varied, however, if 75 per cent of CCU holders approved. CCUs could be issued both to *members* and *non-members*, after the approval, first, of members by way of a special resolution and, second, of the registrar, who could only approve the terms of issue if satisfied that this would not result in a failure of the co-operative to comply with co-operative principles. Disclosure provisions applied to any issue of CCUs and, where the issue was to non-members, the prospectus provisions of Corporations Law applied, with the registrar acting in place of the Australian Securities and Investments Commission (ASIC). Seeking to ensure that member capital was not eroded, the act provided that CCUs could be redeemed only from profits that would otherwise be available for dividends, or out of the proceeds of a fresh issue of shares, or an approved issue of shares. Redemption of a CCU other than by way of a fresh issue of shares required a co-operative to transfer to a capital redemption reserve, profits equal to the nominal amount of CCUs redeemed.[23]

Australian Co-operative Foods (ACF) Chairman Ian Langdon warmly welcomed CCUs believing that '…the structure and terms of CCUs are only limited by the imagination of the boards and management that issue them'. In his guide to the act, however, author Donald Margarey cautioned:

The true nature of a CCU is not easy to discern from the various provisions of the Act… However, what can be said…with some certainty is that a CCU is not a share and the holder of a CCU is not a member…This probably means that CCUs are a form or debt, although a very special form which has some of the attributes of share capital. A CCU is thus probably best described as something between a share and a loan which may have a variety of rights according to the terms of issue authorised by a particular co-operative. [While] the holder of a CCU is not a member of the co-operative…the holder may have certain rights which resemble the rights held by members. The holder of a CCU is not a creditor (in the traditional sense) of the co-operative although [the holder] may have certain rights which resemble the rights held by a creditor.

That is, CCUs might or might not be shares (most likely not shares); might or might not be debt or share capital (although they were unlikely to be share capital); and a CCU holder may or may not be a member with a reasonable likelihood that he or she would be an active member. While CCUs were probably a form of debt and almost certainly not a share, there was no surety that the Taxation Commissioner might not take a different view. Certainly, a CCU holder was not a member, but some of a holder's entitlements *resembled* those of members. Indeed a CCU holder could resemble a shareholder, a member, or a creditor, but was not actually any of these legal personalities. Further, while it was clear that a CCU was neither a loan, nor a share, it was not clear whether a unit was debt, or equity. A CCU could in fact be anything a board and management wanted it to be, within the meaning of the act.

Donald Margarey was only confident that a unit was personal property subject to the rules of a co-operative and capable of devolution by will or the operation of law, concluding:

The act contains a minimum of regulation [concerning the rights of a CCU holder] and allows maximum scope for an individual co-operative to create the terms of issue…It is prudent for a co-operative to obtain proper advice relating to its financial needs and on particular issues such as accounting treatment, tax effect and the status of CCUs in winding-up.

The creation and issue of CCUs (constituting as they do a class of profit and risk-sharing capital separate from that of members of the co-operative) may create a potential difficulty for directors seeking to discharge their duty…Such conflict could for example arise in relation to a decision on a matter where the interest of members may not coincide with the interest of CCU holders. The Act provides that in discharging their duties it is proper for the directors…to take into account that the holders of CCUs have none of the rights or entitlements of…members [and that] in considering the interests of members of co-operatives [they] may ignore the interests of CCU holders.[24]

How were directors, managers and regulators to view CCUs? A solicitor advising northern New South Wales dairy co-operatives, Robert Lovell, thought the definition of a CCU was so broad that a co-operative potentially could confer on a unit holder the rights of a member, particularly for units designed to serve an equity function, and that this raised complex taxation questions:

Should this happen then, as for taxation purposes, the co-operative may have introduced

inactive type members who could work against the co-operative in qualifying as a co-operative
for taxation purposes…In other words its tax status could be in jeopardy.

The hybrid nature of CCUs made them:

…a class of property sui generis (unique; of its own kind: author) which was neither share
debenture, nor debt [and] could be structured anywhere along a continuum from a redeemable
preference share to an ordinary debenture.

Lovell warned that the Commissioner of Taxation was looking at drawing big commercial co-operatives into the tax net and cautioned co-operatives to be very careful in setting up a CCU issue. Certainly, it appeared that interest accruing to a CCU equity instrument would be taxable.

The issue of CCUs was all the more complicated by the fact that Corporations Law did *not* apply to an offer of shares in, deposits with, or CCUs issued by, a co-operative but was regulated by the *Co-operatives Act* in terms similar to those applying to non-bank financial institutions (NBFI), which were now regulated by nationally uniform legislation not yet available to general co-operatives (and unlikely to be in the foreseeable future). Debentures were ordinarily regulated by Corporations Law, directly applied by a clause of the act and, in all other cases of prescribed interest, Corporations Law also applied and ASIC was the regulator.

Such intricate nuances of jurisprudence as CCUs implied required meticulous attention to legal and administrative detail in respect of the interface between co-operatives' and Corporations Law in determining the appropriate regulator. Most co-operative directors, with an eye to duty of care provisions, simply found CCUs 'too hard'. What if regulators in other jurisdictions failed to accept CCUs? What impact might this have upon the quest for nationally uniform co-operatives' legislation? (discussed in Chapter Fourteen)

As seriously for longer-term co-operative development, critics feared that issuing CCUs could dilute member control in situations where capital they provided was of such volumes that its withdrawal, actual or threatened, could jeopardise the viability of a co-operative. External pressure exerted by CCU holders could also influence a co-operative's operations and compromise its autonomy, possibly precipitating a conversion into an investor, rather than member-driven, organisation. Some complained that CCUs were unnecessary and could not understand the administration's apparent fixation with them. Co-operatives were *already* able to raise additional capital from non-members through the issue of debentures or subordinated debt instruments. Now, in the event of a co-operative winding-up, CCU holders had *priority* ahead of shareholders and ranked only behind unsecured creditors. What if the interests of managers, CCU holders and some directors, including external directors, converged and conflicted with member expectations in respect of the rights and entitlements of CCU holders? That could potentially drive a wedge between supplier members, on the one hand, and an 'inner sanctum', effectively controlling a co-operative's policy processes, on the other – a classic 'divide and rule' situation consuming a co-operative's governance, destabilising the organisation and exposing it needlessly to takeover. What might happen, for instance, when, following deregulation, co-operatives could no longer pay suppliers premium prices and charge them lowest prices, but only market-set prices? Notwithstanding the fact that CCU holders had voting rights as a class restricted to matters that affected them as a class (presumably anything affecting a co-operative's profitability), it was not inconceivable that they would find legal ways of exerting rights. Post-deregulation, industry rationalisation would see many farmers wishing to exit an industry and cash in their investments in a co-operative. This could transfer enormous capital pressure to producers choosing to remain in the industry and could concentrate ownership and induce greater reliance upon external investors, who might conceivably seek to dissect a 'hybrid' organisation into co-operative and corporate portions, for instance, compromising the democracy principle and, hence, farmer control.

A poor take up of CCUs

Not surprisingly, given their complexity, possible taxation implications and potential for 'back door' external control, most co-operative directors stayed well clear of CCUs, which were poorly taken up, failed to attract much capital and were used by only a handful of co-operatives. Dairy co-operatives Norco and ACF were two of the first cooperatives to use them. In 1994, hoping to attract funds at less than overdraft rates, Norco used the instrument but found it poorly suited to the task and not understood by members, administrators, banks or financial markets.

Conducting research for the Dairy Research and Development Corporation, Chris Greenwood noted:

> The acceptance and in many cases understanding of CCUs in the market place is still limited, even within the co-operative movement. They will require a significant communications effort to promote them to third party investors, particularly at a time when many conventional share alternatives are becoming available through the federal government's privatisation agenda.

Greenwood pointed out that while it had been established that CCUs did not qualify as shares for taxation purposes because distribution was not deemed to be a dividend, it was unlikely the units would ever be popular with conventional investors. Experience showed that potential CCU holders demanded a 'discount' in respect of curbed entitlements attaching, either in the form of low share prices or a higher yield. There was more interest among co-operatives in most jurisdictions, including New South Wales, in Section 120 of *The Taxation Act*, which was already quite extensively used in Queensland and Tasmania and which allowed co-operatives to claim as deductions amounts paid to shareholders in the form of interest or dividends, rebates, bonuses and deferred payments in addition to deductions on the principle and interest of government loans (discussed below).

Reviewing CCUs later in 2000 New South Wales Registry of Co-operatives Researcher Kerri Grant noted that only *six* co-operatives had issued them. No complaints had been received from members, however, concerning any perceived loss of member control or distribution of profits. Nevertheless, Grant said, the success of CCU issues had been variable and, 'It is hard to avoid the conclusion that the existence of CCUs in New South Wales' co-operative legislation has been something of a non-event'.

'Non-event' they may have been but CCUs were a stumbling block in protracted efforts to achieve nationally uniform co-operatives' legislation (discussed in Chapter Fourteen).[25]

An act for technocrats?

The declared purpose of the *Co-operatives Act* was to engender greater transparency and accountability in co-operatives and provide them with more structural flexibility and regulatory freedom. Admirable as these goals were, for directors of co-operatives, who now faced hefty penalties for a breach of duty (including $5,000 or twelve months' imprisonment for 'oppressive conduct' and a $2,000 fine or five years' gaol, or both, for dishonest conduct or intent to defraud), there were many pitfalls. Some offences were easy for the unwary to wander into. Far from creating 'user friendly' legislation, as the minister had directed consultants reviewing the *Co-operation Act* in 1989, the *Co-operatives Act* was an intricate labyrinth of regulatory and procedural detail. Donald Margarey warned readers not to rely on his book solely, certainly not on telephone conversations with registry officers, and to seek the formal advice of professional advisers. There were many unresolved questions, he said, especially with regard to taxation, and some sections of the act were 'vague', including Section 182, which dealt with voting rights.

Critics described the legislation as paternalistic and over-regulatory, involving a complicated formations and compliance procedure which required high level administrative skills and expensive legal advice. Certainly, the act's complexity, breadth and technicality were forbidding for many farmer directors and neighbourhood groups. For big commercial co-operatives with ready access to the best legal and financial advice money could buy the problem was not so great (albeit costly), but for many small co-operatives or groups trying to set up co-operatives, the complexity of the legislation was forbidding and the expense prohibitive. In seeking to engender greater flexibility, freedom, transparency and accountability for co-operatives, the *Co-operatives Act* saw governmental paternalism give way to professional elitism. Moreover, co-operatives were required by regulation to review their rules over the next three to four years to ascertain any possible conflict with the act, a process complicated by the advent of National Competition Policy, into which many traditional co-operative practices fitted awkwardly and, potentially, unlawfully (discussed below).

Co-ops Now!

In November 1992 the minister released *Co-ops Now!*, a progress report on his department's co-operative development initiatives. The rhetoric was rich, as usual in such promotions, but the deliberateness with which this ambitious centrist agenda was articulated, was new. The government was determined to build on the successes of the New South Wales co-operative movement by developing national and international co-operative strategic alliances. It was no longer a case of 'facilitating' frameworks for co-operative development. The minister, his department and ACDL planned to *guide* the direction of development with the 'involvement' of AAC and the 'assistance' of the ICA. The document drew attention to the Coonamble trials in value-adding to agricultural products and the government's *Co-ops 2000* Strategy which was painted optimistically as a *model for Australia*.

The business of 'talking-up' co-operatives resumed, in earnest. A ministerial press release in December 1992 broadcast that co-operatives were celebrating their most successful year since 1952. The registry had registered some fifty new co-operatives in the past year, mainly in the fields of health, housing, arts and crafts, employment and community advancement. Public interest in the co-operative model demonstrated that 'alternative ways of overcoming the present economic climate' existed. The 'enduring strength' of co-operatives enabled people to 'combine their resources and skills to develop new market opportunities and new undertakings'. Co-operatives existed, the press release said, to restore Australian ownership to Australian businesses, to promote sturdy self-help in achieving prosperity for ordinary Australians, to add value to Australian primary production, to promote sustainable regional development and to create new jobs for Australians. The emphasis was squarely on economic patriotism and the economic importance in this of co-operatives. Including credit unions and building societies, the press release continued, New South Wales co-operatives had a combined membership of approximately five million holding approximately $11 billion in assets and generating $7.5 billion of annual turnover. There were 1,200 co-operatives operating in the state, including building societies, credit unions, co-operative housing societies, friendly societies, community advancement co-operatives and commercial co-operatives, including some very large agricultural co-operatives. Sixteen Australian co-operatives featured in the top 500 of the nation's exporters. The importance of co-operatives to regional New South Wales was inestimable. For example, in the Nambucca Shire on the mid-north coast of the state, numerous co-operatives played a major role in the regional economy, including the Banana Growers' Co-operative, Banana

Coast Credit Union, Norco Dairy Co-operative, Banana Growers' Federation, Nambucca River (Retail) Co-operative and the Mid-Coast Meat Co-operative. The township of Macksville on the Nambucca River was one of the most co-operative in Australia.

The minister said his department hoped that *Co-ops Now!*, which had issued from *Co-ops 2000* Implementation Committee Workshops, would progress to a White Paper officially shaping government policy for long term co-operative development. He stressed that the government was in no way indemnifying or financially supporting any of the *Co-ops 2000* initiatives. That was true, but the Co-operative Development Fund was being used for feasibility studies and other projects associated with the strategy.[26]

The Australian Association of Co-operatives fails

In the midst of this energetic promotion, just weeks before the *Co-operatives Act* was promulgated, in March 1993 the Australian Association of Co-operatives (AAC) was declared insolvent! The crash immediately threatened the solvency of 120 co-operatives, with seventy-four unable to draw cheques or pay wages. The minister initially distanced the government from any attempt to assist AAC but later announced emergency loans for affected co-operatives, eventually wiping off debts amounting to $1.2million (discussed in Chapter Twelve).

Experiencing other reverberations from a scandal involving co-operative housing societies (discussed below), central agencies now appear to have taken a more jaundiced view of co-operatives, seeing them as peculiar relics from a regulated era, as industry busily deregulated. The government declined to officially endorse *Co-ops Now!*, the recommendations of which did not proceed to a White Paper. Clearly, the tide was turning as far as governmental support for co-operative development was concerned.[27]

'Securing the future': the *Co-ops 2000* Strategy

More than four years after the review of the *Co-operation Act*, on 21 May 1993 the New South Wales *Co-operatives Act* was finally promulgated. The legislation's chief protagonists, mainly in the dairy industry, heralded the act as the harbinger of a new chapter in co-operative development.

Quite apart from the AAC collapse, the timing could not have been worse for the implementation phase. Building societies and credit unions were contemporaneously being spun-out of the general co-operatives' administrative framework, severing a century-old link and seeing the departure of administrative staff from an already under-resourced registry. A highly publicised imbroglio involving co-operative housing societies associated with the government's Homefund Scheme and which involved the eviction of tenants unable to meet mortgage payments, was politically embarrassing as a media campaign focused on tenant hardship and the scheme's massive cost to tax payers ($500 million). Press reports deplored the 'substandard, disjointed and uncoordinated administration of co-operative housing societies ... which behave just like loan sharks'. Some reports pointed to the scandal as evidence that mortgagees should stay with 'mainstream' financial institutions and avoid 'risky co-operative alternatives'. Caught in this mire, co-operative housing societies did not migrate to the *Co-operatives Act* but were retained in the *Co-operation Act* with all talk of new legislation for them suspended. Then another political shock came within weeks of the act's promulgation. Following in a ministerial scandal, Premier Nick Greiner resigned and was replaced by John Fahey, well known for his 'dry' financial orientation.

The atmosphere can only have been dismal at a 'Securing the Future Conference' called by the minister to discuss AAC's collapse and the need for a new industry body – talks which eventually saw the re-constitution of the Co-operative Federation of New South Wales as Co-operative

Federation of NSW Ltd and later the Co-operatives Council of Australia (discussed in Chapter Twelve). Minister Peacocke again sought to kick-start the *Co-ops 2000* Strategy, which was directed by Implementation Committee Chair Don Kinnersley with CDB Manager Garry Cronan assisting as Executive Officer. A Legislative Review Committee was formed, chaired by Cronan representing the minister and to which substantial CDB resources were now directed.

Administrative problems

New formations and rules documents complying with the act were prepared by the department's legal division, where, following a comprehensive restructure, knowledge of co-operatives was thin, involving officers in complex and time-consuming liaison with similarly hard-pressed co-operatives' development officers. Lengthy delays in processing clients' business worsened and client dissatisfaction grew, especially in relation to a formations kit in which, applicants reported, it was easy to make time-wasting mistakes. A complex, wordy formation process, the inexperience of many new applicants and uncertainty about director responsibilities and penalties exacerbated this administrative log jam. Indeed the under-staffed registry, lacking appropriate technology to deal with the volume of business being generated by *Co-ops 2000*, was obliged to apply an *administrative cap* on the maximum number of new formations the office could reasonably handle in a year. It is hard to avoid the conclusion that the *Co-operatives Act*, designed to galvanise and propel the co-operative sector towards a new millennium, was actually complicating development.

The co-operatives portfolio is downgraded

In what can only be seen as a governmental change of heart in respect of co-operatives' development, Minister Gerry Peacocke, who had so energetically driven the co-operatives' agenda since 1988, was replaced. Three other ministers followed in quick succession within two years. Indeed, the portfolio became something of a carousel for junior ministers advancing to higher duties. Another departmental staffing reshuffle occurred in a major shake-out of public service positions, precisely as the registry was dealing with a deluge of correspondence in relation to the act. With client dissatisfaction growing, the registry became a target for fundamental review and co-operative development, as such, problematical.[28]

The Co-operative Federation of NSW Ltd reforms

At a meeting instigated by Minister Garry West in August 1993, the Co-operative Federation of NSW Ltd was re-incorporated, following the demise of AAC. Apparently in an attempt to overcome a perceived domination of the policy agenda by agricultural co-operatives, the federation initially consisted largely of personnel associated with *Co-ops 2000* committees. Certainly, the reformed body made a conscious effort to be, and to be seen to be, more representative of the different industries in which co-operatives functioned. Representatives from major industry groupings chaired specific industry committees. A banana grower, Jordan Rigby, chaired the board, which included directors from dairying (Norco), child care, taxi and cultural co-operatives. Don Kinnersley was retained as a consultant. The federation was given 'ownership' of the *Co-ops 2000* Strategy Document with responsibility for implementing this and developing it nationally 'at the appropriate moment'.

Review of the Co-operative Development Branch

After receiving numerous complaints from clients seeking to form co-operatives about the complicated formations procedure and contradictory information issued by the registry, and a worsening work backlog following further rule changes, Minister West requested detailed information with regard to the registry's functions, and in particular CDB.

The review showed that most of the backlog and client dissatisfaction related to dysfunctions in the *Co-operatives Act* with regard to formations and compliance issues *vis a vis* large commercial and small not-for-profit co-operatives. Disclosure provisions for the former were wholly unsuited to the latter. The review said the act needed to be *redrafted* with two tiers: one for large trading (distributive) co-operatives with national and international reach; and another for small, localised non-trading (non-distributive) co-operatives. The legislation also needed to take into account nationally standard accounting practices, National Competition Policy and the *Trades Practices Act*. The review drew attention to considerable CDB resources being directed to *Co-ops 2000*, including travel attending the ICA-Registry project, conferences and seminars, networking and industry liaison. (The registry, in prioritising issues for the review, listed uniform national co-operatives' legislation as 'low priority, not linked to other programmes'.)[29]

The ICA-Registry Agreement is reviewed

Minister West requested a review of the ICA-Registry Agreement. After visiting ICA headquarters in Switzerland and India, the minister agreed to continue the arrangement subject to the registry assuming responsibility for the project from ACDL (which was in decay). In May 1994 the registry organised a Co-operatives Trade and Export Opportunities Seminar, bringing together representatives from ICA and Australian agricultural co-operatives. Regional conferences were also held throughout the state. The registry hosted another visit by Chinese delegates in late 1994 to inspect the Coonamble Wool Processing Co-operative and to meet federal government officials. With these initiatives being poorly supported by the co-operative sector, a cloud hung over the ICA project.

The Key Issues series of conferences

Meanwhile, seeking to fulfil the *Co-ops 2000* mission, CDB was engaged in a public relations exercise accentuating the value of co-operatives to the economy and enhancing their profile in the community and government. From 1993 to 1996, in association with Co-operative Federation of NSW Ltd and the Asia Pacific Co-operative Training Centre (APCTC), the branch organised a series of Co-operatives Key Issues Conferences, which went some way towards filling a vacuum left by AAC's collapse and served as a valuable forum for debate, albeit usually dominated by agricultural co-operatives. Largely self-funding, the conferences nevertheless did involve CDB staff in time-consuming organisational and follow-up duties at a time when the registry was already under strain. The first conference, the 'Co-operative Capital Conference' in 1993, was a relatively small affair preoccupied with the capital-raising requirements of agricultural co-operatives, but subsequent Key Issues Conferences were quite elaborate and are discussed in Chapter Twelve in the context of federal co-operative development.[30]

Co-ops 2000 comes undone

Notwithstanding these valuable Key Issues Conferences, the wheels were falling off the *Co-ops 2000* chariot. The Sydney Cove Authority evicted ACDL and its subsidiary 'Best of Australia Proprietary Limited' from The Rocks premises, harming the league's resources. In December 1994, the new minister (Ted Pickering) directed ACDL to retire as trustee of the Co-operative Development Trust Fund and return all books and money to the New South Wales government. The fund was redirected to the registry for administrative purposes, before being wound up, 'exhausted'.[31]

A change of government

If ever there had been doubts about the future of the Fahey Coalition Government's commitment to a co-operative development programme, these were removed soon after the Carr Labor Government took power in March 1995. A vigorous new broom swept through departments, a 'slash and burn' exercise, some said. For a co-operative sector, which had grown reliant upon government props, this was a precarious situation.

The new government considered two options: move the Registry of Co-operative Societies into a business development department; or split its functions between departments. The outcome was an awkward compromise. The registry was moved from the Department of Local Government and Co-operatives, with no specific portfolio allocation for co-operatives, and came first under the purview of the Minister for Consumer Affairs and later the Department of Fair Trading. The department was located at Parramatta, on the western outskirts of Sydney, and the registry at Bankstown, in the south-western suburbs, where it was lumped with the Building Services Corporation, the Office of Real Estate Services and the Motor Vehicle Repair Industry Council. Additional staff 'savings' were made. A new breed of managers entered the registry with generic information technology-based administrative skills and legal and financial expertise, generally with little knowledge of or sympathy for co-operatives, and targeted for career fast-tracking. Four different officers occupied the registrar's chair in the space of seven months. Departmental knowledge of co-operatives was dwindling.

Responding to a Co-operative Federation of NSW Ltd complaint about the downgrading of co-operatives, the new minister, Faye Lo Po', (the first in a procession of ministers: Langton [1997-98]; Shaw [1998-99]; and Watkins [1999-]) issued a statement in May 1995 on co-operatives' policy and the restructured registry. In a veiled reference to the previous administration's preoccupation with agricultural co-operatives, the minister expected that the reshaped registry would consult more widely, promote the idea of co-operation to a wider audience and address emerging government priorities for co-operation, including disadvantaged workers (such as garment outworkers) and regional and community development. The government understood co-operatives to be simply an 'alternative legal vehicle for individuals to pursue common business and social goals', for which 'a whole of government' approach to public policy, rather than a designated office, was appropriate. That is, co-operatives should enjoy no special treatment. The gist was that so long as co-operatives conducted their affairs in a prudential manner consistent with the act, that was where the government's interest in them began and ended.

The ICA-Registry Agreement is aborted

In respect of primary production, however, the government believed the registry should continue to seek 'strategic co-operative export networks for flexible producer and manufacturer alliances in dedicated export industries' along the lines of the ICA-Registry project. Another survey of the agreement was completed. The Co-operative Federation of NSW Ltd was not particularly supportive of the initiative, reflecting a deliberate shift away from an international focus. In 1996 ICA representatives floated the idea of establishing a trading network in Sydney, joining ICA, the New South Wales government and Australian co-operatives. The registry commissioned consultants to examine the proposal and their report was favourable. A Department of Fair Trading (DFT) consultant's report, however, questioned the proposed project's viability and the idea was dropped in 1998. The Singapore government snapped up the opportunity to host this ICA initiative. Again, the door to international co-operative trade was slammed shut in Australia. The Coonamble Wool Processing Co-operative pilot project stumbled on for a while, produced a few garments and was wound up in 1999. The Feed Lot and Meat Marketing Co-operative was also wound up.[32]

The registry is again reviewed

In April 1996 the DFT Director-General asked the Premier's Department to conduct another review of the registry. This was completed in June and given limited circulation to Co-operative Federation of NSW Ltd and the Co-operatives Council. Many who had contributed to the review were not given an opportunity to sight it!

The report raised concerns about current development strategies. The minister wanted 'clear answers', demanding improved performance in both development and regulatory functions, greater efficiency, lower costs and better, more focused 'quality' policy advice enabling Commonwealth Government and New South Wales Government issues to be more appropriately considered in delivering better services to the sector. A perception that the Registry of Co-operatives was focused excessively on agricultural co-operatives 'mismatched' government's priorities. The Co-operatives Council was clearly dominated by farmer co-operatives, a legacy of the previous administration. A view was held that the registry had become something of a 'fiefdom', not willing to 'fit in' and *earn* government respect. It was accepted that already an urgent review of the *Co-operatives Act* was required because, in its present configuration, the legislation did *not* support co-operatives in new fields. Echoing findings from the 1994 review, the 1996 inquiry noted the need for two-tier legislation to address the development and regulatory needs of different types of co-operatives, not only agricultural Titans, and to take better into account National Competition Policy and the *Trades Practices Act*. The government reaffirmed that a 'whole of government' approach would remove bureaucratic impediments to co-operative development, which in any event, could not work without dispersing the registry's functions across DFT and improving the management structure. Clearly, the registry and CDB, as they existed, were under attack.[33]

The Co-operative Development Branch is abolished

The Registry of Co-operatives was again restructured in September 1996 ignoring CDB Manager Garry Cronan's appeal to keep a focused, well-resourced co-operatives branch operating and protests from sections of the co-operative sector that DFT was not consulting widely enough, seemingly more focused on departmental structure than on co-operatives.

In the rationalisation which followed, policy functions were hived off and shifted, first, to Strategy Division DFT. A Co-operatives Policy Branch was created separate from the registry but within the department's Policy Division with responsibility for policy, legislative review, the Co-operatives Council, formations, strategic projects and research. Market Place Development Division assumed responsibility for co-operative education, communication and marketing, including the publication of a newsletter, *Co-operation*. Ten officers previously engaged in co-operative development were redeployed or took redundancy packages. *Co-ops 2000* was formally ended and the *Co-ops 2000* Implementation Committee was rolled into a Co-operative Development Committee with a broader co-operative development brief specifically *not* focused on agricultural co-operatives. In 1999 the Co-operative Development Committee and the Legislative Review Committee were amalgamated. As noted earlier, the Co-operative Development Trust Fund was terminated and the ICA-Registry Agreement wound down. The future of the Key Issues Conferences also came under a cloud.

'More changes than a super model'

A period of administrative uncertainty followed in the department's co-operatives policy and development sections underlining a diminished priority in a 'whole of government' approach. Initially, the DFT Director-General performed duties as registrar with the Co-operatives Council reporting to him, and not the minister. The first appointee was replaced by the Assistant Director-General, who resigned. The registry remained in Bankstown in Sydney's south-west and the Co-operatives Policy Branch, initially with one staff, Garry Cronan, was first located in the inner city and later shifted to the Office of the Director-General, at Parramatta, in the city's west. Bruce Langton replaced Fay Lo Po' as minister. After he resigned Attorney-General Jeff Shaw assumed the position and abandoned the 'whole of government' approach. As *National Co-op Update* Editor Chris Greenwood noted, co-operative development in New South Wales was being 'pushed from pillar to post [with] more changes than a super model'.

The *Co-operatives Act*: 'A disincentive to development'

A briefing paper was presented to the minister early in 1997, presumably prepared by Policy Branch, focused on bureaucratic impediments to co-operative development in New South Wales. The omnibus nature of the *Co-operatives Act*, the paper argued, lumped together co-operatives of all manner, including agricultural, marketing, supply, trading, consumer, worker, community and other non-profit organisations, and applied the same regulatory regime to all. The act was complicated, acted as a brake on new co-operatives, involved expensive compliance costs, was excessively technical and needed drastic simplification:

> *Representatives from community organisations have indicated that the current legislative requirements for community and non-profit co-operatives [are] severely limiting development opportunities. Compliance costs to co-operatives are also proffered as a reason for the need to have a range of co-operative options within the legislation.*

Groups wanting to form co-operatives were giving up, frustrated by the slow, cumbersome registration process. Many preferred to register as an incorporated association, which, ironically, permitted more flexible, spontaneous co-operation than was possible under the act. For instance, a number of rural Aboriginal groups gave up after repeated applications, frustrated by bureaucratic delays. The very pro-co-operative PACT Theatre, which was formed in 1964, planned to leave the co-operative movement but to keep the 'ideology of co-operation' alive in its new rules:

> *It is often argued that the legislation as presently constructed acts as a disincentive, particularly for community organisations and start-up businesses who would, if simplified plain English co-operative legislation existed, choose to incorporate as a co-operative.*

The ministerial briefing paper said the formation procedure was particularly difficult for first-time users and definitely *not* 'user friendly'. Some groups pointed to the act's paternalistic tone in explaining their rejection of the co-operative option. Policy statements based on the act were said to be vague and unhelpful. Legislative guidelines were not widely available and many professional advisers were not familiar with the act, automatically recommending Corporations Law to groups seeking to co-operate. A lack of nationally uniform co-operatives' legislation and the failure of the New South Wales act to be accepted in other jurisdictions presented enormous practical difficulties for co-operatives seeking to operate or merge across borders and had largely confined co-operative operations to a state level:

As a result, strategic and innovative commercial organisations that are intending to pursue national and international markets or activities have not usually incorporated as co-operatives – it has set a ceiling on development initiatives.

A poor awareness of co-operatives in government was not aided, the briefing paper continued, by abandoning a 'whole of government' approach and the absence of effective promotional materials, including a comprehensive internet site, which added to compliance problems. The public found it difficult to access responsible officers and reliable information in the registry because administrative procedures relating to the act were often poorly understood by public servants, resulting often in the provision of conflicting and erroneous information. The act and its administrative procedures urgently needed to be reviewed and simplified. On the controversial issue of registry inspection powers, the ministerial briefing paper said:

There is a diversity of opinion among co-operatives and government staff on the purpose of inspections of co-operatives. Inspections can be implemented to either **promote** *or* **retard** *[author's emphasis] the development of co-operatives in New South Wales.*

The paper believed that 'a clearly written, unambiguous, pro-active co-operative development policy with an accompanying rationale' would assist in countering such bureaucratic impediments and recommended the formation of an inter-departmental committee on co-operatives policy.

REGISTRATION OF CO-OPERATIVES: NEW SOUTH WALES JUNE 30, 1991–2000[34]				
Year	Total Co-operatives	New Co-operatives	Co-operatives Deregistered	Change %
1991	807	23	0	4.3
1992	842	35	0	1.2
1993	852	46	36	-4.9
1994	810	24	66	1.2
1995	820	37	27	1.6
1996	833	42	29	-0.5
1997	829	24	28	-0.2
1998	827	23	25	1.5
1999	839	17	5	1.2
2000	849	23	13	

'Think Business, Think Co-operatives'

Meanwhile, the business of promoting the new administration's policy priorities for co-operatives had begun. The theme now was: 'Think Business, Think Co-operatives'. Extolling the virtues of co-operatives as small-business structures, Co-operatives Policy Branch Manager Garry Cronan was careful to differentiate commercial agricultural co-operatives from small, not-for-profit co-operatives. The New South Wales co-operative movement was 'thriving', he said, and with over 800 co-operatives and 1,038,000 members (including credit unions), was a major employer producing a turnover in excess of $3 billion (1994/95). In the previous five years 150 new co-operatives had been created; 15 per cent of the total of all co-operatives registered; and Cronan pointed with some justification to the important role CDB had played in this. In addition to agricultural co-operatives, which produced annual exports valued at $608 million (1995), general co-operatives were involved in business, manufacturing, transport, fishing, housing, arts and crafts, tourism and entertainment. There was nothing 'odd' or 'alternative' about co-operatives – a co-operative was simply another form of trading entity the purpose of which was to confer economic benefits on active members. Co-operatives were a 'modern option', not 'antiques' or an option of last resort, as some painted them, and were becoming popular with small businesses contending with competition policy. Co-operatives were a *mainstream* business strategy with a high success rate, so much so, Cronan believed, that the corporate world was now *mimicking* them because they were an 'an easy way to compete better'. Co-operatives empowered the work force, released greater worker productivity, broadened the base of economic ownership, were committed to social responsibility and countervailed market monopolies. Cronan believed a new direction was emerging for the co-operative movement, a new 'social movement' where co-operatives functioned as part of a 'social economy'. A semantic shift was evident in the language in so far as an *a priori* relationship was held to exist between the abstract noun, 'co-operation', and the common noun 'co-operative', Garry Cronan, for instance, saying:

> *Co-operation within business and between business partners is being recognised as the central dynamic which separates a successful business from failure…Co-operation between parties – whether business partners or simply management and shop floor – is being seen as a fundamental element to business success.*
>
> *A natural progression is to take this informal emphasis on co-operation and formalise it into the structure and conduct of the business. This can be achieved as a co-operative, which involves a group of people working together to achieve common economic, social and cultural goals through a jointly-owned and democratically-controlled business enterprise.*
>
> *By becoming a registered co-operative, an organisation can reap the benefits of strategic alliances, shared resources, enhanced market power and a high level of trust in a way not possible under the company or corporate structure.*
>
> *Co-operatives also offer self-help solutions to current social and economic dilemmas. Co-operatives generate productive economic activity, creating wealth for the community and encouraging local employment.*

Ever the optimist, Cronan anticipated renewed public policy interest in co-operatives in the context of continuing moves for nationally uniform co-operatives' legislation. The language was inspiring but there was little evidence of a renaissance of interest in co-operative structure. On the contrary, those co-operatives and mutual societies which had not demutualised or ceased trading had no claim to a monopoly of co-operation – people combining democratically to achieve common social and economic goals. Incorporated associations, co-operative companies and companies with limited liability applying the democracy principle also satisfied this criterion. The weakly organised co-operative sector was no closer to resolving problems, which had retarded its development for years, with vexed questions relating to capitalisation, uniform legislation, deregulation, competition policy and globalisation still unanswered. As always, there was little evidence of sector investment in education, little co-operation among co-operatives and scant evidence of co-operatives' concern for the broader community. Perhaps the problem was not so much a lack of 'public policy interest' in co-operatives, as Cronan believed, but the new government's determination to concentrate on regulation and leave co-operative development where it belonged – with the co-operative sector.[35]

Co-operative development in a vacuum

In early 1997 a DFT inter-departmental committee was formed with a view to developing a Green Paper on Co-operative Policy and Development, contemplating a return to a 'whole of government' approach. Representatives from various departments and central agencies, including State Development, Treasury and Premier's and Cabinet, joined the committee, which was chaired by a DFT representative. A draft paper 'The Role of Co-operatives in Economic Development and Consumer Protection in New South Wales' was prepared, identifying possible roles for government and suggesting co-ordinated development strategies. The paper listed over one hundred issues for public comment and discussion. The government decided to not release the report, however, as a National Competition Policy (NCP) review of the soon to be amended *Co-operatives Act* was due to commence in June 1998 and it was thought that determining policies on co-operatives might pre-empt or confuse the issue. The result was a stalemate. The NCP review was postponed pending resolution of negotiations with other states and territories with regard to nationally uniform co-operatives' legislation – upon which agreement could not be reached. The policy paper fell into a bureaucratic vacuum together with hopes for renewed government support for co-operative development along established lines.

The *Co-operatives Act* is amended

Notwithstanding serious administrative misgivings concerning loop holes in the act which might be exploited to skirt Corporations Law and registry concern about how the scheme was to be maintained, in April 1997 the New South Wales Government agreed to participate in the interstate co-operatives' Common Core Provisions (CCP) Scheme, undertaking to amend the *Co-operatives Act* to achieve compatibility with this (discussed in Chapter Twelve).[36]

Introducing the amendments, the minister carefully pointed out that they were a product of Co-operative Federation of NSW Ltd and Co-operatives Council input. The legislation clarified CCUs, resolved uncertainties about director accountability, addressed the complexity and costs of compliance issues, took into account Victorian improvements to provisions for interstate mergers and transfers, made easier the reporting responsibilities of not-for-profit co-operatives, accommodated NCP and the *Trades Practices Act*, included core consistent provisions already common to co-operatives' legislation in Queensland, Victoria and South Australia, allowed for two classes of shares for trading and non-trading co-operatives on the Victorian model, and permitted co-operatives to issue securities, among other reforms. Still the amended act contained several non-CCP provisions.

In June 1997 the *New South Wales Co-operatives (Amendment) Act* was passed. Watched closely by Cabinet and Co-operative Federation of NSW Ltd Consultant Don Kinnersley, the act became effective later in the year. Given the ancient inability of producer and consumer co-operatives to co-operate there was some irony in the revised legislation coming within the Minister for Consumer Affairs' portfolio. (The act was again amended in 2001.)[37]

Alternative State Support: Section 120 (1) (c)

One of Co-operative Federation's first priorities when it was reformed in 1993 was to lobby the New South Wales government for a facility enabling utilisation of Section 120 (1) (c) of the *Income Tax Assessment Act*, similar to provisions existing in Queensland and Tasmania, by which agricultural co-operatives were able claim tax deductions on repayments of both principal and interest on a loan for capital expenditure relating to the main functions of the co-operative. Assisted by consultant Don Kinnersley, the federation argued for three years that the absence of such a facility put New

South Wales co-operatives in a less competitive position. Already the Namoi Cotton and Norco co-operatives had located manufacturing facilities outside the state (in Queensland) simply to qualify for the facility. ACF planned to do the same in a merger with the Queensland dairy co-operative, Queensco. The Bega Co-operative wished to use the facility for the construction of a major cheese-making plant. Agricultural co-operatives had previously been able to access such finance through state banks and SMAs but these were disappearing. Progress was slow but, in 1997, the Carr Government accepted the argument and created a facility for the use of Section 120 (1) (c).[38]

Co-operatives Policy Branch is abolished

Most Co-operatives Policy Branch officers were transferred back to the registry in 1998 and the branch was disbanded. Remaining staff members were briefed to develop a proposal for the establishment of a Co-operative Research and Development Centre in a tertiary institution. Reflecting on these events, Garry Cronan later observed:

> One view could be that the government…decided not to be directly engaged in co-operative policy and development functions but wished to "outsource" the functions to an external organisation, perhaps the new Co-operative Research Centre. This would…resolve the dilemma for government of promoting policy, based on co-operation, which was seen by some in government as being in possible conflict with the competition policy agendas the state government needed to implement to satisfy the Council of Australian Governments' requirements, or be financially penalised.
>
> Another view might be that the government did not see a role for itself in promoting a particular business model, which was properly a function of industry.[39]

The registry is transferred to Bathurst

In the approach to a state election (which Labor won) in February 1999, Minister Shaw announced that the Registry of Co-operative Societies was to be transferred to Bathurst, a central-western town across the Great Dividing Range in the heart of a marginal seat. Co-operative Federation of NSW Ltd officials lambasted the decision as 'disastrous for New South Wales co-operatives', arguing that a massive loss of expertise would result, client services would suffer further and the shift was ridiculous, in any event, as only 8 per cent of New South Wales co-operatives were in the Bathurst region. Some described the decision as sending co-operation to 'Coventry'. Forty positions were relocated to Bathurst but only one staff member left Sydney to make the transition, representing another loss of 'corporate memory'.

Research and development is 'outsourced'

As the demolition of Policy Branch proceeded and the registry prepared for relocation, Garry Cronan, working with registry officers and the Co-operatives Council Innovation Committee, conducted a survey of New South Wales co-operatives, seeking information on research needs. Nearly half of the respondents indicated they needed information about co-operatives' legislation on a *daily* basis! Many sought research into reasons for particular co-operatives succeeding or failing, on co-operative values and principles, the co-operative image and culture, corporate governance, finance and capital-raising, member communication, directors' responsibilities (particularly external directors) and training and education for compliance issues. Barely half respondents agreed on the *necessity* of establishing a research centre and of those who did several preferred a centre studying 'other areas', not merely co-operatives.

Cronan left for a study tour of Europe to investigate policy and regulatory innovations, returning to advise of 'renewed government interest in co-operatives', abroad. In September 1998 Minister Shaw approved in principle the creation of a research centre for co-operatives and 'similar member organisations based on mutuality', undertaking to fund the organisation some $300,000 annually from the Co-operatives Development Fund, including the salaries of two officers to be seconded from DFT.

The Australian Centre for Co-operatives Research and Development (ACCoRD)

In February 1999 the University of Technology Sydney (UTS) and Charles Sturt University, Bathurst (CSU) were successful in a joint proposal for a research and development centre focused on the 'social economy' (not just co-operatives). In July the centre formally commenced: The Australian Centre for Co-operatives Research and Development (ACCoRD); describing itself as 'Australia's only research and development centre serving co-operatives, mutual and the social economy'. ACF Chairman Ian Langdon was appointed chair. Two part-time co-directors co-ordinated operations: Associate Professor Mark Lyons, a specialist in charities and not-for-profit 'third sector' organisations; and Associate Professor Terry Bishop, an accountant. Departmental officers Garry Cronan and Jayo Wickremarachchi were seconded to the centre as Executive Officer and Senior Research Fellow and Executive Assistant and Research Fellow, respectively. An advisory board was set up consisting of 'senior stakeholders' from the co-operative sector, the wider social economy, government and researchers. An International Advisory Board of leading researchers in co-operatives and the social economy was constituted. The minister intended that ACCoRD should be self-funding after three years.[40]

Conclusion

In barely more than a decade the face of New South Wales co-operation was inalterably changed. The process began in the 1970s in the wake of Britain's entry into Europe, OPEC oil price increases and was accelerated by deregulation and National Competition Policy in the ensuing decades. Many major New South Wales agricultural co-operatives exited the movement and those remaining struggled to reinvent themselves and remain competitive, turning to government for support and the creation of new legislation allowing co-operatives greater fund-raising and structural flexibility. Notwithstanding warnings from traditionalists like AAC's Bruce Freeman that co-operation was in mortal danger by flirting with corporate models and 'back-door' dry-shareholder participation, the Greiner Government heeded the advice of a new breed of co-operative leaders who argued for radical change to co-operative structure, a loosening of the ownership-control nexus, and that external capital need not compromise the democracy principle. The government passed the *Co-operatives Act*, a complicated portmanteau of corporate and co-operatives law, which saw the introduction in statute of 'hybrid' co-operatives. The CDB assumed much of the responsibility for co-operative development work from a disorganised general co-operative movement, which was seriously weakened by the collapse in 1993 of AAC, and launched an ambitious *Co-ops 2000* Strategy. The *Co-operatives Act*, perceived to be a retardant for general co-operative development and quite unsuited to all but a few very large commercial co-operatives, was subjected to a major review. The *Co-ops 2000* Strategy achieved a few successes, principally new co-operative formations and the Key Issues Conferences, but failed to achieve anything like its ambitious agenda. When government interest in co-operatives waned and, after the registry was restructured and CDB was closed down, an organisational vacuum was left in the sector from which it has not fully recovered at time of writing, despite the best efforts of Co-operative Federation of NSW Ltd and ACCoRD. As seriously, elements of the *Co-operatives Act*, particularly CCUs, complicated the vital CCP process.

Nevertheless, a co-operative tradition, albeit unrecognisable from earlier decades, endured in the most populous state. ACCoRD researchers Jayo Wickremarachichi and Andrew Passey found that in 1999/2000 there were 849 general co-ops in New South Wales, excluding financial co-operatives, but including some which were winding up. Approximately 207 were trading co-operatives; 445 were non-trading co-operatives with share capital; and 81 operated without share capital. In the previous decade the registration of co-operatives had risen by 8 per cent, but the rate of formation was slowing. The state's co-operatives now had 1.29 million memberships, down by 3.3 per cent on the previous year and just one co-operative, University Co-op Bookshop, accounted for 892,920 of this. Primary producer co-operatives were showing a strong dollar growth, outstripping membership growth, but other producer (non-farmer) co-operatives and consumer, human services and interest group co-operatives had all declined, some seriously. Culture and recreation co-operatives, however, showed strong growth in membership and assets, but these figures were also distorted by a few star performers.

The sector; 'movement' was certainly no longer appropriate, if ever it had been; was lopsided in physical development with around ten very large co-operatives, mostly farmer-based, and hundreds of significantly smaller ones. A mere 4.1 per cent of the state's co-operatives held assets exceeding $10 million, while 76.2 per cent held assets less than $1 million. There were six fewer primary producer co-operatives at the end of decade than there had been at the beginning, reflecting industry rationalisation, but their total assets had grown by 137.9 per cent (39,791) and membership by 16.2 per cent. In recent years total co-operative assets had grown by 69 per cent in real terms with members' equity almost doubling, mainly in agricultural trading co-operatives. Similarly, an 81 per cent increase in sector turnover across the preceding decade was concentrated in a few farmer co-operatives. The annual turnover of all New South Wales co-operatives amounted to approximately $4.4 billion, excluding foreign co-operatives and interstate trade, up by 11 per cent on the previous year. Over 75 per cent of the state's co-operatives, however, had an annual turnover of less than $1 million. Approximately 60 per cent of total turnover was in regional New South Wales including Newcastle and Wollongong, mainly on the north coast and western districts. The remainder was in Sydney and suburbs, which included by far the biggest of all the co-operatives in the state: the Dairy Farmers Group (DFG) (discussed in Part IV).

(*Postscript*: In 2005, ACCoRD was closed down after the government ceased funding the centre.)

Part 3

NATIONAL

*T*he post-World War II reconstruction period presented excellent opportunities for
co-operatives. The Co-operative Federation of Australia (CFA) (1943-c1985) made
*progress in the 1970s, opening a Canberra secretariat, organising national conventions
and attracting federal government support. Unable to translate conference resolutions into
action, however, and with traditional overseas markets disappearing, more agricultural
affiliates took unilateral action and withdrew support. The CFA stalled and by 1986 was
moribund.*

*The Co-operative Federation of New South Wales (CFNSW), the Co-operative
Federation of Victoria (CFV) and co-operatives in Queensland created the Australian
Association of Co-operatives (AAC). A Standing Committee on Agriculture (SCAWP)
report in 1986 said that co-operatives could be the answer to many agricultural problems,
particularly for dismantling statutory marketing authorities and urged federal government
support. Unsuitable legislation and the inability of states' co-operative movements to agree
on nationally uniform co-operatives' legislation saw this opportunity lost. The AAC never
achieved a truly national mandate and, notwithstanding some notable achievements,
collapsed in 1993.*

*A series of Key Issues Conferences convened from 1993 by the New South Wales
Registry of Co-operative Societies, the Co-operative Federation of NSW Ltd (the reformed
CFNSW) and the Asia–Pacific Co-operative Training Centre (APCTC) provided a
national forum for co-operative debate until the Co-operatives Council of Australia (CCA)
was formed in 1996.*

*Proposals that Canberra assume responsibility for co-operatives were repeatedly rejected
by defenders of states rights. In 1991 a Standing Committee of Attorneys-General Working
Party (SCAGWP) initiated what became the Co-operatives Law Agreement (1996) and
the Core Consistent Provisions Scheme (CCP). The Victorian Co-operatives Act (1997)
was adopted as a basis for the CCP scheme. Progress was slow. A century after federation
the absence of suitable federal or national uniform co-operatives' legislation remained as an
impediment to co-operative development.*

Wheat harvesting begins.
Photo courtesy Co-operative Bulk Handling Limited.

Chapter Ten

The Producers And The Consumers Cannot Co-operate:
THE CO-OPERATIVE FEDERATION OF AUSTRALIA 1943–C1985

Introduction

If ever there was an opportune moment for the Australian co-operative movement to unite, put down solid foundations for growth and locate an influential position in the Australian political economy it was in the post-World War II reconstruction period.

Co-operatives were popular at government level, having played a key role in victualling allied troops in the Pacific with rice, poultry, fruit juice and other products and in orchestrating grain handling for commodity boards set up under war-time emergency conditions, which continued until 1948. A War Time Agricultural Committee was channelling grants to dairy co-operatives, which were seen as 'essential industries' helping to maintain production levels and, with the Commonwealth Government planning massive post-war expansion in food production, funding was available for co-operative extension services.

A Rural Reconstruction Commission Report in 1945 recommended co-operatives for accelerating farm productivity and urged state and commonwealth governments to support co-operatives with research, education, information services, a national financial facility and uniform legislation for co-operatives. The rationale was that agriculture was a national industry, co-operatives operated in all states and territories and therefore required federal support. Co-operatives were seen by state and federal governments as a key to post-war prosperity; vehicles of mutual effort for the common good; 'champions upon which growers should rely to fight their battle'.

The problem was that the co-operators could not co-operate. Producers flatly refused to have anything to do with a national co-operatives' federation created by consumers while the consumer co-operative movement insisted that developments should occur along strict Rochdale lines.[1]

'The producers can do what they like!'

After W D Johnson was elected president of the Co-operative Federation of Western Australia (CFWA) in 1942 he corresponded with the New South Wales Co-operative Wholesale Society (NSW CWS) Board calling for a conference to explore the possibility of a national co-operative wholesale along English Co operative Wholesale Society (CWS) lines – 'One Big Society. The NSW CWS strongly supported the idea, seeing itself as the natural nucleus of such an entity. Westralian Farmers (Western Australia) and Eudunda Farmers (South Australia), both co-operative companies with extensive retail networks, thought similarly about themselves.

Johnson met the board of the Australian Producers' Wholesale Co-operative Federation (APWCF) in Melbourne in early December 1943 to discuss the possibility of joint action in a post-war co-operative reconstruction campaign. Westralian Farmers delegates and other APWCF affiliates, however, were doubtful about the market power such a consumerist organisation might wield, possibly exerting downward pressure on farm commodity prices, and remained non-committal. Johnson therefore announced plans to develop a 'legitimate' national Rochdale co-operative organisation, saying that APWCF was a sectional body and not qualified for this.

At a Canberra conference organised by CFWA and NSW CWS later in December 1943, involving representatives of producer and consumer co-operatives from throughout Australia, delegates had scarcely completed an oath to work for a post-war co-operative new order when bickering erupted on old issues. Rochdale idealists seeking a genuinely democratic national co-operative 'parliament'; a Co-operative Union; criticised both CFWA *and* NSW CWS as 'parochial bodies, not founded on true democratic lines'. CFWA Honorary Secretary T H Bath criticised 'Rochdale doctrinal purists' and 'divvy-hunters of the east':

> There is no point in parading party political puppets as malignant capitalists and ill-used workers [for this is] demagogic claptrap [used by] fanatics who pin their faith to a dogma... Although they have grandiose plans for building fancy schemes for social organisation you will see them incapable of starting a pie stall successfully.

Delegates were unable to agree on virtually anything. Westralian Farmers sought a co-ordinated interstate and international buying and selling agency tied to English CWS, essentially an extension of its own wholesale department, operating on a commission basis. Johnson and George Booth (NSW CWS) argued for a consumer-based co-operative on the Manchester model. Westralian Farmers Chairman Walter Harper then told delegates bluntly that no national body would ever operate without APWCF endorsement. Johnson retorted that the conference was about creating a 'true' Rochdale national structure, which APWCF was not. The situation was complicated by NSW CWS advocacy of national co-operatives' legislation to which the Western Australians (Johnson, Harper and Bath) were implacably opposed, arguing that the idea was 'unrealistic and constitutionally impossible'. Certainly Westralian Farmers did not want any legislation which might impose 'socialistic' Rochdale co-operative principles on operations constraining a corporate flexibility permitted by sympathetic Western Australian law. Opinion was also split on the idea of a co-operative bank with some APWCF affiliates seeking a Raiffeisen (German) model, geared to farm credit, and consumer delegates preferring an English CWS-style co-operative bank.

Two days of inconclusive debate followed with complex splits opening along parochial, ideological and political lines. When, as predicted, APWCF confirmed by telegram from Melbourne that it would have nothing to do with Johnson's 'illegitimate Canberra invention', Johnson told the conference, 'The producers can do what they like! We will carry on without them!' It was not an auspicious beginning to a co-operative 'new order'.

The Co-operative Federation of Australia

A Provisional Committee of the Council of the Commonwealth Co-operative Federation (later, the Co-operative Federation of Australia [CFA]) was formed, briefed to develop a national secretariat in Canberra and operate a national wholesale, 'One Big Society', to which state federations would be eligible for affiliation. NSW CWS President George Booth was elected president, W D Johnson vice president and Eugene O'Neil of the NSW CWS was appointed organiser.[2]

Unsurprisingly, APWCF affiliates refused to endorse CFA as the supreme body of the Australian co-operative movement. The fact was, however, that CFA was eligible for affiliation with the International Co-operative Alliance (ICA) while APWCF, a sectional body representing primary producers, was not. The CFA represented a licence to potentially immense international co-operative trade through ICA and English CWS. Control of the federation, therefore, was seen by APWCF leaders as vital to their affiliates' interests in an anticipated post-war reconstruction boom.

Squabbling tears CFA apart

Early in 1944, NSW CWS executives toured Victoria, South Australia, Tasmania and the Australian Capital Territory under a Rochdale banner attempting to form state federations sympathetic to CFA's proposed 'One Big Society'. Wherever they went, doctrinal rigidity accompanied them. In Victoria they refused to recognise the Christian Co-operative Fellowship (CCF) or the Victorian Co-operative League for purposes of affiliating with CFA. In Sydney they refused to recognise Co-operative Services Limited, a small band of co-operative idealists exploring North American credit union ideas and from which a great credit union movement would later emerge. Rather than tapping into this new wave of co-operative energy, the Rochdale old guard alienated it. At a CFA Provisional Meeting in Adelaide in November 1944 rows erupted on several fronts with the South Australians, particularly Eudunda Farmers' delegates, who saw their co-operative as the natural nucleus of a national wholesale, perfectly placed between eastern and western states and with access to excellent port facilities. The South Australians also strongly resented any 'meddling' in their state, either from CFWA *or* NSW CWS.

When the CFA executive again met in Sydney in December 1944, neither Bath nor Harper of CFWA was in attendance. Instead a declaration was read that CFWA would be reducing subscriptions and reactivating Westralian Farmers' wholesale department in direct competition with CFA's proposed 'One Big Society'. CFA executives defiantly replied that *they* would appoint a commercial administrator, funded jointly by federation affiliates, to develop a national wholesale, co-ordinate trade with English CWS, return Australian co-operation to 'genuine' Rochdale roots and usurp APWCF as the 'proper link' to the British co-operative movement.

Divisions between the various states' co-operative movements deepened when NSW CWS announced plans for a new co-operative insurance society to rival the producer-based Co-operative Insurance Company (CIC) Limited. The APWCF executive was outraged and retaliated in June 1945 by appointing its own commercial administrator, based in Melbourne, and nominating Westralian Farmers' London-based shipping manager, Ken Edwards, as the 'official CFA representative to the ICA'.[3]

Tired of bickering and working for nothing, Eugene O'Neil resigned as CFA organiser. The CFWA promptly nominated W D Johnson as *pro tem* executive officer while a compromise was worked out. Finally A R Small, a 'neutral' Brisbane businessman acceptable to a majority of CFA affiliates, was appointed commercial administrator. After Small travelled to Perth for 'instructions' in late 1945, W D Johnson called for another Canberra conference early in the new-year to 'clear the air'. The NSW CWS board announced that it would not participate and threatened to withdraw all funding from CFA.

Meanwhile another row had erupted between English CWS Agent E H Marsland in Sydney and APWCF affiliates who alleged that the British wholesale was undermining Australian farmers by supporting NSW CWS plans for a rival co-operative insurance company and was also favouring New Zealand farmers. Some APWCF affiliates, including the Gippsland and Northern Co-operative (Victoria), threatened to withdraw supply from English CWS and look to the USA for alternative trading relationships.

Reporting these fractious developments to the English CWS Board on an official visit to Manchester in 1946, Marsland was instructed to return to Australia and refurbish 'traditional' links with Australian farmers affiliated with APWCF and do nothing about the 'One Big Society' idea which might antagonise farmers further. Marsland never reported that message, being killed in a plane crash *en route*, but it arrived nonetheless.

Stunned by this rebuff from 'Mother', the NSW CWS board resolved to proceed independently *without* CFWA; where APWCF held sway; discontinue all trade through CFA, withdraw funding from the federation and close its tiny Canberra office. It appears that A R Small's services were also terminated. NSW CWS executives again took to the road through Victoria and South Australia, seeking 'loyal' branches to retail English CWS goods and sell insurance products. In Victoria they contrived a co-operative association as that state's 'legitimate' CFA affiliate, but this quickly disintegrated. In South Australia they were again given short shrift for unwelcome 'meddling'.[4]

When Marsland's replacement, A F J (Alf) Smith, arrived in Australia in 1947 the agent emphasised that he would renew 'traditional' links with rural co-operatives and seek opportunities for the expanded sale of English CWS goods through 'co-operative outlets', wherever they may be. The 'One Big Society' idea was effectively dead along with hope for a united, national post-war co-operative movement.

Thus co-operators launched their a post-war co-operative 'new order'!

CFWA assumes the lead

CFWA Honorary Secretary Tom Bath now took the position of CFA Honorary Secretary, conducting the federation's business out of CFWA's Perth headquarters. Financially supported by English CWS, Bath toured the Australian states gathering trade data and attempting to develop federations eligible for CFA affiliation. In New South Wales Bath sought a rapprochement with NSW CWS, undertaking to support the wholesale in its struggle with so-called 'socialists' in the New South Wales Co-operative Institute (discussed in Chapter Eight) on condition NSW CWS resumed funding of CFA. In Victoria Bath met the new Registrar of Co-operative Societies, F T Ebbels, instantly falling out with him on the issue of nationally uniform co-operatives' legislation, to which CFWA remained opposed. In association with APWCF, Bath created a Victorian branch of CFA and a similar entity in Hobart. These were largely 'paper' inventions but adequate for purposes of legitimising CFA affiliation with the ICA.[5]

Pointing to Bath's sterling service at a Melbourne CFA meeting in 1949, Alf Smith undertook to continue funding the federation but implored the Australian co-operative movement to put its house in order and capture trade opportunities which English CWS was developing in Asia.[6]

CFA is suspended

The quarrelsome Australians could not achieve unity. Victorian and South Australian affiliates repeatedly threatened to withdraw from the federation in protest against alleged CFWA and NSW CWS interference in their states. The NSW CWS and APWCF and, by association CFWA, continued to be at each other's throats over the Rochdale movement's determination to launch a rival co-operative insurance company and the latter's appropriation of 'CO-OP' brands from English CWS, to which NSW CWS felt entitled as 'natural heir'.

The CFA was 'not working', Tom Bath told a 1951 CFWA conference, announcing his retirement as honorary secretary. In May 1952 Tom Shonk of NSW CWS assumed the position, immediately convening a 'reconciliation' conference in Melbourne. This was a trenchant affair riven with 'Cold War' polemics and acrimonious exchanges. After Westralian Farmers General Manager John Thompson jibed that the Rochdale Pioneers were 'definitely socialist' and consumer co-operatives were '...Labor supporters... and therefore there is something about their ideals unfortunately which we cannot accept', the meeting disintegrated into another slanging match with diatribes on insurance, uniform legislation, a co-operative bank and copyright to brands, ending in disarray and with a motion that CFA should be 'postponed indefinitely'.[7]

English CWS fills the void

For two years CFA lay dormant. In 1954 Alf Smith called affiliates together, advising them that English CWS was planning a massive expansion in South-East Asia and looked to CFA as a springboard facilitating this. Because the Australian co-operative movement seemed incapable of organising itself effectively, Smith said English CWS planned to station managers in key trade positions in Australia and run centralised auditing and management training services, participation in which would be a prerequisite to trade, employment and promotion in the sector.

Over the next few years the CWS Agent worked closely with APWCF and CFWA to build up co-operative trade in (non-communist) international co-operative markets, with grain and dairy co-operatives in particular benefiting from this. The CFA as such was reduced to a statistics-gathering service, supporting this trade. In the interim, NSW CWS and the east-coast Rochdale consumer movement declined, affected by superior competition and doctrinal inflexibility. New South Wales, the largest co-operative movement in Australia, was left rudderless until 1966 when the Co-operative Federation of New South Wales (CFNSW) was formed (discussed in Chapter Eight). Co-operative representative bodies in Victoria, South Australia and Tasmania remained rudimentary and only CFWA and the Co-operative Federation of Queensland (CFQ) were sufficiently well organised to engage in co-operative development work and speak coherently to governments.

Far from uniting and driving a robust post-war national co-operatives development programme, after more than a decade CFA was little more than a 'licence' for ICA membership and a data-gathering ancillary of English CWS-APWCF trade.

'Improving co-operation': the 1957 'All Australia' Co-operatives Conference

In June 1957, under the aegis of English CWS, CFA convened an All Australian Co-operative Congress in Sydney, entitled 'New Moves for Co-operative Expansion'. This landmark conference acknowledged that 'old world' co-operative theory required serious revision for co-operatives to remain commercially and socially relevant. The key issue, one which would dog the co-operative movement for the remainder of the century, was how to achieve capital adequacy in competitive markets while keeping faith with co-operative principles – the 'co-operative dilemma'. More immediately, the problem was how to 'improve' Rochdale principles and methodologies without further fragmenting an already fractious national movement.

NSW CWS President George Booth, presiding over an ailing consumer co-operative movement, came straight to the point: 'We are asking for the power to take over [co-operatives] even without being invited by directors.' After championing voluntary association all of his life, the old Rochdale war-horse was finally acknowledging that in modern commercial conditions this was problematical.

Westralian Farmers General Manager John Thompson could hardly resist saying 'I told you so' in commenting that Rochdale die-hards were at last facing up to economic realities dealt with long ago by his co-operative and Eudunda Farmers – that voluntaryism of itself was insufficient for a co-operative to function in a capitalist market place. 'Many say Westralian Farmers is not "truly" co-operative', Thompson said. 'All I can say is that it is a very good substitute.' The general manager lamented the fact that unity had eluded the post-war co-operative movement, robbing it of many opportunities and laid the blame squarely at consumers' feet. 'If only the whole of us could consolidate, and in one big co-operative combine…, we would indeed be a power in the land.' Agreeing with New South Wales Registrar of Co-operative Societies A R Crosky that education was the key to co-operative development and that better methods of capitalising co-operatives needed to be found if they were to survive modern trading conditions, Thompson said he genuinely doubted that the movement had a capacity for this or knew where it was going.

'The future of the movement', CWS Agent Alf Smith said, 'depends on *improvement* to the original co-operative concept'. This would require minute central planning, resolute unity in co-operative ranks and whatever measures were necessary to match private enterprise efficiency. Was the Australian co-operative movement up to the task?

CFQ Delegate W (Bill) Kidston, while affirming that the democracy principle was the key to understanding co-operative enterprise, agreed that co-operatives needed to conduct their business differently:

> *We must think big. It is a dangerous period for our development. The original flush of enthusiasm is dead. The buoyant expectation of spectacular achievement is dead. We have lost sight of the ideology of our movement and are constantly in danger of becoming just another trading [organisation]... If our movement is to continue as a force, if our movement is to survive, the rebate must be retained. The real purpose...of a co-operative is to prove to people that it is possible to keep the ownership of business and services in the hands of those who buy the goods or utilise the services.*

Kidston agreed with other speakers that co-operatives had a potentially terminal problem – capitalisation – and ways had to be found to *retain* surpluses consistent with co-operative principles enabling a co-operative to build a capital base so that it might remain competitive.

T P Richardson of Eudunda Farmers Co-operative, now with more than 65,000 members, agreed with Kidston and supported NSW CWS moves to centralise operations along the lines of the long-tested and successful Eudunda Farmers' model. Richardson urged co-operatives to place 'compliant' managers wherever they were needed to grow business as Eudunda had done. 'We must join hands...so there will not be any chance of our being destroyed.'

H C Bladwell of the New South Wales Farmers and Graziers Co-operative Company Limited (GRAZCOS), then one of the largest producer co-operative companies in Australia with twenty-one branches in New South Wales and a turnover of £44 million, said that co-operatives must emulate corporate structure to the degree this was possible and still remain a co-operative (presumably for taxation purposes), unfettered by rigid Rochdale principles.

The only dissenting voices came from a few remaining members of the Rochdale Women's Guilds present, who lamented the disappearance of co-operative voluntariness and years of unfulfilled promises, and from an Inverell delegate, Mr Wright, who said he had been in Australia for seven years and had already seen eleven societies fail. 'In rural areas [they] do not know the meaning of co-operation and they are in co-operation for only one reason. You know the reason – money!'[8]

The International Co-operative Trading Organisation (ICTO)

Following the 'All Australia' Congress, CFWA sent A Silsbury to represent CFA at an ICA Conference in Stockholm. There, representatives of forty-one national co-operative organisations met, representing 125 million members (including 15 million farmers) organised in 409,000 co-operative societies. The conference saw planning begin for an International Co-operative Trading Organisation (ICTO), effectively carving the world into communist and non-communist co-operative trading blocs, reflecting 'Cold War' divisions.

Under the aegis of ICA, representatives from co-operatives in Burma, Ceylon, India, Japan, Laos, Sarawak, Malaya, Singapore, Pakistan and Australia met in Kuala Lumpur in late 1958 to

An early Norco truck used for bulk milk collection.
Photo courtesy of Norco Co-operative Limited.

advance the ICTO plan. CFWA Honorary Secretary E T Lotan (who had replaced Tom Bath) represented CFA. An ICA South-East Asian Regional Office was created at this meeting. A secretariat was established in New Dehli to co-ordinate an ICA Committee of Agricultural Trade (South-East Asian Region), which was to be an ICTO zone. Through 'international co-operation', the promotion went:

> *The ICA is continuing the work of the Rochdale Pioneers and, in accordance with co-operative principles, seeks complete independence and by its own methods to substitute for the profit-making regime a co-operative system organised in the interests of the whole community and based upon mutual self-help.*

Support for the ICTO strategy and CFA, however, remained weak in Australia. There were almost 800 general co-operatives and co-operative companies in the commonwealth in 1960 with 640,000 members and an annual turnover of approximately £300 million. Fewer than 20 per cent of these were affiliated with CFA! Major rural co-operatives and co-operative companies were unconvinced of ICTO's practicability and generally proceeded unilaterally with trading arrangements in established UK and European markets. There were a few exceptions, including the (Victorian) Murray-Goulburn Co-operative, but, as it became apparent that ICTO could not deliver on promises, they, too, acted independently. With the New South Wales Rochdale consumer movement now in death throes, no coherent organisation existed to tie that state's co-operatives into ICTO and would not until 1996 when the CFNSW was formed. In South Australia and Victoria all attempts by CFA to get agreement on ICTO, failed. Only CFQ and CFWA succeeded in driving the ICTO agenda in their states but they were unable to achieve a level of commitment at national level which would give ICTO any real chance of success in Australia.[9]

It was clear in any event by the mid 1960s that ICTO's trading partners in South-East Asia had come to resent the scheme's alleged one-sided trade, favouring industrialised nations, with the co-operative movements of poorer nations charging that the so-called 'preference of trade' between ICTO-regional co-operative movements was meaningless, actually benefiting private intermediaries rather than co-operatives. The whole arrangement was perceived by them as little more than a ploy to expand markets for developed countries and in particular English CWS.[10]

By 1963, following two decades of an uncertain and lack-lustre existence, CFA was again moribund and the ICTO strategy was in tatters. Individual Australian co-operatives continued to make solid progress, particularly in the grain, wheat, fishing and dairy industries, but national unity on such issues as a co-operative bank, federal (or uniform) co-operatives' legislation and a federal co-operatives' development service, remained as elusive as ever. Post-war opportunities had been squandered. The legacy would be a retarded Australian co-operative movement wallowing on the margins of mainstream economic and social events.[11]

Bill Rawlinson CFA Executive Officer

Not until the appointment in 1965 of W W (Bill) Rawlinson (1909-1993) as CFA Executive Officer, sharing duties with CFWA, did CFA show any signs of a revival. Over the next two decades Rawlinson and CFA colleagues laboured mightily in seeking to forge a national co-operatives' third-tier organisation bringing direction to a drifting co-operative movement.

A gifted linguist and brilliant organiser, Bill Rawlinson drew upon a distinguished career in the India Army (where he had served as a major in the Field Artillery and won a Military Cross), in the International Commission in the British Zone of Occupied Germany and in the Colonial Government of the Federation of Malaya and Singapore.[12]

Seeking to revive CFA and the ICTO strategy

The two 'Bills', Bill Kidston of CFQ and CFA's Bill Rawlinson, used a Tax Payer Association attack on co-operatives in 1966 (discussed in Appendix One) to rally the federation and draw the recently-formed CFNSW and major Victorian co-operatives and co-operative companies into the fold. With Westralian Farmers' I W Hunter representing CFA on ICA's Advisory Committee and Sub-Committee on Agriculture, the federation organised visits to Australia by ICA delegates and, seeking to revive ICTO, CFA officers regularly attended ICA seminars in Singapore. In 1969, in association with the Department of Foreign Affairs, CFA organised an 'international co-operative study course', the first co-operatives' education program of its kind in Australia and involving twenty-one students from twelve countries in Africa, Asia the South Pacific and Papua New Guinea. The irony was that more reserves were going into foreign co-operatives' education than local.

Backwards Integration

Meanwhile, CFA promoted Westralian Farmers' 'backwards integration' policy, linking co-operatives *or* co-operative-owned businesses all the way through the production-consumption cycle, 'value-adding' from farm-gate to point of sale. Essentially a top-down reversal of Rochdale methodology situating rural co-operatives at the centre of the co-operative universe and, holding that diversification and, where necessary, joint-ventures with non-co-operative partners were necessary, exponents of 'backwards' integration freely adapted co-operative principles to suit commercial realities. Sometimes known as the 'American Rochdale plan', 'backwards integration' in federal Australia implied tortuous taxation problems with regard to the mutuality principle (discussed in Appendix One) and trades practices, in so far as special agreements between suppliers and co-operatives could be construed as anti-competitive and contrary to price-fixing regulations. As dealing with such complex legal and taxation questions was generally beyond the interest or competence of most farmers, 'backwards integration' provided CFA with a *raison d'être*, especially as co-operatives' legislation varied so between states.

Rawlinson's well-crafted strategy was to establish a national CFA secretariat in Canberra, which would co-ordinate 'backwards integration' for co-operatives at federal level, educate politicians and the public and enlist federal support for co-operatives through a farmer co-operative service linked to a Raiffeisen-style land bank, issuing sympathetically-structured finance for co-operatives through ICA affiliates. The question was: would Australian co-operatives support this plan as they grappled with financial problems and erratic commodity markets?[13]

The 1970s: 'a decade of co-operative development'

The ICA proclaimed the 1970s to be 'a decade of co-operative development'. On the contrary, for much of the established Australian agricultural co-operative movement, it proved to be a rout. This was not for lack of opportunity or federal government encouragement, rather the inability of financially-embattled co-operatives to unite around shared objectives and determinedly seek their achievement.

Changing trade patterns in the early 1970s redefined the nature of world agribusiness. Japan was now Australia's largest customer. With the United Kingdom moving into the European Economic Community (EEC), the APWCF arrangement became irrelevant. Since its inception soon after World War I APWCF had handled £1 billion Sterling in trade, 80 per cent of this Australian primary produce. In 1972 the last major Australian shipment through APWCF left for Europe. Australian agriculture was also increasingly being impacted upon by USA and European protectionism. Pricing increases by oil producing exporting countries (OPEC) in 1971 and 1973 saw dramatic changes in patterns of international investment and terms of trade accompanied by a decline in demand for commodities relative to value-added products, and a capital 'drought'. Climbing interest rates and spiralling inflation ate aggressively into co-operatives' assets, rendering them vulnerable to takeover or demutualisation in pursuit of growth capital for which traditional co-operatives fund-raising methods seemed ill-suited, at least to a new breed of co-operative leaders. Co-operatives rapidly lost ground in competition with corporations, which were not so fettered in capital-raising or national trading scope.

'A kind of paralysis in national co-operative development'

Unlike USA, for example, where most co-operatives were regional, state or national and already significantly diversified, Australian co-operatives and co-operative companies were still largely local and industry-specific in nature. In New South Wales, for instance, the rural co-operative movement was concentrated along a narrow coastal strip on the east coast with most co-operatives associated with the dairy industry, which accounted for about 84 per cent of that state's total co-operative turnover. The only regional centre in New South Wales at this time where significant diversified co-operative development had occurred was the Riverina. There fourteen co-operatives in various agricultural industries, including rice, mixed-farming, fruit and vine, accounted for about 12 per cent of the state's co-operative business. Only twenty-one other active rural co-operatives operated elsewhere in the state, most small with an average membership of around 250, providing about 4 per cent of total state co-operative turnover. This was the state with the largest and most diverse co-operative movement in Australia![14]

Studying rural marketing co-operatives in 1969, University of New England Economist R R Piggott concluded that 20 per cent of the gross value of New South Wales state product was marketed co-operatively. While on paper this might seem impressive, the position had not changed for the past eighteen years and the rate of new co-operatives forming was slowing. The academic noted that co-operatives were generally confined to assembling, producing, buying and selling. Wondering why there had been such little impact by co-operatives in Australia compared with the United States, Canada and Europe, Piggott said that the presence in Australia of statutory marketing authorities had retarded the co-operative movement by reducing the need for large marketing co-operatives. Most primary producer co-operatives were still 'price takers', not 'price setters', and they sold to wholesalers rather than to manufacturers, retailers or private companies, unlike co-operatives in the United States, which dealt directly with markets.

Piggott was convinced that the absence of federal co-operatives' legislation was a major inhibitor, pointing to the New South Wales *Co-operation Act*, which prevented 'foreign' co-operatives in other states from registering as a co-operative in that state or becoming a member of an association of co-operatives in that state. An Australian co-operative seeking to trade nationally was required to register as a *foreign society* in each jurisdiction and comply with local regulations, a complicated and expensive process which had produced a kind of paralysis in national co-operatives development. A plethora of state acts relating to co-operatives further complicated matters. Queensland, for example, had one specifically for rural co-operatives (the *Primary Producers Co-operative Associations Act,* 1923), while New South Wales and Victoria each had co-operatives' legislation, company law *and* industrial and friendly society legislation, all impinging upon co-operatives.

Piggott noted how poorly education featured in the primary producer co-operative movement with only 23 per cent of co-operatives surveyed engaging in any educational activity, most of this vaguely described as 'verbal activities'.

He found appalling apathy in the movement, a view corroborated by Commonwealth Department of Primary Industry officers, who reported frustrated attempts to gather quality information on rural co-operation which might aid development. Piggott believed that apathy was underpinned by heavy regulation in primary industry, especially the fresh-milk dairy industry; the dominant co-operative movement in New South Wales; where competition was blunted and farmer co-operatives had grown 'fat and lazy' on the back of guaranteed quotas in prescribed zones. In other industries where co-operatives were also well represented and competition was *strong*, such as potatoes and pumpkins, for example, apathy was not so evident.

The researcher noted how co-operatives behaved individualistically, were uncoordinated and now intense competition existed between them, again, particularly in the dairy industry, especially between Victoria and New South Wales. While agricultural co-operatives had combined well for *foreign* markets, still no national co-operative mechanism existed for *domestic* markets.

Australian co-operatives, generally, were characterised by capital inadequacy, poor management and indifferent selling expertise. What would happen if overseas markets suddenly dried up leaving apathetic and competing Australian co-operatives unready, Piggott asked. (That was about to come, with Britain's entry into Europe.) Piggott thought that the future for rural co-operatives in New South Wales and Australia was uncertain unless they quickly resolved acute capitalisation problems, centralised and co-ordinated activities and asserted a clear position in the political process. Federal legislation for co-operatives, or at least nationally uniform legislation, was absolutely vital.[15]

The CFA makes progress

A poorly supported CFA could do little to remedy Piggott's list of co-operative 'ills': localised growth; economically simplistic; stunted by regulation; hampered by inadequate legislation; lacking federal support; uncoordinated; disunited and competitive; apathetic; poorly educated, inadequately funded; indifferently managed; lacking a domestic marketing system; and bereft of political influence; but it did try.

The federation made some notable progress bringing states' federations into contact, for instance, the Co-operative Federation of Victoria (CFV), which was formed in 1972 after years of effort, and the Co-operative Federation of South Australia (CFSA), which was formed in 1974 with CFA help. The CFA also encouraged state regulators to talk to each other in seeking ways of achieving greater uniformity in the regulation of co-operatives. Bill Rawlinson initiated further meetings of ICA

South-East Asian Regional agriculture and associated committees and CFA continued to support the framework of an ICTO co-operative trade exchange in Singapore. CFA personnel travelled on fact-finding missions and attended international conferences seeking to develop co-operative trade networks. Supported by commonwealth and state governments, the federation brought more trade officials to Australia, for example, in 1971 ICA delegates visited Melbourne, Perth and Sydney. The federation also assisted Inter Co-op Kontakt, a huge conglomerate of European consumer co-operatives based in Hamburg, Germany, to set up offices in Newcastle, Sydney and Melbourne. Federation officials escorted Japanese co-operative leader S Kuwazaka on a visit to Australia in 1970, seeking trade. They helped one of the largest retail co-operatives in the world, UNI Coop Japan, to set up office in Australia.

A 'dawdling' movement

Aided by the Department of Foreign Affairs, CFA President Bill Kidston continued to mount a vigorous co-operatives' education campaign, focused on the Pacific region. In a prolific output Kidston invested great personal effort into co-operatives' education. Co-operators had to change, he wrote, had to adapt to dramatically changing circumstances and learn how to relate to a new *breed* of co-operators, who were wholly unencumbered by history or sentiment and had a purely business outlook. The Australian co-operative movement was dawdling and in danger of being eclipsed by events. The rate of progress had to be accelerated, Kidston warned, and this could only happen if co-operatives supported CFA in efforts to establish a Canberra secretariat which could co-ordinate co-operatives and off-set a serious decline in farmers' political influence. Co-operators must never forget their mission – the democracy principle:

> *Without democratic control we lose our distinction. Co-operatives cannot remain becalmed in a sea of tradition whilst everyone else is riding a current wave of transition. Our new generation of shareholders are more concerned with current achievements than they are with past performance...The lack of co-operation between co-operatives must be realised, identified and remedied.*

Federal government support for co-operatives

The Whitlam Labor Government (1972–1975), ending twenty-three years of Coalition rule, supported CFA's work and the prime minister showed a personal interest in the ICTO idea. After Westralian Farmers General Manager Ken Edwards accompanied Minister for Trade Dr Jim Cairns on an historic trade mission to China in 1972, the minister recommended federal government support for agricultural co-operatives through a Farmers' National Rural Advisory Committee to assist international co-operation 'as canvassed by the CFA' and long supported by the Department of Primary Industry. The Department of Foreign Affairs continued to support CFA's International Co-operatives Training Course. The Attorney-General's Department supported the idea of federal, or at least nationally uniform, co-operatives' legislation. An expansive political atmosphere in Canberra was such that the Australian co-operative movement seemed poised for a great leap forward. Within the movement itself, however, as Piggott observed, conservatism, apathy, parochialism and industry-specific myopia still ran deep.[16]

'To be inert is to be defeated':
The CFA Co-operatives' National Conventions 1973–1975

Seeking to capitalise on Federal Government support for co-operatives, CFA held the first of a series of important national conventions in Canberra in August 1973, organised by the credit union pioneers Kevin Yates and Clarrie Murphy. Because these conventions shed light on Australian co-operation at a moment of historic opportunity, they are discussed in some detail.

The new CFA President, M J Lane, told 115 delegates from government, production and marketing agricultural co-operatives, credit unions and building societies that the convention's purpose was:

> To ascertain government policy towards co-operation and to improve co-operative co-ordination to enable the strong but fragmented co-operative movement...to assume its rightful place in our social and economic system.

Lane described co-operation as a 'broad church with common concerns', including: the principles of co-operation; self-help and mutuality; a desire to cultivate co-operation as a balancing influence between private and public sectors; and a motivation to protect and promote the 'control of our own resources in our own personal and national interests'.

Deputy Prime Minister Lance Barnard spoke of his government's proposed Marketing Research Group in the Bureau of Agricultural Economics, which would have a strong co-operative brief. He warned primary producer co-operatives that they had to find ways of competing efficiently with private-profit enterprise without 'becoming divorced from the needs and wishes of co-operative members' and advised them not to become preoccupied with industry-specific issues but seek to apply co-operation to *new* fields relevant to contemporary community needs, such as health, housing, recreation, information, rural communities, tourism, education and quality of life issues. Barnard continued:

> I hope...the co-operative movement will continue to be a major force in the economic and social life of Australia [but] problems...must be overcome if the world of big business and multi-national corporations is not to swamp us.

Margaret Digby of the UK-based Plunkett Foundation for Agricultural Co-operative Studies, however, cautioned delegates about the proper degree of government aid for co-operatives, saying that co-operatives needed to exercise great care in inviting governments into their affairs. Experience overseas had shown that governments, particularly bureaucrats, were inclined to take over and accommodate only the *biggest* co-operatives with the greatest political and economic sway, to the detriment of broader co-operative development. (Digby's words were prophetic, as discussion in Chapter Nine attests.)

Westralian Farmers General Manager Ken Edwards described what he saw as the *real* reason for co-operatives:

> A co-operative is in the market place to get a better return for the farmer. There is difficulty in establishing the basic philosophies of co-operation amongst farmers, when this is not related to the economic aspect of co-operation.

Agricultural co-operatives had to become more market-orientated and less production driven, Edwards emphasised. Many were now big businesses but they had to get bigger and better, quickly. He detailed the 'backwards integration' strategy, arguing that this was necessary to fend off international agribusiness and replace statutory marketing authorities, which were obstructing the movement of co-operatives into more sophisticated market areas. Co-operatives were closer to producers than statutory boards *and* were based on voluntariness, Edwards continued, while statutory boards hampered competition between marketers and stultified efficiency and competitiveness. They should be replaced by co-operatives! Answering a pointed question about limitations to co-operatives' capital-raising capacity at a state level, Edwards said this was so but he was nonetheless still opposed to national co-operatives' legislation for co-operatives. The reason, he said, was simple – extant Western Australian law suited Westralian Farmers' entrepreneurial style well and it was unlikely the same flexibility would translate into national legislation, which he believed would incorporate rigid co-operative principles.

New South Wales Registrar of Co-operative Societies David Horton considered the role of co-operatives law:

I may lose friends as a result of this talk [by asserting that]…co-operative law may intend to reduce the scope of evolutionary development of the movement, thus causing some degree of fossilisation.

He questioned the need for co-operatives law which 'defined' co-operation, 'leaving no leeway for mutation or experimentation', and keeping the concept tied to nineteenth century standards. Some very successful European co-operative movements had developed *without* co-operatives legislation, Denmark for example. The Rochdale Pioneers, Horton continued, could *not* operate under contemporary conditions and if they were starting out today they would do so differently. Co-operatives law turned co-operation into a creature of statute and complicated it unnecessarily. Silence on a point actually *prevented* co-operatives from functioning in that area, as co-operatives. Much legislation was concerned primarily with penalties for breaches and in this regard registrars were given such wide discretion in the interpretation that they inevitably became targets for criticism and allegations of misadministration. Horton quoted the British nineteenth century co-operative visionary, Dr William King:

Co-operation is a voluntary act and all the power in the world cannot make it compulsory, nor is it desirable that it should depend on any power but its own. The interference of governments would only cramp its energies or misdirect them.

The registrar believed that the co-operative movement urgently needed a co-operatives financial service, but not a co-operative bank, as such. The movement was simply not ready. He raised eyebrows by suggesting that co-operatives should be free to issue bonus shares to members to reflect the revaluation of assets responding to inflation and implored co-operators to invest in education and research to discover new needs relevant to new circumstances 'before [the co-operative movement] is overtaken by difficulties'. In response to a question about uniform national legislation for co-operatives Horton said that, generally, states registrars favoured the idea but it was *not* supported by some major agricultural co-operatives and, therefore, was probably unachievable. Time would prove the registrar correct on this point, to the detriment of Australian co-operation (discussed in Chapter Fourteen).

Discussing the capitalisation question CFA Taxation Consultant E F Mannix agreed with Horton that co-operative members *should* be permitted to sell shares to other members, arguing that a suitable formula for co-operatives' fund-raising was to pay 50 per cent of rebates or dividends in cash to members and distribute the remainder in shares. Tax would be payable only on the cash component. Whatever decision the co-operative movement and legislators finally came to on capitalisation, something radical needed to be done, and soon – time was running out.

Westralian Farmers Financial Manager R M Graham pursued the capitalisation theme further, exploring methods of 'skirting difficulties' in co-operative structure and examining co-operative principles which, he claimed, created capitalisation problems in financing a 'backwards integration' strategy. Graham advocated further restricting dividend distribution, withholding funds to reserves, exploring sophisticated tax-minimisation schemes, paying investors higher interest and providing them with incentives in the form of bonus shares, preference shares, or public shares, *floated on stock exchanges*. Joint-ventures in association with proprietors were another way of overcoming the limitations of co-operative structure, Graham continued, but even *if* the co-operative movement could agree on the desirability of altering co-operative structure, none of the above was possible at national level without significant legislative reform. Both were unlikely.

Delegates were then urged by Queensland Primary Producers' Co-operative (Primaries) Assistant General Manager B A Campbell (then the largest wool and stock agent in Queensland, with sixteen branches and an annual turnover of $100 million) to co-ordinate co-operative efforts and remove undesirable competition between co-operatives. Co-operatives were competing with companies which could trade *anywhere* in Australia, in a way co-operatives could not, Campbell said, and he illustrated the point by reference to Australian Farmers Proprietary (AFP) Limited, a consortium of mainly co-operative companies, which was obliged to incorporate in the Australian Capital Territory as a 'foreign company' because no suitable legislation existed for it to register as a co-operative. AFP constituted an attempt to link 250 co-operatives comprising 80,000 shareholders producing $500 million of annual turnover and marketing 20 per cent of the Australian wool clip through Primaries, Farmers and Graziers, McTaggarts Primary Producers' Co-operative Association (Queensland), South Australian Farmers' Co-operative Union (SAFCU), the Victorian Producers' Co-operative (VPC) and Westralian Farmers. As such, AFP represented a huge part of the co-operative movement and yet it was obliged to incorporate because of inadequate co-operatives legislation. Imagine, Campbell continued, the impact upon the public perception of co-operatives and governments if this Titan could be seen for what it really was – a giant, Australian co-operative of co-operatives! Instead, it was unavoidably part of the corporate world. Co-operatives *had* to co-operate in a national organisation to eliminate duplication and co-ordinate development to their mutual benefit, as in USA, Japan and Sweden, and the movement needed a permanent voice in Canberra, close to government, sending clear and consistent signals:

> If we don't rationalise we risk the judgement of history that co-operatives failed to recognise and grasp opportunities to rationalise their opportunities…and thereby passed the advantage to unsympathetic competitors. To be inert is to be defeated.

Campbell's aphorism could well be an epitaph for the Australian co-operative movement.

Murray-Goulburn Co-operative Managing Director J J (Jack) McGuire, representing 40,000 dairy industry shareholders producing a $100 million annual turnover, warned delegates against 'flirting with private enterprise', as some seemed to be recommending. This was because co-operatives were a *threat* to private enterprise and the relationship could only harm co-operatives. McGuire described farmers as not simply producers but *entrepreneurs*: investors of capital; formulators of production and marketing targets; decision-makers; and executives. Each primary producer was an island and against him were arrayed powerful forces. While a 'get big or get out' strategy might be appropriate in some situations, merger for merger's sake was unwise, simply multiplying inefficiencies. Directors must be properly educated to address these aspects of the farming business, McGuire said. Employ top managers and let them manage!

CFV Honorary Secretary R B (Bob) Maybury also cautioned delegates about co-operatives following the 'corporate trail', arguing that co-operators must keep in mind their *social mission* in determining strategies for commercial success. Co-operation, Maybury believed, was '…a vital force…a middle way between the absolute power of the multinational corporations and the stifling red-tape of bureaucracy' and he deprecated those who saw co-operation narrowly as 'mere economic service'. 'If we accept the benefits of co-operation in one sphere [taxation concessions] it is our responsibility to spread the doctrine of co-operation and assist others.' In short, Maybury implied, if co-operative and co-operative companies were to continue to enjoy taxation privileges at taxpayer expense, they had a duty to serve the broader public good. Maybury also cautioned against the co-operative movement coming to be seen by the public and governments as exclusively a rural domain for farmers and urged *all* co-operators, no matter in which industry they served, to accept a social responsibility for their co-operatives, which was as important and necessary, he believed, as economic success in spreading the co-operative message.

Notwithstanding obviously irreconcilable differences between co-operative idealists and pragmatists, the 1973 convention had an air of cordiality. A welter of resolutions issued from it including: a national co-operatives centre in Canberra; a co-operatives research and development centre supported by the Commonwealth Government; scholarships in co-operative studies for youth; support for CFA's Taxation Committee; and further exploration of capitalisation options. No agreement was reached, however, on a co-operative bank and CFA was authorised only to conduct 'further inquiries' with state registrars with regard to national co-operatives' legislation. Ominously, too, the convention gave only qualified support to the ICTO strategy.[17]

ICTO is restructured

In June 1974 the Singapore-based South-East Asian Region of ICTO (Proprietary Limited!) was restructured. The Australian agricultural co-operative movement, principally Westralian Farmers, provided 50 per cent of the establishment costs in association with co-operatives from Malaysia, Singapore and The Philippines. Applications for shares were received from:

- ❖ *New South Wales*: PDS, Grazcos, Namoi Cotton, the Manning Meat Co-operative and the Newcastle and District Co-operative;
- ❖ *Queensland*: the Co-operative Wholesale Society (QCWS), McTaggarts Co-operative Company, the Primary Producers' Co-operative Association (Primaries), and the South Queensland Tobacco Co-operative;
- ❖ *Western Australia*: Westralian Farmers, the Grain Pool of Western Australia, Co-operative Bulk Handling (CBH); and
- ❖ *South Australia*: the Barossa Co-operative Winery (Kaiser Stuhl).

Significantly, several large dairy co-operative companies, including the Western District Co-operative and the Gippsland and Northern Co-operative (Victoria) and SAFCU (South Australia) stayed out. Murray-Goulburn, the Phosphate Co-operative Company (Victoria) and Eudunda Farmers (South Australia) supported CFA in principle but remained equivocal about ICTO.

Despite this ambivalent Australian support, the ICTO strategy showed promise. Certainly, the Whitlam Government gave strong support to agricultural co-operatives. A Green Paper on Agricultural Policy was prepared, which emphasised the importance of a strong agricultural co-operative sector, the need for a National Rural Advisory Council and identified ways of supporting co-operatives and raising their value for farmers. The government also agreed to a CFA request for a Farmer Co-operative Service to be established in the Department of Primary Industry.

The Coalition opposes a Farmer Co-operative Service

In a major set back for the co-operative movement, however, resisting what it saw as an attempt to 'socialise industry', the Coalition Opposition saw to the defeat of a second reading in the Senate of legislation to rationalise and co-ordinate a plethora of government measures to assist primary industry in a Farmer Co-operative Service and allow the Australian Industry Development Corporation (AIDC) to help agricultural co-operatives.

'The co-operative movement is weary': the 1974 Co-operative National Convention

The 1974 CFA Co-operative National Convention displayed little of the cordiality of its predecessor. Building society and credit union representatives deplored CFA neglect of their interests. A sniping match erupted as it became clear that CFA executives had no intention of acting on any resolution not corresponding with Westralian Farmers' 'backwards integration' priorities. The conversion of many rural co-operatives to capitalist orthodoxy (discussed below) alarmed and depressed many delegates.

Debate amounted to a fundamental reappraisal of Australian co-operation, especially co-operative-government relations and fund-raising problems allegedly implicit in co-operative structure. CFA President M J Lane again reminded delegates that co-operation aspired to *dual* economic and social objectives and was a 'middle way' – partly public and partly private. He described co-operatives as businesses where the elements of ownership, control and use of services were united in one group. This was the co-operative 'difference' and it needed to be proclaimed and celebrated as often as possible. He called for unity, assuring delegates that CFA had sought a co-ordinated dialogue with all sections of the co-operative movement on finance, legislation, education, consumer affairs, insurance and trade, but had found little support and less unanimity. If co-operatives would *not* support their movement and unite behind CFA there was *no alternative* but to look to government. Lane acknowledged that this was risky and threatened co-operative autonomy but there was no other choice for a co-operative movement unprepared to help itself.

In an impassioned address melding idealism and pessimism, PDS General Manager G A J Beytagh further explored the theme of co-operative-government relations reminding delegates that while co-operatives were commercial enterprises they were also 'a small piece of a large social design'. Business, he believed, was simply the outer and visible manifestation of co-operatives' far-reaching objectives which included the subordination of business techniques to ethical ideas. 'Apart from this…the movement has no basic satisfactory reason for existence.' Economists, Beytagh continued, criticised co-operatives for lacking economic theory but he thought this was a *virtue* and precisely the co-operative 'difference' because co-operatives were not just about economics:

> We used to say, "not for charity, not for profit, but for service", but we have fallen into a trap. We too have been dragged into the whirlpool we sought to avoid. The early co-operators wanted to eliminate profit because they knew that no profit can be made except at another's expense. We are not truly democratic. Decisions flow out from managers but not from members. We have lost participation and alienated young and new members, who have become disappointed because they are not getting the inner and personal satisfaction they anticipate because they do not find any great difference that makes it worth the trouble. People will stay with something they call a movement only so long as it serves a deep social and psychological hunger as well as a physical need. Therefore, be successful, but be different in purpose, motivation and pay attention to deeper needs.
>
> The co-operative movement in Australia is weary and fatigued, tired and listless. There is no longer that wonderful feeling of excitement, of co-operators on a journey to a new land. The big co-operatives are losing vision. It is a case of business as usual. The co-operative movement is being left behind by rapid changes in society. The freedom of individuals and co-operation

are not easily reconcilable. I urge Australian co-operators to re-examine their objective. Far too many are motivated by self-interest, not self-help. They remain isolated in their own backyards.

Beytagh urged delegates to rally under the CFA flag and to help it 'harness the collective initiative of the people and to decentralise the base of economic power'. He warned that too much state bureaucracy combined with too little co-operative involvement would produce 'co-operative amnesia' in public policy. Sound public policy for co-operatives would include: a declaration by government that co-operatives were an integral part of its social and economic development policy; sound co-operatives' law; a co-operative department to train people to run co-operatives; and the provision of lines of credit, which the co-operative movement could gradually take over by itself. Beytagh did not say whether this should occur at the federal or state level, but it seems likely he meant the latter. Co-operatives had originally developed in a *laissez faire* environment when it was thought *inappropriate* for governments to meddle, the general manager continued, but now governments were more active in all branches of the economy and therefore it was proper for them to help promote self-governing co-operatives. Beytagh called upon the federal government to encourage the development of co-operatives in all spheres, but this could not and would *not* happen unless the co-operative movement fulfilled its obligations to 'contribute to social reform, human betterment, the quality of life and a just, compassionate Australian society'.

Following Beytagh's appeal for co-operatives to rediscover their original mission, Chairman and General Manager of Co-operative Insurance Society (CIS) UK Limited I I Seeley got to what pragmatists saw as the kernel of the conference: the need to revise co-operative structure. Seeley argued that because of increased competition and costs some Rochdale principles now needed to be discarded. He noted how agricultural co-operatives and the consumer co-operative movement had developed separately, particularly in Australia. Co-operatives were now capital-intensive organisations and the movement must confront and control its major problem – capitalisation. Traditional co-operative structure and the expectation of members that dividends be distributed meant that surpluses were not being ploughed back into co-operatives for modernisation. He detailed ways in which British co-operatives had invested *outside* the movement to overcome this anomaly and said that the Australian movement must do the same if '...it is to be more than a camp follower of the more progressive private-sector and blaze new trails'. About 80 per cent of the British movement's superannuation fund, for example, was invested externally, benefiting from higher interest rates available in the private money-market. He described ways of restricting the rights of members to withdraw funds and detailed a variety of equity securities suitable to the needs of investors and how to 'adapt' ICA principles to attract higher rates of interest. Seeley recommended that co-operatives should not limit themselves to members who 'more often than not [are] in the lower income brackets with only meagre savings potential' and suggested methods by which speculative capital might be attracted into Australian co-operatives, such as selling co-operative property to insurance companies and financial institutions and leasing it back, thereby releasing capital for development. He outlined methods by which managers might foreclose on 'unco-operative' co-operatives and predicted a co-operative movement 'entirely owned by secondary co-operatives', hinting that the English movement was interested in investing in Australian co-operatives, under the 'right conditions':

A secondary organisation could take up non-voting preference shares issued by primary organisations instead of making loans to them. For example, farmer co-operatives, which do not collaborate with larger well-established trading co-operatives, might issue non-voting preference shares to enable the latter to provide capital to the former without giving them control. Co-operatives are different. We try to help each other.

Seeley also called for 'special management shares [so that] outside managers might participate in any success their involvement might have achieved' while *distinguishing* members from shareholders for purposes of capital raising. While ICA principles required open membership he argued that this need not preclude non-voting shareholders from holding 'membership certificates', or non-voting preference shares, which might be quoted on stock exchanges:

Such shareholders might prefer to leave dividends in the co-operative and attract "compensatory votes" or membership certificates or both. This...horrifies some co-operators [but] it should be remembered that the stock exchange is only a specialised market.

These innovations, Seeley concluded, could not be achieved without legislative change and he supported CFA calls for a national secretariat in Canberra to lobby for this. He warned, however, against direct government assistance, saying that no one makes money available 'without strings attached'. Presumably, that also meant the English co-operative movement.

Speaker after speaker suggested possible solutions to the perceived co-operatives' capitalisation dilemma. Representing the Reserve Bank of Australia, A J McIntyre spoke on finance for the rural sector observing that farmers were *already* substantial lenders with an average 36 per cent of their income involved in banks, pastoral houses and government bonds. Many had substantial non-farm assets and had benefited from land sales. Nevertheless, Australian farmers had failed completely to develop rural co-operative credit organisations, had poorly utilised existing rural credit facilities and needed to find better ways of accessing *existing* credit rather than leaning on government or trying to start a new bank.

University of Sydney Academic Dr R L Batterham explored co-operative farm credit systems in the United States relating how the US federal government had established a farm credit system *in 1916*, how this was gradually purchased by farmers and was now run by money experts with the government simply providing inspection and auditing services. There was a great deal of interest in this system, even envy, but that was as far as it went at the convention.

The Caulfield Institute's P Chandler said that co-operatives faced not only a capitalisation problem but the linked problem of *marketing*. Food marketing was undergoing a revolution. Food converters were now integrating backwards to processing *and* farming. Retail chains were going straight to farmers and by-passing intermediaries. Many traditional markets were actually closing down and Chandler cited the Chicago Stockyards. It was important that co-operatives introduce professional directors and managers who were knowledgeable about these trends. Farmer bargaining power was now significantly reduced and buyers, including in many cases huge multi-nationals, were going wherever the cheapest product existed, abandoning traditional suppliers. Even domestic markets were under threat. There were really only three options for co-operatives when it came to marketing: a multi-product market supply co-operative; a co-operative–corporate (hybrid) joint venture; and a single product market co-operative. The first, like 'New Generation Co-operatives' in USA, would have total control, telling farmers what to produce, what quality, how much and when, and would supply all necessary inputs to assure that agreements between the co-operative and producers were fulfilled. It would also exercise strict control over farmers' financial situation and assist with the management of farm operations. In the co-operative–corporate joint venture model, a co-operative would simply supply a corporation, which would market products through jointly-owned processing and distributing facilities. Advantages included access to assured markets (though how this might be guaranteed in deregulated markets was not explained), research, access to joint-stock capital, brand names and a spread of risks. The third option, a specialised single-product marketing co-operative, had been around for a long time and there were successful examples in Australia, in the rice and dairy industries, for instance. They would need to amalgamate further to achieve economies of scale and become more business orientated and politically active if they were to serve farmers' interests best. Did co-operators have a capacity for this?

'It is hard to be optimistic'

Certainly, as co-operatives struggled to stay competitive, as co-operatives, in dramatically altered economic and trading conditions in the 1970s, the Australian co-operative movement was required to deal with two 'monsters': government intervention and; restructuring for capital inadequacy. The inability of many agricultural co-operatives to fund growth from *within* the membership bond sufficient to remain viable, a new breed of managers argued, meant inevitably that their structure needed to be adjusted to accommodate external sources of funding without losing control. This in turn required serious legislative 'surgery', potentially inflaming co-operative movement politics in determining which co-operative principles needed changing. In this way a 'co-operative dilemma' in balancing democracy and capital adequacy was converging on co-operative structure to impel the movement in new and dangerous directions.

CFNSW Director Les Gibbs, an old Rochdale co-operator, lamenting the fragmentation of the Australian co-operative movement, remarked at the convention:

> We must raise the sights of the co-operative movement. We have never really realised out total potential and fragmentation of co-operatives in Australia should concern us all...When it comes to the establishment of a central unifying structure where we can help one another we seem reluctant to do so and are too content to stay in our own backyard or baulk at the expense...It is hard to be optimistic about the future.[18]

The National Co-operative Agricultural Committee

A CFA National Co-operative Agricultural Committee, chaired by G A Beytagh, formed from the 1974 Convention seeking: a Farmer Co-operative Service in the Department of Primary Industry; links to the government's National Rural Advisory Council; better co-operative representation on statutory marketing authorities; improved links to ICA and; solutions to the 'co-operative dilemma'.

Briefly to Canberra

Almost thirty years after CFA first established tiny headquarters in the national capital, in January 1975 the federation re-opened a Canberra secretariat on a trial basis until June 1976. The office was supported by the Commonwealth Government on the understanding that the co-operative movement would take over funding as soon as possible. Bill Rawlinson was employed as full-time executive officer.

This promising start quickly faltered. As some critics of the policy had predicted, the Department of Primary Industry expressed serious concerns about taxation implications with regard to 'backwards integration' and the mutuality principle (90 per cent of business with members). Then, preoccupied with political events leading to the dismissal of the Whitlam Government in November 1975, the department failed to fill a Class 10 position in the Extension Services Branch, specialising in agricultural co-operatives. Another opportunity for development on a national scale was eluding the co-operative movement.

A few CFA papers were issued on capital needs, retaining surpluses, inter-lending and co-operative banking but nothing concrete was done about them. ICTO remained poorly utilised and CFA's National Co-operative Agricultural Committee was seen to be ineffective. The federation seemed incapable of carrying even basic convention resolutions forward prompting previously supportive co-operatives, strapped for cash, to question the value to state federations financially supporting it.

The 1975 Co-operatives National Convention

There was little cordiality evident at the 1975 CFA Co-operatives National Convention. Attendance was well down on previous years and building society and credit union delegates were conspicuous by their absence. It is clear that by now CFA was perceived as primarily a rural 'club' and, in the politically-charged atmosphere of the Whitlam dismissal, perceived to be aligned with conservative forces. Showing some ingratitude, considering everything the Whitlam administration had tried to do to help the movement, often against Coalition opposition, the convention's organisers issued a statement:

> ...regretting the failure of the government to provide the convention with a definition of and clear-cut statement positively setting out attitudes and policies towards co-operatives in Australia as invited by the CFA, and noting the attitude of the alternative government clearly enunciated in the equal time provided for this statement.

Quite possibly imagining that he was talking to a well-organised movement on the European model, the keynote speaker, \, who was secretary-general of the German co-operative and Raiffeisen societies movement, delivered two learned dissertations on 'Mobilisation and Co-ordination of Co-operative Self-help in Rural and Credit Services' and 'Co-operative Banking in the Federal Republic of Germany'. His talks highlighted the features of a mature, integrated and successful German movement. The contrast between the grand sweep and intellectual rigour of Schiffgen's presentations and the narrow concerns of Australian delegates, focused on capitalisation, marketing, taxation and legislation, was glaring.

A paper prepared by a terminally ill CFA President M J Lane was read deploring the fact that state federations seemed reluctant to support CFA's Canberra secretariat and that, therefore, affiliation with the federation was now open to *any* individual co-operative prepared to support it. CFA National Rural Advisory Council (possibly a re-named National Co-operative Agricultural Committee) Chairman S L Ferguson reported that his committee had achieved precisely nothing and that farmers were simply too individualistic and disdainful of regimentation for co-operatives *ever* to co-operate, let alone producers and consumers. Unless they *did* co-operate, however, Ferguson concluded sagaciously, co-operatives would inevitably be pushed towards capitalist orthodoxy and irrelevance.

Isobel Packer, representing the Newcastle Womens' Guild, an ember of the old Rochdale world, said the Australian co-operative movement's history was 'disappointing' and noted how the support of women for co-operation was waning as they became more affluent and independent.

Stating the obvious, Shadow Minister for Manufacturing Industry and Industry Development Senator R Cotton (Liberal-Country Party) noted how the co-operative movement in Australia seemed to be lagging.

A report of progress since 1974 confirmed that little progress had been made except for a research paper on capital formation and studies under way looking at inter-lending and a centralised banking system used by credit unions in New South Wales. Nevertheless, more hopeful CFA resolutions and policy proposals were issued: implement the farmer co-operative service; work towards uniform legislation; explore long-term rural credit schemes; encourage farmer co-operation; utilise existing government and industry training funding; learn more about consumerism; provide equal opportunity for women and so on – more a wish-list than a practical strategy. In seeking to galvanise the Australian co-operative movement and integrate this with government policies, capture new opportunities, overcome the 'co-operative dilemma' and attract public interest, some delegates now thought CFA was embarked upon 'mission impossible'.

The disconsolate 1975 CFA National Convention was the last of its kind for nearly a decade. Meanwhile, the national co-operative movement wallowed.[19]

More co-operatives take unilateral action

In the ensuing years CFA affiliated with the West German Raiffeisen Union and arranged for further visits by German personnel to explore possible inter-lending arrangements. CFA officers were involved in more overseas travel, more reports on key issues and studies of legislation but none of this translated into practical action of immediate benefit to increasingly hard-pressed affiliates dealing with tough markets and capitalisation problems. This point was not lost on affiliates, even co-operatives dedicated to co-operation, who were becoming increasingly impatient with the federation. They flatly refused, for example, to assist in establishing an Australian national co-operatives' education and training centre at the University of New England, despite strong support at institutional level. With UK markets disappearing into the European Economic Union (EEU) and ICTO failing to deliver a suitable alternative, individual co-operatives necessarily took independent action in locating new markets. The Murray-Goulburn Co-operative, for example, successfully sought joint ventures in Japan. PDS opened offices in London, Tokyo and Singapore and Westralian Farmers began joint ventures with foreign meat companies, all virtually without CFA involvement.

Relations with the federal government deteriorate

Meanwhile, relations with the federal government were deteriorating. Fraser Coalition Minister for Primary Industry Ian Sinclair, responding to correspondence from CFA and CFWA seeking action on previous government undertakings with respect to the proposed Farmer Co-operative Service within the Department of Primary Industry and a co-operative bank for farmers, insisted that co-operatives 'should stand on their own two feet', consistent with co-operative principles. Co-operatives were state-controlled, Sinclair emphasised, and outside a federal jurisdiction. State marketing boards were not much different in principle from co-operatives, the minister said, and they were doing much of the work the co-operative movement wanted the federal government to accept. Because co-operatives provided such a wide range of services, this would create administrative problems as responsibility for co-operatives would cross many departments. Sinclair also doubted the value of separating farmer co-operatives from other co-operatives and treating them differently, asked why *non-co-operative farmers* should not also benefit from such services as CFA was requesting and questioned whether services to large commercial co-operatives could be justified at public expense. As for a co-operative bank, Sinclair said that he was prepared to 'catalyse' developments but would involve existing institutions so that any bank which might emerge would *not* be purely co-operative. The minister noted that the Australian Bankers' Association was opposed to a fully-fledged rural bank, arguing instead for an alternative 'refinancing' service with an 'element of public subsidy', because banks were prepared to act only as *conduits* for Treasury loans to rural consumers of long-term concessional interest rate finance, not direct lenders.

The result in August 1978 was the launching of the Primary Industry Bank of Australia (PIBA), a refinancing service involving several banks as shareholders, '...in spite of protracted delays and a lot of farmer criticism concerning its domination by city financial interests'.[20]

Decline of the rural co-operative sector

Farmer co-operatives were still economically significant in the early 1970s, with 452 co-operatives involving 377,530 members generating an annual turnover of $863 million. Co-operatives accounted for a sizeable portion of wheat and coarse grain crops, 95 per cent of rice production, 50 per cent of sugar mills for extracting sugar, 85 per cent of the tobacco crop, 70 per cent of cotton production and processing to milling stage, 40 per cent of vegetable production and marketing, 25 per cent of wine, over 50 per cent of fruit-canning and dried fruit, 20 per cent of the wool clip, 50 per cent of liquid milk, 85 per cent of butter production, 25 per cent of bulk honey, 40 per cent of pre-packed honey and 55 per cent of the fishing industry. In addition, CFA President Bill Kidston estimated that rural co-operatives were directly returning more than $15 million annually to local communities in which they functioned.

By 1980, however, rural products comprised only approximately 40 per cent of all Australian exports; down from 90 per cent in 1950; as metals, minerals and manufactured goods expanded proportionately. While there was no decline in absolute monetary terms, in relative terms the decline of the importance of primary industry to the GDP was dramatic. This was attended by a waning of political influence in rural electorates.

Changes in the economic and political importance of the rural sector were reflected in the decline of the agricultural co-operative movement. By the early 1980s much of the traditional rural co-operative movement had disappeared, a victim of its own disunity together with corrupted overseas markets, decades of protectionism, Britain's entry into Europe, interest rate hikes, a wages explosion, spiralling inflation, radical macro-economic reform and industry reconstruction for which many co-operatives were ill-prepared. Not all co-operatives succumbed, some actually rallied and reaffirmed their position in industries. Nevertheless, several large co-operatives, accepting the advice of corporate finance and management consultants, converted to capitalist orthodoxy – a demutualisation spree began.

Pursuing a path independent of CFA, the South Australian Farmers' Co-operative Union (SAFCU) turned to private consultants, retaining the services of R Seldon and Associates, management consultants of Sydney. Seldon convinced SAFCU directors that there were fundamental flaws in the capital and funding structures of co-operatives, which were only now maturing in contemporary economic conditions. Co-operative philosophy was faulty, Seldon believed, and notions of service and non-profit motivation compromised the '...realism required to maintain a viable and competitive trading operation.' The co-operative image was poor, consultants said, because potential investors saw co-operatives as uneconomic, lacking direction or motivation and hampered by democratic principles and limited interest. Co-operation created corporate apathy and inefficiency with the many leaning on the few creators of opportunities and wealth, awaiting outcomes. There was insufficient 'risk' or involvement in co-operatives to encourage enterprise. The '...maximum returns should be made to those that [sic] create the business opportunities,' Seldon argued, and SAFCU should alter its share structure and interest rate policies to allow *part ownership* by investors and management by specialists. 'Contaminated' co-operatives were prospering, Seldon said, (possibly referring to co-operative companies in Victoria and Western Australia) while 'pure' co-operatives were struggling. The 'co-operators [have] failed to co-operate' he correctly added, 'breaching principle six of the ICA list'. Consequently, Seldon concluded, many co-operatives now faced foreclosure by financial institutions.[21]

Persuaded, SAFCU directors with member approval restructured the co-operative to become 'Southern Holdings'. Ron Brierley of Brierley Investment Limited (New Zealand) and Industrial Equity Limited (IEL) took a 47 per cent share, retaining SAFCU's co-operative structure for its 'cash flow which was…almost as good as a merchant bank'. Southern Holdings then joined with Westralian Farmers and the Victorian Producers' Co-operative Association to form Australian Farmers Proprietary Limited (AFP) (discussed earlier).

Seldon was later invited to restructure the Queensland Primary Producers' Co-operative Association and the McTaggarts Producers' Co-operative Association Limited along the lines of Southern Holdings. The outcome was PRIMAC Holdings, the largest pastoral house in Queensland.

Later, the Victorian dairy co-operatives, Gippsland and Northern Co-operative and Western District Co-operative, which had amalgamated with the Victorian Butter Factories' Co-operative Company Limited in 1967 to create Amalgamated Co-operative Marketers (Australia) Limited (ACMAL), registered a subsidiary in New South Wales: G & N Company Limited. PRIMAC Holdings joined with G & N Company Limited, Southern Holdings and Westralian Farmers to form the Australian Stud, Stock and Land Company Proprietary Limited. The Western District Co-operative Company Limited was retained by ACMAL as a nominal co-operative for 'investment income'.[22]

Meanwhile, CIC (Australia), the Victorian dairy-based insurance co-operative company, which included as shareholders the New South Wales co-operatives PDS and Dairy Farmers (which already held between them $7 million in listed shares), moved into Winchcombe Carson Limited, the Sydney pastoral house, in association with Seldon and Brierley. Shedding workers' compensation, CIC (Australia) was restructured as CIC Holdings, declaring that it 'often pays to act in tandem with Brierley' and with the *Australian Financial Review* reporting that Brierley's IEL 'has a valuable ally in [CIC] in the never-ending takeover wars'. CIC Holdings then invested in PRIMAC Holdings 'taking advantage of the liquidity problems of many co-operative companies' to form Consortium Property and Investment Society Limited, holding 20 per cent of the company's shares with equal parcels taken up by Southern Farmers, IEL and Beneficial Finance Corporation.

Consortium Property and Investment Society Limited then launched a successful takeover of the giant South Australian Fishermen's Co-operative Limited (SAFCUL), which possessed plant in four Australian states, Thailand, Indonesia and The Philippines and restructured this as SAFCUL Holdings, the co-operative retaining 51 per cent ownership for its 'traditional way of buying fish caught by members'. By 1981, this co-operative shell had been stripped away and Brierley's Southern Holdings took a 33 per cent share and the (British) Cold Storage Holdings (an unlisted public company), 33 per cent.

SAFCUL was not the only fishing co-operative to be converted. In 1977 the New South Wales Department of Decentralisation and Development in association with H J Heinz, the multi-national food processor moved to assist the Eden Fishermen's Co-operative on the south coast of New South Wales, then the largest Australian fishing processing plant. The arrangement was that the government would provide financial aid and Heinz would market the co-operative's produce. By 1978 Heinz was the co-operative's major shareholder, which had forfeited its co-operative structure.[23]

By mid-1978 the Brierley pastoral empire constructed on old co-operative assets controlled 15.3 per cent of the market and was the second largest in Australia, behind Elders GM. By 1983 Brierley owned 100 per cent of Southern Holdings, which now including the Adelaide Milk Supply Co-operative (50 per cent), the Farmers' Co-operative Executors and Trustees (100 per cent) and CIC (Holdings) (29 per cent).

In 1980 the mainstay of CFQ, Red Comb Co-operative (Stock Feeds) Co-operative Limited, was taken over by Gillespie Proprietary Limited. In the same year the (South Australian) Barossa Co-operative Winery Co-operative Limited (Kaiser Stuhl), a staunch CFA supporter and then Australia's largest winery, was taken over by Penfolds Proprietary Limited.[24]

In a shock for traditionalists, the old C E D Meares'-inspired distribution co-operative, PDS, an icon of the co-operative movement, fell to Tooth the brewer after a PDS merger with ACMAL fell through. In the process PDS, which did not consult CFA, had registered as a company since no useful state co-operatives legislation existed to allow interstate mergers and, after negotiations stalled, the former assistant general manager of PDS, then employed by Tooth, 'got wind of this' and initiated the takeover.[25]

As noted in Chapter Six, in 1984 Westralian Farmers (Wesfarmers) was listed on the Perth stock exchange, leaving a huge gap in the Western Australian co-operative movement.

The 'conversion syndrome' was far from finished, however. There was another decade for it to run (discussed in Chapters Eleven and Thirteen).

Co-operatives fight back

It was not all retreat and decay for rural co-operatives, however, with scores of smaller co-operatives surviving and some larger long-established societies and co-operative companies adapting successfully to the changed conditions. For example, the Murray-Goulburn Co-operative launched a brilliant initiative to contend with Britain's entry into Europe, developing new foreign and domestic markets and employing the latest technologies (discussed in Chapter Three).[26]

There were also notable victories in the fruit industry. For instance, after an AIDC report called for a major rationalisation of the fruit industry, a 'war' broke out in the Victorian Goulburn Valley between co-operatives and private companies in 1975. In exchange for AIDC financial assistance to restructure the industry, the corporation demanded a consolidation of entities for production and marketing, recommending that the proprietary company, Henry Jones, be sold and that the SPC and Ardmona co-operatives, which were already marketing jointly, join with KY, another regional fruit co-operative, which had been marketing through Henry Jones, to form one big co-operative.[27]

The Harvard-trained general manager of Henry Jones, John Elliot, proposed an alternative plan linking SPC, Ardmona and the South Australian Riverland Co-operative, on the one hand, and Jones, KY and the New South Wales Letona Co-operative, on the other. Progress was halted by the dismissal of the Whitlam Government in November 1975 and, in the political imbroglio which followed, H J Heinz, whose competitors in spaghetti and baked-bean markets included SPC, complained that tax payers' money was being used to assist 'one section of the industry, the co-operative section'. Hearing of this, the Western Australian Manjimup Fruit Growers' Association broke angrily from Henry Jones and formed a rival co-operative. Meanwhile, Australian overseas fruit markets continued to evaporate as South African and US competition intensified. Announcing that he would abandon the original proposal, Elliott moved on SPC, which was vulnerable to 'dry' shareholders (non-suppliers) and had not paid a dividend in seven years. SPC shareholders were attracted to the bid.[28]

The Australian Canning Fruitgrowers' Association (ACFA), which represented 93 per cent of deciduous fruit-growers, bluntly told Elliot, '...forget [the proposal] if you want to stay in fruit'. ACFA threatened to withdraw business from the bank which held 49.99 per cent of Henry Jones' shares and resolved to defend the co-operative basis of the industry:

> *The opposition of growers to the Henry Jones' plan is based on the fundamental belief that growers should control the canning industry and not outside investors, banks, life officers or trading houses...Reliance on companies like Jones is dangerous, we have experienced it in the past. The growers' interests always come last...We will take whatever measures are appropriate to ensure that Henry Jones is not able to disrupt the co-operatively based rationalisation of the canning industry.[29]*

Henry Jones-IXL responded by engaging a former Australian test cricketer, R Cowper, as public relations officer. Cowper said returns to growers would be improved if the Jones' offer were accepted and assured co-operators that, '...if it were to be a fight to the death the proprietary company would survive.'

ACFA responded by boycotting the bank used by Henry Jones. This impacted upon Henry Jones-IXL shareholders, who included Elders-Smith, Goldsbrough-Mort Limited, National Mutual Life and Federation Insurance Limited. Henry Jones-IXL countered by circularising all SPC shareholders, describing the co-operative as 'risky' and arguing that the industry would collapse if the takeover proposal were not accepted. This precipitated '...an emotional response in the Goulburn Valley...because of the historical rivalry existing between the co-operatives and proprietary canners.'[30]

Seeking to drive Henry Jones from the market, SPC announced plans for an SPC-Ardmona-Riverland marketing joint venture, finding support in the Victorian Rural Finance and Settlement Commission. Henry Jones protested that it really only wanted the *marketing* side of the industry – *production* could be left to co-operatives. With growers believing that Jones was simply jockeying for position in order to pick them off, one by one, there was:

> *...much ill-feeling in the Valley against...the Jones takeover bid. The whole matter has become a most sensitive political issue as SPC and Jones fight it out in the Valley, proprietary company versus the co-operative, or someone would say, the city slickers against the country folk...It is all shaping up as a most interesting battle for Australian corporate watchers.[31]*

Henry Jones-IXL withdrew the SPC takeover bid but quickly moved on KY, seeking a 49 per cent interest and anticipating 'substantial future income taxation benefits'. Keen to break the co-operative grip on the Goulburn Valley industry, Jones offered KY shareholders a generous cash offer which, in a tactical *coup*, SPC and Ardmona *encouraged* KY shareholders to accept:

> *...farmers in the Valley stampeded to accept. In two frantic days Jones paid out $2.4 million in cash to shareholders who physically brought their script into the KY office.*

Jones ended up with 76 per cent of KY and, consequently, lost access to the tax act's mutuality principle (90 percent of business with members) and special access to Reserve Bank funds. KY's liquidity position was also weakened when the most profitable line of supply; peaches; was enticed away by SPC. Responding, Jones created a nominee co-operative company 'in friendly hands' and offered shares in this to growers in exchange for fruit supply. In this way Henry Jones-IXL was able to continue trading in the Goulburn Valley, on a nominally co-operative basis. The experience showed that when co-operatives did decide to co-operate, they could be a formidable force. It also demonstrated that the co-operative business model might be opportunistically employed for reasons other than co-operation.[32]

The Standing Committee on Agriculture 1985

In 1985 the Hawke Federal Labor Government convened a Standing Committee on Agriculture (SCA) comprising ministers of agriculture from each Australian jurisdiction. The SCA formed a working party (SCAWP) which explored the scale and significance of agricultural co-operatives in Australia, examined the legislative, financial and management structures of co-operatives and identified obstacles impeding their operation. This promising step in reaffirming links between federal government and the agricultural co-operative sector, reminiscent of the 1945 Rural Reconstruction Commission and initiatives during the Whitlam years, incorporated much of the CFA's agenda. The problem was, after a decade of co-operative attrition and indifferent support for the sector, the federation was on its knees and the movement had been much reduced.

Demise of the Co-operative Federation of Australia
After Westralian Farmers' Co-operative Company was listed as a public company (Wesfarmers) in 1984, CFWA and CFA experienced a dramatic drop in funding. Disagreements erupted between CFWA and CFNSW over the best use of scarce funds, for example, should a proposed world co-operatives' conference planned for Perth proceed, or a tax summit organised by CFNSW? After CFA failed to support CFNSW's successful central banking scheme, the latter resigned and withdrew secretariat support from the federation, which began to fall apart in 1986.

Having failed to achieve virtually all of its objectives: no co-operative 'new order'; no 'One Big Society'; no 'decade of co-operative development'; no ICTO strategy; no federal farmer co-operatives service; no co-operative bank; no uniform national legislation and; no unified Australian co-operative movement; the CFA executive euphemistically announced 'firm progress in the redistribution of its staff and secretariat resources' and began winding up operations in Canberra, 'due to a lack of support'.

Following extensive discussions with ICA in London about ICTO's future, CFA closed the Canberra office and Bill Rawlinson moved to Melbourne to conduct the federation's business there in association with CFV. In 1986 Rawlinson retired as CFA executive officer and the federation was again placed in mothballs until state federations decided to reactivate it. Agricultural co-operatives and co-operative companies continued to develop in an *ad hoc* way, while diminishing as a proportion of total national co-operative membership (10 per cent) in a fractured movement dominated numerically by building societies (45 per cent), credit unions (24 per cent) and consumer or 'general' co-operatives (15 per cent). After more than four decades of talking, travelling, lobbying and reporting the Australian farmer co-operative movement was no closer to resolving vital legislation and capitalisation questions in a rapidly deregulating, global economy. On the contrary, it was more fragmented and vulnerable than ever before.[33]

Chapter Eleven

COMPETITION, DEREGULATION AND THE 'CO-OPERATIVE DILEMMA'

Introduction: a 'new age' economy

Co-operatives do not function in an economic and political void. Before proceeding to consider specifically farmer co-operative development at the national level in the decade to the mid-1990s, therefore, it is useful to digress briefly to consider the 'mood' of the time, which was certainly not conducive to co-operation. Discussion in this chapter is augmented by consideration in Chapter Thirteen of a 'conversion syndrome', by which many co-operatives and kindred societies demutualised, dramatically reducing the size and economic significance of the sector.

A sluggish economy in 1980 deteriorated into a world recession in 1982/83, which saw Australian unemployment climb to near 11 per cent, a wages explosion and interest rates and inflation soar. Blunt instrument monetarist policies impacted on the economy for much of the decade, producing a recession, which was the worst since the Great Depression. In February 1983, the Hawke Federal Labor Government was elected, beginning a thirteen year Labor rule. The new government launched into a sweeping economic reform programme, seeking to transform the Australian economy from a 'closeted, protected and introspective economy into one that is efficient, outward looking and internationally competitive'.

'Ideologies' were unfashionable through most of the 1980s, when ideas (apart from *laissez faire* neo-liberalism) were valued less than practical outcomes. New management and organisational theories emerged challenging 'old world' assumptions based on notions of collectivism, closed systems, choice and freedom of contract and emphasising open systems, transparency, flexibility, bargaining, competition and constant adjustment to endless change. Australia embraced managerialism, developed in USA and perfected in Japan, and was gripped with the idea of subjecting everything to the purifying heat of 'market discipline'. Deconstructionists argued that the industrial economy was over; it had ended in the 1960s but no one had noticed; and now was the time for wholesale radical reform.

If the 1980s was a decade of sleazy deals and conspicuous consumption, the ensuing decade saw a demolition of old values and anything standing in the way of free-market forces. The dismantling of the Berlin Wall in 1989 served as a symbol for an opening of the floodgates, dismantling political and economic rigidities which had congealed since World War II. The concurrent collapse of the Soviet empire delivered a massive fillip to neo-liberal market economics and helped legitimise a shift by governments away from interventionist strategies towards public policies supporting individual freedom, private-profit enterprise and flexibility in responding to market signals. With the 'Cold War' ended, the US economy, freed from a stultifying arms race, boomed, on the back of an information-technology revolution and a share-market bonanza, which spawned 'globalisation', a set of global economic relations constructed on assumptions of trade liberalisation, corporatisation and the uncoupling of geography from profit centres.

With the Hawke Labor Government's deregulation of the Australian financial system driving everything before it, an era of what sociologist Michael Pusey has called 'economic rationalism' began, constructed on notions of competition, deregulation, privatisation, labour-market reform, taxation reform, reduced government spending and a 'user-pays' system, which substituted for public services. Pusey and economist Fred Argey argued that a fundamental shift in the distribution of economic power and resources in Australia, beginning in the seventies, was now seriously eroding old egalitarian and collectivist values, once strong in Australia (and a mainstay of co-operative theory). Resources, opportunities and capability had been transferred disproportionately to the top 10 per cent of the population and from the public sector to the private sector, from wage and salary earners to corporations and from the country to the city. They noted growing social inequality in Australia, little sympathy for the redistribution of wealth not seen to be 'earned' in the market place and an inclination to reward ambitious 'aspirational' people, who brooked no interference in the pursuit of self-advancement through personal initiative and who saw government spending as a waste of money, demanding that income stay in their pockets to spend as they chose. Care and consideration for others; 'other-regarding' values; particularly for the disadvantaged and downtrodden, Pusey and Argey argued, were being replaced by an ethos of 'every man for himself'.

Agricultural protection was seen as a dirty word, a discredited form of 'agro-political protection of sacred cows', notwithstanding the impact upon Australian primary industry of corrupted world markets and such blatant protectionism as the US Farm Bill (Export Enhancement Program), which saw Australian wheat producers lose markets in Sri Lanka and The Philippines and markets diminished in the Republic of Yemen, China and Russia as USA and the European Union (EU) squared off in a $400 billion international trade war. For their part, US trade officials argued Australia's network of centralised statutory marketing authorities (SMAs) not only blurred market signals but constituted 'agrarian socialism' and 'backdoor protectionism', describing the Australian Wheat Board (AWB), for instance, as a 'cartel'.

Economic rationalism was about getting 'overloaded' governments, which had been 'paralysed' by unreasonable public demands, out of the way; dropping protection; facilitating *laissez-faire* markets; and readying Australia for disciplined participation in a global economy. Australia was to be open to the world and the economy transformed into a 'lean and hungry, clean and green' international competitor. Corporations, which streamlined and 'outsourced' many operations, urged governments to emulate them in freeing up markets and engendering flexibility. Driven by economic rationalists in central agencies including Treasury, the Department of Prime Minister and Cabinet and the Industry Commission, federal government industry policy was focused squarely on 'efficiency', a cardinal tenet of free-market faith along with such nostrums as 'streamlining' 'rationalisation' and 'value-adding'.

Simultaneously, the Commonwealth Government relentlessly drove micro-economic reform, a slow but radically transformative process directed to the creation of a truly national economy and extending to rail, electricity, food standards, regulatory standards, environmental protection and uniform state-budget reporting systems. Nothing was sacred and everything was up for change. There was an air of excitement in government where deregulation was seen as a 'shot in the arm' for a stagnant economy. Governments vied to outdo each other in a deregulatory spree, setting up business deregulation units and engaging in the biggest fire sale of public assets ever in Australian history.

Public sector attrition

With over 800 parliamentarians occupying fifteen houses of parliament in addition to 750 municipal and shire councils and over 700 statutory and non-statutory government bodies, Australia was one of the most 'over-governed' nations on earth and the economic-rationalist knives were out in the biggest carve-up of public administration ever in Australia's history. A remorseless 'downsizing' of departments at federal and state levels saw serious dislocation, policy discontinuities and a loss of corporate memory and skills in the bureaucracy, no more so than in departments responsible for co-operatives. In 1983 public service employment accounted for 30 per cent of national jobs. A decade later this figure was 20 per cent and falling. Job security in the public sector was a real issue and 'fearless and independent' advice was at a premium. Bureaucratic management structures, incentive schemes and accounting practices were radically overhauled using new 'tools' to measure effectiveness and emphasising 'outcomes', not 'inputs'. Government programmes for which the rationale was unclear, which showed any hint of 'proprietary interest' or which might be outsourced, were particularly vulnerable. Co-operative development programmes fitted this category, particularly as a perception arose that governments existed to *regulate* co-operatives, not *develop* them – that was the sector's job! An elaborate round of consultation, research, reviews, committee reports, briefings and submissions in respect of National Competition Policy (NCP) and other compliance issues gripped central agencies from which 'service' departments, such as those administering co-operatives, were largely excluded. Co-operatives, unable or unwilling to support a coherent sectoral representative body, ran the risk of disappearing entirely from the public policy agenda.

Increasingly, public policy for co-operatives, which were perceived in some central agencies to be a relic of the 'old world' and slaves of regulation, was made on the run or subject to long delays brought about by reviews often conducted by consultants, who knew little about co-operatives and cared less, or by ministers and officers on a career 'merry-go-round' and not long in the job. In so far as co-operatives were seen to have any distinctive role in economic development it was as an extension of central agency priorities. Ironically, as co-operatives struggled to adapt to dramatically altered regulatory and trading conditions, many turned to government, canvassing sympathetic public policy, in particular legislative reforms to assist fund-raising activities and competitiveness 'on a level playing field'.[1]

Consultants

The 'new age' economy was a bonanza for consultants, accountants, financial advisers, corporate advisers and lawyers, producing years of lucrative work. Increasingly co-operative boards became dependent upon technocrats to guide them through a maze of new compliance issues, legal, financial, taxation and other economic problems. A handful of large accountancy and auditing firms prospered, discovering that the 'real money' lay in management consultancy. Some consultants became virtual *de facto* managers of organisations in which they served, or major shareholders, or both – including co-operatives. A few consultancy firms simultaneously advised governments on running a state, political parties on public policy, departments on managing change, regulators on implementing reform and co-operatives on improving business performance. Unavoidably, much advice was incestuous or narrow in its world view and reflected a corporate paradigm. Hastily prepared 'in confidence' departmental reports on co-operative development strategies were commonplace, full of recommendations for profit maximisation, enhancing share value, external investments and competitive advantage and showing only an esoteric appreciation of co-operation's core values, which were typically seen as outmoded and needy of fundamental change or suited only to small, 'niche' markets.

'Privatisation' of marketing boards

Federal Minister for Primary Industry John Kerin, a poultry farmer, co-operative enthusiast and driving force in Labor's deregulatory agenda, along with Minister for Industry, Technology and

Commerce Senator John Button, had as primary goals the dismantling of SMAs, transferring responsibility from government to industry, increasing the accountability of marketing systems and permitting greater commercial flexibility in exchange for increased 'transparency' and 'accountability'. The methodology included separating SMA marketing functions from policy-making and research and development, creating separate industry policy councils and research and development corporations and removing grower-elected boards and replacing them with members *selected* for commercial expertise along with managers paid what they were worth, not at public service rates.

Some sections of agriculture; in particular wheat and rice growers and New South Wales and Queensland fresh milk dairy farmers; stoutly resisted the dismantling of SMAs. Other sections were suspicious, including leaders of the fruit industry, where co-operatives were strong. The trial corporatisation of a meat and livestock industry board was seen as an expensive flop or, at best, only a partial success. Nevertheless, the dismantling of the old orderly marketing regime proceeded through the 1980s with governments of all stripes eagerly participating. The New South Wales government, for example, overhauled the 1927 *Marketing of Primary Products Act*, to which many agricultural co-operatives had grown accustomed, retaining the pooling idea but making its application more flexible pursuant to a High Court decision against the Barley Market Board, the effect of which was to enable growers to enter contracts with interstate buyers, loosening markets and encouraging 'rebel' producers. In some instances governments sought to employ co-operatives as a transition vehicle in converting SMAs to corporate structure – part of a 'privatisation' process. Three examples are briefly considered below.

(i) The Queensland Cotton Co-operative

The Queensland Cotton Co-operative was formerly a statutory board serving some 250 growers. After a brief experiment with co-operative structure, growers planned to go public because members were reluctant to fund growth from their own pockets and wanted the co-operative's assets valued. Growers agreed to '…shed [co-operatives'] legislative protection' and form a corporate entity in which growers held a majority share and 100 per cent control of a management company governing the new entity. Other agricultural co-operatives watched with interest to see if cotton growers could retain control of their commodity.

(ii) The Egg Producers' Co-operative Limited

In July 1989 the New South Wales Coalition Government axed the Egg Corporation, pushed to action by the commencement of deregulation in Victoria, which ended an interstate 'gentlemen's agreement' on egg production and marketing and threatened a price war. Full and immediate deregulation was effected without consultation with other states and virtually none with producers, who were paid poorly for their licences. Great uncertainty entered the industry. Many producers left and those remaining feared that the industry was about to be grabbed by big retailers. The New South Wales Department of Agriculture ran an 'Options for the Future' programme, which included the possibility of egg producers forming a co-operative. After the Australian Association of Co-operatives (AAC) (discussed in Chapter Twelve) conducted a feasibility study, Egg Producers' Co-operative Limited was registered in August 1989. The co-operative's members voted unanimously to acquire the assets of the defunct Egg Corporation. The outcome was a joint venture with trans-Tasman food conglomerate Goodman Fielder Wattie Australia Limited, which purchased the co-operative's Sydney plant while the co-operative rented premises for the sale of carton eggs. The

Tamworth Egg Farmers' Co-operative purchased and operated the Egg Corporation's processing facility.[2]

(iii) A lost opportunity: the Australian Wheat Board

From the moment it took office in 1983, federal Labor encouraged deregulation in the wheat industry. Progress was slow but in 1989, anticipating a 'value-added' export boom, the domestic wheat market was deregulated. The boom failed to materialise. The Australian Wheat Board (AWB), however, having lost a monopoly to buy and sell the crop, moved into marketing other grains, applying strong deregulatory pressure in sections of the grains industry. The AWB was inundated with commercial offers from overseas and local food manufacturers and grain traders seeking a financial involvement. Subsidiaries of the world's four major grain traders: Cargill; Continental Grain; Louis Dreyfus; and Con Agra Inc; organised in the 'Australian Grain Exporters Association', proposed the privatisation of AWB and the formation of an 'Australian Grain Trading Corporation'.

Alarmed first at a possible industry takeover by overseas interests and then motivated by a need to restructure the AWB board to comply with world trade agreements, talk turned to a grower-owned co-operative to be known as 'NEWCO'. Federal Minister for Primary Industry Simon Crean and Grains Council Australia also explored other options, including a publicly-listed company with grower control retained through a majority shareholding in a holding company, on the Wesfarmers Limited model. The idea was strongly endorsed by food-industry mogul Doug Shears as part of an 'Australian Producers' Corporation' concept.

The NEWCO plan was hampered, however, by the inconsistency of state-based co-operatives' legislation. NEWCO advocates wanted the federal government to support the co-operative with federal legislation and extend to the new entity all of the privileges to which co-operatives had access under states laws. Supportive growers undertook to capitalise the co-operative via a levy on product supplied and the purchase of shares. Some sections of the industry wanted to dump AWB altogether and to form small local co-operatives with access to AWB property. A 1990/91 industry poll, however, showed that 66 per cent of producers were satisfied with AWB and only 62 per cent wanted grower control in a new co-operative with many seeing this as simply a five- to ten-year transition stage in the development of a grain-processing and marketing corporation.

Lengthy parliamentary debates followed considering the relative merits of a co-operative and corporate model. Doubts were raised about the former's capacity to be innovative in marketing and value-adding, about the calibre of people likely to run the co-operative and the willingness of farmers to capitalise the operation. Federal parliamentarians were also dismayed at the inability of states' co-operative federations to agree upon the desirability of nationally uniform co-operatives' legislation!

The NEWCO option was dumped. A proposal to transfer AWB's single desk export monopoly to NEWCO was also rejected. By December 1992 AWB was finalising a five-year corporate plan to transform the authority from a sole exporter into an integrated food company with tradeable equity and a capital base of $500 million.

A great opportunity to extend the co-operative movement to a national level in a major industry at the behest of a supportive federal government was lost, derailed in part by the movement's inability to agree upon co-operatives' legislation. Meanwhile as SMAs were dismantled and National Competition Policy began to take hold (discussed below), the national regulation of financial co-operatives ('non-bank financial institutions' [NBFI]) proceeded. General co-operatives, however, stayed defined in a jigsaw of states' legislation and at a distinct disadvantage to corporate competitors able to operate easily across borders and with ready access to capital.[3]

'Ambivalence will get us nowhere'

An article circulating within the Australian co-operative movement at this time, written by the British co-operatives' analyst, Ted Stephenson, noted apathy, weariness and 'group think' permeating the movement, which tolerated no dissent. Examining the dwindling, once mighty Rochdale consumer movement (which had almost disappeared in Australia), Stephenson said that many co-operatives had become 'prisoners of history', genuflecting to policies set long ago in very different market conditions. Many co-operative boards were no longer really representative of members, but coteries given to group decisions and wearing down the resistance of active minorities. In many cases the democracy principle had deteriorated into nothing more than a 'rubber stamp' in the decision-making process. The co-operative movement persisted in looking inward, engendering a 'persistent isolationism' which sought to ignore competition for fear that co-operation might become 'contaminated' by the ideas of private enterprise. Co-operatives who refused to look at competition realistically, Stephenson argued, would simply watch the world pass them by, because 'ambivalence will get us nowhere'. The co-operative movement was falling a long way behind the private sector and could only catch up if a fundamental reappraisal of what co-operation stood for was urgently completed and translated into effective policies. Co-operatives needed to *understand* markets, not simply *dislike* them:

> *Instead of building hopes and expectations that cannot be fulfilled the co-operative movement should be considering how to create a series of market positions which are realistically based on the resources available to them. There is the belief that market forces should not unduly influence co-operative action [which has] encouraged the notion that scarce resources are readily available if only they can be prised from their present holders on preferential non-market terms.*

The eschewing of market principles was preposterous, Stephenson concluded, and, whether co-operatives liked it or not, markets would continue to determine the value of scarce resources. It was ridiculous also to assume that a co-operative must 'live forever' and absurd to think that a poorly-run co-operative should not go out of business.[4]

Stephenson's challenging article was leapt upon by critics of traditional co-operative values as further evidence that co-operative structure needed to be *completely* rethought and more attuned with markets, including capital markets.

National Competition Policy challenges the concept of co-operation

In April 1995 all Australian governments agreed to introduce National Competition Policy (NCP) to lower business costs, enhance competition and provide for economically sustainable conditions. States and territories undertook to review legislation with a view to removing any anti-competitive implications and were given inducements to do so, including penalties for non-compliance. Regulations, which 'distorted market-signals' and restricted competition or encouraged inefficiencies borne by consumers, were to be removed by 2000. The dairy industry was a prime target. Other agricultural industries, in which co-operatives were strong, including rice, sugar, cotton and grains, also came under close government scrutiny. NCP challenged some traditional co-operative business practices, for example contracts of supply, which appeared to be in direct contravention unless a 'public interest' was demonstrable. Major agricultural co-operatives and co-operative companies,

*Bowraville Butter (and Bacon) Factory (NSW). The Bowraville Co-operative began operations in 1907
and was taken over by the Nambucca River Co-operative Society Limited in 1950.*
Photo courtesy of Nambucca River Co-operative Society Limited.

preparing for deregulation, became preoccupied, even obsessed, with restructuring to comply with
NCP while attracting investments. The democracy principle fitted awkwardly into this equation.
Improved competition and an attendant hunger for capital were fundamentally changing the nature
of agricultural co-operation and there was no guarantee the democracy principle was compatible
with this.

Disagreements over deregulation confound co-operative unity

States varied in their enthusiasm for deregulation, particularly the timing, and the pace of
reform was determined as much by political considerations as economic rationalism. In New
South Wales, for example, any deregulatory step consistent with NCP which might potentially
disadvantage local agriculture was taken very cautiously. Ructions between states on the scheduling
of deregulation spilled into co-operative affairs, particularly in the dairy industry where fresh-
milk producers, enjoying protected markets, generally supported a continuation for as long as
possible while manufactured-milk producers geared to exports sought a prompt end to the old
regime. Disagreements over deregulation confounded all attempts at national unity at this vital
time in co-operatives' history when solving the democracy-capital 'co-operative dilemma', dealing
with a corporate 'conversion syndrome' (discussed in Chapter Thirteen) and achieving uniform
co-operatives' legislation (discussed in Chapter Fourteen) were so important to the movement's
future.

For farmer co-operatives, the combined impact of economic rationalism, deregulation,
unsuitable legislation and NCP exerted powerful pressure upon co-operative principles and

structure. In the event that farmers failed to invest in their co-operatives sufficiently to remain competitive in radically altered markets, was it possible to *retain* control while sharing ownership with outsiders or, alternatively, was it inevitable that a co-operative would go out of business (as a co-operative) simply because it would *not* countenance external investments? Was the co-operative model adaptable to a brave new world of deregulation and competition? Many within and without the co-operative movement thought not. Demutualisation continued apace. These themes are explored further in the following two chapters.[5]

Chapter Twelve

'More Than Making Money':

CO-OPERATIVES SEEK NATIONAL UNITY, 1986–1996

Introduction

In the decade to 1996, while Federal Labor occupied the government benches in Canberra, the Australian co-operative movement faced possibly the greatest complex of challenges ever in its history, dealing with macro and micro-economic reform, deregulation, demutualisation, capitalisation problems, the absence of uniform co-operatives legislation, National Competition Policy (NCP), globalisation and a generally diminishing public profile. If ever there was a time for the movement to rally behind a strong national representative body speaking unequivocally to government and the public and driving co-operative development, it was now.

On the contrary, still riven by parochialism and industry-specific concerns, the co-operative movement remained as disunited and directionless as ever. After the Co-operative Federation of Australia (CFA) ceased operations in 1986, the Australian Association of Co-operatives (AAC), which replaced it, achieved only partial national coverage and failed by 1993. Then, after a three-year hiatus, a 'toothless tiger', the Co-operatives Council of Australia (CCA), resurrected the CFA shell in 1996. Meanwhile, mainstream events passed the co-operative movement by, sweeping it to the brink of irrelevancy.

The Australian Association of Co-operatives

When the Co-operative Federation of New South Wales (CFNSW) resigned from CFA, its dynamic Executive Officer Bruce Freeman, aided by James McCall of the Co-operative Federation of Victoria (CFV) and a few co-operatives in Queensland, formed the AAC in July 1986 designed to:

> create promote, develop and expand a dynamic, vibrant co-operative movement as an extension of a worldwide movement that will satisfy social and economic needs of the people of Australia.

The association's policies were focused on active membership, internal co-operative financing systems (not external investors), federal or national uniform co-operatives' legislation, a federal co-operatives service, adherence to International Co-operative Alliance (ICA) co-operative principles, co-operation between co-operatives (including the ICA) and education. As such, AAC objectives were far broader than a preoccupation with capitalisation and competitiveness characterising the policies of major agricultural co-operatives and co-operative companies. The disparity caused friction. An immediate task, however, was for AAC to arrest a rapid erosion of co-operative assets as corporate raiders continued to target 'dry' shareholders and woo them with lucrative offers.[1]

Bruce Freeman: 'More than making money'

Ever since taking the CFNSW reins in the early 1980s, Bruce Freeman had argued for a national co-operative development agenda and the observance of distinctive co-operative values. He consistently rebutted those who argued that 'too much philosophy is not good for business' countering that in *every* successful business *philosophy* was the guiding light. He railed against those trying to make co-operatives just like other businesses, arguing that co-operatives were *different* and should proclaim and defend this difference. Co-operatives were distinct entities with a discreet structure based on one-member-one-vote, limited return on shares, commitment to member services and profits returned commensurate with business done. In a co-operative, members retained capital for development ensuring continued control of the organisation. Freeman believed that the current crop of Australian co-operative movement leaders did not understand or appreciate the significance of what co-operatives were doing or the traditions upon which they drew. Co-operation, Freeman passionately believed, was essentially about economic democracy – more than making money. There was a vital need for a vibrant co-operative sector in a mixed economy if only for the democratically enriching alternative this afforded competition. Nevertheless, he conceded that an appalling ignorance about the real meaning of co-operation afflicted the movement and the public. How could there be anything but ignorance when rarely had co-operatives invested in co-operative education and, Freeman was wont to say, 'co-operatives which do not educate will last a generation and a half'.

Bruce Freeman was convinced there was nothing wrong in the theory or practice of co-operatives, despite what corporate consultants and some in the movement were saying, only that the current players did not know how to apply them. He deplored the fact that more co-operatives, particularly agricultural co-operatives, were taking individualistic, unilateral action for reasons of self-interest, he alleged, to the detriment of general co-operative development. The co-operatives were not co-operating, Freeman lamented, a deadly formula! Co-operation needed to occur on a national basis, not at a state level preoccupied with parochial concerns. Big co-operatives had become predatory and were 'gobbling' up other co-operatives, instead of co-operating. In so doing they were losing grass-roots involvement and creating thorny communication and relationship problems with members and other co-operatives. Preoccupied with industry specific concerns and simply seeking enhanced competitiveness, such co-operatives were not recognising and affirming their commonality – the democracy principle. All some large co-operatives apparently wanted to do was mimic the corporate sector. The greatest opponents of nationally uniform co-operatives' legislation, Freeman alleged, were those who always had it high on their 'wish list' but actually did nothing about it. There was also the 'mushroom club' in some big farmer co-operatives, who preferred to keep things quiet, unspoken, perpetuating a favourable *status quo* while surreptitiously advancing individual agendas.

As to governmental co-operative development agendas, Freeman believed they were a furphy and warned that where the public and corporate sectors predominated, as was becoming the case, co-operatives inevitably would be squeezed. Where co-operative goals of self-help and democratic control were compromised, he said, a co-operative movement was in mortal danger.

The solution to a demonstrable need for autonomous co-operative development, Freeman argued, was a *co-operative bank*, an institution which understood and recognised co-operative principles and did *not* criticise co-operatives' structure and their capital base, like some 'so-called co-operative leaders with the government's ear'. There were many pseudo-co-operatives in Australia, he said, ripe for take over, and this was only possible because of a generally poorly informed co-operative sector and public, who tended to see capitulation by co-operatives to capitalist orthodoxy as inevitable. 'It is totally immoral that, at any point in time, members or shareholders or both can gain a capital gain at the expense of future generations', Freeman insisted.

Freeman warned that 'interests close to capital' were determined to achieve legislative changes to aid takeover plans and emphasised AAC's equal determination to 'protect the co-operative commercial environment from any attempt to water down legislative protection'. State divisions of the AAC should exist throughout the Commonwealth, Freeman argued, transmitting information about co-operatives and representing co-operatives in a co-ordinated, nationally consistent way and to which federal government must pay heed. These were fine and courageous words but getting co-operatives to unite around anything was quite another matter.

The Standing Committee on Agriculture Working Party Report 1986

In mid-1986 the Commonwealth's Standing Committee on Agriculture Working Party (SCAWP) reported (published in 1988 as *Agricultural Co-operatives in Australia*) concluding that co-operatives and the concept of co-operation could be the answer to many of Australia's agricultural problems. The report noted that there were more than 400 agricultural co-operatives operating throughout Australia, involving approximately 350,000 members holding $2.2 billion in assets. Agricultural co-operatives involved in production, input supply and marketing had assisted farmers to improve marketing performance and achieve economies of scale but had not kept pace with rapid changes in management and financial marketing methods. The SCAWP called upon governments to assist co-operatives achieve a fuller potential and recommended *inter alia*:

- ❖ creating an agricultural co-operative services providing research, data gathering, promotion, development, policy formation and educational services;
- ❖ referring the matter of uniform co-operatives' legislation to the Standing Committee of Attorneys-General (SCAG);
- ❖ exploring innovative fund-raising options for co-operatives consistent with co-operative principles;
- ❖ allowing a sympathetic taxation treatment of co-operative reserve funds;
- ❖ developing co-operative curriculum materials;
- ❖ investigating a co-operative banking system;
- ❖ convening seminars and conferences for agricultural co-operatives; and
- ❖ commissioning research in the fields of co-operative capitalisation, ownership and control, performance, member relations and relations between co-operatives and statutory marketing authorities.

Renewed federal government interest in co-operatives, however, raised many administrative and constitutional questions, for example, which ministries were most relevant to co-operative development: agriculture; attorneys-general; taxation; or should state ministries continue to be responsible for general co-operatives under some national agreement?

The SCAWP was not qualified to answer these questions and, with no widely representative federal co-operatives' body to talk to, and neither co-operatives nor state governments agreeing on what form an Agricultural Co-operative Service should take or even if it should exist, once more the idea stalled. More seriously, the vital federal or national uniform legislation issue became bogged down in interstate bickering (discussed in Chapter Fourteen).

Such legislative reforms as did occur remained at state level, doing little to aid the interstate operations of co-operatives, as co-operatives. Increasingly the emphasis in co-operatives' public policy, particularly in New South Wales, was on capitalisation, competitiveness and, following the passage of the *Co-operatives Act* in 1993, the interface between Co-operatives Law and Corporations Law.[2]

AAC fails to achieve national reach

A paralysis afflicting national co-operative development was not aided by AAC's inability to achieve a truly national affiliate base, particularly in South Australia and Western Australia. Moreover, for much of its short life (1986-1993), the association was at odds with powerful sections of the agricultural co-operative movement on such issues as co-operative principles, national co-operatives' legislation, capital raising and active membership. Nevertheless, by 1989 AAC had 276 affiliates mostly in New South Wales and with only thirty-six in Victoria and fifteen in Queensland. In addition to New South Wales and Victorian divisions, the association had an office in Western Australia, ran a Co-operative Development Unit (CDU) employing three development officers (aided by the New South Wales Government) and provided members with the services of a solicitor and training officer. Its central banking operation, patronised by most affiliates, operated on a $420 million annual turnover allowing the association to post rapid growth in loans, finance and insurance business. New headquarters were opened in Elizabeth Street, Sydney, and a special government relations section was opened (a clue to strained relations with the department). These were noteworthy achievements for an association which enjoyed only the ambivalent support of a splintered co-operative movement and a tribute to those who worked so hard to achieve them. But there were troubled times ahead – non-performing loans and Bruce Freeman's deteriorating health.[3]

The AAC loses Bruce Freeman

Freeman's untimely retirement through illness was a blow to AAC. He was so ill in 1989 that someone had to read his paper at the AAC Canberra Convention. Freeman's replacement, Geoff Ayres, an accountant with a background in commercial finance in the food industry, was considered to have a more 'open mind' on the national co-operatives' legislation question. Berridge Hume-Phillips, emerging from a trade association background in retail, broadcasting and food, was appointed national executive office for trade, government relations, communications and co-operative development. Jim McCall continued to manage the CDU.

The AAC–ICA Asia–Pacific Ministerial Conference and Exhibition 1990

As noted in Chapter Nine, in February 1990 AAC convened the ICA Asia–Pacific Ministerial Conference and Exhibition at Darling Harbour, Sydney. It was the first major national and international co-operatives convention in Australia since the demise of the CFA in the 1980s. Federal and state ministers responsible for co-operatives attended, together with delegates from twenty-two countries, including seventeen Asian and Pacific nations, Canada, UK, Sweden and elsewhere. The purpose of the conference was to showcase the diversity of Australian co-operative activities and encourage growth and trade between co-operatives in the region in 'value-added' primary products. It was CFA's old International Co-operative Trading Organisation (ICTO) in new garb. Thirty-two stalls displayed a wide variety of co-operative goods and services. Opening the conference for Prime Minister Bob Hawke, who was unable to attend, Minister for Industry, Technology and Commerce John Button said:

> *[Co-ops must] recognise the stark realities of doing business which means understanding technological change, product development and marketing... Too often in the past Australian*

co-operatives have made the same old products in the same old ways and expected the world to beat a path to their door.[4]

Federal Minister for Primary Industry and Energy John Kerin described co-operation as a 'middle way between the excesses of capitalism and regulated state-ownership systems' and urged rural industries to engage the strength of the co-operative movement in domestic markets, while expanding export markets. There were splendid opportunities for co-operatives as governments drew back from market intervention, the minister said, but prospects were seriously compromised by 'variations between states in the legislation under which co-operatives operate'. It was imperative that the movement find a way to *agree* on nationally uniform co-operatives' legislation, and quickly, or opportunities would be lost forever.

A welter of ambitious recommendations came from the conference, including a renewed call for a Federal Ministerial Council for Co-operatives with powers to drive a comprehensive co-operative development strategy, 'harmonise' state co-operatives' legislation and better inform the public about co-operatives. The AAC also undertook to examine the feasibility of establishing a co-operative bank for Australia, resurrecting the 'Holy Grail' of financial autonomy for co-operatives (discussed in Appendix Two).[5]

The AAC-ICA Agreement

Later, in September 1989, AAC entered an agreement with ICA to develop mutual co-operative trade, initially in Asia, but potentially in seventy-one countries throughout the world. In the following year ICA established an Australian office in Geelong, Victoria, and appointed a project officer, R Mathimugan. How states rights advocates, particularly in New South Wales, viewed this development is unclear, but it seems unlikely they would have been favourably impressed by an association benefiting from New South Wales government funding entering an agreement with a Victorian-based international trading organisation. Neither would fervent anti-socialists like New South Wales Minister for Co-operatives Gerry Peacocke have enjoyed hearing at the launch of the new venture AAC General Manager Geoff Ayres describe co-operative philosophy as definitely 'socialistic' in that it distributed financial and social benefits and was about:

> *... looking after one another rather than just yourself. Making sure you are all right, but working for the benefit of the co-operative. People in a co-operative make decisions based on the well-being of the co-operative because they are using it.*

The prospects of international co-operative trade through the AAC-ICA agreement, however, was attractive to farmer co-operatives and nothing was to be gained by ignoring it. Indeed, like ICTO, the plan started well with twelve nations reaching agreement on preferential trade for co-operatives, including India, China, Japan, Indonesia, Thailand, Malaysia, Singapore and The Philippines. The AAC prepared to take a prominent role in co-ordinating Australian trade in the region, for example hosting a delegation from the Japanese Consumers Co-operative Union and escorting visitors around co-operatives including the Northern Co-operative Meat Company at Casino in the north of New South Wales. AAC officials travelled to Japan to meet executives from major Japanese co-operatives interested in trade in beef, fresh fruit, vegetables, sea food, horticultural products, wines, woollen and other items, and also travelled to China.

The Asia–Pacific Co-operative Training Centre (APCTC)

In association with Credit Union Services Corporation (Australia) Limited (CUSCAL), ICA Australian Representative Mathimugan and former federal and Victorian Labor politician and minister Race Mathews, AAC created the Asia–Pacific Co-operative Training Centre (APCTC), the first serious attempt in decades to create a genuinely co-operatively based national training and educational body. APCTC Director Tim Dyce, formerly a public affairs manager with the Victorian credit union movement, transferred to Sydney and developed an Australian Certificate in Co-operative Management programme in association with the University of Western Sydney, training managers and directors in law, finance, marketing and management for co-operatives and 'co-operatively-minded' organisations.[6]

Certainly, the need for co-operatives' education was acute after years of neglect. A news poll survey commissioned by AAC in Sydney and Melbourne found that 25 per cent of people interviewed, many of them *members* of credit unions or building societies, said they had *never heard* of co-operatives or thought they no longer existed. Almost half thought they were the same as other companies! Ignorance was not confined to the 'man on the street'. As noted elsewhere, with constant restructuring of state and federal departments, much deep knowledge of co-operatives was disappearing from the corridors of power.

'God Save Co-operatives'

A 'prayer' for co-operatives was circulating around this time, penned by the highly regarded British co-operatives' commentator and Plunkett Foundation (UK) Director, Edgar Parnell, a frequent visitor to Australia through the period. Parnell's prayer well-captured a mood of grim, embattled uncertainty then afflicting the sector:

> *God Save Co operatives*
>
> *Keep them from –*
>
> > *The academics, who wish to pull them apart to see how they work;*
> >
> > *The professionals, who believe that nothing can be achieved by ordinary men and women;*
> >
> > *The advisers, who never tire of finding new problems but never have time to solve any;*
> >
> > *The managers, who want a co-operative to work for them rather than for them to work it;*
> >
> > *The politicians, who seek to use co-operatives as their stepping stone to power;*
> >
> > *The government, that will bury them in bureaucracy;*
> >
> > *The pedlars of dogma, who try to make them fit their view of the world and will not accept co-operatives as economic enterprises;*
> >
> > *The investors, who would take them over and cash in on their assets.*
> >
> > *Help them to deliver benefits working in the interests of their members without transgressing the rights of those outwith (sic) the co-operative.*[7]

Parnell's prayer was not answered, and now – disaster!

The Australian Association of Co-operatives Fails 1993

By 1993 AAC had 339 affiliates, 227 of them based in New South Wales, with Victoria accounting for most of the rest. A staff of thirty ran services for accounting, business plan preparation, submissions, the popular central banking scheme, computing, co-operative buy-out and start-up advice, executive development, overseas study and feasibility studies, government relations, industrial relations, international co-operative relations, international trade, insurance broking, lease broking, letters of credit, management reports, marketing planning and strategies, protocol agreements, rules' reviews and amendments, trade missions and training through APCTC.

Although never achieving anything like national reach and still not supported by some large east-coast co-operatives, the association did nevertheless have some resemblance to a sophisticated third-tier co-operatives' representative organisation.

Just weeks before the New South Wales *Co-operatives Act* was promulgated, in March 1993, AAC was declared insolvent. The association, which had been under a financial cloud for years, was adjudged by the regulator to be operating on a doubtful reserves base and exposed to non-performing loans. Since the late 1980s the association had been extending loans to the faltering Singleton and District Co-operative Society; an eighty-year old Rochdale consumer co-operative with 5,500 shareholders; which was now grappling with high interest rates, improved competition (Woolworths had opened next door), modernisation costs and a failed attempt to set up a branch in Dubbo. By March 1990 the co-operative owed $1.6 million to unsecured creditors, including the association. The AAC extended further loans amounting to $3.9 million in total, but these were not performing. In July 1991 the registrar appointed an independent expert to assess AAC's liquidity and capital adequacy. The conclusion was that the association's future was dependent upon the future of the Singleton co-operative.

In February 1993 the National Australia Bank (NAB), noting AAC interest payments of $1.3 million in arrears, suspended the association's central banking deposit and lending service. Then, early in March, the NSW Aboriginal Land Council withdrew more than $16 million of deposits from the agency (70 per cent of AAC business), presenting the association with a severe liquidity problem. The registrar (Garry Payne) had no power to intervene but did seek the appointment of an administrator to help the Singleton co-operative trade out of difficulties and possibly save AAC. The NSW Labor Opposition called upon the government to shore up the association with a loan.

At an AAC board meeting on 3 March, however, Manager Geoff Ayres and Chairman Ray Ison, a south coast dairy farmer, declared the association insolvent. All banking and trading activities with AAC were frozen. The crash threatened the solvency of 120 co-operatives associated with the central banking service. Suddenly, seventy-four co-operatives were left without any banking facilities and unable to draw cheques or pay wages. The press spoke of 'Co-operatives Reeling', 'Co-operatives Panicky', 'Disaster…A Devastating Blow' and 'Collapse Leaves Investors Facing $13 million Loss'. A report told of how distressed the members of a Gerringong (south coast) milk supply co-operative were because their co-operative was unable to access deeds to its own property or a $130,000 deposit. Farmers told how they had believed AAC was a 'gilt-edged and government-guaranteed' organisation. The Bega Co-operative (dairy) helped some co-operatives to pay wages and the credit union movement assisted ninety of the 120 affected co-operatives after the government rushed through legislation to permit co-operatives to make deposits in credit unions (not previously possible!)

The minister initially distanced the government from any attempt to assist AAC until the association's precise financial position was known. After valuators established that the book value of AAC's assets amounted to $23.5 million and that liquidation could return only twenty-nine cents in the dollar, the minister announced emergency financial support loans for affected co-operatives, including interest-free loans (repayable by December 1994) and other bridging finance. Most co-operatives were not in a position to repay these loans, on time (or at all) and the registrar later recommended wiping off outstanding balances. The government eventually wiped off debts owed by seventeen community-based co-operatives amounting to $1.2 million. Needless to add, the Sydney government was not amused and a bad odour surrounding co-operatives already permeating central government agencies, worsened. The federal government had no time to respond, however, as its attention was distracted by a leadership struggle which saw Treasurer Paul Keating dislodge Prime Minister Bob Hawke and win an election in 1993.

The Australian co-operative movement was wandering into a political miasma.

Former New South Wales Co-operative Development Branch (CDB) Manager Garry Cronan believes that AAC's collapse was the most significant factor in setting the subsequent shape of the Australian co-operative movement. If this is so then the movement must accept much of the blame. Certainly, powerful elements of the agricultural co-operative sector, focused on fund-raising and commercial priorities, never wholeheartedly endorsed the association's crusade to rid the movement of 'dry' shareholders, achieve federal or national co-operatives' legislation and defend co-operatives against 'adaptation' accommodating the interests of external shareholders.[8]

Where to from here?

Jim McCall, formerly an AAC director before becoming a policy adviser to New South Wales Minister Gerry Peacocke and managing director of the Australian Co-operative Development League (ACDL), a quasi-independent industry body (discussed in Chapter Nine), was appointed chairman of a 'National Congress of Australian Co-operatives'. This convened meetings of lawyers, academics, public servants and senior figures from the agricultural co-operative movement in May 1993 (Sydney) and August 1993 (Adelaide) to consider basically the question: Where to from here? A lengthy 'wish list' (couched in loose language reflecting a weak consensus) came from these meetings, including:

- the nature of national representative arrangements including the need for a 'loose' organisation dominated by state federations;
- the cost of 'federalising' co-operatives in Australia, including membership of ICA;
- template legislation for nationally uniform co-operatives legislation;
- the need to ensure that co-operatives were democratic and perceived to be so;
- calls for an annual conference open to all co-operatives and co-ordinated by a congress organising committee;
- clarifying the responsibilities of various co-operative development agencies including the CDB, federations, APCTC and ACDL;
- the role of a re-constituted Co-operative Federation of NSW Ltd in driving the New South Wales *Co-ops 2000* Strategy and identifying issues for a co-ordinated approach to national co-operative development;
- recognising that the diversity of co-operatives prohibited a 'one-size-fits-all' ownership and funding regime;
- a need for consistency in advice given by registry staff, which was often contradictory; and
- more emphasis on the prudential regulation of co-operatives and less on co-operative development.[9]

The 'National Congress' formed the 'National Co-operatives Council', chaired by McCall. Development was slow with further meetings through 1994 and 1995. These were marked by a testiness between regulators and various states' bodies purporting to represent co-operatives on the issue of who really *did* speak for the co-operative movement? A feeling of resentment arose among some participants in these meetings at an alleged tendency by New South Wales delegates to dominate. One particularly thorny issue was nationally uniform co-operatives' legislation and a general view outside New South Wales that that state's *Co-operatives Act* was unsuited for this purpose. Regulators were especially concerned about jurisdictional responsibility where a co-operative's operations crossed borders, particularly with regard to Co-operative Capital Units (CCUs). It was true CCUs were restricted to New South Wales' citizens, but, regulators in other states and territories wanted to know, who *ultimately* had responsibility for a co-operative's actions, or members' or shareholders' actions, where an entity's activities involved interstate trading? Indeed, matters upon which states' and territories' representatives agreed were almost equalled by those upon which they strongly disagreed.

The co-operatives capital adequacy debate

While no agreement could be reached on national co-operatives legislation, another meandering debate proceeded, preoccupying co-operative executives, public servants, economists, consultants, bankers, financial and legal advisers. The issue was co-operatives' capital-raising and ways of modifying co-operative structure to accommodate the expectations of external investors and suit modern trading conditions. Essentially, the capital adequacy debate fell into two camps – supporters of external equity and opponents. At a series of 'Key Issues' Conferences, organised by the New South Wales CDB aided by APCTC and Co-operative Federation of NSW Ltd between 1993 and 1996, which 'showcased' the co-operative movement and helped fill a gap left by AAC's collapse, the capitalisation issue predominated. Indeed, the first Key Issues conference in 1993 was entitled the 'Co-operative Capital Conference'. This was a modest affair but subsequent conferences were quite lavish, providing a rallying point for the co-operative movement, a morale booster and an important forum for debate. Discussion below considers the 1994 and 1995 Key Issues conferences for the light this sheds on the national co-operative movement at the time.

The 1994 Key Issues Conference: people-centred businesses or self-centred capitalists?

The 1994 Key Issues Conference, 'Meeting the Challenge of Competition', examined market pressures as these affected co-operatives and responses to these challenges. The focus was on large, commercial agricultural co-operatives. Presentations made by two key speakers: Australian Co-operative Foods (ACF) Chairman Ian Langdon; and visiting Plunkett Foundation Director Edgar Parnell; indicate just how polarised opinion was with regard to co-operative values and identity.

Langdon's paper, 'Member Control in Perpetuity', impressed the audience with its unashamed acceptance of aggressive commercial goals for co-operatives. The central point, Langdon argued, was that *external* equity need not compromise member control and co-operative philosophy:

> It is the hypothesis of this paper that hybrid structures can be designed to service both co-operative philosophy and the demands of external equity but such structures will not survive over time unless the structure captures and subsequently facilitates the enrichment of the co-operative culture.

Langdon believed that altruistic, people-orientated goals had historically been portrayed as the trademark of co-operatives in comparison with the capital enrichment goals of investor-owned firms. Such perceptions, he said, were no longer consistent with current Australian farmer expectations. Increasingly members were demanding tangible financial benefits from the ownership of co-operatives and he referred to an article in the *Journal of Farm Economics* (Babcock) which, the ACF Chairman said, accurately caught the flavour of a new philosophy defining agricultural co-operatives as:

> ...a legal, practical means by which a group of self-selected, selfish capitalists seek to improve their individual economic position in a competitive society.

Langdon believed such blatantly commercial goals were wholly appropriate for co-operatives and that success was best measured in relation to increased commercial benefit to members, in both income *and* wealth creation. Co-operative philosophy was a *commercial* philosophy, Langdon asserted, and was designed to aggregate the relatively insignificant commercial power of individuals into the substantial aggregate power of a group. For co-operative philosophy to endure, he believed, members must be rewarded not only for *supply* but also for *ownership*:

> *The challenge now is to structure expectations so that they are equitable and fair to the members, affordable to the co-operative and consistent with co-operative principles.*

Langdon spun the patronage principle (dividends commensurate with business done) on its head, arguing that members' individual shareholding should be substantial, reflecting the level of use of a co-operative's services and that this was incompatible with dividend distribution. Compulsory capital investment schemes would mean that members would be inclined to re-evaluate their expectations of a co-operative over time, coming to understand that they were *investors* and not merely *suppliers*. It was inevitable, he argued, that members would demand appropriate financial rewards both in dividends *and* capital appreciation. Nevertheless, Langdon added, external equity was not for every co-operative; particularly those with a poor debt to equity ratio; and should have a legitimate purpose or 'you will lose control'. For co-operatives which needed to stand 'toe-to-toe with large proprietary companies' and fund sustained growth beyond the *capacity* of members, however:

> *There need not be any fear of restructuring to introduce external equity. Handled sensibly member control in perpetuity can be protected, but in the long-term this will always be dependent upon the sustainability of profitable trading and sound commercial decision-making.*

Edgar Parnell's paper, 'People-centred Businesses into the Next Century', seemed to come from another world. The Plunkett Foundation Director also called for the reinvention of co-operatives but along quite different lines. In many parts of the world, Parnell said, general co-operatives were in crisis:

> *People have become prisoners of co-operative history and place too much reliance on dogma rather than looking to the future and adapting their organisations to meet the world as it is today and as it will be tomorrow. I have never heard of anybody winning a race if they are looking backwards when everybody else is looking forward.*

The past was holding co-operatives back, Parnell agreed with Langdon, and co-operatives certainly did need to be 'redesigned'. Co-operatives were not a weapon in a class system but existed to deliver benefits to members and that was their sole reason for being. 'A co-operative is no place for softies because a co-operative is about wielding economic power,' Parnell commented. The 'people-centred' concept the English visitor advocated was indeed about *democracy* but democracy in itself, he added, was no substitute for a clear communication system. A co-operative must ascertain what its members wanted and deliver this. On the vexed issue of capital-raising, Parnell issued a caution on rushing to obtain capital without a strategic plan:

> *We need to create a wholesale capital market which provides a source of investment from institutions and individuals who are prepared to invest money in co-operatives.*

It seems that by this he meant a co-operative bank, or similar institution. This was only achievable, Parnell continued, if co-operatives *co-operated*. There were some in the audience who agreed with Parnell but understood that the 'Holy Grail' of co-operative banking was impracticable in a fragmented Australian co-operative movement. Parnell continued, warning co-operatives against flirting with company structure which, he believed, ultimately only benefited investors, managers and financial advisers and also cautioning against over-regulation:

> *It can stunt growth and it can put brakes on the growth of the co-operative sector. [It] can push people in the direction of company structures when they may otherwise choose a co-operative structure.*

The visitor earnestly urged the adoption of Australia-wide co-operatives' legislation, which, he emphasised 'above anything, gives parity with companies. I am sure you will all have that on your shopping list'. It was a brave hope. Possibly referring to New South Wales co-operative development programmes (discussed in Chapter Nine), the visitor also cautioned against platitudinous 'vision statements', which, he said, were no substitute for the *proper* funding of co-operative development. Employing some rich imagery of his own, Parnell concluded by describing Australian co-operatives as the undervalued 'brown diamonds of the economy' which needed 'repackaging' to ensure they became 'the champagne diamonds of the future'.[10]

The 1995 Key Issues Conference

The 1995 Key Issues Conference, 'Managing Change Into the 21st Century', was a watershed moment in late twentieth century Australian co-operation in so far as it provided a forum for sparring between defenders of the faith, an *enfant terrible*, a high priest of economic rationalism, a crusader for centrally-driven co-operative development and a scalding critic. For this reason, considerable attention is given to this conference.

The conference brought together fifty speakers from around the world and Australia, including regulators from New Zealand, Vietnam, Thailand, Sri Lanka, Malaysia, India, China and Australia. Key speakers included: Professor Allan Fels, Chairman of the soon-to-be-formed Australian Competition and Consumer Commission (ACCC); Professor Hans H Munkner (University of Marburg, Germany), Professor Ian Macpherson (University of Victoria, British Columbia, Canada), Randall Torgerson (Rural Business and Co-operative Services Section, United States Department of Agriculture); local co-operatives' leaders and experts including Ian Langdon (ACF) and David Williams, (Hambros Corporate Finance Limited); and government officials including Garry Cronan (CDB Manager) and Ken Baxter (Director-General of the Premier's Department).

Co-operative Federation of NSW Ltd Chairman Jordan Rigby opened the conference noting that it coincided with the one hundredth anniversary of ICA's formation and commending CDB's work in orchestrating the event. Minister Faye Lo Po' nostalgically recalled memories of co-operatives on the coal fields and spoke of the 'vital' role of co-operatives. Then, it was over to the speakers.[11]

(i) Hans Munkner: The Four Threats

Hans Munkner drew attention to the new ICA definition of a co-operative:

> *…an autonomous association of persons united voluntarily to meet their common economic social and cultural needs and aspirations through a jointly-owned and democratic-controlled enterprise.*

He spoke of radical world change impacting upon co-operatives including political, economic, demographic, social, ecological and technological factors, which would inevitably bring new problems for co-operatives to solve in the twenty-first century. The professor saw opportunities for co-operatives in such areas as employment, health, ageing, child care, the environment, renewable energy, recycling and 'forming agricultural co-operatives for the ecologically sound production of food and cash crops'. He told the assembly that it was not so much a matter of asking what co-operatives could *do* for members, but how, through self-help, individuals could organise to *solve* pressing problems. The goal of co-operatives was not profit but 'long term benefits to the members *and* to the community, provided [it] is economically feasible'. He cautioned delegates against forcing change in co-operatives *without* member support or against the will of members and discussed four dangerous trends threatening co-operative identity.

The first 'threat' was commercialising co-operatives in order to make growth, market-share and competitiveness the priorities of co-operative management:

> *Operations of the co-operative enterprises are expanded [by management] even if more capital is required than the members are willing and able to contribute and therefore preference is given to make profit and to accumulate it in reserves or to seek external funding…This constitutes a threat to co-operative identity because economic success of the co-operative enterprise is becoming the main goal of the co-operative board and management [and] member-promotion rates second.*

Munkner said that managers, lacking a co-operative consciousness, or external directors, *always* found ways of circumventing member priorities, making *growth* an end in itself. Boards and management not motivated by a co-operative consciousness would gradually gain control and, through the administration of a co-operative's capital, incrementally reduce the influence and control of members. Under these circumstances it was almost inevitable that a co-operative would come undone and convert to capitalist orthodoxy.

The second threat to co-operative identity, Munkner believed, was *merger for merger's sake*, for:

> *This brings about large heterogenous membership groups unable to agree on common objectives and to control the management, which in turns forces the board to decide on behalf of the members and to act as their largely uncontrolled trustees.*

The third threat was to *dilute* the idea that the owners and users of a co-operative were *identical* by inviting into an organisation, external investors, members or directors and expanding business with non-members. Munkner was convinced that when a co-operative reached the limits of its ability to raise capital *internally*, it *should* become a company.

The fourth threat was *degrading* member participation by neglecting the nurturing of a co-operative consciousness and a sense of belonging, responsibility and ownership among members, particularly where they had ceased to be the principal financial stakeholders, and failing to invest in education or anything else that did not immediately serve a co-operative's 'bottom line'.

In order to stop the decline of co-operative consciousness, Munkner continued, co-operatives needed to *differentiate* themselves, to concentrate on their *difference* from corporations, not *similarities*, and focus on *members* as the main stakeholders. Efficiency needed to be measured in ways *appropriate* to co-operatives; not corporations; and in all matters, members' interests should come *before* institutional efficiency, no matter what dilemmas this might present managers. Co-operatives should continue to do what they had always done well historically – solve problems which individuals could not solve as isolated beings: 'There cannot be co-operatives without co-operators.'

On the role of government in co-operative development, Munkner quoted the Canadian co-operatives thinker, Alex Laidlaw, saying, 'Government money is the kiss of death to co-operatives.' The academic believed that a proper role for government lay in creating a *facilitative* legal, taxation and research and development environment because, he added, 'special problems arise where co-operatives are used as instruments in development projects initiated by the government'. 'Benign neglect' by government was often better than inappropriate or excessive legislation and regulation. With regard to competition policy, Munkner said it was important to keep in mind that two different kinds of laws often came into conflict: *co-operation law*, which was 'an organisation law, governing the behaviour of people [and including] norms of co-operative behaviour, including equity, open and voluntary membership, democratic management and control'; and *competition law*, which was law governing the behaviour of undertakings in a market economy. The German academic said he believed co-operatives could legitimately be exempted by governments from competition policy if they genuinely complied with co-operative principles because co-operatives were attempting to achieve different things from corporations and, in any event, their presence in markets *improved* competition overall.[12]

Munkner noted the struggle in Australia since the demise of the AAC for a joint co-operative stand on national policy. Politely, wryly, he wondered *who* was representing the Australian co-operative movement and what they were saying. There was much talk in Australia of a co-operative 'sector' and 'industry' but seldom did he hear the words 'movement' and 'co-operation' uttered. The co-operative movement had millions of potential voters in Australia but without a strong national representative body serving as a rallying point it was difficult to influence government and regulatory bodies so that co-operatives risked being pushed aside by radical economic reforms which were sweeping the world.

(ii) Ian Macpherson: The ICA Principles

Ian Macpherson began his address, 'Fellow Co-operators', which some thought quaint, mildly amusing or even optimistic. Noting how ICA had member-organisations in seventy countries and a membership approaching one billion, the Canadian academic spoke of the various co-operative traditions: consumer, worker, banking, producer and services; and reported on a recent Manchester conference where the ICA co-operative principles had been revised. Co-operative principles were not organisational injunctions or 'regulatory maxims', he said, but 'active catalysts' and an integral part of a coherent philosophy underpinning values of self-help, self-responsibility, democracy, equality, equity and solidarity and their application implied honesty, openness, social responsibility and caring for others. Macpherson saw them as *interrelated* and stressed that it was wrong to emphasise just *one* or a *group* of principles over the others. 'I think *each* principle demands a form of minimal behaviour from every co-operative.' The Manchester conference had rejected ideas of 'essential' or 'optional' principles and the notion that they related only to structural or organisational elements of a co-operative, agreeing that co-operative principles related more immediately to members' autonomy, education, co-operation among co-operatives and community.

Macpherson proceeded to describe the ICA revision of co-operative principles in detail. Voluntary and open membership, he said, meant exactly that, regardless of gender, race, class, political affiliation or any other matter relating to an individual's potential use of a co-operative's services. On the other hand, all members needed to understand and abide by the responsibilities of membership. Democratic member control – the democracy principle – meant literally the *active* involvement of members in decisions. The principle of economic participation meant essentially that *members* controlled the capital of a co-operative and were entitled to receive market returns on capital invested. While this did not preclude external capital, the role of external capital in a co-operative needed to be clearly described and understood by all members to avoid serious implications for the autonomy principle, which related to relations between co-operatives and the public sector, political parties and private enterprise. On relations with government, Macpherson said that in many countries co-operatives were often confused as an element of government initiatives and:

> That confusion has often seriously eroded the capacity of those co-operatives to control their own destiny and to respond as they should to their own membership.

Governments and co-operatives must recognise the limits of their respective spheres while co-operatives needed to exercise great care in determining a proper relationship with the private sector. The education principle had been neglected for too long, Macpherson continued, and this had resulted in a 'decline in the public understanding of the organised movement' and a failure to inform the young and public opinion-makers about the 'nature and benefits of co-operation'. Co-operation among co-operatives needed to be taken seriously – currently, in many jurisdictions where deregulation was under way, this principle was being replaced by aggressive *competition* between co-operatives in the same industry. He did not say it but that was precisely the situation in the Australian dairy industry where co-operatives were jousting for market share. The seventh (and new) ICA principle – concern for community – was the most important, Macpherson believed, and he enjoined co-operatives to work for the sustainable development of their communities, emphasising *social responsibility* in their conduct. The Canadian visitor was convinced that this principle would become one of the major advantages of co-operation in future as globalisation proceeded and governments withdrew from many traditional functions:

> The full ramifications of adopting [the principles in totality] are challenging, even intimidating, perhaps because most co-operators instinctively think locally. It is however an approach that is overdue for consideration by most co-operative organisations and I hope it will take firm root.

Co-operatives needed to celebrate the advantage of membership, the academic added; recognise the unique qualities of co-operative principles; empower members, employees, managers and directors; assist other co-operatives to combine their resources prudently; help co-operatives improve their financial strength and; think strategically about the role of the movement, focusing particularly on nutrition, health, housing, finance, employment, women's issues, youth, rural communities and quality of life issues. Dislocating change around the world had made co-operatives more relevant than ever but, Macpherson cautioned, co-operatives 'must do better what they already do'.[13]

Speaking after the presentation, Ian Macpherson agreed with Hans Munkner that competition policy had serious implications for co-operatives and that the Australian co-operative movement must 'stand up and be counted', affirm a co-operative identity, become politically active and more aggressive in promoting co-operatives and make necessary investments in long-term research. On external capital, Macpherson noted that it was also a challenge for Canadian agricultural co-operatives because, inevitably, investor-elected directors 'push the case for higher returns for investors'.

(iii) Randall Torgerson: 'The Means-End Inversion'

Randall Torgerson spoke about co-operative 'takeovers' and 'make-overs', agreeing with Munkner and Macpherson that outside-investment diluted the user-orientation of a co-operative and that there was:

> ...a wave of outsiders who would like to convert co-operatives to investor-owned firms or acquire them. Control of co-operatives can be given away by members, but it cannot be taken away from them.

The issue of external equity had caused great problems of ownership in United States' co-operatives and much litigation, Torgerson said. He warned of a 'means-ends inversion', where managers behaved as if a co-operative was 'theirs' and sought either to preserve the business for its own sake (jobs) or set it up for takeover and a pay out, rather than serve members' needs. In such a context members became alienated and the co-operative prone to a 'sell-out'. Torgerson reiterated the obvious fact that the interests of members and external investors were antithetical in that investors wanted a maximum return while member-producers wanted maximum prices and lowest charges. 'Why,' Torgerson asked, 'would an outsider invest in something whose primary purpose is to enhance returns to members, and he doesn't have a vote?' The trend in United States' co-operatives was now *against* external investors, he said, adding that 'mixed ownership (hybrid) arrangements simply have not worked well and compromise the character of the business as co-operatives'. Torgerson cautioned also against giving management a 'piece of the ownership action', as this diluted the notion of membership-ownership and led to internal disruption. United States' co-operatives were now avoiding this 'pitfall' and were emphasising the importance of finding capital *within* the co-operative movement. Moreover, *less* government assistance, Torgerson affirmed, translated into *more* self-help efforts. Some resources-starved co-operative advocates in the audience dreamed enviously as the American visitor spoke of United States' federal agency promotion of co-operatives, which:

> ...unlike the government functions of the registrars [in Australia], the Co-operatives Service in the United States Agricultural Department is a pure facilitative service unencumbered with any regulatory responsibilities [and] provides continuity and support for a vibrant co-operative business presence in the American economy.

In order to deal effectively with competition policy, Torgerson believed, it was absolutely *vital* that co-operatives become a presence in the national political scene. The co-operative movement was unlikely to receive fair treatment in the application of the policy unless it developed a strong body of information to represent co-operative interests and, he added adroitly, the Australian co-operative movement 'has a major task ahead of it'.[14]

(iv) Allan Fels: Co-operatives and Competition

Professor Allan Fels sent a shiver through the assembly when he declared:

> A co-operative by its very nature represents an agreement between competitors and as such may have anti-competitive consequences in that the agreement may, for example, lead to a substantial lessening of competition. In such instances the agreement is illegal unless authorised on public benefit grounds.

Fels went further by saying that *everyone* was a consumer while only *some* were producers and even fewer, primary producers. The ACCC would look at the rules of individual co-operatives on a case-by-case basis, noting any restrictions on the ability of members to supply customers, other than via a co-operative, which would constitute *exclusive dealings*. In particular ACCC would observe the market power conferred by particular co-operative agreements. Co-operatives would not be given any special treatment and would be treated like any other business. The ACCC would look very closely at mergers of co-operatives and at state co-operative regulators to ensure that compliance with National Competition Policy was being implemented. Potentially, this could cut across a traditional view of farmer co-operation. A competitive market place, Fels continued, delivered benefits to consumers, business and the broader economy and was more important than the *form* an entity took in delivering those benefits; that is, *structure* was less important than *outcomes*. The ideal outcome, Fels believed, was a national allocation of economic resources in perfect markets.

Referring to criticism of the *Trades Practices Act*, which Ian Langdon had described as 'preoccupied with maintaining maximum competition in Australia, even if it means that the players that provide competition are too small to be competitive on an international basis', and Langdon's proposal to 'take on the Trades Practices Commission', the professor said such ideas were misguided, 'old and tired' and 'past their use-by date'. Co-operatives should think more about efficiency, or rather, *inefficiency*. It was not necessary for a co-operative to be *big* to be efficient and deliver a public benefit and rewards for shareholders. A mega co-operative, for example, such as some in the dairy industry were seeking, potentially, could be anti-competitive and Fels concluded:

> In the past many co-operatives have been somewhat protected either in the nature of their business or by tariffs and other forms of protection. But now many are being forced to face the challenge of international competition and others are doing so willingly.[15]

Certainly Langdon was not alone in criticising competition policy. Leading economists were also attacking the reforms as 'broad brush and misconceived', holding that governments were making 'exaggerated claims' about the benefits of micro-economic reforms in lifting national competitiveness. Commercial confidentiality arrangements in the competitive tendering model, critics said, were an open invitation to corruption. The Australian economy was a small one and what might be appropriate for vast North American and European markets did not necessarily apply to Australia, where the same economies of scale did not exist. Moreover, Australia's capital market was inadequate to the task of investing in duplicated efforts and, now, yielding to the 'sacred cow' of competition, the way was opening for foreign domination.

(v) Ian Langdon: Equity or Equality?

Then Ian Langdon spoke. His presentation, 'Member Expectations – Identification and Development', was pugnacious, essentially a lecture on how to encourage co-operative members to think and act like corporate shareholders and a critique of what he saw as the low expectations of the existing co-operative culture. The ACF Chairman saw *ownership* as a primary benefit of co-operative membership, while many boards, he said, still tended to see ownership as simply a residual of *control*. Because members 'expect little', they were content for their co-operatives to be 'marginally better than the next best option'. Consequently, co-operatives 'failed to develop normal business performance criteria of excellence to the…detriment of members'. It was imperative that Boards 'heighten member awareness of their entitlements as owners and deliver carefully articulated expectations'. Boards must also beware of:

> …the aggregation into a set of "sacred cows" [of an agenda] assumed by the members to be their right without due regard to the impact on the co-operative's competitive position and profitability or to equity between members, who may have differing levels of needs and access to co-operative "perks".

In other words, members were not always 'right', even when decisions were democratically arrived at. Examples of co-operative 'perks' Langdon believed, included rebates, subsidies, on-farm services, low cost services and the provision of non-competitive services – virtually everything the traditional agricultural co-operative stood for. Members were simply concerned with farm-gate issues, Langdon argued, and 'unfortunately, some directors pander to these simplistic agenda items'. The ACF Chairman added boldly that members used to such 'perks' could actually *distract* boards from paying attention to fundamental corporate performance criteria. Members needed to be 'educated' to the full range of corporate issues and, with regard to this, Langdon continued, it might become necessary to 'cull' member expectations which had evolved over many years. Because member expectations may 'vary and could even be diagrammatically opposed', it was necessary for boards to take into account *all* members and the impact of their *expectations* on a co-operative in an 'equitable balance'. Boards should regularly audit member expectations and formulate *new* expectations 'of a more demanding financial nature of corporate governance and return'. Co-operative leaders must lead; they must *cultivate* expectations and:

> ...pro-actively build members' expectations [through] detailed communication and constructive education...in the potential of the co-operative in a corporate sense and their reasonable rights in an individual commercial sense.

Such practise, Langdon believed, would eventually create 'its own set of pressures [for] a higher and more demanding set of expectations'. Boards and managers needed to share a *consensus* on a co-operative's corporate direction and strategy and *disseminate* this corporate vision to members:

> It is not always practical to develop such corporate objectives from the bottom [member] upwards but at the very least they should be documented, distributed and debated in forms conducive to interaction between the members' elected directors and senior managers.

It was *not* necessary to 'debate specifics' with members, rather communicate the fundamental assumptions underlying the board's and management's corporate vision. It *was* necessary, however, to get members to own, endorse and commit to this corporate vision and associated objectives. This was an 'educational' process; getting members to agree with you; for better educated members improved performance expectations, which should be focused solely on corporate performance and profitable trading. Members were 'entitled to a premium for ownership [because] they own the business' and, Langdon emphasised, it was a 'misinterpretation' of co-operative philosophy that ownership should not be rewarded:

> Commonsense and commercial reality suggests that in the absence of external equity investments, the fruits of profitable trading should be available for the membership with such rewards being distributed in a manner consistent with co-operative principles...Co-operative purists decry the concept of reward for capital. Purists, have no basis for denying the right for reward for ownership through membership. It is the obligation of boards to ensure that such rewards are measurable, disclosed and evaluated for adequacy.

Ian Langdon believed that boards should never ignore the idea that the capital entitlements of members 'should grow during the term of their membership...even in an environment of apparent or initial member disinterest' and that there was a need to:

> Formalise ownership through growing share possession [so that] members [may] share in the growing accumulated wealth of the business that principally grows through the profitable retention of members' profits.

This needed to be done in a way which rewarded *old* and *new* members equitably and took into account the 'differing rights of members' since, Langdon observed reasonably, co-operative philosophy made no differentiation between rewards for new and long-established members. He was certain that debates on share issues currently swirling through the co-operative movement would create:

> ...inter-member tensions...Cultivating member expectations can be difficult when such expectations may differentiate between members, but it is necessary as an essential aspect of corporate governance...no matter how demanding the result may become over time.

Directors, Langdon continued, must be prepared to stand up to:

...enormous pressure to accommodate special present-day needs [in positioning] their businesses for sustainable long-term growth and prosperity...Unreasonable short-term expectations incompatible with commercial reality do need to be denied....Boards must be prepared to cultivate fresh expectations and to create constructive pressure from the membership for superior performance and realistic membership rewards.

It was the responsibility of directors to sustain the 'co-operative entity' from generation-to-generation because *control* was a 'non-negotiable expectation', but this was only so 'unless, or until, boards are informed to the contrary by the membership'. There was nothing in co-operative theory which said co-operators could not stop co-operating if they wished, Langdon fairly concluded.

Langdon's centralist, top-down notion of corporate governance saw the role of a co-operative's board and management as *directing* members beyond their preoccupation with post-farm gate supply and towards an investor orientation. Where else was a co-operative to obtain the necessary capital to compete? Essentially, it was a restatement of the patronage principle to mean rewards proportionate with supply *and* investments, with the former's volume related proportionately to the latter's level. While this was not inconsistent with a traditional notion of patronage on the supply side, it was stretching the boundary to include capital investments. This was because it was already widely understood – Munkner, Macpherson and Torgeson had just said so – that rewarding members as *investors* inevitably produced 'classes' of shareholders, introduced a divisiveness into supplier – investor relations, diminished co-operative consciousness, appropriated the efforts of past generations in building up the business and jeopardised the expectations of future farmers to have access to a co-operative, simply to reward current stakeholders, not all of whom were necessarily producers or even supported co-operation.[16]

(vi) David Williams: 'Farmers Know Best'

Financial Adviser David Williams spoke on how co-operatives might actually *promote* competition, arguing, contrary to popular belief, that co-operatives were *already* very competitive and that corporate managers *envied* co-operatives for their freedom from having to service shareholder capital. Williams believed that co-operative farmers were the best-informed shareholders in the world and often knew *more* about a business than managers because, not just a job, but their entire business operation depended upon such knowledge. If there was a deficiency in the co-operative business model it was generally agreed that this was at *management* level.

Williams recounted how some statutory marketing boards were converting to co-operatives, while others were not, not because of any perceived flaw in the co-operative model but for other factors, in particular, speedy access to capital in meeting the imperatives of competition policy. Williams might have mentioned the absence of uniform national co-operatives' legislation in the same breath. The expert gave a colourful recount of the growth cycle of a typical co-operative from 'halcyon' early days, where 'we all love each other, we hug each other, we drink in the same pubs and we are making so much money it doesn't really matter', to later in the life-cycle, where 'problems start to emerge' as corporations enter the field and competition intensifies. By building successful businesses and industries, co-operatives inevitably attracted the private profit-sector into the field and 'made a rod for its own back'. This could only worsen as competition policy was more extensively applied. The solution to these 'life-cycle' problems was improved communication (not in a trite sense) involving members at all levels of the operation; improved efficiency in the service of members; and 'altruism and the whole bonding-package that goes with co-operatives'. Contradicting those including Langdon who argued the need for external equity, Williams believed that a *cohesive bond of association* was more important in preparing co-operatives for a competitive 'brave new world'. That could *not* be cultivated by introducing divisive 'classes' of shares.[17]

(vii) Garry Cronan: Mainstreaming Public Policy

Speaking on public policy and co-operatives, CDB Manager and *Co-ops 2000* Executive Officer Garry Cronan described the conference as a 'working model' of what could be achieved between the co-operative sector and government, where the latter was sensitive to the autonomy and independence of the former. In some countries, Cronan said; Belgium and Denmark, for example; there was *no* legislation specifically for co-operatives and yet thriving co-operative movements existed. Getting the public policy–co-operative development 'mix' right was contingent upon the 'capacity and desire of the co-operative movement to fund its own development'. He did not say it, but the historical evidence suggested that the desire was weak.

Cronan's official task was to showcase the recently enacted New South Wales *Co-operatives Act* (discussed in Chapter Nine) and 'market' it to the co-operative movement as a possible template for national legislation. A rule of thumb in understanding the act, he said, was that *external* matters related to corporations' law while *internal* matters related to co-operatives' law. It had been necessary to introduce such an act, Cronan said, to 'delineate the nature of co-operative activity and therefore resolve interface issues between this and other relevant legislation', whether taxation, competition policy, or company law. Cronan sought to explain complicated sections of the legislation, which adopted corporations' law 'in part or whole, sometimes with modifications', or which 'incorporated by reference' the substance of corporations law, or which excluded provisions of corporations law 'that would otherwise apply [including] some fund-raising options'. It was difficult to explain and to understand, complicated by the fact that while corporations' law applied to the *interstate* operations of a co-operative this was not necessarily the case for *intra-state* operations. The responsibility of determining in which jurisdiction a matter rested, or whether co-operative rules were consistent with co-operative principles or not, lay with the registrar and that was why it was so important for regulators to have a true appreciation of the co-operative or mutual nature of organisations they regulated. The inference was that imminent changes in his department reduced the likelihood that such knowledge would exist. 'Hybrid' structures, Cronan continued, seeking 'the best of both worlds'; corporate and co-operative; did present problems for regulators uncertain about which regulator or legislation was relevant, but this problem could be allayed by:

> ...*an agreed common legislative identity across Australia [which] would mean that all governments concerned, state and commonwealth, would understand from a policy viewpoint what was meant by a co-operative organisation. Wider public acceptance would follow leading to a higher profile for co-operatives not only in government but in the general community.*

The public servant saw the *Co-operatives Act* serving as a model for the rest of Australia and the platform for a 'whole of government' approach to co-operative development, crossing all departments, integrating resources, co-ordinating effort and bringing co-operatives' public policy 'in from the margins of the policy debate [to] become part of the mainstream of government economic and social agendas'. Opportunities for co-operative development, Cronan believed, were the 'best they have been for a century' and co-operatives were poised to play a significant role in Australia's future development. It was an optimistic forecast.

(viii) Ken Baxter: 'Get your own act together'

The optimism faded when New South Wales Premier's Department Director-General Ken Baxter addressed the assembly. Baxter, a former chair of the Australian Dairy Corporation, described the co-operative movement's 'message' as confused and said the sector was misguided in remaining obsessed with state ministries for co-operatives. For any real future development, co-operatives must go to the *national* level, to the prime minister, to the federal cabinet. The possibility of uniform co-operatives legislation was unlikely, notwithstanding optimistic talk, particularly in the approach to a federal election in 1996. In remaining fixated on state issues the co-operative movement had squandered a great opportunity for a national presence, which could have assisted in its current capital-raising dilemma. Those opportunities had all but passed the movement by and were unlikely ever to return. The co-operative movement remained fragmented and was sending unclear signals to governments, which did not understand co-operatives and:

> *Part of the reason is that there have been in the past more than one agenda running in the co-operative movement. One was clearly aimed at getting consistent legislation; another was run by some of the major co-operatives which sought to use the co-operative agenda to assist their competitive advantage.*

Co-operatives had to totally rethink their relationship with government and direct their attention to the *federal* sphere and Baxter told them bluntly, 'Get your own act together'.

The official report of the 1994 Key Issues conference did not include Baxter's address but it appeared nonetheless in the first issue of *National Co-op Update (NCU)*, an excellent miscellany of co-operatives news dedicated to a national approach to co-operative development, edited in Victoria by Chris Greenwood (discussed in Chapter Seven).[18]

Commenting later on the conference, Co-operative Federation of NSW Ltd Consultant and *Co-ops 2000* Implementation Chairman Don Kinnersley noted that Professor Fels' delivery in particular:

> *...highlights the lack of understanding of co-operatives amongst politicians and senior bureaucrats and the urgent need for the co-operative sector to mount a case for co-operatives to be understood, respected and assisted to achieve their social and economic objectives.*

If co-operatives were not understood by government, whose fault was this? Had not the sector failed to develop a coherent representative national industry body communicating clearly with state and federal government on co-operatives' legislation, capitalisation and other development issues? Was this not because some large co-operatives had failed to give unequivocal support to a third-tier co-operative body with views at variance from their own and had moulded co-operatives' public policy primarily to enhance their own competitiveness, as Ken Baxter said?[19]

A last hurrah?: the 1996 Key Issues Conference

Given growing uncertainty about CDB's future it is not surprising that the 1996 Key Issues Conference, 'Reinventing Co-operatives – the Next Generation', which formed part of a series of a Co-operative Awareness Week events, lacked the vibrancy of its predecessor. Responding to criticisms that previous conferences had been dominated by agricultural co-operatives, the conference offered participants a flexible format with plenary sessions and session streams. A 'mainstream' conference was held concurrently with an Agricultural Co-operative Leaders' Forum funded by Rabobank and the Department of Primary Industry and Energy. Essentially, the bicameral format symbolised in practical form the gulf existing between big agricultural trading co-operatives and multitudinous community and service-based co-operatives, the heartland of the movement, whose interests in public policy had been largely neglected by the *Co-operatives Act*.

Billed as the biggest gathering of its kind ever held in Australia, the main conference attracted 400 delegates and about fifty local and international speakers from the United Kingdom, Canada,

The number one cream receiving platform at the first Norco Lismore factory (opened in 1902 and closed in 1931). Note the horse drawn wagons and rail trucks to convey cream to the factory and butter to Byron Bay.

Photo courtesy of Norco Co-operative Limited.

Japan, the Netherlands and New Zealand. The conference developed four rather vague themes: 'Innovation and Identity'; 'Globalisation'; 'Democracy, Inclusiveness, Mutuality and Corporate Governance'; and 'Image, Profile and Reality'. The Agricultural Co-operative Leaders' Forum, involving about forty directors and chief executives from agricultural co-operatives and co-operative companies and local and overseas speakers was not so esoteric with practical themes focused on: 'Funding'; 'Value-adding'; 'Global Strategies for Success'; and 'Corporate Governance'. An inaugural Co-operative Researchers' Forum was conducted in conjunction with the conferences, focused on reviewing the current state of co-operatives research in Australia, new co-operatives, worker co-operatives and other co-operative enterprises. The main conference, which ran at a loss, was cross-subsidised by the Agricultural Forum, which produced a surplus. A glamorous affair, the 1996 Key Issues Conference was the last of its kind in Australia in the twentieth century. For reasons of space and because the conference adds nothing new to our discussion, details are not reported here.[20]

The Co-operatives Council of Australia

The Co-operatives Council of Australia (CCA), which finally emerged in 1996 from National Co-operatives Council talks spanning three years, was deliberately framed by co-operative federation delegates from Queensland, Victoria, South Australia, Western Australia and New South Wales to be virtually the *opposite* of AAC, with *no* international brief or commercial functions. Only federations were eligible for affiliation; not individual co-operatives. The council, which incorporated the shell of the defunct CFA, was to be hosted by federations on a rotating basis, with Western Australia first, then Queensland, South Australia and so on. New South Wales was last on the list. CCA would meet twice a year and take action *only* when absolutely necessary and when a *unanimous decision* to do so was reached. Where unanimity did not exist the council would have *no mandate* to speak for

Australian co-operatives. In all other matters, constituent federations were to concentrate wholly on their own jurisdiction, possibly an oblique reference to New South Wales' ambitiousness and an acknowledgment of the parochialism which plagued co-operative development. Certainly, CFWA indicated that it would hotly contest any attempt to introduce legislation leading to an increase in the bureaucratic control of co-operatives as some delegates said had occurred in New South Wales.

Poorly resourced and weakly structured, CCA was effectively a 'toothless tiger' lacking real authority in talking to federal government on such pressing matters as federal or uniform co-operatives' legislation, deregulation, National Competition Policy, financial sector reform and globalisation. Essentially it served as a taxation 'watch dog'. Unwilling to pay the subscription fee, CCA also lacked formal links through ICA to the international co-operative movement.

CCA was occasionally effective in serving the interests of major agricultural trading co-operatives and co-operative companies, including issuing useful discussion papers on the perils of listing on the Australian Stock Exchange (ASX) in 1997 (discussed in Chapter Thirteen) and a successful Senate–lobbying campaign in 1999, which saw the federal government postpone and amend taxation changes affecting co-operatives (discussed in Appendix One). But for general co-operatives' development at national level, CCA had no real mandate.

Conclusion

Here was the Australian farmer co-operative movement on the eve of the new millennium, more than half a century after CFA's invention: smaller (in real terms); asymmetrically developed; dominated by a few big co-operatives; more fragmented than ever; still locked in post-colonial legislative bolt-holes; suffering an identity crisis; invisible to the public; misunderstood in government and the finance industry; and detached from the international co-operative movement in a radically altered and globalising political economy. The sector's chances of ever achieving unity, forging economic and social relevance, capturing the public's imagination and releasing a new wave of co-operative energy, was more remote than ever. Meanwhile, as technocrats and bureaucrats determined the future of a sector which in no real sense could sensibly be described as a broadly based 'self-help' movement, deregulation loomed, National Competition Policy challenged co-operative fundamentals and a demutualisation juggernaut roared on. It is to this ransacking of poorly defended co-co-operatively-owned assets that our attention now turns.[21]

Chapter Thirteen

'Let's Co-operate':
CO-OPERATIVES AND THE STOCK EXCHANGE IN AN AGE OF DEMUTUALISATION

Introduction

In the final decade and a half of the twentieth century some $25 billion of assets held by co-operatives and other mutual organisations, including friendly societies, building societies, mutual insurers and a few credit unions were converted to corporate structure and investor-owned businesses with government blessing, media approval and the overwhelming support of members. This was an age of demutualisation, of an Australian 'shareholder democracy', when members of many co-operatives and mutuals willingly accessed the value of assets built up in some instances over more than a century. In the seven years to 1998 the number of Australians holding publicly-listed shares more than doubled to approximately 50 per cent of the population. For passionate advocates of mutuality and co-operation like former Australian Association of Co-operatives (AAC) Executive Director Bruce Freeman and former federal and Victorian Labor parliamentarian and co-operatives advocate Race Mathews, this ransacking of mutual assets was a morally bankrupt 'abuse of trust', allowing current members to cash in at the expense of past and future generations of co-operators who, in effect, they believed, were being disinherited. After Freeman retired and AAC failed in 1993, Mathews and other activists in Mutuality Australia (discussed in Chapter Seven) maintained the resistance, but it was hopeless and the demutualisation of co-operatives and mutual societies showed little sign of abating. The following chapter resumes discussion begun in Chapter Eleven, where it was established that deregulation and National Competition Policy (NCP) severely exacerbated a dilemma co-operatives faced in bringing the democracy principle and capital adequacy into equilibrium without destroying the distinctive values for which co-operatives stood.[1]

Shedding the co-operative 'chrysalis'

In 1992 officers of the New South Wales Co-operative Development Branch (CDB) compiled a list of recent takeovers and conversions and co-operatives in the process of converting:

Queensland

Tully Co-operative Sugar Milling Association

South Johnston Co-operative Sugar Milling

Babinda Co-operative Sugar Milling Association

Port Curtis Dairy Co-operative

Atherton Tableland Dairy Co-operative

Buderim Ginger Growers' Co-operative Association

Queensland Cotton Producers' Co-operative

Queensland Primary Producers' Co-operative

Queensland Peanut Growers' Co-operative Association

Scarborough Trawlers Fishermen's Co-operative Association

Queensland Independent Wholesalers' Co-operative

The Associated Newsagents' Co-operative

Master Builders' Co-operative

Plumbing Materials Co-operative

Associated Milk Service Co-operative
Master Butchers' Co-operative
Permanent Building Society
Wide-Bay Capricorn Building Society.

Western Australia
Teachers' Credit Society
Plumbers' Co-operative
Westralian Farmers' Co-operative
Perth Building Society
Town and Country Building Society
Permanent Building Society.

New South Wales
Producers' Distributing Society (PDS)
Co-operative
Nepean Dairy Co-operative
Wyong Co-operative Dairy
Farmers' Grazcos Co-operative
Wollondilly Abattoirs Co-operative
Griffith Growers' Co-operative Society
Australian Mushroom Growers' Co-operative
Co-operative Insurance Company (CIC)
Cumberland Cabs Co-operative
Western Districts Taxi Co-operative

NSW Permanent Building Society
United Permanent Building Society
St George Building Society.

South Australia
Berri Fruit Juices Co-operative
Berri Co-operative Winery and Distillery
Renmark Co-operative Winery and
Distillery
Vitor Citrus Co-operative
Red Comb Egg Co-operative
Associated Grocers' Co-operative
Eudunda Farmers' Co-operative
South Australian Fishermen's Co-operative
South Australian Farmers' Co-operative
Union
Co-operative Building Society of South
Australia.

Victoria
Autobarn Co-operative
Drouin Co-operative Butter Factory
Victorian Building Society
Permanent Building Society.[2]

Some co-operatives were lost to the movement through corporate raids on 'dry' shareholders, sometimes welcomed by active members. In New South Wales, for example, the proprietary company, United Dairies, seeking access to the profitable Sydney fresh-milk market, took over the Nepean Dairy Co-operative, offering 'dry' shareholders $43 a share. The Drouin Co-operative (Victoria) was absorbed by the co-operative company, Bonlac, in a similar way. Even co-operatives not lost to corporate raids upon 'dry' shareholders were divided on the issue. For instance when Panfida launched a raid on the Dairy Farmers' Co-operative, (discussed in Chapter Fifteen) and AAC headed this off by seeing to 'active member' amendments to the act, many members favourable to the bid were outraged and sought redress. Some co-operatives were wholly pragmatic, believing that *outcomes* were more important than *ideologies*, for example, the Australian Associated Press (AAP). AAP, formed in 1935 as a co-operative by fourteen Australian newspaper publishers, underwent a corporate transformation in 1992 in a joint venture with News Corporation and Fairfax Holdings.

Occasionally co-operatives strongly committed to co-operative principles were obliged to make a painful conversion to corporate structure for purely commercial reasons or because directors had concluded that the limitations of co-operatives' legislation virtually compelled this. For example, Genetics Australia Co-operative Society Limited (formerly Victorian Artificial Breeders' Co-operative), a long-time co-operative advocate and which now included directors from Queensland, Victoria and New South Wales holding different ideas, began moves in 1994 to review its legal and financial structure, anticipating conversion to corporate structure within two years if legislative impediments could not be circumvented.

The conversion of the Victorian Producers' Co-operative Association (VPC) was particularly stormy and painful. Formed in 1910, VPC conducted wheat and wool sales, a pastoral agency, livestock and real-estate agencies, farm supply and insurance services through fifty branches in Victoria, South Australia and the Riverina and wool stores in Melbourne, Geelong and Portland. In the late 1980s the co-operative had 5,000 members, an annual turnover of $500 million and employed 300 permanent employees and hundreds of casuals. An attempted takeover by 'dry' shareholders, led by the food industry mogul, Doug Shears, was defeated at this time. In the ensuing years, however, the co-operative made mistakes in speculative trading and was damaged by the collapse of the Wool Reserve Price Scheme. Forced to write-off millions of dollars, the co-operative made further losses in the early 1990s and lost 'grass roots' support by conducting business with non-members (amounting to more than 50 per cent of total business!). Following further financial difficulties and a downturn in the industry, the pastoral house Elders launched a takeover bid in 1997, which was challenged in the Federal Court but was formalised in 1999. VPC was lost to the co-operative movement.[3]

Some co-operatives simply gave up, members making the judgement that the nature of markets was such as to not warrant further investments. For example, the long-established Riverina-based fruit and vegetable cannery, Letona Co-operative, decided not to invest further in modernisation and was restructured as a company. In late 1997 the Angaston Fruit Growers' Co-operative, one of South Australia's oldest, simply ceased operating.

'Unlocking' assets: the mutuals

Even mutual societies which were trading profitably, indeed claiming to enjoy a competitive advantage precisely *because* of their co-operative structure, joined the 'dash for cash'. Although falling outside our brief, the mutuals warrant attention. In 1995-1996, for instance, the French insurance company AXA bought and demutualised the highly 'profitable' 125 year old National Mutual Life Society, Australia's second biggest life insurance company, serving 1.2 million policy holders. The Keating Labor Government was delighted, having earlier blocked a proposed merger of this Australian mutual society with ANZ Bank, an Australian bank. The distinguished *Australian Financial Review* market-analyst, Max Walsh, described the deal as 'frankly speaking, a top dollar deal'. No wonder, given that AXA, which controlled 51 per cent of the stock, paid $1.1 billion for an asset valued in late 1996, when the former friendly society was listed, at $38.4 billion! In December 1996 the Colonial Mutual Friendly Society was listed on the Australian Stock Exchange (ASX), followed in January 1998 by the 148-year old Australian Mutual Provident (AMP) Society, Australia's largest life insurance society with assets valued at $92.5 billion, 2.3 million members worldwide and reserves of $11.7 billion.

The seventy-four year old National Road Motorists Association (NRMA), a highly regarded road-service system with 1.8 million members and very profitable insurance operations, valued in total at $4.6 billion, took about five years to demutualise, creating a bonanza of approximately $30 million for lawyers, accountants and bankers. The stated rationale was to remove restrictions on where the mutual could invest and raise capital and a desire by the association's leaders to 'distribute wealth to members'. Opponents argued that distributing wealth through *reduced* insurance premiums and *improved* services was a better option and could be achieved by retaining a 'not-for-profit' mutual structure. The promise to 'unlock' assets, however, swayed members in 1994, who voted to demutualise the association. This was declared invalid by a court ruling that members had not been properly informed. A second attempt at demutualisation in 1999, which avoided the 'D' word (demutualisation) and instead spoke of a 'potential listing' and 're-mutualisation', promised members a $2.4 billion 'give away'. Critics saw the offer as a bribe but it was successful – something for nothing. The popular road service operation was retained on a mutual basis while the profitable insurance arm was privatised.[4]

By 2000 only a handful of mutual societies remained. Former mutual life offices and building societies, now listed on ASX, accounted for approximately 8 per cent of total national domestic market capitalisation and turnover. This was a huge slice of mutually-organised Australia, more than a century in the making and gone forever.

The 'Conversion Syndrome'

The demutualisation juggernaut rolled on, and promiscuously, with company buying co-operative, co-operative buying company, co-operatives up for sale to the highest bidder and 'hybrid' co-operatives listing on the ASX, for instance:

- ❖ United Milk Tasmania merged with Bonlac;
- ❖ Paul's Company Limited acquired the Dairy Fields Co-operative;
- ❖ Australian Co-operative Foods (ACF) acquired the former South Australian co-operative, Dairy Vale;
- ❖ ABC Taxi Co-operative, following a lack-lustre Co-operative Capital Units (CCUs) issue, was up for sale;
- ❖ Warrnambool Cheese and Butter Co-operative (Victoria) prepared to issue preference shares;
- ❖ Darling Downs Co-operative Bacon Association Limited considered floating on ASX;
- ❖ Co-operative Bulk Handling (CBH) (Western Australia) prepared to register as a company while retaining co-operative philosophy and control with a two-tiered share system; and
- ❖ The Bean Growers' Co-operative (Queensland) discarded co-operative structure, adopting company structure and listed.

It would be wrong to assume that co-operatives were the only form of business grappling with structural problems and experiencing difficulties. In the food industry, for example, Australia's two largest producers of branded foods at the time, Goodman Fielder and Pacific Dunlop, were also facing enormous trading problems through this period of intensifying competition and globalisation. It is important also to bear in mind that much of the public sector was being privatised including such icons as the airline, Qantas, and the Commonwealth Banking Corporation and a large tranche of the telecommunications giant, Telstra, was on the selling block. These were days of rampant private-profit.

In a well-constructed paper delivered to an International Co-operative Alliance (ICA) regional assembly in New Delhi in 1994, New South Wales CDB Manager Garry Cronan employed an evocative 'forest' and 'paddock' analogy to explain what he called the 'conversion syndrome'. Once the Australian co-operative landscape had been characterised, Cronan said, by an inter-connected 'forest' of co-operatives of all forms, sizes and functions. Now it was characterised by a mosaic of 'paddocks' with a few large trees left. For instance, the *four* largest of the approximately 800 co-operatives still operating in New South Wales accounted for *50 per cent* of the co-operative movement's total turnover in that state. The top twenty co-operatives accounted for 70 per cent of total turnover. The situation was much the same in other states. The asymmetrical physical development and diverse industry concerns of the co-operative movement made it very difficult to find common interests, develop a united front or speak with a single voice, while the tendency to demutualise was quickening, driven by deregulation, competition, privatisation and globalisation.

Cronan pointed out that it was not his job as a public servant to argue the merits of the situation; simply to give effect to government policy; but he did seek to explain why he thought the 'conversion syndrome' was happening. A key reason, he believed, was the absence of:

> ...*alternative integrated and supportive co-operative structures and networks. Such structures and networks, if present, could well provide co-operatives with greater flexibility to deal effectively with the challenge of a competitive market place without recourse to changes in identity.*

Because the co-operative movement lacked such structures it could not achieve unity and consequently, 'We lack the integration and synergy that characterises more developed co-operative sectors, overseas'. That was true; AAC had failed the previous year; but it was a 'chicken and egg' question for lack of unity was precisely *why* no genuinely nationally-mandated co-operative third-tier body had ever existed, at least not for long. Cronan conjectured upon how many co-operatives might *not* have converted to corporate structure if they had had access to a well supported, professional representative body, which would have provided:

> ...*solutions for some of the structural deficiencies of co-operatives, offered precedents in management approaches and practices,...focused educational and advisory services [and] encouraged greater government support and understanding for the sector.*

A structural void existing in the movement, Cronan continued, meant that co-operatives were obliged to deal with change unilaterally or in an industry context where co-operation was poorly understood or seen as a rival to private-profit enterprise. Indeed, some large agricultural co-operatives *were* obliged to perform unilaterally, but there were also a few which chose to do so for reasons of self-interest and showed no interest in broader co-operatives' development.

Cronan identified twelve factors which he believed had 'helped shape the Australian co-operative movement landscape', grouping these under four headings: structural; management; education and advice; and government facilitation. Seven elements attached to these four factors: co-operative capital; representative co-operative organisations; co-operation among co-operatives; co-operative culture; funding organisations; merger strategies; and deregulation.

The CDB Manager was convinced that a lack of suitable capital-raising options for co-operatives was the main reason for their conversion and, resolving this issue, therefore, was a key to the long-term survival of the Australian co-operative movement. Co-operatives could not continue to operate without competitively managing capital, the public servant argued, referring to a view held by influential Australian Co-operative Foods (ACF) Chairman Ian Langdon, that 'Australian co-operatives have not been sufficiently innovative in encouraging their members to view the investment of funds in their own organisations as worthwhile'. Cronan echoed Langdon's view that permitting a 'proper' return on member investments would help stave off a temptation to 'unlock' the real values of shares in a sale. He commended provisions contained in the recently passed New South Wales *Co-operatives Act* (discussed in Chapter Nine) for capital-raising, including CCUs (acknowledging that they were not popular), commented favourably upon an Irish 'hybrid' co-operative-corporate model (discussed in Chapter Sixteen) and endorsed the idea of dropping the traditional 'limited return on capital' principle in favour of a revised patronage principle relating to investments, arguing in terms reminiscent of Langdon that active-member provisions (for supply) were 'just one side of the equation':

> There is still a need to ensure that current and past members receive value for their participation and investment in the co-operative…To do otherwise is to ignore one of the major motivations for members to convert their co-operative into an investor-owned firm.

Cronan alluded to talks proceeding with a view to forming a new national body, focused entirely on national issues (the eventual Co-operatives Council of Australia [CCA], discussed in Chapter Twelve). He was not overly optimistic about this, however, he said, as co-operation among co-operatives was weak in Australia and, where no commercial gain could be demonstrated, co-operatives behaved as competitors 'rather than organisations with common interests'. Unlike the US system, the CDB Manager added, which '…represents a unique blend of co-operation and competition', co-operative culture was poorly developed in Australia and co-operatives' history poorly regarded, contributing to a general public ignorance about co-operatives and co-operation. Australian co-operatives emphasised wholly-economic functions and saw co-operation's historical roots as a *burden* rather than a source of *strength*. No co-operative bank had ever existed in Australia, a glaring deficit obliging co-operatives to access funds through conventional commercial sources where they were poorly understood, a situation compounded by legalistic limits on credit unions and building societies lending to co-operatives.

While mergers were an understandable response to competition in seeking greater market power, Cronan reiterated, the absence of a 'developed and integrated second- and third-tier co-operative structural option' meant that a few large co-operatives 'soak up the smaller co-operatives around them', adding to a concentration of economic power in a few entities and a tendency among big co-operatives to demutualise upon reaching a certain size in their particular market. Boldly, Cronan suggested *limits* to the size of any one co-operative (although how this might be achieved was not explained) and, with characteristic optimism, saw deregulation as an opportunity for co-operatives to 'develop a comprehensive strategy to establish through new co-operative organisations the necessary building blocks for a working, integrated co-operative system.'

On management's role in the 'conversion syndrome', Cronan conjectured that poorly remunerated managers might be tempted to promote the appointment of external 'professional' directors as a ploy in engineering a conversion to corporate structure. He noted how managers often captured the co-operative agenda *without* sufficient member-support and offered the corporate option as the *only* way ahead because they were 'poorly versed in co-operative culture'.

Co-operatives' education was essential in maintaining a belief in the co-operative system, the CDB Manager stressed, citing former AAC Executive Director Bruce Freeman's adage that a 'co-operative without education will last one and a half generations'. The lack of co-operative education in Australia, Cronan believed, was another major factor in precipitating the demutualisation phenomenon. One consequence was that the movement lacked a supportive infrastructure of informed service providers qualified to provide objective and independent advice and information. Large accounting and legal firms and merchant banks were no substitute for this as they 'generally do not know a great deal about the operation of co-operatives and therefore tend to recommend a corporate strategy'.

On government facilitation, Cronan briefly noted that inconsistent co-operatives' legislation was another important contributor to conversion and related efforts directed at achieving consistency (discussed in Chapter Fourteen).

Frank Bateman beside a bulk milk truck (date unknown).
Photo courtesy of Bega Co-operative Society Limited.

His goal as a co-operative developer, Cronan concluded, was to marry the best of the past with the best of the present and he cautioned that '[as the] critical mass of co-operatives is lost to conversion, [government] resources currently available to support the sector [will be] withdrawn by one or more governments'. Indeed, although Cronan did not say it, his employer, the New South Wales Government, was already looking at ways of rationalising co-operative development functions (discussed in Chapter Nine).[5]

Changing expectations: the hybridisation of co-operatives

Throughout the demutualisation spree, co-operatives and co-operative companies continued to wrestle with the 'co-operative dilemma'; balancing the democracy-capital adequacy equation; hampered in this by the absence of suitable uniform national legislation. In effect, the Australian agricultural co-operative movement was dancing to two rhythms': the ancient beat of 'control – control – control', issuing from a traditional respect for the democracy principle, and a new beat, 'value – value – value', arising from a desire for greater wealth and return on investments. There were four 'beats' in the 'value' tattoo played by a new breed of co-operative leaders: improve shareholder value; restructure co-operatives to accommodate external equity; engender member confidence and; periodically survey members' wishes in respect of their continued attachment to co-operative principles.

Improving shareholder value involved perpetrating a cultural change where members came to *expect more* than simply service from a co-operative but also capital gain. This involved encouraging an appetite for real and realisable wealth not derived from supply alone. The key to changing the farmers' mind set was encouraging them over time to think of themselves as *shareholders*, not simply *members*. Leaders dancing to the 'value' mantra, however, needed to exercise caution in not alienating farmers committed to traditional values like the democracy principle and the measure of control this gave in commodity markets. One approach was to 'hybridise' co-operatives; *separate* supply and processing functions, with the former co-operatively-owned and the latter on a corporate footing, not necessarily listed, with farmers possibly holding a controlling interest. In this way, new breed leaders argued, co-operative *values* and capital *value* might be equitably balanced in 'equilibrium'.

Finally, the 'value' dancers understood a need periodically to take *soundings* of shareholder sentiment in respect of the democracy principle's continuing value. In a market economy *everything* potentially had a price, even democracy. Was selling the co-operative *worth* more to shareholders than retaining control, or the other way around? Shareholders had a right to decide the value of the democracy in which they participated and to consider all options which might serve their interests best. Why be a prisoner of ideology if greater wealth was the price? If retaining democracy meant that the business would become unviable, farmers would lose their co-operatives, anyway. And why would farmers cling to the democracy principle if it meant diminishing shareholder value? Who said that a co-operative must stay a co-operative forever or that the co-operative model necessarily served shareholders' interests best?

In contemplating these questions, co-operators embarked upon a perilous journey of experimentation in the final decade of the century seeking to find a solution to the 'co-operative dilemma'. A case study considering the experience of Dairy Farmers Group (DFG) in this context is found in Chapters Fifteen and Sixteen.[6]

The Australian Stock Exchange discussion papers on co-operatives listing

In October 1996 and May 1997 the Australian Stock Exchange (ASX), itself a 126-year old co-operative association of stockbrokers, prepared to demutualise. In this context, the exchange issued discussion papers canvassing the possibility of other co-operatives listing and exploring how co-operative members might 'quit a holding and realise on that investment'. The declared purpose was to boost agri-business and to assist co-operatives, which in many cases, demonstrably, were experiencing capital-raising difficulties. The ASX proposed that co-operatives either convert to public company structure, through a gradual demutualisation process, or continue to operate as a co-operative but list financial instruments, such as debentures, subordinated debt or Co-operative Capital Units (CCUs) (discussed in Chapter Nine) to form a type of 'quasi-equity instrument', which would be permissible under exchange rules if the instrument were appropriately structured.

As for co-operatives' 'unorthodox' voting and control structures (the democracy principle), ASX expected co-operatives to *phase out* these 'restrictions', or so construct themselves as to enable a later move to 'more orthodox structures, if members or market forces dictate'. The ASX would consider co-operative principles on a case-by-case basis 'for a limited period [five years] after listing', after which their re-adoption would be subject to the approval of *all* shareholders! The ASX thought of co-operatives essentially as a transition phase in a natural progression to an 'orthodox shareholding, based on a one-share-one-vote' basis:

> While the ASX notes that it is prepared to accommodate the co-operative nature of organisations wanting to list, it highlights its desire to see the organisations move towards a more orthodox structure over time.

'Let's Co-operate'

Throughout this dialogue sections of the media amply reported the case *against* the mutual model, arguing that mutualism had outgrown its roots and usefulness in solving market problems because now deregulation and competition policy enabled a truly rational allocation of resources in 'perfect markets'. Co-operatives were *no longer required* and could not hope to compete in the new environment because they were unable to access adequate capital and had limited legal capacities. Deregulation would complete the denouement. The *Sydney Morning Herald* broadcast that only those with 'a desire to place member-benefits above commercial considerations and to maintain the character of an organisation, were…against demutualising'. A *Bulletin* article entitled 'Let's Co-operate', spoke of ASX moves to 'co-operate with the co-operatives', with illustrations showing ASX lubricating and spanner-adjusting an industrial-age machine adorned with brass instruments reminiscent of a nineteenth-century Salvation Army revivalist meeting, into which co-operatively-produced agricultural products were tumbling and from which small change was emerging. Co-operatives, *The Bulletin* opined, were at a 'crucial time in the history of the industry-owned groupings, which run some of the country's key enterprises' and the future of many was in the balance, particularly those seeking to remain competitive.[7]

The Sigma precedent

Media reports predicted an 'avalanche' of co-operatives listing on ASX, particularly after Federal Treasurer Peter Costello in the recently-elected Howard Federal Coalition Government publicly voiced his approval of exempt stock markets, which did not have to meet the tough tests normally required by the exchange. The treasurer pointed to the example of Sigma Company Limited, formerly a pharmaceutical supply co-operative formed in Western Australia in 1912. Seeking to become Australia's leading health-care services company, while retaining a co-operative 'heritage', Sigma issued shares to the public, equal in all respects to shares owned by pharmacist-member shareholders, except for voting rights. Shares sold to non-pharmacists would revert to investor shares, with curtailed voting rights. Sigma did not list on ASX, initially, but appointed a stockbroker to act as a 'stock-exchange', using software enabling participation in an exempt share market. However, Sigma planned to remove restrictions on the holding of ordinary shares by 1998 enabling owners of investor-shares to convert them to ordinary shares (with a 10 per cent individual shareholding limit, for at least five years) while introducing a 'mechanism', which, it was claimed, would ensure continued pharmacist representation on the board.

The success of the Sigma float, which saw investors 'queued up' to access lucrative pharmaceutical markets, acted as a powerful precedent for co-operatives contemplating listing and the gradually shedding of co-operative structure, in the belief that such a device would allow members to *retain* voting control. Under ASX proposed rules, however, this could only be guaranteed for *five* years, after which time *all* shareholders would have to agree to a continuation of the status quo. Here was a real challenge for the democracy principle for the likelihood of all shareholders agreeing to a continuation was remote, particularly where external investors were involved.[8]

The Co-operative Council of Australia discusses ASX proposals

In late 1997 the CCA circulated a discussion paper considering ASX proposals. The Queensland chairman of the council, Jim Howard, cautioned that co-operatives would not be able to list *as co-operatives,* despite what some publicity was saying, stressing that a co-operative simply could not list shares on ASX and remain a co-operative. He urged co-operatives to be careful in proceeding down this path – if ownership and control were important. Re-adoption of a one-member-one-share voting basis after five years was problematical because it 'requires the approval of *all* shareholders, which inevitably means a limited lifespan on their retention'. The AAC paper recommended instead listing debt instruments, such as debentures, which could offer co-operatives opportunities for accessing external capital sources. Even this tactic was problematical, Howard continued, because there was no guarantee that the Taxation Commissioner would not consider such instruments share capital. Howard reminded co-operatives that Division 9 of the *Taxation Act* precluded co-operatives from allowing shares to be sold or purchased on a Stock Exchange or in any public manner. Accepting the ASX proposal, therefore, would almost certainly see co-operatives forfeit valuable taxation benefits and should only '[have] advantages if a co-operative goes down the path of listing and eventual demutualisation [providing] an easier path for co-operatives, who wish to take this major step in restructuring'. In other words, acting on the ASX proposal was the first step to demutualisation.

Co-operative Federation of Queensland (CFQ) President Loui Rateri did not mince words in dismissing ASX proposals saying that they opened the door for some 'finance-industry experts' to jump on an old band-wagon of publicly listing co-operatives because it presented an opportunity to increase their business with the co-operative movement:

> *[What] interests are they really serving?…I would have thought that, if anything, the companies with any sense of mutuality would be moving back into co-operative structures and not away from them.*

Co-operative Federation of Victoria (CFV) Executive Officer Tony Gill was also unequivocal in opposing the idea, which, he believed, would ultimately disadvantage primary producers and further reduce their already limited market power. Pursuing the ASX line, Gill believed, would see the handing over of assets 'built up for the benefit of present and future generations…only to be plundered by short-term investor adrenalins on the stock market'.

Co-operative Federation of Western Australia (CFWA) Executive Officer John Booth said that the papers had created confusion and that the push for co-operatives to list on ASX:

> *…appears to be driven from non-co-operative sectors with an agenda that is not necessarily in the long-term best interests of the user of the co-operative services – the active members.*

Booth agreed with Jim Howard that listing some type of financial instrument presented opportunities for some co-operatives, where this did not impinge upon member control.

Co-operative Federation of South Australia (CFSA) Secretary David Osgood said that ASX existed for investors, seeking profit. Co-operatives existed to provide service and gain market advantage. 'No worthwhile advantage is to be gained by co-operatives listing on ASX, if mutuality is lost.'

Co-operative Federation of NSW Ltd (CFNSW) Consultant Don Kinnersley said that it was impossible in any event for New South Wales co-operatives to list on ASX under current legislation. The suggested reforms, he said, were suitable only for 'companies which have a co-operative-like structure' and would inevitably introduce a conflict of interest between co-operative members and investors, 'which some say is not possible to manage'. Co-operative members sought the best prices and the lowest charges while investors wanted to maximise profits, dividends and share value, Kinnersley concluded. (Amendments, which became effective in September 1997, to the New South Wales *Co-operatives Act* , permitted co-operatives to list securities.)[9]

Co-operatives and the ASX option

The press was full of stories speculating upon co-operatives and mutual societies preparing to list on ASX, for example:

- ❖ Namoi Cotton Co-operative, Australia's largest cotton ginner;
- ❖ Graincorp, New South Wales' biggest grain-storage facility and marketer;
- ❖ Phosphate Co-operative (PIVOT) (Victoria)

- Farm Pride Foods, Victoria's largest egg producer;
- Golden Circle, the Queensland fruit canner.

The experience of three of these is briefly discussed below.

(i) Namoi Cotton

The Namoi Cotton Co-operative, based at Wee Waa, New South Wales, was registered in 1962, comprising mainly immigrant Americans. By 1994 the co-operative had 600 members, twelve gins in New South Wales and Queensland, including some of the most modern in the world. The co-operative generated a $342 million annual turnover (approximately 16 per cent of the total New South Wales co-operative movement), held assets of $232 million, produced exports of $280 million and controlled 35 per cent of the market. It was one of the world's biggest ginning and marketing operations with warehousing, shipping, marketing and operations decentralised in three valleys.

Following a period of turbulence in the late 1980s and early 1990s centring on mismanagement and trading losses on the New York futures market, however, members decided to move away from a decades-old revolving fund system of capital-raising, amounting effectively to a $20 million compulsory loan, which members could ill-afford at that time. Accepting the advice of corporate consultants, directors decided to put a CCU float option on ASX to members, which 'excited... most concern among the purist supporters of the co-operative principles'. The board approved but the rules required 75 per cent approval of members to effect the float. Many members were dismayed by the proposal and some were suspicious of the board's motives. Directors argued that competitors had easy access to equity capital and it was a case of 'damned if you do and damned if you don't'. The float proposal permitted members to 'realise value for at least a portion of their existing shareholding'. Another period of turbulence ensued with the co-operative $40 million in debt, losing market share, appointing four chief executive officers in seven years and embroiled in a bitter board struggle.

In November 1997 members approved a $60 million listing of CCUs on ASX, the first time this had ever been done in Australia. Advocates described the plan as a 'neat solution' to the co-operative's fund-raising problems while retaining member control and providing a vehicle for inactive members to either unlock their capital or realise a dividend on it.

The CCU float was held up as an exemplar with potential to 'reshape' the entire co-operative movement. All of Namoi Cotton's existing shares were cancelled and the co-operative created two new classes of shares: non-tradeable grower shares based on one-member-one-vote for active members; and Namoi Capital Stock Shares listed on ASX. CCU holders were entitled to elect two board members, could freely trade the units with outsiders and had access to between 40 and 60 per cent of the co-operative's profits. A single CCU investor could not hold more than 15 per cent of permissible shares. In addition to non-tradeable growers' shares and CCUs, existing producers were given a further allocation of shares based on their trading history for the past seven years. It was anticipated that members would enjoy 'unlocked' capital and dividends averaging approximately $100,000 per member. The co-operative planned to use funds to strengthen the balance sheet, improve ginning and marketing services and rationalise the industry, for example by taking over grower-owned gins.

Investors flocked to the Namoi Cotton CCU float. However, they took up the instruments at a discount, that is, below their actual value, and the float raised only $44 million, not the $56 million envisaged. Financial markets, unsure of the taxation implications of CCUs (whether debt or equity) in a traditionally risky industry, agriculture, found the instrument 'wanting'. By 1999 the value of Namoi Cotton Co-operative's shares had plunged and, subject to ASX's 'sunset clause' in respect of the democracy principle, the co-operative seemed destined for conversion to company status.[10]

(ii) Graincorp

Graincorp, which was controlled by the unlisted Prime Wheat Association (PWA), comprised 8,000 grain producers operating 250 grain storage sites and export terminals at Newcastle and Port Kembla in New South Wales. Previously PWA owned a majority of full-voting 'A' Class shares, which had been traded on an exempt share market operated by a stockbroker. It also owned a majority of 'B' Class investor shares and 'foundation shares', enabling PWA to determine the board's composition. In order to gain ASX listing for 'A' Class shares, however, Graincorp was required to agree to the exchange's requirements that foundation shares would cease to exist unless shareholders voted for their retention at five year intervals *or* if Graincorp changed its business activities. It seemed only a matter of time before Graincorp left the co-operative movement.[11]

(iii) PIVOT

Following a precedent set by the big Victorian dairy co-operative company Bonlac in 1999, the giant Victoria-based fertiliser and superphosphate supplier, Phosphate Co-operative of Australia (PIVOT), one of Australia's largest farmer-owned co-operative companies with approximately 40,000 members in Victoria, South Australia and New South Wales and a network of 250 distributors, contemplated listing on ASX. The plan was to issue perpetual unsecured notes underwritten by a Melbourne stockbroker. In December 1986 the co-operative company had entered what some commentators described as a legal 'no-man's land', registering under the Companies Code while continuing to apply co-operative principles. The restructured entity involved many 'dry' shareholders, who had a dramatic effect on governance as their number and influence built up. Later, Doug Shears of City Farm Phosphates, made an unsuccessful bid for the company, offering $50 a share to shareholders for shares par-valued at $12.50 and which, Shears emphasised, generated no income for inactive members. Three thousand five hundred mainly 'dry' shareholders sold 33,000 shares, representing 9.5 per cent of PIVOT's issued capital and 8 per cent of the voting power. The deal produced a 'windfall' for 'dry' shareholders and represented a bargain for Shears. The bid was overturned in the courts but Shears remained the co-operative company's largest single shareholder.

Financial pressure built on PIVOT through the early 1990s as competition improved and after the co-operative company borrowed $30 million to acquire Top Australia Limited. A period of board-room turbulence followed, peaking in 1997 when the board proposed to distribute $175 million in retained earnings. The issue was to *whom* should these rewards accrue – members (now referred to as 'customers'), or investors? The co-operative found itself at 'loggerheads' with shareholders including Doug Shears who sought to on-sell his shares to ANZ Securities. Amidst much media attention moves began to re-evaluate shares and re-allocate them, a tactic rejected by PIVOT management. A 1999 note issue sought to reach a compromise, limiting the voting rights of holders to ensure that control stayed with ordinary shareholders while retaining the co-operative company's status for taxation purposes. The taxation position became unclear, however, by dint of increased inputs from non-members. The board elected to frank farmers' share dividends but, by 2000 it seemed likely that ASX's 'sunset clause' on the democracy principle would see PIVOT eventually exit the co-operative movement.[12]

'Misanthropic Corporate Barbarians'

Lawyer Nigel Hill, who helped steer many co-operatives through the demutualisation process, De-Luxe Cabs for instance, spoke of the experience as one characterised by 'misanthropic corporate barbarians', greedy managers, consultants, merchant bankers, lawyers and accountants, who were relentlessly driving the demutualisation agenda while creaming off consultancy fees. Demutualisation, Hill said, had delivered huge benefits to the executive upper-echelons, who stood to gain higher salaries, share options, greater kudos and generous 'golden handshakes'. Any idea that a 'level playing field' existed between the mutual and private-profit sectors was nonsense. The Australian Taxation Office, for example, provided roll-over relief *for* demutualisation but *not for* co-operative mergers! For instance, where co-operatives 'A' and 'B' merged to become co-operative 'C', there was no tax relief. This discrepancy seriously hampered co-operatives' ability to compete, as co-operatives, and had definitely impelled the shift towards corporatisation. Hill thought that politicians tacitly *approved* of demutualisation because it meant an end to taxation concessions and administrative costs associated with their regulation. Competitors also approved because they knew that co-operatives limited their profits by providing consumers with a not-for-profit alternative. In some overseas jurisdictions, co-operatives were encouraged and supported for precisely this reason – to *improve* competition. It was nonsense to argue that co-operatives and National Competition Policy were inimical. It was more that financial institutions, including burgeoning superannuation funds and a proliferating band of money managers, disliked co-operatives because they could not *control* them. As to the furphy that members had generally approved of demutualisation, Hill argued, this was only because promoters had appealed to venal instincts; shareholder aspirations; and it was 'easy to sell a windfall'.[13]

A smaller co-operative movement

It was clear nonetheless on the eve of the twenty-first century that a huge whack of traditionally co-operatively and mutually-organised Australian industry had vanished. Nevertheless, over 300 large and medium-sized rural and agricultural co-operatives survived the conversion syndrome as co-operatives; even prospered. Even so, the distribution of the Australian farmer co-operative movement had shrunk significantly since World War II and was continuing to do so, notwithstanding the emergence of a few Titans, as Garry Cronan so aptly illustrated in his 'forest and paddock' analogy. Indeed, new co-operatives continued to form, particularly in 'niche' and 'boutique' markets in fields previously dominated by statutory marketing authorities in the grain, fruit and vegetable, food and dairy industries. There was also some slight evidence of renewed interest in co-operatives in the water management, energy, specialty farm-product, conservation and agricultural services areas as the full impact of deregulation, competition policy and globalisation swept through Australian agriculture and rural communities. A few ailing companies actually converted to co-operatives to protect jobs.

As noted in the Preface, there were still somewhere between 2600 and 2800 co-operatives operating throughout Australia at the turn of the century and their economic importance was not insignificant with $35.5 billion in total assets, including financial co-operatives (213 credit unions and eighteen building societies regulated by the Australian Prudential Regulatory Authority [APRA]). General co-operatives registered under various states' co-operatives law, together with friendly societies and eight large (mainly) Victorian agricultural co-operative companies, produced an annual turnover of some $10 billion with total assets of around $3 billion.

While the number of Australian co-operatives compared unfavourably with OECD nations, thirteen co-operatives were still listed in the top 1,000 of Australian businesses, albeit some already well advanced in the demutualisation process.[14]

It remained unclear, however, if co-operatives would experience a renaissance. This appeared unlikely in the absence of strongly supported state and national representative bodies, federal or nationally uniform co-operatives' legislation and a solution to the 'co-operative dilemma' not destroying the very thing for which co-operatives stood almost uniquely in business – the democracy principle.[15]

Chapter Fourteen

A Colonial Relic:

SEEKING UNIFORM CO-OPERATIVES' LEGISLATION 1985–2000

Introduction

There were three great deficits in the twentieth century Australian farmer co-operative movement: a co-operative bank to fund co-operatives sympathetically and help solve capitalisation problems; a co-operative representative body with binding powers to integrate, co-ordinate and promote co-operative development; and federal or uniform national co-operatives' legislation affording co-operatives operational flexibility comparable with their corporate cousins. None of these was achieved, essentially because the co-operators failed to co-operate. The following discussion considers frustrated efforts near the end of the century to create federal, or as it was refracted through a state-rights' prism, uniform national, co-operatives' legislation.

Historically, co-operatives' legislation in Australia was enacted in each of the commonwealth's six states and two territories without any determined effort to achieve a uniform code. Apart from taxation, corporations and trades practices powers, and to a small degree foreign policy and trade, the Commonwealth Government had no jurisdiction over co-operatives. The legacy of piecemeal evolution at states' level was separate and inconsistent legislation allowing differing codes to evolve in each jurisdiction, permitting activities in some not permitted in others and making it exceedingly difficult for co-operatives to function at national level, or interstate, as co-operatives.

Opportunities existed for co-operatives in the environment of macro and micro-economic reforms sweeping Australia in the last two decades of the century, for example: filling gaps in markets left by the dismantling of statutory marketing authorities (SMAs); occupying a void in social services left by vacating governments; and providing an alternative structure for businesses, the economic viability of which was challenged by new conditions. In nearly all cases, legislative barriers preventing co-operatives from operating easily interstate and complicating fund-raising, disadvantaged co-operatives while enhancing the comparative allure of alternative structures.

Companies and non-bank financial institutions (NBFI) achieved national regulation in 1992. Responsibility for the formation, development and regulation of general co-operatives, however, stayed defined in inconsistent state and territory laws administered by diverse departments. The problem was straightforward but Australia's federal system was not. Between 1985 and 2000 there were approximately forty elections in Australia, not including by-elections, for thirteen houses of parliament or legislative assemblies. Ministers responsible for co-operatives emerged from disparate portfolios including agriculture, corporate affairs, attorneys-general, treasury, justice, housing, consumer affairs and only in one state, New South Wales, did a ministry for co-operatives exist, albeit of diminishing priority. Administering polyglot co-operatives' portfolios, ministers came and went regularly while departments were shaken by the greatest upheaval ever known in the history of Australia's civil service. Co-operative development programmes and deep knowledge of co-operatives waxed and waned in the public service as government priorities changed, precisely at a time when long-established agricultural co-operatives and co-operative companies were looking to governments for support in coping with deregulation, National Competition Policy (NCP), capital adequacy problems and globalisation. States' rivalries and a disdain of Canberra-centralism, evident in mainstream politics across the century, were reflected in public policy and co-operative movement politics.

The case for and against

States-rights supporters argued that the existing pastiche of co-operatives' legislation gave Australia a legal diversity permitting co-operatives in different jurisdictions to adapt and develop in relation to local circumstances and to do more or less what they wanted, flexibly. Thus in Western Australia, for example, the *Companies (Co-operatives) Act* (1943) had given Westralian Farmers, that colossus of the agricultural co-operative movement until 1984, freedom to 'adapt' co-operative principles to suit the company's entrepreneurial style. In Queensland separate legislation for agricultural and general co-operatives: the *Primary Producers Co-operatives' Associations Act* (1922) and the *Co-operatives and Other Societies Act* (1967); provided farmer co-operatives with commercial flexibility and governmental supports facilitating development of great industries while accommodating the purists' reverence for co-operative principles. The New South Wales *Co-operation Act* (1923), long painted as the 'show piece' of Australian co-operatives' legislation, had sought to encapsulate the Rochdale spirit by affirming 'genuine' co-operation and eliminating 'bogus' co-operation, while its replacement, the *Co-operatives' Act* (1993), enabled commercially-orientated agricultural co-operatives to build 'hybrid' structures and create capital-raising instruments, enhancing competitiveness. In Victoria major agricultural co-operative companies were free to operate outside co-operatives' law altogether, utilising company law for the greater freedom this gave in capital-raising and forming subsidiaries. Such diversity, supporters of the status quo argued, made for a febrile Australian co-operatives' legislation environment enriched by a cross-fertilisation of ideas and regulatory practices, impossible under federal co-operatives' law.

Advocates of federal or uniform national legislation countered that, while a case could be made for supporting the states-rights argument until World War II, when the logistics of travel and communication necessarily kept co-operative movements isolated, the same could not be said for the post-war period, especially after the 1970s. Now, the legal framework was not one of 'enrichment through diversity', but parochial self-serving by powerful co-operatives and co-operative companies seeking to retain a status quo favourable to them, enhancing their competitiveness while doing nothing for general co-operative unity and development.

Notwithstanding such opposed views, a general view from the 1980s onwards was that co-operatives' legislation in all jurisdictions required a drastic overhaul. Common complaints were that extant legislation was 'antiquated', unsuited to modern commercial conditions and social environments, over-regulatory, excessively interventionist, paternalistic, variable in the application of financial and accountability standards and impeded interstate or national trade. Some reformers, like the Australian Association of Co-operative's (AAC) Bruce Freeman, simply sought a more *facilitative* federal or national legislative framework enabling co-operatives to adapt competitively while retaining a distinct identity. Others, principally in primary industries impacted by deregulation, sought fundamental change to co-operative structure, promoting capital mobilisation and resolving interface issues between Co-operatives and Corporations Law.

We have seen in earlier chapters how the co-operative movement gave AAC only qualified support, how it failed to attain national reach and how, after the association failed in 1993, the sector floundered before the Co-operatives Council of Australia (CCA) was formed in 1996, with a very weak mandate. It is not surprising then that only slow progress was made towards achieving federal or national legislation in the last decade and a half of the century. For much of the period, co-operatives wishing to operate interstate were still required to incorporate in the domicile state, achieve 'foreign' status in the jurisdiction where business was sought, change rules to achieve compliance in each jurisdiction and participate in a complicated reporting regime. Understandably, many chose to employ more flexible Corporations' Law.

A jurisdictional smorgasbord

In 1974 there were twenty-two statutes (not including Commonwealth taxation laws) in nine Australian jurisdictions governing co-operatives:

New South Wales

❖ *Co-operation Act 1923-1972*

❖ *Credit Union Act 1959-1971*

❖ *Permanent Building Societies Act 1967-1972*

Victoria

❖ *Co-operation Act 1958-1971*

❖ *Building Societies Act 1958-1971*

❖ *Co-operative Housing Societies Act 1958-1972*

❖ *Industrial and Provident Societies Act 1958*

❖ *Companies Act 1961*

Queensland

❖ *Co-operatives and Other Societies Act 1967*

❖ *Primary Producers Co-operative Associations Act 1922-1957*

❖ *Co-operative Housing Societies Act 1958*

❖ *Building Societies Act 1958*

Western Australia

❖ *Companies (Co-operative) Act 1943-1959*

❖ *Co-operative and Provident Societies Act 1903-1973*

❖ *Building Societies Act 1920-1970*

Tasmania

❖ *Co-operative Industrial Societies Act 1928*

❖ *Building Societies Act 1976*

❖ *Co-operative Housing Societies Act 1963*

South Australia

❖ *Industrial and Provident Societies Act 1923-1974*

❖ *Building Societies Act 1881-1968*

Australian Capital Territory

❖ *Co-operative Trading Societies Ordinance 1939-1963*

Northern Territory

❖ *Co-operative Trading Societies Ordinance 1945-1962*

As noted above, New South Wales was the only state with a government department for co-operative societies headed by a minister, served by an advisory council and registry. Queensland and Victoria also had registries of co-operatives and co-operative advisory councils, but no minister. Tasmania, South Australia and Western Australia had legislation for co-operative societies

Bega Co-operative Store (date unknown).
Photo courtesy of Bega Co-operative Society Limited.

operating under various administrative machinery while co-operative companies were registered under co-operative and/or company legislation administered by the respective state commissioners for corporate affairs. Co-operative acts administered by registrars applied to the Northern Territory and the Australian Capital Territory, which were administered by the Australian government.

By 1981 the number of acts governing co-operatives had grown to twenty-five, with the addition of legislation for credit unions in South Australia and Western Australia in 1976 and 1979, respectively, and for building societies in the Northern Territory in 1979. In New South Wales legislative provision existed for rural, trading, community settlement, community advancement, rural credit, investment, terminating building societies, associations and unions of co-operatives and separately for credit unions and permanent building societies. In Victoria provision existed for producer, trading, community settlement, community advancement, consumer credit, terminating and permanent building societies, associations and federations of co-operatives and for co-operative companies and co-operative societies incorporated prior to 1953. In Western Australia various pieces of legislation provided for co-operative companies, co-operative societies, permanent building societies and credit unions. In South Australia provision existed for co-operative societies, credit unions and permanent building societies. Queensland provisions covered trading, investment, community settlement, community advancement, mutual buying groups, terminating and permanent building societies, credit unions and primary-producer associations. Tasmania made provision for co-operative societies including credit unions and terminating and permanent building societies. The Australian Capital Territory had provisions for trading, building, co-operative credit and co-operative housing and services societies. In the Northern Territory provision existed for co-operative societies including credit unions and terminating and permanent building societies.

Responsibility for administering general co-operatives in New South Wales was shared by the ministry and registry. In Victoria the administrative situation was much more fragmented, shared between the Minister for Housing, the Registry of Co-operative Societies, the Registry of Co-operative Housing, the Attorney-General's Department, the Commissioner for Corporate Affairs, the Treasurer and the Registrar of Friendly Societies. In Western Australia, the Attorney-General's Department, the Commissioner of Corporate Affairs and the Registry of Friendly Societies shared responsibility for co-operatives and co-operative companies. In South Australia the Attorney-General's Department and the Registry of Industrial and Provident Societies administered co-operatives. In Queensland responsibility was shared between the Attorney-General's Department, the Registry of Co-operative Societies, the Ministry for Housing, the Registry of Co-operative Housing, the Minister for Primary Industry and the Registrar of Primary Producer Co-operative Associations. In Tasmania the Attorney-General, the Registrar of the Supreme Court, the Minister for Housing and the Registry of Building Societies shared responsibility for co-operatives. In the Australian Capital Territory responsibility was divided between the Minister for the Capital Territory and the Registrar of Co-operative Societies. In the Northern Territory co-operatives were administered by the Attorneys-General Department and the Registry of Co-operative Societies. Establishing clear lines of communication in this labyrinth was not easy, particularly as the national co-operative movement seldom spoke with one voice.

By 1992 there were still eleven major pieces of legislation governing Australian co-operatives in eight jurisdictions:

New South Wales
- *Co-operatives Act 1992*

Victoria
- *Co-operation Act 1991*

Queensland
- *Primary Producers Co-operative Associations Act 1923-1989*
- *Co-operative and Other Societies Act 1967-1986*

Western Australia
- *Companies (Co-operative) Act 1943-1976*
- *Co-operative and Provident Societies Act 1903*

South Australia
- *Co-operatives Act 1983*
- *Housing Co-operatives Act 1991*

Tasmania
- *Co-operative Industrial Societies Act 1928*

Northern Territory
- *Co-operative Societies Act 1980*

Australian Capital Territory
- *Co-operative Societies Ordinance Act 1939*

New South Wales and Victoria provided for the registration of foreign societies while Queensland, South Australia, Western Australia, Tasmania, the Northern Territory and the Australian Capital Territory did not. Some states and territories placed restrictions on use of the word 'co-operative' in trading names while others did not, for example Western Australia. Some had exemptions or restrictions on trade and others did not. Only in New South Wales and Victoria was a prospectus not required for a merger or transfer of engagements.

Freeing co-operatives from this cobweb of regulation would be problematical, even if co-operative leaders could agree on the desirability of this.[1]

National co-operatives' legislation: not a new idea

The idea of nationally uniform Australian co-operatives' legislation; even federal legislation; was not a new one. Many co-operative leaders, notably John Ross, the Reverend Frank Pulsford, George Booth, Bill Rawlinson, Bill Kidston, Bruce Freeman and others had advocated the idea across the century, seeing it as a prerequisite to significant co-operative development. Even the great free-trader and Dairy Farmers' Co-operative pioneer, C E D Meares, understood the importance of national legislation for co-operatives. At no stage, however, could state federations agree, particularly the Western Australians, so that federal or national co-operatives' legislation stayed a dead letter on the long list of unrealised co-operative objectives.

One of the first serious attempts to address the issue came in the late 1960s when Bill Rawlinson's Co-operative Federation of Australia (CFA) encouraged states' and territories' registrars to participate in regular liaison sessions. Two conferences were held, seeking a uniformity of approach and looking at draft legislation where uniformity would be advantageous to all states. Through the 1970s CFA diligently attempted to put national uniform legislation on the co-operative development agenda, making some progress with the Whitlam Government. Again, the plan fell foul of co-operative politics; mainly Western Australian resistance to Rochdale-inspired 'rigidities' in co-operative structure; and the Fraser Government was not interested.

SCAWP refers the issue to Attorneys-General

As noted in Chapter Twelve, a 1986 Australian Agricultural Council–Standing Committee on Agriculture Working Party (SCAWP) Report, *Agricultural Co-operatives in Australia*, noted that co-operatives had potential to answer many of the agricultural industry's problems but had not kept pace with modern management and financial marketing methods hampering the development of internationally competitive agricultural co-operatives. SCAWP called upon governments to assist co-operatives achieve a fuller potential recommending *inter alia* referring the matter of uniform co-operatives legislation to the Standing Committee of Attorneys-General (SCAG).

AAC conducts a campaign

In line with this, AAC launched a spirited campaign to achieve federal or nationally uniform co-operatives. Bruce Freeman was convinced that this was an absolute priority for co-operatives *along with* greater fund-raising flexibility. At a 1988 AAC meeting in Canberra the association agreed to press for *uniform* legislation, which seemed politically more achievable than *federal* legislation, given disagreements on the issue within the movement. It was agreed that uniform legislation was absolutely essential if co-operatives were to participate in any meaningful way in an 'added-value' export drive in a deregulatory environment.[2]

The SCAG–AAC Working Party

In July 1989 the SCAG–AAC Working Party declared that it was unrealistic to expect further development of the co-operative movement or greater efficiencies in co-operatives until the financial *and* legal environments were 'right'. Capital-raising was just one side of the equation in solving the so-called 'co-operative dilemma' (the democracy-capital balance) – nationally uniform legislation was the other. Co-operatives would continue to be disadvantaged relative to proprietors, who were about to come under a uniform national corporations and securities regime from which co-operatives, non-bank financial institutions (NBFIs), trade unions, professional associations, friendly societies, limited partnerships and incorporated associations would be excluded.

At the AAC Annual General Meeting in 1989 the Federal Minister for Primary Industry and Energy John Kerin noted progress towards achieving uniform legislation but commented on the 'apparent reticence of some state officials' to engage with the idea and 'problems' between the Queensland minister and his New South Wales counterpart. Kerin was also convinced that uniform legislation was the key to co-operatives participating successfully in industry rationalisation and pointed to problems associated with this in the dairy industry affecting co-operatives seeking to move to a national level. It was impossible, for instance, the minister said, under legislation in some cases drafted in the last century, for a wheat co-operative to take over the work of the Australian Wheat Board (AWB). Uniform legislation was *vital* if co-operatives were to have any real chance of mounting a credible alternative to SMAs and was the *key* to Australian trade with the international co-operative movement through an AAC-International Co-operative Alliance (ICA) trading agreement. Uniform legislation was also the key to the financial industry having greater confidence in the sector, *not* changes to co-operative structure as some were arguing. Kerin spoke of a recent meeting of the Australian Agricultural Council where only *two* ministers were in favour of uniform legislation after *six* years of 'nagging' by his departmental officials. A major obstacle seemed to be the prevailing mishmash of interstate departmental responsibility. Only in some jurisdictions, for instance, were co-operatives administered by departments of agriculture. Other sticking points included the insistence by some states and territories upon the inclusion of ICA principles, restrictions on usage of the word 'co-operative' in titles, takeover procedures, voting rights, interstate registrations and amalgamations, accounting and auditing requirements, share practices, *ultra vires* and the responsibilities of office holders. That is to say, there was very little agreement upon anything. Kerin said he would continue to press for uniform national legislation and the Commonwealth Government made $100,000 available to assist the process through the Marketing Skills Division, an innovative agricultural marketing programme.[3]

In March 1990 state attorneys-general again met in Adelaide to consider uniform co-operatives' legislation. New South Wales Minister for Co-operative Societies Gerry Peacocke, however, was concerned that attorneys-general seemed to be taking the running on the issue, questioning their credentials for this and insisting that ministers responsible for *co-operatives* should progress the agenda. But who were they? While Peacocke's complaint was reasonable, ministers responsible for co-operatives came from such diverse portfolios as to make the requirement impracticable.

Nevertheless, the minister's view prevailed (nothing could be achieved without the participation of the largest and most diverse of all the states' co-operative movements) and in June a SCAG Working Party (SCAGWP), consisting mainly of ministers' *representatives* with responsibilities for co-operatives, was established to explore consistency of legislation for co-operatives. Peacocke's deputy, Co-operative Development Branch (CDB) Manager Garry Cronan, chaired the convocation.

The SCAGWP terms of reference were articulated under priority headings:

* ❖ entitlement to use the word 'co-operative';
* ❖ ICA co-operative principles;
* ❖ procedures for dealing with takeovers;
* ❖ voting rights;
* ❖ interstate registrations and amalgamations;
* ❖ intra-state mergers;
* ❖ accounting and auditing requirements;
* ❖ shares and capitalisation;
* ❖ the doctrine of *ultra vires*;
* ❖ the responsibilities of office holders;
* ❖ the definition of a co-operative; and
* ❖ the minimum number of members required to form a co-operative.

Federal-state relations are strained

Opinion was far from unanimous on any of these headings. The possibility of agreement was further reduced by the inclusion of a reference (possibly from New South Wales) for SCAGWP to make recommendations on amendments to the *Corporations Act* to enable the conversion of a co-operative to a company and vice versa, or to exclude provisions from Part 6 of the act dealing with fund-raising and disclosure. Governments were then jittery in the wake of the Pyramid Building Society collapse, notwithstanding AAC reassurances that that debacle was irrelevant to general co-operatives, none of which had failed. The situation was complicated by the creation of the Australian Securities Commission (ASC) (later, Australian Securities and Investment Commission [ASIC]) and the formation of the Ministerial Council for Corporations (MINCO), upon which attorneys-general served. When it became clear that MINCO's brief overlapped the working party's references, SCAGWP officials promptly sought representation on MINCO, straining states-federal relations. The co-operatives' legislation issue became embroiled in a federal-states stand off on powers in respect of Corporations Law powers with Victoria and Queensland supporting the federal position and New South Wales, Western Australia and South Australia opposed. Minister Peacocke was strongly opposed, fiercely resisting any Canberra 'power grab', as he saw it, and stolidly defending his state's corporate affairs commission. Disagreements over who was to have ultimate responsibility for Corporations Law and who would 'own' the system to ensure continued regulatory consistency, spilled into the uniform co-operatives' legislation debate, slowing things down.[4]

Commonwealth Government to assume responsibility for co-operatives?

At a conference of co-operatives' registrars and other regulators from all states in October 1990, delegates recommended that a paper be prepared detailing proposals for the future regulation of financial and other co-operatives. Various options were mooted including the Commonwealth Government's incorporation of co-operatives within Corporations Law, the creation of discreet commonwealth co-operatives' legislation under ASC administration and the regulation of *large* commercial co-operatives under Corporations Law, keeping *small* co-operatives within states' law.

States-rights advocates objected that the co-operative democracy principle was incompatible with Corporations Law and that ASC would inevitably become a 'corporate policeman', incompatible with co-operative governance principles. Indeed, the High Court ruled that the federal government had no constitutional power over the incorporation of companies and a 'co-operative arrangement' based on uniform legislation and a federal court would need to be convened by states' laws, if Canberra were to achieve its goals.

New South Wales seeks a national 'mantle'

It seems clear that by now New South Wales co-operative officials were determined to drive the co-operative development agenda at a national level and to confine Canberra to funding the states for extension work. At a November meeting of a 'national strategy group', convened by Garry Cronan in Canberra, officers from commonwealth and state departments, industry representatives and experts discussed developing a forum for state development of the co-operative sector and to assess the scope for a common direction at national level. Cronan and Stan Rumbel of the New South Wales Registry of Co-operative Societies spoke of resources available for co-operative extension work and of the New South Wales Co-operatives Development Strategy (*Co-ops 2000*) (discussed in Chapter Nine) in arguing that their state was well qualified to lead any future states'-based co-operative development programme. Canberra's role, New South Wales delegates believed, should be restricted to providing a facilitative Corporations Law environment for co-operatives, and funding.[5]

Financial co-operatives achieve national uniformity

Meanwhile, Minister Peacocke was resisting moves by some state governments to create a national board to regulate building societies and credit unions; the Australian Financial Institutions Commission (AFIC) scheme; a co-operative regulatory and prudential arrangement constructed on Queensland 'template' legislation. In an unprecedented Joint Party vote held by the New South Wales Coalition Government the issue was finally resolved in the affirmative with Peacocke tenaciously resisting to the end. The AFIC, based in Brisbane, became operational in July 1992 ending a link between NBFI and general co-operatives going back a century.

Through these proceedings New South Wales and Western Australia were perceived in some jurisdictions to be 'parochial and obstructionist', intervening in such ways as to perpetuate what was widely seen as an inefficient, uncoordinated, duplicative, ineffective and slack state-based NBFI regulatory regime.

The Neil McLeod 'Options' Paper

At another SCAGWP meeting in Sydney in June 1991 researcher Neil McLeod was commissioned to prepare an options paper on co-operatives' legislation. This was seen as important, working party representatives said, without being specific, because 'one or more states are proceeding on a path which may invalidate the SCAG Working Party's progress'. McLeod was briefed to make recommendations with regard to three options:

- ❖ seeking general policy agreement on the twelve priority items already identified with a view to their separate adoption by each state;
- ❖ taking the 'Victoria path', with small co-operatives administered by the state and large commercial co-operatives coming under ASC (later dropped); and
- ❖ a completely national scheme based on the ASC model.

The SCAGWP invited a representative of the Commonwealth Attorney-General's Department onto the committee to liaise with MINCO. The commonwealth now had two representatives on SCAGWP, but still only one vote.

In September 1991 McLeod released a discussion paper arguing the obvious point that uniformity of co-operatives' legislation was desirable and noting the many failed attempts, formal and informal, achieve this goal:

> ...*mainly due to the lack of collective commitment of state supervisors, ministers, or both. This experience over decades contrasts with the commitment to the process of reform of the regulatory system for financial co-operatives which is now evident.*

The states held different views, McLeod reported, on whether co-operatives should be a commonwealth responsibility or whether they should stay state-based but with improved regulatory frameworks. The states and territories disagreed also over whether existing legislation should be simply tidied up and brought up to date or whether co-operatives should have *no* special recognition whatsoever. McLeod dismissed the idea that co-operatives and co-operative companies should come under Corporations Law, arguing that the co-operatives' notion of democratic ownership and control was completely different from companies but, in the matters of external fund-raising and *ultra vires*, there was a case for consistent regulation along corporate lines because these activities extended beyond state boundaries – a Corporations Law interface.

The McLeod Report explored several possible configurations. The first, the 'Corporations Law option', provided a simple 'one-stop shop' solution to the question of uniform legislation but, the researcher commented, this could potentially harm a distinctive co-operative identity. The commonwealth in any event might not be interested or ASC might not accept the idea. Small co-operatives would also find the idea daunting and states would need to confer rights and duties, which some states would resist. A 'Commonwealth Co-operatives' Act' option might not be constitutionally possible *vis a vis* Corporations Law and would obviously impact upon state registries (jobs). A 'state template model' based on the AFIC example was clearly favoured by SCAGWP state representatives and this option, Mcleod believed, would maintain state officers' expertise in co-operatives, retain the unique identity of co-operatives and enable state governments to continue to influence policy. On the other hand, McLeod argued, the option could actually *thwart* a national and global perspective for co-operatives and it would be difficult, if not impossible, to maintain consistency without vigorous ASC oversight. Ministerial changes, state idiosyncrasies, wandering regulation and disagreements over policy direction would inevitably corrode uniformity. A fourth option, 'core consistent provisions' in legislation enacted in each jurisdiction, would not require an exchange of powers by the states, would maintain a commitment to their respective co-operative development programmes but would *not* remove interstate trading problems. Neither could each state, even if they did include identical provisions in co-operatives' legislation, guarantee continuing consistency nor avoid different interpretations in each jurisdiction's courts.

McLeod recommended a 'template option' along AFIC lines; a state-owned, industry-funded (with commonwealth input for national matters), nationally-regulated framework administered and co-ordinated by a Ministerial Council of Responsible Ministers presiding over a national secretariat and national supervisory boards.[6]

New South Wales withdraws from the SCAG Working Party

New South Wales Minister for Co-operatives Gerry Peacocke was opposed to the AFIC model and to the 'AFIC option for co-operatives'. General co-operatives, he argued, had not experienced a collapse of confidence as NBFI had and, therefore, public policy in respect of co-operatives need *not* follow the AFIC example. The minister said he was greatly concerned at the possible 'contagion' of New South Wales regulations and the loss of states' independent co-operative development powers if the model were adopted. He preferred a 'user pays' regulatory scheme for New South Wales co-operatives, building up resources for co-operative development from within the co-operative movement, preserving jobs in New South Wales and preserving regulatory integrity. Under an AFIC model, New South Wales would have voting rights equal only to the *smallest* state. The minister was not prepared to surrender control of what he described as a 'healthy' New South Wales co-operative movement to any AFIC-type scheme.

In October 1991 the minister directed his deputy, Garry Cronan, to withdraw from SCAGWP, explaining that he was not interested in passing *any* responsibility to the commonwealth for the incorporation and supervision of co-operatives. New South Wales would focus on its own co-operatives' legislation and selectively apply the McLeod recommendations.

The SCAG Working Party is moribund

With New South Wales withdrawing from SCAGWP, the Working Party on Uniform Co-operatives' Legislation did not meet again for eighteen months. The federal Department of Primary Industry and Energy (DOPIE) was bitterly disappointed, seeing the delay as only prolonging impediments to the efficient operations of co-operatives at national and international levels and hampering promising industry talks and parliamentary interest in the Australian Wheat Board (AWB) becoming a co-operative. The stand-off was also hampering dairy industry rationalisation, a federal government priority and, possibly, some state officials hinted, this was a political consideration influencing New South Wales' apparent obstructionism. Certainly the New South Wales dairy industry was in no rush for deregulation as discussion in Chapter Three has indicated.

With SCAGWP moribund, DOPIE officials looked to the New South Wales Co-operatives Bill, about to receive a third reading, in the hope that this might remove obstructions to interstate mergers and serve as a model for national application, enabling co-operatives to take over from SMAs. Early in 1992 federal government officials 'strongly urged' state agriculture ministers to convince ministers responsible for co-operatives to rekindle action on uniform legislation allowing co-operatives to assume responsibility for SMAs at a national level. The new minister, Simon Crean, said that he was 'disappointed and frustrated' at the inaction and that industry rationalisation plans were being 'hamstrung' by the states. Crean circulated a letter among co-operatives indicating that AAC supported uniform legislation and calling upon the sector to get behind the issue.[7]

Meanwhile, New South Wales and Queensland ministers continued to squabble over elements of the AFIC scheme, specifically 'ambiguities' in respect of 'due diligence'. Gerry Peacocke was anxious to see the scheme's prudential standards on a par with New South Wales and initiated moves to *oblige* NBFI to lift risk-weighted capital and liquidity requirements in line with Reserve Bank of Australia guidelines and to prohibit 'speculative investments'. New South Wales and Queensland officials traded insults freely, bringing old states' rivalries and jealousies to the fore as officials bitterly questioned each other's motives. Peacocke threatened to take unilateral action and introduce amendments to the AFIC scheme's Queensland draft template bill. This fierce debate proceeded against an unstable political background, with the Victorian Labor Government reeling from the Pyramid Building Society collapse and other difficulties, the New South Wales Coalition Premier Nick Greiner resigning and the Western Australian Burke Labor government rocked by a scandal involving the Registrar of Co-operatives and Financial Institutions and the failed Teachers' Credit Union. In this context, the question of nationally uniform legislation for co-operatives was small beer indeed.

Sector support for uniform or consistent legislation

Matching Simon Crean, in June 1992 Minister Peacocke circulated a letter to co-operatives throughout Australia seeking submissions on co-operatives legislation and comment upon draft Victorian legislation and the not-yet-promulgated New South Wales *Co-operatives Act*. Of the New South Wales co-operatives which replied the Batlow Fruit Co-operative supported national co-operatives' legislation, identifying non-uniform legislation as a major impediment to interstate mergers. The Banana Growers Federation said co-operatives were disadvantaged because of a lack of uniformity and the paternalistic nature of co-operatives' legislation. Australian Co-operative Foods (ACF) said it was experiencing problems in seeking to effect mergers in Queensland and South Australia and strongly supported uniform legislation, 'but in the meantime would like to see arrangements put into place to enable co-operatives registered in one state to operate in other states especially in respect of fund-raising and voting rights'. The ACF submission pointed out that *not one* agricultural co-operative was operating beyond a state boundary in Australia (as a co-operative) and endorsed the forthcoming New South Wales legislation as the basis for national uniform legislation, noting oddly that this could present problems 'in states which want to keep co-operatives small'. The Ricegrowers' Co-operative (RCL) supported consistency, with Chairman Ian Davidge advocating a compromise plan to achieve to the maximum possible extent uniform co-operatives' legislation (core consistent provisions). The Sugar Milling Co-operative supported consistency and commended the New South Wales legislation because it offered better protection against opportunistic takeovers, better active member provisions and no cap on the size of a co-operative, which might serve to discourage the retention of capital. The co-operative doubted, however, that the act's equity instruments, Co-operative Capital Units (CCUs), would work. The Northern Co-operative Meat Company also supported uniform legislation, saying that although the co-operative company operated on the Queensland border it had not moved into Queensland markets because of the 'barrier of incompatible legislation'.

Some Victorian co-operatives and co-operative companies responded to Peacocke's survey: Victorian Producers' Co-operative; Sunraysia Districts Citrus Co-operative; Bonlac Foods; and the Murray-Goulburn Co-operative, for example. All supported moves to consistency in co-operatives' legislation holding that current legislation disadvantaged co-operatives relative to corporations, confused interstate operations, impeded industry rationalisation and inhibited capital formation. Bonlac Foods believed that strong commonwealth action would be needed to overcome chronic states' indecision, however, if the goal of uniform legislation were *ever* to be achieved. The Queensland co-operatives: Darling Downs Co-operative Association; Grainco; South Burnett Co-operative; and the Capgrains Co-operative Association; all strongly supported uniform legislation. Darling Downs saw this as a bridge to federal legislation but Capgrains favoured no development at the expense of states' rights.

Clearly, while co-operatives generally agreed that uniform or at least consistent legislation was desirable, opinion varied greatly upon the *modus operandi* and the extent to which the reforms should extend.[8]

New South Wales returns to the SCAG Working Party process

At a SCAGWP meeting held in the Rural Policy Division of DOPIE in Canberra in July 1992, Garry Cronan from the chair circulated a letter from Gerry Peacocke saying that New South Wales' continued participation in the uniform legislation process was conditional upon the committee working under the supervision of a council of co-operative ministers. The current situation, Peacocke believed, was wholly unsatisfactory as it *precluded* ministers responsible for co-operatives in the Australian Capital Territory and New South Wales. The minister was adamant that attorneys-general should *not* direct progress because they were not necessarily expert in agricultural and pastoral production. Moreover, the SCAGWP brief should be restricted to legislative matters affecting *interstate trade* and it was imperative that the civil service should not be left to run the process as had occurred with the AFIC scheme which, the minister believed, was 'negative and destructive'. Referring to Victorian proposals to impose different regulatory regimes upon small not-for-profit and large commercial co-operatives, Peacocke stressed that he was determined to avoid any possibility of New South Wales legislation for co-operatives 'being infected by some of the damaging proposals...currently before the Victorian parliament (which) might jeopardise a co-operative's progress and the progress of the co-operative sector (in New South Wales)'. The minister was happy for 'relevant' officers from states and territories to resume discussions aimed at achieving 'greater consistency' in co-operatives' legislation and constituting a council of co-operative ministers, including himself, the Queensland Minister for Primary Industries, the Commonwealth Minister for Primary Industry and Energy and the Queensland Treasurer, who also had responsibility for co-operatives. The issue should be addressed at an August meeting of Financial Institutions Ministers (not including attorneys-general) with a view to reaching agreement about shifting reporting arrangements in respect of co-operative development from SCAG to the proposed council of co-operative ministers. Peacocke undertook to contact ministers responsible for co-operatives to outline his proposal.

Some saw Peacocke's proposal as an ultimatum. Nevertheless, SCAGWP agreed to prepare *another* report on uniform legislative options, but no one was really clear as to which minister or ministers the working party should report.

At another meeting in Canberra, five days later, of government officials drawn from DOPIE, Attorneys-General, Corporate Affairs, state and territory registries, departmental legal divisions and business affairs, Chairman Garry Cronan asked the sole co-operative sector representative, AAC's Berridge Hume-Phillips, to leave the room while the Peacocke letter, which had been circulated at the previous meeting, was discussed. Cronan explained that it was inappropriate to involve anyone other than government officials in discussion concerning government representations. Hume-Phillips was not even to be afforded the minutes. The episode was a perfect metaphor for that old Rochdale maxim, 'When government comes in the door, co-operation goes out the window'. After the AAC representative was ushered back into the room, Cronan advised him that 'New South Wales is still considering its position' on participation in the SCAGWP process. The meeting then considered options for uniform legislation, last discussed in October 1991.

On the Corporations Law option Adrian Griffiths (South Australia) said the working party's brief was to look at *consistency*, not the transfer of responsibility to the commonwealth. He argued that a state template co-operative scheme of legislation was the best option with similar acts in each state but believed there was 'little point proceeding without New South Wales', understanding that Minister Peacocke was strongly opposed to the AFIC model. The Victorian representative, Dan Henry, said he thought including co-operatives in Corporations Law was the best option but probably not achievable although it should be kept open for future deliberation. DOPIE's Wayne Ryan agreed with Henry that Corporations Law was the best option for achieving uniformity, emphasising that the commonwealth had no intention of taking over state responsibilities unless the states wanted this and agreed that the option should be kept open. Garry Cronan reported that aspects of Corporations Law applied to the New South Wales Co-operatives Bill and also agreed the option should be retained.

Berridge Hume-Phillips said that the idea of bringing co-operatives under Commonwealth Government control had originated at an AAC Canberra conference in 1988 and the association still considered it a 'good option, but…a lot needs to occur before it could happen'. In a not-too-veiled reference to the impact the option could have upon state registries, Hume-Phillips said that 'funding for co-operatives development might not be forthcoming as states would no longer see it as their responsibility'. He believed it was immaterial who administered co-operatives' legislation 'so long as there is sufficient uniformity to enable national co-operatives to exist and function effectively'.

Garry Cronan suggested an alternative which 'might be to keep the current arrangements but for the commonwealth to legislate to enable particular *national* co-operatives to be established as had been mooted in the case of the Australian Wheat Board'. Wayne Ryan thought it impractical to establish a range of legislated national co-operatives and nothing was agreed on this point.

Discussion followed on the various merits of New South Wales and Victorian co-operatives bills in respect of the national template option. Cronan reiterated Minister Peacocke's position that acceptance of any decision was contingent upon a co-operatives ministerial council having ultimate authority. It was agreed to change the wording of the option 'to make it clear that the power would rest with a ministerial council, not with registrars'.

Adrian Griffiths believed the core consistent provisions option would be a very expensive one, involving numerous meetings of all state representatives '…just to agree on some provision, which when applied out of context, might not work anyway. The process would need to go on interminably as each time one bit is sorted out a new problem will arise.' Wayne Ryan suggested that the option be retained '…because if it is all that can be achieved it is better than nothing', and it was kept in.

Discussion on the template model option precipitated brisk debate. When Dan Henry said that he saw no problem in Victoria taking up much of the New South Wales Co-operatives Bill as a template, Adrian Griffiths said he did not believe the option assumed that New South Wales legislation would be the template, rather that *all* states should have an opportunity to put their position on the table. South Australia had had co-operatives' legislation ready to go for some time but had held it back pending the outcome of the SCAGWP process. Griffiths reminded the group that the ultimate goal was *total* consistency and that consistency in priority areas was simply a stop-gap measure. He proposed a new option that *all* states had an opportunity to table proposals before work on template legislation commenced and that changes to template law in the host state would automatically become law in other states. This new option was added to the list of options for consideration.

Wayne Ryan asked to whom the working party was reporting and told of his minister's growing impatience with the slowness of progress. Cronan replied that New South Wales '…would also like to see things happen more quickly and as such will be looking at facilitating some agreement with SCAG out of session'. He reminded participants that co-operative ministers would be meeting in August to discuss NBFI and, if the proposed council of co-operative ministers was agreed to by those ministers, '...the council could approach SCAG seeking out of session transfer of the working party to the new council'. It was agreed, however, that in the interim the working party should continue to report to SCAG and '...meanwhile New South Wales will look at options for progressing the ministerial council proposal'.[9]

The SCAGWP process, characterised already by impatience, frustration and suspicion, ran the risk of paralysis. Now, in addition to accommodating New South Wales' preferences, two new factors arose to delay progress further. As noted in Chapter Twelve, a few weeks before the New South Wales *Co-operatives Act* was promulgated in May 1993, AAC collapsed. Minister Peacocke was placed in an awkward position, obliged to assist numerous financially-stranded co-operatives quite as the new legislation and *Co-ops 2000* were being launched. Meanwhile, the Victorian co-operatives bill had ended in a ditch, a casualty of political instability which saw the resignation of Premier Cain, a short-lived Kirner government, the dissolution of parliament and the election of the Kennett Coalition. The new administration resolved to completely redraft legislation for co-operatives (discussed in Chapter Seven).

With the New South Wales *Co-operatives Act* in the implementation phase, it appears that that state's main concern in the uniform legislation debate now was resolving interface issues between the legislation and Corporations Law at state and national level. Indeed, uniform legislation appears to have been a low priority in the CDB, coming well behind fund-raising issues. Additionally, the newly-constituted Co-operative Federation of NSW Ltd agreed only to endorse further investigations of 'legislative policy' and, as noted in Chapter Twelve, the Co-operative Council of Australia (CCA) was so constituted as to make it virtually impossible to argue a case to federal government where unanimity did not exist. There was certainly no unanimity on the New South Wales *Co-operatives Act*. The uniform co-operatives' legislation debate again skidded to a halt.

The Model Interstate Division

After Gerry Peacocke was replaced as minister, a procession of New South Wales ministers responsible for co-operatives followed. In this fluid situation, ideas of federal or uniform co-operatives' legislation faded, giving way to a concept of 'similar' or 'consistent' legislation and a 'whole-of-government' approach. In a paper, 'Trends in Co-operatives' Legislation in Australia', Garry Cronan wrote that responsible ministers had agreed to proceed with the development of a 'model interstate division' for inclusion in each state and territory co-operatives' legislation, describing this as the first stage of a process 'which it is hoped will ultimately result in national uniform or consistent co-operatives' legislation'.

The model interstate division idea was constructed around the principle of mutual recognition, with each state and territory enacting provisions recognising co-operatives' legislation in other states and territories. Under the proposed scheme a co-operative registered in one state would be able, subject to prudential standards, 'to operate throughout the country as if the law of its home state applied throughout the country, that is, co-operatives can operate nationally under their home state's legislation'. Cronan added that the interstate division was not a final answer of itself to the problem of inconsistent legislation but '...some consistency will, however, result from requiring similar prudential standards'. For the system to work co-operatives would need to comply with the accountability and auditing requirements of Corporations Law while observing co-operative principles for active membership and voting purposes. This would entail resolving difficulties existing in the interface between Co-operatives Law and Corporations Law, especially in relation to fund-raising. Cronan anticipated that future Victorian legislation would be modelled on the New South Wales *Co-operatives Act* and '…if this occurs, it will, along with the [proposed] interstate division, represent a milestone in the road to national consistent co-operatives legislation in Australia'. Any future trends in legislation, however, Cronan wrote, would '…continue to relate to resolving the dilemma posed by co-operative capital' and ensuring member control in relation to this.[10]

The Co-operatives – Corporations Law 'interface'

In February 1995, a month before the Carr Labor Government ousted the Fahey Coalition in New South Wales, registry officials from various states met with 'peak co-operative bodies' in Sydney to discuss details of the proposed interstate division and 'fund-raising interface issues'. Representatives of large agricultural co-operatives, particularly from the New South Wales dairy industry, wanted co-operatives to be free to accept members across borders *without* implementing the disclosure provisions of Corporations Law, arguing that co-operatives were 'different' and mutual organisations should be exempt from issuing a prospectus. It was proposed that the interface issue should be dealt with in two stages. The first would provide for a model interstate division, which would contain consistent provisions adopted by all jurisdictions including: interstate fund-raising requirements; mutual recognition of foreign societies; co-operative principles; reporting requirements; and mergers and transfers of co-operatives across state borders. It was proposed that each state and territory adopt the model division as part of its existing co-operatives legislation. The second stage would comprise *additional* consistent legislation relevant to the *intra-state* operation of co-operatives. Currently co-operatives were exempt from Corporations Law in their intra-state operations but not for interstate operations. Therefore, proponents argued, for the model interstate division option to operate, 'minor amendments' would need to be made to Corporations Law to accommodate co-operatives, for instance, exempting the issue of unsecured notes, debentures or CCUs. This need not create undue problems, advocates said, because nearly all funds were raised only from members within a state and very little fund-raising was undertaken outside the membership base! The proposal, if accepted, would allow co-operatives to accept members by issuing membership shares across state borders without the expensive business of issuing a prospectus as required by Corporations Law. It was argued that existing supervisory regimes in the states and territories were generally adequate for the purpose of supervising co-operative share issues and that procedures could be formalised and standardised by interstate registrars and reviewed regularly by an interstate registrars' committee, which would also supervise fund-raising from *non-members*.

The proposal amounted to applying 'minimum standards' in relation to fund-raising interstate while circumventing onerous Corporations Law disclosure provisions. Under the plan, new co-operatives seeking to fund-raise interstate would be required to provide the *registrar* with a disclosure statement '…prior to being circulated to the proposed members'. For existing co-operatives '…its members would need to be provided with a simple disclosure statement for additional share debenture, unsecured note or CCU issues, where such issue was to be offered across state borders (subject) to rules of the co-operative'. This information should extend only to the method and timing of issue, whether the issue was voluntary or compulsory and the amount and purpose of the issue proposed. New interstate members would be provided with a simple disclosure statement in the latest annual report, the co-operatives' rules and basic information about the co-operative. With regard to fund-raising from non-members (a thorny administrative issue), information '...similar to Corporations Law' would need to be issued with '...supervising by the registrar to minimise the cost of compliance':

> *It is proposed that the co-operative would be registered in its home state by the home state registrar for operation in other states [and] allowed to operate as a foreign co-operative in the states in which it was registered around Australia. The interstate registrar would be notified and have only a limited ability to lodge a request that the co-operative not be given a foreign registration.*

The boldness of the proposal, tantamount to a circumvention of ASC regulation in the matter of interstate fund-raising by co-operatives, left registrars and attorneys-general in some jurisdictions aghast. Some believed that the proposal, if accepted, would constitute virtually a breakdown of regulation because it would be *impossible* to know who had ultimate regulatory responsibility or authority. The model interstate division option would be unworkable, critics protested, particularly in respect of fund-raising. It was simply designed to allow some large New South Wales co-operatives, involving external investors subscribing to CCU's, for example, to operate in other states with minimum disclosure provisions.

The model interstate division is ditched

The uniform co-operatives' legislation debate lurched into another bureaucratic mire. Predictably, the Co-operative Federation of Western Australia (CFWA) hotly resisted any talk of change to legislation in its state which would increase 'bureaucratic control' as, the federation alleged, had occurred in New South Wales. The New South Wales *Co-operatives Act*, already problematical in the implementation and under extensive review, was quite unacceptable in that state. The Co-operative Federation of NSW Ltd, on the other hand, thought the act was excellent. Clearly, agreement between those states was unlikely. Hopes for deliverance now rested on Victorian legislation, to which the Kennett Government formally committed in late 1995.

In the interim, Garry Cronan reported on the Co-operatives-Corporations Law interface. The interstate model division had failed to come to fruition, he said, because the issue of the break-up of regulatory responsibility for national co-operative fund-raising between the co-operative supervisor and the corporate regulator (ASC) had not been resolved. The CDB Manager and SCAGWP Chair acknowledged that hybrid models, such as were now permissible under the New South Wales *Co-operatives Act*, presented problems for 'government officials responsible for supervising these groups to determine which regulator and what legislation is the most appropriate'. Nevertheless, as was his responsibility, Cronan persisted in promoting the act:

> *...as a model for other states interested in reforming their relevant legislation and it is anticipated that if such changes do occur they should lead to greater consistency between states [but]...it may be necessary to systematically review all the capital provisions of the act to determine if there is further need for amendment.*

At a Co-operative Federation of NSW Ltd meeting in November 1995 to consider the legislation issue, federation consultant Don Kinnersley, then Chair of the New South Wales Legislative Review Committee, said that there were two serious issues to consider: uniformity of legislation across states' borders to allow for national co-operatives; and simpler legislation for not-for-profit organisations. Kinnersley intended to look closely at these issues and make recommendations to the Co-operatives Council for reference to the minister.[11]

There the matter rested while Victorian legislation was framed and the New South Wales *Co-operatives Act* was extensively reviewed to take better account of National Competition Policy and trades practices legislation.

Co-operative development is harmed

As these inconclusive deliberations dragged on at government level, co-operative development in Australia was being harmed. We have already considered the inability of the Australian Wheat Board (AWB) to adopt a co-operative structure due in part to the absence of federal or uniform legislation for co-operatives. Australian Dairy Industry Council Chairman Pat Rowley, in another illustration, noted how some state governments had resisted any attempts through AAC or SCAGWP to adopt uniform national legislation which might facilitate a national co-operative structure. This was harming the dairy industry, Rowley said. Current legislation made a straightforward merger extremely difficult and the chairman renewed calls for national legislation as an urgent matter to enable co-operatives to compete with proprietors, adapt to deregulation and take a more prominent place in world markets. A proposal by the Queensland Prosperine Sugar Co-operative to develop a sugar industry in the Ord River through the Ord River Co-operative (Western Australia) had collapsed because legislation complicated fund-raising. The national Ostrich Farmers Association, seeking to form a co-operative, abandoned the plan for the same reason. A (unnamed) nationally operating co-operative seeking to take on a failed co-operative was unable to do so because of difficulties in accepting members across borders. As noted in Chapter Thirteen, many small to medium-sized enterprises contemplating conversion to co-operative structure abandoned the idea because of the regulatory complexity involved, the high cost of compliance, administrative delays and difficulties in trading across borders.

As soon as a co-operative moved across a border, Corporations Law required 8 to 10 per cent of funds raised on amounts of $10 million or less by way of an indemnity for due diligence and verification checks! Few middling-sized co-operatives could afford that. Possibly the first cross-border merger of agricultural co-operatives in Australia, involving the New South Wales dairy co-operative ACF and the Queensland co-operative Queensco, cost $1 million in consultancy fees and took five years to complete! Many groups inclined to co-operation formed unlisted companies or incorporated associations instead of selecting the co-operative model, more co-operatives converted to 'easier' corporate structure and some SMAs seeking to adopt a co-operative structure, even those with Federal Government encouragement like AWB, were unable to do so because of deficient co-operatives' legislative arrangements.[12]

The Core Consistent Provisions Scheme

In framing new legislation for co-operatives, the Victorian Government drew upon the New South Wales act, but not solely, also referring to SCAGWP recommendations in respect of the Corporations Law interface and MINCO recommendations (discussed in Chapter Seven). It was proposed that the Victorian legislation should serve as a template for national legislation, providing a base model for a Core Consistent Provisions (CCP) Scheme comprising 95 per cent agreed provisions for fund-raising, active membership, co-operative principles, reporting requirements, director responsibility and winding-up, and leaving 5 per cent for state peculiarities. The bill contemplated distinct *trading* and *non-trading* categories of co-operatives each with different fund-raising capacities and disclosure provisions in an effort to remove the 'dead hand of bureaucracy' from smaller not-for-profit entities.

The legislation would also introduce different *classes of shares* and various equity instruments for members, but *not* CCUs, which were seen to present jurisdictional problems outside New South Wales. It would clearly articulate a process for the interstate registration, operation and merger of co-operatives and would *not* include a supreme ministerial body like the New South Wales Co-operatives Council.

In April 1996 the Victorian Government appointed an officer to achieve inter-governmental support for the bill.

Back to the 'drawing board'

As Victorian legislation was prepared, SCAGWP and MINCO met periodically to resume discussions on the problem of co-operatives wishing to trade across borders. *Nine* possible legislative structures were now considered, paraphrased below:

❖ Structure One: complementary commonwealth - state co-operatives' legislation. The commonwealth passes legislation and each state or territory passes legislation which interlocks with it and which is restricted in its operation to matters not falling within the commonwealth's constitutional powers.

❖ Structure Two: complementary or mirror legislation. For matters which involve overlapping or an uncertain division of constitutional powers, essentially identical legislation is passed in each jurisdiction.

❖ Structure Three: adopted complementary legislation. A jurisdiction enacts the main piece of legislation with other jurisdictions passing acts, which do not replicate but merely adopt that act and subsequent amendments, as their own.

❖ Structure Four: referral of power. The commonwealth enacts national legislation following a referral of relevant state power to it under Section XXXVII of the Australian Constitution.

❖ Structure Five: alternative consistent legislation. Host legislation in one jurisdiction is utilised by other jurisdictions which pass legislation stating that certain matters will be lawful in their own jurisdictions if they would be lawful in the host jurisdiction. The non-host jurisdictions cleanse their own statute books of provisions inconsistent with the pertinent host legislation.

❖ Structure Six: mutual recognition. Where goods or services comply with the legislation in their jurisdiction of origin they need not comply with inconsistent requirements otherwise operable in a second jurisdiction into which they are imported or sold.

❖ Structure Seven: unilateralism. Each jurisdiction goes its own way, the antithesis of uniformity.

❖ Structure Eight: non-binding national standards model. Each jurisdiction passes its own legislation but a national authority is appointed to make decisions under that legislation. Such decisions are, however, variably applied by the respective state or territory ministers.

❖ Structure Nine: adoptive recognition. Where one jurisdiction may choose to recognise the decision-making process of another jurisdiction as meeting the requirements of its own legislation regardless of whether this recognition is mutual.

The Co-operatives Law Agreement 1996

In July 1996 the Victorian Government released an exposure bill for perusal by federal, state and territory governments. In October, a decade after the Australian Agricultural Council Standing Committee recommended to the federal government the enacting of federal or uniform national co-operatives' legislation, SCAGWP resolved that the best way of achieving 'substantially uniform co-operatives' legislation' was through an inter-governmental agreement incorporating 'core' provisions consistent across all jurisdictions with changes effected by a ministerial council for co-operatives' law. Accordingly, the states signed a Co-operatives' Law Agreement designed to achieve 'common core provisions' based on the forthcoming Victorian *Co-operatives Act*. There was to be *no* commonwealth involvement apart from 'rolling back' Corporations Law in respect of co-operatives interstate fund-raising.

The CCP Scheme sought to achieve 90 to 95 per cent consistency in legislation with the remaining 5 to 10 per cent 'unique' to each state to allow for local circumstances. *Core* provisions extended to incorporation, the powers of a co-operative, democratic voting, co-operative principles, accounting standards, recognition of the registration and operation of interstate co-operatives, active membership and stronger investigation and enforcement powers. *Non-core* provisions included stamp duty, appeals and penalties. In order to avoid the problem of 'drift' as jurisdictions altered legislation, all parties to the Co-operatives' Laws Agreement undertook to use '…best efforts to ensure that the administration of the legislation remains reasonably consistent'. Under the 'roll-back' plan, co-operatives would not be subject to Corporations Law for share issues to existing or new members, rather they would be regulated by state law using modified Corporations Law referred to the relevant co-operatives act in the states and territories. Corporations Law, however, would *still* apply to prescribed interests in profitable undertakings. All legislation enacted by parties to the agreement was to be consistent with CCP and amendments could proceed only by the *unanimous agreement* of parties, who were to be represented by ministers responsible for the regulation of co-operatives.

'The journey to national consistent co-operatives legislation may have begun'

In December 1996 the Victorian *Co-operatives Act* was passed (but not promulgated for nearly a year). Minister (Attorney-General) Jan Wade said the act formed the basis for an historic agreement between the commonwealth and states to adopt a state-based national scheme for consistent co-operatives' legislation, heralding the beginning of a new stage of co-operative growth. Co-operative Federation of Victoria (CFV) Secretary Tony Gill, who had played a key role in drafting the bill and guiding its development, commented, 'With the new Victorian act…to become a reality there are encouraging signs from a number of the other states that the journey to national consistent co-operatives legislation may have begun'.[13]

The Commonwealth Government proceeded to draft amendments to Corporations Law to incorporate a co-operatives' interface, contingent upon all parties to the Co-operatives' Law Agreement passing complementary legislation. The South Australian Co-operative Federation supported the main thrust of the CCP Scheme, released a draft bill for comment and anticipated adoption of core provisions by July. The Co-operative Federation of Queensland (CFQ) was interested but suggested amendments. Queensland Registrar Paul Kerr, who saw New South Wales' CCUs as inconsistent with other CCP Scheme provisions and a stumbling block, began moves to bring community and agricultural co-operatives within the one bill. Tasmania, a state which had also agreed to participate, proceeded with a new bill. Northern Territory Registrar Barbara Bradshaw, who chaired a Registrars' Group supervising the Co-operatives' Law Agreement, said she would promote the legislation in the Northern Territory and hoped it would be ready by July. The Australian Capital Territory reported no action. The CFWA undertook to discuss the proposal in detail with the co-operative sector, but no further progress was reported. In April 1997 the New South Wales Government agreed to participate in the CCP Scheme. The official reason for the delay was that the *Co-operatives Act* was under review. While that government did sign the Co-operatives' Law Agreement with bipartisan support, serious misgivings were voiced at an administrative level about weaknesses in the scheme which might be exploited to avoid Corporations Law requirements. The registry, undergoing serious restructuring, remained uncertain about the proposed scheme, with senior officers concerned that 'devilish questions' remained to be answered and wondering how the CCP Scheme, to commence in July 1997, was to be maintained.[14]

The New South Wales Co-operatives' Act Amendment Bill

In May 1997 Minister Fay Lo Pò introduced in parliament the New South Wales Co-operatives Act Amendment Bill to enact core provisions found in the Victorian *Co-operatives Act*. The amendments, the minister emphasised, were a product of Co-operative Federation of NSW Ltd and Co-operatives Council input. This legislation would retain extant provisions for ICA principles, active membership, the abolition of *ultra vires*, director responsibilities and orderly takeover, but embrace Victorian provisions for trading and non-trading co-operatives, classes of shares, processes for foreign co-operatives registering, operating and merging procedures, enhanced enforcement powers, consistent offence and proceedings provisions and increased disclosure requirements.

Several non-core CCP Scheme elements remained in the legislation, however. Provisions for CCUs and the Co-operatives Council were retained. Other 'non-core' elements related to curing procedural irregularities, double jeopardy, civil liability arising under the co-operatives law of New South Wales and another jurisdiction, offences committed partly in and partly outside a jurisdiction, reciprocity in relation to offences, applications to the Supreme Court to resolve 'transit difficulties' and uniform disclosure and reporting arrangements for all co-operatives to avoid an element of public risk. Minimal level disclosure, the minister said, would not impact greatly on the interstate operation of the CCP Scheme as most *non-trading* co-operatives operated solely within a state. The legislation also retained 'at the request of the industry' current provisions allowing *fewer* than five members to constitute a co-operative. In a blow to the democracy principle, the registrar could also approve of an alteration to the rules of a co-operative by its *board* if satisfied that approval by *members* was not necessary and alteration by the board was appropriate and a matter of commercial convenience. The power of the New South Wales minister to approve of greater than one in four non-active member directors on a board was also retained and the registrar retained powers to appoint an administrator. The minister anticipated further amendments as the CCP Scheme took effect.

At the bill's second reading in June, J H Turner (Myall Lakes) said he would not oppose the amendments but doubted that the CCP Scheme could succeed, noting that various states and territories had not proceeded with the idea. Turner doubted also that uniformity could be retained and regretted that the amendments preserved a 'great deal of bureaucracy' and were still very complicated. For example, fund-raising by members was governed by Co-operatives Law while for non-members it was governed by Corporations Law. Under the CCP Scheme co-operatives would continue to be registered by state and territory registries of co-operatives while prescribed interests would be registered with ASC. This was a 'bureaucratic set-up', Turner believed, which needed further streamlining and did not represent a *truly* uniform national co-operatives legislation regime.[15]

CCP Scheme uncertainty

As New South Wales amending legislation proceeded through parliament, months of intense and sometimes heated debate on the CCP Scheme continued between 'co-operative officials', almost entirely government personnel. The states were unable to agree on versions of CCP amendments and registrars were increasingly uncertain about their interstate responsibilities. A blizzard of facsimiles and terse correspondence passed between members of the CCP Registrars' Group and patience was wearing thin.

Then, when the Commonwealth Treasury learned that the New South Wales co-operative, Namoi Cotton, was preparing to issue CCUs on the Australian Stock Exchange (ASX), Treasury officials wrote to CCP officials to canvas their views, reminding them that a MINCO resolution with regard to the interface between Corporations Law and the CCP Scheme rested on an assumption that co-operatives would *not* be listed on ASX or any other stock market. The Treasury letter also noted that ASX was continuing discussions with a number of co-operatives about listing (discussed in Chapter Thirteen) and indicated in strong terms that the issue would need to be resolved and a joint commonwealth/state/territory approach agreed before draft complementary commonwealth legislation 'rolling back' Corporations Law in respect of co-operatives' fund-raising could be finalised.

In August Barbara Bradshaw wrote to the New South Wales Department of Fair Trading (DFT) Trading Strategy Division, which now had responsibility for co-operatives, calling for an urgent telephone hook-up to discuss CCP provisions in the New South Wales Co-operatives Amendment Bill, many elements of which seemed inconsistent with the scheme and might need repealing. New South Wales' officials took exception this, saying that their state was not prepared to rush consideration of the issue and that introducing amending legislation would probably result in further lengthy delays. The division did, however, undertake to prepare a detailed response to concerns raised, circulate this and participate in a 'phone hook-up.

Bradshaw then wrote to the ASX Managing Director expressing concern at misunderstandings caused by the release of ASX guidance notes for co-operatives which had proceeded '...in spite of the attempts by members of the [Co-operatives Registrars' Group] to explain matters to your staff'. Bradshaw emphasised that co-operatives were mutual organisations with one vote per member and strict active membership provisions and were *unsuitable* for listing on ASX.

After another squall of correspondence between Bradshaw and the New South Wales department, a meeting of 'co-operative officials' was held in Adelaide on 15 September 1997, focused on the New South Wales Co-operatives Amendment Bill. The CCP Scheme at that stage was supposed to start on 1 September but this now seemed impossible with New South Wales' amendments yet to be proclaimed and uncertainty lingering over the Namoi Cotton CCU issue and the Commonwealth's response to this. On the vexed issue of CCUs the New South Wales delegation said it would be impossible to effect amendments before the Autumn Session (in 1998) and that therefore CCUs would remain part of their state's non-core provisions in the CCP Scheme.

Some participants doubted the genuineness of the New South Wales position. The South Australians said they were frustrated by years of delay. Queensland Registrar Paul Kerr said that New South Wales should have raised such non-core issues while other states were considering the CCP – not now! Was New South Wales a participating jurisdiction, or not? Some accused New South Wales of arrogance and wanting to dominate. New South Wales representatives replied that, because of ministerial directives on work priorities, they had not had the opportunity to participate for about ten months while other jurisdictions were discussing CCP matters. They added that they would consider 'grandfathering' (extending the life of) existing CCU share issues and bringing provisions for the instrument into line with the subordinated debt provisions of the CCP Scheme through further amendments to the New South Wales act. There were *thirty-four* parts and sections of the act to consider in relation to CCP, New South Wales officials conceded, some needing amendment, some needing to be repealed and some for other jurisdictions to adopt. The meeting agreed to segregate New South Wales provisions into: those that the state should amend, defer proclamation or repeal; those which other jurisdictions should consider; and those for which no action was required.

The meeting then considered the state of readiness of the various states and territories to meet a SCAG deadline for the compliance with Co-operatives Law Agreement – December 1997. Queensland had forms and circulars ready. South Australian law acknowledged New South Wales, Victoria, Queensland and Northern Territory laws. Victoria was experiencing some difficulty with a 'whole of government' approach, then favoured by New South Wales. The Northern Territory was ready, but still Western Australia, Tasmania and the Australian Capital Territory had not proclaimed new laws. Barbara Bradshaw undertook to write to the Commonwealth Government with regard to CCP matters arising from New South Wales amendments and emphasised the need to be '…seen to be speaking with one voice'.[16]

The Co-operatives Council of Australia's limited role

CCA affiliates also wished to discuss the CCP Scheme in respect of New South Wales amendments but could not do so because, under the association's constitution, the required unanimity did not exist. The Co-operative Federation of NSW Ltd, for example, fully supported the amendments as they stood. Some other federations did not. CCA Chairman Jim Howard (Queensland) was therefore confined to issuing a commentary paper pointing out that Queensland, South Australia, Victoria and the Northern Territory had already adopted CCP Scheme provisions pursuant to the Victorian act and it was expected that other states would follow, although progress in New South Wales was bogged down in administrative changes. Howard anticipated a widespread shift to co-operative structure as a result of the CCP Scheme with companies joining together in second-tier co-operatives or becoming active members of existing co-operatives. He believed that the proposed legislation would enable boards and managers to act in accordance with modern corporate principles while keeping member-benefits and jobs largely in Australia. The CCP Scheme also created the possibility of listing a range of financial instruments with special (non-voting) rights, which could create opportunities for finance and investment bodies to invest in co-operatives.[17]

The CCP Scheme comes unstuck

Nothing could happen if the CCP Scheme stalled, however. Just before New South Wales amendments were proclaimed on 1 December 1997, the Namoi Cotton Co-operative proceeded with an issue of CCUs on ASX. Under existing provisions, the New South Wales registrar was obliged to approve!

The Namoi Cotton issue was seen by the CCP Co-operative Officials Group (as the committee was now named) as patently incompatible with the Co-operatives' Law Agreement and likely to provoke a commonwealth reaction. The move rekindled state and territory registrar concerns about their responsibility in respect of interstate co-operatives' fund-raising activities and the mistrust of New South Wales' intentions deepened, especially among Queensland and Western Australian officials. New South Wales officials repeated earlier assurances given at the Adelaide meeting, explaining that the Namoi issue was permissible under extant law, the Amendments Bill had not yet been promulgated, and that *amendments to the amendments* to make such a thing as Namoi Cotton's share issue impossible, already proceeding through parliament, were not possible until the Autumn Session of 1998.

Early in November 1997, a Commonwealth Treasury official wrote to the DFT Trading Strategy Division asking whether New South Wales had adopted, or was intending to adopt, CCP Scheme provisions and, if so, whether co-operatives regulated under New South Wales legislation would be able to issue CCUs and to list on ASX. Treasury was of the view that co-operatives would *not* issue CCUs under CCP legislation and that the *listing* of co-operatives was not possible. The letter emphasised the relevance of the matter to proposed 'roll-back' amendments to Corporations' Law with regard to CCP legislation, which MINCO had resolved to do at a meeting in 1996. In reply, the division pointed out that New South Wales was the only jurisdiction with CCUs, that they were a non-core CCP element, that existing law had obliged the registrar to proceed with the Namoi Cotton issue and that the CCP Scheme remained a 'high priority' for New South Wales. The director proposed a meeting early in 1998 to resolve the issue.[18]

The Commonwealth Government thereupon declined to proceed with the Corporations Law 'roll-back' amendments, leaving the CCP Scheme in a shambles.

By 1999 uniformity still had not been achieved. Northern Territory, South Australia, Queensland and Victoria each recognised the legislation of the other jurisdictions, but Victoria had not yet recognised New South Wales law. CCP arrangements remained on hold in Tasmania and the Australian Capital Territory. Western Australia was not involved in the scheme.

With Queensland Registrar Paul Kerr to the fore, more meetings were held and discussion papers circulated seeking a way through the impasse. CCUs were considered as a possible element of the CCP Scheme. MINCO again considered ways in which Corporations Law might be amended to accommodate an interface with Co-operatives Law with regard to co-operatives' ability to list securities. A series of amendments to the *Queensland Co-operatives Act 1997* went through the Queensland parliament (consisting of one house only), eagerly awaited by other states wishing to effect consistent amendments.

'The greatest impediment to co-operative development'

Still unanimity on the issue could not be reached. Speaking at a Co-operative Federation of NSW Ltd conference in 1999 the British co-operatives' analyst Edgar Parnell described the absence of uniform legislation in Australia as the greatest impediment to co-operative development and a deterrent to people choosing the co-operative model as a solution to organisational or market problems. The CCP Scheme as it stood, the visitor observed diplomatically, was '…still a little heavy-handed compared with quite a lot of legislation in other countries'. Australian co-operatives' legislation, Parnell said, was a legacy of the colonial era: prescriptive, inflexible, patronising; 'like Africa'; diminishing the attractiveness of co-operatives to the public, complicating capital-raising and creating a dysfunction between large trading and small not-for-profit co-operatives.

Indeed, tortuous accountability, auditing and regulatory questions remained unanswered in the incomplete CCP Scheme, requiring states' legislation to resolve. It was also becoming apparent that compliance was complex, expensive (involving a new schedule of fees and charges), duplicative and cumbersome. For instance, if a co-operative wanted to solicit for members, issue shares or provide goods and services in another state or territory, it was required to register as a 'foreign co-operative' in that jurisdiction where the regulator could declare the co-operatives act of another state to be 'Co-operatives' Law' under the scheme, sufficiently similar to enable the co-operative to register as a 'participating co-operative'. A co-operative was required first to apply to ASC for a business number and, if successful, then apply to the registrar in the home state for a compliance certificate and, finally, apply to the registrar in the foreign state for registration. Both registries were to be informed of developments and changes and reporting information was to be made available to both. If the co-operative sought to operate in several states and territories, the registration and reporting procedures simply multiplied. The problem of legislative 'drift' was never satisfactorily dealt with and the Corporations Law interface remained unresolved. It was unlikely that groups seeking ways to develop national co-operatives would find such a convoluted scheme helpful.

The Co-operatives National Working Party

This complex, legalistic arrangement was the best a historically fractured Australian co-operative movement largely reliant upon government support could hope for. Some existing co-operatives did use the CCP Scheme, for example some grains co-operatives in various states and also Victorian co-operatives and co-operative companies such as Consolidated Herd Improvement Services, Genetics Australia and Co-operative Purchasing Services and the New South Wales co-operatives Netco, Plumbers' Supplies, Australian Wine Consumers and the University Co-operative Bookshop.

In July 2000 a Ministerial Council on Consumer Affairs, convened by New South Wales Department of Fair Trading Assistant Director Brian Given, brought together a Co-operatives' National Working Party (CNWP) to review the CCP Scheme. The CNWP was directed to articulate proposals to replace the scheme's existing foreign registration provisions with a 'mutual recognition' scheme for other jurisdictions and to develop proposals for nationally co-ordinated and consistent policies and developmental and implementation processes by all jurisdictions, including legislative consistency with consumer protection laws.

In November CNWP met CCA where, it is reported that '...regulators and state groups (which have been dragging their feet on a number of issues of concern to those co-operatives wishing to trade across borders and/or seek members and raise funds in other states) (*sic*) were deprecated'. The CNWP tabled yet another list of options for uniform co-operatives' legislation including: agree to adopt consistent legislation; mutual recognition; template legislation; transfer administrative responsibility to the commonwealth or; incorporate co-operatives legislation under Corporations' Law. The CCA supported mutual recognition and template legislation, recognising that this would require further legislative changes. The CNWP then invited additional input from co-operatives which were experiencing difficulty in cross-border operations, particularly in relation to CCUs. The Victorian representative indicated his government's willingness to review legislation and, where possible, expedite the process of achieving national legislation. Co-operative Federation of NSW Ltd Consultant Don Kinnersley sought views from the New South Wales co-operative sector on the direction legislation should take as the *Co-operatives Act* was again amended to deal with disclosure issues relating to a takeover bid by Italian company, Parmalat, in respect of the Dairy Farmers' Group (DFG) (discussed in Chapter Sixteen). Again, events in New South Wales necessitated urgent amendments to CCP legislation.

In this context CNWP sought to improve the CCP Scheme by adopting fund-raising provisions in *all* jurisdictions, permitting co-operatives to issue CCUs based on New South Wales' legislation and to replace foreign registration provisions with a mutual recognition system designed to reduce as much as possible the expense and bureaucratic complexity of operating interstate.

Progress was slow. By early 2003 CNWP had again adjusted its focus. Rather than seeking to 'improve' the CCP Scheme, the working party now recommended to the Ministerial Council on Consumer Affairs a 'longer-term strategy' involving template legislation to *replace* the CCP Scheme. Council Convenor Brian Given explained that if governments adopted the template legislation, a model act would be passed in one jurisdiction and applied to all other states and territories through 'Application of Laws' acts passed by their respective parliaments. This would ensure that future-agreed amendments to the template legislation would be applied throughout Australia simultaneously and through a speedier process. The drafting of amendments was expected to be completed soon, Given said, and ministers had agreed to seek to secure their passage in the parliaments of each jurisdiction as soon as possible.

Conclusion

More than a century after the federation of Australian states, and after nearly two decades of great effort, first by AAC executives working with federal officials and later by 'co-operative officials', from state and territory governments, the saga of nationally uniform co-operatives' legislation continued. In 1989 the SCAG-AAC Working Party had reported that two things needed to be achieved for national co-operative development to proceed: uniform legislation and fund-raising flexibility. The latter had been achieved but arguably at the cost of stymieing the former. That a cornerstone of national co-operative development should not be in place at the beginning of the twenty-first century was something for which the co-operative movement might still pay the supreme price.[19]

Part IV:

CASE STUDY – THE DAIRY FARMERS' GROUP

In 1960 'dry' (non-producer) shareholders unsuccessfully attempted to take over Dairy Farmers' Co-operative (Dairy Farmers), an icon of the Australian co-operative movement, arguing that the co-operative had grown 'fat and lazy'. A 'siege' mentality gripped New South Wales fresh-milk producers at this time as Victorian producers assailed protected markets. Dairy Farmers sought to rally New South Wales' co-operatives in resisting this 'foreign invasion' but was hampered by the unwillingness of co-operatives to work together and distracted by another takeover raid.

A report by consultant Ian Langdon recommended serious industry rationalisation, leading to the formation of Australian Co-operative Foods (ACF), joining Dairy Farmers and co-operatives in the Hunter Valley and Shoalhaven regions. Faced with the expensive business of redeeming 'dry' shares to meet the Co-operation Act's active member provisions, ACF urgently required capital for growth competitiveness. The now ACF Chairman, Ian Langdon, sought the co-operation of dairy co-operatives in forming 'one big society' north of the Murray River. The unwillingness of co-operatives to co-operate and ACF members to adequately fund their co-operative frustrated the chairman, who saw an urgent need to solve a 'co-operative dilemma' in co-operative structure found in tensions between capital adequacy and democracy.

Various capital-raising options were mooted and in 1993 ACF members approved a compulsory bonus share-acquisition scheme linked to volume of supply. ACF then engaged in an expansive growth programme seeking to build a 'mega' co-operative capable of meeting intense competition and adapting to deregulation. Overseas models were studied including an Irish 'hybrid' model, theoretically capable of bringing capital and democracy into 'equilibrium'. The idea of raising external equity was also flagged. Many members were hesitant, unconvinced that external investors and perpetual control were reconcilable. In 1995, however, the board approved a five-year plan of vigorous investments and market development in preparation for deregulation.

The Dairy Farmers' Group (DFG) which emerged from this comprised a geographically-dispersed heterogeneous membership, radically altering the bond of association. With an executive hungry for capital and driving growth, a grassroots reaction began. A ballot to divide the co-operative into co-operative supply and proprietary processing and marketing divisions was scrapped. DFG continued to court mergers and takeover proposals, precipitating a showdown with dissenters. Another ballot to partially demutualise the co-operative failed to attract the required number of votes.

When DFG encountered difficult trading conditions soon after deregulation in 2000 the executive remained as determined as ever to press on with a partial-demutualisation restructure and, as a first step, divided the organisation into two co-operatives.

Dairy Farmers Co-operative Show parade entry (c1950s)
Photo courtesy of Australian Co-operative Foods Ltd.

Chapter Fifteen

'Dry' Shareholders, Deregulation and Capital Adequacy: THE DAIRY FARMERS' CO-OPERATIVE TO 1993

Introduction

Like 'book ends', our discussion of Australian farmer co-operatives in the twentieth century begins and ends with the dairy co-operative movement. In the first three chapters (Part I) we considered how co-operation in that great industry evolved from the end of the nineteenth century through to deregulation in 2000. By way of a case study the following two chapters consider the experience of one of Australia's largest co-operatives, one which operated for virtually all of the twentieth century and continues to operate successfully at the time of writing: the Dairy Farmers Milk Co-operative Company Limited (Australian Co-operative Foods [ACF]; Dairy Farmers Group [DFG]; hereafter 'Dairy Farmers').

What is particularly interesting about Dairy Farmers from an historical perspective is that it evolved across the century from a tiny, regionally-based, passionately free-trade organisation into a hugely successful, heavily-regulated entity between the world wars, before reinventing itself in the 1980s as a 'lean and hungry' national conglomerate in the approach to deregulation and globalisation. For the co-operative's most recent incarnation a 'co-operative dilemma' needed to be solved: how to attract and retain sufficient capital to maintain and capture market share in order to remain competitive while remaining faithful to the democracy principle? Discussion in Chapters Fifteen and Sixteen examines stages through which Dairy Farmers passed after World War II, first in identifying the 'co-operative dilemma', second in seeking to solve it and finally how the co-operative sought to stay true to the democracy principle.

Ironically, considering the co-operative's historical opposition to government intervention, Dairy Farmers prospered from regulated-New South Wales' fresh-milk markets before and after World War II. Indeed the co-operative was deemed by the federal government to be a 'protected industry' under war-time emergency regulations. Aggrieved producers outside metropolitan zones lacking quotas, however, were critical of the co-operative arguing that technological and transport improvements made the regulated system redundant. A perception arose that Dairy Farmers had become complacent, was not matching farmer productivity improvements and was infested with 'dry' shareholders. Nevertheless, with Victorian suppliers knocking on the door of Sydney markets, everyone in the industry understood that if Dairy Farmers were wrenched from farmer hands as dairying was deregulated, New South Wales farmers would be in jeopardy. With 'milk wars' continuing within and between states, New South Wales co-operatives failed to unite and rationalise sufficiently to match Victorian efficiencies. Certainly, as more co-operatives fell to corporate raiders, Dairy Farmers sought to join with other co-operatives but the process was slow and expensive with members generally unwilling to fund this.

Utilising active-member provisions introduced into the *Co-operation Act* in 1987, Dairy Farmers fended off a corporate raid, resolving to pay out 'dry' shareholders. Their expulsion, however, meant that new ways of attracting and retaining capital needed urgently to be found, consistent with co-operative principles. Further debt was not an option. In this context, an integral relationship existed between the co-operative's survival and an enhanced fund-raising capacity.

After Dairy Farmers merged with Hunter Valley and Shoalhaven co-operatives in 1989 to form ACF, the co-operative launched an ambitious mergers and acquisitions programme and was hungry for capital. Even so, essential industry-wide rationalisation could not be achieved. ACF Chairman Ian Langdon therefore argued that the co-operative must grow strongly and independently while being restructured to bring member equity and the democracy principle into equilibrium. In 1993 members approved a compulsory bonus-share scheme. Now more adequately capitalised, ACF launched an ambitious expansionary programme in the countdown to deregulation.

Dairy Farmers and 'dry' shareholders

Some New South Wales dairy co-operatives tended to look down on Victorian counterparts as 'quasi' co-operatives; 'impure' co-operative companies registered under the Companies Code. For their part, Rochdale purists, such as New South Wales Co-operative Wholesale Society (NSW CWS) President and state Labor MP George Booth, were disdainful of some New South Wales farmer co-operatives, especially Dairy Farmers, which for years had resisted efforts by NSW CWS to sell fresh milk in metropolitan markets. Booth railed in parliament against Dairy Farmers as 'bogus' and undemocratic for using a weighted voting system, which, he said, gave control of the co-operative to non-producers and city interests. Dairy Farmers, he charged, was 'sucking the life blood' from both producers and consumers by exploiting the regulated marketing system.

The Australian Taxation Office (ATO) was also of the view that Dairy Farmers was not a 'mutual' organisation for purposes of the act. Most of the co-operative's 5,952 (post-war) share-holders, who held a majority of the co-operative's £473,000 share capital, the ATO claimed, were not suppliers, meaning that the co-operative failed to satisfy the mutuality test for purposes of Division 9 of the act (90 per cent of business done with members, discussed in Appendix One). The ATO said that unless the co-operative took immediate steps to correct the situation it would be facing a massive taxation pay-out as debentures, mostly held by 'dry' shareholders, matured. It is not known how the co-operative dealt with this.

Meanwhile, producers in dairying areas excluded from metropolitan fresh-milk markets complained that the co-operative was a Sydney-centric organisation of little benefit to them or the industry. When a New South Wales Labor government sought to extend metropolitan milk-supply zones to include the Hunter Valley and Illawarra districts, in order to pool the fresh-milk supply and share the market equitably at fixed prices, Dairy Farmers' parliamentary friends objected, arguing that 'one big co-operative' was preferable, with sufficient market power to manage liquid and manufactured milk markets equitably. But how to achieve this?[1]

The Co-operative Dairy Association of New South Wales Limited

Nothing came of the 'one big co-operative' proposal for the usual reason that dairy co-operatives could not co-operate. In 1947, however, the Co-operative Dairy Association of New South Wales Limited (CDA) was formed, designed to represent the dairy co-operative movement to state government, seek improved representation on the Commonwealth Dairy Produce Equalisation Committee and the Australian Dairy Produce Board and work for the general advancement of the dairy industry through the co-operative movement. Privately, it was understood that CDA existed to resist 'foreign' (interstate) takeovers of New South Wales' co-operatives and to join battle for the Canberra fresh-milk market, targeted by Victorian producers and the Far (New South Wales) South Coast Co-operative Factories Association, centred on the Bega Co-operative. The CDA was divided into twelve zones with one nominee from each zone represented on the board, including the general managers of Norco, the Producers' Distributive Society (PDS) and Dairy Farmers.[2]

Friction over regulation

In 1950 Dairy Farmers took over the Albury District Rural Co-operative on the New South Wales-Victorian border and began selling Victorian milk from co-operative factories at Eskdale and Tallangatta into New South Wales metropolitan zones. This was a controversial move with many Dairy Farmers' members protesting that the co-operative was 'selling out' co-operative principles. Dairy Farmers' executives replied that the move had been necessary to head off Bega Co-operative's designs on the Canberra market, then the only free (unregulated) market for fresh milk in Australia. Dairy Farmers opened a bottling plant in Griffith, in the state's south west, to supply Canberra and the Monaro region and began shipping in milk from Norco (then numerically the largest New South Wales dairy co-operative with 10,012 members).

Quite apart from underlining a lack of co-operation between co-operatives and highlighting that Dairy Farmers' suppliers could not reliably meet seasonal supply shortages, the new arrangements demonstrated that transport improvements really had rendered the regulated zonal system redundant. Those aggrieved producers who sought an easing of supply zone regulations were disappointed, however, when the New South Wales Milk Board introduced new quotas in 1955, seeking to overcome seasonal shortages, allocating them exclusively to farmers in established milk zones and cutting out non-zone suppliers without warning or compensation. As the gap in prices paid to fresh and manufactured milk suppliers widened; with the former significantly better off; bitter disagreements began between producers in zone and non-zone areas, which continued for years. When the Cahill Labor Government attempted to allow fresh milk from outside milk zones to enter metropolitan markets, it met stout resistance in parliament and backed down.

'Dries' attempt to take over Dairy Farmers

In 1960 rumours circulated that Dairy Farmers was about to be taken over by proprietors (including Peter's Ice Cream). At that time thirty per cent of the co-operative's shareholders were 'dry', 25 per cent of suppliers were not members and only 45 per cent of shareholders were active producers. Rumours were circulating that 'dry' shareholders had stacked the Dairy Farmers' board in order to orchestrate takeover offers and 'let shares find their true market value' (impossible under the *Co-operation Act*). Some shareholders wished to trade shares, lodging them as bank securities or leaving them to family members on retirement. Others accused the board of secretive and underhand behaviour, claiming that directors' primary aim 'seemed to be to build from the farmers' money a colossus of wealth in which the farmer is not permitted to share and about which he is given the minimum of information'. The Dairy Farmers' board came under sustained attack in the press, with allegations resurfacing that the co-operative was a 'bogus' organisation denying shareholders free choice. Some reports described co-operatives as 'pampered' and a 'cost of living' issue. Members were deeply divided between those seeking access to the co-operative's asset wealth and those demanding that it continue to provide traditional farmer services, fearing that Dairy Farmers falling into proprietary hands would see a return to market chaos.

A formal takeover bid was made in March 1961 by a consortium of Sydney corporate heavyweights, including W J Smith, Frank Packer, the D Macarthur-Onslow family, Randolph B Carpenter and C W Neill. The co-operative's own solicitor was involved in the bid, which involved cash for shares and shares in a new proprietary company. The proponents argued that co-operative structure was obsolete, that the Milk Board was the true guardian of producers' interests and had rendered co-operation irrelevant. The consortium formed a holding company to list Dairy Farmers on the Sydney Stock Exchange. The city press supported the bid, saying that a joint-stock company was as 'good as a co-operative [because it is] developed to pool the resources of the many for the benefit of the many'.

Minister for Co-operatives Abe Landa and Registrar of Co-operatives A R Crosky rushed to assist Dairy Farmers, believing that the proposed takeover threatened the New South Wales milk industry and milk supply. They saw to hurried amendments to the *Co-operation Act* giving co-operatives greater commercial freedom in respect of issuing bonus shares on a voluntary basis and protection from hostile takeover, including:

- ❖ limited share holding per member;
- ❖ limited dividends on share capital;
- ❖ proxy voting;
- ❖ non-supplier votes on issues other than special resolutions seeking the termination of a rural society or its co-operative structure;
- ❖ 75 per cent approval vote by active members with ministerial approval acting on Co-operative Advisory Council recommendation for any proposal to sell a co-operative or terminate its co-operative status; and
- ❖ the ability to re-value assets and distribute bonus shares if agreed to by co-operative members.

Predictably, Rochdale consumer movement purists were opposed, arguing that the amendments made a mockery of co-operative principles, particularly those permitting weighted voting and 'classes' of shares. From retirement, former Registrar Alf Sheldon observed that the 'limited interest on share-capital [co-operative] principle is definitely abrogated'. Many suppliers were also opposed, wanting cash in hand, not locked up in 'co-operative aggrandisement' and believing there were serious taxation implications in the new arrangements. The amendments had the desired effect, however, and the takeover bid failed. The question of 'dry' shareholders gaining control by stealth, however, remained unanswered, particularly as farmer shareholders were reluctant to support the co-operative voluntarily through the device of bonus shares.[3]

The Co-operative Federation of New South Wales

Intense discussions between New South Wales co-operatives proceeded over the next few years seeking solutions to the dual challenges of 'foreigners' invading markets and raids by 'dry' shareholders. These talks occurred against the background of moves to create a new state in the north of New South Wales, which was only narrowly averted in part because of farmer opposition in Newcastle and Hunter Valley dairy districts, who were fearful of losing access to Sydney fresh-milk markets. Dairy Farmers unsuccessfully sought a merger with Norco, negotiations foundering on the latter's demand for a portion of metropolitan milk-zones and Dairy Farmers' refusal of this.

The Co-operative Federation of New South Wales (CFNSW), however, emerged from these meetings through 1966 and 1967, however, establishing a forum for debate on such matters as protecting co-operatives from takeover, achieving equity in the distribution of accrued co-operative assets, capital raising, and, in particular, meeting Victorian competition, which many farmers were now convinced threatened to destroy the New South Wales dairy industry (also discussed in Chapter Eight).

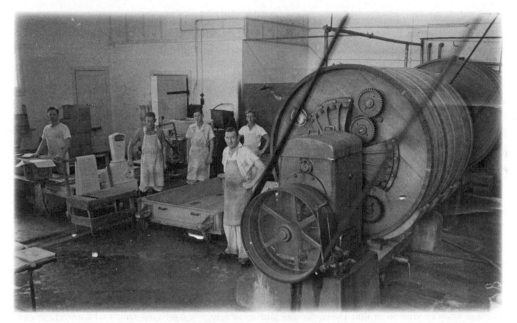

Cheese making (date unknown).
Photo courtesy of Bega Co-operative Society Limited.

'Milk Wars'

The dairy industry remained as split as ever on the issue of quotas and zones. With the press complaining about so-called 'pampered' dairy producers and the high cost of milk in Sydney, in 1970 the Askin Coalition Government passed the *Dairy Industry Authority Act* seeking to revitalise the industry and end the milk-zone 'war'. The act granted some quotas to producers outside established zones but did little to help north coast and remote area farmers. The Norco and Bega co-operatives were furious to have been left out and challenged the act's constitutionality. In October 1970 the High Court ruled that the act was indeed unconstitutional (Section 92, Free Trade). Immediately, Jewell Food Stores announced plans to place generic brand Victorian milk on New South Wales supermarket shelves. Milk-zone producers successfully challenged the retail chain in the courts and the 'southern invasion' was again postponed.

Now the attack came from northern New South Wales. Norco saw to the formation of a Dairy Farmers' Action Group early in 1976, pointing to the high prices of Sydney milk and arguing that this was because productive farmers were being denied equal opportunity. Another 'milk war' began with tankers hauling north coast milk into metropolitan markets. The press extensively covered the issue, alleging that prominent parliamentarians held milk-quotas and that co-operatives were 'a waste of taxpayer money', delivering only high prices benefiting powerful sectional interest groups. Labor Opposition Leader Neville Wran picked up the issue in the approach to an election, demanded an inquiry and used this to drive divisions in government ranks. Wran won the election in May 1976 with a narrow majority, delivered to him in part by 'milk war' issues.[4]

The new government immediately dismantled the *Dairy Industry Authority Act*, abolished geographic boundaries and introduced an equitable share of the liquid milk market for all producers. The established pricing and quota system stayed in place however; only geographical barriers were removed. With the dairy industry in decline on the north coast (85 per cent of producers leaving the industry!), remote area producers complained that the Wran formula distorted markets and was actually more favourable to *Victorian* than to New South Wales producers. Irate farmers conducted noisy rallies in Sydney protesting the 'iniquitous situation'.[5]

A communication gap

It was clear by the second half of the 1970s that divisions in the co-operative dairy industry were not confined to New South Wales and Victorian co-operatives and co-operatives *within* states but extended to relations between members in their *own* co-operatives. With serious rationalisation at farm level proceeding in New South Wales, fewer farmers were supplying virtually the same number of processors; mainly co-operatives. Farmer rationalisation was not being matched by processor efficiency and, farmers believed, this was being reflected in declining returns. A perception arose among farmer-suppliers that co-operatives had become indolent on the back of decades of protection and guaranteed prices. Now these same co-operatives were demanding more capital from members to engage in what some saw as 'empire building'. A communication gap was opening between farmer co-operative shareholders and co-operative boards and management. Some farmers alleged that processors were manipulating the regulated system to protect inefficiencies while taking the largest cut of price increases. Others claimed that co-operatives were stifling innovation and change because they existed to exploit the *status quo* and serve largely city-based sectional interest groups. Co-operatives, they said, were slow and unresponsive and had become virtually tranquillised by years of regulation. Victorian co-operative companies, on the other hand, critics claimed, had easy access to capital and were engaged in massive rationalisation, the efficiency of which New South Wales producers could only dream of. *Farmers* were adapting to change in New South Wales – but what about their *co-operatives*? How could New South Wales co-operatives, restricted to shareholder funds, ever hope to compete? The New South Wales industry was not only physically small in comparison with the Victorian industry but years off the pace in industry modernisation and lacked the discipline and efficiency necessary to sell into highly contested foreign markets. Co-operatives must shape up or the New South Wales dairy industry would be wholly proprietorial in a few years – if it survived at all.

The whole question of co-operatives' suitability to modern business practise came into focus. PDS General Manager A W Walker, for example, speaking about his co-operative and Norco co-operating in the use of shared delivery vehicles (Marketing Co-operative Limited), questioned whether co-operatives were 'up to it' in the changing circumstances. Marketing was a *science* now, Walker said, and co-operatives had to re-examine their role, find ways to co-operate and attract sufficient capital to develop a marketing role, while retaining farmer involvement and control, or they would go out of business as co-operatives. Walker's words were prophetic, but not in the way intended, for soon after, PDS, a co-operative movement icon and part of C E D Meares' old grand vision, was lost to the movement, taken over by Tooth, the brewer, following a failed merger with ACMAL (Victoria) brought on by the absence of suitable legislation allowing interstate co-operatives to merge as co-operatives.[6]

Deregulatory pressures build

With the Wran Government's mind focused on the possible political consequences of a collapse of the New South Wales dairy industry in the approach to a 1978 election, amendments to the *Co-operation Act* were confirmed permitting co-operative shareholders to access capital appreciation through bonus shares on a *voluntary* basis. While in theory this enabled co-operatives to retain capital to aid rationalisation and enhance competitiveness, it did nothing to alleviate the problem of asset-stripping, where assets were perceived to be more valuable than shareholdings, while serving to whet shareholder expectations of future wealth in the event of a co-operative demutualising or accepting a takeover bid. In fact it was a non-event for the provision was not widely used, most farmers continuing to insist co-operatives pay them dividends rather than locking up money in the organisation.[7]

At the end of the decade, most New South Wales dairy farmers, especially fresh-milk suppliers, favoured a continuation of the existing regulated system, so long as this achieved orderly marketing and regular, reasonable incomes. It was plain, though, with Britain going into Europe and domestic butter consumption declining, that the regulated system was becoming dysfunctional.

'Foreign' invaders

A 'siege' mentality gripped New South Wales fresh-milk producers supplying Dairy Farmers Co-operative when, in April 1984, after a long court battle, the New South Wales Supreme Court confirmed the legality of Jewell Food Stores bringing Victorian milk into Sydney. The supermarket was able to provide consumers with milk at nine cents a litre *less* than the regulated price! Sections of the New South Wales dairy industry saw Jewell's action as nothing less than a declaration of war. When competitor supermarkets threatened to go to Victoria for cheaper milk, the long-established 'gentlemen's agreement' confining fresh-milk supply to state boundaries (skirting Constitutional difficulties) threatened to unravel.

Crisis meetings of New South Wales dairy industry leaders followed, seeking ways to deal with the southern invasion. A Dairy Industry Conference was formed, designed to present a unified voice to government and the public and argue the importance of a viable local industry. Seeking to remove the incentive to go to Victoria processors, Dairy Farmers offered discounts to big buyers. These were paid for by cutting vendors out of the supply loop, precipitating an angry reaction. Vendors demonstrated outside Parliament House, Sydney, demanding that the government withdraw support for the Commonwealth Government's Domestic Market Support (DMS) Scheme (discussed in Chapter Three), which protesters believed was subsidising the cross-border invasion. There were violent scenes in September when a road-blockade organised by New South Wales dairy farmers physically prevented tankers carrying Victorian milk from entering New South Wales. With Jewell suffering adverse publicity centred on a so-called betrayal of 'loyal, local producers', the supermarket withdrew Victorian milk from its shelves.

New South Wales producers had gained another reprieve, which Dairy Farmers described as a 'victory for orderly marketing'. This latest 'milk war', however, simply highlighted the increasingly untenable position of the New South Wales fresh-milk industry. Australian Dairy Industry Council (ADIC) Chairman Pat Rowley warned:

> *Unless the New South Wales and Queensland co-operatives and processors regroup behind a couple of banners, they will be run down by the purchasing power of the supermarkets and the strength of the Victorian co-operatives.*

With many New South Wales' farmers convinced they were being let down by their processors, including co-operatives, which appeared to lack the incentive to innovate and modernise, co-operative managers argued that there were too many small, inefficient co-operatives, the product of nearly a century of parochial development, and many would have to go. The industry was clearly set for a painful rationalisation.

Dairy Farmers and industry rationalisation

Dairy Farmers Managing Director Murray Mead and Deputy General Manager Don Kinnersley worked assiduously to bring New South Wales processors together under the Sydney-based co-operative's banner. Through mergers and acquisitions, more co-operatives and companies were brought into the fold: Dungog (1981); Illawarra (1984); Central Western Dairy (Dubbo) (1985); and Manning Valley Co-operative (1984-1987). Rationalisation was costly. For instance, the Illawarra arrangement cost Dairy Farmers $32 for each share and the Manning Valley deal cost $5 million to top counter offers from Norco and Hunter Valley co-operatives.

Some co-operatives resented Dairy Farmers' expansionary strategy, describing it as predatory and divisive. Co-operatives at Nowra and Gerringong on the south coast would have nothing to do with it, merging to form the Shoalhaven Co-operative. The Norco and Bega co-operatives were also determined to proceed independently with Norco purchasing the Logan and Albert Co-operative in southern Queensland and courting a merger with another southern Queensland co-operative, Queensco. (Discussions foundered on the issue of where headquarters should be situated – Lismore or Brisbane.)[8]

Mead and Kinnersley argued that New South Wales co-operatives must grow 'big and strong' or they would disappear under the dual assaults of Victorian competition and corporate raiders. Western Australia and Tasmania were losing co-operatives at a rapid rate and, in the South Australian and Queensland dairy industries, co-operatives already accounted for less than 50 per cent of production. There were still twenty-two co-operatives in New South Wales – far too many and the industry needed to rationalise urgently or be swamped by 'foreigners'. New South Wales prided itself on being the most 'co-operative' state in the commonwealth and, Dairy Farmers leaders said, that 'heritage' must be protected. Indeed, executives regularly reminded suppliers that Victorian co-operatives were not 'co-operative' at all, but co-operative companies and, because of this, could not trade in New South Wales as co-operatives without serious taxation consequences. For the time being, they were locked out. Now was the time to act, Mead and Kinnersley argued, while New South Wales co-operatives still enjoyed a legislative 'firewall' and before they were picked off one by one. Already Nepean Milk Co-operative had been taken over by Dairy Farmers greatest proprietary rival, United Dairies, which paid $43 per share to 'dry' shareholders. Farmers' GRAZCOS Co-operative had been sold to proprietors after a $15.6 million offer to 'dries' had been accepted. The restructured entity, 'Panfida Foods' (1987), was preparing to list on the Australian Stock Exchange (ASX) and, Mead and Kinnersley warned, the company was eyeing Dairy Farmers' assets. How would suppliers fare in metropolitan markets if proprietors gained control, buying whatever suited them?

Don Kinnersley and the 'co-operative advantage'

After Murray Mead died in 1986 Don Kinnersley became Dairy Farmers Managing Director. The former industrial chemist took the helm at a crucial moment in the co-operative's history. The issue was nothing less than survival. With producers leaving the industry in droves, 'dry' shareholders covetously contemplated the co-operative's assets. Kinnersley knew all too well that 'dries' were a real risk to the retention of producer-control – yet he desperately needed their capital. Without capital, Dairy Farmers had no chance of expanding on the scale required to achieve efficiencies and keep raiders – Victorian competitors and corporate asset-strippers – at bay. It was risky leaving 'dries' on the shareholder register but equally risky to pay them out. The co-operative needed to find new ways of securing capital *consistent* with co-operative principles. If Dairy Farmers were to survive as a farmer-controlled co-operative, greater volumes of capital must be accessed, the deregulatory process needed to be 'managed' to the degree this was politically achievable and the co-operative's structure needed to be adjusted to lift profitability – all this while retaining farmer confidence and staying true to co-operative principles. Such an agenda was only achievable through legislative reform and that would not be straightforward. Kinnersley believed that securing member support for the upheaval Dairy Farmers needed to pass through to remain competitive was as much about changing *attitudes* and raising *expectations* as it was about continuing to do what the co-operative had always done – paying suppliers best prices and keeping costs low. Most farmers simply wanted to farm and expected only the highest prices and best services possible from their co-operative. In a looming deregulatory climate, however, a co-operative might not be able to be everything all of its members expected. Nevertheless, a co-operative did have something to offer farmers which proprietors could not match– democratic control of the business – the 'co-operative advantage'. Kinnersley launched the co-operative into a period of enormous change.

Enter Ian Langdon

In seeking a 'lightning rod', one with the intellect, quicksilver skills and energy necessary to reshape his co-operative's fortunes, Kinnersley's attention was drawn to a dynamic academic accountant who had been engaged by the Queensland Minister for Primary Industry to prepare a discussion paper on the rationalisation of the dairy industry in that state – Ian Thomas Langdon. Born in Melbourne, Langdon was a specialist financial and business-administration expert, then Dean of Business Studies at the Gold Coast College of Advanced Education (later Griffith University). A strategic thinker of immense drive and determination, Langdon was precisely the attitudinal 'circuit breaker' Kinnersley sought, capable of pushing aside the sentiment of past decades and driving the co-operative forward into a new, competitive world.[9]

Langdon showed his mettle in August 1987 when addressing a disgruntled audience of dairy farmers at Warwick, where he argued the need to rationalise Queensland co-operatives into a single entity. To a barrage of questions from irate and confused farmers worried about a loss of local autonomy and possible taxation implications, Langdon replied that traditional co-operatives would fail in any event if they did not radically restructure and that a new generation of co-operatives was needed, capable of flexible fund-raising. It was imperative, Langdon stressed, that co-operatives redefine the notion of *returns* and not limit this simply to dividends on *supply*, if farmers were to retain control and not be at the mercy of markets. Capital was needed and capital must have its rewards. Moreover, the accountant said, there was only limited value in having a co-operative sector at *all*, if it were not strong and competitive.[10]

In December 1987 six large New South Wales dairy co-operatives (Dairy Farmers, Hunter Valley, Shoalhaven, Norco, Bega and Hastings) engaged Langdon to analyse the benefits of 'one big co-operative' in that state and to make recommendations on timing, mergers and possible new structures for a fresh start to the industry, consistent with a commitment to co-operative principles. The consultant prepared a sweeping review of the New South Wales industry noting significant factory over-capacity and a need for draconian rationalisation.

The Centre for Co-operative Studies in Agriculture

The Victorian dairy industry also engaged Langdon's services and, through his consultancy and research expertise, Langdon quickly located a key role in national debates on co-operative structure and co-operative development. Aided by a $1 million grant from the Commonwealth Department of Primary Industry and Energy (DOPIE) Marketing Skills Programme, which had the dairy industry as a prime target, Langdon established the Centre for Co-operative Studies in Agriculture (CASGU) at the Gold Coast College of Griffith University. Before it was closed down in 1993,

CASGU provided an influential co-operative finance and business administration service for the Australian Agricultural Council, publishing extensively on the role of co-operatives in promoting agriculture.[11]

Active member provisions

Meanwhile, in October 1987, New South Wales Minister for Co-operatives Frank Walker moved to head off further 'dry' shareholders takeovers of co-operatives. Accepting the advice of dynamic CFNSW Manager Bruce Freeman, a former GRAZCOS Co-operative employee, the minister introduced active member amendments to the *Co-operation Act*, the effect of which meant that shareholders who had not supplied a co-operative for a period of two years would have their shares *compulsorily* redeemed at par value. Further, it was confirmed that a co-operative could not be sold to outsiders without the approval of 75 per cent of active members.

Dairy Farmers' official historian, Jan Todd, noted:

> *Dairy Farmers was ambivalent about the...changes. In theory it was fine to suggest that the company should be totally controlled by suppliers...In practice there was the thorny issue of capital and the loyalty and sentiment of the old-timers. Many of those who were now dries had once been the life-blood of the company and this was a heritage not lightly overthrown.*

Dairy Farmers proposed an alternative scheme involving the introduction of *two* classes of shares: voting shares for active members; and non-voting shares for inactive members. The idea of shareholder 'classes' was contentious in the co-operative movement, however, where many believed this would see a 'watering down' of the democracy principle and it would only be a matter of time before non-voting shareholders demanded more rights. Bruce Freeman and the Australian Association of Co-operatives (AAC) (which had recently replaced CFNSW, discussed in Chapter Twelve) were strongly opposed.

The government proceeded with the active member provisions, which tested Dairy Farmers' capital position and created much discontent among shareholders. Co-operatives in the Shoalhaven, Nowra and Jamberoo districts, and Bega and Norco co-operatives, for example, had been buying up 'dry' shares in Dairy Farmers since the 1950s and were now major shareholders in the co-operative. There was no love lost for Dairy Farmers in sections of the New South Wales co-operative dairy industry but real concern about the impact of a proprietary company gaining control of its metropolitan markets as deregulation approached.

The press followed the situation closely. The *Sydney Morning Herald* charged that Dairy Farmers was not a 'traditional' co-operative because, first, it did not directly transact with members, since all New South Wales milk was vested in the Dairy Corporation and, secondly, because 5,450 of its 8,100 shareholders, that is approximately 80 per cent, were 'dry'. The *Herald* argued that the co-operative delivered no benefits to consumers that private competitors could not provide and that New South Wales consumers were paying too much for milk, when Victorian producers were ready and willing to supply cheaper milk, resisted tooth and nail by Dairy Farmers. The regulated system of fresh-milk supply was costing New South Wales' consumers $1.4 million a week, the *Herald* alleged, and Dairy Farmers' 'dry' shareholders were the chief beneficiaries.

The Panfida raid on Dairy Farmers

As Dairy Farmers prepared for the expensive business of shedding 'dry' shareholders, Panfida Foods Limited watched and waited. Through a subsidiary, Bodalla Company Limited, which was a major Dairy Farmers' shareholder but which supplied little milk to the co-operative, the company offered

$5 a share to mainly 'dry' shareholders, who were holding 124,500 shares at par $2 value. The offer was below Dairy Farmers' asset value but attractive to many retired farmers and those planning to leave the industry. Panfida mounted a media campaign describing the bid as a 'mission of justice' to save co-operatives from their own inadequacies as 'irrelevant business entities'.

Some Dairy Farmers supplier-members supported the bid arguing that the co-operative was inefficient, had neglected valuable export markets, squandered opportunities for value-adding, was not commercially-driven and that productive producers were being penalised by the co-operative's conservative 'old boys' network. Some offered shares to Panfida. On the other hand, many 'dry' shareholders remained loyal to co-operative principles and refused the offer (at the price being offered). In a show of pragmatic support, Bega Co-operative offered $5 a share for 620,000 shares in Dairy Farmers, urging other co-operatives to rally behind the movement and to do the same. There was an element of co-operative solidarity in this but it appears the offer had as much to do with access to Sydney markets as altruism.

To further complicate the issue the New South Wales Dairy Farmers' Association was again calling for a *single* New South Wales dairy co-operative; one big society; requesting the government to assist by allowing the industry a 'breathing space' and to continue protection for at least twelve months, while leaders worked out a way to *reform* the regulatory system in the best interests of farmers. The alternative, association spokesmen said, was possibly the wholesale destruction of the state's co-operative dairy industry.

New Labor Minister for Co-operatives Bob Debus, Dairy Farmers Managing Director Don Kinnersley and the AAC's Bruce Freeman worked closely to fend off the Panfida raid, seeking high level corporate financial and administrative advice. The minister agreed to the Dairy Farmers' Association request for a 'breathing space' on deregulation but insisted that active member provisions be proceeded with and that the New South Wales dairy industry take all steps necessary to expedite deregulation, once the Panfida crisis was over.

Dairy Farmers Co-operative convened a Co-operatives' Conference in February 1988, a 'rallying of the clan'. Here, leaders called for a united front in a two-pronged battle with corporate raiders and southern invaders noting that Norco and Bega co-operatives were also resisting Panfida overtures, with company agents cruising co-operative supply areas urging shareholders to join the bids, wooing them with promises of access to metropolitan fresh-milk markets.

Bodalla then made a counter bid to the Bega offer, offering $5 for 50 per cent of Dairy Farmers' shares. A third of the co-operative's shareholders supported the bid!

In March a Dairy Farmers Special General Meeting in Newcastle agreed to accept into the rules the *Co-operation Act's* active membership provisions, effectively disenfranchising 'dry' shareholders. The meeting also directed the co-operative to redeem shares at par value of $2. The die was cast. In order to fend off Panfida and preserve the democracy principle (farmer control), Dairy Farmers was prepared to alienate a major source of capital and much 'heritage' support.

Panfida appealed to the courts, unsuccessfully. In April the co-operative's Special General Meeting decision was ratified. A long-running court battle ensued in which Bodalla sought a court order to prevent the forfeiture of Dairy Farmers' shares. Bodalla also appealed to the new Greiner Coalition Government Minister for Co-operatives Gerald (Gerry) Peacocke, a National Party member for Dubbo in the state's central west. Bodalla officials told Peacocke that private enterprise could do a better job in the New South Wales dairy industry than co-operatives, a view with which many of the minister's cabinet colleagues agreed.

Peacocke stayed action for twenty-eight days while Bodalla sought a legal remedy to the share pay-out. 'Dry' shareholders organised noisy rallies outside Parliament House demanding that the Bodalla bid be accepted and attacking Dairy Farmers' 'forced acquisition', which they said discriminated against an 'oppressed minority'. Active member amendments to the act, they said, were 'unfair, un-Australian and undemocratic', a 'kick in the teeth' for years of loyal support. Bodalla argued that shareholders should have access to the full market value of shares and sought an independent inquiry to establish if 'dry' shares could be maintained as a permanent class of non-voting share.

With the media speculating on the relative merits of private-profit business and co-operatives, AAC placed full-page advertisements in newspapers defending active-member provisions, which, the association said, would help protect the assets, benefits, diversity and importance of co-operatives, which so 'enriched the lives of six million Australians'. The association also attacked the idea of non-voting shares, which were 'not in the spirit of co-operation since co-operative shares did not exist for capital gain'.

Caught in this cross-fire, the minister directed the Registry of Co-operatives to investigate the merits or otherwise of different classes of shares in co-operatives. A registry representative took a seat on the Dairy Farmers' board, heralding a closer relationship between the minister, his department and the co-operative.[12]

Dismissing Bodalla's request for a special inquiry, the minister retained active member provisions with only one class of share relating to business done with a co-operative, but introduced amendments permitting 'dry' shareholder access to capital gains from the sale of co-operative assets for *three* years after becoming inactive (not the two years argued by AAC, or five years sought by some). Other amendments were hurried through parliament allowing Norco to proceed with merger talks with Queensco in Queensland. The minister also promised a fundamental review of the *Co-operation Act* with a view to completely redrafting the legislation (discussed in Chapter Nine).[13]

Following further litigation, in April 1989 Dairy Farmers reached a confidential out-of-court settlement with Panfida Foods Limited. The court found that, while it was true that Bodalla was a major shareholder, the company supplied only 4 per cent of the milk which Dairy Farmers processed and therefore under the act's patronage principle (dividends proportionate with business done), Bodalla wielded only a very minor influence.

Bodalla was expelled from Dairy Farmers. Panfida sold the company and left the fresh-milk field. Dairy Farmers' Historian Jan Todd reports:

The victory of the Dairy Farmers Co-operative was a victory for the co-operative system of country supply to the city. Therefore, the message inherent in that victory said that no one should ever underestimate farmer power when rallying to protect the co-operative structure that had been evolving since the struggles at the beginning of the century.

The Dairy Co-operatives' Association

Business analysts continued to highlight an alleged lack of commercial and marketing expertise among co-operatives, claiming they were conservative and lacked the drive to enter new markets. Forecasting the wholesale collapse of the New South Wales dairying industry, analysts alleged that farmer supply co-operatives had become apathetic, simply producing milk for consumption in cosseted markets with no more economic significance than that. Co-operatives were superfluous in modern markets and holding back progress on deregulation.

Stung by such criticisms, in July 1988 twenty-two New South Wales dairy co-operatives convened the 'Dairy Co-operatives' Association' (perhaps the 'Co-operative Dairy Association', formed in 1947, renamed) to consider further rationalisation of the industry. Ian Langdon addressed the association, arguing against any government-driven model in facing the dual threats of Victorian competition and deregulation. Farmers should drive the political agenda, Langdon believed, apprised of all the facts and, when a way forward had been determined, move swiftly and decisively. Whatever the future of the industry, or pace of change, there would be *pain*, with closures and the enforced alteration of old habits and attitudes. A single, combined co-operative was probably the best way of meeting competition while ensuring farmer control, but this almost certainly would be confounded by parochialism and vested interests. The association was greatly impressed – and chastened – by Langdon's candour and clarity of vision, commissioning him to investigate further the New South Wales co-operative dairy industry, especially capital-raising and how to achieve economies of scale.

The AAC and Dairy Farmers

Jan Todd tells us that AAC was 'no real friend of Dairy Farmers'. What does she mean? No friend of dairy farmers in general or Dairy Farmers Co-operative, in particular? There seems little doubt that the act's active member provisions for which AAC had so strenuously fought, reinforced farmer control of co-operatives and probably saved Dairy Farmers from the Panfida raid. This surely cannot be what Todd is referring to. Certainly many of Dairy Farmers' 'dry' shareholders resented AAC's opposition to non-voting shares and its efforts to confine to two years an entitlement to a share of a co-operative's assets in the event of it being wound up or corporatised. Indeed, AAC repeatedly warned farmers that 'takeover strategists', such as Doug Shears' ICM Group, which was attempting to take over the Victorian superphosphate co-operative company, PIVOT, and the Victorian Producers' Co-operative, were orchestrating a media campaign to appear to be genuinely interested in farmer welfare and their co-operatives while simultaneously portraying co-operatives as 'outdated anachronisms' and gradually eroding confidence in them. The AAC had no quarrel with the idea that co-operative structure should be improved but was adamant that this should not occur at the expense of co-operative philosophy and rejected any idea that co-operatives were old-fashioned relics, pointing to statistics indicating that more private enterprises were failing than co-operatives. The New South Wales *Co-operation Act* could also be improved; of that there was no doubt, the AAC believed; and fund-raising for co-operatives made more flexible, but not to the extent of allowing external investors into a co-operative's governance machinery, as some consultants were now advising.

Above all, AAC was opposed to any capitalisation scheme carrying a co-operative towards an investor-orientated model by adapting 'more flexible' capital-raising options while discarding traditional co-operative principles. The association believed that an answer to a so-called 'co-operative dilemma' (adequate capitalisation *versus* continued democratic control) was *not* accessing external investments, but greater *co-operation between co-operatives* facilitated by federal or nationally uniform co-operatives' legislation. The AAC was convinced that existing state-based legislation fragmented the co-operative movement and complicated the operations of individual co-operatives. Ideally, AAC Executive Director Bruce Freeman argued, the co-operative movement should have a minister in each state with the Commonwealth Government ultimately responsible for co-operatives. The Federal Labor Minister for Primary Industry and Energy John Kerin agreed, repeatedly arguing that the absence of uniform national co-operatives' legislation was impeding the co-operative movement's development and hampering the process of co-operatives adapting at a national level to nationally-focused industry restructuring (also discussed in Chapters Eight, Twelve and Fourteen).[14]

Dairy Farmers also sought improved legislation and appears not to have been averse to uniform national legislation, in so far as this served the co-operative's strategic goals, but disagreed with AAC as to the *content* and *timing* of this. It was obvious at a Canberra AAC National Seminar of Co-operative Development in October 1988 that Dairy Farmers' (now) chief adviser Ian Langdon was at odds with AAC on several fronts. With characteristic boldness he confronted the assembly:

> *My views are definitely inconsistent with the association. The co-operative movement must pull its head out of the sand and become far more commercially-orientated. If we are not careful in another decade...the room will only be half full because there will be only half the number of co-operatives.*
>
> *Perhaps it's time that the co-operative movement did become more assertive and started to look at buying the farm, started looking at buying into the proprietary company. Why should it be all one way? What's wrong with the co-operatives buying back into some of those public companies that have been making inroads into them? Why on earth do you think the public companies are wanting to buy into co-operatives...?*
>
> *I hold a number of opinions which seem to be in conflict with the co-operative principles. Let me say that you won't find anywhere an individual who believes more strongly in the right of co-operatives to exist, to expand the right of the farming communities and other members of co-operatives to have their finger in all the profits earned, all the way down the line, with the production, collection, processing and marketing of their products...I am a true believer in the strength and potential of the co-operative movement [but] co-operatives will not survive unless they rationalise and rid themselves of inefficient practices.*
>
> *Co-operatives don't have access to external paid-up capital. They are not permitted to be floated on stock exchanges and that is correct and I believe that should be maintained.*

Ridding co-operatives of 'dry' shareholders was essential, Landon continued, but this obviously placed a strain on co-operatives' capital. By way of adapting, therefore, co-operatives would need to *retain* profits for development and issue bonus shares or debentures to reflect the true asset value of a co-operative. How else could co-operatives access capital and retain control? Capital had to come from the *producers* and, with regard to this, Langdon continued, the 'limited return on shares, if any' co-operative principle was obsolete. There should be a fair return on shares. How could a co-operative attract sufficient capital otherwise? Co-operatives were vulnerable to takeover because they had been lulled into a false sense of security by years of doling out dividends to shareholders in deference to taxation concessions rather than finding ways of retaining capital for growth and positioning themselves strategically in rapidly changing markets. Co-operatives must plan ahead carefully, take a long-term view and act definitively in 'one big step'. Langdon was convinced: everything necessary to their survival involved co-operatives in improved fund-raising activities. Dairy Farmers, he said, had no intention of going out of business as some commentators were predicting. On the contrary, it was planning a major expansionary phase designed to protect markets from 'foreign' invaders and if that meant adapting hallowed co-operative principles, so be it.[15]

The Langdon Report

Ian Langdon's report for the Dairy Co-operatives' Association, investigating the New South Wales co-operative dairy industry with regard to capital-raising and achieving economies of scale, detailed big savings *if* a rigorous schedule of rationalisation extending to the industry's peak bodies could be achieved. The consultant detailed a possible programme of accelerated mergers while emphasising that economic *performance* was more important than a 'mega co-operative', *per se*. Even if some co-operatives were not interested in merging, for example Norco and Bega, substantial savings could still be realised if the Dairy Farmers, Hunter Valley and Shoalhaven co-operatives merged.

The Dairy Co-operatives' Association then asked Langdon to devise a scheme whereby a merged entity could attract and retain the necessary capital (as 'dries' were paid out) while ensuring producer control 'in perpetuity' The consultant was also asked to make recommendations on a possible representative base for the new entity, the removal of inefficiencies and duplication, the introduction of improved business methods and ways of achieving an on-going rationalisation of the dairy co-operatives' sector in preparation for deregulation.

Australian Co-operative Foods

In July 1989 Ian Langdon was appointed head of a joint committee with references from Dairy Farmers, the Shoalhaven Co-operative and the Hunter Valley Co-operative, briefed to supervise their merger. Langdon was interviewed about his possible interest in becoming independent chairman of the merged entity. He agreed, demanding absolute authority, direct communication with shareholders and government and the appointment of Don Kinnersley as executive officer. These terms were agreed.

In December, following a lengthy process to achieve 75 per cent member approval, the Dairy Farmers, Hunter Valley and Shoalhaven co-operatives agreed to merge and form Australian Co-operative Foods (ACF). The Hunter Valley and Shoalhaven co-operatives transferred their net assets and business to Dairy Farmers. Care was taken not to mention 'Dairy Farmers' in the title. Describing itself as a 'lean and hungry' organisation, the merged co-operative's mission was to achieve leadership in core markets in the approach to deregulation, remove inefficiencies and be competitive – summarised by some directors as 'survival at all costs'. The chair and deputy chair of each co-operative moved onto the new board.

The Bega Co-operative supported the ACF merger but opted to stay out, purchasing instead a 10 per cent shareholding of the Sydney-based United Dairies and, in so doing, gaining access to 30 per cent of the regulated Sydney fresh-milk market in the expanding western suburbs. Norco continued talks with Queensco. The Dairy Farmers' Association was disappointed that not all of the state's dairy co-operatives had united and reiterated the need for a strong co-operative structure or 'private enterprise will rule the roost'.

Redeeming 'dry' shares

The first challenge ACF faced was the awkward, expensive and painful business of redeeming 'dry' shareholders' shares. It did so with a business-like adroitness, redeeming shares at $2 par value and paying no interest on 'dry' investments for fifteen months, at a time when interest rates were very high. The process was costly, slashing the merged entity's total issued share capital from 3,824,842 shares held by many thousands of share holders to 1,108,049 shares held by 2,336 shareholders. And this was just the beginning![16]

Mergers, acquisitions and an urgent need for capital

Commanding 21 per cent of the Australian fresh-milk market and 59 per cent of the Sydney market, ACF in 1991 was the largest market-milk co-operative in Australia. Major local and interstate fresh-milk competitors included: United Dairies (25 per cent of New South Wales); National Foods (65 per cent of South Australia; 45 per cent of Victoria; and 75 per cent of Tasmania); Associated Dairies (Victoria); and QUF (Paul's) (14 per cent of the national market; 49 per cent of Queensland; and 17 per cent of Victoria).

A seemingly endless process of mergers and acquisitions was under way in preparation for the expected deregulation of the industry, with processors, including ACF, jockeying for position. Of the many co-operatives still operating in the New South Wales industry ACF was most rapidly effecting change, rationalising plant and taking an aggressive approach to alliances, mergers and acquisitions. The fact was, however, the co-operative simply lacked capital to match its expansionary programme. The strategic game was very costly, particularly where a change of ownership of more than 50 per cent was involved, attracting capital gains tax, stamp duties, other government charges and professional fees.

Dairy Farmers and United Dairies submitted a joint tender for Midland Milk, a Victorian company which was leading the push for southern milk into New South Wales, but were trumped in this by the Victorian co-operative company, Bonlac, which maintained supply to Sydney supermarkets. Now, with sales of New South Wales milk declining in metropolitan areas, Victorian Sandhurst Dairies announced plans to enter the Sydney fresh-milk market in association with the major retail chain, Coles-Myer, offering cheap milk as a 'loss leader' to lure customers into stores. In 1992 ACF explored a joint venture with Bonlac for the purchase of Sandhurst but, lacking funds, was beaten by Paul's. ACF, Murray-Goulburn Co-operative and Bonlac explored a possible merger but talks stalled on 'milk war' issues and old enmities. ACF nevertheless did purchase from Murray-Goulburn a parcel of shares in Associated Dairies by way of a strategic positioning ploy, precipitating a reaction from some members about possible taxation implications and the appropriateness of co-operatives buying shares in public companies. Rumours circulated that ACF was about to make a counter bid to National Foods for United Dairies but again, the co-operative could not afford this and there were trades practices difficulties. The Bega and Norco co-operatives also made an offer for United Dairies but were trounced by National Foods, which now controlled 30 per cent of the Sydney market and became Australia's largest market-milk processor. The co-operatives were losing ground.

The New South Wales Dairy Farmers' Association warned that if co-operatives north of the Victorian border, from 'Cairns to Bega,' did not get together and merge, the dairy industry north of the Murray River would simply lack the commercial viability to cope with deregulation.[17]

Australian Premium Foods

Ian Langdon's early efforts to encourage co-operation between interstate dairy co-operatives in exports, cross-border mergers and broader collaboration were largely thwarted, but the campaign continued. Through 1991 and 1992 ACF and four other co-operatives (South Coast and West Co-operative Dairy Association [Gold Coast, Queensland]; the Atherton Tablelands Co-operative Dairy Association; Dairy Vale Co-operative Limited [South Australia]; and Queensco-Unity Dairy Foods Co-operative Association [South East Queensland]) formed Australian Premium Foods (APF) Proprietary Limited. On paper APF commanded a turnover of $830 million and operated thirty-five factories in three states and two territories. The group appointed the Singapore-based

Indian Ocean Export Company to handle sales in the South-East Asian region. These promising developments, however, bogged down on equity issues dividing old and new co-operative members and APF was ineffective. ACF left first, forming its own international division in October 1992.

'Perpetual farmer control' in harnessing capital power

The unwillingness of members to adequately fund their co-operative for the modernisation and expansionary agenda Ian Langdon believed was necessary for ACF and co-operatives in general to have any chance of survival, let alone prosper, and the apparent inability of co-operatives to co-operate, frustrated the chairman and he castigated co-operators at an Agricultural Co-operative Update Conference in Queensland in September 1992. Alluding to provisions in the New South Wales Co-operatives Bill, then well advanced through parliament (discussed in Chapter Nine), the ACF Chairman told the assembly that co-operative structure as it stood was *unsuitable* for modern conditions; that the equity base of share capital and unallocated reserves was generally inadequate; that co-operative shares needed to be truly valued and investors rewarded; that the co-operative principle of limited interest on shares was a deterrent to co-operative development; and that co-operatives must take urgent steps to *link* share ownership and patronage. Essentially, Langdon was arguing for a restatement of the co-operative model, which was traditionally built on principles of voluntariness, service, democracy and the patronage principle. Langdon well understood that achieving acceptance of such reforms would require a determined effort but, the alternative to meeting the challenge of mergers and acquisitions head on, the ACF Chairman believed, was to stand by and watch co-operative markets further erode.

The ACF Board agreed that the key to solving the problem of declining market share was *accessing capital* and quickly. But farmers were already struggling to keep their businesses viable in a bad season. How could appropriate capital power be harnessed within membership? In seeking to answer this riddle directors considered how to:

❖ overcome nearly a century of 'tribalism' in one of the most emotionally-charged industries in Australia with deep local roots about which farmers felt so passionately?

❖ reconcile co-operative ideals and member expectations with modern commercial realities?

❖ adapt co-operative fund-raising methods to modern conditions?

❖ educate farmer directors to deal with complex questions of accountability, marketing and finance?

❖ redefine the nature of co-operative shares so that the *form* distribution took became irrelevant?

❖ grow individual farmer wealth equitably while retaining democratic farmer control and solidarity?

❖ persuade members to be more than 'entry-fee' passengers but long-term investors with a greater interest in the organisation than simply supply?

❖ reshape the organisation from a traditional service-orientation to a profit-driven orientation without converting it into an investor-driven entity and losing farmer control?

❖ fund growth and position the co-operative advantageously without alienating shareholders?

❖ 'manage' the deregulation process, allowing ACF sufficient time to consolidate and remain competitive?

Possible answers to every question were measured against one bedrock proposition: perpetual farmer control. Was market competitiveness in a fluid market environment really achievable while the organisation remained co-operatively structured? ACF leaders spent much of the ensuing decade finding out.[18]

Solving the 'co-operative dilemma': an investor culture

A dramatic jump in ACF profitability vindicated the direction in which Langdon and the board were moving and built confidence in the leadership's views. Pointing to a survey of 207 co-operatives completed by the Centre for Co-operative Studies in Agriculture, the ACF chairman said this indicated that *retaining profits* for future development, modernisation and dealing with corporate raiders were absolute priorities for most co-operatives preparing for deregulation. He was convinced that ACF needed to radically *restructure* if it wanted to solve the 'co-operative dilemma' and achieve capital adequacy while retaining farmer control. The co-operative would also have to re-evaluate its debt to equity gearing and fund future growth through retained earnings. There was no other way – if control mattered. The only alternative was external equity, and that was risky. The co-operative must develop a new *member investment culture* while simultaneously cultivating loyalty and developing co-operative philosophy. Members should see as part of their commitment to the co-operative the acceptance of an *additional* financial obligation strengthening the organisation's equity position by converting profits into investments and not dissipating them in dividends. Investing in ACF, Langdon argued, was as important to farmers as investing in their own *farms* because the co-operative was simply an *extension* of the farm and underpinned farm value. The chairman called upon members to *voluntarily* reinvest dividends so that their true capital power might be harnessed. Essentially, the message was that if members valued the democracy principle, they would have to *pay* for it.

The appeal for voluntary investments failed to produce the desired result. Jan Todd tells us that retirees actually took *out* more share capital from the co-operative than the appeal realised. Clearly, if ACF were to attract and retain sufficient capital to grow and meet competition in the approach to deregulation, voluntarism was not enough.

'Manage' deregulation and grow

Meanwhile a 'shaky truce' with Victorian producers in relation access to Sydney milk markets continued while governments sought ways to establish a workable national pricing formula for liquid milk *vis a vis* manufactured milk. The New South Wales Government was also preparing to reform that state's dairy industry by removing regulated pricing beyond the farm gate and abolishing all distribution zoning over two years.

In this context, Dairy Farmers' Website history tells us, ACF decided to take pre-emptive action, accusing the government of creating uncertainty in the industry and lacking long-term vision, which threatened the industry's future. In 1992 the co-operative decided to meet the Victorian milk challenge '…head on, taking action to ensure that regulation in New South Wales was kept intact while the co-operative continued upon a major internal rationalisation of production, products and distribution'. The co-operative's new Chief Executive Officer Alan Tooth, who replaced Don Kinnersley, developed a national strategic plan designed to provide a broader base for battling deregulation and creating greater product diversity, committing ACF to a plan which would see the co-operative generating half of its revenue outside New South Wales by 2000.

Remodelling co-operative structure

Ian Langdon now floated various capital-raising options with the ACF Board seeking a much *larger* capital base for the co-operative devolving on *shareholdings commensurate with milk supplied*. Capital expenditure, he reiterated, ultimately, could *only* be funded either by debt *or* new share issues. Was ACF ready for more debt? Pointing to 'New-Generation Co-operatives' (NGCs) in the United States, where an equation existed between a member's usage of a co-operative and his/her investments in it, and to the new New South Wales *Co-operatives Act* (discussed in Chapter Nine), Langdon sought *compulsory* contributions to shares in the form of revolving funds and rebates linked to business done and structured to capture more member capital over the long-term. When farmers reached the upper limit of shares permissible under the act (20 per cent), contributions would shift into a revolving capital scheme or 'Co-operative Capital Units' (CCUs), permitted by the new legislation.

The board was cool to such ideas, especially the compulsoriness, and, at the Annual General Meeting, members approved only a proposal to introduce rebates linked to supply and rejected the compulsory share plan. Most directors and members also doubted the potential of CCUs to raise much capital, which in any event would be subscribed to at discounted rates. (Indeed, Norco, which was one of the first co-operatives to use CCUs in 1994, when the co-operative sought $10 million from external investors, realised only $2 million from the float, with investors demanding a discount in exchange for curtailed voting rights.)

Langdon persisted, arguing the merits of lining up *ownership* through shares commensurate with the *supply* of milk and thereby *equating* the interests of shareholders *and* suppliers. The chairman was convinced the plan would resolve the 'co-operative dilemma', equitably reward loyalty, guard against takeover and strengthen ACF's merger position. Employing various media outlets to promote what he described as a 'survival message', Langdon observed that Australia was littered with co-operatives which had foundered because they failed to invest in capital expansion and raised questions about the capacity of co-operatives to survive – as co-operatives – in a deregulated industry. Focused wholly on large commercial co-operatives, of which ACF was one of the greatest, the chairman said the finance world was sceptical about co-operatives, seeing them as irrelevant in mainstream business, inept at fund-raising, poorly directed by amateurs. Only a few had been able to grow beyond $100 million in assets. Unless farmers matched the corporate sector's economic performance they would inevitably lose their co-operatives and 'farmer control over their own destiny'. ACF had four weaknesses, Langdon argued: a low equity base, which represented a cheap buy for a corporate raider; poor access to equity capital; dividend dissipation; and (taxation) disincentives to invest in the co-operative through the purchase of shares. Getting the 'right balance' (equilibrium) between the *value* a co-operative returned to farmers in the form of dividends and the *value* farmers could realise through shares in their co-operative was absolutely essential in breaking 'the circularity of the co-operative dilemma'.

There was no doubt, either, Langdon reiterated, that the Rochdale tradition of limited interest on co-operative shares was irrelevant in a contemporary market economy:

> *While this accorded with the original co-operative ethic that denied investment value to shares, it also denied full farmer ownership rights to the assets of their co-operative and denied the co-operative the farmer investments it was seeking...Dairy Farmers [has] managed to moderate the limited interest principle, pushing co-operative legislation over the years to increase the allowable dividends.*

The ACF Chairman saw co-operative shares as an investment, *not* an entry fee and:

...in effect an extra means to an old co-operative end to establish formal farmer ownership rights to the returns won from the product of [farmer] labour. It was this which had brought farmers together in co-operatives a century before, only now the processing and marketing [are] much more sophisticated and expensive.[19]

With the *Co-operatives Act* through parliament, but not yet promulgated, in the first quarter of 1993 Langdon, ACF Deputy Chair Philip Bruem and Chief Executive Officer Alan Tooth tirelessly toured dairy centres in New South Wales, Victoria, Queensland and South Australia seeking support for the idea of a powerful, multi-state co-operative. Wherever the officials went they spoke of the new act, noting how it gave co-operatives powers to *compulsorily* withhold dividends in the form of bonus shares linked to business done, where members approved. They spoke of the new CCU equity instrument, how the act permitted 'natural persons' including co-operatives and corporations to become members of a co-operative and how provisions for interstate links between co-operatives now existed. Langdon related how co-operatives were losing ascendancy in market milk and how 75 per cent of the market was now controlled by five companies, only one of them a co-operative. Rationalisation attending deregulation would see this reduced to three companies and, the ACF Chairman insisted, at least one must be a co-operative. Co-operatives, however, were developing more slowly than competitors and needed to embrace some of the flexibility of private enterprise without compromising co-operative principles and ideals.

In many locations ACF executives encountered scepticism, indifference, even hostility. Members of the Bega Co-operative, for example, were interested in strategic alliances with private enterprise improving access to Sydney markets and would have nothing to do with ACF's proposal for a 'mega co-operative'. Norco supported the idea of a national co-operative but disagreed with ACF as to the means of achieving this and proceeded independently, undertaking to pay out 'dries' in a 'principled' manner while pursuing trading links with Unity Dairy Foods Co-operative Association (QUD) (South Queensland). As for QUD, the board strongly disapproved of ACF's 'predatory' style and accused the latter of meddling in Queensland affairs, specifically, ACF talks with co-operative leaders on the Atherton Tableland, which had led to disagreements.

ACF members approve compulsory bonus shares

In a persuasive address to ACF Members in May 1993 Ian Langdon argued that the compulsory purchase of shares was necessary to bring the co-operative's membership structure into 'balance', so that the co-operative could compete effectively, make valid performance comparisons, relieve debt and free-up capital for growth. Security, Langdon believed, could only be achieved through commitment and that meant something *different* from traditional ideas. ACF must carve out a national presence, the chairman continued, or be systematically picked off by private enterprise. The co-operative was still a market force to be reckoned with but it must act *now* if it were to defend co-operative industry and preserve farm-gate prices while retaining co-operative principles. The voluntary system of capital-raising, demonstrably, had not worked. The ability to acquire bonus shares voluntarily had existed since 1979 but had done very little to improve the co-operative's capital position. Langdon understood that farmers preferred to invest directly in their farms but now the *Co-operatives Act* allowed for co-operatives to *compulsorily* withhold dividends for purposes of issuing bonus shares. Langdon urged members to approve a new scheme whereby they would receive *one* share (the same class as existing shares) for a *set unit* of supply. Employing such a scheme, the chairman reckoned, the average member-shareholding would grow to 100 000 one dollar shares over the next five years. Historically, the co-operative's average was less than 4 000 shares per member!

ACF members responded overwhelmingly in support of Langdon's appeal. In a postal vote, 95 per cent approved of the compulsory share acquisition plan on the basis of *volume* of milk supplied. Members also approved of ACF issuing CCUs, which were described as 'non-voting, tradable equity instruments' and which were capped at 10 per cent per individual. The thinking at this stage was to keep fund-raising wholly within the existing bond of association and did not include external investors. That would soon change.

Critics of the compulsory scheme

Not surprisingly, ACF's move to a compulsory share-acquisition scheme attracted criticism both within the co-operative and from the broader co-operative sector. Some believed that the co-operative movement had been irreversibly changed by the *Co-operatives Act* and insisted that ACF's compulsory scheme was antithetical to co-operative voluntariness. Others described the resolution as an enforced, authoritarian measure which would inevitably divide members into 'classes': new and long-term members and large-suppliers and small-suppliers; while whetting an expectation of realising upon the future value of the co-operative's assets – potentially takeover by stealth. The scheme would gradually convert the co-operative into an investor-organisation at farmer expense while promising farmers 'control in perpetuity', a promise which could not possibly be kept in deregulated markets. Describing farmer co-operatives as custodians for future generations of farmers, critics argued that the compulsory share scheme, potentially, could leave farmers in *debt* because there was no guarantee that the co-operative would be able to *redeem* shares at the appointed time. Some were also worried about CCUs for, while the issue was initially restricted to ACF Members, under the legislation ACF could *hold open the option* of offering them to non-members. Overall, critics believed, the new capital-raising scheme would cultivate an investor mentality and skew member aspirations *away* from collective solidarity and *towards* self-interest. Some members, unconcerned about philosophical issues, simply resented a compulsory levy on supply of five cents a litre, rising to ten cents a litre, to fund shares, seeing this as just another impost, a deduction from farmer payments to fund management 'empire building'. Sceptics were convinced that the co-operative was on the 'slippery slope' to corporatisation.

The fact was ACF now had a capacity to fund-raise in a way it had never before possessed and members had agreed to this. The co-operative was better placed to participate in the remorseless merger and acquisition game in readiness for deregulation. But could ACF really perform a 'balancing act' on a tightrope between capital adequacy and the democracy principle while maintaining farmer control in perpetuity?

Chapter Sixteen

'Hazy Horizons':
THE DAIRY FARMERS GROUP AND 'PARTIAL' DEMUTUALISATION 1993–2004

Introduction

Discussion in the following chapter considers how attempts were made to 'hybridise' (part co-operative, part corporation) the Dairy Farmers Co-operative (Australian Co-operative Foods [ACF], Dairy Farmers Group [DFG]) after members authorised a compulsory bonus share acquisition scheme to fund growth and achieve improved competitiveness in 1993. The discussion is arranged in four sections considering: events leading to a first failed attempt to partially demutualise the co-operative in 1990; a second unsuccessful attempt in 2001; a third attempt which, at time of writing, remains unresolved; and, finally, DFG and the democracy principle.

Section One
Dairy Farmers' Group and the Equilibrium Model 1993-1999

'Hazy horizons, exciting challenges'

When reporting developments in ACF in the last decade of the twentieth century, the co-operative's Official Historian Jan Todd observed:

> Those co-operative visionaries who had gazed towards the dawn of the twentieth century could not have hoped for more...For a century co-operation had proved itself a living thing, adapting to a changing world, surviving to carry on its main purpose – to mobilise collective farmer power in pursuit of the best return for their product. Now it (sic) must press on with innovative responses...to new demands. Co-operative ideals had won their place in the market but co-operative idealists still had a job to do to find equity structures which could take dairy co-operatives into the twenty-first century. New horizons were still hazy but full of exciting challenges.[1]

Indeed horizons were 'hazy' for the New South Wales dairy industry and co-operatives were bracing themselves for deregulation in a global economy with no certainty about what was in store, only that they must be ready and that it would be 'challenging'. Could the 'co-operative dilemma' in respect of balancing capital adequacy and the democracy principle be resolved enabling ACF confidently to take its place in that world while retaining farmer control? Could the 'Siamese twins' of ownership and control be separated without mortally wounding co-operative structure?

Co-operatives consider various business models

Emboldened by overwhelming member approval of a compulsory issue of bonus shares by way of surplus distribution in 1993, ACF leaders accelerated the co-operative forward in a vigorous growth spurt, renewing attempts to establish links with other co-operatives and build a 'mega' co-operative capable of meeting Victorian and proprietary competition head-on while adapting to deregulation.

Queensland co-operatives on the Atherton Tableland (Milanda Dairy Foods) and at Port Curtis and South Australia's Dairy Vale, however, remained unimpressed with the proposed share bonus plan in merger talks with ACF, many members eager to realise their co-operative's cash value; to 'sell out' and pursue other options. Milanda Dairy Foods, for example, was actively considering non-co-operative options and looked to the (Western Australian) Wesfarmers' model (discussed in Chapter Six) for inspiration.

Milanda Dairy Foods had engaged the services of Macquarie Corporate Finance advisers, who had been involved in the demutualisation of a building society. The co-operative briefed them to track social and economic change in the industry, to solicit and suggest strategies for *managing peoples' expectations* and to devise a solution to suit a possible ACF-Milanda merger. The consultants asked directors to rank their priorities. A high priority was given to supplier milk-security, profit-sharing, share capital appreciation, ability to trade shares and access to *external* equity capital. Medium priorities were listed as farmer control, co-operative ideals, democratic voting and the role of the co-operative in community development. Low priorities were tax credits attached to share dividends and the appointment of external directors.

In ensuing merger talks with ACF, Jan Todd tells us, the Milanda Board presented the Sydney-based co-operative with three essentially non-co-operative options: tradeable shares; share capital appreciation; and external equity. The ACF Board was not interested in proceeding on this basis, believing that co-operative shares were not a commodity to be traded and that limits on capital gain was a basic co-operative tenet. Any idea of ACF 'buying co-operatives' was also dismissed as unethical and inequitable, the rationale being that existing ACF Members had already forgone a pay-out option when earlier merging to form the co-operative, so why should Milanda be any different?

Co-operatives lose ground in the fresh-milk market

As talks with co-operatives in Queensland and South Australia slowly proceeded, ACF sought to purchase 50 per cent of Associated Dairies (Victoria). ACF's solicitor detailed how the co-operative could make a bid through an ACF Dubbo subsidiary (Central Western Dairy Limited). By November 1993, however, ACF was out of the race, trumped by Queensland United Dairies Association (QUD) (Paul's), which now became the second-largest fresh-milk processor in Australia, ahead of ACF.[2]

Restating the 'co-operative dilemma': external equity?

ACF Chairman Ian Langdon was convinced the challenge lay in finding a practical response to current commercial pressures and that this was as much about *survival* as about co-operative philosophy. The 'co-operative dilemma', as he now interpreted it, was thus: by restricting funds to *members* the co-operative could certainly retain *control* but would almost certainly cease to be *competitive*. That is to say, farmers would *lose* their co-operative and any semblance of commodity control anyway because it would be driven from markets by superior competition. Langdon reasoned that an ACF, which did not capture a major market share at national level and diversify into value-added products, would inevitably go out of business or be taken over. *External* equity certainly risked the possibility of losing farmer control but the *absence* of it inferred a loss of commercial viability. How did farmers intend to resolve this dilemma?

At an ACF Special Board Meeting in September 1993 Langdon told directors that the 'cheap' merger with co-operatives strategy was not working. The failed bid for Associated Dairies, he said, had demonstrated a need for capital greater than the co-operative's capacity to provide it *internally*.

ACF needed to make *acquisitions* to gain market share and to position itself for deregulation and intensified competition. The chairman reiterated that the finance industry would not take co-operatives seriously, did not understand them and believed they would not survive deregulation. There were only two ways to proceed, he repeated: debt, or external equity. Both Langdon and Chief Executive Officer (CEO) Alan Tooth were opposed to further debt but had different views on suitable alternatives with Tooth preferring to *list* the co-operative in order to 'release co-operative wealth to the farmers' while the chairman sought an innovative structure which would 'bring the best of both worlds', for example 'golden shares', which attracted external equity but did *not* carry voting rights. Was this not just 'dry' shareholder control by another name, some directors wondered? But what was the answer?

'Control is everything'

Notwithstanding such disparate views on how to fund expansion, the ACF Board elected to push ahead aggressively in a determined search for capital, 'hungry' for mergers and acquisitions. The plan was to position the co-operative to produce 50 per cent of profits *outside* New South Wales by the year 2000. A long list of investment opportunities was drawn up and the board invited Macquarie Corporate Finance and Gresham Partners to suggest possible alternative capital options.

Some directors expressed misgivings about inviting in corporate advisers who might have a poor understanding of co-operatives and flagged their reluctance to deviate from traditional co-operative methods. Co-operatives, they emphasised, existed to provide *services*, not to make *profits*; operated to bring the best prices for suppliers; worked for members, not outsiders; and functioned to protect farmers from speculators, takeover merchants and outside control. *Control* was everything. Whatever corporate consultants might say, dividends and capital return were *not* a priority and, some directors insisted, co-operative shares had *no* market value and could *not* be traded. Very deliberately, they said, limits had been imposed in co-operative structure upon share yields and the number of shares an individual could hold. That was the whole point of co-operatives – the democracy principle: one-member-one-vote; democratic ownership *and* control! It was wholly appropriate, traditionalists argued, to fund co-operatives from member funds, bank debt and debentures. To go looking for external investments was just courting trouble.

Would farmer-members provide adequate capital for the co-operative to remain viable, post-deregulation? Ian Langdon did not think so. Did that leave only Alan Tooth's option of listing? Even if that were desirable, and Langdon had an open mind on anything serving shareholder interests, members would never allow it. The chairman, therefore, looked for a compromise, something potentially agreeable to all parties.

The Irish 'hybrid' model

ACF Executives, including Ian Langdon, travelled to Europe and the United States to study alternative co-operative models. In the United States they investigated 'New Generation Co-operatives' (NGCs). In Ireland they studied four Irish dairy co-operatives which had adopted public-equity structures in an effort to 'marry' commercial objectives and co-operative principles, creating 'hybrids'. NGCs presented problems under Australia's trades' practices legislation. The Irish 'hybrid' model, however, was examined closely.

Essentially the 'hybrid' model devolved upon *separating* a farmer-owned-and-controlled supply co-operative from a farmer-controlled processing company. In Ireland the Kerry Co-operative Group had listed on the London and Dublin stock exchanges. By 1993, when ACF Executives visited, co-operative ownership had been watered down to around 50 per cent and many farmers were making more money from *shares* than from farming. Share price and profitability were replacing milk as principal wealth creators. Sceptics, however, pointed to falling milk prices in Ireland, elite management teams allegedly driving co-operatives toward capitalist orthodoxy and tensions already growing between farmers and investors in the industry. It seemed only a matter of time before farmers lost control.

Sections of the ACF Executive, including Ian Langdon, however, were 'converted', Jan Todd tells us, by what they saw in Ireland and began exploring ways to adapt the 'hybrid' model to include a supply co-operative holding 'golden shares' in a processing company, which conferred special rights on the co-operative.

External investors and co-operation

The ACF Board authorised the chairman to make an in-principle statement on the matter of external investors to the 1993 Annual General Meeting (AGM). Langdon employed all of his persuasive powers in arguing that it was possible to reconcile external investments *and* farmer control. The chairman's commitment to co-operation, he said, was unswerving and co-operation was unquestionably a part of the ACF 'heritage'. There was something inherently valuable in the co-operative principles of farmer ownership and control, equality and democracy, and it was *precisely* these values, Langdon emphasised, which were driving ACF policies. He was convinced the 'do-nothing' option would not work. It was not simply a matter of further rationalisation or consolidation – ACF had to *grow*! The dairy industry had changed forever and when, as seemed likely, full deregulation came, ACF needed to be ready or go out of business. That was the choice. The co-operative must *add value* to products and *acquire assets* for it to compete effectively with private enterprise. ACF must achieve *scale* and *market share* or it would be devoured by proprietors. It truly was a case of 'Get Big or Get Out. The whole issue of reconciling co-operative principles and capital-raising options had to be fundamentally re-examined. There was no time for delay. The magnitude of competitors' access to capital was far greater than the capacity of ACF Members to supply capital. Members had overwhelmingly agreed to the compulsory issue of bonus shares. Now the matter of raising *external* equity needed to be confronted; the 'co-operative dilemma' must be resolved. The alternative was to be driven gradually from the industry with farmers losing control to proprietors and 'foreigners'. It was not a matter of forlornly *hoping* that co-operatives would co-operate to achieve the necessary scale to remain viable – they would *not* co-operate! Regional perspectives and jealousies were preventing the timely rationalisation and growth of the dairy co-operative sector and producing unnecessary and wasteful competition. *All* options needed to be considered; anything potentially in the interests of farmer shareholders; and *nothing* beneficial to farmers should be precluded by philosophical rigidities.

Not surprisingly, Langdon's candid presentation precipitated a strong reaction from some members, especially the idea of external investors. Some believed that the co-operative was being strategically set up for a takeover and questioned the 'growth for growth's' sake philosophy. Some ACF Directors and many members doubted senior management's commitment to co-operative philosophy and structure observing that, while they argued for co-operation as part of a farmer 'heritage', they seemed hell-bent on *dismantling* co-operative structure. ACF Historian Jan Todd, however, believes that Langdon was truly dedicated to ACF remaining a co-operative, the chairman passionately believing that farmers were custodians for future farmers and emotionally committed to the same long-term ideals that motivated farmer directors. At times, she says, Langdon seemed more passionate about co-operative ideals than many of the farmers themselves because he was searching for a solution to the 'co-operative dilemma' *within* a co-operative framework so that ACF could 'have its cake and eat it too':

> As they deliberated on new challenges ACF's board and senior management were conscious of the long history and strength of co-operative agriculture. At the same time they were forced to confront certain shortcomings in the existing equity structure. Could present shareholders provide sufficient capital in equity form to enable ACF to compete unhindered in a broad Australian-wide market and in the even more exacting export markets of the world?[3]

Equality or equity?

Notwithstanding doubts about the motives of sections of the executive, the 1993 AGM endorsed Langdon's precept that all options should be 'on the table'. Accordingly, at a Special Meeting in November General Manager Tooth was given an opportunity to address the board on his preferred option – listing the co-operative. The guiding principle in serving shareholder interests, Tooth said, was that *all* possibilities should be considered; all the way from 'do nothing' to a publicly-listed company. What was at issue was the *economic welfare* of farmers and the best and most equitable ways of achieving this. It was not simply a matter of preserving a philosophy preoccupied with *equality* but of finding ways of achieving farmer *equity*. Two central questions needed to be examined with a view to discovering ways of achieving equity for members: how to bring into equilibrium the relationship between co-operative principles and capital adequacy; and how to structure co-operatives as a vehicle for capital growth while simultaneously performing processing and marketing functions for farm products. It was vital, Tooth continued, that ACF review *all* equity options with regard to co-operative principles and develop a share culture to make the co-operative more like an investor-organisation and, if necessary, *modify* the co-operative model. The Irish 'hybrid' model definitely should be studied further to find ways of separating milk supply from processing and attracting private investment to the processing arm so that share price and dividends from profits became more important to farmers than the price of milk, as was the case in Ireland.

Some members and directors supported the idea of creating separate organisations for supply and processing and were drawn to Tooth's argument. Others believed the ACF Executive was embarked upon 'mission impossible'. Grudgingly the board did agree, however, to examine other fund-raising and equity options including tradeable shares and how it might be possible to mesh these with co-operative principles while guaranteeing farmer control. A Share (later 'Equity') Committee was formed.[4]

ACF continues to expand

Meanwhile, ACF continued to post excellent trading results aided by the bonus share scheme. The co-operative showed exceptional profit (surplus) growth – 432 per cent between 1991 and 1994 and turnover *doubled* in the seven years to 1998! Farm-gate milk prices rose through the period and, deploying member capital and borrowed funds in constructing manufacturing equipment, ACF made progress with new products in New South Wales and Victoria, including cholesterol-free milk and yoghurt products.

Nevertheless, debt remained a nagging problem. Talks concerning possible interstate alliances and mergers with co-operatives proceeded but generally were slow, complicated by the incompatibility of state-based co-operatives' legislation. ACF assisted the company, National Foods, to work up a proposal for a possible merger with the co-operative but talks faltered on issues of control and structure. Clearly all options *were* on the table.

In a bold move in November 1993, seeking a beach head in Victoria, ACF purchased Bonlac's Midland Milk (Shepparton), a factory which had been sending milk into Sydney since 1984. This, the co-operative's first operational expansion outside of New South Wales, gave access to the Melbourne fresh-milk market and was heralded as a successful step in the co-operative's national strategy and important in developing value-added export markets. It was certainly a confidence-booster – New South Wales producers were retaliating! Critics, however, doubted the wisdom of ACF using member money to engage in speculative ventures, thought the factory was poorly placed for post-deregulatory trade into Melbourne and said it was wrong in principle to be using non-member milk supply.

By 1994, well ahead of schedule, ACF had more than doubled business outside New South Wales, especially in soft dairy food products and, in that year, acquired Wyong, Kempsey and Orange (New South Wales) milk businesses from National Foods and proceeded with a vigorous rationalisation and infrastructure development process. The compulsory bonus share scheme was clearly working. The question of financing their redemption, however, remained.[5]

A balancing act: the Equilibrium Model

Over the next few years the ACF Executive floated numerous 'hybrid' models, essentially derivatives of the Irish Model, for the consideration of the board and members, detail of which is beyond our brief and well covered in Jan Todd's *More Than Milk*. We will look, however, at the main contender, the 'Equilibrium Model', of which there were at least two versions.

Against a background of rumours that ACF was preparing for a $150 million float on the Australian Stock Exchange (ASX); which Ian Langdon vociferously denied; in March 1994 the ACF Board appointed corporate advisers, briefed to identify a practical model which would deliver the co-operative a commercial orientation while retaining co-operative principles and farmer control in perpetuity. The advisers were asked specifically to recommend an *improved* capital structure which would overcome co-operative rigidities (*sic*) while rewarding shareholders and recognising the value of their equity. They were also asked to identify and recommend methods for dealing with *other defects* in the co-operative model including the differing expectations of shareholders and the influence of member-politics in restricting long-term strategic thinking and a commercial focus.

Pursuant to their report, in mid-1994 the executive mooted a tripartite structure, referred to as the 'Equilibrium Model'. This consisted of a supply co-operative, which *guaranteed* to take member milk; a listed proprietary limited company (PLC) for processing; and an investment vehicle to be owned initially 100 per cent by ACF, but eventually, 70 per cent by the co-operative and 30 per cent by individual farmers. As capital was required, more shares in the PLC would be offered to the public. A 'rule of fifty-one' obtained, however, by which the co-operative at all times was to own no less than 51 per cent of PLC shares, the board of which was to be numerically controlled by the co-operative.

'Marketing' the Equilibrium Model

ACF Executives who endorsed the Equilibrium Model launched a vigorous campaign to 'market' the idea. At the 1994 Co-operatives Key Issues Conference in Sydney (discussed in Chapter Twelve), for example, where Ian Langdon (after Babcock) defined a co-operative as a 'legal means by which a group of self-selected, selfish capitalists seek to improve their individual economic position in a competitive society', the ACF chairman argued powerfully that hybrid structures could be designed to service *both* co-operative philosophy *and* the demands of external equity, without necessarily compromising member-control or co-operative philosophy. Co-operative philosophy was simply a *commercial* philosophy, Langdon emphasised, and members should be rewarded for *ownership* as well as supply. It was inevitable, he believed, now that members of his co-operative had subscribed to compulsory capital investment schemes, that they would *demand* appropriate financial rewards both in dividends *and* capital appreciation.

At an international dairy congress later in Melbourne ACF Executives highlighted the poor investment performance of Australian agricultural co-operatives, arguing that this was because co-operative structure *impaired* capital-raising and gave no incentive to external investors. The asset-base of large trading co-operatives, they said, was not reflected in the share value and consequently co-operatives could not keep pace with markets and were losing business opportunities. It is difficult to avoid from this the conclusion that they saw the existing co-operative model as a defective one.[6]

'Be prepared for conflicts'

Not all experts agreed that 'hybrid' models and inviting external investors into co-operatives were desirable. For example United States Department of Agricultural Economics Cornell University Professor Bruce Anderson, then visiting Australia, was *surprised* by the apparent fixation with tapping public equity markets, citing the experience of irreconcilable conflicts between public shareholders and farmer members in Ireland and elsewhere which had arisen when the industry hit hard times, obliging farmers to *buy back* public stock at a premium or risk their *farm businesses* failing! Anderson also saw listing on ASX as a highly expensive mistake and warned Australian dairy co-operators – 'be prepared for conflicts'.

ACF Board scepticism grows

The issue of external equity polarised opinion on the ACF Board where reverberations from the 1993 AGM were still rumbling. How would the Equity Committee guarantee that farmer ownership would not be gradually watered down? How was it possible to limit the voting rights of outsiders without offering shares at a discount or yielding to demands for a greater say? Tinkering with the democracy principle was dangerous. The 'rule of fifty-one' was not watertight, as the Irish experience and Professor Anderson suggested. Co-operative Capital Units (CCUs) were already seen to be ineffective, attracting little new capital and presenting thorny taxation problems. Why persist with these ideas?

The board directed the Equity Committee to explore 'hybrid' models further with a view to reworking various options and providing *better* guarantees of farmer control in perpetuity.[7]

A five-year plan

In March 1995 the ACF Board approved a five-year plan of vigorous investments and market development in preparation for deregulation. That was well and good – but how to fund it? Ian Langdon was convinced that farmers would *be obliged to* invest in that part of their business which extended beyond the farm gate – the co-operative – formalising ownership:

> ...to ensure that this organisation and its farmer owners maintain a position of strength and competitiveness in this sector so crucial for dairy farmer income...further investments will be needed...To better recognise members' formal ownership of the business through a progressive increase in issued capital, through share acquisition, bonus issues and share rebate issue... Progressively the portion of profit distributed to members in the form of dividends will increase consistent with the rapid growth of share capital. Provided this share capital increases pro rata

with milk supplied by individual members, then such distributions will remain consistent with
co-operative principles and simultaneously build the individual wealth of the member to be
realised after exit from the industry.[8]

The issue is control

Heated debates continued at board level through 1995 and into 1996 on the issue of funding and various 'hybrid' models inviting external equity while purporting to guarantee farmer control in perpetuity. Critics of 'hybrids' persisted in arguing that ACF existed to maximise the milk price and that farmers did not *want* to share profits with external investors; they simply wanted premium prices and tax benefits, which a tried and tested traditional co-operative model could deliver. Farmer control was non-negotiable. Adopting a 'hybrid' model meant that suppliers would no longer be equal in the co-operative but rewarded *variously* for investments along with other investors. Was this not capitalism masquerading as co-operation? Moreover, it was wrong in principle and anti-co-operative to reward large suppliers with a greater proportion of the co-operative's ownership simply because they were large suppliers. The idea smacked of joint-stock orthodoxy. What about small suppliers who had supported the co-operative for generations? What was their loyalty worth?

Supporters of the 'hybrid' model and external investments argued that the *value* of farmer control was being overstated and that co-operatives' taxation benefits, which acted as an incentive to dissipate profits, were simply 'not worth it'.

This lively debate was temporarily submerged by broader industry events in the approach to deregulation and by more ACF mergers and acquisitions. But it would resurface.[9]

The ACF-QUD merger

Following nearly five years of inconclusive talks, in which a lack of uniform co-operatives' legislation proved to be a stumbling block, in February 1996 ACF and the Queensland United Dairy Foods Association (Queensco-Unity) (QUD) finally merged on a share-swap basis. The New South Wales *Co-operatives Act* allowed co-operatives to merge either by transfer or engagements, or by both co-operatives transferring their assets into a new co-operative, the latter option having significant capital gains tax implications. Queensland legislation, however, permitted only the latter option with no provision for an interstate co-operative to become a registered processor in that state, as a co-operative. For years the merger was mired in red tape meeting bureaucratic and political resistance and with the Queensland Registrar of Co-operatives gravely concerned about a possible lack of jurisdiction. The Australian Taxation Office also was slow to approve the scheme.

A way was found around these problems when ACF bought a farm, which became a supplier to QUD! New South Wales active membership provisions meant that ACF, first, had to receive milk and, second, forward this to the QUD plant in Queensland. ACF was also required to register in Queensland under dairy industry legislation. Finally, proceeding without reference to the New South Wales *Co-operatives Act,* the ACF-QUD merger proceeded. The episode, which eloquently demonstrated the inadequacy of Australian co-operatives' law and the disincentive this could be in co-operative development, cost about $1 million to realise and is generally considered to be the first cross-border merger of its type in Australia.[10]

The Dairy Farmers' Group (DFG)

The ACF-QUD merger saw new personnel with different ideas enter the long-running ACF capital-raising debate, altering expectations within the co-operative. While 'Australian Co-operative Foods' remained the registered name of the new entity, the ACF-QUD merger was known as

'Dairy Farmers Group' (DFG), omitting any reference to 'co-operative' in the title. This angered some long-term ACF Members, particularly on the south-coast of New South Wales, the birthplace of Australian dairy co-operation, who argued that the co-operative was losing its identity and were unhappy with the direction in which the executive was taking the organisation. Possibly this was why, from July 1996, ACF began trading under its former operating name of 'Dairy Farmers', or it simply might have been a good marketing move.

Diluting the bond of association

More seriously for future member relations, many ACF shareholders who were anticipating leaving the industry after deregulation had by now reasonably come to expect *access* to the co-operative's share value at some stage as recompense for forgoing income in the form of compulsory bonus shares. As critics of the scheme had predicted all along, divisions opened in the membership. The bond of association; that spirit of common identity and solidarity binding a co-operative together; was changing from one born of locality and heritage values, to a geographically dispersed *consensus* built upon expectations of capital gain and wealth accumulation. Confirming this attitudinal shift, Jan Todd reports that 'there was now…[a] certain expectation that members would at some stage be given the option of taking the money from a portion of their shares', observing that Ian Langdon had 'courageously embraced' the PLC model in seeking to develop a 'share culture' in the co-operative so that shareholding was prized.[11]

'Why fix what ain't broke?'

With a reshaped DFG Equity Committee tabling various 'hybrid' restructure models, fierce camps of opinion developed at board level and among the membership. Traditionalists wanted to preserve co-operative identity. Pragmatists wanted access to the co-operative's wealth, partially or fully. Many remained non-committal but suspicious, wondering why the Equity Committee seemed so determined to 'fix what ain't broke'. Some continued to be bitterly resentful of what they saw as a compulsory share levy which they believed was not only antithetical to co-operation but was being used simply to aggrandise an executive elite. The issue of equitably rewarding long-established members and new members was particularly thorny. Opponents of the bonus scheme argued that the spectre of shareholder 'classes' was fracturing the co-operative's solidarity and that it was, and always would be, impossible to reconcile the antithetical principles of economic *equity*, determined on the basis of a member's supply and investments, on the one hand, and *equality* pursuant to the democracy principle, on the other. Shareholder 'classes', which whetted investor expectations, and farmer control on a one-member-one vote basis, were inimical, the critics insisted. Opponents of the various 'hybrid' models being mooted argued that 'unbundling' prices paid for milk from returns from investments, as advocated by the executive, was a dangerous, divisive strategy because deregulation would inevitably see prices tumble and suppliers go to wherever the best returns were available, not necessarily the co-operative. Inevitably, investors would come to control the PLC side of the proposed operation and, by dint of that, obtain surrogate if not actual control of the co-operative itself. The 'rule of fifty-one' was also unsafe, potentially setting up a situation for another Panfida-type raid. Some members seriously doubted the executive's motives.[12]

'Keeping faith with co-operative philosophy'

Ian Langdon replied that it *was* necessary to 'unbundle' prices paid for a raw commodity from returns on investments, even though this might be unpopular with farmers. Reassuring the DFG Equity Committee that his commitment to co-operative philosophy was 'absolute' and that 'traditional and farmer-focus would not permit structural change to compromise co-operative philosophy', the chairman prepared a seven-point plan: 'Keeping Faith With Co-operative Philosophy'. This was designed to assuage doubters while promoting structural flexibility consistent with co-operative philosophy. Langdon's road map, comprising long-held views and a few new ones, included:

1. A philosophically strong co-operative:
   - shares aligned with patronage;
   - shares not tradeable;
   - shares redeemed at par value upon exit;
   - a realistic dividend paid on capital;
   - a member shareholding of at least 50 per cent of the co-operative's net worth;
   - reward shares by dividends *and* premium returns for farm outputs;
   - dividend income to grow through share rebates from profits and effective capital appreciation of ownership, *without* the need for tradeable shares or a move away from paying face value on shares.
2. Value the entire business at market value.
3. List an outside arm of the co-operative to attract outside equity, without compromising co-operative legal or taxation status.
4. Allow for the partial liquidation of member equity – a 'spin-out' of accumulated wealth.
5. Build a package of rewards for member equity, including dividends on shares, premium prices, farm services and retaining profits to build up the co-operative's share in the PLC.
6. Any structural change to require 75 per cent member approval at *two* consecutive meetings.
7. Maintain farmer involvement to create incentives and encourage the type of behaviour which fosters the spirit of co-operation.[13]

The DFG-Malanda merger

Again, the capital-structure debate was subsumed within growth issues when, after five years of strenuous effort, in January 1997 DFG and Malanda Dairy Foods in far north Queensland merged. This was celebrated as a vital step in consolidating DFG's market power in fresh-milk markets. DFG now controlled milk supply in northern Queensland and a large part of south-eastern Queensland. The QUD and Malanda mergers also saw DFG develop a significant cheese manufacturing capacity, augmented in October 1997 by the purchase of Kraft's cheddar cheese business. The co-operative now occupied 22 per cent of that market.

Considering listing

The merger saw Malanda suppliers enter the DFG Board and Equity Committee, again altering perceptions in respect of ownership and control. In May, with a controversial discussion paper on co-operatives issued by the ASX circulating (discussed in Chapter Thirteen), DFG considered the listing option. Ian Langdon was now of the view that listing would allow monetary recognition of the co-operative's spectacular growth in revenue and profits and unlock several hundred millions of dollars, giving farmers access to this value. It was a tempting prospect but the board remained unconvinced, pointing to an ASX 'sunset' clause in respect of the democracy principle and with some directors perturbed by continued press speculation that DFG was about to list and sell 49 per cent of its assets! Where did these rumours come from?

For the remainder of 1997 sections of the DFG Executive persisted in arguing that it was necessary to access external investments and canvassed possible options for the board's consideration. The co-operative also invited Irish directors of 'hybrid' co-operatives to Australia to address the board and DFG Directors travelled abroad to study the Irish Model.

Member dissent grows

Meanwhile, a strong reaction to the executive's apparent determination to 'hybridise' or list the co-operative was building at grass-roots level. Some members claimed that vested interests had infiltrated the board and Equity Committee and were setting up the co-operative for a takeover. They described the board as a 'closed shop' on which it was impossible to gain representation unless you were very wealthy or agreed with the general direction in which the executive was taking the organisation. Some members doubted that senior managers were even *listening* to them, simply using farmers' funds to advance personal agendas and demanded that the board obtain further information, give greater emphasis to farmer control and investigate other models, not *only* the Irish Model.

The Dairy Vale merger

As dissent fomented, DFG proceeded on an expansionary programme, purchasing Dairy Vale Co-operative Limited, a South Australian 'hybrid'. Carrying serious debts, caught in a supermarket price-war and with the South Australian Government accelerating deregulation, Dairy Vale had been seeking ways to 're-invent' itself. Earlier, lengthy talks with ACF had lapsed, foundering on legislation, states' rights and managerial issues. A new manager, who saw co-operative structure as a liability and democracy as an anachronism for investors, pruned Dairy Vale's operations and argued the need for the co-operative to list on the ASX. Farmer-members, concerned at a possible loss of control, were reluctant. After a drawn out and expensive consultation process in 1994, member talk turned to a 'hybrid' structure, something akin to the Victorian co-operative company, Bonlac, which had been modelled with reference to New Generation Co-operative (NGC) structure. In March 1995 Dairy Vale Co-operative, as such, was dissolved and the business transferred to Dairy Vale Foods Limited, a processor and marketing company. Dairy Vale Limited was set up as a holding company, which owned Dairy Vale Foods through a trust, Dairy Vale Investment Trust. Former members of Dairy Vale Co-operative were *obliged* to sell through Dairy Vale Foods Limited, which was *obliged* to receive supply from them. Dairy Vale Investment Trust was listed on ASX on a five-year trial after which, under ASX rules, *all* farmer investors were required to vote for a continuance of co-operative structure.

Dairy Vale Investment Trust, in which ACF was a major shareholder, raised $14 million through the float. Through 1996 and 1997, however, facing improved competition from National Foods (constructed partly on former co-operative assets absorbed by Southern Holdings) and New Zealand exporters, and with prices to farmers falling, Dairy Vale share prices fell from $1.20 to approximately eighty cents. Locked in expensive litigation with vendors and with investors jittery, the issue of farmer ownership and control became problematical as ASX urged resolution of an 'irregular' situation where the trust owned nearly 90 per cent of the holding company's shares but only sent *two* representatives to its eight-member board.

The former co-operative became a takeover target. ACF offered to buy Dairy Vale Foods Limited for $36 million. In November 1997 Murray-Goulburn Co-operative offered $45 million. Early in January 1998 ACF offered to go as high as $50 million, 'both directly as ACF and also through nominee companies'. After some initial uncertainty among Dairy Vale suppliers about whether this amounted to a takeover or a friendly merger, in May 1998 Dairy Vale integrated with ACF to become part of DFG. The DFG Executive made much of the fact that the merger had seen Dairy Vale Co-operative return to the co-operative fold – co-operatives were fighting back!

Dairy Vale introduced cheddar production mainly for exports and was an important element in DFG's goal to achieve national leadership in the core markets of milk, cheese and yogurt, reducing a dependence on market-milk.

The *Co-operatives Act* is amended

Meanwhile, in December 1997 the New South Wales *Co-operatives Act* was amended in an attempt to resolve Core Consistent Provisions (CCP) issues in respect of nationally uniform co-operatives' legislation (discussed in Chapter Fourteen). The amendments allowed New South Wales co-operatives to issue securities to 'outsiders', introduced provisions for two classes of shares (trading and non-trading) on the Victorian model and enabled co-operatives to gain access to tax-deductible government loans.

Former ACF General Manager and now Co-operative Federation of NSW Ltd Consultant Don Kinnersley called for an international conference on NGCs at this time, arguing that younger farmers did not see co-operatives as appropriate to the contemporary economic environment because, he said, co-operatives were slow in making decisions and carried 'free-riders', who did not commit themselves in the long term. Kinnersley also wanted to see further investigation of investments in co-operative shares and voting rules which gave small suppliers as much power as larger ones.[14]

'A dairy giant on a spending spree'

With deregulation of the fresh-milk industry now widely seen as inevitable, DFG accelerated its expansionary programme. General Manager Tooth and Chairman Langdon endorsed a proposal by National Foods that DFG purchase Paul's Victorian operations, but, constrained by money, they watched the Italian food giant, PARMALAT, snap the company up for $436 million. In May 1998 DFG bought all of the former New South Wales Dairy Marketing Board's brand names at auction for the bargain price of $7 million! DFG proposed a $50 million merger with Norco, but it is reported that this fell foul of National Competition Policy (NCP) rules. DFG was also involved in a failed merger attempt with the Gold Coast Dairy Fields Co-operative and became involved in a joint venture with the Bega Co-operative in the Australian Capital Territory and in south-eastern New South Wales. In January 1999 DFG acquired the *Danone* yogurt licence and, later in the year, major capital works were undertaken, amounting to $65.9 million.

In this context, Jan Todd tells us, 'Dairy Farmers recognises that there is a need to improve the funding flexibility of the co-operative through access to external capital by a capital restructure'.

'Almost free of heritage restrictions': Equilibrium Model Version Two

Amidst suspicion and rumour in some sections of DFG's Membership, the board, which now included representatives from three states, sought to revive the 1994 Equilibrium Model. Ian Langdon argued:

> *Many members are wondering why the co-operative needs to continue to grow and why it needs to change its structure to attract outsider capital. DFG must keep pace with the competition or lose its commercial relevance and capacity to compete in the market place. The aim of the Equilibrium Model is to strengthen the business and the co-operative philosophy that is so*

important and essential to the membership…There is no need to abandon, nor weaken the commitment to co-operative philosophy and farmer ownership.

Equilibrium Model Version Two was described as virtually 'heritage free', a unique opportunity to preserve control while attracting investors and keeping the competing interests of all 'stakeholders' (not 'members' or even 'shareholders') in balance, bringing 'equilibrium' to their expectations of the co-operative. Theoretically, the model, which was targeted at a deregulated industry where relations between processors (including co-operatives) and suppliers would be fundamentally redefined, would enable a supply co-operative to offer a processor a competitive price for (required) milk and a 'spot price' for milk surplus to requirements. It would also enable the conglomerate to provide farmers with a capital return on ownership while gaining access to short-term liquidity through a 'spin out' of 25 per cent of the shares based on a supplier's current shareholding, in a new PLC which he or she could keep as 'superannuation' or sell on ASX. Members could also buy PLC shares on ASX and exercise voting rights both as individual shareholders and members of the supply co-operative, which would command a powerful bloc vote. The supply co-operative, owned by active farmers, would initially own 75 per cent of the PLC shares but this proportion would be progressively reduced as the PLC issued new shares to raise capital, as the need arose, and could fall *below* 50 per cent – it was up to the co-operative's active members to retain the 'rule of 51', if they valued it. There was nothing in co-operative theory, proponents argued, which said co-operators should continue co-operating indefinitely – that was purely sentiment. It was *assumed*, however, that co-operative members would continue to hold a controlling bloc of shares in the PLC through 'vigorous investments', but for this to be achieved farmers might be required to *borrow* against future cash-flows, that is go into debt, themselves. Control in perpetuity, like everything else in a deregulated market economy, had a *price* and it was up to farmers, not co-operatives, to pay that price.

Statements of the proposed PLC Board's composition varied over time, but the 1998 'heritage free' model contemplated a board of ten: five farmer-appointed directors; four independent directors appointed by the PLC; and one CEO, appointed by the company.

The proposal was that a new supply management system would be negotiated between the supply co-operative and the PLC processor. In this the co-operative would undertake to *guarantee* dependable supply and the PLC would undertake to buy milk from the co-operative *before* it approached the open market. It was envisaged that farmers could expect a production expansion of about 5 per cent per annum. The PLC would be 'transparent and market-driven' and would continue to pay 'regulated' prices for market milk *unless* the farm-gate price was deregulated (which was now widely seen as inevitable). The processor company, however, would only pay commercial prices for manufactured milk. Farmer investors would benefit from a 'cascade' of financial rewards in several streams, including dividends on shares in the co-operative and the PLC, premium prices for milk, returns on equity in the co-operative, bonus shares and retained earnings – all contingent upon the PLC being profitable.

Perpetual control cannot be guaranteed

Touring DFG Membership areas in three states, the executive faced a barrage of questions especially when telling members that the 'rule of 51' was 'not magic [nor] as important in the control issue as many people believe' and that the democracy principle was 'political' rather than 'commercial'. Farmers throughout the world, executives said, were voting to abandon the principle. With characteristic candour Ian Langdon told members that if the proposed PLC had the opportunity to make a strategic acquisition, which would push members' equity *below* 51 per cent and, if minimum supplier-shareholder rules (the democracy principle) required the co-operative to go back to members to do this, valuable time would be lost and, in a corporate culture like that of the late 1990s, opportunities could be lost in a lengthy approval process. Were farmers really about losing opportunities or were they in business to make money? He related how large single shareholders in listed companies exercised effective control with as little as 20 to 25 per cent of shares. Effective farmer control, Langdon believed, could actually be maintained with 'probably around 35 per cent' of the shares. If the PLC raised funds for an acquisition, which pushed the co-operative shareholding below 35 per cent, '...it would be up to the members to look at ways of raising the necessary capital to ensure its shareholding remained unchanged'. If they could not, then that was the business reality of the situation. Farmers were businessmen, not ideologues. In any event the supply co-operative would *always* have first opportunity to buy shares in any public issue of PLC shares and regulations existed to ensure a ceiling of 15 per cent was kept on shares owned by one party other than the co-operative. Nevertheless, Equilibrium Model Version Two could *not* guarantee continued control of the PLC by the co-operative – it was up to farmers to do that. The structure was almost completely free of 'heritage' factors, Langdon continued, for example, there were no voting 'restrictions' and few legislative or co-operative rules to restrict shareholding. For this reason, it was unlikely that PLC shares would be *discounted* in share markets for the company would be seen to be like any other public company with a strong family bloc shareholding.

The DFG Executive announced that it was seeking about $200 million of fresh capital and, if Equilibrium Model Version Two were approved, proposed a $150 million 'spin out' of shares to individual farmer owners.

'The greatest threat to co-operative principles'

Equilibrium Model Version Two attracted much criticism from traditionalists who saw the scheme as another ploy in a takeover gambit and the 'spin out' as simply a 'bribe'. The proposed supply management system, critics argued, would almost certainly fall foul of NCP regulations, notwithstanding reassurances to the contrary. The proposal, guaranteeing premium prices for fresh-milk supply, was also constructed on assumptions relevant to regulated markets – which were ending. Only the most optimistic or uninformed farmer could assume that the old sureties would continue after deregulation. Despite the executive's reassurances to the contrary, it was probable that financial markets *would* perceive the 'hybrid' as farmer-controlled and demand a discount on shares by way of compensation. The PLC processor *would* go wherever best prices were available in the interests of investor shareholders and there was absolutely *no guarantee* that any supply agreement would endure, potentially placing the supply co-operative in an invidious situation. Moreover, critics said, using farmer money to play the stock market was not only unethical but unwise. The proposal made it plain that the price for maintaining control of the PLC was *further* investment, possibly causing farmers to incur unsustainable debt and putting ownership of the family farm at risk. And how could the supply co-operative afford to redeem compulsory bonus shares if it had investments tied up in a PLC, which was unprofitable or for other reasons was prevented from returning those investments as required? The whole idea, traditionalists believed, was grandiose, unworkable and reckless.

Not only farmer critics had problems with the model. *National Co-op Update* Editor and Co-operatives' Analyst Chris Greenwood, studying 'hybrid' capital-raising models for Monash University, concluded that most 'hybrid' solutions '...appeared to threaten over time the co-operative philosophy as the trickle (or even flood) of external equity swamps the co-operative spirit among members'. Considering DFG's Equilibrium Model Greenwood said:

> *The mechanism is vulnerable in that it is heavily dependent on the continued commercial success of the Dairy Farmers' PLC. The Dairy Farmers' supply co-operative, to maintain its controlling percentage ownership in Dairy Farmers' PLC, must keep receiving significant dividends from its holding in the PLC. If the company faces tough times the PLC's performance may wane with subsequent flow-on effects for the dividend to the supply co-operative.*
>
> *Deregulation has put extreme pressure on margins in the fluid milk business while takeover activity has done the same in the dairy dessert/yoghurt business, both strong areas for the Dairy Farmers' Group. While in a strong position now it is fair to say that, along with its competitors, Dairy Farmers' is in for a torrid time in the next couple of years.*
>
> *This pressure may reveal a weakness in the structure in that if intense competition drives margins and therefore profits down in the PLC its flow of dividends will be correspondingly reduced. This may impinge on the supply co-operative's ability to maintain its investments. If, for example, the PLC identifies that a major acquisition is required to improve its performance the required injection of outside equity may well dilute the co-operative's shareholding well below that required for notional control.*[15]

The DFG Executive presses ahead

The DFG Executive pressed ahead with the restructure, announcing in August 1998 that the co-operative had plans to float a new processing company in twelve to eighteen months time, to be known as 'Dairy Farmers Limited'. This would be almost completely free of 'heritage' restrictions. It was reported that DFG would make a large equity issue to non-farmer investors, involving possibly a market investment of $800 million! Initially, the proposed supply co-operative would own about 60 per cent of the PLC shares, individual farmers 20 per cent and outside investors about 20 per cent. Ian Langdon drew attention to the fact that the listed company would *not* have voting restrictions, 'golden shares' or other constraints which entrenched control with farmers and that it would be up to the supply co-operative to maintain a stake above 50 per cent if it wanted to retain control. In careful language, the chairman claimed strong support for the proposal from those farmers who understood that the restructuring was purely commercially motivated.[16]

Turbulence in 1998

At a September 1998 DFG Board Meeting, with Langdon and Tooth out of the room, a 'wide-ranging discussion' considered many unresolved issues affecting the co-operative, in particular Equilibrium Model Version Two. The board was sorely divided on the issue about which great uncertainty prevailed.

At the 1998 DFG AGM in November Alan Tooth put the Equilibrium Model Version Two partial-demutualisation proposal to members. The general manager argued that farmers must be part of a total supply management system that included processors and retailers to the mutual benefit of all stakeholders. He fielded a welter of probing questions from the floor about the co-operative 'selling its soul', the taxation implications of the proposed scheme and ASX concerns about a co-operative holding a majority shareholding in the proposed company. Some members made pointed references to executive salaries and the difficulty of filling casual vacancies on the board. DFG Official Historian Jan Todd, however, notes that there seemed to be greater acceptance of the PLC idea than previously with some members supporting a complete float. It was agreed at the AGM that a vote would be taken on the Equilibrium Model in March 1999.[17]

Preparing DFG for partial-demutualisation

As rumours spread among suppliers that DFG was preparing to 'go public', Ian Langdon talked up the proposed partial-demutualisation plan proclaiming:

> We will not be restricted by lack of funding flexibility. We will drive business so much that we have visions that we will, from a co-operative base, maintain farmer ownership and control, be the Nestlè of tomorrow…That is not the vision of a company that will fall over post-farm gate deregulation.[18]

A vote of no confidence

The AGM resolution to put the Equilibrium Model Version Two proposal to members in March was delayed while complex Trades Practices Commission (TPC) implications were ironed out. Then there were further delays as doubts about the relationship between the proposed PLC and the supply co-operative were clarified, particularly the composition of the board. Some members complained that senior management seemed to be trying to wear down the resistance of directors, to have them accede to their point of view, and pointed to what was now common knowledge that Irish dairy farmers, albeit wealthier, had lost control of their industry so much so that it was unclear how the next generation of farmers would be able to *afford* to co-operate or benefit from the existing arrangement.[19]

As preparation for the vote proceeded, rumours circulated that the giant Italian food company PARMALAT had DFG in its sights for a takeover. Indeed, DFG Executives had visited Italy and PARMALAT had corresponded with Alan Tooth. It is reported that the general manager did not show the correspondence to the chairman at this time, nor was it communicated to the board or members, with Tooth of the view that disclosure was not required as talks were only conceptual.

A dissenters group

Following disclosure of these developments, however, a dissenting group of fifty-six members, mainly from the Southern Highlands of New South Wales, formed to focus a growing hostility toward elements of the executive and simmering discontent in sections of the membership going back to 1993 on such issues as the compulsory share levy, milk prices, the admission of interstate members, long-term suppliers disadvantaged by interstate mergers and the role of the co-operative, post-deregulation.

At a meeting of the dissident group in the Burrawang Hotel in July 1999 a vote of no confidence was carried in Langdon, Tooth and Deputy Chairman Philip Bruem. Dissenters alleged that the DFG Board comprised an 'inner' and 'outer' circle, was serving the interests of management, not members, and Ian Langdon was said to 'have taken producers on a roller-coaster ride of decreasing returns', determined to have his way, no matter what. The Burrawang Hotel group demanded a vote on *alternatives* to Equilibrium Model Version Two, a moratorium on executive salaries and fresh, independent advice. The group circulated minutes of the meeting widely among members, claiming that farmer wealth, which had been extracted compulsorily from members in the bonus share scheme, was now largely to be 'locked up' in a supply co-operative at $1 per share, in perpetuity.

> They did not believe Ian Langdon's argument that the supply co-operative was the key to channelling continuing wealth from the PLC to the farmers and did not accept that the proposed structure of governance gave effective control to the supply co-operative's board. Rather they suspected that the board would be run by a small group of insiders dominated by the non-farmer independents.[20]

Over the next three months a vigorous tussle continued at board and executive levels involving four main camps of opinion: the 'do-nothing' option; Equilibrium Model Version Two; the PARMALAT takeover offer; and the Burrawang Hotel dissenters.

The PARMALAT fiasco

In July 1999 Ian Langdon called a special meeting to brief the board on discussions with PARMALAT.

Two days later the New South Wales Supreme Court approved the structure proposed for Equilibrium Model Version Two. On 9 August ballot papers for the Equilibrium Model proposal and information were sent to members. The closing date for the ballot was 9 September. Through August the press carried stories speculating on DFG's talks with PARMALAT, the probity of which Langdon defended saying that a co-operative was entitled to speak with whomsoever it wished, including competitors, who could 'put an offer on the table at any time'. That did not mean it would be accepted!

PARMALAT informally proposed to acquire control of DFG for $471 million. The Burrawang Hotel group wrote to the board on 11 August in relation to this 'offer' demanding to know if the board was disclosing everything members needed to know and was it a 'red herring' to frighten members into accepting the Equilibrium Model? Notwithstanding a reply to the effect that the PARMALAT offer was nothing more than an indicative concept, on 24 August seventy dissenters demanded a Special General Meeting and sought to suspend the Equilibrium Model ballot while the PARMALAT issue was resolved. The executive refused to call such a meeting, inflaming dissenters. The issue was followed closely in the press.

On 31 August, just over a week before the ballot closing date, PARMALAT furnished figures to the DFG Board amounting to what was described as a 'reverse' takeover offer involving $402 per co-operative share, equivalent to a bid of $472 million. The bonus share levy was to be abolished and control of processing would revert to PARMALAT leaving a supply co-operative to negotiate the sale of milk. It was the 'hybrid' model with a foreign twist and no pretence of farmer control in perpetuity.

On 3 September, less than a week before the ballot closed, directors met to discuss the PARMALAT offer, some still wondering whether it was simply designed to confuse and disrupt the Equilibrium Model option and how it might affect the ballot's legality.

Meanwhile, PARMALAT alleged in the press that DFG Directors were seeking to control the future of their members. Why was General Manager Tooth complaining about the timing of the offer and loss of control, company officials asked, when *he* had visited PARMALAT headquarters in Italy?

Three days before the ballot closing date, on 6 September, Ian Langdon sent a letter to members through the press explaining both the Equilibrium Model and the PARMALAT bid, emphasising that the issue was *control*. The closing date for the ballot was extended by a fortnight to 23 September 1999. The chairman pointed out that those who had already voted would need to do so again, if they wished to change their vote, and that the PARMALAT offer would be considered *after* the ballot was concluded. The issue of farmer control – whether this was a prerequisite for the future, or not – would be discussed at the November AGM.

It is reported that both the Burrawang Hotel dissenter group *and* supporters of the PARMALAT bid urged members to reject the Equilibrium Model and vote *first* on the PARMALAT offer. Indeed, on 15 September dissenters took legal action to stop the 'hybrid' ballot alleging that DFG Directors had engaged in 'misleading, deceptive and invalid conduct'.

The ballot is scrapped

On 20 September the issue of the legality of the Equilibrium Model ballot went to the New South Wales Supreme Court. The court ruled that not all members could have been apprised of all the facts necessary to reach a valid conclusion and that the court therefore could not be confident that the ballot as it stood would reflect the true will of members. The ruling said that some materials used in conducting the ballot were misleading and deceptive, especially the use of combative and emotional language by directors in disapproving of the PARMALAT offer. Members were entitled to an objective presentation of factual information. The court reconvened on 21 October and ordered DFG to allow members to consider the PARMALAT offer fully *before* any further restructure plans were proceeded with. The extended 'hybrid' vote was declared invalid, particularly as it violated the privacy of those who wished to change their vote. The court found that directors had acted in a 'misleading and combative way' and ordered a fresh ballot with greater disclosure of all salient facts. There was no finding of dishonesty or bad faith but costs were awarded against DFG Directors.[21]

Defending the democracy principle

Hostile divisions opened between pro- and anti-board camps at the 1999 DFG Annual Convention in Surfers Paradise. Lengthy, animated debate ranged over issues pertaining to farmer control. Some members claimed that nothing less than a century of democratic control by farmers was at stake. Supporters of the democracy principle argued that farmer ownership *and* control were inextricably linked and that a clear line of communication between members and directors was absolutely essential in the business of maintaining and cultivating democracy. How clear were the signals being transmitted to members by the DFG Executive? Who in the executive was actively campaigning *for* the democracy principle and to keep the co-operative intact? Why was official talk seemingly always about accessing greater and greater capital and splitting up the co-operative. The message persistently was that the *only* way the co-operative could hope to compete with corporations was to become *like* them, a self-fulfilling prophecy amounting to, 'if you can't beat them, join them!' Was not the idea of a partial demutualisation reckless, threatening a century of co-operation? Hadn't the Irish experience amply demonstrated this?

Many continued to be irritated by the bonus share scheme, which they saw as nothing more than a burdensome levy to fuel managers' ambitions. The Equilibrium Model, they said, whatever version, was complex, threatened producer control and needed to be extensively modified to take into account *exit* value for farmers leaving the industry. Some warned of taxation problems if the co-operative became an investor-organisation by default. Farmers historically left a co-operative when they had no further use for its services and active membership provisions in the act now required this but many were *expecting* to leave and to realise the full value of compulsory loans which had been extracted in the form of bonus shares. The exit value of DFG shares was now a sum 'worth fighting over' and members *expected* to be rewarded fully for their loyalty. How could the co-operative afford to do this if surpluses were to be tied up in investments in a PLC?

There was little support at the convention for the PARMALAT offer but a few demanded a vote on this before any restructure ballot proceeded. There were calls for Ian Langdon and Alan Tooth to resign, but insufficient support for this. There was support, however, for a four-part motion put by Langdon to affirm farmer control, discuss the PARMALAT offer at board level, disclose all information in respect of the offer and explore the exit value of shares in the Equilibrium Model.

Equilibrium Model Version Two is ditched

The DFG Board decided to defer the capital restructure vote for twelve months. Resolving to deal with the PARMALAT offer first, on 25 November directors sought further information. On the following day DFG officials informed the Supreme Court that it was *not* proceeding with the Equilibrium Model restructure vote. With the press speculating about DFG's 'declining value', PARMALAT was invited to forward a formal proposal to be put to a vote by farmer-owners. The company declined to do so, alleging a 'breach of trust'.

'The co-operative has run its course'

A voluble dissenting group on 3 December again called upon the chairman and general manager to resign and proceeded with court action seeking damages against DFG Directors, individually, undertaking to withdraw the action if Langdon and Tooth departed and new directors were elected. The group circulated to members court judgements in respect of the dispute and a questionnaire focused on farmer control and access to the co-operative's full value. The circular claimed that DFG was no longer delivering benefits for which the co-operative had been established and alleged that it had 'run its course'.

On 28 January 2000 the dissenting group filed further allegations relating to the remuneration of top executives, alleged that cliques existed on the DFG Board who were engaged in misleading and deceptive conduct and wastage of money in forcing an *unwanted* restructure upon the membership.

In February the group's survey results were published in the press. Of the 1,076 replies received (from 5,084 active members):

- 72.7 per cent thought realising *value* was more important than *control*;
- 82.6 per cent wanted to *access* the full value of their shareholding;
- 74.7 per cent wanted the board to negotiate with PARMALAT; and
- 58 per cent sought the removal of Langdon, Tooth and Deputy Chairman Bruem.[22]

DFG continues to court mergers and takeover proposals

Meanwhile, through the turbulence, DFG merger talks with Bonlac proceeded. The merger, if successful, would create an entity equal to 40 per cent of the Australian dairy industry. With both DFG and Bonlac heavily in debt, Bonlac experiencing internal strife and old antipathies lingering, however, talks collapsed. DFG then began talks with National Foods with Alan Tooth seeking a takeover proposal including a *premium* for the loss of farmer control. Discussions were suspended until late 2000, however, as everyone's attention shifted to 'D-Day' – Dairy industry deregulation, scheduled for 1 July 2000 (discussed in Chapter Three).

A showdown with dissenters

At another Special Meeting between the DFG Executive and dissenters on 18 April 2000, further motions were put to remove Langdon, Bruem and Tooth. Dissenters alleged that the trio had failed to inform the board of the PARMALAT takeover proposal and had then engaged in a cover-up. The three leaders were accused of bad corporate governance, misleading and deceptive behaviour and, it was asserted, they were unworthy of member trust. Profits were plunging, the co-operative's market value was declining and the organisation was unstable. Large executive bonuses received particular attention. An exhausted Ian Langdon countered that he and the board had fought hard to bring unity and vision to the disunity of the co-operative movement and insisted that a co-operative was free to talk to anyone, any time, on any matter beneficial to members. Indeed, dissenters replied, but not without proper disclosure. There the matter rested while deregulation proceeded, to be resurrected early in 2001.[23]

Section Two
The 'Big Milkshake': DFG post-deregulation 2000-2004

A divided membership

In 2000 the New South Wales-based Dairy Farmers component of DFG was a century old. In revenue terms, the group was the largest dairy business in Australia.

When deregulation of the dairy industry finally came on 1 July 2000, removing regulated prices and quotas and fundamentally changing the relationship between farmer-suppliers and processors (discussed in Chapter Three), DFG Membership was torn between those who wanted to remain in and those who wished to exit the industry, taking the co-operative's share value with them into retirement or another vocation. It was common by now for individual DFG Members to hold in excess of 100,000 shares. One shareholder had 500,000 shares and controlled approximately 25 per cent of the New South Wales fresh-milk supply! Realising share value and capital gain were topical issues, especially as rumours were circulating about the co-operative's alleged insolvency and uncertainty grew about its ability to redeem shares *before* farmers exiting the industry were deemed to be *inactive* by the *Co-operatives Act* and ineligible for a share of the proceeds of a sale or takeover. Of the co-operative's 5,400 members approximately 600 were already technically inactive. Indeed, about 25 per cent of the membership was actively soliciting a takeover bid valued at $793 million from National Foods. The DFG Board elected, however, not to support the proposal and invited National Foods to put a proposal direct to farmer-owners. National Foods declined to do so and talks lapsed.

The Woolworths' contract

Submitting a low-priced tender, DFG won a supply contract with the major retail supermarket-chain Woolworths in Victorian and Queensland fresh-milk markets, retained the South Australian market but lost New South Wales to National Foods. DFG now commanded 65 per cent of fresh-milk distribution in Australia. On the other hand, wholesale prices plunged by 25 per cent and farmer incomes in New South Wales and Queensland in particular declined commensurately, notwithstanding DFG's efforts to provide Queensland producers with a three months 'soft landing' by retaining pre-deregulation prices.

Five weeks after deregulation, on 5 August 2000, DFG announced price cuts to suppliers and introduced a three-tier payment system for dairy milk, year-round milk and seasonal surplus milk. Supplier allocations were also tied to a three-year supply performance formula.

With Paul's and National Foods now *refusing* milk from DFG Members, disagreements resurfaced between farmers close to and remote from markets and those in seasonally advantaged and disadvantaged areas. It was like those unruly times before co-operatives were invented. More DFG Members could no longer see any advantage in continued membership of the co-operative or indeed in DFG's continued existence. Dairy farmers, including DFG Members, picketed Woolworths in four states demanding a fair price for their produce and criticising processors, including DFG, for 'caving in' to the big retailer's demands. Dairy industry leaders spoke disappointedly about processors who had failed to stand united in dealing with the supermarket assault on prices, including the Chair of the Australian Dairy Industry Council (ADIC) Pat Rowley, who described the successful DFG bid for Woolworths' contracts as a 'tragedy' and said:

> I was disappointed that the co-operatives were either unwilling or unable to stand up there on behalf of farmers and try and hold that (supermarket contracts) price better than where it went to. I've always been concerned that the argument for market share would be fought out with farmers' money and it has been. The premium that has been lost has been lost probably forever…and it is a national tragedy that it has happened. What has happened to market milk will happen to other products unless processors, particularly co-operative processors, work out a way to do something better than they have done.

Ian Langdon defended the Woolworths' tender, claiming that it was a strategic decision to cut competitors' margins and that DFG was, and intended to continue to be, a 'lean and aggressive competitor in the domestic dairy market'. The contract was seen pragmatically as simply an investment in gaining market share and market leverage. The problem, Langdon believed, was not co-operatives nabbing the best deals available under the new conditions but an 'unrealistic price being paid for milk, which should be paid for what it is worth'.[24]

The National Foods takeover bid

After suspended talks resumed, in December 2000 National Foods proposed a merger with DFG. The bid, amounting to $793 million, 75 per cent to be paid in cash and 25 per cent in shares, was virtually a takeover with references to the Equilibrium Model. The proposal contemplated a farmer-owned supply co-operative holding negotiated supply agreements with but *no* shares in a processing and marketing PLC. National Foods also undertook to acquire all DFG CCUs.

The DFG Board was divided on the offer with some directors keen to put the proposal to members while others argued that it failed to provide sufficient guarantees of control for those continuing in the industry. Moreover, opponents said, the deal was based on a *promise* of supply agreements which was impossible to guarantee under Australia's trades practices laws. Without the surety of a guaranteed acceptance of supply, which *only* a farmer-owned co-operative could provide, the farm operations of many producers could be rendered worthless. In other words, only a co-operative could securely underpin farm property values. Were farmers ready to test the market and put their farms at risk?

The National Foods offer lapsed with the company charging that DFG was 'insincere'. Some DFG Members reacted angrily, threatening a class action against the co-operative. Another vote of 'no confidence' was moved against Langdon, Tooth and Bruem in November, attracting only 300 votes indicating approximately 80 per cent support for all three. Dissenters vowed to fight on and early in 2001 yet another move was made to remove the trio and also Director Girgenson. Again members supported the executive, although this time approval fell below 80 per cent.[25]

The Equilibrium Model is resurrected

DFG took another version of the Equilibrium Model back to the Supreme Court in April 2001, better taking into account members exiting the industry who were seeking to access share value. The judge noted that both active and inactive members were seeking to unlock the co-operative's value but that the latter were at a greater risk because if they were not paid within the period permitted by the act they would not receive the full value for shares. The judge ordered that DFG conduct a plebiscite of inactive members in conjunction with a postal vote of active members, with regard to the proposed restructure. The court also ruled to permit a creditors' meeting of CCU holders. (At that meeting, unsubstantiated allegations were again raised that DFG was technically insolvent.)

DFG subsequently changed the rules so that directors were obliged to put a proposal to members *regardless* of the views of directors and to ensure that all information would be provided in a neutral and factual manner, standardised and according to agreed guidelines. With board power so qualified and grower control reasserted, an out-of-court settlement was reached between the DFG Board and dissenters whereby the latter agreed to cease action and the former to cover costs.

'No' to the Equilibrium Model

A hurried ballot proceeded. Members were supplied with two thick volumes of detailed information and ballot papers covering 'No Change', 'Sell Everything' and 'Equilibrium Model' options. A busy schedule of member meetings was arranged where it was noticeable that big shareholders generally urged a 'No Change' vote and a return to the National Foods offer. Members demanded more information but, DFG's History Website notes, 'directors [were] under strict conditions imposed by the court on what they [could] say in answering…questions'.

When the ballot closed on 15 June, 73 per cent of active members had voted. After more than seven years of urging by the executive, a clear majority supported the Equilibrium Model proposal (63 per cent), but this was well below the 75 per cent approval required by the act. The 'Sell Everything' option similarly failed to attract the required vote.

Jan Todd tells us that the DFG Board was 'dismayed' by the result. The Equilibrium Model, Todd believes, had simply 'run out of time' after deregulation changed conditions and sentiment and made it worthwhile for competitors to exploit farmer fears. 'Democracy' did not work, Todd says, because:

> In all the legalistic constraints, prescriptions, precautions and requirements for detail the capacity to make a simple statement of the essence of choice had been lost…The Dairy Farmers' Co-operative was more than milk, more than a dairy processor, it was also a community. The ethos of "each for all and all for each" had been sorely tested, frayed and fractured by deregulation, but in 2001 it still meant something. The most pressing future challenge for the board was to repair the fissures, restore the collective spirit and unite the membership once again behind the programmes and progress of their co-operative.

Ian Langdon pointed to the repeated failure of 'no confidence' motions as a vindication of the executive's policy, optimistically describing the ballot result as heralding new opportunities:

> The commercial vision with a restructured capital base was aggressive. The commercial vision without a restructured capital base, although more conservative, is still exciting. It is one of consolidation rather than expansion but consolidation with internally-generated growth.

A 'manager thing'

Some observers were not quite so philosophical. One Gerringong farmer, for example, believed that the ballot had failed because members were suspicious of the DFG Executive, that the co-operative had become a 'manager-thing' and 'farmers feel they have no control over the co-operative any more and that dealing with it is no different to what it would it be like dealing with a public company'. A visiting Netherlands scholar, Onno-Frank van Bekkum, who was investigating co-operative models and farmer policy reform in Europe, Australia and New Zealand, noted that of all the co-operatives in the world he had looked at DFG was exceptional for the *limited* influence of members on company affairs. The researcher believed that DFG's expansion programme had *of itself* generated a heavy investment need which had exceeded the capacity of members to finance this internally and had inevitably driven the co-operative toward an investor model. Moreover, van Bekkum argued, inappropriate investment signals existed in the DFG system and the co-operative's heavy investment campaign, which might have been appropriate in a *regulated* market, in a *deregulated* market introduced incentive problems, which had been masked through an earlier period of sustained growth.[26]

Section Three
Splitting the Co-operative: A Ten-Year Vision

DFG strikes hard times

In 2001/02 DFG's Membership fell by nearly 1,000, the surplus plunged to $700,000 and debt rose to $222 million, plus investments of approximately $80 million. The co-operative nevertheless enjoyed a robust cash-flow of $1.4 billion and rising and, in that sense, was the top dairy business in Australia. Certainly the industry was required to take DFG seriously. DFG had also achieved 1993 goals of 50 per cent revenue from manufacturing milk and 50 per cent of business, not merely outside New South Wales but outside Australia!

A major cost-reduction program was begun designed to eliminate $90 million in business costs over four years while, on the growth front, $77 million was expended on major up-grades to milk-processing plants in South Australia, Queensland and Victoria and on a mozzarella plant at Malanda, geared to exports. The industry was also surprised to learn that DFG had acquired a 9.2 percent holding in National Foods. How could the co-operative afford all of this?

With CEO Alan Tooth planning retirement a major management restructure began. Sounding a little exasperated, the general manager detailed how DFG intended to abandon low-profit business (including milk-supply contracts), prune jobs (which precipitated strikes) and abandon any industry rationalisation initiatives, especially with co-operatives. Tooth now acknowledged that co-operating farmers had 'priorities of their own', which did not necessarily coincide with conventional expansionary agendas:

> *If we were all public companies [rationalisation] would have happened a long time ago. But farmer security, farmer growth, prosperity and the value of their farms are far more important to our members than the value of their shares in the co-operative.*[27]

In 2002 the co-operative lost Woolworths' contracts in some states in a tendering process which saw National Foods gain a much greater share and now control 40 per cent of the total national drinking-milk market. With farmers dumping milk surplus to requirements, DFG was required to *import* Victorian milk to honour supply agreements.

Partial-demutualisation: a 'ten-year' vision

Notwithstanding earlier rebuffs, Alan Tooth and Ian Langdon were as determined as ever to achieve a partial-demutualisation restructure, still arguing that DFG's capital position was unsustainable and that it was impossible to 'grow' the organisation reliant upon internal capital. Langdon promised to rule out nothing 'involving benefits to the dairy farmers of Australia,' continued to hold discussions with potential corporate partners and sought bank advice on restructuring debt and financing further expansion.

Alan Tooth's replacement as Managing Director and CEO, Calvin Boyle, had been with DFG for more than a decade. At the 2002 AGM, which saw rule changes by special resolution to provisions for elections, casual board vacancies and increases to directors' remuneration, the chairman told the assembly of a new 'ten-year vision' for DFG. The co-operative's need for a substantive capital base and a more flexible capital structure was as vital as ever, Langdon reiterated, and the board intended to revisit the capital restructure option for a *third* time:

> *Dairy Farmers has built up considerable momentum over the past ten years during a period of considerable growth. Now we have to reinvest in that momentum if we are to sustain the growth in the business that is called for by our new vision…We still have a long way to go to deliver the returns that our farmer/members demand. As a co-operative 100 per cent Australian owned we have to respond to our farmers who insist that we provide them with security and growth for their future…Over the next few months the board will work on new plans which will be different from the Equilibrium Model that was presented eighteen months ago. Circumstances have changed…but one thing that is constant is our need for a substantive and flexible capital base to allow us to meet the growth requirements set by our new vision.[28]*

A 'de-merger' proposal

A protracted drought through 2003 saw production levels fall and farm gate prices for milk decline. With DFG's cost-cutting and debt reduction programme in full swing and some analysts concerned at the co-operative's debt level ($302 million), the board's attention was briefly diverted from the ten-year vision. DFG, however, continued to operate as Australia's second-largest fresh-milk processor, behind National Foods but ahead of the PARMALAT Australian operation.

In March 2004 Chairman Langdon began an intensive round of member meetings with a view to a partial-demutualisation of the co-operative and an ASX listing later in the year. Fifty meetings were held in a fortnight involving DFG's 3200 members! The rationale was to corporatise Dairy Farmers' processing arm to enable the co-operative to be 'more pro-active in consolidating Australia's $11 billion dairy industry'. Langdon employed all of his persuasive skills to encourage members to agree to splitting DFG into *two* co-operatives, a new one for milk supply (Dairy Farmers Milk Co-operative Limited [DFMC]) and one for processing (the original Australian Co-operative Foods [ACF]). In Stage 1 existing ACF members would have all of their shares cancelled and be issued with one DFMC share for each original ACF share cancelled, paid out at the original price of $ 1.00 per share. This stage was seen as the first step in a two-year plan to convert ACF into a company; Dairy Farmers Limited; and pursue public listing (Stage 2).

The chairman remained convinced that ACF could more easily acquire assets (in PARMALAT's Victorian business, for instance) if it were structured as a company and would be able to raise equity capital from financial markets and not be restricted to the membership base. He believed that a 'de-merged' structure would permit investors in Dairy Farmers Limited to come to 'directly own' (through listed shares) an entity which they had formerly owned only 'indirectly' (co-operatively), without changing the underlying ownership structure of the original group of companies. Theoretically, the 'de-merger' would permit existing ACF shareholders to own 100 per cent of the new supply co-operative, DFMC, and 80 per cent of the restructured processor, which would initially be 20 per cent owned by DFMC with existing ACF members holding 80 per cent of shares which would become available for trading at market value over time. The size of the board was to be reduced to nine, including five farmer-directors and four independent directors, including the managing director.

Feedback from these meetings was incorporated in Supreme Court briefings and the court approved the holding of a ballot. In June 2004 members overwhelmingly (85.5 per cent) supported Stage 1 of the restructure which split ACF into separate milk supply and processing co-operatives.

The supply co-operative, DFMC, commenced operations on 29 June 2004, with responsibility for negotiating milk supply terms with ACF and was designed:

> ...to secure a long term, dependable outlet at commercial prices for milk produced by farmers/ members of the supply co-operative which takes into account their on-farm growth. The Annual General Meeting [saw] the finalisation of Stage 1 of the Restructure, with the election of the reduced numbers of farmer/directors – three ACF farmer/directors, two in common farmer directors with the Dairy Farmers' Milk Co-operative and four independents.

Flat sales and a subsequent plunge in profits, however, saw plans for Stage 2 postponed. Listing was now not thought likely until 2007. In the interim Dairy Farmers sold its 9.2 percent stake in National Foods and Calvin Boyle resigned as Managing Director and CEO. He was replaced by Rob Gordon, formerly with Goodman Fielder Consumer Foods.

At time of writing the democracy principle survives in Dairy Farmers, after more than a century. Nevertheless, Ian Langdon sensed that there was a:

> ...growing desire amongst many members for greater access to liquidity of ownership of equity as well as a desire to achieve growth in the value of such equity.[29]

Certainly the 'hybrid' model had borne surprising fruit.

Section Four
DFG Member-Executive Relations and the Democracy Principle

It would be tempting to conclude from the foregoing that DFG Members were driven over several years by a leadership bent on growing the co-operative at farmer expense before partially-demutualising or selling the operation outright, regardless of member sentiment. This would be a simplistic and misleading view. Numerous factors need to be taken into account in understanding DFG's Member-Executive relations through this torrid period, including: geography; the heterogeneity of membership; the impact of deregulation; an inability of co-operatives to co-operate; and a practical need to resolve a 'co-operative dilemma' found in capital adequacy-democracy tensions.

An heterogeneous membership
ACF/DFG's far-flung membership base was heterogeneous, comprising long-term and new members, young and old farmers, large and small suppliers, pro-co-operative and anti-co-operative elements, regionally-focused producers and farmers with opposed views on deregulation. As the co-operative expanded interstate, the membership naturally reflected a greater diversity of traditions and expectations, affecting communication. It was inevitable that this should surface in governance where the interests of all shareholders needed to be taken into account. If nurturing a close bond of association had been a priority, possibly outcomes might have been different. Whether they would have served members' interests better, however, is debatable.

The role of deregulation
With impending deregulation driving everything before it in dairy industry politics, it was hardly surprising that differences on strategic responses should surface at board level and at AGMs. The fear of deregulation occurring *before* the co-operative was ready to deal with it and the disastrous impact this could have on farm values and dairying communities created a 'siege mentality' where the co-operative's survival at all costs shaped policies, even to the extent of considering an abandonment of the democracy principle. Why else would members overwhelmingly have approved the compulsory

issue of bonus shares in 1993? Farmers understood that deregulation would divide the interests of suppliers and processors; co-operative or not; because old guarantees and supports would disappear, sellers and buyers had inimical interests and because it was pragmatically recognised that, in a contest between principle and self-interest, the latter would usually prevail. Farmers *and* processors independently would seek the best prices available, wherever they might be found in free markets. How could control in perpetuity be guaranteed in this scenario? Was not a 'hybrid' compromise sensible, efficiently locking in farmer investments and providing them with a modicum of commodity control in markets to the degree farmers were willing to fund this? In seeking to answer these questions, members, directors and managers, severally and individually, offered solutions ranging from 'do nothing' to 'sell up and leave everything to markets'. In a democratic business like DFG, these opposed camps naturally vied for ascendancy, creating tensions and occasionally conflict. That is how a democratic business functions. It was not merely a case of an executive asserting a particular line redolent of the corporate world; although some tried; but a situation where commercial judgement was always tempered by the democratic participation of the organisation's owners – farmers. That is not to say that growth for growth's sake was not without risks for an organisation genuinely seeking to retain a co-operative identity. But the opposite was equally true – doing nothing in the approach to deregulation was potentially disastrous.

The co-operatives will not co-operate

If co-operatives were to have any real chance of retaining a significant market share post-deregulation, there were really only two choices: co-operate through a council of co-operatives wielding critical mass sufficient to influence markets; or individually grow as large as possible so as to be taken seriously. ACF did initially seek to join with co-operatives but this proved to be slow, expensive and exasperating. A labyrinth of states' rights, parochialism, ancient enmities, inadequate legislation, disagreements over deregulation, National Competition Policy and trades practices laws existed to complicate co-operation between co-operatives. Cases in point were the 1997 rejection by the Australian Competition and Consumer Commission (ACCC) under NCP rules of a proposed ACF-Norco merger and complex and expensive jurisdictional problems attending the QUD merger. Facing such obstacles in fluid and highly contested markets it is perhaps understandable that co-operative leadership might occasionally act unilaterally in conducting a growth programme. What is not so clear, however, is why a leadership committed to co-operative principles would drive so ambitious a strategy that it required more capital than members could reasonably provide themselves without recourse to external investors.

Restating the 'co-operative dilemma'

Resolutely economic rationalist, Ian Langdon saw co-operation as purely a commercial philosophy, a vehicle for creating wealth in a competitive world. His emphasis in policy formulation lay unashamedly on the amassing of individual wealth. He deprecated co-operative 'purists' for perpetuating rigidities in co-operative structure, based on what he saw as narrow and inflexible 'rules'. To the degree co-operative principles supported wealth creation, they were efficacious. To the extent they did not, they were dispensable. Even the sacred democracy principle where this hampered wealth accumulation was 'political', not 'commercial', and needed redesigning. The mutuality principle, allowing co-operatives favourable taxation consideration (discussed in Appendix One), was similarly disposable if it cut across wealth creation. Insisting he was keeping faith with co-operative principles, the chairman nevertheless lost no opportunity to critique co-operative structure which, he argued, not entirely unreasonably, dissipated capital, was flawed in equity principles, laboured under inadequate legislation, was prone to 'lack-lustre' performance and was motivated more by sentiment and 'tribalism' than good business sense. Langdon was convinced that ACF must 'Get Big or Get Out' and, with co-operatives losing the ascendancy to companies in fresh-milk markets, there was evidence supporting this view. There was also evidence confirming a 'Small is Beautiful' philosophy, the Bega (New South Wales) and Tatura (Victoria) co-operatives, for example, but this option seems not to have been seriously considered by ACF Members, perhaps reflecting leadership's commitment to growth.

Ian Langdon resolutely linked ACF/DFG's survival to growth and significant capital-raising. The choice in fund-raising, he correctly said, was either *internal* or *external* and both were risky. Convinced that deregulation would compel a shift by co-operatives toward an investor-model as they lost dominance in markets, the executive was successful first in obtaining approval for the compulsory bonus-share scheme, notwithstanding doubts about creating 'class' divisions and the co-operative's capacity to redeem shares. Subsequently, senior executives argued the need for external capital. If capitalists were not permitted to invest in the co-operative, Langdon believed, farmers would lose control anyway because ACF/DFG would inevitably become unviable in deregulated markets. That is, the justification for external investment was the inevitability of non-viability in its absence – it was better to invite external investors in and retain a degree of farmer control to the extent members were prepared to fund this, than to lose control entirely. However, the argument went, capitalists would not invest in co-operatives without discounts with 'heritage' values like the democracy principle encumbering their interests. This was the 'co-operative dilemma', restated. It was not simply a matter of *balancing* democracy and capital adequacy, but of *diluting* the former to attract *sufficient* of the latter. As Onno-Frank van Bekkum observed, however, the ambitious investment and acquisitions programme driving DFG's insatiable appetite for capital was possibly as important a reason for the farmers' inability to provide adequate funds as alleged deficiencies in the co-operative business model.

Uncoupling ownership from control

The executive advocated a 'hybrid' Equilibrium Model, almost unique in Australian corporate history, in the belief that financial markets (investors) would take this seriously. While the model evolved over time, the basic premise was that through its application *ownership* might be uncoupled from *control* in co-operative structure. The assumption was that the latter could possibly exist in the absence of the former; that perpetual control and shared ownership were reconcilable. Many members simply did not believe this, but some did – a majority in the 2001 ballot. In response to complaints that the 'hybrid' model was simply a return to 'dry' shareholder days, DFG leaders challenged opponents to *fund* the retention of the democracy principle and other 'heritage' values if they valued them so much.

As profits fell, member concern arose about alleged cliques on the board, an 'inner sanctum' deaf to their concerns. By 1997, for example, the board and the Equity Committee were divided, with some directors arguing that it was fanciful to split the co-operative into sections performing opposed economic functions – buyer and seller – and impatient with the apparent fixation of some directors with the 'hybrid' model, which they believed would merely smooth the way to demutualisation. Inevitably questions arose. What did a profitable co-operative of active members really have to fear if it continued to provide services at cost and return surpluses equitably? What guarantees were there, really, that a new breed of 'dry' shareholder would not emerge in the investor part of the 'hybrid' and, in hard times, press to sell off the co-operative and realise on its assets? Was the executive really trying to solve a 'co-operative dilemma' or was it more a management problem and a question of commitment to co-operation? Simultaneously the executive grew weary of what it saw as membership indecision and procrastination, which confounded good business judgement.

A question of style: the democracy principle

Many communication problems experienced by members and the executive stemmed from: the co-operative's sheer size and spread; a bold, even 'predatory', expansionary agenda; the hectic pace of change; and a perception that managing this was more a matter of executive prerogative than member will. Certainly, tension existed between an executive frustrated by a need to manage with 'one hand tied behind its back' and a membership equally determined to see a proper observance of the democracy principle. Determined that DFG should not 'fall over' post-deregulation; as many in the industry expected; the executive was sometimes perceived as overbearing, employing a 'top-down' centralist style of management. Indeed, some elements gave every appearance of believing that the co-operative was 'theirs', rather than a vehicle for the expression of members' democratic will. Occasionally, the executive ignored cautioning by members and international visitors against accepting the advice of corporate consultants and the shortcomings of 'hybrid' structures. Leaders often justified strategic positions as if they were self-evident truths, for example: partial demutualisation was inevitable post-deregulation; farmers could keep control but the co-operative would cease to be viable; and listing on ASX was a desirable thing for a co-operative to do. Information to which members were reasonably entitled was occasionally not made available in a timely manner. The executive seemed also to be engaged in development 'creep': first, internal capital sourced from a compulsory bond-share scheme was adequate; then, external capital was vital. 'Control in perpetuity' was reconceived to mean *only if* farmers were prepared to pay for it. Seeking to release wealth for DFG's 'stakeholders', everything was placed 'on the table', including options to sell outright, or list. Some members understandably asked if this was how leaders committed to co-operation really behaved?

In seeking to make the co-operative more like an investor-organisation, DFG leaders challenged members to develop a share culture, to swap the notion of *equality* for *equity*, enabling the co-operative to source new income streams, rework the patronage principle and discard other 'rigidities' like the 'limited interest on shares' principle. Certainly, there was nothing in the *Co-operatives Act* contrary to this. Moreover, ICA principles permit members to allocate surpluses for co-operative development, through reserves for example, benefiting members in proportion to their transactions with the co-operative in support of other activities approved by members.

There is no question that DFG was a democratic business in the sense used here: owned and controlled jointly by members who actively participated in setting policies and making decisions. When Ian Langdon took the helm, the co-operative's democracy was shaky, recovering from the Panfida raid and a purging of 'dry' shareholders. While Onno-Frank van Bekkum noted in 2000 that DFG was exceptional for the limited influence upon policy of members, this problem was addressed by an extensive ward system of representation, improved transparency and a more inclusive process of filling casual vacancies on the board. In this sense DFG's democracy was *stronger* at the end of the period than the beginning, albeit sorely tested in the intervening years.

For a big trading co-operative, the interface between markets and members *is* the board and executive and it is their job to keep both sides of the equation satisfied. To the extent that the DFG Executive creatively managed this relationship and grew the co-operative, their efforts were successful. It cannot be overlooked that the co-operative was drawn back from the brink of destruction in the late 1980s and was turned into a major player in national dairy product markets, with successful interstate and international operations. The board and executive must take much of the credit for this and, in particular, Chairman Ian Langdon. Finally, however, through support of their co-operative and democratic participation, it was the members who curbed the excesses of those who would 'sell out' to the corporate world and who delivered that success.

Part V

OVERVIEW

CBH Group, Metro Grain Centre. An aerial view (date unknown).
Photo courtesy of CBH Limited.

Chapter Seventeen

'Missing in Action':
FARMER CO-OPERATIVES IN TWENTIETH CENTURY AUSTRALIA

Traditional primary co-operatives are business entities with a distinctive structure based on one-member-one-vote (the democracy principle), commitment to member service, limited return on shares, and profits returned to members commensurate with business transacted (the patronage principle). While modern business practice has made limited return on capital and the patronage principle less a feature of co-operative structure, the democracy principle is crucial to an understanding of economic co-operation.

It is conventional wisdom that 'democracy and business do not mix'. Curiosity about this dichotomy motivated the study. A corollary was, if the democracy principle is such a good idea, why did it not achieve a greater potential in the economy through the Australian farmer co-operative movement? Seeking to answer this question, the book has explored how external and internal forces played upon tensions between the democracy principle and capital adequacy (the 'co-operative dilemma') and how this impacted upon the credentials of co-operatives as democratic businesses.

Physically and institutionally the Australian farmer co-operative movement remained immature relative to other OECD nations at the end of the twentieth century, notwithstanding a long and colourful history and the presence of a few giants. The future of the movement hung in the balance, with many 'icons' disappearing in the final quarter, or so restructured as to be borderline co-operatives. After a century of effort, there was no economically powerful producer-consumer wholesale business exercising market power and providing a countervailing force in a food industry increasingly dominated by retail chains and international agribusiness. Very few innovative farmer co-operatives operated in secondary and tertiary sectors of the economy. There was no co-operative bank issuing sympathetic finance to a united and prosperous co-operative movement differentiated in markets under a distinctive banner. No resolutely-supported co-operative 'parliament' existed, representing a wide spectrum of co-operative opinion, democratically determining policy nationwide, resolving co-operative disputes and speaking to governments with a single voice. There was no federal co-operatives extension service for development work co-operating with state registries in the administration of uniform (or federal) co-operatives' legislation, which also did not exist. Neither did a tertiary co-operatives research and development institution, one primarily funded by the co-operative movement, exist. The Australian farmer co-operative movement remained adrift from the international co-operative movement. Why?

In drawing conclusions about the role of the Australian farmer co-operative movement in the twentieth century, reference is made to the external and internal factors.

External factors include:

❖ Australia's vast distances and the thinly scattered dispersal of co-operatives;

❖ the relative lateness, historically speaking, of co-operation's introduction into antipodean agriculture;

❖ dramatic changes in world trade conditions across the century;

❖ states rights issues;

- governmental opportunism in respect of co-operative development;
- unhelpful legislation;
- the absence of a strong federal government hand in co-operative affairs;
- macro- and micro-economic reform at odds with co-operative principles;
- the impact of ideological and market opponents;
- a lessening of agriculture's economic and political importance; and
- a general perception that co-operatives lay outside public and private-profit mainstream traditions, encapsulated by a suspicion of co-operatives within both the labour movement and the finance industry.

Internal factors include the unavoidable conclusions that farmer co-operatives were:
- more given to competition than co-operation;
- owed their first allegiance to industries in which they functioned, rather than to a co-operative movement as such;
- failed to co-operate with each other, let alone with co-operatives of other descriptions, particularly the consumer co-operative movement;
- neglected to build or adequately support durable co-operative umbrella institutions;
- failed to invest in co-operative education;
- failed to capture the imagination of younger generations; and
- in seeking to solve the 'co-operative dilemma', fell foul of Hans H Munkner's 'four threats' thesis (discussed in Chapter Twelve), explaining how co-operatives may lose sight of their unique identity.

The first threat, which Munkner posits, is commercialising co-operatives to prioritise market share and competitiveness. The second is growth for growth's sake, so diluting the bond of association and creating a membership so heterogeneous that it is impossible for members to agree on anything. The third threat is inviting external investors into a co-operative's structure, diluting the ownership-control equation. If a co-operative needs to do that, Munkner believes, it is time to convert to a company. The fourth threat is degrading membership by neglecting to cultivate a co-operative consciousness in everything a co-operative does, particularly education.

Considering external factors first, Australian rural co-operation began late in the nineteenth century when the dual impacts of 'middle men' and improved productivity upon farmer incomes virtually compelled it. The co-operative idea spread quickly, albeit piecemeal, throughout Australia's far-flung agricultural areas. Industries and rural communities sprang up around co-operatives, which developed largely in isolation from each other. Until well into the twentieth century, late by international standards, there were few sedentary rural communities in a still developing nation where a co-operative culture might take root. Distance, parochialism and post-colonial state jealousies, encapsulated in a free-trade–protectionist schism, militated against co-operative unity, ensuring that the nascent movement stayed scattered and poorly organised. Very few farmer co-operatives thought of themselves as national entities, but rather operating at regional or state level, and most were small and local in nature – rudimentary businesses with only a few involved in value-adding.

Farmer co-operatives evolved through a century of stupendous change when the socio-economic environment was transformed from one conducive to co-operation to one which was inhospitable, even hostile, placing conventional co-operative values under enormous strain. The national economy, conforming for much of the period to a rural division of labour, passed through four major phases: nineteenth century *laissez faire*, characterised by an exploitation of farmers; industry self-regulation, which saw unruly markets develop; rigid statutory control, which stifled co-operative development; and, near the end of the century, *laissez faire* neo-liberal globalisation. A shambling farmer cooperative movement, at best reflexive to each phase, except for the first, coped haphazardly.

The importance of protectionism and state socialism in shaping Australian co-operative development cannot be overemphasised. The golden period for farmer co-operatives expansion was between the world wars, ironically coinciding with the expansion of regulation. While it is fair to say that co-operatives enhance farmer marketing power, their capacity to do so was significantly modified by the presence for much of the century of statutory marketing authorities (SMAs), which cocooned co-operatives and tended to make them 'lazy' and, generally, production-driven. SMAs did much of the work done by co-operatives in other nations and, historically speaking, their creation sealed the fate of Australian farmer co-operation.

SMAs, not co-operatives, insulated farmers from market vicissitudes, provided countervailing power, put a floor under market prices, controlled supply, smoothed price fluctuations, identified export opportunities, achieved economies of scale, conducted industry extension services and spoke coherently to government. An historic opportunity existed for farmer co-operatives to develop many of these functions in the first quarter of the century but, still primitively organised and parochial, they failed to do so. For over half a century SMAs quarantined co-operatives from market forces so that, after the 1970s, when co-operatives were exposed to inflation, corporate raids, changing consumer habits, improved competition, deregulation and globalisation, many were ill-prepared and exited the movement or were so restructured as to be unrecognisable as co-operatives. Essentially, as regulation first expanded and then contracted, like a statutory ice age, farmer co-operatives generally failed to adapt quickly enough, leaving opportunities for SMAs and for corporations at opposite ends of century. The historic price for co-operatives was marginalisation.

The Canadian co-operative thinker, Alexander Laidlaw, warns that government money is the 'kiss of death' for a co-operative movement, which becomes as a result a mere instrument in development projects. Australian co-operative leaders who were knowledgeable about co-operative theory and history well understood that when co-operatives give governments responsibility for solving their problems, a co-operative movement is doomed. Too much bureaucracy and too little co-operative involvement is prone to produce 'co-operative amnesia' in public policy and a degrading of co-operative consciousness. The problem for Australian co-operative development was that some major agricultural co-operatives, early and late in the century, desperate for support from whatever quarter, actively courted government patronage. While SMAs stunted co-operation's economic development, even well-intended centralist co-operative development programmes tended to anaesthetise the movement's capacity for independent institutional development (not that this was often evident). Some government programmes were successful, such as fishing co-operatives, building societies and credit unions, which fall outside the scope of this study, but many failed and most underachieved. Political support for co-operatives was always conditional and, some believed late in the century, more about setting them up legislatively to be *taken over* or to be *listed* on a stock exchange, than about promoting them as a distinctive form of business. Indeed, some central agencies, persuaded to economic rationalism and competition, saw co-operatives as 'fossils' from a bygone era and the best thing that could happen to them was to be absorbed into the corporate world.

It is a truism that law can facilitate or obstruct. For much of the last century Australian state-based co-operatives' legislation was deficient: variously vague, archaic, slack, complicated, paternalistic or excessively regulatory and heavy-handed. One of the great themes in Australian co-operatives' history has been tension between 'bogus' (investor orientated) and 'genuine' (services orientated) co-operatives. Co-operatives' legislation long tolerated 'bogus' co-operatives and accommodated the interests of 'dry' shareholders, diminishing the incentive for 'genuine' co-operation and sullying co-operation's credentials as a democratic movement. A jig-saw of state-based legislation hampered co-operation at national level, 'pigeon-holed' co-operatives, complicated their institutional development and proscribed financial autonomy. A great problem, too, for governmental co-operative development agencies, was accommodating the legislative and institutional needs of an asymmetrically-developed sector characterised by a few commercially-orientated giants and a multitude of community-based not-for-profits. Registries were required simultaneously to perform 'policeman' and development roles and, as resources were diverted elsewhere in the bureaucracy, officers faced a quandary: how to balance co-operative development with a capacity for sound administration. More development inevitably placed the bureaucracy under strain, effectively putting a cap on development. Once having gained a grip on co-operative development, bureaucracies tended to retain their hold. There was rough justice in this, however, for how could a co-operative movement unwilling to nurture its own organisational needs, *not* be subsumed within government? By late in the century such dwindling public resources as existed for general co-operatives development were concentrated upon implementing radically new legislation enhancing the competitiveness of farmer co-operatives and largely unhelpful to community-based co-operatives, the heartland of the movement, or to a new 'social economy-third sector' movement. After government interest in co-operatives waned, an organisational vacuum was left in co-operatives development from which the movement has still not recovered.

A notable feature of Australian co-operatives' history has been the absence of a strong federal presence other than for taxation and trade. Periodically, however, the federal government did seek to encourage co-operative development, in the contexts of wartime essential services, deregulation and foreign aid, for example. Such efforts were repeatedly thwarted by states' rights advocates, 'anti-socialist' elements, particularly in the National Party, and individual co-operatives chary of referring powers to Canberra, which might disadvantage them in markets.

Notwithstanding campaigns by co-operative activists and government officials, who understood the critical need for federal or uniform national co-operatives' legislation, this was not achieved after nearly a century of effort, although some painfully slow progress was made late in the period. This contributed to the squandering of historic opportunities, for instance, co-operatively organising the dairy industry nationally early in the century. It also hampered the utilisation of the co-operative business model as SMAs were being dismantled in the final quarter, and remains a major stumbling block.

As to the role of competitors, it would be naïve to discount the impact of ideological and market opponents upon co-operative development, although the study has not delved into this in a systematic way. In a virulent Australian capitalist environment characterised for much of the period by a strong element of state socialism, farmer co-operatives were not operating in a benign situation. For half a century they sheltered behind statutory regulation, which 'carved up' market functions between proprietary, co-operative and government players in a state-based 'co-operative' arrangement, all that was possible under the Australian Constitution. To the degree that farmer co-operatives improved competition in orderly markets and confined themselves to legislatively prescribed roles, they were politically accommodated, even encouraged, and perceived to have a valid role in a mixed economy. Nevertheless, co-operatives were seen by ideological opponents as a rival to the capitalist model and viewed suspiciously by market competitors, especially their favourable taxation position. Occasionally this translated into political attacks (discussed in Appendix One).

With regard to internal factors impinging upon co-operative development, at industry level co-operatives demonstrated that they were more given to competition than co-operation. Co-operatives' first allegiance was to their industry, with the co-operative movement running a poor second. Usually content to rely upon sectional industry bodies for development work, farmer co-operatives generally showed low-level support for broader co-operative development issues and were reluctant to adequately fund co-operative third-tier organisations, which might have nurtured solidarity, cultivated a co-operative consciousness and provided a stable forum for debate and representation. They also often failed to co-operate *within* an industry, let alone *across* industries – the dairy industry is a good example. Industrial fractiousness was exacerbated by states'-rights bickering, ensuring that the movement stayed disunited and directionless. Numerous co-operative institutions arose and fell, confounded by ideological disputation and ambiguous support from the sector. The failures of the Co-operative Federation of Australia (CFA) and the Australian Association of Co-operatives (AAC), in the 1980s and 1990s respectively, were colossal blows. Failing to construct an enduring 'parliament' united around a common core of agreed principles and strategies, large commercial farmer co-operatives assumed leadership and looked to government and investors for a solution to the 'co-operative dilemma', a risky strategy for a professedly 'self-help' movement and of little relevance to most co-operatives.

Failing to invest adequately in co-operatives' education (product advertising is not education), farmer co-operatives allowed the run-down of co-operative consciousness to continue, one of Munkner's most serious 'threats'. Not withstanding efforts by a few gallant souls, this neglect guaranteed that the general understanding of co-operative culture among the public and members alike remained superficial. Another consequence was that most co-operators did not know *how* to co-operate, how to make reciprocity work, how to help interdependence bear fruit, how to effect timely strategic decisions, how to deal with selfishness, egos and a lust for power or how to learn from mistakes. Indeed, Garry Cronan has observed that most co-operatives saw their historical roots as a *burden* and not a source of strength. Not surprisingly a perception arose that co-operatives were the 'poor cousin' of corporations: poorly managed; lacking access to adequate capital; with the majority of members leaning on the few; risk averse; technologically backward; and poor performers. Co-operatives came to be seen by some as contrary to Australian individualism, vulnerable to the 'human factor', flawed in theory and managing a cost structure and operating in ways relevant to an economic and regulatory environment which was passing.

Validly or otherwise, co-operatives were thought of as inherently 'unprofitable' and risky, slaves of regulation, administratively 'expensive', relics of a bygone era which had exceeded their 'use by' date and would 'fall over' as soon as the props of regulation were stripped away. Seldom did farmer co-operatives rally to refute such allegations, or to argue coherently the special qualities and benefits of co-operation, leaving that task generally to government departments and a few dedicated advocates. No wonder co-operatives lost the hearts and minds of a generation and became largely invisible to the masses, baffling to government, reliant upon experts and corporate consultants unversed in co-operative ways and confined to the margins of economic and social mainstream events.

As for nurturing a support base within agriculture, farmer co-operatives, whatever principles they might have espoused early in the century, when they enjoyed widespread rural support, lost sight of their original purpose and forgot the co-operative maxim, 'Each for All and All for Each'.

Far from proclaiming the democracy principle as a quintessential element of a farmer ethos, this was hidden away as if it were an embarrassing family secret from a radical past. Apart from wealth creation, which corporations also stood for and did well, farmer co-operatives ultimately stood for nothing. Why should anyone particularly care about them? The price was a further decaying of community support.

Farmer co-operatives, historically, generally refused to co-operate with Australian co-operative consumers, seeing their interests as inimical and, in so doing, squandered their greatest potential support base while, ironically, co-operating with British co-operative consumers for much of the century through English CWS. Indeed, in the labour movement, they were commonly perceived as little more than agents of a native rural hostility towards urban consumers. This crucial flaw in the farmer co-operative movement's preparedness for economic and social leadership reaped bitter fruit late in the century when retail conglomerates dominated food markets and farmers again became price takers. Indeed, the recent phenomenon of Farmers Markets, where producers and consumers trade directly, is redolent of the old co-operative wholesale idea espoused by Rochdale idealists – but the markets are still small, scattered and not usually structured as co-operatives.

Farmer co-operatives seldom worked harmoniously with Labor or the labour movement and were generally identified with the conservative side of politics, anomalous for a so-called apolitical movement. Of all major political groupings, the Country (National/Nationals) Party did most to promote agricultural co-operatives, seeing them as a natural element of their support base and a bulwark against 'socialism'. Across the century, agriculture shrank significantly as a percentage of GDP and the nature of agriculture changed, becoming more concentrated and capital intensive. Naturally, this impacted upon co-operatives, changing the demographic while necessitating hefty investments to match competition. With economic pressure building on family farms, a trend to corporate farms accelerated after the 1980s as agriculture's political influence waned. Nevertheless, the farmer co-operative movement continued to exercise political influence through 'back door' access to government via co-operative advisory councils, for example. Co-operative leaders occasionally used this 'card' to go straight to the relevant minister, bypassing industry bodies (or co-operative associations) whose policies conflicted with theirs. Certainly, agricultural co-operatives strongly influenced public policy for co-operatives and not always beneficially. Examples of this are found in Western Australia between the world wars and New South Wales in the early 1990s, where the state virtually took over co-operative development at the behest of politically powerful agricultural co-operatives.

When, in the wake of OPEC price increases and Britain's entry into Europe in the 1970s, the tide of history turned against co-operatives, long established societies began a frantic scramble for capital and, in the process, fundamentally changed the nature of co-operation. Unable to achieve financial autonomy through a co-operative bank (a prerequisite for a 'self-help' movement), co-operatives remained beholden to the good will of capitalist financial institutions. In the quest for competitiveness, indeed, survival, they turned to corporate consultants, who tended to see co-operatives either as anachronisms or as serving purely pecuniary interests, with no other meaning or purpose. A new breed of leaders arose, briefed by farmers to resolve the 'co-operative dilemma'. Holding that co-operation was purely a commercial philosophy, new leaders confronted farmer directors with a conceptual challenge: radically alter co-operative structure or go out of business. They argued for the adaptation of co-operative principles to suit new business realities, the flexible reconfiguration of co-operative structure and the exposure of the democracy principle to market forces, in order to ascertain its true value to farmers. By offering rewards for supply *and* investments,

Murray Goulburn Factory, Leongatha (November 1978).
Photo courtesy of Murray Goulburn Co-operative Co. Limited.

new wave leaders sought to convert co-operatives from a service orientation to a wealth-creation orientation. By linking supply to shareholding, they dismissed the idea that co-operative shares were merely a licence to participate and attached to them a value beyond any traditional understanding of the patronage principle. Disregarding local advice and international evidence to the contrary, they advocated the *separation* of ownership from control, theoretically enabling farmers to access multiple income streams *without* surrendering control, even to the extent of sharing ownership with external investors.

Only the democracy principle braked their enthusiasm. Flirting with external investors was always risky and farmers knew it, observing many co-operatives in Australia and abroad already struggling to maintain equilibrium on the 'slippery slope' to capitalist orthodoxy – but what was the alternative? Slowly becoming non-viable? There is no rule which says a co-operative should live forever. Co-operators decide whether to continue or discontinue co-operating and, like all businesses, uncompetitive co-operatives go out of business. Farmers also knew that a 'Get Big or Get Out' philosophy, promoted by some leaders, would inevitably exacerbate the 'co-operative dilemma', rendering co-operatives vulnerable to a paralysis in governance and to external investors, Munkner's second and third 'threats'. Farmers knew that the larger a business grows the more technology, equipment and supplies it needs to operate and the more difficult it becomes to mobilise large amounts of capital, building pressure to demutualise. Onno-Frank van Bekkum tells us, that as 'village' (small agricultural) and commodity co-operatives evolve towards value-added markets, they become more 'individualised', more efficient, more involved in domestic markets, more compact in membership, less likely to co-operate with other co-operatives and require higher levels of member investments. Agency and transaction theories also suggest that organisations whose members have little individual stake in them when they become *too large* for direct member control, become vulnerable to competitors able to access equity in contestable markets, begging the question: is there a point when a co-operative becomes too large for participative member control?

Certainly, as co-operatives merged and grew larger, cannibalising each other, the problems of retaining a febrile bond of association and maintaining clear lines of communication grew. With a heterogeneous membership drawing upon diverse traditions and with different expectations operating upon a 'mega' co-operative, agreement on policy direction became difficult. For many farmers, membership of a co-operative was part of a folkloric identity, but when that special relationship was dissolved, it became simply a matter of convenience, straining loyalty. In this context the democracy principle was held by some leaders to be an actual *obstacle* to good governance, a hindrance, acting against shareholder interests, and dispensable. With leadership elites orchestrating a 'guided' democracy, more members became alienated, conflicts arose and the few co-operative conglomerates surviving the attrition of the seventies and eighties were subjected in the nineties to demutualisation pressures from within and without.

Considering these external and internal factors, it seems reasonable to conclude that while farmer co-operatives achieved less than the potential their strong presence in great Australian agricultural industries would suggest possible, they achieved more than critics supposed. Co-operatives drew small local enterprises into district, regional, state and, in a few cases, national networks. They made a major contribution to the development of pioneer agricultural industries. Co-operatives developed successful export industries, particularly in the wheat, grain, rice, sugar, dairy, fruit and fishing industries. They played an important role in developing intrastate, national and international commodity markets. Co-operatives underpinned the value of family farms and contributed to the prosperity of many farming and rural communities. At the end of the century some co-operative companies were among the mightiest businesses in the land.

Far from uniting under a distinctive banner proclaiming the democracy principle, however, co-operatives concealed this essential difference from other businesses while ironically emphasising precisely that which made them invisible – individualism and the pursuit of wealth. Certainly, co-operation's most distinctive feature; democracy; was seldom as compelling a feature of co-operative management as the pursuit of individual wealth and, generally speaking, only the fear of losing taxation privileges and such control as farmers exercised in commodity markets sustained loyalty to the principle, essentially negative reasons.

Australian farmer co-operation was reflected more in form than substance. Relations between co-operatives were normally characterised by self-interest, parochialism and unilateralism, rather than by community-interest, universality and multilateralism, the essence of co-operation. Rather than co-operate with each other, farmer co-operatives tended to merge with or take over other co-operatives, driven by the pressure of industry rationalisation, or they engaged independently in 'backwards integration' policies through subsidiaries, joint ventures and partnerships. Farmers generally were inclined to squeeze every last 'drop' from their co-operatives and neglected to invest in them adequately or in anything not immediately enhancing the 'bottom line', such as education or federations. With few exceptions, it was a short-sighted and stingy movement.

Efforts to educate the public and opinion makers, particularly the young, were paltry. Apart from occasional rhetorical flourishes, for instance in support of existing taxation privileges and appealing to 'little guy' sentiment, there was scant evidence of farmer co-operatives encouraging a co-operative consciousness. On the contrary, new breed leaders, in commercialising co-operatives and making market share and competitiveness priorities, invited farmers to forget traditional co-operative principles and think of themselves not as 'members' but as 'shareholders' or 'stakeholders' in an industry. They presided over a dilution of the collective bond-of-association 'glue' (giving rise to governance and communication problems), recast traditional co-operative structure, emphasised the capital power of individuals over the collective power of the group, wooed external investors and flirted with stock exchanges, where the democracy principle was not only poorly understood but spurned as 'unorthodox' and subject to a 'sunset' clause.

Similarly, there is little evidence of farmer co-operatives espousing a sense of social responsibility or a concern for the wider community, apart from sponsoring a few sporting events or funding advertising. Pursuing a wholly commercial agenda, farmer co-operatives gradually lost touch with the concerns of mainstream society and became concentrated upon the financial interests of a relatively small and declining number of aging, predominantly male shareholders, of little relevance to broader public issues and concerns.

At the end of the twentieth century, the Australian farmer co-operative movement was institutionally feeble, asymmetrically developed, and co-operatives were decreasing in number and the rate of new formations was slowing. Nevertheless, a fragile tradition of farmer co-operation had survived the century and continues at the time of writing. To this very limited extent, the experience of Australian farmer co-operatives suggests that democracy and business *can* 'mix' in a capitalist society, albeit fraily and atomistically. The historical evidence suggests, however, that in the absence of co-operative unity, an effective third-tier body, financial autonomy, national or federal co-operatives' legislation and a willingness by co-operators to promote a co-operative consciousness not focused simply on money – all of the things which co-operative idealists had long argued for and which had been comprehensively quashed by pragmatists – a broadly supported, robust farmer co-operative movement cannot exist.

The future of the Australian farmer co-operative movement and the democracy principle it ambiguously embodies, hang in the balance. With regard to this precarious situation, Queensland Co-operatives Community Council (CCC) activist Anthony Esposito cautions:

>...there hasn't been a lot going on in recent years. There was a real high point through the mid to late 90s and into the early 90s and then it sort of tapered off gradually from there, and I think it's at a bit of a low ebb. And in the broad conservatism of our time... other players have sort of stepped in ...because they are favoured by government. At the moment, the climate suits them more than it suits us. They have resources, we don't.

>...Some of it is cyclical (but) I think we... have to pay more attention to some of the more fundamental shifts. This is where the co-op movement is lacking – on this whole demutualisation front. This is an organised, large scale, multilateral assault on some of the fundamentals of social democracy, of co-operation and community, of notions of commonwealth, of participation and equity, of a broader set of values than merely economic instrumental values, and you know, the co-operative movement in this country is missing in action. It fights limited rear-guard defences, and is usually only mobilised where something affects them directly – like a tax concession is lost, or something of that sort...I think the co-op movement and co-op ideas (are) a powerful counter to (the extremes of economic rationalism) but its advocates are not. And a lot of the co-op movement is based historically on the philosophy, that if you get out there and create the examples, just by the sheer goodness of them, people will be persuaded to come and join. Ah, it's naïve at best. It was then. It's even more so now.[1]

Appendices

Norco stall displaying products.
Photo courtesy of Norco Co-operative Limited.

Appendix One

Australian Co-operatives and Taxation:
AN HISTORICAL OUTLINE

Introduction

The following discussion is intended only as a descriptive sketch to assist the general reader better understand the historical evolution of tax provisions as these affected co-operatives in twentieth century Australia and is not intended as an authoritative analysis, for which the present researcher is not qualified and for which specialist expertise need be sought.

Federation to the Great Depression

At the time of Federation in 1901, all states were collecting income tax and continued to do so until 1942, when the Commonwealth Government began collecting the tax on a uniform basis throughout Australia. The first *Commonwealth Income Tax Assessment Act* of 1915 did not contain any specific provisions for taxing co-operative companies. In 1918 the definition of 'income' contained in the act was amended to include, in the case of a co-operative company or society, all sums received from its members in respect of commodities, animals, valuables or land sold or supplied to or on behalf of members. At that time *all* companies were entitled to a deduction in respect of amounts distributed as dividends to shareholders or members.

The amendment to the definition of 'income' was thought necessary to prevent the possible loss of taxation revenue on the income of a co-operative company which could have occurred had not the law made specific provision for its inclusion. Doubts had arisen as a result of a High Court judgement that members' subscriptions received by a club did not constitute *income* of the club. It was thought that the judgement also applied to co-operative associations and would render them exempt from tax on amounts received from trading with members. The amendment to the definition of 'income' prevented this effect.

In 1921 the definition of 'income' was again amended to exclude rebates received by members of a co-operative based on their purchases from a company, where the company was one which usually sold goods only to its members. This provision was amended in 1922 to exempt rebates of a kind where the Taxation Commissioner was satisfied that 90 per cent of a co-operative's sales were made to its own members.

Acting on the recommendations of a 1922 Royal Commission on Tax the deduction in respect of amounts being distributed as dividends was removed by an amendment to the act in 1923 so that companies were taxed on the *whole* of their income regardless of the amount of dividends distributed to shareholders. This basis of assessment proved to be a heavy burden on many co-operatives and in 1925 a provision was inserted to allow consideration to co-operatives for amounts distributed among shareholders as interest or dividends on shares. For the purposes of that provision, however, a definition of 'co-operative company' was inserted. To qualify, the rules of a company had *to limit the numbers of shares that could be held by, or on behalf of, members and prohibit the public sale or purchase of shares*. In addition, it was necessary that the company be established for the purpose of carrying on a business, industry or trade, having as its primary object or objects one or more of the following:

(a) the acquisition of commodities or other goods for disposal or distribution among members;

(b) the acquisition of commodities or animals from members for disposal or distribution;

(c) the storage (later, marketing, packaging or processing) of commodities for members.

The provisions particularly benefited retail and agricultural co-operatives. These conditions were subsequently extended to include the rendering of *services* to shareholders and the obtaining of funds from shareholders for lending to co-operative shareholders in order to enable them to acquire land or buildings to be used for the purpose of residence and business. The amendments benefited financial services co-operatives including building societies and professional associations co-operatives. In any financial year in which *less* than 90 per cent of the total business was conducted with its members a company would fail to qualify as a co-operative.

In 1927 rebates and discounts were added to the specific deductions of interest or dividends on shares that had been provided for by the 1925 amendments. The reasoning was that rebates and discounts distributed by co-operatives to their shareholders based upon business done with the company should be regarded as deductible from the assessable income derived by the company, similar in nature to a share discount granted by an ordinary business to a customer.

With the effects of the Great Depression being felt in 1930, provision was made for the allowance of deductions for co-operatives which claimed certain commonwealth or state government loans to enable them to borrow assets required for the purpose of carrying on business or taking over such assets from the government. The purpose of the amendment was to assist co-operatives to withhold moneys borrowed from governments to acquire such primary production plant as sugar mills, butter factories and bacon factories and came in recognition of the co-operatives' limited ability to access external capital. Responding to Opposition objections and complaints from business that this amounted to 'featherbedding' and an elaborate 'tax dodge', a further amendment was made in 1930 restricting rebates to those not based on 'purchases for the purposes of a business'.

The Ferguson Royal Commission

A Royal Commission on Tax in 1932-1934 (the Ferguson Royal Commission) noted variations between the states in concessions made to co-operatives, observing that in some cases concessions allowed had been based *not* on settled principles but for reasons of political expediency.

Commissioners noted that in New South Wales, for example, the income of co-operative companies registered under the *Co-operation Act* (1923) was taxed but that the taxable income did not include any undistributed profits or profits paid to members by way of rebates or bonuses based on the business done with the company where 90 per cent of its business was done with its own members. Other co-operative companies registered under different legislation, however, were assessed on a similar basis to that contemplated by a proposed Commonwealth Income Tax Assessment Act, subject to the reservation that interest in respect of, or dividends on, shares and amounts applied to the repayment of loans from governments were not allowed as a deduction.

On the other hand, the relevant Queensland act exempted the profits of any co-operative company whose memorandum and articles of association provided that profits should *not* be distributed amongst shareholders as dividends and which was declared to be exempt by the Governor-in-Council. Co-operative companies consisting of shareholders who produced primary products used for food purposes were liable to taxation only upon their undistributed profits. Certain other primary producer associations were also liable to tax on undistributed profits, while dividends and interest on shares were not allowed as a deduction. The shareholder or member of a company, however, was taxable on amounts received by him or her. The Queensland situation was administratively complex.

The relevant sections of the South Australian act were based on the same principle as that of the proposed commonwealth act except that dividends on shares and moneys applied to the redemption of loans were not allowed as deductions. Moreover, if rebates paid by a co-operative company to a tax-payer arose out of purchases made by him or her for the purpose of conducting business, such amount was taxable in his or her hands as income from personal exertion.

Western Australia adopted an entirely different principle. That state exempted rebates or discounts received by *shareholders* of a co-operative company as a consequence of their trading with the company, but apparently made no concessions to the *company*.

The acts of Victoria and Tasmania contained *no* provisions which dealt specifically with co-operative companies.

The Royal Commission concluded that, nationally, the situation *vis a vis* co-operatives and taxation was problematical and reported *inter alia*:

> In considering the liability of a co-operative company a clear distinction must be made between the payments to persons because they are shareholders and payments made to persons because they are customers. For example, interest paid on or in respect of shares is to all intents and purposes a dividend as it arises from the possession of a share interest and not because of a business transaction with the company. Rebates to persons who deal with the company are in a different category. If the co-operative company charged the exact price for the goods which it sold, or paid the exact price for those which it bought, no rebates would be payable. But the societies for good reasons prefer to fix a scale of prices which gives them a margin. Thus an adjustment has to be made periodically to so much of the balance as the Directors think fit to divide or distribute among the members or customers in proportion to the value of the business they have done with the company. This rebate is clearly not profit but merely an adjustment of the sale or purchase price.

Leaders of primary producer co-operatives argued that if a co-operative company was to be regarded in the same light as any other *company*, there was no reason why the interest paid on or in respect of shares or dividends should be allowed as a deduction to the company for it represented a distribution which should be subject to tax in the hands of the *recipient*. But Commissioners could not see why an exception should be made in the case of co-operative companies, nor any justification for allowing as a deduction to a company profits applied in repaying loans as this would be a concession denied to other taxpayers.

The Mutuality Principle

The resultant *Consolidated Income Tax Assessment Act* of 1936, Division 9, Sections 117-121 inclusive, however, redrafted taxation conditions for co-operatives and mutuals, making provision for rebates and bonuses distributed by a co-operative to shareholders based on business done with the co-operative as deductible items from the assessable income derived by the co-operative, seeing these as similar to a trade discount granted by other forms of business. Taxation for co-operatives (and co-operative companies) was now based on the mutuality principle, which, paraphrased, meant for taxation purposes that 'you cannot make profit from doing business with yourself' and that, as a person's income consists only of moneys derived from sources other than him/herself, an entity in which *owners and users are identical* applies the mutuality principle.

Section 117 defined co-operatives for purposes of the act:

❖ limiting the number of shares held by any one shareholder;

❖ prohibiting the quotation of shares for sale or purchase on a stock exchange or in any public manner; and

❖ requiring that the primary objects of a co-operative must be to acquire, dispose, store, market, pack or process the commodities of its shareholders or render services to them.

Section 118 reinforced the mutuality principle by requiring that 90 per cent of the services provided, or the storage, marketing, packing or processing of commodities by a co-operative must be provided to the members or shareholders (while recognising that some co-operatives had no shares).

Section 119 required co-operatives to declare as assessable income all sums received by the co-operative for rendering of services or storage, marketing, packing or processing of commodities from all sources, including members.

Section 120 allowed deductions to those co-operatives who met the primary objects defined in Sections 117 and 118 for distributions among shareholders or members in the form of rebates or bonuses based on business done with shareholders or interest or dividend on shares. The second part of Section 120 (S12[1][c]) allowed co-operatives which complied with Section 117, and where 90 per cent of the value of the co-operative was held by *active* members, deductibility for government-sourced loans raised with the primary object of acquiring commodities or animals from shareholders for disposal or distribution. Co-operatives were able to deduct the principle (not only interest) of loans for capital equipment. This provision was inserted to compensate for co-operatives' perceived poor fund-raising ability (a function of having no fixed capital base) and to assist co-operatives retain internal funding for tax effective investments. The desired effect was to provide lower cost capital to co-operatives involved in agricultural production and to permit increased investments and job creation in regional Australia. Some state governments, including Victoria and Queensland, utilised this provision early to assist co-operatives but others did not, New South Wales for example did not utilise it until the 1990s, possibly because that state tolerated 'dry' shareholders (inactive members) until the late 1980s.

The definition of 'co-operative company' was also extended to include one providing services to its members as, for example, shearing or any similar activity. Co-operative companies *without* share capital were also included in the definition in order to meet the requirements of co-operative companies under Queensland's *Primary Producers' Co-operative Associations Act*. Companies qualifying as co-operatives under the act were allowed the following deductions in respect of assessable income:

❖ amounts distributed amongst shareholders as rebates or bonus on business by shareholders; and

❖ amounts distributed among shareholders as interest or dividend on shares.

Rebates or bonuses based on purchases made by a shareholder were also not included in the shareholder's assessable income except when the price of such purchase was allowable as a deduction in ascertaining his or her taxable income in any one year.[1]

Tax attacks on co-operatives through the 'Cold War' period

After the states referred income tax collection powers to the Commonwealth Government in 1943, the application of Division 9 to co-operatives and co-operative companies became uniform throughout Australia. With governments of all persuasions looking to co-operatives to enhance food production during and after World War II, a spate of agricultural co-operatives development occurred. This provoked a reaction from private-profit business, often of a strident anti-socialist nature redolent of 'Cold-War' sentiment then dividing Australia. For example, representatives of shopkeepers, retail trades and small business complained about the alleged 'unfair trade and tax position of co-operatives', which was giving co-operatives an unfair advantage. Co-operatives were 'anti-capitalist', critics said, the public was subsidising them and they would be uncompetitive without tax concessions because they were inefficient and had passed their zenith.

The industry journal *Retail Trade* linked co-operatives, regulated markets and communism, alleging that co-operative shareholders were unwilling to invest in and grow their businesses or 'share proceeds' with the community. The journal called upon 'whistle blowers' to help determine exactly how much the public was subsidising co-operatives. 'Private enterprise', *Retail Trade* shouted, was 'massing resources to fight...preparing for preliminary skirmishes':

> *In the butter industry the co-operatives are fighting a losing battle against private enterprise...*
> *It is proposed to sharpen up this attack and work the remaining co-operatives out of business, already limping along behind private enterprise, and they will find the going more and more difficult.*

Many co-operatives were 'bogus', *Retail Trade* alleged not unreasonably, and a 'gentlemen's agreement' between the states, limiting dairy industry producers to their home state and stifling free competition, was 'eye-wash', repugnant to the Australian Constitution and 'fleecing consumers'. The journal described at length how 'business' deeply resented the favourable taxation treatment of co-operatives, demanded equal treatment for 'free enterprise', called for a royal commission into the co-operatives' tax advantage and planned to make 'revelations which could lead to action which will result in co-operatives being *forced* to contribute to tax in a more normal way'. Treasury was losing millions, the journal said, because co-operatives were 'not paying up' and yet no government was prepared to do anything 'because shareholders are farmers' and governments were terrified of the political consequences in rural seats. *Retail Trade* called upon the Commonwealth Government to adopt a Canadian practice of limiting co-operatives' tax concessions to a set period and then taxing them at the full rate so that they might 'compete on equal terms with private enterprise'.

A Fair Tax League, established in 1950, described a co-operative as a 'capitalistic institution which uses capital equipment to make profits' and maintained a spirited attack on the alleged 'unfair' tax concessions given to co-operatives, arguing that these pertained to their humble origins around the turn of the century and were no longer appropriate. 'Today some of our most capitalistic undertakings enjoy tax-free privileges because they are registered under co-operative movement legislation.' Co-operatives distributed tax-free profits, the league alleged, under the guise of rebates and discounts, and provided a convenient tax dodge for inactive ('dry' shareholder) members. Taxation would not harm genuine co-operatives but only bogus co-operatives and, the league charged, pointing at 'dry' shareholders, 'It is interesting that in Australia that an individual's interest in many of the larger co-operatives exceeds £10,000 and £15,000 in asset values.' Tax concessions *were* acceptable for small not-for-profit co-operatives, the league maintained, but *not* for large commercially-orientated producer co-operatives, which had grown into wealthy capitalist bodies at taxpayer expense. Big producer co-operatives had powerful political links through the Country Party to the Commonwealth Treasury and it was by exercising this political patronage, the league argued, that co-operatives were able to 'legally avoid tax':

> *The Country Party has seen to laws over the past quarter century favourable to the agricultural co-operative sector, for example low interest loans with little incentive to pay them off. These co-operatives and co-operative companies distribute surpluses in a number of ways, including the highest prices, all tax-payer subsidised and distorting markets. Big co-operatives are capitalistic, being used by business managers as a means of avoiding tax on behalf of the wealthy graziers, farmers and other land holders who own them.*

A 'Save Democracy League' joined the attack. League Secretary Ben Doig charged that co-operatives were luring business away from private enterprise by offering higher prices or discounts 'subsidised by tax exemptions'. He analysed the accounts of a 'large New South Wales co-operative', which had allowed rebates of £79,059 in one financial year. The tax payable by that organisation, if it had been operating under company law, Doig reckoned, would be £62,370. The actual tax paid was £1,400! The co-operative's surplus, therefore, was subsidised to the extent of £60,970. Doig then compared two businesses, each with fifty shareholders and net profits of £50,000, one a co-operative and one a company. The company, he said, paid £22,500 in tax while the co-operative paid £7,425. Taxpayers were obliged to pay more tax, Doig alleged, so that some privileged shareholders were enabled by tax law to pay less. 'By allowing such deductions the commonwealth conspires with the co-operatives to defraud itself of tax.' In addition, Doig continued, using government loans at discounted rates, a co-operative could buy assets which themselves were subject to a *second* deduction – depreciation! Co-operatives were *not* an efficient alternative to private enterprise, the league secretary claimed, but were 'privileged capitalist enterprises'. Private companies, 'no matter how efficient', could not compete with them under the existing tax discrepancies. Some immigrant farmers, Doig added, who had escaped from Soviet tyranny, saw the regulated system of Australian agriculture as a 'police state' and co-operatives reminiscent of the communist regimes from which they had fled. Many farmers resented being *compelled* to supply co-operatives while the co-operatives were *free* to sell anywhere. The Leeton fruit cannery, for example, Doig alleged, was a 'socialist' enterprise, enjoying large, virtually interest-free loans from the government while it remained inefficient, produced no profits and was incapable of handling the crop. The Save Democracy League demanded that agriculture be left to private-profit enterprise, which was 'not averse to paying tax'.[2]

Periodic attacks upon co-operatives along these lines continued, occasionally attracting Commonwealth Government attention. Delegates at the Taxpayers' Association 1966 Perth Conference, for instance, protested that 'quasi' co-operatives were still enjoying taxation privileges when they were not in fact genuine co-operatives, naming a Queensland co-operative milling entity, which had been benefiting for thirty years from the tax act's provision and proposing:

> *That the practice of co-operatives in distributing rebates in the form of shares be made reasonable by preventing a distribution of shares to cover payment of such repayment being considered a tax deduction to the co-operative concerned except where the amount distributed is made at least half in cash and the remainder in shares.*

'No unfair advantage'

Economist and University of New England agricultural researcher, R R Piggott, agreed in the early 1970s that the *Income Tax Assessment Act* provided a stimulus to the co-operative movement through its 'rather liberal definition of a co-operative'. Tax laws had encouraged the payment by co-operatives of surpluses to shareholders as rebates and farmers had traditionally used these as an *offset* against on-farm expenses rather than allow them to be allocated as 'retained earnings', which would be subject to tax at normal rates. The result was that co-operatives were starved of capital in order to match competition from proprietary companies, which paid tax but enjoyed easy access to finance and, to this degree, co-operatives enjoyed 'no unfair advantage'. Co-operation was just another way of doing business, Piggott said, with its own peculiarities, and was legitimate in its own right. Moreover, periodically, the Federal Commissioner of Taxation compelled co-operatives to *restructure* to remain eligible under Division 9. For example the Renmark Fruit Growers' Co-operative had been obliged to form a separate company from the parent co-operative, so there was no question of 'cosy molly-coddling', as some alleged. Nevertheless, Piggott continued, in 1971 when the Commissioner of Taxation assessed 3,623 companies defined as co-operatives for tax purposes, he found that they had 2,173,800 members, an average membership of approximately 600, and that 2,174 of these companies had a taxable income less than $2,000!

Division 9 was not amended until 1973 and 1974 by the Whitlam Labor Government – which extended the mutuality principle to credit unions!

Complaints continue

Complaints about the alleged 'unfair' tax position of co-operatives continued. A Tax Review (the Asprey Committee) received submissions about the trading position of co-operatives including one recommending the withdrawal of S120 (1) (c), allowing deductibility for government loans in certain circumstances. This was strenuously fought by the Co-operative Federation of Australia (CFA), which rallied co-operative federations in New South Wales, Queensland, Victoria, Western Australia and wine producers in South Australia to ensure this recommendation was not acted upon (for political reasons), demonstrating that when the co-operatives pulled together nationally, they could be effective. It would not be the last time the co-operative movement rallied around the issue of a tax attack. Indeed, there was little else around which it would unite.

In 1976 a competitor hauled the Kaiser Stuhl Co-operative (wine) before the Trades Practices Commission, alleging unfair trade in respect of taxation liability. The outcome is unknown. In the following year New South Wales Minister for Co-operatives Sydney Einfeld harangued sections of the co-operative movement for becoming an 'elaborate tax dodge' and promised to take co-operatives in hand, particularly big primary producer co-operatives, which, he claimed, were manipulating the system at taxpayer expense.

With public disquiet mounting over general taxation evasion and the uneven application of tax laws, culminating in a 'bottom of the harbour' scandal in 1982, involving tax-avoidance rorts, which Federal Treasurer John Howard estimated were costing taxpayers hundreds of millions of dollars, the issue of consistency in taxation became politically sensitive. There is no suggestion that any co-operative was associated with such a scheme, but in this context, Division 9 came under closer attention. Treasurer Paul Keating in the Hawke Labor Government (1983-1993) favoured a broad-based services tax but this idea was scuttled for political reasons (later to be refloated as the Goods and Services Tax [GST] by a John Howard Coalition). The Hawke Government did however introduce dividend imputation provisions, providing franked dividends for investments in corporations, affording them taxation treatment similar to co-operatives and, coincidentally, neutralising much of the latter's attraction in respect of tax effectiveness.[3]

The mutuality principle is questioned

By the early to mid 1990s the capital-raising needs of large trading co-operatives were such that many of them developed policies for the retention of earnings, for example distributing earnings to members in various equity forms, including compulsory shares. These schemes were not particularly popular among farmers, who preferred cash in hand and because they posed complex taxation problems. Acceptance of the mutuality principle as a legitimate basis for taxation deductibility was by now wearing thin in the Australian Taxation Office (ATO) where a view had formed that the concept was vague and imprecise and that while some co-operatives – most co-operatives – exemplified the principle, not all did, particularly 'hybrid' agricultural co-operatives and co-operative companies, some of which were among the largest businesses in the land. The ATO sought consistency and equity in applying tax laws to all entities in respect of their economic substance, *not* their form. While Labor governed, however, nothing precipitative was done in respect of general co-operatives.

A threat to Section 120 (1)(c)

In 1996 the newly-elected Howard Coalition Federal Government Treasury reached a budget decision to *remove* benefits accruing to co-operatives under Section 120 (1)(c) of the act. Under the provision, if a co-operative or co-operative company could establish that in addition to the mutuality principle in relation to business done by a member with the co-operative, 90 per cent or more of its *issued capital* was held by active members, then repayment and associated interest on government loans for the acquisition of assets was tax deductible (in states where this facility existed). Numerous co-operatives and co-operative companies complained that their viability would be seriously challenged by the removal of the provision, for example, several Queensland co-operatives borrowing funds through the Queensland Industrial Development Corporation. The Mackay Sugar Co-operative, based in a marginal north Queensland electorate, estimated that loss of the benefit would cost the co-operative $16 million in the next season. The Budget decision also brought a quick response from the 'National Co-operative Council' (a forerunner of the Co-operatives Council of Australia [CCA]), which argued that the change threatened regions, held that co-operatives were already disadvantaged when seeking to borrow funds in the marketplace and led a national lobbying campaign in key marginal seats where a rural revolt was in progress led by an expelled Liberal Party candidate, Pauline Hanson. The Budget decision was deferred in the Senate.

The Business Tax Review (Ralph Committee)

Determined to achieve a consistent tax regime, the Howard Government prepared for a White Paper and in August 1998 appointed a Business Tax Review (the Ralph Committee) to review the taxation system. The review passed through several stages but a primary goal throughout was to achieve a unified entity taxation regime, including the abolition of Division 9.

The CCA submission to the Business Tax Review

Calling upon co-operatives to 'stand united behind the CCA', the association prepared a submission to the Business Tax Review entitled 'Australians Extending Their Own Business' and launched a political campaign in 1999, targeting all parties. The submission spoke as if all co-operatives were service-orientated and not-for-profit; appealed to economic-nationalism by describing co-operatives as a community-based, Australian-owned 'way of wealth creation'; and drew a parallel between co-operatives and small business, a Howard Government priority:

> *Co-operatives are formed by many small businesses and individuals based on a mutual relationship that enables the small Australians to compete on the world economy...The market reality is that most small businesses (including primary producers) are not of a sufficient size to compete effectively with larger corporations or gain access to overseas markets...Co-operatives play a vital role in enabling small business to be a player in the market.*

The submission alluded frequently to 'the Co-operatives Act', and referred to the Co-operatives' Law Agreement (discussed in Chapter Fourteen) as if uniform national co-operatives' legislation was already a reality:

> *All states and territory governments have recognised the unique character of co-operatives and their importance to their economies by adopting in 1996 a national scheme for consistent co-operatives legislation around Australia.*

The submission's central argument, which was focused on farmer co-operatives rather than small business *per se*, was two-pronged. First, Division 9 should stay because co-operatives, which lacked fixed capital, were disadvantaged in raising finance and existing tax provisions offset this. Second, the Business Review Committee had failed to take into account co-operatives' distinct identity. Co-operatives *did* contribute to the tax revenue base through improved farmer incomes. Therefore, tax deductibility of rebates and bonuses for co-operatives was logical because farmers did not *know* the selling price of a commodity when they delivered it. A co-operative was required to decide, when the selling price was known what to do with surpluses accruing, if any – either to retain them in part or full (taxed), distribute them in part or full as dividends (taxed in members' hands), or return surpluses as rebates, bonuses or back pays in part or full in proportion to business done with a member (sharing tax liability). The message was that it was wrong to tax co-operatives *twice* – once at entity level and again in members' pockets.

The CCA argued that abolishing Division 9 would represent a 'serious threat to the principles of fair treatment for co-operatives'. Co-operative surpluses were different from company profits, because a co-operative's primary purpose was to provide *services*, not make profits. Co-operatives were an extension of a member's business and rebates represented a *refund* on goods or services bought or sold by the co-operative. Division 9 did not convey special privileges to co-operatives but enshrined a long-established and accepted principle of mutuality, 'which is intrinsic to the nature of all co-operative enterprises' and should be retained with *improvements*, including:

❖ distributions by way of a rebate or bonus based on business done by the members with the co-operative should be an allowed deduction in the year in which the business was done in order to earn the rebate or bonus;

❖ the issuing of shares to members of a co-operative out of retained earnings should not be treated as taxable income in the hands of the members;

❖ members should be taxed only when shares were sold by the member and proceeds received;

❖ Section 120 (1)(c) should be enhanced to allow *all* co-operatives the same deduction, not only those which complied with Section 117 (1)(b); and

❖ the Taxation Department should work with the co-operative movement to determine a set of guidelines for the operation of Division 9 and subsequently release a public ruling which supported the guidelines.

There were some problems with the CCA submission. First, not-for-profit co-operatives were lumped with trading co-operatives, which clearly existed to make profits, by whatever name. Certainly, for farmers, a co-operative *was* an extension of the primary business but the same could not be said for members of a community advancement co-operative, for example. Linking such disparate entities was stretching a long bow. Theoretically, co-operatives did exist to provide services and not to make profits but that could not be said of 'hybrid' co-operatives and co-operative companies which were encouraging members to think of themselves as *investors* as well as suppliers and actively courting external investments.

The mutuality principle, where owners and users were identical, was a long established co-operative tenet. Co-operation and the mutuality principle were indivisible. Co-operatives and taxation consideration in respect of the mutuality principle, however, were *not* indivisible. Neither was taxation consideration intrinsic to an understanding of co-operation, rather a concession acceded to for political reasons and, equally, withdrawable for political reasons. While the argument reasonably applied to co-operatives genuinely applying the mutuality principle this was not necessarily the case for those structured so as to optimise shareholder value, exactly like corporations. The provision of services at cost to members might still be a primary goal of such co-operatives but it was not the *only* goal individual wealth creation was just as important. Far from affirming a distinctive co-operative identity, some co-operatives were *mimicking* corporations right through to listing. Why should they not be treated the same as corporations for taxation purposes?

The CCA's special pleading for co-operatives was reasonable to the extent that the vast majority of genuinely not-for-profit co-operatives dedicated to member service and observing the democracy and mutuality principles warranted special treatment as entities distinct from and with motives different from profit-making, investor-owned businesses. In lumping genuine, not-for-profit co-operatives with commercially-orientated co-operatives, however, the submission ran the risk of exposing *all* co-operatives to an adverse finding.

On Australian ownership the submission also overlooked the fact that the management of at least one large agricultural co-operative was courting a foreign suitor in a takeover deal which, ostensibly, would best serve the interests of shareholders. One of Australia's greatest mutual insurance societies had already been sold to an overseas company with government blessing. There was nothing intrinsic to co-operatives quarantining them from foreign ownership.

Given CCA's unpreparedness to affiliate with the International Co-operative Alliance (ICA), the submission included an astonishing recommendation:

> *That any new tax act recognises the principles of co-operation as adopted by the International Co-operative Alliance as defining a co-operative enterprise for the purposes of the act.*

The strategic purpose appears to have been to suggest an alternative to the mutuality principle, should Division 9 be abolished. Such a recommendation, adopting ICA principles for purposes of determining tax liability, if accepted, would have constituted nothing less than a revolution in Australian tax law in respect of co-operatives, clearly demarcating organisations which did *not* comply from those which did.

On the matter of retaining Division 9, however, there is no question that CCA was effective. In April 1999 the association organised a Public Policy Conference in Canberra to which seventy delegates, principally from the rice, grain and sugar industries attended. The conference was told that if Division 9 'free-kick' taxation consideration went, so too would many of the co-operative movement's 'icons'. Attention was drawn to the existence of numerous farmer co-operatives in key marginal seats. A function was held in Parliament House to which several senators were invited and CCA ran a successful lobbying campaign. Deputy Prime Minister Tim Fischer (National Party) undertook to support the co-operatives in the business tax inquiry.[4]

The Review of Business Taxation reports

In September 1999 the Business Taxation Review Committee reported on general issues affecting taxation, noting that the existing system was complex, uncertain and imprecise and needed simplification and clarification. The report noted how the *timing* of distribution by co-operatives could produce significantly different taxation outcomes for entities. On the mutuality principle the committee noted that the 'hybridisation' of co-operatives' capital-base required adaptation of tax rules for co-operatives. Co-operative shares traditionally had constituted a 'qualification' enabling the use of a co-operative's services and had *not* been designed to yield dividends. The principle of 90 per cent of business done was sound only to the degree that 90 per cent of the *value* of a co-operative was also held by members. While Division 9 treated co-operatives differently on the basis of the mutuality principle, the committee recognised that co-operatives which might have originally been established on such a principle were in many cases *mutating* to emphasise value to shares rather than the provision of services to members and that therefore the mutuality principle could not be said to apply to all co-operatives. The committee believed that the solution was a full imputation system ensuring that all distribution of profits would be taxed at the company rate at the entity (co-operative) level rather than at shareholder level with the result that all distribution of profits would be fully franked. Specifically the proposals were to:

- ❧ tax trusts, life insurers, co-operatives and limited partnerships as companies;
- ❧ simplify the imputation system;
- ❧ refund excess imputation credits to resident individuals and superannuation funds to improve equity between taxpayers; and
- ❧ provide consolidation for groups of companies and trusts while addressing value shifting and achieving a constant treatment of entity distributions.

These redesigned arrangements, the Business Taxation Review Committee said, would *supersede* unique tax rules for co-operatives. A reformed tax system would emphasise what people *do* rather than the *structures* they employ, because structure was less important for tax consideration than economic substance and profit outcomes.[5]

Co-operatives to be taxed like companies

With a federal election looming and the Hanson rural revolt in full swing, the recently appointed Deputy Prime Minister John Anderson, leader of the National Party, issued a media release on 21 September 1999, soon after the report's release entitled: 'A Better Deal on Company Tax for Country Australia':

> *The government has listened to the concerns of rural and regional Australians and put their interests at the forefront in a tax reform package that is good for small business and the bush.*

One of the highlights of the package, Anderson said, was that all primary producer-specific tax concessions had been *retained*. Trusts, life insurers, co-operatives and limited partnerships would be taxed like companies but the new regime would not commence until 1 July 2001, giving businesses time to adjust. Section 120 (1)(c) would be retained but subject to a review. The Review Committee's proposal to impose fringe benefits tax on benefits not subject to income tax would not proceed. It was proposed that the company tax rate would be cut from the present 36 per cent to 30 per cent in 2001/02. Unincorporated farm businesses would benefit from personal tax cuts, 99 per cent of primary producers would keep their access to accelerated depreciation and the compliance burden would be simplified.

The CCA again called upon co-operatives to rally at the national level, to forget state rivalries and deliver a clear voice to the Commonwealth Government on appropriate recognition and representation for co-operatives. In this campaign, the association met with only moderate success.

In August 2001 the federal government proposed to provide co-operatives with an *option* to frank dividends to members as an alternative to having these payments treated as deductions from assessable income. Co-operatives would be free to continue to treat dividends and rebate payments as deductions from assessable income, but the franking option was seen as particularly suitable to agricultural co-operatives which had retained earnings for growth and it applied to securities and Co-operative Capital Units (CCUs) listed on the Australian Stock Exchange (ASX). This put commercial co-operatives on a par with corporations in that the former paid tax but the entity retained co-operative status. Effectively, the option would allow for *separate* taxation treatment of co-operatives *with* and *without* share capital.

In December 2002 the Taxation Laws Amendment Bill (No. 8) was introduced into the federal parliament to enable co-operative companies to frank distributions out of the current year's assessable income and allow co-operative members to claim the corresponding franking credits. The bill was referred to the Senate Economics Legislative Committee in March 2003, which recommended passage. The bill was passed as Bill No. 3 in September 2003 and assented to in October as Act No. 101,2003.[6]

Appendix Two

The 'Holy Grail' Of Australian Co-operation: A CO-OPERATIVE BANK

The brief summary below highlights some of the many attempts made to create that 'Holy Grail' of Australian co-operation: financial autonomy through a co-operative bank.

In 1864 the *Industrial and Provident Societies Act* of New South Wales specifically banned co-operative banking as 'too risky' and 'not in the public interest'. In the 1870s the Victorian Co-operative Association advocated the development of 'a Co-operative Commonwealth', financed through a co-operative bank, but producer and consumer co-operators disagreed on this and nothing happened. In the 1880s there were plans for 'People's Banks' in Victoria on the European Credit Co-operative model. In the 1890s building societies, 'genuine' and 'bogus', were decimated in a financial and property crash, particularly in Victoria. Decades passed before confidence in the idea of co-operative banking returned. In the last decade of the nineteenth century the Rochdale consumer-influenced Federal Co-operative Association, linking co-operatives in South Australia, Victoria and New South Wales, sought trade union support for a co-operative bank. The plan foundered on state rivalries and bitter memories trade unions had of Owenite failures in Britain, which had harmed working-class organisations.

In the first two decades of the twentieth century Christian Socialists and Worker Educational Association (WEA) activists in New South Wales and Victoria again sought a trade union-co-operative alliance for a co-operative bank, channelling funds for co-operative development. Farmers and trade unions were mutually suspicious, however, and unable to work together, paralysing development. At an All Australian Co-operatives Congress in 1920 the bank idea resurfaced before disagreements over which model to apply: Raiffeisen (German), or (Manchester) English CWS? To the ban on co-operative banking going back to the 1860s, the New South Wales *Co-operation Act* (1923) added a ban on co-operative insurance. Labor plans to nationalise the banking system saw interest in a co-operative bank diminish further. In the period to World War II the British co-operative movement and local commercial banks adequately served agricultural co-operatives' financial needs. Between the end of the Great Depression and World War II, Christian groups urged a co-operative 'new order' based on financial co-operation, specifically credit unions. The Victorian Young Christian Workers (YCW) and the Australian Christian Fellowship, for example, advocated financial co-operation based on credit unions to develop the co-operative sector but this idea was resisted by the Rochdale consumer movement 'establishment', which held cash trading to be a cardinal rule.

The Co-operative Federation of Australia (CFA) (1943) advocated a co-operative bank on the English CWS model but again the federation's consumer and primary producer affiliates could not agree. In 1944 the New South Wales Registrar of Co-operative Societies Alf Sheldon sought trade union support for a co-operative bank to be developed from a permanent building society. Trade unions were not interested, the building society movement was opposed and, as usual, consumer and primary producer co-operatives squabbled. In 1949 New South Wales Minister for Co-operatives

Martin raised the issue of a co-operative bank in parliament. The idea was destroyed in 'Cold War' faction fights and lapsed. In 1969 a Queensland banking licence became available and the credit union pioneer, Tom Kelly, and sections of the credit union movement sought the support of friendly societies, trade unions, clubs and associations in association with European co-operative banks. The idea stalled when credit unions withdrew support and Labor forgot election promises. In the 1970s CFA again sought a co-operative bank for rural co-operatives but the plan was dropped, this time by the Fraser Coalition Government, which created instead the Primary Industry Bank of Australia (PIBA), subsequently purchased by Rabobank. Later in the decade, under the direction of Bruce Freeman, the Co-operative Federation of New South Wales (CFNSW) created the Australian Financial Administrative Group, seeking to link co-operatives operating in different industries into a coherent financial bloc, forming the basis of a co-operative bank. Poorly supported by the co-operative movement, this initiative disappeared with the collapse of the Australian Association of Co-operatives (AAC) in 1993. The Australian Co-operative Development League (ACDL), a quasi-independent co-operatives development agency, also tried unsuccessfully to rally support for a co-operative bank in 1992 (discussed in Chapter Nine).

Notes

Bega butter factory workers (1937)
Photo courtesy of Bega Co-operative Society Limited.

Notes:

THE DEMOCRACY PRINCIPLE

PREFACE

1   Hans H Munkner *Chances of Co-operatives in the Future: Contribution to the International Co-operative Alliance Centennial 1895-1995,* Institute for Co-operation in Developing Countries, Marburg, Germany, 1995; Mervyn Pedelty, 'Capital, Democratisation and Governance' International Co-operative Banking Association, Journal No 11, 1999; H H Bakken, Basic Concepts, Principles and Practices of Co-operation, Mimir, Wisconsin 1963; Robert Axelrod, *The Problem of Co-operation,* Basic Books, New York 1984; Peter McKinlay, 'Innovations in Co-operation for the 1990's: Trade and Capital', Paper to Asia Pacific Ministerial Conference on Co-operatives, Sydney, 9 February 1990; Onno-Frank van Bekkum, *Co-operative Models and Farm Policy Reform,* Van Gorcum, The Netherlands, 2001; Daniel Cote, 'The Future of Co-operatives: Managing the Specifics', Paper to Monash Agribusiness Co-operatives Seminar, 1 November 2002; John Watson, 'Things I wish I had known', Paper to Monash Agribusiness Co-operatives Seminar, 1 November 2002; Ian Langdon, *Agricultural Co-operatives: An Australian Perspective,* Working Paper No 6 Centre for Agricultural Co-operative Studies, Gold Coast University College of Griffith University, November 1991; David Griffiths, 'Capital and Agricultural Co-operatives in Australia', 22 April 2003; Australian Centre for Co-operatives Research and Development (ACCoRD) Newsletter, October 2003; Jayo Wickremarachichi and Andrew Passey, 'State of the Sector New South Wales Co-operatives, 1990-2000', Australian Centre for Co-operatives Research and Development (ACCoRD), June 2003; Lee Alan Dugatkin, *Co-operation Among Animals: An Evolutionary Perspective,* Oxford University Press, New York/Oxford 1997; International Co-operative Alliance, Geneva, Switzerland, *Website.* In Singapore, 32 per cent of the population, 1.4 million people, were members of co-operatives and consumer co-operatives accounted for 55 per cent of supermarket purchases and had a turnover of US$700 million. In Korea agricultural co-operatives had over two million memberships, representing 90 per cent of all farmers and produced an output of US$11 billion. Other definitions which were helpful in scoping the study include:

❖   *Co-operatives are incorporated service organisations serving the needs of members.*

❖   *A co-operative is an organisation owned and controlled by the people it serves who combine for a common purpose.*

❖   *An association of primary producers combining to achieve common economic objectives more effectively than they could as isolated, competing individuals.*

Between 30 and 40 per cent of the adult population of Canada and USA held co-operative memberships in 2001. In the United States in 2003 more than thirty co-operatives had annual revenue in excess of US$1 billion, the top 100 co-operatives had combined revenues of US$117 billion and approximately 30 percent of farm products were marketed through 3,400 farmer-owned co-operatives. In Belgium there were 29,933 co-operative societies and in France, 21,000 co-operatives employed 700,000 people. In the UK, one of the largest farmers and the largest independent travel agency were co-operatives. In Norway, 1.5 million people out of a population of 4.5 million were members of co-operatives, dairy co-operatives commanded 99 per cent of the milk production, consumer co-operatives held 25 per cent of the market and forestry co-operatives were responsible for 76 per cent of timber. Finnish co-operative groups accounted for 74 per cent of meat products, 96 per cent of dairy products, 50 per cent of egg production, 34 per cent of forestry products and handled 34.2 per cent of total deposits in Finnish banks. In Japan, one third of all families were members of co-operatives, 91 per cent of all Japanese farmers were members of co-operatives and agricultural co-operatives' output amounted to US$90 billion.

CHAPTER ONE

1   For a description of the spread of dairy farming in the Illawarra, see W A Bayle, *Illawarra Pastures: Diamond Jubilee of the Illawarra Central Dairy Society Limited, 1899-1957*, Wollongong 1959; G Davidson, *et al*, (eds.) *Australians*, Sydney 1987, pp 162-4, 301-3; Stuart Piggins, *Faith of Steel: A History of the Christian Churches in Illawarra Australia*, Wollongong 1984, pp 12, 38, 77-8, 80, 87-90, 99, 144, 303; T C Kennedy, *Twenty Years of Progress, 1895-1915: North Coast Co-operative Company Limited*, Sydney 1915, p 13; C C Singleton, *Railway History in the Illawarra*, Wollongong 1964, p 48.

2   Kennedy, 'The Rise and Fall of the Farmers' and Settlers' Co-operative Company of New South Wales,' in *Brief History of Co-operation as Applied to the Dairy Industry*, Lismore, *c* 1910, pp 5, 13, 16; A C Murray, *Norco Co-operative Limited, 1897-1970*, Lismore, 1970, p 10. A L Dymock, J Hanrahan, S Marks, W Gray and others were appointed to tour the district and attract interest in co-operation. South Coast and West Camden Co-operative Company Board June 1880, A C Dymock, J Weston, J Black, H Honey, Thomas Mort, J Graham (Manager). Thomas Mort was a pioneer of refrigerated and frozen beef.

3   Kennedy, 'Rise and Fall', *op cit*, pp 20, 28-29. North coast co-operative dairy factories included Perseverance(Clunes), Federal Eureka, Newbar, Alstonville, Rous, Brooklet, Byron Creek (Bangalow), Dunoon, Pearces Creek, Woodburn and Bexhill.

4   Murray, *op cit*, p 5; T C Kennedy 'Rise and Fall', *op cit*, pp 34-35. Directors: Illawarra Central Co-operative Factory: A C Alcorn, F H Bartlett, S R Cook, C J Gibson, A Johnson, J B Kelly, W M Moses, W Marks, G Pearson. For further discussion on Norco see A C Murray, *Norco Co-operative*, *op cit*.

5   Kennedy, 'Rise and Fall' *op cit*.

6   Newspaper cuttings: visit of CWS to Australia 1896, Vol 58, Mitchell Library, 46; the *National Advocate*, 10 June 1986.

7   Newspaper cuttings, *op cit*, pp 13, 23; *The Argus*, 8 April 1896; *Sydney Morning Herald*, 14 February 1896. Plummer notes that forty-eight rural co-operatives were registered under friendly society legislation in New South Wales in 1896, while eighty-four were registered under company law. *Co-operative Federation of Victoria: Annual Report*, February 1983.

8   Newspaper cuttings, *op cit*, pp 23, 31.

9   *Sydney Morning Herald*, 8 May 1896; *The Age*, 14, 17 March 1896; *Wagga Express*, 25 February 1896; *The Hillgrove Guardian*, 28 February 1896; *The Monaro Mercury*, 3 March 1896; *The Inverell Times*, 10 June 1896; *The National Advocate*, 10 June 1896.

10 See Gary Lewis, *The Quest for a Middle Way: Rochdale Co-operation in New South Wales, 1859–1984*, Brolga Press, Curtin, ACT, 1992.

11 Newspaper cuttings, *op cit*, Vol 59, p 35; *Forbes Times*, August 1896; *Lismore Chronicle*, 1 August 1896; *Maitland Daily Mirror*, 8 July 1896; *Barrier Mail*, 23 July 1896; *Clarence Examiner*, 15 April 1896; *Bathurst Times*, 8 July 1896. The Citizens' Committee consisted of Premier G Reid; Minister for Lands, J H Carruthers; Opposition Leader M McGowan; representatives of the AWU; the United Labourers' Protection Society; W Butler of the Surplus Workers League; J Medway Day, editor of *The Worker* Co-operative Printery; Mrs Armstrong, president of the Silk Workers' Co-operative Society; A Tremayne, founder of "Co-operative Irrigation Colonies", probably the Chaffey settlement at Caldera or Narrandera; delegates from the Co-operative Refrigeration Society, the Co-operative Tailoring Company and the Civil Service Co-operative Society.

12 *The Co-operator*, February 1897; B P McEvoy, New South Wales Registrar of Co-operative Societies, *Notes on Co-operation Act 1923-1936*, Sydney, Government Printer, 1937; Directors of the

Woolgrowers' Co-operative Association: D F McMaster (Darling Point), A F McCaughey (MLC), F C Bacon, J Atkinson, D McMaster and T W Waddell.

13 *The Co-operator*, February, November, December 1897, March 1898; *Farmers' Co-operative* News, October 1898.

14 Sydney *Morning Herald*, 4 August 1898; W Kidston, 'Co-operative Movement in Australia', Study Paper No 3, Co-operative Federation of Queensland, n.d.; *Farmers' Co-operative News*, January 1900: Directors of the Farmers' and Settlers' Co-operative Company Limited were: W M McMillan, D L Dymock, A Campbell, J Stewart, H M Osborne, E R Evans, J Monoghan, J Cork, J Fraser. Dairy factories consigning supplies to Farmers' and Settlers' included Albion Park, Druewalla, Gerringong, Woodstock, Smithtown, Barrengarry, Jamberoo, Kangaroo River, Unanderra, Lower Manning, Ulladulla, Berry Central, North Coast Fresh Food and Cold Storage (Norco), Foxground, Marshall Mount, Martinsville, Wattamolla, Burrandulla.

15 R S Maynard, *His Was the Vision: The Life of C E D Meares*, Sydney 1941, pp 56-8; *Farmers' Co-operative News*, October 1898.

16 *Farmers' Co-operative News*, March 1900; Maynard, *op cit*, pp 57-58.

17 T C Kennedy, 'Rise and Fall', *op cit*, pp 27-28; *Farmers' Co-operative News*, March 1900. Reports of this meeting vary. T C Kennedy says that Meares was not present, that he was plotting with others in an upstairs room of the Grand Hotel, Kiama. The Fairbairn-controlled *Farmers' Co-operative News* implies that Meares did attend the meeting and that only six in the packed hall supported him.

18 Dairy and bacon co-operatives and private companies then consigning to McMillan's included: Illawarra Central, Ulladulla Central, Camden Park Estate, Duckenfield Park Estate, Woodstock Central, Foxground Dairy Company, Kangaroo Valley Butter and Bacon, Smithtown Dairy Federation, Blayney, J C Huttons, North Coast Co-operative (Foley Brothers), Barrengarry, IXL (Henry Jones) Butter, Barnes Bacon, Hicks Bacon.

19 Maynard, *op cit*, pp 10-12; E Sommerland (ed) *Fifty Years of Co-operative Service: a Survey of Co-operative Distributors, Dairy Farmers' Co-operative Milk Company Limited, 1900-1950*, Sydney 1951, p 15; *Coastal Farmers' Gazette*, April 1901, March 1902. Subscribers to Meares' capital drive included: K Noble (Byron Bay), Geoff Tait (Kangaroo Valley), David Thorburn (Jasper's Brush), M J Hindmarsh (Gerringong), George Couch (Dunmore), W Thompson (Cambewarra). Managers who left McMillan's included: Messrs Bryce, Mathison, Armstrong, Murphy, Cooper and Hill.

20 The English CWS subsequently became more deeply involved in South Australian wheat exports and later developed an intensive interest in Western Australian wheat.

21 *The Co-operator*, September 1900, December 1901, August 1902; *Farmers' Co-operative News*, September 1904; W Kidston, 'Co-operative Movement in Australia', Study Paper No 3, Co-operative University of Queensland, 1960.

22 *The Co-operator*, December 1901.

23 Sommerland, *op cit*, p 18; *Farmers' Co-operative News*, October 1898; Co-operative Dairy Conference, Albion Park Town Hall, 29 August 1901. Two earlier conferences of dairy co-operators had been held, one in 1897 and another at the Oddfellows Hall, Kiama on 7 September 1898. Co-operatives which supported Meares' plan included: North Coast Fresh Food (Norco), Illawarra Central, Woodhill (Berry), Albion Park, Meroo Meadow, Bombaderry, Candelo, Kangaroo River, Berry Dairy, Foxground, Dapto, Glenn Innes, Singleton. Twelve co-operative factories in the Byron Bay, Illawarra, Berrima and Bega districts did agree to experiment with an informal 'butter council' to regulate prices co-operatively, but there was little conviction or purpose about it, underlying a prevailing lack of confidence in co-operative methods at the time.

24 *Shepparton News*, 5 November 1954. Creameries were established at Mooroopna, Kialla, Kialla West, Tallygaroopna, Pine Lodge, Pine Lodge North, Pine Lodge South, Cobram, Boosey, Dunbulbalane, Numurkah, Congupna and Katamatite. First board of directors: Messrs James

Fairley (Shepparton) (Chairman), Joseph Hillier (Pine Lodge), Joseph Jacon (Arcadia), Charles Norton (North Mooroopna), George Gordon (Kalimna), Thomas Geddes (Shepparton) and E E Green (Shepparton).

25 Sommerland, *op cit*, p 23.

26 *Coastal Farmers' Gazette*, February 1903, January 1904.

27 *Coastal Farmers' Gazette*, September, November 1903, February 1903, January 1904; Royal Commission into the Butter Industry (Victoria): Reports 11 April, 24 June, 2 November 1904, 24 January, 1 June 1905. VPp 1904, No. 42 (V 2); 1905 No. 3 19+ 10a (V 2); Royal Commission on the Butter Industry 11 April 1904–5, August 1905, Pp II: 1621; 1905 II, 1210–1291.

28 *Farmers' Co-operative News*, September 1898, September 1899; *Coastal Farmers' Gazette*, November 1904, February, May, October 1905, January 1907. Late in 1906 Fairbairn retired from the Gloucester Dairy Co-operative after 'bookkeeping' discrepancies were discovered. Manifest of RMS *Macedonia*, which sailed for London on November 12, 1904: Coastal Farmers' – 2705 boxes of butter; Farmers' and Settlers' – 1967 boxes. Co-operative dairy factories consigning through Coastal Farmers' in September 1904 were: Illawarra Central, Nowra, Casino, Aberdeen, Cobargo, Woodstock (Jamberoo), Woodhill (Berry), Foxground, Upper Kangaroo River, Candelo, Dapto, Nambucca, Raymond Terrace, Lismore, Pambula, Coralline, Argyle (Goulburn), Southgate, Glenn Innes, Crookwell, Grabben Gullen and Laggan (Goulburn), Bellingen, North Coast (Byron Bay), Hastings, Barrengarry and others from Ulmarra and Palmer's Island.

29 H W Osborne, 'The Story of the Career of Harry W Osborne, Municipal Officer, Merchant, Printers' Apprentice, Journalist', Terang, Victoria 1939, pp 21, 28-32; *The Age*, Melbourne, 3 June 1905; *Federal Co-operative News*, October 1904; N T Drane and H R Edwards (eds) *The Australian Dairy Industry, An Economic Study*, Melbourne 1961, p 31.

30 Osborne, *op cit*, pp 22-24, 26-29, 32-34.

31 Cathedral Hotel Meeting, 29 July 1905. Representatives of the following butter factories attended: Bloomfield, Crossover, Dumbbell, Foster and District, Heyfield, Leongatha, Mirboo North, Bowen, Sale, South Gippsland, Stony Creek, Traralgon. Directors: J McKenzie, P Johnson, J L Murdoch, G H Stellen, H Smith, R S Overend, J R Rahilly. The board of directors comprised three representatives from each of the founding companies. Chairman Mr James McKenzie, who represented Gippsland and Northern, Messrs P Johnson and A W Wilson. Representing Western District were Messrs T McCullough, J Rankin and H W Osborne.

32 In 1944, G & N started a superannuation fund. By 1950 it had 400 employees and £47,000 capital.

33 *Federal Co-operative News*, April 1906; John Ross, *From Competition to Co-operation: Socialism in the Making*, Melbourne, 1906, p 83.

34 *Federal Co-operative News*, September 1912; Osborne, *op cit*, p 35; *Coastal Farmers' Gazette*, July 1909; Maynard, *op cit*, p 29; Conference, Sydney 15-16 July 1909. Present were: Victoria: A J Black and H W Osborne (Western District); J McKenzie, A Wilson (Gippsland and Northern), Colonel W B Pleasants (Victorian Butter Factories Co-operative and Victorian Co-operative Association); Queensland: A M Stevens, H Sharpe (Farmers' Co-operative District); New South Wales: W Watts, C E D Meares (Coastal Farmers'); J Alcorn, N A Throsby (Berrima District Farmers and Dairy Company), F Reading, W A Clifford (North Coast Co-operative). The annual turnover of those co-operatives was £3 million. There was some tension between the Gippsland and Northern Co-operative and Western District Co-operative at this time, after the former, responding to rumours spread by proprietors that the latter was underselling it, opened a rival selling floor in Melbourne.

35 W M Smith, *The Marketing of Australian and New Zealand Primary Production*, London, 1936, p 259; C M H Clarke, *A History of Australia, op cit*, pp 339, 343; Royal Commission of Inquiry as to Food Supplies and Prices, *Reports*, 30 January, 8 October, 29 November 1913; NSW Parliamentary

Papers 1913, V 4, First Session, pp 243-263; V 3, Second Session, pp 107-566, 567-663; Maynard, *op cit*, pp 32, 54.

36　Maynard, *op cit*, p 33; Osborne, *op cit*, pp 30-33; Smith, *op cit*, p 1. By 1912, following amalgamations, 126 co-operative dairy factories were producing 195 million pounds of butter, virtually doubling production in a decade.

37　H C Wilkinson, *State Regulation of Prices in Australia*, Melbourne 1917, p 83; W M Smith, *The Marketing of Australian and New Zealand Primary Production*, London 1936, p 4. Relevant legislation included: (Commonwealth) the Customs Act 1910-1914; (New South Wales) the Commodity Control Act (1914), the Wheat Acquisition Act (1914); (South Australia) the Prices Regulation Act (1914); the Foodstuffs Commission Act (1914), the Grain and Fodder Act (1914), Loans to Producers Acts 1917; (Western Australia) the Control of Trade in Wartime Act (1914); (Queensland) Meat Supply for Imperial Uses Act (1914), the Control of Trade Act (1914), the Co-operative Agricultural Production and Advances to Farmers Act 1914-1919, the Co-operative Sugar Works Act (1914); (Victoria) the Cold Stores for Fruit Act (1914), the Primary Producers Advances Act 1919-1922; (Tasmania) Advances to Fruit Growers Acts 1918-1919

38　Wilkinson, *op cit*, pp 84-6; Smith, *op cit*, pp 5, 16.

39　Maynard, *op cit*, pp 45-6; *Royal Commission of Inquiry on the Rural, Pastoral, Agricultural and Dairy Industries with Particular Reference to Share Farming*, New South Wales Government Printer, August 1917; Wilkinson, *op cit*, p 218.

40　Parliamentary Debates NSW V 82, 1929, p 687; V R Ellis, *History of the Australian Country Party*, Melbourne, 1963, p 81.

41　R S Maynard, *op cit*, pp 30, 52, 65; Osborne, *op cit*, pp 40, 45, 48; Commonwealth Dairy Produce Equalisation Committee Limited, *Report*, 1937, p 1. New South Wales delegates included: J McGregor and W A Clifford (Norco), C F Williams, J H Bate (Primary Producers' Union), W Watts, C E D Meares (Coastal Farmers').

CHAPTER TWO

1　R S Maynard, *His Was the Vision*, *op cit*, p 61; V R Ellis, *AustralianCountry Party*, *op cit*, p 81.

2　Federal Co-operative Conference *Report*, Athenaeum Hall, Melbourne, 14 May 1918, pp 9, 10, 13. Co-operative companies and companies represented included:

Victoria: the Victorian Producers Co-operative Company, the Western District Factories Co-operative Production Company, G & N Co-operative Selling and Insurance Company, the Victorian Butter Factories Co-operative Company, the Victorian Orchardists Co-operative Association, the Geelong District Farmers Co-operative Association, the Western and Murray Co-operative Bacon Curing Company, the Goulburn Valley Industries Company and the Wimmera Inland Freezing Company;

New South Wales: the Coastal Farmers' Co-operative Union and the Farmers and Settlers Co-operative Grain Company;

South Australia: South Australian Farmers Co-operative Union (SAFCU) and the Farmers Producers Co-operative Limited;

Queensland: Downs Co-operative Bacon Company, the Queensland Co-operative Fruitgrowers' Company, Rural Industries (Queensland) Limited, the Queensland Cheese Manufacturers Association;

Western Australia: Westralian Farmers;

Tasmania: the Tasmanian Orchardists and Producers Co-operative Association, the Farmers, Stock-owners and Orchardists Association.

There were also delegates from New Zealand. Provisional Committee of the Australian Producers Wholesale Co-operative Federation in 1918: Messrs P H Ibbott and B Wilson (Victoria); C E D

Meares and Gorman (New South Wales); B Murray (Western Australia); Galbraith (Queensland) and Badcock (South Australia).

3   Maynard, *op cit*, p 64. Co-operatives present at the 1919 conference included: South Australian Farmers Co-operative Union, Murray River Wholesale Co-operative, Farmers' and Graziers' Co-operative Grain and Insurance Agency Company, Coastal Farmers' Co-operative, Farmers' Co-operative Distribution Association of Queensland Limited, Tasmanian Orchardists and Producers Limited, Co-operative Dried Fruit Sales Proprietary Limited, Gippsland and Northern, Victorian Butter Factories Co-operative Limited, and Westralian Farmers. The combined turnover of these organisations was £18.5 million. Coastal Farmers' turnover was £3.25 million. Provisional Board of the Australian Producers' Wholesale Co-operative Federation November 1919: P H Ibbot (Victorian Producers' Co-operative Company), A W Wilson (G and N Co-operative Selling and Insurance Company Limited), B L Murray (Westralian Farmers), C E D Meares (Coastal Farmers' Co-operative), E A Badcock (South Australian Farmers' Co-operative Union), T E Yelland (South Australian Farmers' Co-operative Association), A C Galbraith (Rural Industries Co-operative [Queensland] Limited), R McWhinney (Farmers' Co-operative Distribution Company of Queensland).

4   H W Osborne, *Career of Harry Osborne*, *op cit*, p 50. Overseas Farmers' developed branches at Glasgow, Liverpool, Manchester, Cardiff, Birmingham, Nottingham, Bristol, Leeds and Belfast. In 1921 A E Gough of the English CWS revisited Australia leading a conference of 'Co-operative Federations' from South Africa, New Zealand and Australia. The theme of the conference was a 'Co-operative Commonwealth', but not in the Rochdale sense – in an imperial sense.

5   Producers' Co-operative Distribution Society (PDS) *Report*, Sixth Annual Conference, Sydney, September 1932; Maynard, *op cit*, p 68; D H McKay, 'History of Co-operation in South Eastern Australia', MA Thesis, University of Melbourne, c1942, p 106; W Kidston, History and Economic Background of Foreign Affairs in Australia', in International Training Course, Perth, 1969.

6   F J Foster, *Broad Principles of an Australian Producers' Co-operative Party*, Pamphlet, Burwood, NSW, 1917.

7   L J Lewis and I Turner (eds), *The Depression of the 1930s*, Cassell 1968, p 12; C B Schedvin, *Australia and the Great Depression*, Sydney 1990, pp 63-73.

8   Royal Commission of Inquiry into the Rural, Pastoral, Agricultural and Dairy Industries with Particular Reference to Share Farming, New South Wales, August 1917, p 1; V Ellis, *op cit*, p 10.

9   Commonwealth Dairy Produce Equalisation Committee Limited, *Report*, 1937, p 1; H W Osborne, *op cit*, pp 40, 45, 48.

10 J A Morey, 'The Role of the Statutory Marketing Board', MA Thesis, University of Sydney, 1959, p 26; W M Smith, *The Marketing of Australian Primary Production*, *op cit*, pp 7, 9, 14, , 45, 98; C B Schedvin, *op cit*, p 68; Ellis, *op cit*, p 81. Examples of post-war legislation regulating trade include: (Queensland) Profiteering Prevention Act, 1920; (New South Wales) Necessary Commodities Control Act, 1919, Profiteering Precautions Act, 1920; (Victoria) Necessary Commodities Control Act, 1919; (South Australia) Prices Regulation Act, 1919; (Western Australia) Prices Regulation Act, 1919 and 1920; (Tasmania) no action. In W A McArthur v State of Queensland [1920], 28 CLR, 530, the legality or marketings boards was questioned.

11 Morey, *op cit*, pp 52-54; E O Shann, *Quotas and Money*, Sydney, 1935, p 5; Osborne, *op cit*, p 54. The main drive at Ottawa came from the British delegation seeking a sheltered home market for British farmers. The Australians sought protection for Australian industry and continued access to British markets. Agreements were reached in an atmosphere of 'sordid bargaining' and bitter struggles ensued, damaging empire relations.

12 Osborne, *op cit*, p 54.

13 R R Piggot, 'Aspects of the Organisation of Rural Marketing Co-operation in New South Wales', University of New England, Armidale, NSW, 1969; Osborne, *op cit*, p 58; E O Shann *op cit*, p 5.

14 C Ashton (ed), *Dairy Farming in Australia: Victoria Edition*, Commonwealth Department of Commerce and Agriculture, Sydney, 1949, p 34; Commonwealth Dairy Produce Equalisation Committee Limited, *Report*, 1935, p 1; Commonwealth Dairy Produce Equalisation Committee Limited, *Report*, 1940, p 3; Commonwealth Dairy Produce Equalisation Committee Limited, *Report*, 1946, p 4; Morey, *op cit*, p 91; Smith, *op cit*, p 73, 113-117, 233; Producers' Co-operative Distribution Society (PDS), *Report*, 1931, *op cit*, p 9; Commonwealth Parliamentary Debate 14/156, Geo V Vol 109, p 17-35; *Co-operative News*, November 1929, February 1933; Osborne, *op cit*, p 58; Maynard, *op cit*, p 79; PDS, *Annual Report*, 1932, p 3; Australian Institute of Political Science Pamphlet Series, Sydney 1937, pp 28-29. South Australia elected to participate in the Equalisation Committee only for cheese production. Western Australia influenced by political friends of that state, conducted an independent market regulatory system until 1946, despite a majority poll of producers favourable to the equalisation scheme. The Australian Dairy Produce Board consisted of sixteen members: one commonwealth representative; one representative from the Federal Council of Australian Factory Managers and Secretaries Association; two representatives from proprietary companies; two representatives of co-operatives and co-operative companies from each of the major producing states (New South Wales, Victoria, Queensland); and three representatives of co-operatives and co-operative companies from South Australia, Western Australia and Tasmania.

Results of the Dairy Producers' Poll, 11 October 1934

State	Number of Votes in favour of continuance of Act	Number of Votes not in favour of continuance of Act	Number of Votes rejected as informal	Majority of Votes in favour of continuance of Act
NSW	15,799	188	21	15,591
VIC	15,120	346	24	14,774
QLD	16,114	152	28	15,962
SA	1,346	233	7	1,113
WA	1,339	16	4	1,323
TAS	1,049	481	3	568
Totals	50,747	1,416	87	49,331

In James v Commonwealth, 1935, the Privy Council reversed a High Court Decision of 1920 in respect of the act's constitutionality. The commonwealth unsuccessfully sought constitutional powers to regulate through referenda in 1936, 1944 and 1946. State legislation complementing the Commonwealth Dairy Produce Act: Queensland Dairy Products Stabilisation Act, 1933; New South Wales Dairy Products Act, 1933; Western Australian Dairy Products Act, 1934, Victorian Dairy Products Act, 1933, Tasmanian Dairy Products Act 1933. In 1932 Major Russell replaced Meares as managing director of PDS. Meares died in 1934. Russell had spent more than twelve years in London for APWCF and had also represented the Australian Dairy Products (Exports) Control Board. In 1932, E Hardy Johnston, an attorney for the English CWS, briefed the Co-operative Advisory Council on dairy exports. Some of his recommendations were carried in the New South Wales Dairy Products Act. In 1929, Dairy Farmers Co-operative absorbed the Camden Vale Milk Company Limited, and the Farmers' and Dairymen's Milk Company. In 1932, eleven of the fifty-two affiliates of PDS were non-co-operative. In 1934, Dairy Farmers acquired the Singleton–Waratah Milk Company Limited, McNamara Limited and the Woodstock Milk and Cream Company Limited.

15 Gary Lewis, 'Co-operation, Carruthers and Community Settlement: the *Co-operation Act* 1924', a sub-thesis for the Bachelor of Letters Degree, Australian National University History Department, 1980; Gary Lewis, *A Middle Way, op cit*, pp 93-101; Parliamentary Debate NSW 92 LA First Reading, 18 October 1923, pp 1651-1658; Parliamentary Debate NSW 94 LA Second Reading, 29

November 1923; 5 December 1923, pp 2901-1922, 3053-3117; Parliamentary Debate NSW 94 LA Committee, 6 December 1923, pp 3149-289; Jan Todd, *Milk for the Metropolis*, Hale and Iremonger, 1994, pp 83-97, 101, 138.

16   *Co-operative News*, July 1927.

17   *Co-operative News*, May, October 1924, January, February 1925, June 1928, January, July, August, November 1929, May 1930, February 1931, March 1932, February, November 1935, February, March, May, September 1939, October 1940; *Westfarmers Gazette*, 13 January, 27 June 1939, 23 February 1939; Morey, *op cit*, pp 53-55; Smith, *op cit*, pp 70-73. In James v South Australia (1927), 40 CCR, it was held that 'compulsory' powers vested in state marketing authorities were obnoxious to the constitution. Poultry farmers had used the Berrima District and Coastal Farmers' distribution system prior to 1929 when the Egg Marketing Board was set up. The NSW CWS complained that poultry farmers were ignoring the welfare of consumers, but poultry farmers replied that the Rochdale movement had ignored them for twenty-five years and told the NSW CWS to 'wake up to itself', that it had co-operated the 'wrong way around: the producer, not the consumer, comes first'. The Commonwealth Dried Fruits Act was passed without reference to growers and was complemented by the NSW Dried Fruits Act (1927), giving the Commonwealth Dried Fruits Board authority to acquire crops, determine quotas for export, issue licences for interstate trade, reject and regulate trade. This arrangement was subject to court challenges but was able to function virtually up to World War II when the New South Wales Dried Fruits Board was constituted. In 1939, PDS merged with Queensland Producers' Co-operative Distributive Society.

18   F R Mauldon in *Annals of the American Academy of Political and Social Science* (ed). D B Copland Professor of Commerce, University of Melbourne, Philadelphia, 1931, pp 189, 190-1.

19   *Co-operative News*, January 1925.

20   NSW Registry of Co-operative Societies, *Annual Report*, 1928; McKay, thesis, *op cit*.

21   New South Wales Registrar of Co-operative Societies, Address to the Third Annual Conference of the Co-operative Federation of New South Wales, 22 November 1967; *Westfarmers Gazette*, 27 January 1939; *Co-operative News*, March 1936; Morey, *op cit*, Chapter 3.

CHAPTER THREE

1   *Dairy Industries International*, April 2001. Average land size of farms in 1975 had been 77 hectares. By 2000 the average size was 170 hectares. In 1950 the average annual cow production was 1,746 litres of milk and by 1996 this had risen to 4,481 litres.

2   Jan Todd, *More Than Milk: Dairy Farmers and the Co-operative Response to Industry Deregulation*, Hale and Iremonger, 2001, p 15; J Todd, *Milk for the Metropolis, op cit*, pp 140-144, 147; *Westralian Farmers' Gazette*, October 1948; *Weekend Australian*, 11-12 January 2003.

3   C Watson, *Just a Bunch of Cow Cockies: the Story of the Murray-Goulburn Co-operative*, Murray-Goulburn Co-operative, 2000, p 140; Murray-Goulburn Co-operative Limited, *Twenty Seven Years at the Helm: Jack McGuire 1952-1999: A Memento to the Retirement as Managing Director of Murray Goulburn Co-operative Company Limited*, 31 March 1979; Gary Lewis, *Interview*, Jack McGuire, 19 June 1983. A new version of the refrain in the 1970s reflects a change in sentiment:

    Murray-Goulburn, a dairy farmer co-operative owned by Australian dairy farmers and residents of the rural communities in which they live, controlled by Australian dairy farmers using the collective strength of the many to build and protect the welfare and security of each one, giving an equal voice to dairy farmers in every area in which it operates.

4   Watson, *op cit*, pp 112-113, 127, 140.

5   R R Piggott, 1969, *op cit*, pp 118, 120; Watson, *op cit*, pp 137-141.

6   C Greenwood, *Australian Dairy Co-operatives: Planning for the Future*, Dairy Research Development Corporation, February 1996, p 30; Gary Lewis, *Interview*, C W Gerrish, 17 June 1983.

7   Watson, *op cit*, pp 142, 162-173, 182, 185; Todd, *Milk for the Metropolis, op cit*, p 217; CFNSW, *Newsletter*, January-February 1973; Australian Dairy Industry Corporation Incorporated, *Annual Report*, 2002, pp 10-12. In 1979 the Murray-Goulburn democratic delegate voting system was redesigned to include ten supplier zones with each zone represented by a supplier director who maintained contact with other suppliers through twenty to thirty delegates selected by dairy farmers in the zones, which were determined by the quantity of butter fat supplied, not production volume alone.

8   CFNSW, *Newsletter*, January-February 1975; Watson, *op cit*, pp 190-191, 193-194.

9   Gary Lewis, *Interview*, J J (Jack) McGuire, 17 June 1983; Gary Lewis, *Interview*, C W Gerrish, *op cit*; Gippsland and Northern *Co-operator*, 28 July 1966; *Australian Financial Review*, 27 April 1976, 21 July 1977,16 March 1978; Watson, *op cit*, p 962; CFNSW, *Newsletter*, March 1974; Murray-Goulburn Co-operative Limited, *Annual Report*, 1982; Murray-Goulburn Co-operative Limited, *Twenty-Seven Years at the Helm, op cit*. Ian Wood, with a Reserve Bank background, became General Manager.

10 Watson, *op cit*, pp 220-226, 228, 230; Todd, *More Than Milk, op cit*, p 29.

11 ACMAL, *Annual Report*, 1972; CIC, *Annual Report*, 1969; Gippsland and Northern, *Co-operator*, 28 July 166; Watson, *op cit*, p 229; Todd, *More Than Milk, op cit*, p 29; *Australian Financial Review*, 23 March 1971; Brad Plunkett and Ross Kingnell, 'Co-operatives for Agricultural Marketing and Processing', in *Agribusiness Review*, Vol 9, Paper 9, 2001. The co-operative company acquired the Australian operations of Unigate Australia. CIC Insurance Proprietary Limited began trading in Perth and Westralian Farmers and Sunnywest Co-operative Dairies directed business through Bonlac.

12 Victorian Artificial Breeders Pamphlet, 'VAB Through the Years; Gary Lewis, *Interview*, T N D Stevens, 17 June 1983. Board of Directors Victorian Artificial Breeders 1985: J D Gardiner, W R Selzer, J T Reid, H L Martin, R M Noble, C H Chamberlain, J Peach.

13 Todd, *More Than Milk, op cit*, pp 6-17.

14 Watson, *op cit*, p 198.

15 Watson, *op cit*, pp 223, 227; Todd, *More Than Milk, op cit*, pp 23, 29.

16 Watson, *op cit*, pp 233-238; Bill Pritchard, 'Global Trends in the Dairy Industry', Economic Geography Department, Sydney University, February 2001, pp 16-18, 29; Greenwood, *Australian Dairy Co-operatives, op cit*, pp 19, 25; *Australian Financial Review*, 6 November 1989; Todd, *More Than Milk, op cit*, pp 23-29.

17 *Australian Financial* Review, 1 February 1990; *Australian Dairy Foods*, Report 1999, p 18; Todd, *More Than Milk, op cit*, p 113.

18 *Bulletin*, 16 January 1990, 16 July 1991; *Western Magazine*, (Dubbo), 25 June 1990. The New South Wales' industry was in serious decline. A Rural Adjustment Scheme was assisting many farmers to exit the industry with many of those remaining forced to survive on social welfare payments.

19 National *Co-op Update*, May-June 2002; Chris Greenwood, 'Capital Raising Issues and Options for Australian Dairy Co-operatives, Masters of Business (Agribusiness) Thesis, Monash University, Victoria, March 1999, p 41; Watson, *op cit*, pp 249-251.

20 *Sydney Morning Herald*, 1 February 1995, 19 February 1999; *Australian Financial Review*, 13 June 1995.

21 Chris Greenwood, *Thesis, op cit* pp 25-26, 30, 44, 62-64, 68, 72; Michael O'Keefe, 'Co-operatives: Opportunities and Dilemmas', Agribusiness Research Unit, Monash University, 1996; James Evans, 'Innovative Funding Sources', in *Report, New South Wales Registry of Co-operative Societies 1996 Key Issues Conference*.

22 *Australian Financial Review*, 31 July 1998; *National Co-op Update*, May-June 1998; *Bulletin*, 18 August 1998. Bonlac was required by the Australian Securities and Investments Commission

(ASIC) to issue a supplementary prospectus making clear Bonlac's obligations to pay interest on the notes. The co-operative company's chairman and deputy chairman were removed in 1999. Bonlac's Managing Director was recruited from Coca-Cola Amatil Limited.

23 Commonwealth Parliamentary Papers, *Dairy Industry Adjustment Bill 2000*. The Reverend F J Nile (Christian Democratic Party) was opposed to the Dairy Industry Adjustment Bill, claiming that it would drive farmers out of business, lead to a Victorian milk invasion and see a greater concentration of farm ownership. Already, he said, in the New South Wales Legislative Council, one dairy farmer with 27,000 cows controlled 27 per cent of the New South Wales market.

	Current Dairy Farm Incomes ($)	Annual Full Income per Farm ($)	Adjustment per Farm ($)
New South Wales	83,510	46,210	169,408
Victoria	44,690	16,270	95,061
Queensland	56,470	32,940	123,914
South Australia	55,520	31,550	160,159
Western Australia	89,510	53,500	237,254
Tasmania	53,740	28,350	118,192

CHAPTER FOUR

1 T Fisher *A Short History of the Adelaide Co-operative Society, 1867-1924*, Adelaide 1924; *Port Adelaide Industrial Co-operative Society Ltd: The Story of its Foundation and Progress*, Adelaide, 1920, C Hill, *Fifty Years of Progress: A History of the South Australian Farmers' Co-operative Union*, Adelaide, 1938, pp. 5, 9-10, 16-17, 21-23. Hill refers to 'Langlois defalcations'.

2 C Hill, *op cit*, pp 23, 26, 46. In 1903 SAFCU was involved in litigation with former English CWS agent R J Fairbairn on the matter of wheat quality.

3 C Hill, *op cit*, pp 35-36; *Co-operative News*, January 1925, November 1927. Factories were at Murray Bridge, Woodside, Milang, Naracoorte, Glencoe, Hindmarsh Island, Eudunda, Orroroo, Stansbury, Meadows.

4 C Hill, *op cit*, pp 5, 8, 36, 73, 82; *Co-operative News*, 1 January 1925; *Westfarmers Gazette*, 25 October 1934, 20 June 1935; *National Advocate*, 10 June 1986. Branches were at Port Adelaide, Wallaroo, Port Pirie, Port Lincoln, Mount Gambier, Kapunda, Bilaclara, Jamestown, Murray Bridge, Clare, Pinnaroo, Wirrabara, Millicent, Thevenard, Snowtown, Burra, Maitland, Minlaton, Strathalbyn.

5 C Hill *op cit*, p.95.

6 *Path to Prosperity: Abridged History of Eudunda Farmers' Co-operative Society Limited 1896-1946*, Adelaide, February 1946; *Co-operative News*, January 1948. Eudunda Farmers First Executive: G H Lurke, W Knight, A Schiller, J Schmidt, H Schwartz, J F Kennedy, J Foroton, J F Michel, T Roberts.

7 *Path to Prosperity*, *op cit*, p 19-23.

8 *Co-operative News*, June, September 1923; October 1927; February 1931; May, November 1933; July 1934; June 1936; November 1937; November 1939, April 1941; September, December 1943; May 1946; June, November 1947; January, May 1948; May 1950; January, May, November 1951; May, November 1952; May, December 1953; July, December 1956; May, July, December 1957; June, December 1958; May 1959; *Adelaide Advertiser*, 21 October 1981.

9 *Select Committee on Village Settlements Paper 113 of 1895, South Australian Parliamentary Debates 1895*, p. 1,446, *Paper 10 of 1900, Vol. 1.1 & 11, Papers 37 of 1900, Final Report of Committee on Murray River Settlements, Paper 93 of 1900*, p. 508, *1901*, pp. 114-6, *South Australian Lands Report 1907*, p. 9, *1913*, p. 27; Leroy-Beaulieu in *Les Neuvelles Societies Anglo Saxonnes (1901)*; H J

Finniss, 'Village Settlements on the River Murray', in *Proceedings of the Royal Geographical Society, South Australian Branch*, Vol. 69, 1959; L A Kerr, *Communal Settlements in South Australia in the 1890s*, University of Melbourne, 1952; W P Reeves, *Village Settlements in Australia*, New Zealand Parliamentary Papers 1895, C.6, pp. 6-8; J E March, *Settlement of People on the Land*, New Zealand Parliamentary Papers 2895, pp. 11-14; S H Roberts, *History of Australian Land Settlement 1785-1922*, Melbourne, 1927; M Davitt, *Life and Progress in Australian, Part II: The Murray River Labour Settlements*, London, 1898, pp. 75-104; *Register*, 15 September 1895, 14, 17 December 1901. For further information on the village settlements see *Advertiser*, 7 October 1893, 30 November 1893, 23 September 1895, 27, 31 July 1897. By 1951 it was estimated that co-operation and irrigation combined had added 40,000 to the population of the Sunrasia and fruit growing regions along the Murray.

10 D C Winterbottom, *Co-operation in the Dried Fruit Industry*, Queensland Co-operative Union Conference, 1957, p 1-3.

11 Winterbottom, *op cit*, 41; *South Australian Parliamentary Debates 1923*, Vols 1 and II, pp 300, 328-332, 714-716, 742-744; *Co-operative News*, August 1929.

12 Rivergrowers Co-operative Limited, *Annual Report*, 1983; *Co-operative News*, August 1929; *Adelaide News*, 9 March 1976; Co-operative Federation of New South Wales, *Federation Newsletter*, May 1972; Berri Co-operative Winery, *Kaiser Stuhl: The First Fifty Years 1931-1981*; *Australian Financial Review*, 23 January 1976.

13 Queensland Co-operative Union, *Annual Conference Report*, 1951, p 167; Berri Fruit Juices Co-operative Limited, *Leaflet*, n.d.; *Australian Financial Review*, 3 May 1978; W Kidston, *Study Paper No. 4*, Queensland Co-operative Union.

14 *Co-operative News*, May 1952. Committee of Management Nuriootpa Co-operative: A J Chapman (Orchardist), C E Maine (Cannery Manager), H B Scholz (Masseur), C B Robin (Orchardist), S B Denton (Chartered Accountant).

15 *Co-operative News*, May 1952; August 1954; *Westralian Farmers' Gazette*, November 1950; T H Bath in Westralian Farmers' *Annual Conference*, Perth, 1951.

16 *Co-operative News*, December 1949; March 1956.

17 Alice Womesley in *Co-operative News*, November 1950.

18 *The Valley of Barossa: A Township Starts to Live: South Australia's New Community*, Commonsense Publications, Adelaide, c.1949, pp 3, 29-31.

CHAPTER FIVE

1 Gavin Souter, *A Peculiar People: The Australians in Paraguay*, Sydney, 1968; S H Roberts, *History of Australian Land Settlement, 1788-1922*, Melbourne, 1924; *Cosme Monthly Homestead Village Press*, Gloria, Cosme, Paraguay, November 1902; Queensland *Parliamentary Debates*, Volume 70, 1893, pp 391-421, 443-467; Volume 74 1895, pp 1858-1879; *Courier*, 2 December 1895; *Worker*, October 1891; *Farmers Co-operative News*, October 1899; *Co-operative News*, September, November 1923, January 1924; Ian Stewart, *A History of Dairying on the Atherton Tableland*, Co-operative Dairy Association, Malanda, Queensland, 1983, p 2; W Kidston, *A Co-operative Study Course: The Co-operative Movement in Australia*, Co-operative Federation of Queensland 1965.

2 K Saunders, *Workers in Bondage: The Origins and Bases of Unfree Labour in Queensland, 1824-1916*, University of Queensland Press, 1982, pp 147-8, 172, 174; International Co-operative Alliance, Geneva Convention 1966 in *Co-operatives in Australia*, Australian Information Service, *op cit*, p 8; *Co-operative News*, September 1954; Co-operative Federation of Queensland, *Report 1951 Annual Congress*, Brisbane, April 151. The Colonial Sugar Refinery (CSR) maintained its monopoly of refining.

3 *Co-operative News*, July 1920, July 1935; 'Green Folder' T H Bath Memorial Library, Perth *op cit*. McGregor was later an Australian Trade Commissioner in London.

4 *Co-operative News*, January, July 1925.

5 *Co-operative News*, July 1925.

6 *Co-operative News*, November 1923, July 1925.

7 *Co-operative News*, June 1939; Kidston, *Co-operative Study Course, op cit*, Australia, June 1989.

8 *Co-operative News*, January, December 1923, July, September 1932, Co-operative Union of Queensland, *Congress*, 1951. The co-operative's turnover quadrupled in the decade to 1953.

9 *Co-operative News*, August, November 1923, September 1924, July, August 1930, December 1931, July, September 1932, July 1933, October 1935, March 1954; Queensland Poultry Farmers' Co-operative Society Limited, *Our First Thirty Years 1922-1951*, Co-operative Press, Brisbane, 1951; Co-operative Union of Queensland, *Report of Conference*, Red Comb House, Brisbane, 16 August 1945.

10 Queensland Poultry Farmers', *Our First Thirty Years, op cit*; Co-operative Union of Queensland, *Report of Congress*, 1951; *Co-operative News*, May, October 1951, May 1952, September 1956; Co-operative Wholesale Society of Queensland, 'Story of a Successful Co-operative' in Co-operative Union of Queensland, *Report Eighteenth Annual Congress*, Brisbane, March 1963.

11 Co-operative Federation of Queensland, *Managers' Conference*, Brisbane 19-20 March 1960 and 24-25 March 1961; Registration of Co-operative Housing Societies Queensland, *Report*, 1960.

12 *Co-operative News*, September 1944, June, October 1945, May 1946, October 1947, May 1951, July 1953, May 1958; *Our Home*, Australian Association of Permanent Building Societies, March 1948, March 1949; *Queensland Co-operator*, October 1948; Co-operative Union of Queensland, *Report Conference*, 1951, pp 31, 136-137; Co-operative Union of Queensland, *Report Conference*, 1953; North Queensland Co-operative Conference Ingham, *Report*, April 1963; *Credit Unions: A Co-operative Solution to the Credit Problems*, Co-operative Press, Brisbane, 1948.

13 Co-operative Federation of Queensland, *Report Managers' Conference*, Brisbane 25-26 March 1961, 17-18 March 1962.

14 Co-operative Federation of Queensland, *Annual Congress Report*, Brisbane, 1965; W Kidston, *Co-operative Study Course Number One: Introduction to the Co-operative Movement*, Co-operative Federation of Queensland, Brisbane, c 1965.

15 Co-operative Federation of Queensland, *Seventeenth Annual Congress Report*, Brisbane, 1962; Co-operative Federation of Queensland, *Eighteenth Annual Congress Report*, 22-23 March 1963; Co-operative Federation of Queensland, *Managers' Conference Report*, March 1963.

16 *Australian Financial Review*, 1 May 1992; *Land*, 31 August, 28 September, 31 November 1989, 30 August, 20 September 1990, 18 February, 6 August 1992; *Australian*, 24 September 1991; *Queensland Graingrower*, 15 August 1990; *Southern Rural*, 6 July 1990; *Cootamundra Herald*, 16 August 1991.

17 Registrar of Co-operative Housing Societies, Queensland, *Report*, 1967; Co-operative Federation of Australia, *Report*, June 1970; W Kidston, *The Role of Co-operatives*, Co-operative Federation of Queensland, November 1971; W Kidston, *The Extent and Impact of Co-operatives in the Pacific Region*, p 171; W Kidston, *Let's Give It A Go: Being an Interpretation of the Present Day Size and Importance of the Co-operative Movement in Queensland*, p 171; Co-operative Federation of New South Wales, *Federation Newsletter*, March 1969, July 1972, April-March 1973; Correspondence J E Urqhart from Secretary Red Comb Stock Feeds Co-operative Limited, 22 April 1982. In 1967 was an amendment to the act made permitting married women to legally become directors of a co-operative society! Ann El Khoury, *Interview*, Anthony Esposito, CCC Member, August 2003

CHAPTER SIX

1 Robert Gottleibsen, *10 Best and 10 Worst Decisions of Australian CEOs 1992–2002*, Viking, 2003, pp 200-211.

2 *Australian Financial Review*, 2 November, 3, 20 December 1977, 5, 13, 18, 20, 26 January, 15 February, 10, 31 March, 4, 5, 6, 7, 10, 11, 12, 20 April, 17 July, 6, 18 September 1978; 18 October 1989; *Australian* 27 September 1989; *Business Review Weekly*, 18-24 August 1984. Westralian Farmers' Co-operative Limited associated companies, 1980: Westralian Farmers' Transport Proprietary Limited (Melbourne), Westralian Farmers' Transport Limited (London), Wesfarmers Europe Limited (London). Subsidiary companies: Advance press Proprietary Limited, Bonestock Proprietary Limited, CSBP and Farmers Limited, Cuming Smith and Company Limited, Farmers Stores of WA, Gascoyne Trading Proprietary Limited, High Nickel Alloys Proprietary Limited, Masters Dairy Limited, Sunnywest Co-operative Dairies Limited, Wesfarmers Kleenheat Gas Proprietary Limited, Wesfarmers Linley Valley Meats Proprietary Limited, Westralian Farmers Superphosphates Limited, Westralian Fruit Exports Proprietary Limited. Associated Companies: Albany Woolstores Proprietary Limited, Alexandra Bridge Wines Proprietary Limited, Australian Stud Stock and Land Company Proprietary Limited, Detroit Engine and Turbine Company (WA),Fremantle Dumpers Limited, Liquid Air WA Proprietary Limited, Wesdelf Limited, Wesfarmers Hassall Proprietary Limited, Wesfarmers Tutt Bryant, Wesfeeds Proprietary Limited, Wesmilk Proprietary Limited, Wool Exchange (WA) Proprietary Limited.

3 Kevin Smith, *A Bunch of Pirates: The Story of a Farmer Co-operate*, Westralian Farmers' Co-operative, Perth, c.1984, p 10; J Sandford, *Harper and the Farmers'*, Westralian Farmers' Co-operative, Perth, 1955.

4 Western Australian *Hansard* 1876, p 36; 10 April 1895; Western Australian *Year Book*, 1902-04, 1015 ff; *Morning Herald* (Perth), pp 4, 6, 7, April 1896.

5 Harper and M H Jacoby were involved in a tussle for control of the Western Australian fruit industry.

6 T H Bath Memorial Library, Perth, 'Green Folder', 1984 (uncited). Farmers and Settlers Association of Western Australia members included: M H Jacoby, J Gardiner, J Deanne-Hammond, C W Harper, A J Monger, G Patterson, D Munro, M Padbury, C Penny, T H Wilding, R Maitland Leaks.

7 'Green Folder', *op cit*.

8 'Green Folder', *op cit*; *Co-operative News*, 1926; Sandford, *Harper and the Farmers*, *op cit*, p 294; J Sandford, 'Sixty Eventful Years', Pamphlet, Co-operative Federation of Western Australia, n.d.; Westralian Farmers Co-operative, *Annual Report*, 1974.

9 F R Mercer, *On Farmers Service: A Short History of Farmers Organisations in Western Australia*, Perth 1955, pp 55, 57-58, 110, 111; Sandford, *op cit*, p 294.

10 *Western Australian Parliamentary Debates*, Vol 82, 1929, pp 687-88; *Special Committee of the Legislative Assembly on Wheat Marketing Report*, 2 November 1916, 29 November 1916; *Western Australian Parliamentary Debates*, Vol 2, viii, 1916/17; Sandford, *op cit* pp 36, 294.

11 *Co-operative News*, January 1926.

12 'Green Folder', *op cit*; Mercer, *op cit*, pp 58, 110.

13 *Co-operative News*, January 1926; 'Green Folder', *op cit*; Westralian Farmers' Co-operative Limited, *Annual Report*, 1974.

14 Co-operative Federation of Western Australia, *Minutes*, 9 October 1919; Sandford, *Harper and the Farmers*, *op cit*, p 37.

15 Co-operative Federation of Western Australia, *Minutes*, 29 January, 27 May, 11 August, 27 September 1920.

16 *Primary Producer* (Perth), 6 February 1920, 18 November 1921.

17 Sandford, *Harper and the Farmers*, *op cit*, p 54; First Australian Congress of Consumer Co-operatives, *Report*, Melbourne, p 7; Co-operative Federation of Western Australia, *Minutes*, 4-5 October 1921; Mercer, *op cit*, p 5.

18 Co-operative Federation of Western Australia, *Minutes*, 8 October, 2 November 1921. The company also agreed to appoint a CFWA delegate to its board. Only £10 was sent by CFWA to support the Reverend Frank Pulsford's planned Co-operative Union Congress in Melbourne in 1922.

19 Co-operative Federation of Western Australia, *Minutes*, 6 March, 12 April, 16 June, 13 July, 8, 26 October, 2 November 1921; 22 February, 3 May, 10, 27 October, 6 December 1922; *Co-operative News*, July 1922; 'Green Folder', *op cit*.

20 Co-operative Federation of Western Australia, *Minutes*, 3 May, 17 July, 2 August, 27 October, 6 December 1922; 6 June 1923; Co-operative Federation of Western Australia Annual Conference, *Minutes*, 10-12 October 1923; 'Green Folder' (Co-operative Bulk Handling). Johnson was angry that the company would not support the State Implement Works, a 'socialist' construct that gave Westralian Farmers' Country Party supporters the horrors. In 1927 The Trustees of the Wheat Pool acquired a block of shares in this company and seat on the directorship.

21 Co-operative Federation of Western Australia, *Minutes*, 6 June 1923; *Co-operative News*, June 1923, December 1956; 'Green Folder', *op cit*.

22 Co-operative Federation of Western Australia, *Minutes*, 12 March, 16 April, 9 July 1924; Sandford, *Harper and the Farmers*, *op cit*, p 68.

23 Co-operative Federation of Western Australia, *Minutes Fifth Annual Conference*, 10-11 September 1924.

24 *Co-operative News*, October, November 1924; August, November 1925; June 1926; Co-operative Federation of Western Australia, *Minutes*, 2-3 August 1923, March 1924; Co-operative Federation of Western Australia, *Minutes Fifth Annual Conference*, *op cit*; Sandford, *Harper and the Farmers*, *op cit*, pp 59, 64, 66; Sandford, 'Sixty Eventful Years', *op cit*, p 21; Co-operative Institute of New South Wales, *Jubilee Co-operative Handbook*, Sydney 1952, p 129.

25 *Co-operative News*, January 1926, October 1927; H E Braine, formerly of Westralian Farmers' managed the Pool while Harper was involved in a lengthy Royal Commission investigation into the failure of British immigrant settlements (the BAWRA Scheme) in mainly the south-west dairy districts. See *Argus*, 6 September 1923 for a report of the Royal Commission into Group Settlement.

26 Co-operative Federation of Western Australia, *Sixth Annual Conference*, 9-10 September 1925; *Co-operative News*, November 1925.

27 Sandford, *Harper and the Farmers*, *op cit*, pp 68, 70, 78; *Co-operative News*, January 1926; Westralian Farmers' Co-operative Limited, *Annual Report*, 1974; J S Teasdale was associated with Australian Outturns Proprietary Limited

28 J McNeil Martin to Mr Sutcliffe, 4 August 1939 in Archives Producers Markets Limited, Perth; *Co-operative News*, August, October, November 1924; November 1925; April 1950; Co-operative Federation of Western Australia, *Minutes Sixth Annual Conference*, 10-11 September 1924. The H J and J Simper buy-out gave Westralian Farmers' depots in Java, Singapore and Malaya and stands at Bridgetown, Sunnybrook, Argyle, Capel, Balingup, Manjimup and Albany.

29 Co-operative Federation of Western Australia, *Minutes Seventh Annual Conference*, 25 August 1926, *Minutes Eighth Annual Conference*, 31 August 1927; Co-operative Federation of Western Australia, *Minutes*, 2 June 1926; *Co-operative News*, January 1926, August 1929.

30 Co-operative Federation of Western Australia, *Articles of Association*, 1927.

31 *Co-operative News*, August 1929; Sandford, *Harper and the Farmers*, *op cit*, pp 68, 70, 111.

32 Western Australian Parliamentary Debates, Vol 13, 4 October 1944, pp 921, 928; Co-operative Federation of Australia Group Study Course in the Establishment and Management of Co-operatives in Australia, 1969. Johnson was nominated as a Westralian Farmers' Director and given an ex-officio role in Central Council.

33 Co-operative Federation of Western Australia, *Minutes Annual Conference*, 9-10 September 1925, 25 August 1926, 31 August 1927, 22-23 August 1928, 11-13 March 1930; Co-operative Federation of Western Australia, *Minutes*, 2 June 1926, 6 April, 2 June 1932; Parliamentary Debates Western Australia, Vol 82, 11 September 1929, pp 684, 690, Vol 113, 6 September 1944, p 435, 4 October, 1944, p; 921, 914, 928; 'Green Folder', 'Towards Maturity', *op cit.*

34 Co-operative Federation of Western Australia, *Minutes Annual Conference*, 11-13 March 1930.

35 Sandford, *Harper and the Farmers, op cit*, pp 111-113; Gary Lewis, *Interview*: N Tidy, Co-operative Bulk Handling Limited, Perth, 31 May 1983. Westralian Farmers' wrote off £440,000 as 'bad debts'. The company remained in debt to English CWS until at least 1937. A Merchant and Farmers' Protection Association formed which successfully pressed the coalition government for debt adjustment legislation which prevented Westralian Farmers from foreclosing or repossessing.

36 Co-operative Federation of Western Australia, *Minutes Annual Conference*, 19 February 1931.

37 *Westralian Farmers' Gazette*, January, May 1932; 'Green Folder', Co-operative Bulk Handling, *op cit.*

38 Co-operative Federation of Western Australia, *Minutes Annual Conference*, 19 February 1931. Mr Spillman of the Eastern District Council, noting the high cost of bags, moved that pooling be investigated and the motion was carried. By 1934, 100 per cent of the Western Australian and Queensland crop was pooled; 80 per cent in South Australia; 43 per cent in Victoria; 25 per cent in New South Wales

39 *Westralian Farmers' Gazette*, July, October, November 1932.

40 Westralian Farmers, *Annual Report*, 1974; Sandford, *Harper and the Farmers, op cit*, p 12. Experimental bulk handling installations were developed at Penjabberrino, Korrelocking, Nembudding, Yelberri and Trayning. After the success of the experiment, Westralian Farmers submitted a proposal to the state government for a statewide bulk handling facility based on horizontal storage bins and mobile elevators.

41 Sanford, *Harper and the Farmers, op cit*, 77.

42 Co-operative Federation of Western Australia, *Minutes*, 6 April, 2 June 1932; Sandford, *Harper and the Farmers, op cit*, pp 62, 123-124, 127, 144, 146, 148, 264; *Westralian Farmers' Gazette*, 23 March 1933; J A Morey, *The Role of the Statutory Marketing Board in the Marketing of Australia's Primary Products, op cit*, p 119. Sandford's explanation of the 'strike' supports Westralian Farmers' case. When the Wheatgrowers' Union instituted the wheat hold-ups, they called on Westralian Farmers for assistance, asking the company to refuse to receive wheat at sidings. Westralian Farmers, under contract to the Pool, referred the matter to that body and the Pool instructed the company to receive wheat because of its commitments to those growers who wanted to cart. 'Between the devil and the deep blue sea, the two co-operative organisations were not in a position to further the strike, and consequently they incurred an enmity among many growers'. Under the International Wheat Agreement, twenty-two importing/exporting countries set quotas to protect markets.

43 *Westralian Farmers' Gazette*, 19 October 1933.

44 'A Co-operative Enterprise', Perth 1942, p 6; Sandford, *Harper and the Farmers, op cit*, p 71, 172, 179; C W Harper, 'A Brief Outline of Co-operative Achievement in Western Australia with Answers to Typical Criticisms', Perth 1933. The Royal Commission took evidence from A J Monger, J S Teasdale, T H Bath, J A Diver, C W Harper, W Marrick, W D Johnson, H W A Tanner, T C Boyd, H E Braine and J Thomson.

45 Sandford, *Harper and the Farmers, op cit*, pp 118, 143-146, 153, 156, 183.

46 C W Harper, 'A Brief Outline', *op cit*; 'Green Folder', Co-operative Bulk Handling, *op cit*; *Wheatgrower*, 10 October 1934.

47 *Westralian Farmers' Gazette*, 9 March 20 November 1935; *Wheatgrower*, 28 June, 10 October 1934; 'Green Folder', Co-operative Bulk Handling, *op cit*.

48 *Westralian Farmers' Gazette*, 17 October 1955; *Co-operative News*, September 1951; Sandford, *Harper and the Farmers*, *op cit*, p 159; Western Australian *Minutes and Votes of Proceedings of the Parliament*, Vol 1, 1935.

49 *Westralian Farmers' Gazette*, 26 September, 21 November 1935, 30 January, 12 March 1936; Westralian Farmers' *Annual Report*, 1974; *Co-operative News*, February 1947, April 1950, May 1956; Sandford, *Harper and the Farmers*, *op cit*, 1974; *Westralian Farmers' Gazette*, 9 May, 20 November, 5, 26 December, 1935; P S King (pub.) *Proceedings of the Imperial Conference on Agricultural Co-operation*, 18-20 July 1938, London 1939. English CWS delegates included Messrs Penny, Pickup and Williams. In addition to wheat handling and shipping, Westralian Farmers' at this time had interests in marketing bags, superphosphate, insurance, income tax services, merchandise, livestock, wools, skins and hides, farm produce, fresh and dried fruit, machinery and dairy products. After several milk producers withdrew from the company's 1925 fresh milk arrangement, the Western Australian Milk Board was formed, around 1933, and Westralian Farmers created Dairy Farmers' Co-operative Company Limited. The company also had fruit packing sheds at Bridgetown, Balingup, Boyanup, Brook, Manjimup, Donnybrook, West Swan and Geraldton, cool stores in Perth and Bridgetown, two flour mills and what was widely regarded as the best motor garage in Perth.

50 *Westralian Farmers' Gazette*, 3 March, 15 September 1938, 19, 23 January, 6 February, 21 September 1939, 29 February 1940, March 1951; *Co-operative News*, February 1935, August 1936; Co-operative Federation of Western Australia, *Minutes Annual Conference*, 22 February 1937; Sandford, *Harper and the Farmers*, *op cit*, pp 171, 175, 176, 179, 181, 185; *Newspaper Clippings*, 26 August, 15 November 1935, T H Bath Memorial Library, Perth; *Western Australian Parliamentary Discussions*, Vol 1134, October 1944, p 918; *Bulletin*, 22 February 1939.

51 Special Committee of the Legislative Assembly into Wheat Held in Storage, by Western Australian Merchants, *Western Australian Parliamentary Discussions*, 1940, No 15, Vol 2, p 42; *Report*, 11 November, 15 November 1939, No AL, Vol 2, p 12; *Western Australian Parliamentary Discussions*, 1947, No. 8, Vol 1, p 19; Morey, *op cit*, pp 20, 94; *Westralian Farmers' Gazette*, 19 January 1939; Sandford, *Harper and the Farmers*, *op cit*, pp 220-221, 228-229. The Wheat Pool's function was changed from receiving, selling and directing proceeds from wheat sales to simply providing services for the Australian Wheat Board.

52 *Westralian Farmers' Co-operative Gazette*, June 1951. South West Co-operative Dairy 'Sunnywest', then the largest dairy co-operative in Western Australia, processed half the state's butter. It was formed in 1908. In 1944, the co-operative had factories and depots at Bunbury, Busselton, Boyanup, Bridgetown, Harvey, Manjimup, Margaret River, Northcliffe, Perth; stores at Bunbury, Margaret River, Northcliffe, Boyanup, Case Mill and Dandalno; cold stores at Bunbury, Busselton, Harvey, Manjimup and Margaret River; an engineering depot at Bunbury; export floors in Perth; and two subsidiaries, Cowaramup Co-operative and Transport Proprietary Limited.

53 Sandford, *Harper and the Farmers*, *op cit* 104; Westralian Farmers' Co-operative Limited, *Annual Report*, 1974; T H Bath, *Statistical Survey of Co-operative Progress*, CFA, Perth, 1950; CFWA, *Minutes and Report*, Annual Conference, 20-22 February 1950; *Westralian Farmers' Co-operative Gazette*, December 1948; January 1949, July 1950.

54 Sandford, *Harper and the Farmers*, *op cit*, p 240.

55 CFWA, *Minutes and Report*, Annual Conference, 20-21 February 1951.

56 Sandford, *Harper and the Farmers*, *op cit*, p 34; CFWA, *Minutes*, 31st Annual Conference, 1951; Queensland Co-operative Union, *Minutes*, Conference, Brisbane, 16-17 April 1951.

57 Co-operative Federation of Queensland, *Minutes*, Conference, Brisbane, 17-18 March 1962; Sandford, *Harper and the Farmers, op cit*, p 288.

58 *Australian Financial Review*, 18 October 1989; *Australian*, 27 September 1989; Kevin Smith *op cit, p 10;* Gottleibsen, *op cit*, pp 200-211. In 1999 Co-operative Bulk Handling announced demutualisation plans. CFWA Affiliates 2004:

Albany Gateway Co-operative Limited

Albany Organised Primary Producers Co-op Ltd

Associated Newsagents of (WA) Co-op Society Ltd

Beacon Co-operative Limited

Bindoon Chittering Growers Co-operative Ltd

BKW Co-operative Ltd

Boyup Brook Co-operative Ltd

Brookton Farmers Co-operative Ltd

Capricorn Society Ltd

Carob Growers Co-operative Ltd

Caxton Co-operative Ltd

Challenge Dairy Co-operative Limited

Community Co-operative Travel Ltd

Co-operative Bulk Handling Ltd

Co-operative Purchasing Services Ltd

Cunderdin Farmers Co-operative Co. Ltd

Denmark Co-operative Co. Ltd

Esperance Organised Primary Producers Co-op Ltd

Gascoyne Water Co-operative Ltd

Geraldton Fishermen's Co-operative Ltd

Geraldton Organised Primary Producers Co-op Ltd

Kalgoorlie Taxi Owners Co-operative Ltd

Kojonup Co-operative Ltd

Midland Forestry Alliance Co-operative Ltd

Milling Co-operative Company Ltd

Mount Barker Co-operative Ltd

Nungarin Farmers Co-operative Co. Ltd

Octaviat Co-operative Limited

Ord Irrigation Co-operative Ltd

Ord River Districts Co-operative Ltd

Pindar Tardun Farmers Co-operative Ltd

Poultry Farmers of WA Co-operative Ltd

Preston Valley Irrigation Co-operative Ltd

Quairading Farmers Co-operative Limited

South West Irrigation Management Co-op Ltd T/As Harvey Water

Supermarket Transport Co-operative Ltd

Swan Taxis Co-operative Ltd

Sweeter Banana Co-operative Ltd

Tambellup Co-operative Ltd

The Wagin District Farmers Co-operative Co. Ltd

United Crate Co-operative Ltd

United Farmers Co-operative Company Ltd

Western Australian Meat Marketing Co-op Ltd

Western Inland Fisheries Co-operative Limited

Westonia Community Co-operative Limited

Wheatbelt Growers Co-operative Ltd

Wildmovers Co-operative Limited

York & District Co-operative Ltd

Chapter Seven

1 T H Bath, *Statistical Survey of Co-operative Progress, op cit*; Tony Gill, Co-operative Development Services Ltd, 'Demutualisation: Another Perspective', 26 July 2003. The author gratefully acknowledges Tony Gill's contribution to discussion on Victorian co-operatives. Gill believes that agricultural co-operative companies cannot be considered to be mutual organisations because they have *user* and *investor* shareholders, whereas a mutual society is an organisation where there is a complete identity between participants in the entity and its members and where the entity's income is derived from members.

2 W W (Bill) Rawlinson, Discussion Paper, 'Promotion of Co-operatives, Victorian Co-operative Advisory Council, 1983; Registry of Co-operative Societies, Victoria, *16th Annual Report*, June 1970. Over the next thirty years 654 government guarantees were extended to co-operatives, the vast majority going to schools and recreation societies. CFA Executive Officer Bill Rawlinson believed that the scheme's potential benefits had been squandered and misunderstood and, instead of driving co-operative development, had become 'a convenient structure...to obtain a gilt-edged security against which a bank might advance funds without any awareness of the true nature of co-operatives'.

3   Rawlinson, Discussion Paper, *op cit*; David Griffiths, *Co-operation Between Co-operatives*, Co-operative Federation of Victoria Website *www.australia.coop*.

4   David Griffiths, *op cit*; *Melbourne Age*, 28 February 1978, 25 June 1981; *Australian Financial Review*, 14 June, 2 July, 29, 30 September, 1, 2, 30 October, 1975, 16, 28 February, 5 May, 8 April, 10 July 1978; *Canberra Sunday Life*, 21 May 1978; *Bulletin*, 9 August 1989; *Ronald Anderson's Primary Industry Newsletter*, Collingwood, Victoria, 15 March 1978.

5   Gary Lewis, *Interview* T D Stevens, (HISCOL), June 1983; Ministerial Advisory Committee on Co-operatives (MACC) Report, *The Co-operative Way: Victoria's Third Sector*, Ministry of Housing, Victoria, July 1986, pp 85-86.

6   MACC *Report*, *op cit*, pp 3-4, 23, 61-63, 89, 97, 119, 13-141; David Griffiths, *op cit*.

7   Australian Association of Co-operatives, *Co-op Courier*, August-September 1987.

8   David Griffiths, *op* cit; Co-operative Federation of Victoria, *Report to Members*, 23 October 1987. Victorian legislation was changed to permit Friendly Societies to purchase shares in companies satisfying certain criteria for security and public benefit. Large societies launched managed funds and developed new equity benefit funds.

9   *Australian Financial Review*, December 1989. See Gary Lewis, *People Before Profit: the Credit Union Movement in Australia*, Wakefield Press, 1996, pp 327-336 for a discussion on the development of the Australian Financial Institutions Scheme (AFIC).

10 *National Co-op Update*, September-October 1986; Co-operative Federation of Victoria, *Victorian Co-op News*, Autumn, June-July, December-June 1999, October 2000; Gary Lewis, *People Before Profit*, *op cit*, pp 316-318.

11 Victorian *Parliamentary Debate*, Vol 432, 16 October, 14 November 1996, pp 900, 1013, 1194; Gary Lewis, *Conversation*: Tony Gill, Co-operative Development Services Limited; *Victorian Co-operative News*, September-October 2000; David Griffiths, *op cit*.

12 Social Enterprise Partnerships Website Home Page; Tony Gill, 'The Golden Years: A History of the Co-operative Federation Ltd 1993-1999', Co-operative Federation of Victoria Website; Co-operative Development Services Ltd Website *www.australia.coop*. In 2002 Tony O'Shea became CFV chairman.

Co-operative Federation of Victoria Affiliates 1999

Abalone Fishermen's Co-operative Ltd

Amalgamated Taxis of Wodonga Co-operative Ltd

Apollo Bay Fishermen's Co-operative Ltd

Architeam Co-operative Ltd

Ardmona Foods Limited

Australian Venison Producers Co-operative Ltd

Ballarat Child Care Co-operative Ltd

Ballarat Community Education Centre Co-operative Ltd

Ballarat Taxis Co-operative Ltd

Beaumaris Motor Yacht Squadron Co-operative Ltd

Bonlac Foods Ltd

Cape Volney Co-operative Society Ltd

Carlton Rental Housing Co-operative Ltd

Central Highlands Co-operative Ltd

Central Shires Co-operative Ltd

CEPA Co-operative Ltd

Cobden Artificial Breeders Co-operative Ltd

Colac Herd Improvement Co-operative Ltd

Consolidated Herd Improvement Services Co-operative Ltd

Co-operative Development Services Ltd

Co-operative Energy Ltd

Co-operative Purchasing Services Ltd

Dandenong & District Aboriginal Co-operative Ltd

Down To Earth (Victoria) Co-operative Ltd

Emerald & District Co-operative Society Ltd

Emu Farmers Co-operative Ltd

Essendon Rental Housing Co-operative Ltd

Euroa Co-operative Society Ltd

Frankston Rental Housing Co-operative Ltd

Geelong Radio Cabs Co-operative Ltd

Genetics Australia Co-operative Ltd
Gippsland Tip Truck Hiring Co-operative Ltd
Green Valley Co-operative Ltd
Greenlands Co-operative Ltd
Herd Improvement Co-operative (Maffra) Ltd
Hopetoun Community Hotel Co-operative
Society Ltd
Hopetoun Courier Co-operative Ltd
Kensington Children's Co-operative Ltd
Keysborough Freedom Club Co-operative Ltd
Lakes Entrance Fishermen's Co-operative Ltd
Macalister Research Farm Co-operative Ltd
Macaulay Community Credit Co-operative Ltd
Melbourne Co-operative Bookshop Ltd
Mirboo North Newspaper Co-operative Ltd
Moonee Creek Co-operative Ltd
Moorabbin Rental Housing Co-operative Ltd
MSA Co-operative Bookshop Ltd
Mt. Murrindal Co-operative Ltd
Murray Goulburn Co-operative Co. Ltd
Muslim Community Co-operative
(Australia) Ltd
New Market Co-operative Ltd
North East Forest Growers Co-operative Ltd
Northcote Rental Housing Co-operative Ltd
Northern Herd Development Co-operative Ltd
Para Park Co-operative Game Reserve Ltd
PBE Water Supply Co-operative Ltd
Primeat Co-operative Society Ltd
Progressive Broadcasting Service
Co-operative Ltd
Ruach Community Co-operative Ltd
Rupnorth Co-operative Ltd
Rural Industries Co-operative Ltd

San Remo Fisherman's Co-operative Society Ltd
Skye Children's Co-operative Ltd
South Barwon Rental Housing Co-operative Ltd
South Gippsland A.B. Co-operative Ltd
South Kingsville Health Services
Co-operative Ltd
Southern Energy Co-operative Ltd
St. Albans Community Centre Co-operative Ltd
Sunshine/St. Albans Rental Housing
Co-operative Ltd
Swinburne Bookshop Co-operative Ltd
Terang & District Co-operative Society Ltd
The Western Vic Dairy Research &
Demonstration Farm Co-operative Ltd
Timboon Herd Improvement Co-operative Ltd
Toora & District A & B Co-operative Ltd
Urban Camp Melbourne Co-operative Ltd
Victorian Producers' Co-operative Co. Ltd
Warm Corners Co-operative Ltd
Wathaurong Aboriginal Co-operative Ltd
Waverley Trading Co-operative Ltd
West Gippsland Herd Improvement
Co-operative Ltd
Wholefoods Co-operative Ltd
YCW Co-operative Society Ltd
Yinnar Community Hotel Co-operative Ltd

CHAPTER EIGHT

1 Australian Association of Permanent Building Societies, *Our Home*, July 1943; Gary Lewis, *A Middle Way*, op cit, pp 156-204, 343.

2 Gary Lewis, *A Middle Way*, op cit, pp 190-199.

3 New South Wales Co-operative Institute, *Jubilee Handbook*, Sydney, 1952, p 40; Gary Lewis, 'Co-operation, Carruthers and Community Settlement', op cit.

4 Piggott, 'Aspects of the Organisation', op cit, p 8; Gary Lewis, *A Middle Way*, op cit, pp 200-202. A surge of new registrations occurred in the following five years, including some co-operatives which became major players in the movement such as the Namoi Cotton Co-operative, formed by a group of Americans at Wee Waa in 1961.

5 Co-operative Federation of New South Wales (CFNSW), *Newsletter*, 8 September, 15 December 1967. The CFNSW Board included: M P Dunlop, Major Russell King, Mr Broadhead, J L Shut, G M Dart.

6 **CFNSW Affiliates, 1967-1968.**

Banana Disease Control and Development Co-operative Ltd
Banana Growers Federal Co-operative Ltd
Batlow Packing House Co-operative Ltd
Bodalla Co-operative Cheese Society Ltd
Casino Co-operative Dairy Society Ltd
Central Dairy Co-operative Society Ltd
Certificated Seed Potatoes NSW Co-operative Ltd
Cessnock District Co-operative Society Ltd
Clarence River Fishermen's Co-operative Ltd
Comboyne Rural Co-operative Society Ltd
Conargo District Rural Co-operative Society Ltd
Co-operative Insurance Company of Australia Ltd
Curlewis Farmers' Co-operative Society Ltd
Curlwaa Co-operative Packing Society Ltd
Dairy Farmers Co-operative Ltd
Dorrigo Co-operative Dairy Company Ltd
Dungog Co-operative Dairy Company Ltd
Eastwood Co-operative Society Ltd
Gerringong Co-operative Dairy Ltd
Gloucester Co-operative Dairy Company Ltd
Gosford Co-operative Citrus Packing House Ltd
Griffith Co-operative Cannery Ltd
Griffith Producers Co-operative Ltd
Hastings River Fishermen's Co-operative Ltd
Hawkesbury District Co-operative Ltd
Hawkesbury Potato Growers Co-operative Ltd
Hunter Valley Co-operative Dairy Company Ltd
Illawarra Co-operative Central Dairy Society Ltd
Jamberoo Co-operative Dairy Society Ltd
Laurieton Fishermen's Co-operative Ltd
Leeton Co-operative Cannery Ltd
Lisarow Fruitgrowers Rural Co-operative Society Ltd
Macleay Co-operative Ltd

Manning Park Fishermen's Co-operative Ltd
Manning Co-operative Meat Society Ltd
Manning River Co-operative Dairy Society Ltd
Master Butchers Co-operative (NSW) Ltd
Mid-Coast Co-operative Meat Society Ltd
Moruya Co-operative Dairy Society Ltd
Narrabri District Co-operative Ltd
National Co-operative Insurance Society Ltd
Nepean Co-operative Dairy and Refrigerating Society Ltd
Newcastle & District Co-operative Ltd
Newcastle District Fishermen's Co-operative Ltd
Newcastle Permanent Co-operative Building & Investment Society Ltd
New England Co-operative Society Ltd
New South Wales Co-operative Wholesale Society Ltd
Northcote Co-operative Ltd
Northern Co-operative Meat Company Ltd
Nowra Co-operative Dairy Company Ltd
Pacific Growers Rural Co-operative Society Ltd
Pioneer Mutual Fund Co-operative Ltd
Producers' Co-operative Ltd
Producers' Co-operative Distributing Society Ltd
Shire of Mitchell Ratepayers' Co-operative Ltd
Upper Hastings Co-operative Society Ltd
Upper Wallamba River Co-operative Dairy Society
Wallis Lake Fishermen's Co-operative Society Ltd
Wingham Rural Co-operative Society Ltd
Wyong Co-operative Citrus Packing House Ltd
Wyong Co-operative Dairy Society Ltd
Yarrahappinni rural Co-operative Society Ltd
Yenda Producers' Co-operative Society Ltd
Young District Producers' Co-operative Society Ltd

7   CFNSW, *Newsletter*, September 1970, February 1971. Interview: Co-op Kontact (Australia) Association Incorporated, R Woolnough (CIS) Chairman, A J O'Neill (Graziers) Secretary.

8   CFNSW, *Newsletter*, March 1972; New South Wales Registry of Co-operative Societies, *Annual Report*, 1971-72; Gary Lewis, *A Middle Way, op cit*, pp 214, 223, 228.

9   CFNSW, *Newsletter*, July, August, November-December 1974, December 1976, June-July 1977.

10 CFNSW, *Newsletter*, December 1976, June-July, August-September 1977, January-March 1978; CFNSW Report, *17th Annual Conference*, 26-27 October 1981; Gary Lewis, *A Middle Way, op cit*, pp 228-229.

11 Gary Lewis, *A Middle Way, op cit*, pp 229-232. Rawlinson reported on the Australian Development Assistance Course in the Establishment and Management of Co-operatives which was supported by the Commonwealth Government. GRAZCOS was taken over by ADSTEAM PANFIDA.

12 CFNSW, *Newsletter*, August-September 1980; CFNSW Report, *Annual Conference* 26-27 October 1981; Cronan and Wickremarachchi, *A Study of Co-operative Development and Government-Sector Relations in Australia*, ACCoRD, Sydney, November 1995, pp 23, 45-47.

13 Cronan and Wickremarachchi, *op cit*, pp 47-48, 51; J Todd, *Milk for the Metropolis, op cit*, p 232; *Sydney Morning Herald*, 15 April 1989; New South Wales Public Service Board, *Review of the Organisational Structure of the Department of Co-operative Societies*, New South Wales Government, Sydney, 1987, pp 3, 12, 15.

CHAPTER NINE

1 Australian Association of Co-operatives, *Co-op Courier*, August-September 1989; *Bulletin*, 16 January 1990; *Daily Telegraph*, 8 January 1989; Australian *Rural Times, 1993; Manning River Times*, 17 March 1989. The Work Co-operative Programme was launched in 1978, targeting youth unemployment. An allocation of $3 million was made available. Approximately twenty-one collectives were formed, only nine of them registered under the *Co-operation Act*. In 1984, the Registrar of Co-operative Societies described the programme as a failure. The Worker Enterprise Corporation was established to assist skilled individuals to work co-operatively and to assist the conversion to co-operatives of enterprises facing closure. The Co-operative Development Trust Fund was created to assist this. Approximately twenty-six worker enterprises started under the programme, only three of these co-operatives. By 1987, approximately 340 jobs had been created or saved. By 1993, only six of the enterprises in the programme survived.

2 *Sydney Morning Herald*, 11 March 1993; *National Co-op Update*, January-February 1989; *Land*, 4 May, 6 July 1989; *Sunday Telegraph*, 8 January 1989.

3 John Kerin to AAC General Meeting, in Australian Association of Co-operatives, *Co-op Overview*, August-September 1989; Mary Donnelly, *Co-operatives* (Booklet), Australian Assocation of Co-operatives, Sydney, 1989; New South Wales Government, *Directions in Government*, April 1988.

4 *Australian Financial Review*, 24 March 1989; *Land*, 4 May 1989; Garry Cronan and Jayo Wickremarachchi, *A Study of Co-operative Development, op cit*, pp 51-52, 60-61. The author gratefully acknowledges the New South Wales Registry of Co-operatives for support in helping to publish *A Middle Way: Rochdale Co-operatives in New South Wales 1859-1986,* Brolga Press, Canberra, 1992 and *An Illustrated History of the Riverina Rice Industry*, Ricegrowers' Co-operative Limited, Leeton, 1994.

5 New South Wales Public Service Board, *Review of the Organisational Structure of the Department of Co-operative Societies*, Sydney, 1987; Cronan and Wickremarachchi, *A Study of Co-operative Development, op cit*, p 48. In 1983/84 there were 845 co-operatives in New South Wales. A survey of the top 100 general co-operatives in 1990/1991 indicated that they had 695,892 members generating a total turnover of approximately $1.9 billion. The four largest co-operatives, with 6,052 members; 1 per cent of the total New South Wales co-operative membership; produced 90 per cent of the turnover. The 'big four' were Australian Co-operative Foods (Dairy Farmers) (2,771 members), Namoi Cotton (587 members), Ricegrowers' Co-operative Limited (1,854 members), and Norco Co-operative (dairy) (840 members). The other ninety six general co-operatives in the top 100, with approximately 600,000 members, generated an annual turnover around $800 million. In 1993/94, there were 810 co-operatives in the state. Some examples of new co-operatives in the rural sector included:

    1988   Manning Dairy Co-operative, North Clarence Co-operative, Biological Farmers of Australia Co-operative, Mohair Producers of Australia Co-operative;

    1989   Central Coast Milk Vendors' Co-operative, NSW Egg Producers' Co-operative;

1990   Tamworth Egg Producers' Co-operative, Tea Tree Oil Research Co-operative;

1991   Brunswick Valley Harvesting Co-operative, Australian Oyster Manufacturers' Co-operative, NSW Fish Merchants' Co-operative, Arajoel–Kywong Rural Co-operative, GrenfellRural Producers' Co-operative;

1992   Mudgee Creative Yarns Co-operative, Coonamble Beef Feed Lot and Marketing Co-operative, Coonamble Wool Processing Co-operative, Totally Organic Producers' Co-operative, Orange Fruit Export Co-operative.

6   Gerry Peacocke, New South Wales Minister for Business and Consumer Affairs, *Opening Address*, New South Wales Dairy Industry Association Annual Conference, May 1989; *Australian Financial Review*, 22 March 1989.

7   Blake, Dawson, Waldron (Solicitors) and Dominguez, Barry, Samuel, Montagu Limited (Investment Bankers), *Review of the New South Wales Co-operation Act: Executive Summary to the Minister for Business and Consumer Affairs*, May 1989; *Australian Financial Review*, 22 March 1989. Ian Langdon and colleagues, Derek Wilde, Andrew Kew, Andrew Gibson and Damien Wood, contributed to the review. The consultants' description of CCUs was complex:

CCUs may only be redeemed if fully paid-up and only out of profits available for dividend or a fresh issue of CCUs or ordinary shares made for the purpose, or if redeemable at a premium the premium on redemption may be provided for out of profits or out of the share premium accounts for shares or CCUs.

8   *Review of the Co-operation Act, op cit*. The *Co-operation Act* already permitted an entry fee for membership, regular subscriptions by members, compulsory loans by members if authorised by members, external borrowing, one class of share of fixed amount and limited dividend.

9   Gerry Peacocke, *Opening Address, op cit*; *Sydney Morning Herald*, 15 June 1989; *Land*, 15 June 1989; *Australian Financial Review*, 15 June 1989.

10   J Todd, *Milk for the Metropolis, op cit*, p 264; Bruce Freeman, *Interview: Country Hour*, Radio 2FC, transcript Media Monitors, NJP Proprietary Limited, 12:30 p.m., 28 June 1989; Correspondence: B P V Pezzutti, Jon M Axtens, Bruce Caldwell, J Raymond, Norco Co-operative, August-September 1989 in ACCoRD Archives.

11   Australian Association of Co-operatives, *Co-op Courier*, August-September 1989; Gary Lewis, *Interview*: Bruce Freeman, 2 May 1984. AAC Assistant General Manager Reg Nichols retired in June 1989.

12   *Land*, 6 July, 12 October, 21 December 1989, 8 August 1991; *Land Review*, 1995; Australian Association of Co-operatives, *Co-op Courier*, January-February 1989; *Successful Horticulture*, July-August 1990; *Australian Financial Review*, 28 August, 30 October 1989; New South Wales Government, *Directions in Government*, August 1989; *Business Review Weekly*, 10 November 1989.

13   *Sydney Morning Herald*, 1 June, 12 December 1990; *Daily Telegraph*, 6 February 1990; *Weekly Times*, 7 November 1990; *Wagga Wagga Advertiser*, 18 September 1990; Australian Association of Co-operatives, *Co-op Courier*, January-February 1990; *Western Advocate*, 22 August 1990; *Port Macquarie News*, 22 August 1990; *Narromine News*, 31 January 1990; *Inverell Times*, 31 January 1990; *Daily Advertiser*, 29 March 1990.

14   Premier of New South Wales *Memorandum* and *Review of Programs*, 1991, pp 91-97 in ACCoRD Archives; Australian Association of Co-operatives, *Co-op Courier*, January-February 1989; *Successful Horticulture*, July-August 1990. Registrar David Horton was replaced by Garry Payne. Deputy Registrar Uri Windt left the registry.

15   For a detailed discussion of the New South Wales Co-operatives Act see D M Margarey, *Guide to the NSW Co-operatives Law*, CCH Publishing, Sydney 1994.

16   New South Wales Ministerial Council for Co-operatives, *Securing the Future: Recommendations*, April 1993; *Co-ops 2000 Development Strategy*, December 1991, April-May 1992, p 3; Cronan and

Wickremarachchi, *A Study of Co-operative Development, op cit*, pp 10-12, 64, 110-111; New South Wales Registry of Co-operatives, Co-operative Development Branch, *Co-ops 2000 Newsletter*, April-May 1992.

17 Australian Co-operatives Development League (ACDL), *Newsheet*, January 1992; *Newsletter*, No 2, January-February 1992; Credit Union *Bulletin*, 21 January 1992; *Australian Financial Review*, 28, 29, 30 January, 10 August 1992. Rabobank accounted for 40 per cent of the Dutch savings bank market, 33 per cent of life insurance, 25 per cent of residential mortgages and was Europe's premier co-operative bank, owned by 850 local Dutch banks and with offices in thirty-five countries.

18 Cronan and Wickremarachchi, *A Study of Co-operative Development, op cit*, pp 55-56, 60, 62-63, 65. In 1992 Austrade, the federal government's international trade promotion and support agency, surveyed possible links between Australian dairy co-operatives and Japanese producer co-operatives in developing products targeted at the Japanese market. The survey found that there was more Japanese interest in fruit and vegetable products, particularly stock feed. The Austrade survey also noted that the necessary links between co-operatives in the two nations did not exist and appeared to be some way off.

19 New South Wales Parliamentary Debates, 9 April, 1992, Vol 229, p 2476, 30 April 1992, Vol 230, pp 3166-3185.

20 Garry Cronan, *Trends in Co-operative Legislation in Australia*, Department of Local Government and Co-operatives, Sydney, c 1994, pp 6, 8, 10; Cronan and Wickremarachchi, *A Study of Co-operative Development, op cit*, pp 43, 50, 64-65; Gary Lewis, *Conversation*: Garry Cronan, 28 January 2003; Garry Cronan 'Legislation and Disclosure Issues Relating to Co-operatives Legislation', Key Issues Capital Raising Conference, Sydney, 1993; *Australian*, 5 March 1995.

21 Todd, *Milk for the Metropolis, op cit*, p 264; Margarey, *op cit*, p iv.

22 Australian Co-operative Development League, *Newsletter*, No 5, 1993.

23 Australian Co-operative Development League, *Newsletter*, No 5, 1992; Department of Fair Trading, Information Paper, 'Co-operative Capital Units', November 2000; Margarey, *op cit*, p 115; Chris Greenwood, *Australian Dairy Co-operatives: Planning for the Future*, Dairy Research and Development Board, February 1996, p 42.

24 Margarey, *op cit*, pp 73, 103, 105, 110, 114-117, 139, 209.

25 Robert Lovell, 'Co-operatives – the New Regime: Accounting and Taxation', Lismore, 1993; Kerri Grant 'Co-operative Capital Units', New South Wales Registry of Co-operatives, November 2000. Other co-operatives to issue CCUs included Namoi Cotton, Walgett Special One, ABC Radio Taxi and Longyard Golf Course co-operatives.

26 ACDL *Newsheet*, January 1992; Cronan and Wickremarachchi, *Study of Co-operative Development, op cit*, p 69.

27 *Sydney Morning Herald*, 19 January 5, 11 March 1993; *Telegraph Mirror*, 5 March 1993; *Australian*, 5 March 1993; *Goulburn Post*, 7 March 1993; *Kiama Independent*, 17 March 1993; *Australian Financial Review*, 29 January, 10, 11 March 1993; Gary Lewis, *Conversation*: Garry Cronan, 28 January 2003. In February 1992, AAC launched the Australian Co-operative Management Certificate Course, co-ordinated by Tim Dyce in association with the University of Western Sydney and the Australian Institute of Management; a twelve-day certificate course funded by the New South Wales Education and Training Foundation.

28 Cronan and Wickremarachchi, *A Study of Co-operative* Development, *op cit*, pp 64, 65; Todd, *Milk for the Metropolis, op cit*, p 264.

29 New South Wales Registry of Co-operative Societies, *Co-operation*, Special Edition, January 1994; New South Wales Registry of Co-operative Societies, *Review of Co-operative Development Branch*, in ACCoRD Archives. A survey of CDB functions revealed:

Co-ops 2000: 5 per cent of staff; consumed a high level of branch resources, including 41 per cent of management time.

Formations, including new formations: 34 per cent of staff; over-extended as the *Co-operatives Act* bedded down, occasioning a cap on new formations.

ICA/Registry Project: 3 per cent of staff; funds from the Co-operative Development Fund allocated for research into joint ventures and international trade involving staff in travel.

Publications: 10 per cent of staff; funding a *Guide to the Co-operatives Act*, formation kits, newsletters and conference research papers.

Co-operatives Council: 4 per cent of staff and a financial allocation.

Conferences/Seminars/Education: 12 per cent of staff; CDB involved in helping to organise an international dairy conference in Melbourne and Key Issues Conferences.

National Legislation: 1 per cent of staff; low priority not linked to other programmes; CDB Manager chair of Standing Committee of Attorneys-General (SCAG) Working Party.

Policy Advice: 3 per cent of staff; Section 120 (1)(c) an important issue.

Networking/Industry Liaison: 10 per cent of staff; facilitation including travel.

Research: 8 per cent of staff; Ian Langdon Sector Analysis Study; capital-raising; education of directors; Co-operative Capital Units.

Co-operative Development Fund: 2 per cent of staff; administering $350,000 per annum Co-operative Development Fund for feasibility and industry studies.

In 1992/93 thirty six co-operatives were deregistered, mainly for failing to comply with regulations but also because some had dissolved or ceased trading. The following year the number was sixty-six.

30 Cronan and Wickremarachchi, *A Study of Co-operative Development*, op cit, pp 67-69.

31 *Sydney Morning Herald*, 29 November 1994.

32 Cronan and Wickremarachchi, *A Study of Co-operative Development*, op cit, pp 62-64, 70; *Australian Financial Review*, 24 February 1992; *Daily Advertiser* (Wagga), 7 February 1991; *Tumut and Adelong Times*, 25 January 1991; *Land*, 8 August 1991; New South Wales Registry of Co-operative Societies, *Co-ops 2000 Newsletter*, Sydney, April-May 1992.

33 *National Co-op Update*, July 1996; CFNSW, *Newsletter*, April, December 1995; Cronan and Wickremarachchi, *A Study of Co-operative Development*, op cit, pp 74-75.

34 Department of Fair Trading, *Annual Report*, 1995/96, p 20; *National Co-op Update*, January-February 1998, Cronan and Wickremarachchi, *op cit*, pp 60, 66; Jayo Wickremarachichi and Andrew Passey, 'State of the Sector New South Wales Co-operatives 1990-2000', ACCoRD, June 2003, p42.

35 *National Co-op Update*, July-August, September-October 1991; *Sydney Morning Herald*, 22 April 1997; Cronan and Wickremarachchi, *A Study of Co-operative Development*, op cit, pp 69, 74-76.

36 *Victorian Co-operative News*, September/October 1996, 1999.

37 New South Wales Parliamentary Debate, Vol 258, Co-operatives Act Amendment Bill, pp 9478, 10427, 10371, 10866, 10870; Denis Burke, *Correspondence*: Minister, 20 June 1997, in ACCoRD Archives; *Australian*, 20 June 1997; *Australian Financial Review*, 18 March 1997.

38 Cronan and Wickremarachchi, *A Study of Co-operative Development*, op cit, pp 57, 66. By 1996 the federation had ninety members, including the thirteen largest co-operatives in New South Wales.

39 Cronan and Wickremarachchi, *A Study of Co-operative Development*, op cit, pp 53, 70-71, 76-77.

40 *National Co-op Update*, January-February, September-October 1998, March-September 1999, March-April 2000, May-June 2002; Cronan and Wickremarachchi, *A Study of Co-operative*

Development, op cit, pp 71-72. Jayo Wickremarachichi and Andrew Passey, 'State of the Sector, *op cit*.

CHAPTER TEN

1   J S A Hunter and J C Wood *International Economics: An Australian Perspective*, Sydney 1983, pp 129, 153-4; *Westralian Farmers' Gazette*, July-August 1952; H J Hynes, 'The Economics of Co-operation' in *Agricultural Gazette*, NSW, Vol LV, No 12, December, 1944, p 517; *Co-operative Building Societies Gazette*, 18 December 1944, p 6; Rural Reconstruction Commission, *Farming Efficiency and Cost Factors Relating Thereto (6th Report)*, Government Printing Office, Canberra, 1945, p 83; Gary Lewis, *A Middle Way, op cit*, pp 181-3, 301.

2   *Westralian Farmers' Gazette*, 16, 23 February, April, July 1939, April 1940, August 1941, May, June November 1943, September 1947; CFWA *Minutes*, Annual Conference, 20-22 February 1939; *Co-operative News*, January 1944; Report: *Commonwealth Consumers' Co-operative Conference*, Canberra, December 6-8 1943, pp 18, 21-22, 26-29, 39, 41, 45-46, 73, 78; *Workers' Pioneer Co-operative Labour Journal*, Brisbane, 1944, Delegates: **Western Australia:** W D Johnson, MLA (CFWA; Director Westralian Farmers'; Chairman Co-operative Wholesale Section, Westralian Farmers'; Director Producer and Citizens Co-operative Assurance Company); T H Bath (CFWA; Chairman Co-operative Bulk Handling, Director Tammin Farmers' Co-operative); C W Harper (Chairman CFWA; Chairman Westralian Farmers'; Director Producer Markets Co-operative Limited); E C Barnett (Manager Co-operative Wholesale Section, Westralian Farmers'); J H Worthington (CFWA, Assistant Secretary Westralian Farmers'); F Howie (President Collie Industrial Co-operative); F Nisbet (Manager Collie Industrial Co-operative). **New South Wales:** G Booth MLA (President NSW CWS); F Clarke (General Manager NSW CWS); T Silcocks (Director Woonona Industrial Co-operative); T Shonk (Director NSW CWS; Editor *Co-operative News*); H Head (Economist representing Registry of Co-operative Societies). **Queensland:** S Lloyd (Chairman of Directors Poultry Farmers' Co-operative; Director Queensland Board of Co-operative Insurance Company); C Kidd (Assistant Manager and Secretary Poultry Farmers' Co-operative; Editor *Red Comb*). **Victoria**: H A Elliot (Gippsland and Northern Co-operative; Managing Director Bloomfield Butter and Cheese Co-operative Company); W Purvis (Director Wonthaggi Industrial); I M Kelly (Education Secretary Melbourne Rochdale Consumer Co-operative Society; Director Northern Suburbs Co-operative Society). **South Australia:** H S Hatwell (Chairman Adelaide Co-operative Society); A W James (Secretary Adelaide Co-operative Society); E J Trowbridge (Chairman Edunda Farmers' Co-operative); T P Richardson (Secretary Edunda Farmers' Co-operative Society). **Tasmania:** J R Hilder (Chairman Tasmanian Farmers' Co-operative); C Mitburn (Manager Tasmanian Farmers' Co-operative); a representative of King Island Co-operative Society. Co-ordinated Interstate Buying Committee: Clarke, Richardson, Barnett, Elliot, Kidd, Milburn. Council of the Commonwealth Co-operative Federation (renamed the Co-operative Federation of Australia [CFA]) December 1943: G Booth (President); W Johnson (Vice President); H Elliot (Secretary); Mr Thorton – not mentioned in delegate list – (Assistant Secretary and Treasurer); F Clarke (New South Wales); C Kidd (Queensland); T Bath (Western Australia); J Hilder (Tasmania); H Hatwell (South Australia); I M Kelly (Victoria *protem*). The CFA Canberra Secretariat was to be run on a £2,000 budget; New South Wales contributed £600, Western Australia £500, Queensland £300, Victoria £300, Tasmania whatever was possible.

3   *Co-operative News*, January, March, April, June, August, November, December 1944; January, February, April, May, June, July, August, October, November, December 1945. CFA Meeting, 27-28 March 1944 at the Club Room, Co-operative Services Limited, Sydney. Present were Messrs Bath (Western Australia), Hatwell (South Australia), Kidd (Queensland), Holder (Tasmania), Elliot (Victoria), Clark, Shonk, Booth (NSW CWS) and H Head representing the Registrar. Agenda items at the November 1944 meeting included: national co-operative legislation, education, co-operative between producers and consumers, co-operative home building, 'One Big Society', rehabilitation,

'benevolent' co-operatives and co-operative production. K W Edwards represented the CFA at ICA conferences in Scotland, France and Sweden.

4   *Co-operative News*, March 1950, October 1951, March, June, July, September 1952; *Bulletin*, 9 January 1952; *Westralian Farmers' Gazette*, December 1951. CFA Council Meeting Brisbane, April 16-17 1950. Present: Booth, Clark, Silcocks (New South Wales), Lloyd, Kidston (Queensland), MacDeonnell (Victoria), Bath (Western Australia). Queensland delegates sought a reduction of the subscription fee. The South Australians signalled that they were preparing to withdraw. Victoria was funded by Wonthaggi Industrial to the amount of £12.10.0. New South Wales contributed £200, Queensland £150, Western Australia £125, South Australia £25.

5   *Co-operative News*, February, June, July, August, September, December, 1947, February, May, October, December 1948, April, May, August, October, November 1949, May 1954, January 1956. A Victorian, F S Nurse, was briefly employed by the CFA as commercial manager. CWS Public Relations Division, *All About the CWS: The World's Largest Co-operative Organisation*, Manchester, 1901; *Westralian Farmers' Gazette*, December 1948.

6   *Co-operative News*, May, July, August, December 1954, May, July 1955. CFA Meeting, Sydney, June 4-5, 1954, President: Booth, Shonk, Silcocks (New South Wales), Lotan (Western Australia), Kidston (Queensland), Lowe and MacDonnell (Victoria), Kentish (South Australia). K W Edwards, E T Lotan and F W Richards of Westralian Farmers' attended the 1956 Blackpool (England) Co-operative Congress.

7   *Co-operative News*, November 1949, October 1953, January, March, April, October, December 1956, April, June, September 1957. CFA Meeting organised by the Co-operative Federation of Queensland, Sydney, September 12, 1956. Present: Smith, Booth, Clark, Shonk (New South Wales), Kidston (Queensland), Lowe (Victoria), Lotan, Bath (Western Australia). Agenda items: changing trade conditions, taxation, accountancy practices.

8   Report: *The Proceedings of the All Australia Co-operative Congress*, Sydney 14-15 June 1957.

9   *Co-operative News*, November 1957, April 1958, July 1959.

10   P E Weereman, *The ICA in South East Asia*, New Delhi, 1971.

11   Gary Lewis, *Interview* W W (Bill) Rawlinson, 17 June 1983.

12   *ibid*.

13   *Canberra Times*, 9 July 1977; *Canberra Sunday* Life, 21 May 1978; *Australian Financial* Review, 10 July 1978; *Bulletin*, 9 August 1983. In the 1970s the Trades Practices Commission (TPC) moved against a number of major primary producer market co-operatives alleging restraint of trade, monopolistic practices and exclusive dealings. There was a positive side to this. For example, the CSR sugar monopoly responding to TPC complaints urged New South Wales cane growers to purchase the company's three New South Wales mills which were unprofitable and 'enjoy the tax benefits of co-operation'. The New South Wales government provided $3 million and CSR technical support for five years.

14   J B Rutter, *Agricultural Co-operatives in Australia*, Department of Primary Industry, Marketing Division, Canberra, August 1957. There were twenty-six co-operatives in the County of Cumberland, nineteen on the south coast, eighteen in the Hunter and Manning River districts and fourteen on the north coast.

15   R R Piggott, *Aspects of the Organisation of Rural Marketing Co-operatives in NSW*, University of New England, February 1969.

16   Co-operative Federation of New South Wales, *Newsletter*, March, April 1971, March, June 1972; *Victorian Co-operative News*, December 1998, January 1999; CFA Report: *National Convention*, Canberra, 1975.

17   CFA *Report* Year Ended June 1973; CFA Report, *National Convention*, Canberra August 1973. I Hunter of Westralian Farmers' was the Australian Member of the ICA South East Asia Regional

Office Committee for Agriculture and Trade in New Delhi in 1971O, which involved more than thirteen countries.

18 CFNSW *Newsletter*, August-September 1973, November-December 1974; CFA Report, *Annual Convention*, 1974, CFA *Report* Year Ending 30 June 1971G. The National Agricultural Committee of the CFA 1975: G A Beytagh (PDS Chairman), J R Shultz (Murray-Goulburn), G C Rogers (Barossa Co-operative Winery), R M Graham (Westralian Farmers'), later joined by R G Sutherland (CFWA), W Kidston (CFQ); Finance Committee of the CFA 1975: R M Graham (Westralian Farmers', Chairman), R A Litchfield (Barossa Co-operative Winery), W H Lugg (Phosphate Co-operative Company [Victoria]), C J Robinson (NSWCUL), the Finance Committee was later expanded to include W Kidston (CFQ), G F Scarth (CIC [Victoria]).

19 CFA *Report*, Annual Convention, October 1975; CFA *Report* Year Ending 30 June 1975, 30 June 1976; CFNSW *Newsletter*, January-February 1975. CFA Executive 1975: M J Lane (President), I H Hunter and W W Rawlinson (Western Australia), R J Woolnough and A J O'Neill (New South Wales), N Studt and W Kidston (Queensland), W J Lyons and B Machintosh (Victoria), B R Litchfield and P C Bagley (South Australia).

20 CFWA *Minutes 56th Annual Conference*, 1976. The Commonwealth Bank, the Rural Bank of New South Wales, the State Savings Bank of Victoria, The State Savings Bank of South Australia, the Rural and Industrial Bank of Western Australia and seven trading banks participated in PIBA as shareholders.

21 CFWA Report, *56th Annual Conference*; CFWA Report, *60th Annual Conference*; CFA *Report* Year Ending June 1976, June 1977, June 1978; CFNSW *Newsletter*, May, June 1976, April-May 1977, Jan-March 1978; *Australian Financial Review*, 5 May 1977; Ronald Anderson, *Primary Industries Newsletter*, No 629, September 1978. This was in addition to 1.5 million members of 6,500 general co-operatives including building societies, credit unions and community co-operatives, many in rural areas.

22 *Bulletin*, 9 August 1983; *Australian Financial Review*, 17 February 1975; 8, 22 May, 10, 15 July 1978; CFNSW Report, *13th Annual Conference*, November 1977; CFNSW *Newsletter*, May, October-December 1977; Amalgamated Co-operative Marketers (Australia) Limited, *The Story of Seventy-Five Years, 1905–1980*, Melbourne, 1980.

23 *Australian Financial Review*, 17 February 1975, 31 May, 1 June 1976; *Canberra Times*, 9 July 1977; *Sydney Morning Herald*, 26 September 1983; South Australian Fishermen's Co-operative Limited (SAFCOL), *27th Annual Report*, June 1971; CIC Holdings, *Annual Report*, 1975, 1976. CIC (Australia) had 204 affiliates in 1975 in the dairy, woolbroking, fruit, cattle, sheep, pig, stock and station, poultry and eggs, honey, livestock, milling, feed, tobacco, cold storage, sugar, bean, cane, maize, potato, credit union, wholesaling, building society and hotel industries. Approximately 300 co-operatives in Papua New Guinea were shareholders. Subsidiary companies of CIC Holdings Limited in late 1975 included CIC, CIC Insurance Proprietary Limited, NCIS Insurance Proprietary Limited, CIC Insurance (Pacific) Proprietary Limited, CIC marine Investment Proprietary Limited (Queensland), Nova Holdings Proprietary Limited (Queensland), Redco Holdings Proprietary Limited (Queensland). CIS Superannuation, the giant off-shoot of CWS (UK) Limited retained a nominal 4 per cent shareholding.

24 *Australian Financial Review*, 9, 30 June 1978. Kaiser Stuhl became the largest winery following a 1976 merger of several smaller co-operative wineries. Correspondence: J E Urquhart, Assistant Manager, Gillespie Brothers Proprietary Limited, 22 April 1982 and R Schiller, former Chairman, Barossa Co-operative Winery, 1 July 1984.

25 Gary Lewis, *Interview*, W W (Bill) Rawlinson, 17 June 1983.

26 *Australian Financial Review*, 24 March, 27 April 1976, 21, 24 February, 1, 21 July, 23, 24 August, 8 September, 25 October 1977,9 January, 25 July 1978, 9 January 1979. Gary Lewis, *Interview* J J McGuire, Managing Director, Murray-Goulburn Co-operative Limited, 18 June 1983.

27 *Australian Financial Review*, 24, 25 March 1976. The Federal Government through its agencies had loaned SPC, Ardmona and KY co-operatives $38 million.

28 *Australian Financial Review*, 24 March 1976, 21, 24 February 1977.

29 *Australian Financial Review*, 1 July, 23 August 1977; *Farmers and Graziers*, 5 May 1977.

30 *Australian Financial Review*, 23, 24 August, 8 September 1977.

31 *Australian Financial Review*, 25 October 1977, 9 January 1978; *Australian*, 24 August 1977.

32 *Australian Financial Review*, 25 July 1978, 9 January 1979.

33 Australian Information Service Reference Paper, *Co-operatives in Australia*, Government Printing Office, 1976; CFNSW *Newsletter*, May, December 1976, April-May 1977, January-March 1978; *Australian Financial Review*, 17 February 1992. Parliamentary Committee to Investigate a 'Co-operative Bank for Farmers': J Short, B Simon and H Thomas (Liberal), D McVeigh (National Country Party).

CHAPTER ELEVEN

1 *Sydney Morning Herald*, 21 March 1998, 3 June 2003; Phillip Ruthven and Jennifer Mead in 'Industry Towards 2000' Series, *Australian Financial Review*, 10, 12 April 1996; 23 March 1998, 24 April 2001; *Australian*, 22 April 1996, 10 March 1997; *Australian Farm Journal*, February 1999; *National Co-op Update*, September/October 1996; *The Age*, 3, 9 April 2003; Evatt Foundation Website, 'Economic Rationalism Twenty Years On', 3 June 2003. In October 1992 Treasurer Paul Keating commissioned Professor Fred Hilmer to establish a consistent national framework for competition, applying to everything and everyone, and to make recommendations suitable to neo-liberal market-driven policies directed at improving social welfare through the promotion of competition, fair trade and consumer protection. Hilmer's 1993 report was focused on any form of government regulation lessening competition and recommended pressuring regulators to enter 'the new age economy', rid the economy of redundant laws, regulations and standards and establish a nationally standard set of business rules – a 'level playing field' of 'competitive neutrality'.

2 *Sydney Morning Herald*, 13 August 1989, *Sun Herald*, 13 August 1989; *Daily Telegraph*, 28 August 1989; *Australian Financial Review*, 7 August 1989; *Land*, 6 July, 21 December 1989; *National Co-operative Update*, January/February 1998; *Country Leader*, 11 June 1990; *Northern Daily Leader*, 25 January 1991.

3 *Land*, 12 September 1991, 9 April 1992; *Daily Telegraph*, 16 December 1992; *Australian Financial Review*, 9, 19 January 1990, 9, 13 April, 17 December 1992; New South Wales, *Farmers and Graziers*, October 1987; *Australian*, 15 August 1991; *National Co-operative Update*, September/October 2000. Brad Plunkett and Rose Kingnell, Department of Agriculture, Western Australia, 'Co-operatives for Agricultural Markets and Processing in Australia: Principles, Practicability and a Case Study', *Agribusiness Review*, Vol 9, Paper 9, 2001. For further discussion on Australian Financial Institutions Commission legislation for non-bank financial institutions see Gary Lewis, *People Before Profit: The Credit Union Movement in Australia*, Wakefield Press, South Australia, 1996. For further discussion on deregulation in the rice industry see Gary Lewis, *An Illustrated History of the Riverina Rice Industry*, Ricegrowers Co-operative Limited, Leeton, 1994.

4 Ted Stephenson in *Co-operative News* (UK), 28 June, 23 August, 20 September 1988.

5 *Weekly Times*, 4 April 1990; *Land*, 15 February, 19 November 1990; *Business Review Weekly*, 15 June 1990; R Moss-Kantor, *The Change Masters*, Allen and Unwin, 1983; *Australian Financial Review*, 7 September 1974; *Queensland Graingrowers*, 8 August 1990.

CHAPTER TWELVE

1 Australian Information Service Reference Paper, *Co-operatives in Australia*, Government Printing Office, 1976; CFNSW *Newsletter*, May, December 1976, April-May 1977, January-March 1978;

Australian Financial Review, 17 February 1992. *Weekly Times*, 4 April 1990; *Land*, 15 February, 19 November 1990: *Business Review Weekly*, 15 June 1990; R Moss-Kantor, *The Change Masters*, *op cit*, 1983; *Australian Financial Review*, 7 September 1974; *Queensland Graingrowers*, 8 August 1990; Gary Lewis, *Interview* W W (Bill) Rawlinson, 17 June 1983; Standing Committee on Agricultural Working Party, *Agricultural Co-operation in Australia*, AGPS, 1988; Garry Cronan and Jayo Wickremarachchi, *A Study of Co-operative Development, op cit*, pp 82-3.

2   Standing Committee on Agriculture Working Party, *Agricultural Co-operation in Australia*, AGPS, 1988; Cronan and Wickremarachchi, *A Study of Co-operative Development, op cit*, p 82-3.

3   CFNSW, *Newsletter*, April-September 1981; CFNSW, *Annual Report*, 1983. Subsidiaries owned by AAC included Co-op Trade Proprietary Limited, AAC Insurance Brokers Proprietary Limited and AAC Financial Services Limited.

4   Australian Association of Co-operatives, *Co-op Courier*, September-October 1989; *National Co-op Update*, December 1995; Cronan and Wickremarachchi, *A Study of Co-operative Development, op cit*, pp 50, 65.

5   *Daily Telegraph*, 6 February 1990; *Brisbane Sun*, 14 February 1990; *Land*, 7 December 1989, 15 February, 1 March 1990; *Bulletin*, 16 January 1990; *Melbourne Herald*, 18 January 1990; ICA, *News*, Issue 2, 1990.

6   *Land*, 15 February 1990; *Daily Telegraph*, 6 February 1990. AAC sought links with the All China Federation of Supply and Markets Co-operatives at the Foreign Trade Corporation of Zheijiang Co-operative. AAC representatives invited key Japanese co-operative organisations including JCCU, Unico-op Japan, Nadakobe Consumer Co-operative Society and Kanagana Consumer Co-operative Society.

7   *Australian Rural Times*, 19 April 1990; *Manning River Times*, 17 March 1989; Edgar Parnell in *ICA News*, n.d.; Greenwood, *Thesis op cit*, p 9, 34; SWOT Analysis, Brisbane, Uncited in ACCoRD Archives; For discussion on Edgar Parnell's poem see Gary Lewis, 'Edgar Parnell's Prayer: An Australian Perspective', in ICA, *International Review of Co-operation*, 2001

8   *Sydney Morning Herald*, 19 January 5, 11 March 1993; *Telegraph Mirror*, 5 March 1993; *Australian*, 5 March 1993; *Goulburn Post*, 7 March 1993; *Kiama Independent*, 17 March 1993; *Australian Financial Review*, 29 January, 10, 11 March 1993; Gary Lewis, *Conversation* Garry Cronan, 28 January 2003.

9   'Summary of recommendations arising from a group discussion session at the National Congress of Australian Co-operatives', 6 May 1993.

10 New South Wales Registry of Co-operative Societies, 1994 Key Issues Conference, *Report*, Sydney 1994.

11 *Australian*, 4 October 1995; *Australian Financial Review*, 3 October 1995; *Sydney Morning Herald*, 15 February 1995; *Land*, 31 July 1994; CFNSW, *Newsletter*, December 1995; *National Co-op Update*, December 1995; New South Wales Registry of Co-operative Societies, 1995 Key Issues Conference, *Report*, Sydney, 19-20 October 1995.

12 1995 Key Issues Conference, *op cit*, pp 25-30, 129-134.

13 1995 Key Issues Conference, *op cit*. pp 31-37.

14 1995 Key Issues Conference, *op cit*, pp 143-147.

15 1995 Key Issues Conference, *op cit*, pp 38-46.

16 1995 Key Issues Conference, *op cit*, pp 47-51.

17 1995 Key Issues Conference, *op cit*, pp 126-128.

18 *National Co-op Update*, December 1995.

19 CFNSW, *Newsletter*, December 1995.

20 New South Wales Registry of Co-operative Societies, 1996 Key Issues Conference, *Papers*, Sydney 1996; 1996 Agricultural Co-operative Leaders' Forum, *Budget as at 25 February 1997*, in ACCoRD Archives; 1996 Key Issues Conference, *Budget as at 25 February 1997*, in ACCoRD Archives; *National Co-op Update*, July/August, September/October 1996. Overseas speakers included Charlie Cattell (UK), Dr Lou Hammond Ketilson and Professor Murray Fulton from the University of Saskatchewan, Canada, Professor Gert Van Dijk (Netherlands), Isaro Takamura (Japan), Dr Glenn Webb (USA), John Newland (New Zealand) and Dr Johnston Birchall (Brunel University, UK).

21 CFNSW, *Newsletter*, April 1995; Gary Lewis, *Conversation* Garry Cronan, 28 January 2003.

Chapter Thirteen

1 Garry Cronan and Jayo Wickeremarachchi, *A Study of Co-operative Development*, op cit, pp 202-3; 'Demutualisation' is used in a general sense in that some 'demutualising' organisations were not 'mutual' in the first place, in that they did not conduct 90 per cent of their business with members.

2 Jim Manwaring, Manager Rural Co-operatives, 'Report to Co-operative Development Branch', 23 June 1992; Garry Cronan, *The Conversion Syndrome: Australian Co-operatives into Investor-owned Firms*, ICA Regional Assembly for Asia and the Pacific, New Delhi, India, 5-7 October 1994.

3 Co-operative Federation of Victoria, *Victorian Co-op News*, December 1998-January 1999; June-July 1999.

4 *Sunday Telegraph*, 25 September 1994; *Sydney Morning Herald*, 19 February 1999.

5 Cronan, *Conversion Syndrome*, op cit, pp 1, 7, 14-15, 17, 19-20.

6 Greenwood, *Thesis*, op cit, p 56, 192-195; Jan Todd, *Milk for the Metropolis*, op cit, p 292.

7 *Bulletin*, 18 August 1998.

8 *Business Review Weekly*, 27 June 1997; *Business Sydney*, 23 June 1997.

9 Co-operative Council of Australia, 'Commentary on ASX Proposal', 5 September 1997.

10 Namoi Cotton *Media Release*, 1 November 2001; Namoi Cotton Co-operative Limited (1997) ACLC 498; *National Co-op Update*, January-February, March-April, May-June 1998; *Australian Financial Review*, 22 June 1994, 22 August 1998; *Sydney Morning Herald*, 17 November 1992; *Land*, 26 October, 30 November, 21 December 1989; Co-operative Federation of New South Wales, *Newsletter*, June 1970; 3 March 1994; Chris Greenwood, *Thesis*, op cit, p 34, 43.

11 *Bulletin*, 18 August 1998; *Business Sydney*, 23 June 1997. Under the Farm Pride plan no group could own more than 20 per cent of the company for a three-year period. Ron Brierley's Guinness, Peat Group immediately took a 12.4 per cent stake.

12 *Weekly Times*, 18 April 1990; *Western Advocate*, 3 May 1990; *National Co-op Update*, September-October 1999; Chris Greenwood, *Thesis*, op cit, p 36.

13 *Sydney Morning Herald*, January 1999.

14 *Sydney Morning Herald*, 19 February 1999; *National Co-op Update*, July-August 1999, May-June 2000.

15 Tony Gill, Co-operative Development Services (CDS), Victoria. Some of the many successful primary producer co-operatives operating in addition to those already mentioned included (courtesy Tony Gill):

Fishing

Abalone Fishermen's Co-operative Limited
Clarence River Fishermen's Co-operative Limited
Fremantle Fishermen's Co-operative Limited
Geraldton Fishermen's Co-operative Limited
Gloucester Native Fish Growers
Co-operative Limited

Lakes Entrance Fishermen's Co-operative Limited
Sandgate Fishermen's Co-operative
Society Limited
San Remo Fishermen's Co-operative Limited
Fruit and vegetable
Banana Growers Federation Co-operative Limited
Batlow Fruit Co-operative Limited

Hunter Olive Co-operative Limited
Mildura Co-operative Fruit Co. Limited
Queensland Chamber of Fruit & Vegetable
Industries Co-operative

Grain/seed

Capgrains Co-operative Association Limited
Co-operative Bulk Handling Limited
Excello Co-operative Limited
Gilgandra Marketing Co-operative Limited
Netco Co-operative Limited
Seedco Australia Co-operative Limited
South Australian Co-operative Bulk Handling
Limited
Shepherds Producers Co-operative Limited.
United Farmers Co-operative Limited
Walgett Special One Co-operative Limited

Livestock

Bluegum Co-operative Limited
Gloucester Gourmet Foods Co-operative
Limited
Goat Meat Producers Co-operative Limited
Orana Choice Group Co-operative Limited
South Table Goat Meat Producers
Co-operative Limited
Western Australian Meat Marketing
Co-operative Limited
Timber Cooloola Forest Growers
Co-operative Limited
North Queensland Timber Co-operative Limited
North West Treegrowers Co-operative
Society Limited
Western Timber Co-operative Limited

Other

North Coast Native Foods Co-operative Limited
NSW Egg Producers Co-operative Limited
New South Wales Sugar Milling
Co-operative Limited
The Tobacco Co-operative of Victoria Limited

Dairy

Bega Cheese Co-operative Limited
Butter Producers' Co-operative Federation
Limited
Challenge Group Co-operative Limited
Hastings Co-operative Limited

Fibre

Australian Alpaca Co-operative Limited
Omeo Fine Fibres Co-operative Limited

Fruit

Appledale Processors Co-operative Limited
Australian Fruit Marketing Co-operative
Limited
Berri Fruit Juices Co-operative Limited Meat
Northern Co-operative Meat Company Limited

Other

Australian Bush Foods and Products
Co-operative Limited.
Neem Trees, Processing and Neem Products
Co-operative Limited

Input supply

CEPA Co-operative Limited
Gerringong Co-operative Dairy Society Limited
Mildura Co-operative Fruit Co. Limited
Nungarin Farmers Co-operative
Company Limited
Quairading Farmers Co-operative Limited
Rural Industries Co-operative Limited
The Tobacco and Associated Farmers
Co-operative Limited
Wamuran Co-operative Limited
Yeppoon District Co-operative Society Limited
Agricultural services
Biological Farmers Co-operative Limited
Central Highlands Regional Resource Use
Planning Co-operative Limited
Colac Herd Improvement Co-operative Limited
Coleambally Irrigation Co-operative Limited
Genetics Australia Co-operative
LimitedGippsland Herd Improvement
Co-operative Limited
Herd Improvement Services of SA
Co-operative Limited
Lenswood Cold Stores Co-operative Society
Limited
National Agricultural Data Co-operative
Limited
South West Irrigation Asset Co-operative
Limited
South West Irrigation Management
Co-operative Limited
Tasmanian Machinery Ring Co-operative
Society Limited
United Crate Co-operative Limited
Victorian Dairy Research & Demonstration
Farm Co-operative Limited

CHAPTER FOURTEEN

1   Australian Information Office, 'Co-operatives in Australia', Reference Paper, July 1976, pp 4-5; Co-operative Federation of Australia, 'Co-operatives Legislation in Australia', June 1982.

2   New South Wales Registry of Co-operative Societies, *Annual Report*, 1968-1969; Tony Gill, Co-operative Development Services, Website; Garry Cronan and Jayo Wickremarachchi, *A Study in Co-operative Development*, *op cit*, pp 82-83, 119.

3   *Co-op Courier*, August/September 1989; *Sydney Morning Herald*, 4 October 1989.

4   *Australian Financial Review*, 4 July 1990; *Sydney Morning Herald*, 4 July 1990; *Daily Telegraph*, 9 February 1990; Cronan and Wickremarachchi, *op cit*, p 64.

5   National Strategy Group on Co-operatives Development, *Minutes*, Meeting, Canberra, 23 November 1990, in ACCoRD Archives. Attendees:

Garry Cronan	New South Wales: Office of Registrar of Co-operatives
Stan Rumble	New South Wales: Business and Consumer Affairs
Jane Reynolds	Victoria: Office of Registrar of Co-operatives
John Lightowlers	Western Australia: Legal Division
Peter McDade	Queensland: Registrar of Agricultural Co-operatives
Matti Mattimugan	Australian Association of Co-operatives
Jim McCall	Australian Association of Co-operatives
Wayne Ryan	Director, Marketing Section, Department of Primary Industry and Energy
Phil Goode	Marketing Section, Department of Primary Industry and Energy
Peter Slobodian	Marketing Section, Department of Primary Industry and Energy

6   Neil McLeod, 'Options for the Reform of the Regulatory Structure of General Co-operatives', New South Wales Registry of Co-operative Societies, September 1991, p 15.

7   Departmental Correspondence, 27 September 1991, 22 May 1992, in ACCoRD Archives.

8   *Australian Financial Review*, 3, 18, 27 March 1992; Uncited document, 'Summary of Responses to Minister's Letter to Co-operatives', 1992, in ACCoRD Archives.

9   Standing Committee of Attorneys-General Working Party on Consistency in Co-operatives Legislation, *Minutes*, Rural Policy Division, Department of Primary Industry and Energy, Canberra, 8 July 1992, in ACCoRD Archives. Attendees:

Garry Cronan (Chair)	Manager, Co-operatives Development Registry of Co-operatives, Department of Local Government and Co-operatives, Parramatta, New South Wales
Roosie de Baros	c/- Registrar of Commercial Acts, Brisbane, Queensland
Dan Henry	Office of the Registrar of Co-operative Societies, Melbourne, Victoria
Adrian Griffiths	Senior Corporate Regulator, State Business and Corporate Office, Attorney-General's Department, Adelaide, South Australia
Bill McMillan	c/- Registrar of Co-operative Society, Australian Capital Territory Government, Canberra, Australian Capital Territory
Berridge Hume-Phillips	Australian Association of Co-operatives
Wayne Ryan	Rural Policy Division, Department of Primary Industries and Energy
Phil Goode	Rural Policy Division, Department of Primary Industries and Energy

Apologies:

Peter Richards	Legal Division, Office of State Corporate Affairs, Perth, Western Australia
Barbara Bradshaw	Registrar of Business Affairs, Office of Business Affairs, Department of Law, Darwin, Northern Territory

10 Garry Cronan, 'Trends in Co-operative Legislation in Australia', Department of Local Government and Co-operatives, n.d., *circa* 1994, pp 11-12, in ACCoRD Archives.

11 CFNSW, *Newsletter*, December 1995; Uncited Draft Report, 'The Co-operatives Interface', 1995, in ACCoRD Archives; Garry Cronan, Key Issues Conference 1995, *Report*, pp 77-79.

12 Chris Greenwood, *Thesis*, *op cit*, pp 25-26, 30; *Victorian* Parliamentary Debate, Vol 431-433, 14 November 1996, p 1195.

13 Greenwood, *Thesis*, *op cit*, pp 25-26, 75-80; Western Australian Parliament Standing Committee on Uniform Legislation and Inter-governmental Agreements, 'Co-operatives Law', 21 May 1998.

14 *Victorian Co-operative News*, September/October 1996, 1999.

15 New South Wales Parliamentary Debates, Vol 258, Co-operatives Act Amendment Bill, pp 9478, 10427, 10371, 10866, 10870; Departmental Correspondence, 20 June 1997, in ACCoRD Archives, *Australian*, 20 June 1997.

16 *Australian*, 20 June 1997; Uncited, 'Minutes of Meeting Co-operative Officials', Adelaide, 5 September 1997, in ACCoRD Archives. Attendees: Andrea Sherko (Victoria); Garry Cronan, Peter Boland (New South Wales); Paul Kerr, Time Beale (Queensland); Peter Richards (Western Australia), Stewart Chapman (Australian Capital Territory), Adrian Griffiths, Imelda Bradley, Regan Burnell (South Australia). Correspondence: Commonwealth Treasury to Barbara Bradshaw, 13 August 1997; Barbara Bradshaw to Director, 14 August 1997; Barbara Bradshaw to Australian Stock Exchange, 28 August 1947, in ACCoRD Archives; Co-operative Federation of Victorian, *News*, November-December 2000; *National Co-op Update*, May-June, November-December 2000, July-August 2001; Gary Lewis, *Conversation*, Tony Gill, 27 January 2003; Gary Lewis, *Conversation*, Garry Cronan 28 January 2003.

17 Co-operatives Council of Australia, 'Commentary: New Co-operatives Legislation and the Australian Stock Exchange', 5 September 1997.

18 *Australian Financial Review*, 18, 19 November 1997; Co-operative Federation of Victoria, *News*, November-December 2000; *National Co-op Update*, November-December 2000; Gary Lewis, *Conversation*, Garry Cronan, 28 January 2003; Correspondence, 3 November 1997, in ACCoRD Archives. CCP officials: Imelda Bradley, Attorney-General's Department, Adelaide; Barbara Bradshaw, Office of Business Affairs, Darwin; Peter Maloney, Department of Justice, Hobart; Michael Monaghan, Attorney-General's Department, Sydney; Peter Richards, Office of Corporate Affairs, Perth; Kerin Turner, Office of Fair Trading, Melbourne; Tim Beale, Department of Justice and Attorney-General, Brisbane.

19 *National Co-op Update*, May-June, September, 1998, January-February, May-June, July-August, November-December 1999; Co-operative Federation of New South Wales, *Annual Report*, 1997-1998; Cronan and Wickremarachchi, *A Study of Co-operative Development*, *op cit*, pp 76-77; Western Australian Parliament, 'Uniform Legislation', *op cit*; Tony Gill, Co-operative Development Services, *Website*; Gary Lewis, *Conversation*, Garry Cronan, 28 January 2003; Co-operative Federation of Victoria, *Website*.

CHAPTER FIFTEEN

1 *Sydney Morning Herald*, 6 September 1941; J Todd, *Milk for the Metropolis*, *op cit*, pp 140-144, 147. Booth claimed that conservative interests in parliament, for example Colonel Playfair MLC, had a conflict of interest and should not be involved in setting government policy for co-operatives or the

industry. Dairy Farmers retained the services of E C Sommerland MLC, the manager of *Country Press*, to monitor parliamentary developments and represent the co-operative's interests.

2   M Ryan, *A Centenary History of Norco, 1985-1995*, Norco Co-operative Limited, Lismore, 1993, p 321; Todd, *Milk for the Metropolis, op cit*, pp 173-179. Renegade dairy producers and vendors in the Penrith and Nepean regions formed United Dairies in opposition to Dairy Farmers.

3   B H Macintosh, 'Dairy Co-operatives: What is their Future?' Talk given at Morwell, 18 April 1969; R R Piggott, 'Aspects of the Organisation of Rural Marketing Co-operatives', *op cit*, pp 118, 120. Not until 1979 was the legality of allowing capital appreciation in co-operatives via the device of bonus shares finally confirmed.

4   *Sydney Morning Herald*, 14, 22 March, 1961; *Daily Telegraph*, 22 March 1961; CFNSW, *Newsletter*, 15 December 1967; New South Wales Department of Co-operatives, *Annual Report*, Year Ending June 1961; Todd, *Milk for the Metropolis, op cit*, pp 173, 179, 180-191. C M Barker of Dairy Farmers Co-operative and Chair of the Co-operative Federation of New South Wales took a position on the Co-operative Advisory Council. In 1967 Dairy Farmers won a Tax Board of Review appeal. In 1972 the former Chair of CFNSW resigned to go to Dairy Farmers.

5   Ryan, A Centenary History of Norco, *op cit*, p 321; CFNSW *Newsletter*, August 1970, February, June 1971, July 1972, July-August 1974, May 1977; *Australian Financial Review*, 17 February 1975, 31 May 1976, 10 July 1978. The Producers' Co-operative Distributive Company (PDS) and Norco formed Marketing Co-operative Limited, endeavouring to rationalise transport costs by delivering products in the same vehicles. After fifty years of service, including periods as chair of CFNSW and on the executive committee of the Co-operatives' Advisory Council, Dairy Farmers' General Manager C Barker retired. He was replaced by Murray Mead. Don Kinnersley, a trainee chemist who joined the co-operative in 1957, was appointed assistant general manager.

6   Ryan, *A Centenary History of Norco, op cit*, pp 333-335.

7   *Australian Financial Review*, 1 February 1990; *Australian*, 17 February 2001.

8   Ryan, *A Centenary History of Norco, op cit*, pp 333-5; Todd, *More Than Milk, op cit*, pp 9-10, 16-18, 29; Greenwood, *Thesis, op cit*, pp 19, 25; Todd, *Milk for the Metropolis, op cit*, pp 218-230; Gary Lewis, *Conversation*, Garry Cronan, 28 January 2003.

9   Australian Association of Co-operatives, *Co-op Courier*, August-February 1989; *Australian Financial Review*, 30 January 1989; *Land*, 30 January 1989; Todd, *More Than Milk, op cit*, pp 23, 25-27, 29.

10 Todd, *Milk for the Metropolis, op cit*, p 25. Langdon at various times also served as a director on the boards of PIVOT, Primary Industry Bank of Australia (PIBA) and Rabobank Australia Limited.

11 *Land*, 21 April 1988, 20 July 1989; Cronan and Wickremarachchi, *A Study of Co-operative Development, op cit*, p 86; *Queensland Dairy Farmer*, May, December 1986; Todd, *More Than Milk, op cit*, pp 29, 59-82 (for a discussion on the Queensland dairy industry); Todd, *Milk for the Metropolis, op cit*, pp 245-253.

12 Uri Windt (for the Registrar), 'Submission to the Minister for Business and Consumer Affairs on Dairy Farmers Co-operative Limited Active Membership Provisions', 7 July 1988; Jan Todd, *Milk for the Metropolis, op cit*, pp 241-245, 250.

13 Australian Association of Co-operatives, *Co-op Courier*, September-October 1988; Gerry Peacocke, *Opening Address* to the New South Wales Dairy Industry Authority Annual Conference, May 1989; *New South Wales Dairy Digest*, March 1988; Todd, *More Than Milk, op cit*, pp 31-35; Todd, *Milk for the Metropolis, op cit*, pp 231-144, 247-248.

14 *Sydney Morning Herald*, 15 April 1989; New South Wales Government, *Directions in Government*, April 1988; Todd, *Milk for the Metropolis, op cit*, pp 232, 235; Todd, *More Than Milk, op cit*, p 32.

15 Todd, *Milk for the Metropolis, op cit*, pp 244-245, 250.

16 Chris Greenwood, *Australian Dairy Co-operatives: Planning for the Future, op cit*, pp 9, 19, 25. Seven smaller co-operatives later joined ACF. Some co-operatives redeemed shares in what they described

as a 'principled way'. Bega Co-operative, for instance, paid out $350,000 in 1983. Between 1983 and 1988 the Hunter Valley Co-operative paid out $3.4 million. Between 1987 and 1990, Norco paid out $3 million and COD Co-operative Haulage paid $2 million between 1983 and 1990.

17   Watson, *Just a Bunch of Cow Cockies, op cit*, pp 243, 245; *Australian Financial Review*, 1 February 1990; *National Business Review*, (New Zealand), 17 September 1990; *Land*, 8 November 1990; Todd, *More Than Milk, op cit*, pp 37-39. Queensco, Darling Downs Co-operative Bacon and Dairy Vale and Mount Gambier co-operatives in Queensland and South Australia, co-operatively merged functions.

18   *Land*, 8 November 1990; Todd, *More Than Milk, op cit*, p 257.

19   ACF Limited, *News*, February 1990; *Land*, 4, 18 January 1990; Todd, *More Than Milk, op cit*, pp 49, 82-83, 200-201, 234-236, 260-262; *Australian Rural Times*, 19 April 1990; Dairy Farmers, 'History of Events', www.dairyfarmers.com.au.

CHAPTER SIXTEEN

1   Jan Todd, *Milk for the Metropolis, op cit*, p 284.

2   *Land*, 3 March 1994; Todd, *Milk for the Metropolis, op cit*, pp 204-211, 272-278, 281, 284. David Featherston and David Jones advised Milanda Dairy Foods.

3   Todd, *Milk for the Metropolis, op cit*, pp 276-281.

4   Ian Langdon, 'Capital Raising Options for Co-operatives', in New South Wales Registry of Co-operative Societies, *Co-operation*, Special Edition, January 1994; Garry Cronan, 'USA/Australian Experience', in *Australian Dairy Foods Journal*, June 1994; Chris Greenwood, *Australian Dairy Co-operatives: Planning for the Future*, Dairy Research and Development Corporation, February 1996, pp 33, 59; Todd, *Milk for the Metropolis, op cit*, pp 199-200, 204-207, 264-266, 281-282.

5   Todd, *Milk for the Metropolis, op cit*, pp 276-278, 281; Todd, *More Than Milk, op cit*, pp 207-209. Port Curtis Co-operative was sold to private-profit enterprise.

6   Ian Langdon, 'Member Control in Perpetuity', New South Wales Registry of Co-operative Societies, *1994 Key Issues Conference*, Sydney.

7   *Land*, 3 March 1994; Chris Greenwood, Interview: Ian Langdon, September 1998; Cronan and Wickeremarachchi, *A Study of Co-operative Development, op cit*, pp 83-84; Catherine Watson, *Just a Bunch of Cow Cockies, op cit*, pp 249-251, 254, 257; Greenwood, *Australian Dairy Co-operatives, op cit*, pp 30, 46; Todd, *Milk for the Metropolis, op cit*, p 284; Todd, *More Than Milk, op cit*, pp 209-211, 240-241.

8   Australian Co-operative Foods, *Annual Report*, 1995.

9   Todd, *More Than Milk, op cit*, pp 85, 89-91, 211-212, 249; *Land*, 18 February 1993; Australian Co-operative Foods, *News*, January 1996.

10   *Queensland Dairy Farmer*, March 1995; Co-operative Federation of New South Wales, *Newsletter*, December 1995; Todd, *More Than Milk, op cit*, pp 91, 96-98, 100, 103-104.

11   Todd, *More Than Milk, op cit*, pp 136, 213-214, 223, 257-259.

12   Greenwood, *Australian Dairy Co-operatives, op cit*, 62, 66-68.

13   Watson, *Just a Bunch of Cow Cockies, op cit*, p 254; Greenwood, *Thesis, op cit*, pp 25-26, 32, 50; Todd, *More Than Milk, op cit*, pp 105-106, 136; 213-214, 223, 274.

14   Watson, *Just a Bunch of Cow Cockies, op cit*, pp 254, 258, 265; *Australian Dairy Foods*, February 1998; *Business Queensland*, 9 June 1978; *Australian Financial Review*, 2 July 1997, 1, 31 July 1998; *Land*, 12 November 1998; *Bulletin*, 18 May 1998; Greenwood, *Thesis, op cit*, pp 48-49; *National Co-op Update*, March-April, May-June 1998, July-August 1999; *Australian*, 17 February 2001; Todd, *More Than Milk, op cit*, pp 120, 124-125, 129, 177, 215-217, 221-224, 240-242, 249.

15 *Weekly Times*, 1 April 1998; *Australian Dairy Foods*, October 1998; *Australian Financial Review*, 31 July 1998; Todd, *More Than Milk, op cit*, pp 124, 189. DFG turnover had doubled to $1.35 billion since 1991, total assets amounted to $587 million and the co-operative produced a surplus of $35 million. DFG purchased the Lite White, Shape, Hi-lo and Moove brands from the New South Wales Marketing Board. It was estimated that regulation delivered an annual subsidy to individual farmers of $44,000 and $11,000 in Queensland and New South Wales, respectively.

16 *Bulletin*, 18 August 1998; *National Co-op Update*, May-June 1998.

17 *Land*, 12 November 1998; Todd, *More Than Milk, op cit*, pp 220-221.

18 Todd, *More Than Milk, op cit*, pp 220-221.

19 Will Hughes, University of Wisconsin Center for Co-operatives, December 1999; Todd, *More Than Milk, op cit*, pp 220-223.

20 *Australian Dairy Foods*, June 1999; *Australian*, 20 August 1999; Todd, *More Than Milk, op cit*, pp 221-5, 264. Dissenters included Murray Sowter, Max Cochrane, Cathy Cleary, Sherylene Cole, Trevor Parrish, Jo Curcuriot. Sydney merchant banker Leon Carr assisted.

21 *Australian Financial Review*, 31 July, 1998, 30 August 1999; Todd, *More Than Milk, op cit*, pp 177, 217, 223-229, 249.

22 *Australian Financial Review*, 20, 30 August 1999, 31 March, 17, 18, 23, 24, 25 August, 3, 6 October 2000; *Australian*, 3 September, 20 August, 3 September, 2, 3 December 1999, 2, 10 March, 20 October, 5 December 2000, 2 February, 19 June 2001; *Business Review Weekly*, 15 January 2000; *Age*, 19 April 2000; *Sydney Morning Herald*, 23 October 1999, 19 January 2000; *Australian Dairy Foods*, June 1999; *National Co-op Update*, May-June, November-December 1999, January-February 2000; New South Wales Supreme Court, *Cleary v ACF*, 1999, pp 45, 57, 75-76, 81; Onno-Frank van Bekkum, *Co-operative Models and Farm Policy Reform*, Van Goreum, Netherlands Institute of Co-operative Entrepreneurship, 2001, p 230; Todd, *More Than Milk, op cit*, pp 221-229, 231-238, 251, 264.

23 New South Wales Supreme Court ACF Limited Application of 2001, p. 382 at www.lawlink.nsw. gov.au/sc; Todd, *More Than Milk, op cit*, p 253.

24 *Australian Dairy Foods*, October 2000, October 2001, October 2002; *Australian Financial Review*, 3, 7, 6, 10, 23, 24 August 2000; Todd, *More Than Milk, op cit*, pp 243, 246-250, 257-259.

25 Todd, *More Than Milk, op cit*, pp 251-252.

26 Onno-Frank van Bekkum, *op cit*, pp 189, 215-217, 230; Todd, *More Than Milk, op cit*, p 223.

27 Dairy Farmers Group, *Annual Report*, June 2001; *Sydney Morning Herald*, 18 June 2001; Todd, *More Than Milk, op cit*, pp 221-224, 234, 249. The *Co-operatives Act* was amended requiring external disclosure for the issue of CCUs above $5 million to non-members and information sheets for issues below that amount.

28 *Australian*, 17, 28 February 2001; *Age*, 10 October 2002; *Australian Financial Review*, 2 May 2002; *Information*, 17 May 2002; *Weekend Australian*, 11-12 January 2003; *Land*, 24 August 2000; *Australian Dairy Foods*, April 2000; *News Weekly*, 12 July 2000; Todd, *More Than Milk, op cit*, pp 240, 243, 245, 260; *National Co-op Update*, March-April, May-June 2000; Watson, *Just a Bunch of Cow Cockies, op cit*, p 265; Robert Gottleibsen, *Ten Best and Ten Worst Decisions of Australian CEOs, 1992-2002, op cit*, 2003, pp 25-26, 228; Wayne Whiting, 'Changing Face of Australian Dairy Industry', Shainwright Consulting and Research Group, 2003; Onno-Frank van Bekkum *op cit*, pp 48-57, 184-189

29 Dairy Farmers 'What's New', 28 November 2003, 2 June 2004; Dairy Farmers 'History of Events 2004', www.dairyfarmers.com.au

Chapter Seventeen

1   Hans-H Munkner *Chances of Co-operatives in the Future: Contribution to the International Co-operative Alliance Centennial 1895-1995,* Institute for Co-operation in Developing Countries, Marburg, Germany, 1995; Onno-Frank van Bekkum, *Co-operative Models and Farm Policy Reform,* Van Gorcum, The Netherlands, 2001; Daniel Cote, 'The Future of Co-operatives: Managing the Specifics', Paper to Monash Agribusiness Co-operatives Seminar, 1 November 2002.

Appendix One

1   W W Rawlinson, Executive Officer, Co-operative Federation of Australia, *Correspondence*: J P McDermott, Senior Assistant, Commissioner of Taxation, 25 March 1977; Australian Information Service Reference Paper, *Co-operatives in Australia*, Canberra 1976; (Ferguson) Royal Commission on Taxation, 1932-1934, Part III, pp 146-7; Gary Lewis, *Discussion*: W W Rawlinson, 1983; W W Rawlinson, 'Study Course in the Establishment and Management of Co-operatives in Australia', 1967; F Bock and E F Mannix, *The Guide to Australian Income Tax*, 13th edition, Butterworth, Sydney, 1967; R R Piggott, 'Aspects of the Organisation of Rural Marketing Co-operatives in New South Wales', *op cit*; Jenni Mattila, Tress, Cocks and Maddox, 'Income Tax Consultancy – Co-operatives', Sydney, 16 May, 1991; Robert Lovell, 'Accounting and Tax Issues for Co-operatives', Thomas Noble and Russell Chartered Accountants, 27 October 1993; Berri Co-operative, Packing Union v Federal Commissioner of Taxation, 1930, 44, CCR, p 236.

2   *Retail Trade*, 13 May, 9 June, 28 November 1947, 19 November 1948, 8 September, 13 October, 1950, 24 August, 7 December 1951, 25 April, 25 June 1952; New South Wales Parliamentary Debate, 1950-1952, pp 4123-4142; Employers Mutual Indemnity Association v Federal Commissioner of Taxation, 2 AITR 1943, p 502; Ardmona Fruit Products Co-operative v Federal Commissioner of Taxation, 5 AITR, 1952, p 342.

3   Co-operative Federation of Australia National Convention, *Report*, Canberra, August 1973, pp 60-62; Gary Lewis, *A Middle Way, op cit*, pp 228-229; R R Piggott, *Aspects of the Organisation of Rural Marketing Co-operatives, op cit*, p 34; *Australian Financial Review*, 26 June 1967; Renmark Fruit Growers' Co-operative v Federal Commissioner of Taxation, 1 AITR, 1969, p 385; Revesby Credit Union Co-operative Limited v Federal Commissioner of Taxation, 9 AITR, 1964, p 459.

4   *Sydney Morning Herald*, 9 March 1999; Chris Greenwood, *Thesis, op cit*, pp 15-17; *National Co-op Update*, September-October 1996, November-December 1998, May-June 1999; Co-operative Council of Australia, National Conference, Canberra, 20-21 April 1999.

5   *National Co-op Update*, November-December 1998; May-June, September-October, November-December 1999; March-April 2000.

6   *National Co-op Update*, September-October, November-December 1999, March-April 2000; John Anderson, Minister for Transport and Regional Services, *Media Release*, Parliament House, Canberra, 25 September 1999; Co-operative Federation of Victoria, Website.

Index

C